BANNED BOOKS

LITERATURE SUPPRESSED ON

Political Grounds

Third Edition

NICHOLAS J. KAROLIDES

Preface by
KEN WACHSBERGER

An Infobase Learning Company

Facts On File, Inc.
An imprint of Infobase Learning
132 West 31st Street
New York NY 10001

Library of Congress Cataloging-in-Publication Data
Karolides, Nicholas J.
Literature suppressed on political grounds / Nicholas J. Karolides ; preface by Ken Wachsberger. — 3rd ed.
p. cm. — (Banned books)
Includes bibliographical references and index.
ISBN 978-0-8160-8231-5 (acid-free paper)
1. Censorship—United States—History—20th century. 2. Censorship—United States—History—21st century. 3. Censorship—History. 4. Prohibited books—United States—Bibliography. 5. Prohibited books—Bibliography.
6. Communication in politics—United States—History—20th century.
7. Communication in politics—United States—History—21st century.
8. Communication in politics. I. Title.
Z658.U5K37 2011
363.31—dc22   2010030413

Facts On File books are available at special discounts when purchased in bulk quantities for businesses, associations, institutions, or sales promotions. Please call our Special Sales Department in New York at (212) 967-8800 or (800) 322-8755.

You can find Facts On File on the World Wide Web at
http://www.infobaselearning.com

Text design by Cathy Rincon
Composition by Publication Services, Inc.
Cover printed by Yurchak Printing, Landisville, Pa.
Book printed and bound by Yurchak Printing, Landisville, Pa.
Date printed June 2011

Printed in the United States of America

10 9 8 7 6 5 4 3 2 1

This book is printed on acid-free paper.

*T*o the University of Wisconsin–River Falls
Chalmer Davee Library staff,
particularly
Brad Gee, Valerie Malzacher, Michele McKnelly,
reference librarians,
as well as Mary Augustine and Ann Welniak, interlibrary
loan librarians,
for their knowledgeable and persevering assistance
and their dedication to freedom of inquiry

Democracy is more stable, and people are more free, when the press is free.
—William Jefferson Clinton

If all mankind minus one were of one opinion, and only one person were of the contrary opinion, mankind would be no more justified in silencing that one person, than he, if he had the power, would be justified in silencing mankind.
—John Stuart Mill

The free press is the mother of all our liberties and of our progress under liberty.
—Adlai E. Stevenson

If knowledge is power, access is empowerment.
—Mark R. Hamilton

We are not afraid to entrust the American people with unpleasant facts, foreign ideas, alien philosophies, and competitive values. For a nation that is afraid to let its people judge the truth and falsehood in an open market is a nation that is afraid of its people.
—John F. Kennedy

So long as books are kept open then minds can never be closed.
—Gerald R. Ford

I grew up understanding that the greatness of our democracy is the difference of opinion and the ability to voice it freely.
—Jane Alexander

CONTENTS

ACKNOWLEDGMENTS

Credit and appreciation are due to university colleagues, Marshall Toman, Cecilia Bustamante-Marré, and Joseph K. M. Fischer; former students and my daughter, Mitchell Fay, Jane Graves, Alexis Karolides, Laurie Pap, and Eric P. Schmidt, who read texts, researched censorship histories, and wrote fine, meaningful essays found in this volume. Their names follow their individual writings. My thanks also go to colleagues who offered advice and scholarship on individual entries: Herbert R. Cederberg, historian; Tracey L. Gladstone-Sovell, political scientist; J. Michael Norman, journalist; John R. Walker, economist; and C. B. Brohaugh, for language expertise. In the preparation of this third edition, I am immeasurably indebted to Joseph K. M. Fischer for his dedication and research expertise in establishing censorship data for new material as well as updating the entries for the first and revised editions. Also, I am comparably grateful to Gretchen Toman who researched and translated German periodicals and newspapers about censored German authors with finesse and clarity. In addition to the librarians to whom this volume is dedicated, I applaud the cooperation of librarians and school personnel in communities across the country who have readily researched newspaper reports of censorship and school district files for me. I am particularly grateful to Inga Karolides for her advice about language clarity and nuance throughout, and to Ken Wachsberger for his expert editing of the original volume. My gratitude as well goes to Sharon L. Fowler and Doreen Cegielski for efficient and conscientious preparation of the revised manuscripts and the original edition, respectively.

—N. J. K.

PREFACE

We Americans are proud of our Constitution, especially its Bill of Rights. The First Amendment right to freedom of speech and religion has inspired dissenters and nonconformists everywhere. Censored writers such as Salman Rushdie, Pramoedya Ananta Toer, and Aleksandr Solzhenitsyn have looked to our country's example for strength as they battled for their rights to express their own thoughts and that of others to read them, even at the risk of their lives.

Yet, censorship has been a major part of American history from the time of Roger Williams and other early colonial freethinkers. Many of the richest literary works—*Adventures of Huckleberry Finn, The Color Purple, The Grapes of Wrath, The Jungle, Uncle Tom's Cabin, Tropic of Cancer*—have been censored at one time or another. Even today, school boards, local governments, religious organizations, and moral crusaders attempt to restrict our freedom to read or learn alternative viewpoints. Witness the Texas State Board of Education's attempts to revise American history and tear down the wall separating church and state through its revisionist textbooks. Advancing technology has provided more diverse targets—the record, film, and television industries and the Internet—for the censors and would-be censors to aim at, as they work their strategies to restrict free expression and the freedom to read, watch, and listen, dumbing down material in order to shield their children, and you, from original or disturbing thoughts.

In this third edition, Nick Karolides adds to his illuminating collection of censorship histories from around the world with examples from eight different countries. While political censorship of books in the United States is not as widespread or open as in some other countries, alternative, subtler methods of political censorship can also affect what books get published or read. Examples from the new millennium include opening up library records to government officials under the PATRIOT Act in the name of fighting terrorism; branding opponents of certain government policies, no matter how misguided, as traitors and unpatriotic; and threatening religious organizations with revocation of their nonprofit status if leaders express antiwar views, even when they do not endorse specific candidates or political parties.

Fortunately, our country has a strong tradition of fighting censorship as well. Groups such as the National Coalition Against Censorship, the

American Library Association's Office for Intellectual Freedom, People For the American Way, the American Civil Liberties Union, the PEN American Center, and the National Writers Union exist to defend the First Amendment and support independent writers, through legal action and by raising public awareness.

The first edition of the Facts On File Banned Books series came out as a four-volume hardcover set in 1998. The second edition, which was published in 2006, added 50 additional titles to the list. The four volumes in this dynamic revised and expanded third edition add to our rich First Amendment tradition by spotlighting approximately 500 works that have been censored for their political, social, religious, or erotic content, in the United States and around the world, from biblical times to the present day. While many of these have been legally "banned,"—or prohibited "as by official order,"—all indeed have been banned or censored in a broader sense: targeted for removal from school curricula or library shelves, condemned in churches and forbidden to the faithful, rejected or expurgated by publishers, challenged in court, even voluntarily rewritten by their authors. Censored authors have been verbally abused, physically attacked, shunned by their families and communities, excommunicated from their religious congregations, and shot, hanged, or burned at the stake by their enemies. who thus made them heroes and often enough secured their memory for posterity. Their works include novels, histories, biographies, children's books, religious and philosophical treatises, dictionaries, poems, polemics, and every other form of written expression.

It is illuminating to discover in these histories that such cultural landmarks as the Bible, the Qur'an, the Talmud, and the greatest classics of world literature have often been suppressed or censored for the same motives, and by similar forces, as those we see today seeking to censor such books as *Daddy's Roommate*, and *Heather Has Two Mommies*. Every American reading these volumes will find in their pages books they love and will be thankful that their authors' freedom of expression and their own freedom to read are constitutionally protected. But at the same time, how many will be gratified by the cruel fate of books they detest? Reader-citizens capable of acknowledging their own contradictions will be grateful for the existence of the First Amendment and will thank its guardians, including the authors of this series, for protecting us against our own worst impulses.

It is to Facts On File's credit that it has published this new version of the original Banned Books series. May the day come when an expanded series is no longer necessary.

***

To prevent redundancy, works banned for multiple reasons appear in only one volume apiece, based on the judgment of the editor and the volume authors. The alphabetical arrangement provides easy access to titles. Works whose titles appear in Small Capital Letters within an entry have entries of their own elsewhere in the same volume. Those whose titles appear in *ITALICIZED SMALL CAPITAL LETTERS* have entries in one of the other volumes. In addition, each volume carries complete lists of the works discussed in the other volumes.

—Ken Wachsberger

Ken Wachsberger is a long-time author, editor, educator, and member of the National Writers Union. He is the editor of the four-volume Voices from the Underground series, a landmark collection of insider histories about the Vietnam era underground press (www.voicesfromthundergroundpress.com).

INTRODUCTION

The phrase *suppressed on political grounds* casts a shadow of a heavy-handed government blocking its citizens from receiving information, ideas, and opinions that it perceives to be critical, embarrassing, or threatening. This image, unfortunately, is too often reality. It is not, however, limited to dictatorships such as those of Adolf Hitler's Nazi Germany, Joseph Stalin's Communist Soviet Union, Suharto's Indonesia, Augusto Pinochet's Chile, and Sani Abacha's Nigeria. The political turbulence of the 1990s dismantled several dictatorships, establishing more open government in Indonesia, Chile, Nigeria, and Russia. The governments of democracies, however, also participate in attempts to censor such critical material in order to protect their own perceived state security. Indeed, repression of freedom of expression has been a significant operative factor in South Africa of the apartheid era, in pre-1990 South Korea, in Turkey, in postcommunist Ukraine, and recently in Russia. It is a factor, as well, in the United Kingdom and the United States today.

Further, the impression that censorship for political reasons emanates only from national governments is mistaken, Another common source of such activity, notably in the United States, is at the local community level, generated by school board members or citizens, individually or in groups, who attack textbooks and fiction used in schools or available in school libraries. In contrast to censorship challenges at the national level, challenges at the local level are aimed at the political values and images that children are receiving. In past decades, the chief targets were socialism, communism, and the portrayal of the Soviet Union. A companion concern was the portrayal of the United States. At the center of such objections was the fear that the Soviet Union would be viewed too positively or the United States too negatively. Continuing in the present, examining flaws in American society is deemed unpatriotic to critics, who become concerned when past and present policies of their government are questioned in school textbooks and library books. Expressing flaws in behavior of its citizens is deemed inappropriate for students. Books conveying the dynamics of war situations are targets of censoring challenges as well.

The titles discussed in this book vary considerably in subject and form. Some texts have extensive or impressive censorship histories. Other works appear to have had comparably limited censorship exposure. *The Grapes of*

Wrath was challenged and burned within months of its publication in 1939 and has been subject to attacks for more than 60 years. The censorship of Solzhenitsyn's books by the Soviet government gained international notoriety. Four other novelists whose works are included have had their entire oeuvre censored by their respective governments: Nobel Prize winners Miguel Angel Asturias of Guatemala and Gao Xingjian of the People's Republic of China; Duong Thu Huong of Vietnam; Pramoedya Ananta Toer of Indonesia, and, more recently, Liao Yiwu, of the People's Republic of China. Harriet Beecher Stowe's antislavery novel, *Uncle Tom's Cabin*, was broadly censored in the South in the 19th century, and *My Brother Sam Is Dead*, the antiwar, nonromanticized Revolutionary War novel by James Lincoln Collier and Christopher Collier, has drawn considerable fire since its publication in 1974. Some works have faced significant court cases: *Decent Interval*, by Frank Snepp; *I Am the Cheese*, by Robert Cormier; *Slaughterhouse-Five* and *Cat's Cradle*, by Kurt Vonnegut; *Spycatcher*, by Peter Wright; and United States–Vietnam Relations, 1945–1967 (*The Pentagon Papers*), issued by the U.S. Department of Defense.

Not all objections are formalized or publicly announced; some are reported only in local newspapers. Self-censorship by teachers and librarians is common. I recall the comment of a librarian who accounted for the lack of challenges to her collection through her tactic of not ordering books that were censored elsewhere. Further, not all attacks are identified forthrightly; it is apparently more difficult to protest the politics of a text than it is to protest its offensive language. Lee Burress, who has conducted five state and national surveys of censorship of school library and classroom materials, referred to this mask as the "hidden agenda" of censorship.

The accounts of these attacks at local levels may seem to the glancing eye diversified and transient; those at the national and international levels may appear remote and arcane. These multiple streams of curtailed thought, however, combine to form a treacherous current. Its undertow can ensnare the mind in the tangled weeds of ignorance and irrationality. Denied both in individual incidents and en masse is the sine qua non of democracy, the right of fundamental inquiry, the ebb and flow of thought.

NOTE ON THE SECOND EDITION

This revised edition is updated in two ways. First, 10 entries have been added. These books spotlight the international scene. One, *Did Six Million Really Die?*, is set in western Europe. The others are dispersed around the globe: Chile (*El libro negro de la justicia Chilena*), China (*Bus Stop*, *Fugitives*, and *Waiting*), Nigeria (*The Man Died* and *The Open Sore of a Continent*), Kurdistan (*After Such Knowledge, What Forgiveness?*), Palestine (*The Politics of Dispossession*), and Israel (*The Patriot* and *The Queen of the Bathtub*). Two of the authors, Wole Soyinka and Gao Xingjian, have been awarded the Nobel Prize in literature, bringing the total of such prestigious authors included in this volume to seven.

The second strategy entailed a research review of each entry of the original edition, primarily focusing on censorship events since the first edition's publication. The results are assorted updates, some of them extensive, notably for *All Quiet on the Western Front* (the additions pertain to the censoring of the film), *The Jungle* (additional insights have been drawn from the discovery of the original manuscript), and *Mein Kampf* (more state censorship has taken place since the publication of the first edition). Other entries were amended with the addition of a recent school challenge, such as *The Grapes of Wrath* and *Black Boy*. In a few cases, occasional clarifications were made to texts' summaries.

NOTE ON THE THIRD EDITION

The 12 works added to this expanded and updated edition of *Banned Books: Literature Suppressed on Political Grounds* are entirely international. Indeed, several represent nations that have not heretofore been included in this collection. Alphabetically, they are: Argentina (*Kiss of the Spider Woman*), Czech Republic/Czechoslovakia (*The Joke* and The Vaněk Plays), Saudi Arabia (*Cities of Salt* and *Girls of Riyadh*), and Turkey (*The Bastard of Istanbul* and *Snow*). Germany is representd by an historical memoir (*A Woman in Berlin: Eight Weeks in the Conquered* city) and Romania by a novel set and censored there (*The Appointment*). The last three are nonfiction: one a memoir from Nigeria (*A Month and a Day: A Detention Diary*) and two from China (*The Corpse Walker: Real Life Stories: China from the Bottom Up* and *Yangtze! Yangtze!*). Two of the authors, Herta Müller and Orhan Pamuk, have been awarded the Nobel Prize in literature, bringing the total number of these laureates in this volume to nine.

As with the first revised edition, several electronic databases and online resouces were searched to ascertain if any of the entires in the previous edition had received new censorship challenges. *Mein Kampf* was the focus of a controversy in Germany, as was the publisher of *Did Six Million Really Die?*, who was accused of inciting racial hatred and Holocaust denial. Other entries, such as *Slaughterhouse-Five* and *The Things They Carried*, were amended. An intriguing about-face in Russia with regard to *The Gulag Archipelago* is also notable.

—Nicholas J. Karolides
University of Wisconsin–River Falls

WORKS DISCUSSED IN THIS VOLUME

MY BROTHER SAM IS DEAD
James Lincoln Collier and Christopher Collier

MY NAME IS ASHER LEV
Chaim Potok

MY PEOPLE: THE STORY OF THE JEWS
Abba Eban

NELSON AND WINNIE MANDELA
Dorothy Hoobler and Thomas Hoobler

1984
George Orwell

NOVEL WITHOUT A NAME
Duong Thu Huong

OIL!
Upton Sinclair

ONE DAY IN THE LIFE OF IVAN DENISOVICH
Aleksandr Solzhenitsyn

*ONE PEOPLE, ONE DESTINY: THE CARIBBEAN AND
CENTRAL AMERICA TODAY*
Don Rojas

*THE OPEN SORE OF A CONTINENT: A PERSONAL NARRATIVE
OF THE NIGERIAN CRISIS*
Wole Soyinka

OUR LAND, OUR TIME: A HISTORY OF THE UNITED STATES
Joseph Robert Conlin

PARADISE OF THE BLIND
Duong Thu Huong

*THE PATRIOT (HA PATRIOT)
THE QUEEN OF THE BATHTUB (MALKAT AMBATYA)*
Hanoch Levin

THE POLITICS OF DISPOSSESSION
Edward W. Said

THE PRINCE
Niccolò Machiavelli

THE THINGS THEY CARRIED
Tim O'Brien

THIS EARTH OF MANKIND
CHILD OF ALL NATIONS
Pramoedya Ananta Toer

365 DAYS
Ronald J. Glasser

TODAY'S ISMS: COMMUNISM, FASCISM, CAPITALISM, SOCIALISM
William Ebenstein

THE UGLY AMERICAN
William J. Lederer and Eugene Burdick

UNCLE TOM'S CABIN
Harriet Beecher Stowe

UNITED STATES–VIETNAM RELATIONS, 1945–1967
(THE PENTAGON PAPERS)
U.S. Department of Defense

THE VANĚK PLAYS
Václav Havel

WAITING
Ha Jin

WHY ARE WE IN VIETNAM?
Norman Mailer

A WOMAN IN BERLIN: EIGHT WEEKS IN
  THE CONQUERED CITY
Anonymous

WORDS OF CONSCIENCE: RELIGIOUS STATEMENTS
  ON CONSCIENTIOUS OBJECTION
A. Stauffer Curry, editor (first edition)
Shawn Perry, editor (ninth edition)

YANGTZE! YANGTZE!
Dai Qing

LITERATURE SUPPRESSED ON POLITICAL GROUNDS

THE AFFLUENT SOCIETY

Author: John Kenneth Galbraith
Original date and place of publication: 1958, United States
Publisher: Houghton Mifflin
Literary form: Nonfiction

SUMMARY

". . . [T]he experience of nations with well being is exceedingly brief. Nearly all throughout all history have been very poor." The exception, "great and unprecedented affluence," is found in Europe and the United States in the last few generations. With this stark assertion, John Kenneth Galbraith sets the stage for his analysis of the economic attitudes and behaviors of this affluent society. Essentially, he attacks current economic thinking. An underlying point is that the standard economic ideas (i.e., "conventional wisdom") were developed in a world where poverty was normal, where scarcity of goods and services was accepted as the way of life.

In the late 18th century, Adam Smith, a key figure in the "central economic tradition" (a phrase used to denote the classical tradition, the main current of ideas in descent from Smith), posited a hopeful vision of an advancing national community in *An Inquiry into the Nature and Causes of the Wealth of Nations*. In his view, the economic society was regulated not by the state but by competition and the market, the market consisting of small entrepreneurs; people, using their resources, worked for the enrichment of society. Smith perceived that the distribution of wealth depended on bargaining power that favored merchants, manufacturers, and landlords; workers, subject to market forces, "could not for very long rise very far above the minimum level necessary for the survival of the race." This concept became a basic premise— with some qualifications—of economists David Ricardo and Thomas Robert Malthus, Smith's successors in the central tradition; it also served as the crux of Marx's attack on capitalism. According to Galbraith, by the onset of the 20th century, the severity of this position was diminished but not altogether negated.

A presumption of inequality was inherent to the competitive model of the central tradition, defended by the rich, whom it benefited, and conservatives. The competitive, efficient entrepreneur was rewarded as was the comparable worker, but the rewards were not equal. In dissent from the central tradition, some economists, including Marxists, have argued that the redistribution of wealth and income was possible—and necessary. Indeed, some leveling, achieving a reduction of inequality in advanced countries, has occurred. Some credit for this reduction is given to the progressive income tax but, more so, to an increase in production (i.e., an expanding economy). This progress has caused a decline of interest in and attention to the issue of inequality, though equality has not been achieved and a self-perpetuating margin of poverty still exists.

Galbraith points out that comparable tension exists between the insecurity also inherent in a competitive system and the search for security. Businesses attempt to reduce risks; individuals, when their stake is high enough, seek job and social security. Modern corporations through their size and wealth have significantly minimized insecurity; government intervention (e.g., unemployment insurance, price supports for farmers, fair trade laws), unions, and trade associations have mitigated the dire effects of insecurity for individuals and small businesses. Stabilizing the fluctuations of the business cycle, held by the central tradition to be inevitable, became a principal goal of public policy, including the control of depressions. Despite the long-held belief that economic security was the enemy of production, the reverse seems to have become the case. Galbraith identifies two interlocking ideas: "A high level of economic security is essential to maximum production. And a high level of production is indispensable for economic security."

A third, predominant concern is production. A focal factor for the central tradition theorists because goods were scarce, production was also meaningful in providing basic comforts. In modern times it has become a requisite in maintaining economic security; it established and ensures the American standard of living. Loss of production is taken very seriously. However, whereas in the past, production was geared to needs, it is now oriented toward economic security: employment and income. Galbraith claims that the measures used to manage the problems of production are traditional, harking back to those relevant in the last century, and irrational. In the context of production, he asserts that the main task of his essay is the "concern . . . with the thralldom of a myth—the myth that production, by its overpowering importance and its ineluctable difficulty, is the central problem of our lives."

Linking production to consumer demand, which is further linked to advertising, Galbraith promulgates two important ideas: the source of demands has shifted from needs to wants; in contrast to the theory of consumer demand that wants are generated by the individual, production itself "creates the wants it wants to satisfy." Consumption is driven principally by the social goal for a higher standard of living, as abetted by emulation of others, and the availability, thus accumulation, of new products. "The urge to consume is furthered by the value system which emphasizes the ability to produce. The more that is produced the more that must be owned to maintain the appropriate prestige." Advertising's central function is to create desires where they did not exist. Advertising (thus wants) is induced by the producer, establishing production as the prime urgency. The demand for goods is artificial; the things produced are not of great urgency. The assumption that wants are unlimited, justifying unrestrained production, Galbraith argues, may have dangerous consequences to the economy.

A related discussion is that of social balance, that is, what the society produces. The great emphasis is on privately produced goods, which can be sold, to the detriment of public services, which depend on tax outlays. Goods privately produced are not often balanced by equal regard for public services they might require: good and sufficient streets and roads and parking for cars, traffic control and safety, and breathable air. Goods are superfluous, often frivolous, while human needs—schools, parks, hospitals, housing—which at least indirectly relate to production, are neglected. The factor of inequality is operative in this regard, and inflation is a causal agent in the deterioration of public service since it favors the private economy.

Galbraith proposes solutions. Since steady jobs and a steady income are needed and desired rather than production of unnecessary and oversupplied goods, a substitute for production as a source of income is required. A system of unemployment compensation is proposed: Cyclically Graduated Compensation (CGC). Under this system, unemployment compensation would increase to a large percentage of normal income during periods of recession when jobs are hard to find; compensation would increase as unemployment increases, and it would decrease to a minimum level during periods of job availability. This procedure would break the connection between production and income security and would provide comparative stability of income.

Reversing the social balance to provide support for public services can be accomplished by a sales tax. "The relation of the sales tax to the problem of social balance is admirably direct. The community is affluent in privately produced goods. It is poor in public services. The obvious solution . . . by making private goods more expensive, public goods are made more abundant." In addition to upgrading such universal services as roads, schools, hospitals, and the environment, addressing public service requirements would have the meritorious effect of meeting the needs of the poor, reducing self-perpetuating poverty through investment in the children of poverty.

A concluding discussion focuses on the nature and extent of toil. The workweek has been drastically reduced over the last century, evidence of the acceptance of the lessened urgency of goods, of production. The attitudes toward work and leisure have also changed. Galbraith suggests that work can be made easier and more pleasant, that hours may be shortened, and that fewer people could work—the latter two related to lower production needs. In the context of the emergence of a "New Class," for whom work is satisfying and enjoyable, offers prestige and the opportunity to apply thought to work, and does not involve toil in the ordinary labor sense, Galbraith proposes "the greatest prospect . . . what must be counted one of the central economic goals of our society—to eliminate toil as a required economic institution." Education is the qualifying entrance mode.

These suggestions offer a commonality that projects a unifying force for the text: a concern for the human perspective, an investment in individuals. "A society has one higher task than to consider its goals, to reflect on its pursuit of happiness and harmony and its success in expelling pain, tension, sorrow, and the ubiquitous curse of ignorance. It must also, so far as this may be possible, insure its own survival." This closing statement is a goal distant from that expressed by Adam Smith and his successors.

CENSORSHIP HISTORY

On June 14, 1972, the board of education of Roselle, New Jersey, voted to remove *The Affluent Society* from a high school library list. It was among 520 titles identified as reference texts for a federally funded course in American studies. The removal was initiated by John Everett, president of the board, who lined out this title and three others—THE AGE OF KEYNES by Robert Lekachman, *The Struggle for Peace* by Leonard Beaton, and TODAY'S ISMS: COMMUNISM, FASCISM, CAPITALISM, SOCIALISM by William Ebenstein—just before the board took action to approve the program. Everett claimed that every board member had received the list of books and had been invited to make deletions. Only he took this action.

"I will do anything to thwart permissive liberalism," he was quoted as saying in the *Newark Star-Ledger*. "I violently disagree with them. . . . If I'm in a position to stop these books from being distributed then I think it's my political right."

Three days later, he was quoted in the *New York Times* as saying, "I guess I'm known around here as a book burner, but it doesn't bother me. In my opinion, the books were too liberal and I disagree with their points of view. . . ."

Galbraith and Lekachman's books were specifically earmarked as advocating "too much permissiveness." Everett said, "I deny their right to tell me that their theories are correct." In deleting the book *The Struggle for Peace*, he noted that he objected less to its contents than to its author, "Cecil" Beaton, whom he described as a "kook." (Another board member, Brother John Tevlin, pointed out that the author was Leonard Beaton, a reporter for the *London Times*.) The vote seems to have identified *The Struggle for Peace*, by "Cecil" Beaton, as the text to be deleted. Referring to Ebenstein's *Today's Isms*, Everett noted that the author "finds nothing wrong with communism, but his big bugaboo seems to be fascism" and "he beats up on capitalism." The four books were deemed far too "astute for tender minds that are not able to distinguish between right and wrong when reading such texts."

The board voted 4-3 in support of removing the titles. One of the four, Judith Solujich, indicated she had voted to ban the books because "they didn't agree with my political philosophy." She and one other of the book banners admitted they had not read the books. Among the dissenters, Brother John Tevlin asserted the action was based on "nothing more than the whim of one board member. It is the most blatant example of repression. . . . something out of the McCarthy era." Another dissenter, Garvey Presley, said, "If we were debating the merits of a textbook to be used in class it would be one thing, but these books were part of a reference library for the new humanities course."

In subsequent weeks educational groups spoke out against the actions of the Roselle Board of Education. The New Jersey School Boards Association rejected the action as the "use of naked power to subdue legitimate points of view" and "unethical behavior for those entrusted with advancing education." In parallel language the New Jersey Education Association deplored the banning as "contrary to the ideals of education to try to limit or censor ideas because one disagrees with them."

A New Jersey Department of Education official, Clyde Leib, special assistant to the commissioner, indicated that if a complaint were filed, the rule of law might recognize that banning the books was within the purview of the board of education. However, "Philosophically, we strongly disapprove of Everett's action, depriving the young people varying points of view. We live in a society that values dissent and I doubt if the republic would crumble as a result of a few unpopular books in the library. . . . The republic is surely in far greater danger by the banning of books than exposing young people to them."

In an interview of June 22, Everett said, "I want equal time and I want it known that our libraries are filled with liberal books and very few books reflecting the conservative point of view."

On July 5, the superintendent of schools, Robert F. X. Van Wagner, announced that he had placed rush orders for the books and that they would be on the library bookshelves. The four books would be purchased for the school system's libraries "administratively" even though the board had voted not to include them among those funded under the federal grant. They would be "balanced by at least four books with conservative viewpoints," a provision that Everett had offered. He indicated that he had read the books and had not found them objectionable.

FURTHER READING

Cohen, Robert. "Educational Groups Deplore Roselle Book Ban." *Newark Star-Ledger,* June 23, 1972, p. 17.

———. "Roselle Board President Defends Book Bannings." *Newark Star-Ledger,* June 15, 1972, p. 11.

———. "State Education Official Assails Book Bannings." *Newark Star-Ledger,* June 27, 1972, p. 15.

Moffatt, George. "Book 'Ban' Challenged in Roselle." *Newark Star-Ledger,* June 28, 1972, p. 18.

———. "Roselle Will Buy 'Banned' Books and 4 'Balancers.'" *Newark Star-Ledger,* July 6, 1972, p. 20.

"A School Board Head in Jersey Orders 'Liberal' Books Deleted." *New York Times,* June 18, 1972, p. 50.

"Success Stories." *Newsletter on Intellectual Freedom* 21 (1972): 147.

AFTER SUCH KNOWLEDGE, WHAT FORGIVENESS?—MY ENCOUNTERS WITH KURDISTAN

Author: Jonathan C. Randal
Original dates and places of publication: 1997, United States; 2001, Turkey
Publishers: Farrar, Straus and Giroux; Aresta
Literary form: Nonfiction

SUMMARY

In the last several pages of *After Such Knowledge, What Forgiveness?*, Jonathan Randal remarks: "Yes, I confess the gambler in me was rooting for the Kurds to make something of the situation they'd inherited in 1991," a sympathetic posture evident throughout his text. After introductory chapters of compact geographic data, a basic historical overview, and a general portrait of the Kurds, Randal focuses on the significant situations and actions of the Kurds themselves and on the attitudes and behaviors of several nations' leaders toward them, principally Iraq, the United States, Israel, and Turkey.

Kurds populate a broad expanse of the Middle East, a contiguous core area, spanning from northwestern Iran across northern Iraq and southeastern Turkey to the Syrian border; there are isolated communities elsewhere in these countries and in neighboring Armenia and Azerbaijan, for example. The Kurds are the Middle East's fourth largest community, the top three being Arabs, Iranians, and Turks. Kurdish society is multilingual, multiracial, and multireligious, yet the Kurds share a common historical experience and political aspirations. They are a recognizable ethnic community, the "world's largest ethnic group without a state of their own."

Modern Kurdish history begins in 1918 with the end of World War I. In the 19th century "Kurdistan had declined into an isolated 'mountainous irrelevancy.' . . . When peace returned in 1918, Kurdistan was a land with its infrastructure wrecked, its society in utter disarray, its intelligentsia dispersed, and the tribal chieftains and sheikhs in full control of what was left." During the war President Woodrow Wilson in the 12th of his Fourteen Points had "promised the Kurds a vaguely defined country of their own, to be carved out of the carcass of the defeated Ottoman Empire"; however, resurgent Turkey, under the leadership of Mustafa Kemal Atatürk, rejected this proposal, as did the British who had been entrusted with a League of Nations mandate for the territory that became Iraq. The Kurds' territory was divided up among Iraq, Iran, Syria, and Turkey. The thwarting of Kurdish nationalist ambitions—the Kurds "virtually alone of the Ottoman Empire's subjects [being unable to] establish their own state"—was based in part on Western notions of a modern centralized state (an idea used by various Middle Eastern governments to suppress Kurdish revolts) and in part that "Britain was more interested in safeguarding Kirkuk's oil [in the Kurdistan area] for itself than in Kurdish nationalist aspirations."

Over the intervening years between 1918 and 1997, the Kurds from time to time experienced a sense of freedom, particularly in their mountains, remote from the centers of power, before planes and helicopters bridged this impediment. They resisted assimilation with constancy and maintained their goal of achieving nationalist rights: for the Iraq Kurds—autonomy within a democratic Iraq. "The Kurds realized no one was willing to accept an independent Kurdistan carved out of Iraq—or Iran or Turkey." The Iran Kurds were of like mind; the Turkish Kurds were separatist rebels, focused on independence from Turkey. Given the active aggression of this group, Turkey was particularly fearful of any attempt of these three groups to unify to create a country of their own. This united front seemed unlikely, given the evidence:

> So strong were traditional Kurdish tribal rivalries that one tribal leader's decision to join a nationalist uprising often prompted another to remain aloof or even accept arms and money to fight for the government. Even clans within a given tribe have ended up fighting each other. . . . But Kurdish history is also replete with Kurds betraying fellow Kurds. This cast of warring stock characters at times starred illiterate tribal leaders arrayed against the urban intelligentsia as well as villains drawn from both categories and willing to play the government's game for their own short-term tactical purposes.

Three nationalist groups emerged: Kurdistan Democratic Party (KDP) in Iraq, initially led by Mullah Mustafa Barzani and later by his son, Massoud; Patriotic Union of Kurdistan (PUK), led by Jalal Talabani; and Kurdistan Workers Party (PKK) in Turkey, led by Abdullah Öcalan. These groups participated in warfare against one another, but in 1991, the KDP and PUK did organize genuinely free elections, agreeing to split power when the results were inconclusive. By 1994, however, the two groups resumed their feuding, the results being disastrous. Amnesty International reported in February 1995 that both the KDP and PUK were "fully responsible" for most of the abuses: torture and arbitrary arrest; deliberate killing of political opponents, peaceful demonstrators, and rival militiamen captured in battle; and the "abandonment of fundamental human rights principles to which the Kurdish leadership had committed itself."

Randal dips into earlier centuries, expressing a long tradition of nationalist spirit and revolts. Examples in the 20th century abound: In early 1925, Sheikh Said of Piram led a short-lived revolt in Turkish Kurdistan, covering a third of the region; he and four dozen lieutenants paid "on the gallows." Before the harsh, specially instituted

> Independence Tribunal was disbanded two years later, 7,440 Kurds were arrested and 660 executed. Hundreds of Kurdish villages were burned, and between 40,000 and 250,000 peasants died, in the ensuing "pacification."

Over the next dozen years or so, perhaps a million Kurdish men, women, and children were uprooted and shipped to western Anatolia. Sixteen more Kurdish revolts in Turkey ensued at irregular intervals over the next decade and a half, and all of them were brutally repressed.

In August 1945, Mullah Mustafa Barzani led a general revolt that initially gained considerable success against Iraqi troops. However, after rival tribes were paid off to join the Iraqis, "Barzani's forces—some ten thousand followers, a third of which were fighters—retreated into Iran." Fighting between Barzani forces and the government started again in September 1961 and lasted until 1975, excepting periods of extended cease-fires. In May 1966, facing a major offensive to deprive him of vital logistical access to Iran, Barzani won his most important victory at Mount Hendrin; however, peace talks failed because Barzani refused to negotiate if Talabani was a participant. When fighting resumed in 1969, Saddam Hussein having achieved power, the Iraqi forces again were defeated. Subsequently, on March 11, 1970, Iraqi president Ahmed Hassan al-Bahr announced Iraqi recognition of "the existence of the Kurdish nation." The Kurds, however, were outmaneuvered several years later, in 1974. The fifth Kurdistan war erupted in response to Baghdad's having reclaimed much of the Kurdish area. "The fighting was by far the most devastating and demoralizing yet, prompting an agonizing reappraisal in Kurdish nationalist ranks. Barzani's [guerrillas] from the start gave up ground, abandoning more territory in six months than the government had controlled since 1961," writes Randal.

During the 1991 Persian Gulf War to rescue Kuwait from Hussein's occupation, which had occurred on August 2, 1990, U.S. president George H. W. Bush, on February 15, 1991, urged the Iraqi military and the Iraqi people "to take matters into their own hands." Yet, in the weeks before and during the invasion, the Bush administration had not consulted or coordinated with the Kurds. After the American-led coalition forces had liberated Kuwait and abruptly ended hostilities, "from President Bush on down, no one in the administration made any pretense of hiding the fact that its number-one priority . . . was to declare victory and ship the troops home," based, as Randal notes, on a fear of getting involved in a Vietnam-type situation. Despite repeated protestations by the Bush administration that it had misled no one, "Talabani said, the Kurds had been set up by the Bush administration. First, Washington encouraged them to revolt, then by not shooting down the helicopter gunships gave Iraq the green light to attack Kurdistan." In the aftermath, Hussein put down a Shia uprising in the south (U.S. troops actually stood by as Iraqi army units moved in) and then crushed the Kurd insurrection in the north. Once again the United States had let the Kurds down.

In the book the United States and specifically Presidents George H. W. Bush and Richard Nixon and National Security Advisor/Secretary of State Henry Kissinger are significantly criticized regarding two other situations: humanitarian aid to the Kurds in the post–Persian Gulf War period and the May 1972 arms deal with Iran. In the first, humanitarian aid was delayed, despite "tireless lobbying" by U.S. ambassador to Turkey Morton J. Abramowitz; calls from the British, French, and other European allies, including Turkey; domestic critics; and mounting evidence of need.

> Among the Kurds, exhaustion, exposure, not to mention lack of food, clean water, and sanitation, produced epidemics of diarrhea, dysentery, and other communicable diseases. The death toll rapidly mounted, although probably never reaching the sustained rate that American officials and a U.N. spokesman in Iran in late April estimated at 1,000 to 2,000 a day. Most of the victims were under five or elderly. U.S. health authorities estimated that 6,700 Iraqi Kurds along the Turkish border died during the three weeks of exodus—which was 6,200 more than would have been considered normal in northern Iraq. The U.N. High Commissioner for Refugees estimated that 12,600 of the Kurds who sought refuge in Iran also succumbed.

It was not until "April 16, more than two weeks after the exodus began, [that] Bush reversed himself," having been "forced to consider abandoning his stubborn heartless refusal to deal with the Kurds."

Comparably, Nixon and Kissinger, during a 22-hour stopover in Tehran, gave the shah of Iran a free hand to purchase U.S. military weapons, reversing two U.S. policies: discouraging the shah's military and geopolitical ambitions and opposing aid to Barzani's rebellious Kurds.

> Leaked in early 1976, [the report of the Select Committee on Intelligence, chaired by Otis G. Pike] revealed how the Shah, with American connivance, first inveigled Barzani to resume hostilities against Iraq, while purposely depriving the Kurds of the wherewithal to win, then, (without a peep out of Washington) abruptly abandoned them to Baghdad's tender mercies when he got what he wanted in March 1975. The report concluded that for Tehran and Washington the Kurds were never more than a "card to play," a "uniquely useful tool for weakening" Iraq's "potential for international adventurism."

Barzani's forces experienced one of the most decisive defeats in history, having been "driven into the trap laid by the Shah and Washington." Randal calls it "a textbook case of betrayal and skullduggery," principally naming Kissinger.

Toward the end of the Iran-Iraq War, 1980–88, the tide of battle having turned against Iran, Saddam Hussein turned against the Iraqi Kurds, labeled "saboteurs" and "traitors," with repeated use of chemical weapons, starting in April 1987, against civilians and guerrilla soldiers. Over a period of a year and a half, his regime gassed at least 60 villages. At Halabjah in March 1988, thousands of Kurdish civilians succumbed to chemical weapons, thousands more died in the final months before the August 20 cease-fire, and thousands more died afterward. Although Secretary of State George P. Shultz issued a rebuke denouncing the use of these weapons as "unjustifiable and abhorrent" and "unacceptable to the civilized world," "Washington took no punitive action against Saddam Hussein's use of poison gas." The flight of 60,000 Iraqi Kurds in August 1988 across the border into Turkey at last obligated Western governments to react. Other tactics used by Hussein included reneging on agreements with Kurdish leaders when his regime gained strength, "attempted assassinations, the razing of villages, and collective deportation to the south." Also, in July 1983, "he rounded up between five thousand and eight thousand Barzani males—a few under ten, but most aged fifteen or more, including forty-two of Massoud's close relatives—and they were never seen again."

Meanwhile, Israel's "periphery policy" was designed to create problems for Arab regimes in order to give Israel space; it involved clandestine contacts with non-Arab minorities inside Arab countries and with non-Arab Muslim states. In the mid-1960s it helped Barzani with Iran's approval, which also provided aid, in conducting a war against Iraq. Israel supplied money, weapons, ammunition, military advisers, training, agriculture experts, doctors, dentists, and a field hospital. The Kurds' 1961 Mount Hendrin victory—the destruction of an entire Iraqi brigade, a hundred Iraqi tanks in half an hour—resulted from an ambush devised by Israel's colonel Tsuri Saguy. The betrayal occurred in 1975. An agreement between Iran and Iraq, announced on March 6, caused the abrupt withdrawal of Iranian support troops, artillery, and antiaircraft guns. The Israeli team also departed immediately. Unwarned, the Kurds were left at risk: "hundreds of Iraqi Kurds were massacred and thousands driven into exile either in Iran or in arid southern Iraq." In 1991 Massoud Barzani "made [it] clear that he believed . . . that the Israeli connection had led his father, his tribe, his family, his party, and the Iraqi Kurds in their entirety down a disastrous path."

Modern Turkey's basic policy after the creation of the Turkish Republic was to deny the Turkish Kurds their culture, their language, and their political identity—indeed, their identity. A policy of assimilation—"turkification"—was pursued, while those who lived in the east and southeast were referred to as "mountain Turks." This denial of their existence—the Kurdish minority, the largest in any state, is estimated at 20 percent of the Turkish population—did not quell the nationalist fervor of the Turkish Kurds.

At the end of the 20th century the Kurdistan Workers Party (PKK), led by Öcalan, mounted in 1984 an insurrection to achieve independence. Turkey had "heavy-handed[ly] suppressed one Kurdish revolt after another": "Some 3,200 Kurds disappeared in 1993 and 1994 in so-called mystery killings, which foreign and Turkish human rights activists nonetheless often linked with officially protected death squads." In March 1993, Öcalan, encouraged by Jalal Talabani, proposed a cease-fire, promising that his guerrillas would fight only in self-defense, instead opting for a negotiated settlement. Öcalan's published demands no longer included self-determination; rather, his goals shifted to "cultural freedoms and the right to broadcast in Kurdish, abolition of the village guards, lifting of the emergency regulations, and 'recognition of the political rights of the Kurdish organizations.' " Unfortunately, Prime Minister and President Turgut Özal, who reportedly was ready to participate in the negotiation, died on April 17 of a heart attack. With no evidence of Turkish willingness to proceed and parliament hawks announcing that the state would never negotiate with terrorists, the cease-fire broke down.

Randal's sympathy aside, his accumulated portrait of the Kurdish people, principally those from Iraq, reveals them as he sees them. Witness these snippets: "At first glance, many Kurdish acts of resistance and heroism by themselves impress, then, all too often, detailed examination reveals repeated faultlines"; "Never a politically unified people, they have suffered greatly from deep divisions and an entrenched penchant for treachery in their own ranks;" "the Kurds are both stubborn survivors and steady losers, likable for their warmth, humor, courage and charm and distinguished by a streak of unpredictable violence." Their naiveté and humanitarianism are evident, as is their personal and tribal loyalty, their constancy toward their nationalist ideals, exhibiting a dogged persistence. Evident also is their seeming inability to learn from their mistakes and to perceive potential, or even probable, disastrous outcomes and act accordingly—that is, their misjudgment and intransigence. The internecine fighting between the KDP and the PUK time and again is witness to these traits.

CENSORSHIP HISTORY

Abdullah Keskin, a Turkish publisher of Kurdish extraction, was charged in 2002—his trial opened on April 3—with "Separatist propaganda through publication in order to sabotage the indivisible integrity of the state and nation of the Republic of Turkey," a crime under Article 8 of Turkey's Anti-Terror Law. (He had faced criminal charges five times in 1999 and twice in 2001 for publishing historical and academic books that referred to the Kurds' struggle to maintain their identity, language, and traditions.) The Turkish edition of *After Such Knowledge* had been issued in 2001 and confiscated on January 15, 2002, by order of a state security court. Keskin faced a sentence of up to three years in prison or a $2,500 fine.

The accusation refers to pages where the words *Turkish Kurdistan* are mentioned, which is a taboo in Turkey, and concludes: "This book taken as a whole constitutes separatist propaganda by evoking a distinct Kurdish nation and a state of Kurdistan within the territory of the Republic of Turkey, by mentioning provinces and districts within the territory of the state of the Republic of Turkey and by in a certain way drawing a map of Kurdistan." Examples of offending passages are the following:

> On page 22, ". . . then following the meandering Tigris river through endless plains to Diyarbakir, the unofficial capital of Turkish Kurdistan."

On page 23, "I've been awakened at dawn in a cheap city hotel in Turkish Kurdistan by sustained shooting only a few hundred yards away, then watched Turkish security forces go through neighborhood after neighborhood with all the violent efficiency of colonial troops answerable to no one. I've trudged through winter snows along smugglers' mountain paths to listen to the nationalist fervor lurking beneath the relentlessly inculcated, half-baked Marxism of young, jejune Turkish Kurds who would have died by the thousands for an independent state."

On page 25, "At one recent point, Kurds in Iran, Iraq, and Turkey were all in simultaneous but noncoordinated revolt. . . . In 1991, the first Kurds in seven decades were elected to Turkey's parliament as genuine representatives of Kurdish interests. Unsurprisingly, they lacked sufficient political skills to avoid isolation, arrest and imprisonment at the hands of a government dominated by Turkey's armed forces. Their inexperience inadvertently helped prolong the very conflict in Turkish Kurdistan that they had hoped to end."

On page 27, "Modern Turkey has pursued policies aimed at obliterating the Kurds' cultural as well as political identity for more than 70 years. In March 1924, less than a year after the creation of Mustafa Kemal Ataturk's Turkish Republic, Kurdish culture, language, and even place-names were banned. Elevated to dogma was the assimilationist credo that any Kurd outside physical Kurdistan accepted the regime's central ideological objective of 'turkification' and in effect ceased being a Kurd, or, at least, a nationalist Kurd. . . . For decades Turkey insisted that the Kurds were 'mountain Turks' who lived in the 'east and southeast,' not in any Kurdistan."

On page 309, "All these hopes evaporated as successive governments after 1984 failed to end a burgeoning and ever more expensive civil war in Turkish Kurdistan."

An amicus curiae brief was submitted by four press freedom groups—the Committee to Protect Journalists, the World Press Freedom Committee, the Independent Journalism Foundation, and the Reporters Committee for Freedom of the Press—in support of Keskin. It argued that the prosecution of Keskin violates Article 10 of the European Convention on Human Rights of which Turkey is a signatory, and thus is illegal. Further, the brief stated, "The European Court for Human Rights has held repeatedly that simply describing, explaining or providing opinions on the Kurdish situation in southeastern Turkey cannot constitute a risk substantial enough to outweigh the rights of the publisher and the public to free expression."

On July 31, 2002, the Istanbul State Security Court sentenced Abdullah Keskin to six months in jail but then converted the sentence to a fine of

830 million Turkish lira (about $500). Keskin's attorney indicated that the sentence would be appealed and that a complaint would be lodged with the European Court of Human Rights. The book remained banned after the trial.

The International Freedom to Publish Committee selected Keskin as the 2005 recipient of the Jeri Laber International Freedom to Publish Award. He was recognized for his long commitment to Kurdish writings in the face of great political obstacles—and personal peril—over the past decades.

FURTHER READING

Riding, Alan. "Book by American Leads to Charge Against a Turk." *New York Times,* July 21, 2002, sec. 1, p. 12.
"Turkish Publisher Fined for U.S. Book on Kurdish Conflict." Agence France Presse (August 2, 2002).
"Unofficial Translation of Turkish Indictment Against Abdullah Keskin." Committee to Protect Journalists CPJ News Alert 2002. Available online. URL: http://www.cpj.org/news/2002/Turkey03apr02na.html. Accessed September 16, 2010.

THE AGE OF KEYNES

Author: Robert Lekachman
Original date and place of publication: 1966, United States
Publisher: Random House
Literary form: Nonfiction

SUMMARY

This study is divided into two parts, their titles revealing the book's structure and content: "Keynes and Keynesian Economics" offers a biographical sketch representing John Maynard Keynes's early life, focusing on the evolution of his theories, and the General Theory itself; several chapters reflect its application. "The Keynesian Era" provides four chapters that discuss economic issues and events in relation to Keynesian principles and practices.

After graduating from Cambridge University, Keynes served initially in the British civil service in the India Office and then as a lecturer at Cambridge. His writings that applied economic theory to practical problems brought him recognition; during World War I, after publishing two articles on war finance, he was appointed to the Treasury Office. Rising rapidly through the ranks, at the end of the war he served as Treasury's representative to the Paris Peace Conference. Keynes became convinced that the evolving treaty was unjust, unworkable, indeed, potentially calamitous. He resigned his office and published in 1919 *Economic Consequences of the Peace,* his indictment of the Versailles settlement and its lead negotiators. It and he were both condemned and acclaimed. The result: Keynes became a pariah to government service, a situation that lasted until World War II.

Early in the intervening years, Keynes was awarded a chair in economics at Cambridge. As a faculty member and in publications, he began to delineate his economic principles, which were predictive of his later theories. In 1931, in *Essays in Persuasion*, he expressed his concerns about inflation: "There is no subtler, no surer means of overturning the existing basis of Society than to debauch the currency." Expressing, however, the active role of government in economic expansionism, he favored the proposal of Lloyd George to establish a public works program to promote employment, denouncing the existing government doctrine that employment could not be created by borrowing and expending funds by the state. This position was a precursor to his theory of aggregate demand espoused in the General Theory. In other essays, he hints at the need for government regulations because he perceived large corporations taking on "the status of public corporations rather than that of the individualistic private enterprise," whose managers would value "the general stability and reputation of the institution" rather than "the maximum of profit for the share holders." Keynes further hints at the use of regulation in the economy as he sees corporations not operating efficiently. He also promotes the idea of a central bank—control of currency and credit by a central agency, coordinated activity to solve investment and savings disequilibriums.

The General Theory of Employment, Interest and Money, one of the more influential 20th-century books, was published in 1936. According to Robert Lekachman, Keynes rewrote the "content of economics" and had a "liberating impact" on public policy. "Keynes informed the world that fatalism toward economic depression, mass unemployment, and idle factories was wrong." He argued against the assumption that competitive markets had the ability to expand employment and production through flexible prices. For Keynes, prices were not flexible; thus, it is possible for the economy to settle into equilibrium below full employment. As a result, in the face of economic downturn, aggregate demand would not be restored through lower prices (as Say's Law of Markets suggests). Keynes insisted that government had the responsibility to play an active role to boost aggregate demand and to restore the economy to full employment (or capacity).

What emerges from the General Theory (in contrast to orthodoxy) is the concept that aggregate demand plays a dominant role in the determination of employment and income in the short term. Along with this emphasis on aggregate demand, Keynes posits that in addition to the full-employment equilibrium, the economy may settle into many possible equilibriums that are below full employment. In fact, he points out that Say's Law—which affirmed only one possible equilibrium (full-employment equilibrium)—is only a special case. Thus, Keynes's theory is the "General Theory."

The core of Keynes's theory of aggregate demand is his theory of consumption, as expressed in his Fundamental Psychological Law, which states "that men are disposed, as a rule and on the average, to increase their consumption as their income increases but not by as much as the increase in their income." That is, as income increases so does consumption; however, a portion of that increased income goes to savings. Important here is the emphasis on income, not prices, in the determination of consumption and savings.

Investment is another key component in the Keynesian system. He saw the need for a healthy private sector. Applying the multiplier concept (developed several years earlier by R. F. Kahn—it acknowledges a proportionate increase in national income with each stage of consumption) increases in investment spur multiplied increases in income; that is, a new investment provides income equal in size to the investment, but as the recipients of that income spend it, the national income increases by a multiplication factor.

Keynes proposed a public policy shift: public spending financed by government deficits. An activist government was required to stabilize the economy; flexible prices could not be relied on. This proposal was argued in relation to the understanding that "unemployment and depression were consequences of a deficiency of aggregate demand for goods and services." Increasing government expenditure would result in employment, which would lead to further output and labor. Keynes favored projects of social utility, but he recognized that "pyramid building," earthquakes, and wars would have the effect of increasing national wealth in desperate times (e.g., the Great Depression). While critics argued he was promoting policies anathema to free markets (capitalism), Keynes saw himself as promoting policies that would save capitalism.

The three succeeding chapters of *The Age of Keynes* express the influence of Keynesian economics during the Roosevelt New Deal administrations in attempting to reverse the 1930s depression, during World War II and subsequent to the war. Evaluated from a Keynesian perspective, the Roosevelt administrations' policies are perceived as "too timid, too wavering, and too often contradicted by other measures. . . ." When Keynes's principles were employed, the effects were positive, as in the deficit spending practices of the Works Progress Administration. The war period, however, effectively demonstrated the effect of greatly increased government expenditures in stimulating the economy. Postwar policies of the Eisenhower administrations reduced the application of Keynes's principles, resulting in unemployment and semistagnation, until they were reasserted in 1961–62 by the Kennedy administration, the economy falling and rising accordingly.

The postwar decades are the "Age of Keynes"; though not universally applied, his theory was to be reckoned with. In the second part of the book, the author discusses its relevance to new problems in the postwar decades: growth of the population and the economy, automation and its effect on unemployment and modern inflation (as differentiated from classic inflation). The text's concluding chapter, "The Triumph of an Idea," looks to the fiscal policy of the future. The author's enthusiasm for Keynes's doctrines is manifest both in its specific formulations and in its general "search for increased rationality in economic policy. In its contemporary applications, Keynesian economics is essentially a description of the ways in which an alert government, by taking thought, can tame the business cycle and alleviate the miseries of personal insecurity."

CENSORSHIP HISTORY

The Age of Keynes by Robert Lekachman was one of four books challenged and temporarily censored by the board of education of Roselle, New Jersey, in 1972. This event is detailed in the discussion of THE AFFLUENT SOCIETY by John Kenneth Galbraith.

FURTHER READING

Cohen, Robert. "Educational Groups Deplore Roselle Book Ban." *Newark Star-Ledger,* June 23, 1972, p. 17.

———. "Roselle Board President Defends Book Bannings." *Newark Star-Ledger,* June 15, 1972, p. 11.

———. "State Education Official Assails Book Bannings." *Newark Star-Ledger,* June 27, 1972, p. 15.

Moffatt, George. "Book 'Ban' Challenged in Roselle." *Newark Star-Ledger,* June 28, 1972, p. 18.

———. "Roselle Will Buy 'Banned' Books and 4 'Balancers.'" *Newark Star-Ledger,* July 6, 1972, p. 20.

"A School Board Head in Jersey Orders 'Liberal' Books Deleted." *New York Times,* June 18, 1972, p. 50.

"Success Stories." *Newsletter on Intellectual Freedom* 21 (1972): 147.

ALL QUIET ON THE WESTERN FRONT

Author: Erich Maria Remarque
Original dates and places of publication: 1928, Germany; 1929, United States
Publishers: Impropylaen-Verlag; Little, Brown and Company
Literary form: Novel

SUMMARY

He fell in October 1918, on a day that was so quiet and still on the whole front, that the army report confined itself to the single sentence: All quiet on the Western Front.

He had fallen forward and lay on the earth as though sleeping. Turning him over one saw that he could not have suffered long; his face had an expression of calm, as though almost glad the end had come.

This final passage of Remarque's renowned novel enunciates not only the irony of death of this unknown soldier, but also the irony of the wartime communiques that announced that there was nothing new to report while thousands were wounded and dying daily. (The German title of the novel, *Im Westen nichts neues*, translates as "nothing new in the West.") The final passage also signals the irony of the title, a bitterness that pervades the entire work.

There are many unknown soldiers in the novel on both sides of the trenches. They are the bodies piled three deep in the shell craters, the mutilated bodies thrown about in the fields, the "naked soldier squatting in the fork of a tree . . . his helmet on, otherwise he is entirely unclad. There is one half of him sitting there, the top half, the legs are missing." There is the young Frenchman in retreat who lags behind and then is overtaken, "a blow from a spade cleaves through his face."

The unknown soldiers are background. The novel focuses on Paul Baumer, the narrator, and his comrades of the Second Company, chiefly Albert Kropp, his close friend, and Stanislaus Katczinsky, the leader of the group. Katczinsky (Kat) is 40 years old; the others are 18 and 19. They are ordinary folk: Muller, who dreams of examinations; Tjaden, a locksmith; Haie Westhus, a peatdigger; and Detering, a peasant.

The novel opens five miles behind the front. The men are "at rest" after 14 days on the front line. Of the 150 men to go forward, only 80 have returned. A theme—and the tone of disillusionment—is introduced immediately, the catalyst being the receipt of a letter from Kantorek, their former schoolmaster. It was he who had urged them all to volunteer, causing the hesitant ones to feel like cowards.

> For us lads of eighteen [adults] ought to have been mediators and guides to the world of maturity. . . . in our hearts we trusted them. The idea of authority, which they represented, was associated in our minds with greater insight and a manlier wisdom. But the first death we saw shattered this belief. . . . The first bombardment showed us our mistake, and under it the world as they had taught it to us broke in pieces.

This theme is repeated in Paul's conversation with adults at home during a leave. They evince deep ignorance of the nature of trench warfare and the living conditions and the dying. "Naturally it's worse here. Naturally. The best for our soldiers. . . ." They argue about what territories ought to be annexed and how the war should be fought. Paul is unable to speak the truth to them.

Vignettes of the solders' lives pile up in the first several chapters: inhumane treatment of the recruits at the hands of a militaristic, rank-conscious corporal; the painful death of a schoolmate after a leg amputation; the meager food often in limited supply; the primitive housing; and glimpses of the fear and horror, the cries and explosions of the front. The experienced men reveal their distance from their youth, not merely the trench warfare smarts in contrast to the innocent unready replacement recruits. Gone was the "ideal and almost romantic character" of the war. They recognized that the "classical conception of the Fatherland held by our teachers resolved itself here into a renunciation of personality." They have been cut off from their youth and from the opportunity of growing up naturally; they cannot conceive a future.

After a major battle, Paul narrates: "Today we would pass through the scenes of our youth like travellers. We are burnt up by hard facts; like trades-men we understand distinctions, and like butchers, necessities. We are no longer untroubled—we are indifferent. We long to be there; but could we live there?"

Paul experiences the depths of this alienation during his leave. Beyond recognition and a vivid yearning, he knows he is an outsider. He cannot get close to his family; of course, he is unable to reveal the truth of his terror-filled experiences, so he cannot seek their comfort. Sitting in the arm-chair in his room, his books before him, he tries to recapture the past and imagine the future. His comrades at the front seem the only reality.

Rumors of an offensive turn out to be true. They are accompanied by a high double-wall stack of yellow, unpolished, brand-new coffins and extra issues of food. When the enemy bombardment comes, the earth booms and heavy fire falls on them. The shells tear down the parapet, root up the embankment and demolish the upper layers of concrete. The rear is hit as well. A recruit loses control and must be forcibly restrained. The attack is met by machine-gun fire and hand grenades. Anger replaces fear.

> No longer do we lie helpless, waiting on the scaffold, we can destroy and kill, to save ourselves, to save ourselves and be revenged . . . crouching like cats we run on, overwhelmed by this wave that bears us along, that fills us with feroc-ity, turning us into thugs, into murderers, into God only knows what devils; this wave that multiplies our strength with fear and madness and greed of life, seeking and fighting for nothing but our deliverance. If your own father came over with them you would not hesitate to fling a bomb into him.

Attacks alternate with counterattacks and "slowly the dead pile up in the field of craters between the trenches." When it is over and the company is relieved, only 32 men answer the call.

In another situation the relative anonymity of trench warfare is erased. On patrol to scout out the enemy lines, Paul becomes separated from his own troops and finds himself in French territory. He hides in a shell hole, surrounded by exploding shells and sounds of activity. He is strained to the utmost, armed with fear and a knife. When a body crashes in upon him, he automatically slashes at and then shares the shell hole with the dying Frenchman who has become a person. He tries to dress the stab wounds. He is devoured by guilt:

> Comrade, I did not want to kill you. If you jumped in here again, I would not do it, if you would be sensible too. But you were only an idea to me before, an abstraction that lived in my mind and called forth its appropriate response. It

was that abstraction I stabbed. But now, for the first time, I see you are a man like me. I thought of your hand grenades, of your bayonet, of your rifle; now I see your wife and your face and our fellowship. Forgive me, comrade. We always see it too late.

There is a respite for the company, and then it is sent out to evacuate a village. During the march, both Paul and Albert Kropp are wounded, Albert seriously. Hospitalized, they fear the amputation-prone doctors; Kropp loses his leg; he does not want to live a "cripple." Paul hobbles around the hospital during his recovery, visiting the wards, increasingly aware of shattered bodies:

And this is only one hospital, one single station; there are hundreds of thousands in Germany, hundreds of thousands in France, hundreds of thousands in Russia. How senseless is everything that can be written, done, or thought, when such things are possible. It must all be lies and of no account when the culture of a thousand years could not prevent this stream of blood being poured out, these torture-chambers in their hundreds of thousands. A hospital alone shows what war is.

Back at the front the war continues, death continues. One by one the circle of comrades is killed. Detering, maddened for home by the sight of a cherry tree in bloom, attempts to desert but is captured. Only Paul, Kat, and Tjaden are alive. In the late summer of 1918 Kat sustains a leg injury; Paul attempts to carry him to a medical facility. Near collapse, he stumbles and falls as he reaches the dressing station. He rises only to discover that Kat is dead; en route he has sustained a splinter in the head.

In the autumn there is talk of peace and armistice. Paul meditates about the future:

And men will not understand us—for the generation that grew up before us, though it has passed these years with us here, already had a home and a calling; now it will return to its old occupations, and the war will be forgotten— and the generation that has grown up after us will be strange to us and push us aside. We will be superfluous even to ourselves, we will grow older, a few will adapt themselves, some others will merely submit, and most will be bewildered;—the years will pass by and in the end we shall fall into ruin.

CENSORSHIP HISTORY

When *All Quiet on the Western Front* was issued in Germany in 1928, National Socialism (Nazism) was already a powerful political force. In the social political context a decade after the war, the novel generated a strong popular response, selling 600,000 copies before it was issued in the United States, but it also generated significant resentment. It affronted the National Socialists, who read it as slanderous to their ideals of home and fatherland. This resentment led to political pamphleteering against it. It was banned in Germany in 1930. In 1933, all of Remarque's works were consigned to the infamous bonfires. On May 10, the first large-scale demonstration occurred in front of the University of Berlin: Students gathered 25,000 volumes of Jewish authors; 40,000 "unenthusiastic" people watched. Similar demonstrations took place at other universities; in Munich 5,000 children watched and participated in burning books labeled Marxist and un-German.

Remarque, who had not been silenced by the violent attacks against his book, published in 1930 a sequel, *The Road Back*. By 1932, however, he escaped Nazi harassment by moving to Switzerland and then to the United States.

Bannings occurred in other European countries. In 1929, Austrian soldiers were forbidden to read the book, and in Czechoslovakia it was barred from military libraries. In 1933 in Italy, the translation was banned because of its antiwar propaganda.

In the United States, in 1929, the publishers Little, Brown and Company acceded to suggestions of the Book-of-the-Month Club judges, who had chosen the novel as the club's June selection, to make some changes; they deleted three words, five phrases, and two entire episodes—one of makeshift latrine arrangements and the other a hospital scene during which a married couple, separated for two years, has intercourse. The publishers argued that "some words and sentences were too robust for our American edition" and that without the changes there might be conflict with federal law and certainly with Massachusetts law. A spokesperson for the publisher explained:

> While it was still being considered by the [BOMC's] judges, the English edition was published, and while most of the reviews were favorable in the extreme, two or three reviewers condemned the book as coarse and vulgar. We believe that it is the greatest book about the war yet written, and that for the good of humanity it should have the widest possible circulation; we, therefore, concluded that it might be best not to offend the less sophisticated of its potential public and were, therefore, wholly satisfied to make the changes suggested by the Book-of-the-Month Club after the judges had unanimously voted for the book.

Another kind of publisher's censorship was revealed by Remarque himself. Putnam's had rejected the book in 1929, despite the evidence of its considerable success in Europe. According to the author, writing decades later, "some idiot said he would not publish a book by a 'Hun.' "

Nevertheless, despite its having been expurgated, *All Quiet on the Western Front* was banned in Boston in 1929 on grounds of obscenity. In the same year, in Chicago, U.S. Customs seized copies of the English translation, which had not been expurgated. Lee Burress, in *Battle of the Books: Literary Censorship in the Public Schools, 1950–1985*, reveals challenges on the grounds of its being "too violent" and for its depiction of war as "brutal and dehumanizing." A more recent example is identified in *Attacks on Freedom to Learn, 1987–1988*, the annual survey of school censorship of People For the American Way, in which the charge was "foul language" (California). The suggestion is, however, that censors have shifted their tactics, using these charges instead of such traditional accusations as "globalism" or "far-right scare words." It is identified in *The Encyclopedia of Censorship* as one of the "most often" censored books.

The 1930 U.S. film, *All Quiet on the Western Front*, acclaimed as one of the greatest antiwar films and the winner of Oscars for best film and best director, has been both banned and significantly expurgated. The leaders of the Reichswehr, the German army, protested its being filmed because of the negative portrayal of the army. On the opening night of its screening, December 5, 1930, brown-shirted Nazis demonstrated in the theater, causing the film not to be shown. This event and others on succeeding days, all orchestrated by Joseph Goebbels, effectively barred the screenings. While the German Left applauded the film, criticism by the political Right was "intense and uncompromising"; the Nazis identified the film as a "Jewish lie" and labeled it a "hate-film slandering the German soldier." A cabinet crisis ensued; within a week the film was banned for the reason that it "removed all dignity from the German soldier" and perpetuated a negative stereotype. According to historian Joel Simmons, nationalistic critics focused on "the film's anti-war theme and its characterization of German soldiers and the German army. In effect they condemned the film for being true to the novel. To them, its portrayal of German soldiers as frightened by their first exposure to gunfire and so disillusioned by the battlefield carnage as to question their superiors and the ultimate purpose of the war, denigrated the bravery and discipline of German fighting men and undermined the nation's confidence in its armed forces." Parallel reactions in Austria led to violent street confrontations after the film's preview on January 3, 1931; on January 10 it was banned. It was also denied exhibition in Hungary, Bulgaria, and Yugoslavia. However, in September 1931 as a result of a changed political situation, authorities in Germany permitted a moderately edited *All Quiet on the Western Front* to be screened; there were no demonstrations or evident outrage.

Universal Studios began cutting the film as early as 1933, removing important scenes in the United States and abroad, these exclusions resulting from censorship, politics, time constraints (to shorten the film so that it would fit into a double bill), and film exhibitors' whims. When *All Quiet on the Western Front* was reissued in 1939 as an anti-Hitler film, it included narration about the Nazis. Another version added music at the film's conclusion, a segment that was originally silent.

FURTHER READING

Attacks on Freedom to Learn: 1987–1988. Washington, D.C.: People For the American Way, 1988.

Burress, Lee. *Battle of the Books: Literary Censorship in the Public Schools, 1950–1985.* Metuchen, N.J.: Scarecrow Press, 1989.

"Censorship Continues Unabated; Extremists Adapt Mainstream Tactics." *Newsletter on Intellectual Freedom* 37 (1988): 193.

Geller, Evelyn. *Forbidden Books in American Public Libraries, 1876–1939: A Study in Cultural Change.* Westport, Conn.: Greenwood Press, 1984.

Green, Jonathon, and Nicholas J. Karolides, reviser. *The Encyclopedia of Censorship, New Edition.* New York: Facts On File, 2005.

Haight, Anne L., and Chandler B. Grannis. *Banned Books: 387 B.C. to 1978 A.D.* 4th ed. New York: R. R. Bowker, 1978.

Hansen, Harry. "The Book That Shocked a Nation." In *All Quiet on the Western Front,* by Erich Maria Remarque. New York: Heritage Press, 1969.

Simmons, Joel. "Film and International Politics: The Banning of *All Quiet on the Western Front.*" *Historian* 52, no. 1 (1999): 40–60.

Tebbel, John. *A History of Book Publishing in the United States.* Vol. 3. New York: R. R. Bowker, 1978.

AMERICA IN LEGEND

Author: Richard M. Dorson
Original date and place of publication: 1973, United States
Publisher: Pantheon Books
Literary form: Nonfiction

SUMMARY

America in Legend's subtitle, *Folklore from the Colonial Period to the Present,* reveals the nature of its content. Its intent, however, is deeper: to use folklore, as Dorson explains in his foreword, as "one means of redressing the inattention to the common folk in American life and history." History as it is generally written focuses on the elite, the major events and personalities; the lives of common men and women in relation to the cultural, economic, and social changes of their times are largely neglected. The thesis of this book is that "the vital folklore and especially the legends of a given period in American history reflect the main concerns and values, tensions and anxieties, goals and drives of the period. We may well find in the folk legends a statement of the common man's outlook denied us in conventional documents."

America in Legend is divided into four sections or periods, each representing a dominant lifestyle. A period's lifestyle is characterized by its dominant goals and aspirations as reflected in the "prevalent social philosophy, in the landmark writings, in the cultural and popular heroes, and in legends and folklore." In general terms "American lifestyle has sought to express a freedom of action and belief against an enemy of freedom, against the Establishment of its day."

The lifestyle of the colonial period is identified as oriented toward religion with the Church of England as the oppressor. This period extended from the first settlements through the mid-18th century. Comparable to the religions of the day, the folk legends and beliefs also were copies of English folklore though they expressed New World experiences. Two differences were the inclusion of Native Americans and the exclusion of the fairy belief, that is, such unnatural creatures as elves, sprites, and hobgoblins.

The folklore was used by the theocrats to uphold the mission of establishing a holy community in the wilderness and to demonstrate the Lord's support against their enemies, those with false doctrines, the savages, sinners and heretics, demons, witches, and Satan. The accepted folklore focused on providences, judgments, witchcraft, apparitions, specters, poltergeists, and compacts with the devil. A providence was an event affecting either the community at large or an individual, which held special meaning as a factor of God's will, expressing His pleasure or displeasure. Many providences incorporated supernatural beliefs—ghosts, witchcraft, the powers of the devil. Among the common motifs were lightning and thunder as evidence of God's intent; bloodstains or bleeding corpses; ghosts appearing to make known the circumstances of their deaths; and apparitions who make accusations of witches. Judgments are represented by the occasions when blasphemers are struck dumb or lifeless, adulterers are punished, and by various phenomena like earthquakes and deaths of livestock. Witchcraft, involving agreements between witches and the devil, reflected more complex episodes. These colonials saw witches as dangerous to the holy community. The witches had in their possession specters or devils with which they bewitched and tormented the innocent; they could also take on the shapes of innocent people and become invisible.

The early nationalist period stretches from the American Revolution to the Civil War and reflects the democratic impulse. The folklore of this period breaks away from English patterns, featuring regional types, urban and rural, reflecting American folk humor. Essentially the butt of this humor is the foppish, aristocratic upper-class type. Reflecting the thesis of Frederick Jackson Turner in "The Significance of the Frontier in American History" (the frontier shaped the American character and democratic institutions), these tales celebrated the daring, the prowess, and the achievements of the rustic common man.

The folktale patterns are represented by five personages, three of whom were real people, two of whom were created: Davy Crockett, the Tennessee backwoodsman who was first elected to the Tennessee legislature and then to Congress before fighting for Texas and dying at the Alamo; Mike Fink, a Mississippi keel-boatsman who also joined a fur trade enterprise to ascend the Missouri River; Sam Patch, who gained fame as a jumper from cliffs and bridges into rivers; Mose the Bowery B'hoy, a stage character modeled on a notorious Bowery brawler and volunteer fireboy; and Yankee Jonathan, a stereotyped figure representing the rustic New England farmer. Backwoods heroes, Crockett and Fink, are endowed with physical prowess and skills; fighters and marksmen, they become larger than life. Boasting exuberantly

(Crockett, a clever storyteller, boosted his own image), they are trickster heroes, using cunning and deception; they are, however, good-hearted and open-mannered. Comparably, Mose, at once tough, rough, and elegant, is a prankster, clown, and hero. He displays his prowess in fights and in fires—rescuing women, saving babies, outwitting villains. The Yankee farmer, a country bumpkin, is nevertheless clever and crafty. Though a figure of ridicule, inside his gawky appearance and his unsophisticated manner and speech, he is proudly independent and both morally strong and physically brave.

The hundred years from 1860 to 1960, the later national period, encompass the economic impulse.

> Folk legends have fastened onto the master workman, in his role as cowboy or lumberjack or railroad engineer, to the neglect of the captain of industry and the laborer on the assembly line. Something of the democratic, egalitarian spirit of the common man folk heroes of the early national period has transferred to the occupational heroes, but these later swashbucklers command attention, not for their eccentricities of character, but for their prodigies of work.

The choices of these, along with the miner and the oil driller, are a reflection of American history.

These men are revealed as fearless individualists with abundant skill and physical daring—sometimes self-sacrifice. They are proud of their abilities, hardworking, and loyal to their employers. The songs and tales, often borrowed from one occupation to another, reveal the occupational lives and habits of the men: the loneliness of the cowboy, his "he-man drinking and eating habits," his gambling and spending; the hardships faced by the lumbermen and oil drillers, their whiskey-fighting orgies when out of camp. Along with the attributes of fearlessness, pride, courage, and heroism, the miners' lore includes "a litany of hardship, deprivation, suffering, and despair, punctuated by mine disasters and strikes." An extension, emanating from discontent and frustration and the bitter, violent strikes, is the vision of the miner as hero fighting for his rights; the parallel opposite vision is of the miner as law-breaker and destroyer of life and property.

By the turn of the century, the tensions caused by shifting economic and occupational conditions are reflected in the folklore. The hero's image becomes besmirched. Casey Jones, the railroad hero who lost his life to save the crew and passengers, becomes a scab, a victim of labor's attitude toward the company man. Casey also, not uniquely among occupational folktypes, becomes a super-virile hero, a mighty lover. "Instead of representing the solid economic virtues of sobriety, piety, thrift, love of family, and support of church and community, he becomes the gay deceiver, the libertine and profligate. In this second role he does indeed represent the underside of the Gilded Age, the public and private immorality of the era."

The human impulse is the keystone of the contemporary period, beginning in the 1960s, initiated, in the author's mind, by the expression of the counterculture of the Berkeley free speech movement. "The folklore of the counterculture proves to be largely a druglore. Cycles of legends have grown around potheads and acidheads, narcs and busts." The lore presented is from the perspective of the "head" (a habitual drug user) community: dopers are the trickster-heroes. They are pitted against cops-narcs and other straight-world enemies, often in the stories getting the better of them, though at times getting busted. The cops are fooled and seen as fools. The doper is reaffirmed. Distinctions are drawn between hippies as drug users and pseudo hippies: The hippie values "the essential brotherhood of man, the sacredness of the individual, and the identification of the good by the simple sensation of feeling good. True hippies live in families, communes, and cooperatives"; the pseudohippie does not share these values.

Another facet of contemporary youth culture lore focuses on the draft dodger. As an antihero outwitting the establishment, the draft dodger assumes the role of clever trickster reminiscent of earlier folk heroes. This hero's confrontation is with the military personnel, outwitting them to avoid service in the military or to avoid a jail sentence. He is applauded while, comparable to the cop or narc, the system's representatives are fooled. "So in this spate of legendary tales the draft dodger takes his place with other admired antiheroes of the youth culture bucking with their wits and guts a relentless, implacable, but dull-minded System."

CENSORSHIP HISTORY

Local political figures and several parents of Cobb County, Georgia, instigated the charges against *America in Legend*. School officials removed several copies of the book from library shelves because of "objectionable" passages. Mary Lu Armstrong, supervisor of media and information services, who was in 1977 a middle school media specialist, recalls being "directed to remove the book from general circulation available to students and place it in the professional collection available only to teachers."

The concerns were twofold: Bobby Waters, former mayor of Power Springs, charged that the book "condones draft dodging" and is "terrible for children"; several parents and a former city councilman, Glen Thrash, objected to stanzas of the song "Casey Jones," which describe Jones's sexual prowess. Thrash compared *America in Legend* unfavorably to *Playboy*. When Thrash asked to read passages aloud at the Cobb County school board meeting, board member John McClure protested that this would "make more students want to read the book."

Subsequently, Waters asked the school board to hold "screening sessions" during the summer to "ferret out" any other objectionable books in the libraries. While the school board did not formally vote on this request, they took it "under advisement." McClure indicated he would try to have the board meet in the next month to review book-purchasing procedures. He declared that any book purchased in the future should be "reviewed in its entirety" because "you're going to get freaks in the American Library Association just like any place else" (a reference to the professional publications used as book review sources). The school district records do not reveal what steps were then taken.

FURTHER READING

Armstrong, Mary Lu. Letter to the author. December 19, 1994.
"Cobb County, Georgia." *Newsletter on Intellectual Freedom* 26 (1977): 133.
Crawford, Tom. "Ferret out Books, Cobb Board Told." *Atlanta Journal*, May 27, 1977, p. 8A.

AMERICAN CIVICS

Authors: William H. Hartley and William S. Vincent
Original date and place of publication: 1967, United States
Publisher: Harcourt Brace Jovanovich
Literary form: Textbook

SUMMARY

American Civics, a traditional textbook in its format, is organized into eight units, each subdivided into two to five chapters with appropriate pedagogical tools, including a "special feature," "What do you think?" Significant issues, such as "Women's Liberation," "Growing Old in America," and "Health Care: A Right or Luxury," are briefly explored. The authors, signaling that answers are not easily arrived at, ask a series of textual questions to provoke thought and debate.

"Citizenship in Our Democracy," Unit I, establishes who the people of the United States are, that is, where we have come from and how we become citizens. Immigration history has been long; initially narrow in its acceptance of people of the world, it has broadened. However, there has been bias in the past, notably, against American Indians, African Americans, and Chinese.

Another focus is government, its purposes and roles. The Constitution's ideal, "government by consent of the governed," serves as the keystone. The explanation of the federal system, the division of powers between the national and state governments, and the distribution of powers among the three branches of government reveal the checks and balances incorporated into the Constitution. The rights and freedoms of Americans, established by the Bill of Rights, are explained. Units II and III outline the workings of the federal, state, and local governments, illustrating the division and distribution of powers. Discussion of the federal government is more detailed, attention given to the committees of Congress, the president's cabinet, executive agencies, and the types of courts.

Citizenship, that is "The Citizen in American Government" and "Citizenship in Home, School and Community," is the focus of Units IV and V. An overview of the political two-party system, with historical reference points, provides a view of purposes and activities of the parties. Citizens participate in the political process, particularly as voters; they are also obliged to help pay for the costs of government through taxes.

Family citizenship is discussed in the context of changes that have occurred in family structures and relationships, as well as outside-the-home influences—schools, peers, and television. A parallel discussion of types of communities and their purposes and services establishes the critical roles citizens play in serving their communities.

Against a backdrop of the history and structure of the American school system and a broad expression of the goals of education, school citizenship is expressed as learning to think: how we think and how we learn to improve our thinking so we can understand and be resistant to propaganda. Censorship is identified as a potential tool for controlling propaganda but is perceived as dangerous in relation to the basic freedoms of speech and press. Articulated is the importance of learning about a variety of ideas and viewpoints and being able to think responsibly about them.

Unit VI addresses the American economy, that is, how it works. A key word is *free:* free enterprise, free competition among business firms, free markets, free competition among workers, freedom to earn profits, and freedom to acquire private property. The government role is that of "referee" in the economy because it makes some economic decisions, but most such decisions are made by individuals. Other aspects of the economic system discussed are the organization of American business, the system of mass production, money management, and credit.

The contradictions and challenges of the American economy are shown in the "pockets of poverty" in this "Land of Opportunity." While about half of the poor people live in urban areas, there are poor people in almost every part of the country. They are of all ages, almost half being under 21 years of age; nearly one of five persons over 65 years old is poor. The identified causes of poverty are lack of education or training; unemployment caused by changes in industry or slumps in the economy; discrimination; misuse of national resources; and old age, insufficient income, and illness. In this context government efforts to deal with poverty are presented, and the welfare system is discussed. Among the other challenges to the economy presented are the problems of labor and management, primarily an historical perspective; the farm problem, recognizing the plight of the small farmer and efforts to alleviate it; and the "boom or bust," inflation and depression, cycles of the economy.

A brief introduction to foreign policy makes up Unit VII. The role of the president and of Congress is presented along with the development of

American foreign policy. Highlighted are the isolationism of the first decades of the nation; the Monroe Doctrine; the "good neighbor" policy; and involvement in world affairs—the world wars, World War I having been followed by an isolationist stance, and the United Nations.

An brief introductory history of the Soviet Union and its communist system provides the background for the foreign policies of containment in Europe and, after the victory of communism, in China, Korea, and Vietnam. Discussed briefly are the "Truman Doctrine" of aid to countries threatened by communism and relief (through the Marshall Plan) to victims of World War II; the Peace Corps, proposed by President Kennedy; and the "Nixon Doctrine" of "limited withdrawal" from worldwide commitments.

The concluding unit, "Improving Life for All Americans," reveals some critical problems of American society. These cluster around three foci: urban living, social issues, and environmental pollution. In many respects American cities are in a crisis state. Utilities, such as electric power, water supply, sewage disposal, garbage and trash removal, and public transportation, are either in short supply or in need of major overhaul. Housing, particularly in inner-city (slum) areas, is rundown, dirty, and crowded; other problems are magnified in slum areas. Poverty is prevalent—unemployment is a constant; disease, overcrowded schools, insufficient child care facilities for working mothers, undernourished and neglected children, crime and violence, juvenile delinquency, and drugs are all pressing problems.

In the early 1970s, almost 6 million serious crimes were reported each year in the United States. There was a murder every thirty minutes, a robbery every 2 minutes, and an auto theft every ½ minute. On an average, ten crimes take place every minute of each day and night. The annual cost of these crimes is over $25 billion.

These statistics introduce the discussion of types of crime and juvenile delinquency. Also discussed are the role of police and the methods of punishing and treating lawbreakers.

Violence is another significant social concern. By definition and example, the authors distinguish among dissent, civil disobedience, and violence, the second being illustrated by John Peter Zenger in colonial times, Henry David Thoreau in 1849, and Rosa Parks in 1955. Urban riots and campus disorders in the 1960s are the points of comparison.

The drug abuse problem is similarly contrasted to the beneficial uses of drugs as medicine. Abusive drugs are briefly described, primary attention being given to narcotics, hallucinogens, depressants, stimulants, and marijuana. However, the problems of alcohol abuse and smoking are also introduced.

Health and safety, disease control, highway safety, and fire prevention are attended to with brief presentations of agencies that provide rules and prevention-inspection procedures. Health and safety of the planet—and, of course, its life-forms—are projected in discussions of air and water pollution. Human activities from cutting down forests to mistreating farm and ranch lands and misusing fertilizers and pesticides, have upset the balance of nature. The text concludes with discussions of methods of conservation of farmlands, controlling population, cleaning the air, and controlling water pollution.

CENSORSHIP HISTORY

American Civics was challenged in Mahwah, New Jersey, in September 1976 by several local residents and a school trustee. Trustee Richard Mech attacked the book, arguing that it "promotes socialized medicine and considers government a big machine with the people having no voice." He and several residents attested that it gives a distorted picture of American life. A contending opinion defended the emphasis on city life and problems.

The deciding vote on the issue was split, 4-4, in effect denying the use of *American Civics* as a textbook for ninth grade.

FURTHER READING

Dixon, Ron. "A Book Debate Splits Mahwah." *Paterson News*, September 14, 1976, p. 17.
"Mahwah, New Jersey." *Newsletter on Intellectual Freedom* 26 (1977): 8.

THE AMERICAN PAGEANT: A HISTORY OF THE REPUBLIC

Author: Thomas A. Bailey
Original date and place of publication: 1956, United States
Publisher: D.C. Heath and Company
Literary form: Textbook

SUMMARY

Thomas A. Bailey's foreword proposes a focus on the human actors in American history, his purpose being to stimulate a "sense of pleasure and excitement" and, more important, "to create a sympathetic understanding of the problems confronting our statesmen and to implant a more lively concern for the lessons of the past." He emphasizes causes and effects and underlying trends and movements.

As might be expected, the text is chronologically organized, encompassing "New World Beginnings" (chapter 1) through "Korea and the Challenge of the West" (chapter 46). The initial chapter expresses the activities of discovery and exploration, the Europeans seeking routes and establishing their claims to territory; though they are certainly critical actors in the text, the claims of the "Indians" to the lands are not identified, their rights not discussed. A European mind-set so revealed, the focus on the emergence of the United States is established. A final short chapter, "The Long View," expresses a sense of the future, that is, danger signals, dilemmas, and national and international issues.

The early strands plaited into the text are those of the tension between aristocracy and democracy, the rise of democracy and independence, the seeds of unity and the rebellious attitudes toward England and her aristocratic representatives. These are illustrated in the 1676 rebellion of angry Virginia backcountry men against the tidewater gentry; the ease with which persons might rise from a low to a high status; the rejection of doctrinaire states by outcasts and religious dissenters who formed the colonies of Rhode Island, North Carolina, and Pennsylvania; and the frequent quarrels with the Crown.

Intercolonial disunity persisted throughout the colonial period and the Revolution, but seeds of unity were planted by need. An early planting was the New England Confederation of 1643, "essentially an exclusive Puritan club," primarily intended as a defense measure. Later, notable instances grew out of the French and Indian Wars. Disunity, effected by distance, geographic barriers, varied religious and national origins, different types of government and social-economic class, was eroded by the coming together of statesmen and soldiers. The Revolution itself cultivated and nurtured the sense of unity.

The Revolution is described without patriotic blinders: the disunity of states regarding themselves as "sovereign"; the badly organized rebels—actually only a select minority; unreliable militiamen; American profiteers putting gold above patriotism; brutality against Loyalists, whose case as "tragic figures" is presented. The Second Continental Congress initially asked in 1775 for a redress of grievances, not independence. The idea of independence grew out of a realization of inconsistency of England's treatment of the colonies and the fiery pen of Thomas Paine in *Common Sense.*

Divisiveness did not disappear with either the signing of the Declaration of Independence or the adoption of the Articles of Confederation and subsequent ratification of the Constitution. Indeed, the opposing factions in the ratification struggle, representing those who favored a strong federal government and those who feared the loss of states' rights—the latter group joined by backcountry men, artisans, and other less educated persons who perceived the Constitution as a stratagem of aristocrats—evolved into the first political parties, the Federalists and the Democratic-Republicans. The North-South cleavage, evident in the colonial period, also reemerged in the debate over the Bank of the United States, with support coming from the commercial and financial centers of the North and opposition from the agricultural South. Thus, sectionalism—the North, the South, and the West—and the tension between states' rights and federal power have been constants in the American political spectrum. "Wild talk of secession" grew out of such differences, an early event emanating from New England Federalists' opposition to the War of 1812 and discontent with the operation of Congress. The doctrine of secession was also foreshadowed in 1828 by South Carolina's declaring (without formal endorsement) that it had the right to declare a tariff as null and void within its borders. This sense of the right of nullification was cultivated by other tariff issues and fertilized by the slavery issue. Its full blossoming occurred when South Carolina seceded in 1860, initiating the "save the Union" Civil War.

Nationalism has been an often passionate counterpoint. It served to discredit sectionalism and to foster unity. The "spirit of nation-consciousness or national oneness" was intensified by war emergencies and revitalized by war successes: The War of 1812 was an early case in point; World Wars I and II were 20th-century examples. The Civil War dramatically illustrates the conflict between national and state loyalties. Nationalism also was rooted in greater economic and political independence from Europe, in the development of American industry, in the transportation connections between states, and in Supreme Court rulings that promoted the precedence of the central government.

Upon the success of the Revolution, the United States was the black sheep in the fold of nations. "The most consistently dangerous 'isms' of the late 18th century, in the eyes of European royalty were American republicanism, constitutionalism, and liberalism." Political independence created by the Revolution and personal independence fostered by the frontier promoted international independence. Another factor was needed: survival and national protection. There were two sides to this coin: neutrality in the conflicts of Europe and resistance to foreign intervention on the American hemisphere. The former, proclaimed first by President George Washington, kept the United States essentially free of foreign entanglements and bred the strong and lasting strand of isolationism that has permeated American thought and policy. The latter, formally declared by President James Monroe, established a basic posture of defense and independence.

Political freedom effected by the Revolution and personal freedoms expressed by the Bill of Rights did not spell democracy. The framers of the Constitution, like their predecessors, were "well born" and conservative, "virtually unanimous in agreeing that manhood-suffrage democracy— government by 'democratick blabbers'—was something to be feared and guarded against." Voting was limited to males who owned property; only the House of Representatives was chosen by direct vote. President Thomas Jefferson advocated the rule of the people, but he did not include every adult white male—only those literate enough to inform themselves. By the 1820s and 1830s, a shift toward white male suffrage became pronounced; the impact of the western frontier states was felt, partly due to the availability of land, partly the result of the individualism and demands of the westerners. National women's suffrage was not granted by constitutional amendment until 1920, though the Territory of Wyoming granted unrestricted suffrage to women in 1869.

There were other democratic triumphs. The will to arbitrate and compromise preserved, excepting the Civil War, the union and the government during political crises. The Missouri Compromise of 1820, the reduction of the Tariff of 1832—both engineered by Senator Henry Clay—and the Compromise of 1877, which broke the election deadlock between Hayes and Tilden, are meaningful examples. Others arise out of efforts in behalf of the public welfare, notably by the administrations of Presidents Jefferson, Grover Cleveland, Woodrow Wilson, and Franklin D. Roosevelt.

However, the "cradle of democracy" was flawed. The aristocratic-commonfolk tension continued through the decades. With the election in 1828 of Jackson, the "view of the New Democracy that 'Every man is as good as his neighbor'—perhaps 'equally better' " took hold. Class differences, of course, did not die out, as represented by the plantation system's hierarchy of the South; such differences were also evident in the business-labor confrontations of the 20th century. Continuing racial discrimination reflects a comparable human flaw within democracy.

Another aspect of flawed democracy is the evidence of corruption in government and of public and private greed at the expense of the public domain. Particularly affected by the impact of cronyism were the administrations of Andrew Jackson (1829–37), Ulysses S. Grant (1869–77), and Warren Harding (1921–23). Other administrations also suffered from the effects of the spoils system, introduced on a large scale in President Jackson's term; curbs on this system were initiated by act of Congress in 1883. Graft among officeholders was commonplace: the buying of positions through campaign contributions; the "purchasing" of judges and lawmakers; the deeding of acres of the public domain as well as timber, mineral, and oil resources to cattle barons, railroads, and business titans with and without the profit-based intervention of officeholders.

The doctrine of Manifest Destiny significantly influenced international relations both on the North American continent and abroad. Expressing the overreaching attitude of expansion, it drove the United States to the Pacific Ocean, enforcing the departure of European powers, trampling over the territorial rights of (and treaties with) Indians, and undercutting the territorial claims of Mexico. Attitudes engendered by Manifest Destiny coupled with a variant interpretation of the Monroe Doctrine led the United States on the "path of empire." The empire began to take shape in the 1880s, driven by a new internationalism and by expanding economic and diplomatic interests in Latin America, the Far East, and the Pacific. These led to ventures both defensive and offensive in South America, the Pacific islands of Samoa and Hawaii, and, after the Cuban uprising against Spain and the Spanish-American War, in Cuba and the Philippines. President Theodore Roosevelt's "big-stick" approach augmented this policy at the outset of the 20th century. Imperialism had overtaken isolationism.

The 20th century reflects a mix of internationalism and isolationism. Contradictory forces and values were at play in the periods preceding both world wars: the avoidance of entanglements, pacifism and the rejection of war; sympathy for the Allies and downtrodden peoples; outrage at atrocities; and recognition of the United States's international presence and responsibilities. In both 1917 and 1941, acts of aggression inflamed a war mentality and mobilized—unified—the nation. An important difference in the two postwar periods—the rejection of the League of Nations versus the acceptance of the United Nations—reflects a significant direction for the United States in the second half of the 20th century.

The American Pageant's 950 pages are replete with intriguing vignettes and details of the highways and byways of historical events. Also revealed are nuances of character and personality as well as philosophies of the players who hold the historical stage. These are sometimes complimentary, sometimes not. These revelations express, both directly and indirectly, the impact of these traits on actions taken, thus affecting the course of the nation.

Chapters expose the significant changes in social and religious thought, mores and behavior, including attitudes toward slavery, suffrage, education, and immigration. These are often hinged to reform movements. Revolution in industry, transportation, and agriculture in concert with technological developments are presented, their discussion further expressing social and cultural shifts.

CENSORSHIP HISTORY

The John Birch Society's chapter in Glen Burnie, Maryland, condemned *The American Pageant: A History of the Republic* and demanded in February 1966 that it be banned in the Anne Arundel County, Maryland, public schools. The book was used as a basic text in two advanced history classes at Annapolis High School taught by Christiana Alexander. She and Dorothy Noble, Anne Arundel County supervisor of social studies, defended the book for its high readability and for stirring the interest of high school seniors.

The basis of the society's complaint was a review of the book by Clarence B. Carson, an "announced conservative" and a Grove City College professor of history. Carson, who represented America's Future, a conservative group operating out of New Rochelle, New York, described it as "a parody of the findings of historical research, a vulgarization of the men and events of the past, a cheapening of history and a distortion of the record." He objected to the book's "liberal orthodoxy" and, for example, to passages that portrayed businessmen negatively as "industrial monarchs," as "manipulators," and as "heartless" and the statement "[business] trusts with their thirst for power, had neither souls nor social consciences." Further, he objected to the depiction of President Franklin Delano Roosevelt as a "gifted leader" and a passage in which he is likened to both President Thomas Jefferson and Alexander Hamilton.

The American Pageant was also one of five books removed from the state-approved textbook list in March 1981 by the Alabama State Board of Education; a sixth book previously had been removed from the list by the State Textbook Committee. Originally, 11 texts on the approved list had been challenged. The board meeting was held in the governor's mansion; it was organized and attended by Governor Fob James, who supported the removal of the books.

These actions grew out of complaints of four parents, apparently led by Leo and Betty Yambrek. Generally, the complaints against the social studies texts refer to "profanity," the authors' "negative" portrayal of the United States, and their "failure to prescribe firm values." Particular objections to *The American Pageant* included the assertion that passages are "consumed with vulgar profanity"; objection to a quotation of President Grover Cleveland—"I made a mistake from the party standpoint, but damn it, I was right" (the context of Cleveland's remark was his determination to be principled and honest); and objection to a Watergate-tape statement of President Richard Nixon in which he described Harry Truman as "an old bastard who many had admired for standing by people who were guilty as hell" (the text, concluding with the Eisenhower administration, does not include Nixon at all).

In June 1984, the Racine (Wisconsin) Unified School Board voted 5-3 to ban three social studies textbooks. *The American Pageant; Portrait of America*, volume II, edited by Stephen B. Oates (1973); and *American Foreign Policy: A History/1900 to Present*, by Thomas G. Paterson et al. (1983). The texts had been designated for use in a new college preparatory course on United States and world history. Board member Marilyn L. Langdon, who supported excluding the texts, said that one of them contained "judgmental writing" and "a lot more funny pictures of Republicans and nicer pictures of Democrats." She also claimed that one book did not present an adequate analysis of the Vietnam War. Of the three books, only *The American Pageant* contains caricatures and political cartoons; the comment about the presentation of the Vietnam War clearly relates to one of the other books, most likely *Portrait of America*. At the succeeding week's meeting, the board voted (5-4) to reverse its decision to ban the books. In the interim, James Ennis, head of the Racine Education Association, threatened to sue to prevent the board from carrying out the ban.

The two other challenged books do each contain a segment about Vietnam. *Portrait of America* includes an essay by Ronald Steel entitled "Chinese Checkers and Vietnamese Chess." (This is a nontraditional text, which provides a series of essays chronologically organized about the major periods and events of American history.) Steel's focus is United States policy that led to the origin and escalation of its involvement in Vietnam. He cites the containment of China and the prevention of the spread of communism as the basic posture and expresses the crudity of analysis and the mistaken presumptions that led to the failure of U.S. policy. One of these presumptions was involvement in a civil war in South Vietnam, one faction of which was aided by the North Vietnamese government. Steel quotes a *New York Times* journalist: "The communists, despite their brutality and deceit, remain the only Vietnamese capable of rallying millions of their countrymen to sacrifice and hardship in the name of the nation."

American Foreign Policy provides a quite extensive chapter, "Bearing the Burden: The Vietnam Years, 1961–1969." Its discussion initiates with the Indochina war and diplomacy before 1961, and provides the development of American involvement in the Kennedy and Johnson administrations. The Americanization of the war is discussed, followed by expression of political dissent and efforts to achieve peace.

FURTHER READING

Dowe, Kelly. "Conservatives' Sword Mightier Than Textbooks." *Birmingham Post-Herald*, April 9, 1981, p. C1.

Gillespie, Scott. "Racine Board Bans 5 Books from Curriculum." *Milwaukee Sentinel*, June 12, 1984, pp. 1, 11.

Harris, Kate. "Parents Group Trains Guns on Number of Textbooks." *Birmingham News*, February 12, 1981, p. 2A.

Jarnigan, Bill. "Board, Committee Hear Textbooks Denounced." *Birmingham News*, March 26, 1981, p. 10A.

Kurtz, Bill. "Book Ban Reversed in Racine." *Milwaukee Journal*, June 19, 1984, p. 3.

Newsletter on Intellectual Freedom 15 (1966): 28; 30 (1981): 67–68, 92–93; 33 (1984): 158.

Runkel, David. "Book Controversy in Anne Arundel: Antibusiness, Class-Struggle 'Facts' Hit." *Baltimore Evening Sun*, February 17, 1966, p. D1.

Wolfe Bell, Stephanie. "State Education Board Drops Several Social Studies Books." *Alabama Journal*, March 17, 1981, p. 13.

ANDERSONVILLE

Author: MacKinlay Kantor
Original date and place of publication: 1955, United States
Publisher: World Publishing Company
Literary form: Novel

SUMMARY

Andersonville is a novel of war—the Civil War; it does not, however, fit the stereotype of war novels, for it offers little action on the battlefield, strategies and troop movements, or individual responses to such situations in the manner of Stephen Crane's *The Red Badge of Courage* or Erich Maria Remarque's ALL QUIET ON THE WESTERN FRONT. There are essentially two settings: Ira Claffey's Georgia plantation and Andersonville, a prison for captured Yankees.

Episodic in structure, the novel provides access to Ira's life and his emotional and intellectual reactions to the war and the prison. These episodes, interspersed among those that focus on Yankee prisoners and Confederate officers and guards, provide plot movement.

Managing his plantation from the outset of the war without the help of an overseer, Ira Claffey is perceived as capable and honest. In this last year of the war, he nurtures his family with compassion. Only two live on the plantation with him: Veronica, his wife, and Lucy, their daughter. They are joined during this year by surgeon Harry Elkins, formerly a comrade-in-arms of the Claffeys' eldest son. This son and another have already died in battle; their third son is reported dead early in the novel. This final bereavement casts a shroud over the mind of Veronica. She gradually distances herself from the living and fades into the past. Lucy bears these burdens and the death of her fiancé with pain and anger and courage.

Ira is not a secessionist; he does not favor the war. Initially angry and embittered, he grieves for his sons. His philosophy and nature help him to acknowledge the reality of war's destruction and that families in the North also grieve for their lost sons.

Deploring cruelty, Ira treats his slaves, now totaling 12 including children, with paternalistic kindness. He will not allow them to be mistreated by the Confederate soldiers; and when he must sell them, he assures himself that they will not be mistreated. At the end of the war he informs them of their freedom and their right to leave; however, out of concern for their safety and welfare, he urges them to remain on the plantation as salaried employees. When one couple decides to leave, he gives them a mule and cart so their young children won't have to walk.

Ira's sense of compassion is intensified with the advent of the stockade. At first he disbelieves the deliberate intent, as voiced by Captain Winder, to mistreat the prisoners by providing no shelter from the elements, to cause their deaths. He is increasingly horrified by the brutality and miserable conditions. He attempts to help—protesting to the officers, joining his neighbors to bring food and clothing for the prisoners (these are rejected), traveling to Richmond to gain the ear of President Jefferson Davis, a friend from his military days—but realizes his helplessness.

Others join him in these attitudes. Chief among them is Surgeon Elkins, who, having come to investigate the health conditions, returns out of a humane sense of obligation to tend the sick. The post commander, Lieutenant Colonel Persons, of like mind, puts his career on the line to protest the actions of Confederate brigadier general John H. Winder and his son, Captain Sid Winder. Other inspectors follow suit; Dr. Joseph Jones concludes his highly critical report with the following:

> This gigantic mass of human misery calls loudly for relief, not only for the sake of suffering humanity, but also on account of our own brave soldiers now captives in the hands of the Federal government. Strict justice to the gallant

men of the Confederate armies, who have been or who may be so unfortunate as to be compelled to surrender in battle, demands that the Confederate government should adopt that course which will best secure their health and comfort in captivity; or at least leave their enemies without a shadow of an excuse for any violation of the rules of civilized warfare in the treatment of prisoners.

In counterpoint to these beacons of humanity are Brigadier General Winder and Captain Winder, whose intentions are revealed in this statement by the captain in response to Surgeon Elkins's concern that there are no shelters built or trees left to shield the prisoners from the hot Georgia sun: "What the hell's the use of coddling a pen full of Yankees? I've got a pen here that ought to kill more God damn Yankees than you ever saw killed at the front." The general demonstrates a more rabid expression of these intentions.

General Winder assigns Captain Henry Wirz as superintendent of the prison. Wirz, a doctor by profession, made intensely irritable and vituperative by an arm wound, brutalizes the prisoners: they are tyrannized; their diet is insufficient in both quantity and nutrients; their living conditions are abominable. A failure as an administrator, his efforts are ineffectual. Wirz is in part victim of a situation he cannot control: the vindictiveness of the Winders; the overloading of the compound; lack or denial of food and medical supplies.

The stockade and the prisoners are, however, the core of the novel. The stockade's 27 acres, intended for some 10,000 men, held upward of 30,000 at one time. (Of the 50,000 prisoners received there, about 16,000 died.) With no sanitation facilities, the area soon becomes putrid, its limited water supply polluted, its stench befouling the surrounding neighborhood. The Yankees die from dysentery, scurvy, and polluted water; wounds, scratches, and stings festered into gangrene. Others die of starvation and violence, groups of "raiders" attacking and stealing from the weak, the innocent, the unprepared among them.

Against the background of ever-increasing privation and brutality, decay and death, individual prisoners are spotlighted. Their origins and childhoods, their initial responses to the war are counterpoints to their immediate situation. How they survive—whether they survive—reveals their natures. Edward Blamey, a New England fisherman, survives, though he initially resists, by selling his extraordinary eyesight to the raider, Willie Collins, in return for protection and creature comforts. Blamey spies goods among the other prisoners that can be stolen. Collins, surly and corrupt since childhood, uses his brute strength and amorality to build a power structure in which the "raiders" within the stockade terrorize fellow prisoners. He is finally tried, condemned, and hanged, along with others of his ilk, by a group of prisoners organized by Seneca MacBean and Nathan Dreyfoos, a semieducated midwesterner and an upper-class easterner. The Iowan Eben Dolliver's childhood is filled with a consciousness of birds, with birdsong; he is driven by starvation to attack a swallow for food. At age 13, Willie Mann of Missouri had rescued several immigrant German children from a bully; subsequently he fell in love with one of them and now is sustained by dreams of returning to her. He survives because his doctor father had taught him the health value of pure water; he refuses to drink except when it rains.

A minor plot strand, the story of the poor white Tebbs family, particularly a vignette of the eldest son, brings the novel to fruition. Having enlisted at age 17, Coral returns home without a foot. Embittered, depressed, he flails at his family and at his life. While searching for a bird he has shot, he discovers an escaped prisoner lacking a hand, just about dead from starvation and weariness. Both have lost their limbs at Gettysburg. Coral on an impulse decides to help him with food and a hideout; the Yankee boy, Nazareth Strider from Pennsylvania, helps Coral in return by shaping a "peg-leg-foot" for him, with knowledge gleaned from his father's craft and using tools borrowed from Ira Claffey. When Ira discovers their secret, he shocks them both by helping. Again, Ira's humanity emerges; he muses as he works on the wooden foot, "It seemed odd to be performing a service for a wounded Yankee and a wounded Confederate in the same act and in the same breath." Acts of humanity unite the two boys.

The novel continues for another 40 pages beyond this episode to encompass the defeat of the Confederacy, the release of the prisoners, and the military arrest of Wirz. Two of Ira's adult slaves with their children take advantage of their freedom and leave; Coral Tebbs finds employment as their replacement. However, the crescendo of the novel is in the mutual salvation of Coral and Nazareth and in the symbolic healing and reunification it expresses.

CENSORSHIP HISTORY

Andersonville was challenged by Laurence Van Der Oord, the father of an Amherst (Ohio) High School student in 1967. Identifying the novel as "filth," he claimed his 16-year-old daughter could not read it because she did not understand the obscene words. He asserted that the book was 1 percent history and 99 percent filth and demanded that Donald Hicks, the history teacher who had assigned the novel as an optional choice, be dismissed.

Hicks countered that the relative worth of the novel outweighed the objectionable parts; about 30 of the 795 pages contain slightly obscene language. Defense of the novel was also offered by the school board president, Mrs. Clem Rice: ". . . maybe we should not shield high school students. . . . Perhaps they should know these facts exist even though they are bad and may not exist in our community." On August 24, the school superintendent announced that he would not order the removal of the book.

In 1973, a Buncombe County, North Carolina, school board member, Edna Roberts, removed several books, including *Andersonville*, from the high school library, claiming they were "unsuitable" for school libraries because they contained objectionable language. Subsequently, she introduced a resolution to the board that would have "expunged 'unsuitable' books from school libraries." The board rejected it, reaffirming its "Policies for Selection." Mrs. Roberts's efforts were supported by the Christian Action League and Answer for America.

Buncombe County in 1981 was the scene of another controversy over classroom and library books, including, among others, *Andersonville*. The protest was initiated by a group of citizens meeting at Asheville's Owens High School in January; the meeting was led by several fundamentalist ministers, a chief spokesperson being Wendell Runion, who had organized the Concerned Citizens of Owens District group. The books on the list were labeled obscene. The group planned to file a grievance with the Buncombe County schools' administration to get the books removed. In February, an opposition group, calling itself "Books," was organized to provide an alternative perspective. On February 19, more than 1,000 residents attended a forum to air the two positions. Those opposed to the current book selection policy called for closing loopholes that "promote immorality." Pastor Randy Stone noted, "The use of God's name in vain, whether it be in a Pulitzer-prize winner or a book from an adult bookstore, is offensive to us and demands some sort of attention." Books's spokespersons included Loretta Martin, the president of the North Carolina Association of Educators, and Elsie Brumbeck, the director of educational media for the State Department of Public Instruction. Martin said, "Our schools are the only institution today that seeks to free the human mind." Brumbeck read a letter from the North Carolina Library Association in support of Buncombe County's current selection policy. Receiving the strongest accolade, however, was Pastor Fred Ohler, who, in support of the book selection policy, asked, "Why is immorality seen only as profanity and sexuality in Steinbeck, Salinger or Kantor and the larger issues of grinding poverty and social misjustice, of adult hypocrisy, of war camp atrocities never faced?" Referring to the list of quotations from the challenged books, he continued, "To read the Bible as some folks read *The Grapes of Wrath* would be like going through the Gospels and only seeing tax collectors, wine-bibers and Mary Magdalene." In March the Buncombe County Board of Education voted (5-2) to support the book selection policy.

Andersonville was withdrawn from the 11th-grade reading list at the Whitehall, Michigan, high school on December 12, 1963. An "unspecified number of unidentified complaints" were received by Superintendent of Schools Melvin Lubbers and County Prosecutor Harry J. Knudsen; the latter indicated he did not care if the book had won 20 Pulitzer Prizes; it was not fit reading for high school students. One parent, Jane Moog, angry about the dropping of the book, termed the act a "violation of civil liberties." Lubbers indicated that they did not quarrel with the author's message, but it was not of "sufficient benefit to justify putting it before the young mind." Despite a defense of the book by a school board member, Evelyn Robinson, and Circuit Judge John H. Piercy, the board of education voted 6-1 in support of Lubbers.

In 1961, under the leadership of J. Evetts Haley, Texans for America, a right-wing group, supported by the Daughters of the American Revolution (DAR) and the John Birch Society, attacked the language and concepts of a range of history books. They succeeded in causing the State Textbook Committee to reject 12 books opposed by the Texans for America and four opposed by the DAR. In addition, substantial changes in their texts were required of publishers for specific books.

These textbook battles spilled over to affect library books. *Andersonville* was banned from the four Amarillo high schools and at Amarillo College. The stated reasons were its political ideas and that its author was cited by the House Un-American Activities Committee. In 1962, a committee of inquiry, instigated by a Texas House of Representatives resolution, investigated the content of school books, searching for subversion of American principles and traditions. At an Austin hearing, excerpts from *Andersonville* were read as examples of obscenity and filth.

An attempt to ban *Andersonville* was also reported in Rock County, Wisconsin, in 1969.

FURTHER READING

Blake, Barbara. "Who Is the Rev. Wendell Runion and Why Does He Want Those Books Banned?" *Asheville Citizen*, January 31, 1981, [n.p.].

Burress, Lee. *The Battle of the Books: Literary Censorship in Public Schools, 1950–1985.* Metuchen, N.J.: Scarecrow Press, 1989.

Campbell, John, Jr. "Concern Expressed over Books in Schools." *Asheville Citizen*, January 23, 1981, [n.p.].

———. "Large Crowd Gathers for Sessions on Books." *Asheville Citizen*, February 20, 1981, p. 17.

Grisso, James L. "Amherst High Keeps *Andersonville*." *Cleveland Plain Dealer*, August 25, 1967, [n.p.].

Hoyle Bolick, Sandy. "Book Issue: Pros, Cons." *Asheville Times*, February 20, 1981, [n.p.].

Nelson, Jack, and Gene Roberts, Jr. *The Censors and the Schools.* Boston: Little, Brown, 1963.

Newsletter on Intellectual Freedom 13 (1964): 14; 22 (1973): 52; 30 (1981): 74.

"Official Removes 'Objectional' Books." *St. Louis Post Dispatch*, March 28, 1973, 22A.

"Pro Books Group Is Organized in County." *Asheville Citizen*, February 14, 1981, 7.

"Rock County Librarians United to Battle Would-Be Banners." *Beloit Daily News*, April 17, 1969, [n.p.].

ANIMAL FARM

Author: George Orwell
Original dates and places of publication: 1945, England; 1946, United States
Publishers: Secker and Warburg; Harcourt, Brace and World
Literary form: Novel

SUMMARY

The subtitle of George Orwell's *Animal Farm,* "A Fairy Story," reveals that he is not focusing on reality in the traditional sense. Indeed, his characters are animals who rebel against humans and take over Manor Farm, renaming it Animal Farm. Orwell, as quoted by C. M. Woodhouse, from the *Times Literary Supplement,* in the preface (dated August 6, 1954) to the Signet Classics 29th edition, wrote "Every line of serious work that I have written since 1936 has been written, directly or indirectly against totalitarianism . . . *Animal Farm* was the first book in which I tried, with full consciousness . . . , to fuse political purpose and artistic purpose into one whole."

The animals' rebellion can be traced back to old Major, the prizewinning boar who assembles the animals one night to communicate to them his strange dream. He sermonizes about the low state of animals at the hands of humans, a life of hard work for which there is no reward except bare rations and a stall; since Man consumes without producing, animals must resolve to bear enmity toward humans. Through his dream he predicts that Man will be vanquished and animals will reign in freedom.

Inspired to a new outlook, the animals secretly begin planning for a rebellion. The pigs, deemed the cleverest, take charge, under the leadership of Snowball and Napoleon. Several months later, when Mr. Jones gets drunk and sleeps through the day, forgetting to feed the animals, they respond to their hunger and angry frustration by taking action. They gain control of the farm.

At first, all is bliss; that is, equality among the animals is practiced. Seven commandments are identified and painted on the barn wall, expressing that "All animals are equal" and other tenets, chiefly reflecting animosity toward humans and their ways. The animals work hard together, completing farm tasks for the good of the community. Boxer, the horse, is foremost with his energy and power, establishing for himself an "I will work harder" motto. The animals also fight off, under the leadership of Snowball, a counterattack from Jones and his men. After this, an even greater spirit and sense of dedication prevail.

The bliss and equality, however, are marred: First, the pigs quietly take the daily milk for themselves; then, they commandeer the windfall apples. It seems natural that they should take charge and direct the farm's activities and should work at organizing and planning, rather than laboring in the fields. The less clever animals accept this and are confused by the quarrels between Snowball and Napoleon.

Their disputes come to a head over the windmill proposed by Snowball. When he appears to have carried the vote, Napoleon gives a high-pitched whimper; nine enormous dogs, which he had secretly trained, dash into the barn and attack Snowball, who only barely manages to escape. Napoleon's autocratic regime is thus initiated, the troubled animals too shocked and terrified to react to the new edicts. The new code words now are "loyalty and obedience."

The animals adhere to their duties while Napoleon tightens his control, exacting more work from them, giving them less food and less relaxation time. When Napoleon establishes trade relations with the enemy, there is vague uneasiness among the animals; however, they accept the assurances made by Squealer, Napoleon's mouthpiece. They also accept the scapegoating of Snowball for everything that goes wrong, a pattern that begins with moderate accusations but escalates to denouncing his past purposes, putting him in secret league with the enemy. At an assembly, Napoleon, surrounded by his snarling dogs, demands "confessions" of all disloyal animals; hearing these, he orders the guilty animals slaughtered on the spot by his dogs.

Suffering these indignities, the animals, frightened and disturbed, are mournful. They perceive that their dream of a "society of animals set free from hunger and the whip, all equal, each working according to his capacity, the strong protecting the weak" is somehow in jeopardy. The more astute of them, Boxer and Clover, the horses, and Muriel, the goat, note that some of the commandments seem changed—"without cause" has been added to "no animal shall kill any other animal"—but cannot be certain, cannot quite remember how it had originally read.

In the succeeding months, another invasion is fought off, but less successfully. Napoleon, unlike Snowball, directs the animal forces from the rear. Boxer, who is injured in the attack, continues to work but collapses from overexertion. He is presumably being taken to a veterinarian for treatment but is picked up by a truck labeled "Horse Slaughterer and Glue Boiler." This reading is forcibly denied by Squealer as "wicked rumour."

Years later, only a few of the original animals live. The rebellion has faded in their memories; the succeeding animals don't know anything about it. Three startling events conclude the fairy story: the pigs start walking on their hind legs; only a single commandment remains on the barn wall—"All animals are equal but some Animals are more equal than others"; Napoleon hosts a party, the guests being the neighborhood human farmers. Clover and other animals watch through the window as a farmer toasts Napoleon for his discipline over the "lower animals," for getting them to do more work yet feeding them less. Napoleon announces in his return toast the changed name of the farm, from "Animal Farm" to "Manor Farm." As the creatures outside watch, the pigs and men inside become indistinguishable—"from pig to man, and from man to pig, and from pig to man again; but already it was impossible to say which was which."

CENSORSHIP HISTORY

Animal Farm was one of 64 books of literature banned from classroom teaching at Bay and Mosley High Schools in Panama City, Florida, on May 7, 1987. The action was taken by Bay County School Superintendent Leonard Hall. Although six days later the Bay County School Board reinstated all 64 texts, the controversy did not end. The situation and issues are detailed in the censorship history discussion of I AM THE CHEESE by Robert Cormier.

A survey of censorship challenges in the schools, conducted in DeKalb County, Georgia, in 1982 for the period 1979 to 1982, revealed that *Animal Farm* had been objected to for its political theories. (The survey's list does not provide details.)

A comparable study of censorship in New York State English classrooms was conducted in 1968 by the New York State English Council's Committee on Defenses Against Censorship. Its findings, based on 160 returns, identified *Animal Farm* to be high on its list of "problem books"; the reason cited was that "Orwell was a communist."

A Wisconsin survey in 1963 revealed that the John Birch Society had challenged the use of *Animal Farm;* it objected to the words "masses will revolt."

The novel has also been challenged internationally. It was among eight titles (also including Orwell's *1984*) suppressed from being displayed at the 1977 Moscow international book fair.

In 1986, objections persisted; the stage production of *Animal Farm* was banned from the Theatre of Nations Festival in the United States. Eastern bloc pressure—the Soviet Union had insisted that Poland, Hungary, Bulgaria, and Czechoslovakia would withdraw from the festival if the play were performed—had caused the suppression. A reversal occurred in 1988 when *Izvestia* published two chapters of the novel.

A production of *Animal Farm* was banned in 1991 by Kenyan authorities, allegedly because it criticizes corrupt leaders who abuse political power. (Kenya was a one-party state.) The novel was banned in 2002 from schools in the United Arab Emirates, along with 125 others. The Ministry of Education banned it on the ground that it contained written or illustrated material that contradicts Islamic and Arab values—in this text, pictures of alcoholic drinks, pigs, and other "indecent images."

FURTHER READING

Burress, Lee. *The Battle of the Books: Literary Censorship in Public Schools, 1950–1985.* Metuchen, N.J.: Scarecrow Press, 1989.

Fransecky, Roger B. "Censorship and the Teaching of English." *Newsletter on Intellectual Freedom* 17 (1968): 39–40.

Kegler, Sissy, and Gene Guerro. "Censorship in the South." *Newsletter on Intellectual Freedom* 35 (1986): 29, 56.

Orwell, George. *Animal Farm.* New York: New American Library, 1946.

THE APPOINTMENT

Author: Herta Müller
Original dates and places of publication: 1997, Germany; 2001, United States
Publisher: Rowohlt Verlag; Metropolitan Books/Henry Holt
Literary form: Novel

SUMMARY

I've been summoned. Thursday at ten sharp. Lately I'm being summoned more and more often: ten sharp on Tuesday, ten sharp on Saturday, on Wednesday, Monday. As if years were a week, I'm amazed that winter comes so close on the heels of summer.

The subtle shuddering of this opening paragraph of *The Appointment* suggests, beyond mystery, something troubling and dark. (The German title translates to *Today I'd Rather Not See Myself.*) The unnamed female narrator is feeling threatened for good reason. Employed in a clothing factory, having separated from her first husband, anxious to find a way out of the country (Romania), she slipped a note into the pocket of ten suits bounds for Italy: "Marry me, *ti aspetto*" including her name and address. She is denounced. At the "meeting," which she is not allowed to attend, the notes, apparently ideologically offensive, were judged to be "prostitution in the workplace"; her supervisor, Nelu, whose advances she had rejected, had argued for "treason." Since this was her first offense and she was not a Party member, she was reprimanded. Following the discovery of three notes in trousers scheduled for Sweden: "Best wishes from the dictatorship," of which she is falsely accused, she becomes the object of the summonses from the secret police.

The novel in its entirety, in a stream-of-consciousness style, reveals the thoughts of the narrator during her walk from her apartment and ride on the tram to her meeting with her interrogator, Major Albu. She observes and considers the landscape and her fellow passengers; she reflects on family and her first and second husbands; she contemplates the nature of the world around her and herself. There is no sequential order or connectedness among her thoughts. The surface confusion it portrays represents her view of the world itself.

Two strong strands of thought and emotions, however, emerge: the representation of the dictatorial, malicious, and corrupt government and the demoralized repressed people who have been affected by the hollowness, constraints, and terror of their lives.

Bits and pieces of the brutality of the government are interspersed among the personal experiences and thoughts. Examples include: The narrator's good friend Lilli is shot while trying to escape to Hungary with her army officer lover. She is downed by one bullet but several more follow; five dogs shred her body. Only two factory coworkers—aside from Nelu and the narrator—attend the funeral. Others out of fear of association "refused to have anything to do with an escape attempt and the way it ended." Comparably, the narrator is fearful of missing her appointment with Alba: The summons is delivered orally. She worries that she may have misheard the date and will suffer consequences. During his session with her, Albu reveals that she is being shadowed; he knows of her activities with Paul, her second husband. Her shoemaker acquaintance whose wife was in a "mental home," apparently afflicted with senility, refers to two young women in the same institution "who lost their wits after what the police did to them. These women hadn't done anything either—one swiped a little candle wax from the factory, the other took a sack of corncobs that were lying in a field."

Paul also becomes a victim, first of clothing theft at his factory workplace and, subsequently, a political target. Stealing clothing while the owner is showering is apparently not unusual, but Paul is frequently a prey—indeed sometimes all of his clothes. This rationalization is expressed: Stealing isn't considered a bad thing in the factory. "The Factory belongs to the people, you belong to the people, and whatever you take is collectively owned, anyway—iron, tin, wood, screws, and wire, whatever you can get your hands on." However, in response to jokes about his "naked" situations, Paul remarked, "Socialism sends its workers forth into the world unclad. . . . Every week or so it's as if you were born anew. It keeps you young." This political statement is reported; Paul is required at the Party meeting (he is a Party member) to stand in front and "deliver public self-criticism for his quip." The narrator comments that if Paul had not made this blunder "some other pretext would have been discovered. False steps can always be found, unlike stolen clothes." This prediction presages Paul's clash with government inspectors.

A circumstantial family story reveals expropriation practices. The narrator's grandfather years before her first marriage was the victim of her father-in-law, a Party operative. He confiscated her grandfather's gold coins and jewelry; he had him and her grandmother deported to the harsh Baragon Steppe where her grandmother died under cruel, disheartening conditions. When her grandfather returned, his house having become state property, he had to go to court several times before he could reclaim his house. Her father-in-law, a danger to others, would ride a white horse from house to house, demanding that his horse be fed and watered, searching each house for grain and gold.

> First he rounded up the farmers with large holdings and turned them over to the security services, after that he went after medium-sized farmers, then he moved on to smallholders. He was a hard worker, after a while he was rounding up too many farmers, and ones who were too poor at that, so the gentlemen in the city sent whole groups of them back to the village on the next train.

This repressive persecution and brutal social-political environment are the backdrop to the chilling expression of the impoverished lives of the people and their inhumanity toward each other, mirroring, in effect, the government's behavior toward them. Given the prevailing threatening surveillance of the state, the constant awareness of needing to protect herself, given also the invasion of her privacy, the narrator trusts no one—even family and husbands. She begins to feel safe with Paul, but at the end of the novel a questions is raised in her head. Personal relationships are fraught with betrayals: the narrator's father daily, seemingly, meets a young woman—a girl the narrator's age—from the market for sex—a great loss for the narrator who discovers them; her father-in-law, when his son reported for military duty, makes sexual overtures toward her to help her get over her husband's absence and when she resists him, he grumbled, "You rack your brains to come up with ways of helping your children, and this is what you get for your pains"; at a New Year's Eve party, the married couples by "mutual agreement had turned a blind eye to each other's whereabouts"; Lilly repeatedly urges her new stepfather to have sex with her when her mother/his wife is shopping, a plea to which he succumbs on a daily basis.

The overall impact upon the narrator of the political and social-personal environment is numbing, except in her careful scrutiny of everything about her. The events and images are dislocating and at times oppressive. She talks almost hopelessly about happiness and seems haunted by death. Her sanity may be at the brink. Suggestively, at the end of the novel when she accidentally sights Paul where she doesn't expect him to be, she thinks: "The trick is not to go mad."

CENSORSHIP HISTORY

Herta Müller's early career advocacy of freedom of speech and overt opposition to the Ceauşescu dictatorship in Romania started during the 1973–1976 period when she was a student at the university in Timişoara (Temeswar). She associated with Aktionsgruppe Banat, a circle of German-speaking authors who sought freedom of speech. (Müller's father served in the Waffen SS during World War II. After the war in 1945, her mother was deported to the Soviet Union to a work camp in present-day Ukraine for five years.)

Müller's first collection of short stories, *Niederungen (Lowlands)*, also titled *Nadirs*, was published, though heavily censored, in Romania in 1982; it was held by the publisher for four years. The Romanian press was very critical. An uncensored copy of *Niederungen* was smuggled into Germany and published in 1984. The German press gave it positive reviews; it was well received by the German public. In 1988 she published her first novel, *Drükender Tango*, in Romania where it experienced the same fate as her earlier work. (It was published in Germany in 1996.) These works spotlight life in a small German village in Romania, depicting the difficult life and harsh treatment of Romanian Germans under the repressive Ceauşescu regime. Major themes are corruption and intolerance. Indeed, because Müller had publicly criticized the dictatorship of Nicolae Ceauşescu, her works were banned from publication in Romania.

After her studies in Timişoara, Müller worked as a translator in a tractor factory. However, when she refused to work for the Securitate (secret police), she was fired. Subsequently, she was harassed by the Securitate, subjected to threats, house searches, and bugging. She emigrated to Germany in 1987.

These practices are still active, the Securitate (CNSAS) only having been renamed—the Romanian Information Service (SRI)—40 percent of whose personnel are former secret police. On her visits back to Romania, as recently as spring 2009, Müller has experienced the bugging of her telephone, being shadowed, having an interview with a reporter interrupted, and the reporter also shadowed. Every year, she asked to see her file but was denied access. In 1999, as a result of the European Union's requirement, personnel files being held by CNSAS were released to the SRI, but her requests were denied; ostensibly the file was "still being worked on."

In 2004, "suddenly" her file was found under the name Cristina—three volumes totaling 914 pages. According to Müller, the reason given for opening the file was her "tendentious distortions of reality in the country particularly in the village environment," as depicted in her book *Nadirs*. The entry in the file for November 30, 1986, stated: "Every trip that Cristina takes to Bucharest and to other parts of the country, is to be reported in a timely fashion to the inland and counterespionage services, so that permanent control can be guaranteed" in order to "carry through with the appropriate control measures in connection with West German diplomats and West German citizens."

Müller also recounts a few incidents of physical abuse to herself and to other persons who planned to contact her, including a *Die Zeit* journalist who was "brutally" beaten, ending with broken toes on both feet. She notes, "My file also shows that a surreal punishment process was laid out because of spying for the BND (German police). I have the resonance of my books and the literary prizes to thank that the plan was not activated and I wasn't arrested."

Herta Müller was awarded the Nobel Prize in literature in 2009. Previously she won the German Kleist prize in 1994 and the International IMPAC Dublin Literary award in 1998 for her novel *The Land of Green Plums* (1993).

FURTHER READING

Baskin, Jason M. Review of *The Appointment*, by Herta Müller. *Chicago Review* 48, no. 4 (Winter 2002/2003): 136–138.

Eder, Richard. "Allegory of Oppression in Ceaucescu's [sic] Romania." *New York Times*, September 12, 2001, E8.

Filkins, Peter. "Betrayal as a Way of Life." *New York Times Book Review*, October 21, 2001, 18.

Müller, Herta. "The Secret Police Is Still in Service." *Die Zeit Online*. Available online. URL: http://www.zeit.de/2009/31Securitate. Accessed October 15, 2010.

Zaleski, Jeff. Review of *The Appointment*, by Herta Müller. *Publishers Weekly*, August 6, 2001, 61.

AREOPAGITICA

Author: John Milton
Original dates and places of publication: 1644, England; 1888, United States
Publishers: [s.n.]; Cassell and Company
Literary form: Nonfiction essay

SUMMARY

Considered seminal in the defense of freedom of expression, *Areopagitica*, published in 1644, has been frequently cited by anticensors in promoting freedom of the press and of speech.

The title of John Milton's most famous prose work was derived from Areopagus, the hill of Ares in Athens named after Ares, one of the 12 major gods of ancient Greece. (In mythology, Ares, who had killed Poseidon's son for his having raped his daughter, was tried for murder by a council of the gods on this site; he was acquitted.) At this site the highest judicial court of ancient Athens met to debate political and religious matters. Its nearly 300 members were elected by a vote of all the free men of the city. Since the site Areopagus is identified with the glory of Athens's democratic institutions, Milton's title, *Areopagitica*, reveals his inclinations. The subtitle, *A Speech for the Liberty of Unlicensed Printing to the Parliament of England*, identifies his intent. In his "The Second Defense of the People of England," published in 1654, Milton noted:

> I wrote my *Areopagitica* in order to deliver the press from the restraints with which it was encumbered; that the power of determining what was true and what was false, what ought to be published and what to be suppressed, might no longer be entrusted to a few illiterate and illiberal individuals, who refused their sanction to any work which contained views or sentiments at all above the level of vulgar superstition.

It was specifically directed against the Order of Parliament of June 14, 1643, an ordinance requiring the licensing of all books and pamphlets in advance of publication. It also expresses significant ideas of religious liberty, interrelated with those of freedom of the press; however, these will not be discussed here.

Milton recognized the great concern the "Church and Commonwealth" had about the contents of books "for books are not absolutely dead things, but do contain a potency of life. . . . they do preserve as in a vial the purest efficacy and extraction of that living intellect that bred them." However, he argued that "Who kills a man kills a reasonable creature, God's image; but he who destroys a good book, kills reason itself, kills the image of God, as it were in the eye."

Milton decried censoring activities that represented what is now termed *prior restraint;* indeed, this becomes a basic tenet of his discussion. He likened the impulse to license to the prohibitory attitudes and actions of the papal court, which led to the Spanish Inquisition. He noted that their censoring acts spread from the heretical to any subject they found unsuitable, thus expressing a warning about the pattern of censorship. Before this "tyrannous inquisition," books were allowed to be born into the world, judgment about them reserved. Continuing this metaphor, rather than stand before a jury prior to birth to be judged in darkness without any public scrutiny, books should be examined more openly after publication.

Historical examples are used to support this position. He identifies practices in classical Athens and early Christianity, finding them free of control prior to publication and in all instances after publication except atheism, blasphemy, and libel. One example is the burning of the books of Protagoras and the banishing of the author himself upon command of the judges of Areopagus; Protagoras had written that he did not know "whether there were gods, or whether not."

The value of knowledge and learning forms a cornerstone of Milton's discussion. Books enhance our understanding of the known and introduce us to the new. The Order of Parliament would "suppress all this flowry crop of knowledge . . . to bring a famine upon our minds again" and allow the people to know only what the licensers permit. He likens this to the state of ignorance to which the decree of Julian the Apostate reduced the Christians, forbidding them to study the heathen texts. Thus, licensing would greatly discourage learning by reducing access to information and discussion. Restraining the freedom to write and the liberty of printing nullifies the privilege of the people and shackles the freedom to learn.

Knowledge thrives on the mind's exercise as does the discovery and affirmation of truth. His illustrations encompass the religious and scientific, attaining the truth by examining all opinions, even errors, so they may be known and evaluated. Individuals who base their beliefs solely on what they are told by their pastors or as determined by the assembly without knowing reasons cannot be said to understand. Even if the doctrine is true in an objective sense, it is not believed in the right way. It has not been questioned or examined, thus not really understood; the belief is superficial. An unlicensed press can propose challenges to cause thinking, thus enhancing the understanding of accepted beliefs or revealing new truths. Milton proposes these concepts for both the nation and individuals.

Extending this position, Milton promotes the reading of all texts, the good as well as those of "evil substance." The latter to a "discreet and judicious reader serve in many respects to discover, to confute, to forewarn, and to illustrate." Truth and virtue are attained by including all opinions, even errors, so they may be known and reasoned. Individuals are put in positions of having to make moral choices between the good and evil that surround them.

> Since therefore the knowledge and survey of vice is in this world so necessary to the constituting of human virtue, and the scanning of error to the confirmation of truth, how can we more safely, and with less danger, scout into the regions of sin and falsity than by reading all manner of tractate, and hearing all manner of reason? And this is the benefit which may be had of books promiscuously read.

Milton drew a cause-and-effect connection between the actions of government and the nature of the populace. An "oppressive, arbitrary and tyrannous" government breeds a "brutish, formall, and slavish" people. A mild and free human government promotes liberty, the liberty of free writing, and free speaking. These in the past have enlightened the spirits, enfranchised and enlarged the apprehensions of the English people, making them more capable, more knowing, and more eager to pursue the truth. These attributes would be suppressed by the enforcement of this order.

The effectiveness of the order is also questioned. One aspect is the licensers themselves: They need to be above all other men to accomplish the task without bias, but are apt to be ignorant, corrupt, or overworked. Another is the assumption that books themselves are the sole source of ideas and behaviors that are perceived by the authorities to be censorable. Milton refutes both of these, arguing, as summarized above, the efficacy of books, thus the requirement of unlicensed printing.

CENSORSHIP HISTORY

Licensing of books, which should be understood as the suppression of undesired publications, was a frequent policy in England. As early as 1408, confirmed by Parliament in 1414, Archbishop Arundel's constitution forbade the reading of any book that had not been examined and approved by the University of Oxford or Cambridge. Henry VIII forbade the printing of any book concerning holy scripture unless it had been examined or approved. This was spread to the licensing of books of any kind. This policy was reasserted by the monarchs who succeeded him—Edward, Mary, Elizabeth, James, and Charles.

The practice and procedures of censorship had been developed in England over the 16th and 17th centuries, including the incorporation of a Stationers Company charged with the administration of the system. In 1637, in Charles's reign, the Star Chamber decree of July 11 established a broad range of censorship measures that forbade the printing, importing, or selling of seditious or offensive books; required the licensing of all books before being printed or reprinted; limited the number of master printers, specifying the number of presses and workers each might have; forbade the providing of space for unlicensed printers; and empowered the Stationers Company to search houses for such unlicensed printers.

In 1641, the Star Chamber had been abolished, an outcome of the defeat of Charles in the English Civil War. Though the Stationers Company was not abolished, its powers were diminished; for about 18 months there were no statutory restrictions on the press. Gradually, the openness was narrowed. In 1643, the Puritans through a series of regulations, preceded by a 1642 regulation mandating that every publication bear the name of the printer, reinstated censorship practices until they were in full force. A significant factor underpinning these actions was the religious toleration controversy of the time.

In this context, John Milton published in 1643 *Doctrine and Discipline of Divorce* without benefit of authorization, registration, or signature, by then required. It was reprinted in February 1644, again without being authorized or registered, though it was signed. At this time the Royalists suffered a defeat, causing the Westminster Assembly (an advisory body to Parliament about reformation of the church, dominated by Presbyterians) to condemn tracts favoring toleration. A sermon on this subject, preached before Parliament, spoke against illegal books and identified *Doctrine and Discipline of Divorce* as immoral. Further, booksellers, united in a corporation, complained about illegal books to the House of Commons, denouncing Milton among others.

These were the direct catalysts of *Areopagitica*. Issued on November 23, 1644, it also was published without benefit of authorization or registration and in defiance of the restraining ordinance. (It was also delivered orally before Parliament.) On December 9, the booksellers complained to the House of Lords, but the lords took no action.

Milton's attack on licensing had no effect on Parliament's policy. Indeed, licensing was reasserted several times and continued to be practiced until 20 years after Milton's death, in 1694. Frederick Seaton Siebert notes that *Areopagitica* had "very little effect" on Milton's contemporaries; it "went unmentioned by most of the writers and public men of the times."

After the execution of Charles I and the abolition of the monarchy, Oliver Cromwell, named as lord protector in 1658, condemned *Areopagitica* as did the "Little Parliament" of Protestant England that had succeeded the expelled House of Commons.

Areopagitica appeared in only one edition and was not republished until 1738. At this time it aroused public support for the concept of freedom of the mind. According to Siebert, a significant factor in this change in public opinion was the Peter Zenger trial in a colonial courtroom in New York. Zenger's acquittal of libel of the royal governor was perceived as a freedom of the press issue; the publication of the trial transcript, four editions in London in 1728, notes Siebert, "undoubtedly set an example for English juries."

FURTHER READING

Green, Jonathon, and Nicholas J. Karolides, reviser. *Encyclopedia of Censorship, New Edition.* New York: Facts On File, 2005.

Haight, Anne Lyon, and Chandler B. Grannis. *Banned Books: 387 B.C. to 1978 A.D.* 4th ed. New York: R. R. Bowker, 1978.

Hunter, William B., ed. *A Milton Encyclopedia.* Lewisburg, Pa.: Bucknell University Press, 1978.

Saillens, Emile. *John Milton: Man, Poet, Polemist.* Oxford, England: Basil Blackwell, 1964.

Siebert, Fredrick Seaton. *Freedom of the Press in England, 1476–1776.* Urbana: University of Illinois Press, 1965.

Sirluck, Ernest. "Preface and Notes." In *Complete Prose Works of John Milton,* Vol. 2. New Haven, Conn.: Yale University Press, 1959.

THE BASTARD OF ISTANBUL

Author: Elif Shafak
Original dates and places of publication: 2006, Turkey; 2007, United States and Canada
Publisher: Metis Yayinlari; Viking Penguin
Literary form: Novel

SUMMARY

Against the backdrop of the century-old antagonism and bitterness between Armenia and Turkey, stemming from the "Armenian genocide" of 1915, three generations of two families are introduced, their culture and lives experienced. The Kazanci family—four daughters, their mother, and grandmother—live in Istanbul; the son, Mustafa, left Turkey to study at the University of Arizona. The youngest daughter has a daughter, Asya, born out of wedlock; the father is not revealed until the end of the novel. The Armenian family, the Tchakhmakchians—three daughters and one son, their mother, Shushan—live in San Francisco. The son is divorced from an American woman, Rose, who is now married to Mustafa; their daughter, Armanoush, divides her time between Tucson and San Francisco. Asya and Armanoush are both about 20 years old.

The novel principally expresses the lives of two generations of both families with significant flashbacks to the grandparents and, occasionally, the great-grandparents. Told in temporal sequence, the chapters generally alternate from one family to the other until Armanoush travels to Istanbul to connect with her Armenian forebear, but as a guest in the home of her stepfather's family.

While the two families are politically, culturally (though their cuisines overlap as do family attitudes), and linguistically distinct, there is a surprising connection. Shushan, the matriarch of the Tchakhmakchians, the

Armenian grandmother of Armanoush, is also the mother of Levant Kazanci, the patriarch of the Turkish family, father of Mustafa, and grandfather of Asya. During the forced exodus from Turkey, Shushan at the age of three had been separated from her brothers. First, she was rescued by two Turkish women who saved her life, and later, she was adopted by a Turk from an orphanage; subsequently he married her and fathered Levant. When she was found by her brothers, Shushan made the difficult decision to abandon her son and Turkish husband; and emigrated to America. Thus, she is the great-grandmother of Asya. And as we learn in the penultimate chapter, Armanoush's stepfather is Asya's father; he had, in a show of power and authority, raped his sister before leaving for America.

Armanoush's life is relatively calm. She does feel overprotected by her mother, who needs to know what is going on in her daughter's life, especially when she is visiting her father's family in San Francisco. Comparably, her doting aunts and grandmother attempt to control her life, partly protective, partly to assure her growing up as an Armenian. Especially, they ensure that she knows about the forced exodus from Turkey, the diaspora that separated families and caused many deaths.

A computer group, Café Constantinopolis, is a sanctuary for Armanoush. A regular member, she joins the online discussion on almost a daily basis. The focus of these sessions is on their common history and culture—and their common enemy, the Turks. It is during one of these sessions that Armanoush decides to go to Istanbul to track her family's roots. And she does during spring break, secretly, pretending via cell phone that she is with the other half of her family.

Asya's life is more tumultuous, as is she. Like her mother, Auntie Zeliha, a relatively free spirit, who refuses to conform to traditional rules and codes in dress, behavior, and religion, Asya expresses her rebellion from her overbearing, nagging aunts, feeling suffocated by the love and attention of her four "mothers." She found out she is a bastard, initially accidentally, and then from derisive schoolmates' taunts. She is distressed about not knowing who her father is and, further, aggrieved that her mother won't tell. She identifies herself as an outcast.

In a conversation with Armanoush she says "with a glint of rage in her eyes, '. . . if my father were deceased, this vagueness would be over once and for all. That's what infuriates me the most. I can't help thinking he could be anyone. When you have no idea what kind of man your father is, your imagination fills the void.'"

Asya's depth of depression is evidenced in her attempted suicide two days before her 18th birthday. At 19, however, she realized that "from now on she could not possibly be treated like a kid."

Like Armanoush, Asya is an adherent of a group that meets at the Café Kundera, a small coffee shop, where lethargy prevails. Its members, disparate and argumentative, meet to talk and drink. They seem at once superficial and intellectual, but not serious. They see themselves as outsiders from society, bored, pessimistic, nihilistic, and seemingly without purpose. Asya unloads her resentment toward her family there, finding inner peace. She sees herself as a nihilist and composes a Personal Manifesto of Nihilism. Example articles: "One: If you cannot find a reason to love the life you are living, do not pretend to love the life you are living. Two: the overwhelming majority of people never think and those who think never become the overwhelming majority. Choose your side."

Armanoush's arrival in Istanbul is welcomed by the Kazanci aunts and mother; it is the first living connection with their brother/son in 20 years. Asya, however, is distant and resistant; she does not want to befriend the American, expecting her to be there to analyze them, but she comes to understand her mission. The two develop respect for each other, recognizing similarities in their lives though not in their attitudes toward life. The Armenian history, related through her family's history, seems to help them to bridge the chasm. Asya knows the facts but has never heard it from the lips of a "survivor."

This history, told partly by flashback and partly by Armanoush, is expressed in several venues. The Turkish-Armenian tension about the event, including the evident unawareness of ordinary Turks, is quite apparent when Armanoush relates her family's history to the Kazancis. They seem to disconnect from it. Even Auntie Cevriye, a Turkish national history teacher at a private high school,

> declared without comprehending that the repercussions could be far more complex than she would care to acknowledge. . . . she was so accustomed to drawing an impermeable boundary between the past and the present, distinguishing the Ottoman Empire from the modern Turkish Republic, that she had actually heard the whole story as grim news from a distant country.

The Ottoman government's targeting of writers, poets, and intellectuals to be "eliminated" is introduced in the context of Armanoush's love of reading. As such, it is a prelude to her compelling narrative.

> My grandmother's father, Houhannes Stamboulian, was a poet and a writer. . . . But unfortunately his name was on the list . . . the list of Armenian intellectuals to be eliminated. Political leaders, poets, writers, members of the clergy. . . . There were two hundred and thirty-four people total.

An extended commentary about the forced march follows, including beatings, inadequate food, and other harrowing details.

The subject is broached again in Asya and Armanoush's conversation about the value of history. It is detailed in Auntie Banu's mystical memory tour and argued at the Café Kundera when Armanoush is introduced as an Armenian American. There is immediate denial of the event, but Armanoush stands her ground; Asya supports her defense. The narrative of Shushan's calamity offers another repetition from the perspective of her eldest brother's search for her.

CENSORSHIP HISTORY

Charged under Article 301 of the Turkish penal code with insulting "Turkishness" in *The Bastard of Istanbul*, Elif Shafak appeared in court on September 21, 2006, to defend herself. This was her second appearance. She had escaped a court date earlier by asserting that the statements objected to were made by fictional characters. In June, a public prosecutor in Istanbul accepted this argument and dismissed the case.

A lawyer, Kemal Kerinçsiz, filed a new complaint. (He is the leader of the Unity of Jurists, a rightist group opposed to Turkey's membership in the European Union.) A high criminal court in Istanbul overruled the lower court's decision, thus leading to the trial.

The plaintiffs objected to the utterance of the word "genocide" with reference to the 1915 exodus of the Armenians from Turkey. Also, the statement of Uncle Dikran about the upbringing of his young niece, Armanoush, by an American woman and potentially a Turk who she is dating, is offensive:

> What will that innocent lamb tell her friends when she grows up? My father is Barsam Tchakhakchian, my great-uncle is Dikran Stamboulian, his father is Varvant Istanboulian, my name is Armanoush Tchakhakchian, all my family tree has been Something Somethingian, and I am the grandchild of genocide survivors who lost all their relatives at the hands of Turkish butchers in 1915, but I myself have been brainwashed to deny the genocide because I was raised by some Turk named Mustafa!

Turkey asserts that the mass evacuation and deaths of about 1.5 million Armenians from 1915 to 1917 was not genocide. The issue has been a taboo subject in Turkey; naming it "genocide" is a criminal offense under Article 301. Insulting Turkishness under this article carries a penalty of up to three years in jail.

Elif Shafak was acquitted of charges that her fictional characters "denigrated" the Turkish nation. Judge Ifran Adil Uncu noted in his ruling that "freedom of speech is a priority."

FURTHER READING

Fowler, Susanne. "Turkey, a Touchy Critic, Plans to Put a Novel on Trial." *New York Times*, September 16, 2006.

Freely, Maureen. "Writers on Trial." *New York Times*, August 13, 2006.

Newsletter on Intellectual Freedom. "Istanbul, Turkey" 56 (2007): 35–36.

Turgut, Pelin. "Novelist Acquitted after Trial for 'Insulting Turkishness.'" *Independent*, September 22, 2006.

BLACK BOY

Author: Richard Wright
Original date and place of publication: 1945, United States
Publisher: Harper and Row
Literary form: Autobiography

SUMMARY

"My days and nights were one long, quiet, continuously contained dream of terror, tension and anxiety. I wondered how long I could bear it." So concludes chapter 13 (there are 14) of Richard Wright's autobiography, expressing the crescendo of his feelings before finally in the last chapter achieving his secret dream of escaping the South to the North.

Subtitled "Record of Childhood and Youth," the memoir begins when he is four years old and takes him into his 19th year. His accounts of his experiences and relationships reveal how he has been shaped and conditioned, the person he has become.

Wright's childhood was one of trauma and indignity, narrowness and poverty. The family moved frequently, first from the plantation of his birth, where his father was a sharecropper, to Memphis. Other moves resulted from his father's abandoning his wife and two sons for another woman. These moves took the family to lower-rent accommodations, to new locations in search of jobs or to relatives where they lived on their sometimes grudging charity. Such dependence became virtually permanent after his mother at quite a young age suffered a stroke that caused paralysis of her legs.

Wright's dominant childhood memories are of hunger, deficiency, and fear. With his father's departure, there was no income until his mother was able to find work. Hunger, constant and gnawing, haunted the family; when food was available, it was insufficient in both quantity and nutrition. Often there was not enough money to heat their shack. Sometimes young Richard's mother brought the two boys to work with her; they stood in the corner of the kitchen where she was a cook, smelling the food but unable to eat. There was not enough money for clothes; ashamed of Richard's destitute appearance, his mother would not send him to school.

Beatings appear to have been "automatic" responses of adults toward children for misbehavior or stubborn resistance. Young Richard, an intractable, willful child, is often birched or strapped by his mother (before her illness) and relatives. Uncles and aunts attempt also to browbeat him into submitting to their wills. A parallel violence is evident in contacts with neighborhood gangs and in schoolyards. Richard, the new kid, the outsider, has to prove himself before he can gain entrance.

The sense of abandonment, exacerbated by being placed in an orphanage when his mother could not afford to take care of the two boys, and the feelings of loss—though perhaps not understood—were effective in forming

Richard's personality. These dovetailed with his frequent outsider status; opportunities for deep and lasting relationships were thwarted by both the frequent moves and the suppressive attitudes of the significant adults. Warmth, tenderness and encouragement were lacking, except sporadically from his mother.

Religion was another source of agony and emotional browbeating, particularly during the period when he lived in his grandmother's house. Despite his young age, he resisted his grandmother's efforts to commit him to her fear-evoking religion, refusing to be bullied into submission. When his equally rigid and devout aunt, who is also his teacher, struck him across the knuckles with a ruler because she assumes he, rather than a devout classmate, is guilty of littering the floor, he vowed not to allow it a second time. When she came at him at home with a switch, he fought her off with a kitchen knife, fighting, in effect, for his sense of justice and independence.

A contrasting strand is woven through the autobiography: young Richard's curiosity, his eagerness to learn to read and the rapidity with which he learned. He began to pick out and recognize words in his playmates' schoolbooks at age six; in about an hour's time, the coalman taught him to count to 100. He questioned everything. His school attendance started late and was erratic; he was past 12 before he had a full year of formal schooling. But once fully enrolled, he excelled, graduating as the valedictorian of his class. Books became his salvation, both an escape from his tormenting environment and an avenue to a dreamed of future: "going north and writing books, novels." Books opened up the world of serious writing, opened up for him the life of the mind and encouraged his conviction to live beyond the constraints of the South.

Richard Wright acknowledges his limited contacts with whites during his early years. By age nine, a dread of whites had grown in him, fueled by frightening tales of repression, of the Ku Klux Klan, and of his family's experiences. His first jobs with whites when he is a young teenager corroborate his impressions of their meanness and mistreatment, projecting their view that blacks are children or idiots and less than human. A significant realization is his understanding that "the entire educational system of the South had been rigged to stifle" the aspirations of the black citizens.

As he gains experiences in the white world, Wright learns to keep secret his dream of going north and becoming a writer. It takes him considerably longer than his school and work acquaintances to learn appropriate obsequious mannerisms, language, and tone. His ignorance causes him to lose employment and to suffer harm. Part of his "problem," as a friend notes in his sixteenth year: "'You act around white people as if you didn't know that they were white.'" Wright silently acknowledges this truth:

> . . . it was simply impossible for me to calculate, to scheme, to act, to plot all the time. I would remember to dissemble for short periods, then I would

forget and act straight and human again, not with the desire to harm anybody, but merely forgetting the artificial status of race and class.

His friend continues: "You know, Dick, you may think I'm an Uncle Tom, but I'm not. I hate these white people, hate 'em with all my heart. But I can't show it; if I did, they'd kill me."

Richard Wright did learn to control his public face and voice to a greater extent, but not without a sense of shame, tension, and mental strain. While the latter dissipated somewhat in the more urbane atmosphere of Memphis, he was frequently reminded of the need to be guarded. These experiences and responses reveal Wright's growth and cultural assimilation. They also reveal the survival training induced in blacks by the white threat: deception, dishonesty, lying, and irresponsibility.

When contemplating his present life and his future, Wright sees four choices: rebellion, organizing with other blacks to fight the southern whites; submitting and living the life of a genial slave, thus denying that his "life had shaped [him] to live by [his] own feelings and thoughts"; draining his restlessness by fighting other blacks, thus transferring his hatred of himself to others with a black skin; and forgetting what he's learned through books, forgetting whites and finding release in sex and alcohol. In this context, he continues:

> I had no hope whatever of being a professional man. Not only had I been so conditioned that I did not desire it, but the fulfillment of such an ambition was beyond my capabilities. Well-to-do Negroes lived in a world that was almost as alien to me as the world inhabited by whites.

Finally, however, "sheer wish and hope prevailed over common sense and facts." Planning with his mother, brother, and aunt, he takes the step; he boards the train bound for Chicago.

CENSORSHIP HISTORY*

Richard Wright was not unfamiliar with the threat of censorship. A member of the Communist Party in 1940 when *Native Son* was published, he was threatened with expulsion because at least one party leader sensed a fundamental disagreement between the party's views and those expressed in the book. Wright had been saved by its popularity and acclaim, making Wright too important a member to lose. Wright had recognized other attempts by the party to constrain his thinking. In 1940 he renounced his affiliation with the party.

The Special Committee on Un-American Activities, the Dies Committee, had investigated him and called him subversive. Wright had also been the target of a top-priority investigation of the FBI regarding his

---

*This censorship history was augmented by the research and writing of Dawn Sova.

affiliation with and activities for the Communist Party. Wright knew that his neighbors had been questioned. These events had preceded the publication of *Black Boy*. In the 1950s Richard Wright was identified unfavorably before the House Un-American Activities Committee and cited by the committee as belonging to one or more "fronts." According to existing directives, his work should have been withdrawn from U.S. libraries overseas.

Black Boy as originally submitted, titled *American Hunger*, included Wright's Chicago experience. Although it was initially accepted by Harper and Row, his editor later informed Wright that the book would be divided: The first two-thirds, the experiences in the South, would be published separately from the experiences in the North, Chicago, and New York. Initially, Wright accepted this suggestion without question; Constance Webb, Wright's biographer, notes, however, that subsequently he felt "in his whole being that his book was being censored in some way." He considered the possibility that Harper and Row did not want to offend the communists, since the United States and the Soviet Union were then allies, or that the Communist Party itself was exerting some influence over the publisher. He determined to find a way to publish the omitted final segment of his manuscript.

At the time of publication, despite its being a Book-of-the-Month Club selection and achieving both broad readership and significant acclaim in reviews, Mississippi banned it; Senator Theodore Bilbo of Mississippi condemned the book and its author in Congress:

> *Black Boy* should be taken off the shelves of stores; sales should be stopped; it was a damnable lie, from beginning to end; it built fabulous lies about the South. The purpose of the book was to plant seeds of hate and devilment in the minds of every American. It was the dirtiest, filthiest, most obscene, filthy and dirty, and came from a Negro from whom one could not expect better.

The autobiography has been met with controversy in school districts in all regions of the United States. Most of the challenges have been of mainly local interest, while one case received national attention and created precedent. In a 1963 school censorship survey of Wisconsin, *Black Boy* was reported removed because it was deemed unsuitable for high school students; a 1966 national survey reported the book challenged on the grounds of obscenity and that it teaches blacks to hate whites. In 1972, parents in Michigan objected to the book's sexual overtones and claimed it was unsuitable for impressionable sophomores, which resulted in its removal from the classroom. It was banned in Baltimore in 1974. In 1975, the book was removed from Tennessee schools for being obscene, instigating hatred between races, and encouraging immorality.

Complaints against five books, including *Black Boy*, were filed in November 1975 in East Baton Rouge, Louisiana, by Babs Minhinnette, chairperson of Concerned Citizens and Taxpayers for Decent School Books. This complaint emerged out of a controversy over the removal of two books, one by the school board and the other by the principal. This controversy had led to the adoption in May 1975 of a policy to handle objections. Subsequently, however, in September 1975, the school board had ordered a search for books and materials containing obscenity, filth, or pornography. Teachers and librarians criticized the search order, claiming it was a reversal of the policy adopted in May. The challenge to the five books by the Concerned Citizens chairperson was perceived as an attempt to test the new review procedure. The committee voted 6-1 to reject the request to remove the books after a review conducted in late November.

A comparable situation developed in Nashua, New Hampshire, in 1978. As a result of a complaint against the use of *Black Boy* in the ninth grade of the high school in Nashua, a review committee recommended that the book be removed from this grade level and that it be used only in elective courses in grades 11 and 12. The controversy over *Black Boy* gave rise to questions about the appropriateness of certain textbooks in schools across the state and gave impetus to the formation of a new organization, Concerned Citizens and Taxpayers for Better Education. This group's intention was to monitor books used in classes of several communities, from which its members were drawn, in order to safeguard "traditional Judeo-Christian values" in the schools.

The Anaheim (California) Secondary Teachers Association in September 1978 charged the Anaheim Union High School Board of Trustees with having "banned thousands of books from English classrooms of the Anaheim secondary schools." The trustees, acting on a recommendation of the district's administration, had removed more than half of the reading material available to English teachers. *Black Boy* was among the books banned from the classroom and from school libraries. The board's president, James P. Bonnell, claimed that the 270 books remaining on the grade 7 to 12 list were "adequate." Teachers were instructed to simply store the book, along with others, and cautioned that they were not permitted to provide the books for supplemental reading or to discuss the books with students. The local school board warned teachers that they risked dismissal if they taught any of the banned books. The result of the confrontation was the mounting of a recall campaign: Petitions were circulated to enforce a reelection ballot for Bonnell and another trustee, and "Notice of Intent to Recall" papers were served on these individuals. The recall election was successful in unseating these trustees.

In September 1987, Nebraska governor Kay Orr's "kitchen cabinet" met with leaders of a citizens' group, Taxpayers for Quality Education. The group made recommendations to the governor regarding curriculum, strategies for teaching reading, and school administration. It also indicated it would monitor books in school libraries and recommend reading lists. George Darlington, president of Taxpayers for Quality Education, identified *Black Boy* as one of the books that should be removed, asserting it had a "corruptive obscene nature" and citing the use of profanity throughout and the incidents of violence. He noted that such books "inflict a cancer on the body of education we want our children to develop." The book was removed from library shelves, then returned after the controversy abated.

Objectionable language was the basis for challenges in California (1977) and New York (1983); both failed. In Oxford, North Carolina (1994), objections focused on "filthy words," "lustful talk," and "immoral sex"; "the putting down of ALL kinds of people: the boy's family, the white people, the Jew, the church, the church school and even his friends." Also in 1994, a complaint in Fillmore, California, pointed to violence—the killing of a kitten—and profanity; the parent stated that the book is "not conducive to teaching what civilized people are supposed to behave like." The autobiography was also challenged in Round Rock, Texas, in 1996, for graphically describing three beating deaths and for having been "written while the author was a member of the Communist Party." The charges against the book in Jacksonville, Florida, in 1997, were made by a minister complainant, who alleged the book was profane, could stir up racial animosity, and was not appropriate for children; he urged the school board to ban the book and to fire the teacher who had assigned it.

In a landmark case, the autobiography was one of nine books that the school board of the Island Trees (New York) Union Free District removed from the junior and senior high school libraries in 1976; two books were removed from classrooms. The other books were *The Best Short Stories by Negro Writers*, THE FIXER, GO ASK ALICE, SLAUGHTERHOUSE-FIVE, DOWN THESE MEAN STREETS, A HERO AIN'T NOTHIN' BUT A SANDWICH, LAUGHING BOY, THE NAKED APE, SOUL ON ICE, and *A Reader for Writers*. Condemned with broad generalizations, the books were charged with being "anti-American, anti-Christian, anti-Semitic, or just plain filthy." As entered in the court record, the specific objections to *Black Boy* concerned the use of obscenity and the anti-Semitic remarks and other ethnic slurs, in such passages as the following: "We black children—seven or eight or nine years of age—used to run to the Jew's store and shout: . . . Bloody Christ Killers/Never trust a Jew/Bloody Christ Killers/What won't a Jew do/Red, white and blue/Your pa was a Jew/Your ma a dirty dago/What the hell is you?"

The controversy began in March 1976 when the chair of a Long Island school board, Richard J. Ahrens, using a list of "objectionable" books and a collection of excerpts compiled by Parents of New York United (PONY-U), ordered 11 books removed from the Island Trees School District High School library. Teachers indicated that two of the books, Bernard Malamud's *The Fixer* and *The Best Short Stories of Negro Writers*, had been removed from classrooms, where they were being used in a literature course. The local teachers' union did file a formal grievance against the board, alleging a violation of the provisions of academic freedom in the union contract. A group of residents also objected to the censorship, stating they would protest to the state commissioner of education.

In defense against the protests of parents and students, the school board appointed a committee made up of parents and teachers to review the books and to determine which, if any, had merit. The committee recommended that seven of the books be returned to the library shelves, that two be placed on restricted shelves and that two be removed from the library, but the school board in July ignored these recommendations and voted to keep all but two of the books off the shelves. It authorized "restricted" circulation for *Black Boy* and circulation without restriction for *Laughing Boy*. The others would be "removed from . . . libraries and from use in the curriculum," that is, not to be assigned as required, optional, or even suggested reading, although the books might still be discussed in class. The vote was unanimous on most titles. Ahrens said, "It is not only our right but our duty to make the decision, and we would do it again in the face of the abuse heaped upon us by the media."

Five students—one junior high school student and four senior high school students—filed suit on January 4, 1977, against the school district, seeking an injunction to have the books returned to the library shelves. The students challenged the censorship, claiming that the school board had violated their constitutional rights under the guise of protecting their social and moral tastes.

A federal district court decision handed down in August 1979 (*Pico v. Board of Education*) favored the school board. U.S. District Court judge George C. Pratt rejected what he termed *tenure* for a book; in effect, he ruled that school boards have the right to examine the contents of library materials in order to determine their "suitability." At the center of the controversy was the constitutional role of the school board in public education, particularly in selection of content in relation to the perceived values of the community.

> In the absence of a sharp, focused issue of academic freedom, the court concludes that respect for the traditional values of the community and deference to the school board's substantial control over educational content preclude any finding of a First Amendment violation arising out of removal of any of the books from use in the curriculum.

After a U.S. Circuit Court of Appeals decision to remand the case for trial—in a 2-1 vote—the school board requested a review by the U.S. Supreme Court, which was granted. The appellate court had concluded that the First Amendment rights of the students had been violated and the criteria for the removal of the books were too general and overbroad.

The Supreme Court justices, sharply divided in a 5-4 decision (*Board of Education, Island Trees Union Free School District v. Pico*), upheld the appeals court. The Supreme Court mandated further trial proceedings to determine the underlying motivations of the school board. The majority relied on the concept that the "right to receive ideas" is a "necessary predicate" to the meaningful exercise of freedom of speech, press, and political freedom. Justice William Brennan, writing for the majority (which included Justices Thurgood Marshall, John Paul Stevens and Harry Blackmun; and Justice Byron White with qualifications), stated: "Local school boards have broad discretion in the management of school affairs but this discretion must be exercised in a manner that comports with the transcendent imperatives of the First Amendment."

> Our Constitution does not permit the official suppression of *ideas*. Thus whether [school board's] removal of books from their school libraries denied [students] their First Amendment rights upon the motivation. . . . If [school board] *intended* by their removal decision to deny [students] access to ideas with which [school board] disagreed, and if this intent was a decisive factor in [school board's] decision, then [school board] have exercised their discretion in violation of the Constitution. To permit such intentions to control official actions would be to encourage . . . officially prescribed orthodoxy. . . . [emphasis in original].
>
> [W]e hold that local school boards may not remove books from school library shelves simply because they dislike the ideas contained in those books and seek by their removal to "prescribe what shall be orthodox in politics, nationalism, religion, or other matters of opinion." . . . Such purposes stand inescapably condemned by our precedents.

In their dissenting opinion, Chief Justice Warren Burger and Justices Sandra Day O'Connor, Lewis Powell, and William Rehnquist issued a warning as to the role of the Supreme Court in making local censorship decisions: "If the plurality's view were to become the law, the court would come perilously close to becoming a 'super censor' of school board library decisions and the Constitution does not dictate that judges, rather than parents, teachers, and local school boards, must determine how the standards of morality and vulgarity are to be treated in the classroom." Thus, in their reluctance to place the Supreme Court in the position of local censor, the conservative justices recommended that the task of setting local community standards remain in local hands.

The controversy ended on August 12, 1982, when the Island Trees school board voted 6-1 to return the nine books to the school library shelves without restriction as to their circulation, but with a stipulation that the librarian must send a written notice to parents of students who borrow books containing material that the parents might find objectionable. The board also delayed action on whether *The Fixer* would be returned to the curriculum.

In February 2007, a citizens' group, the Livingston Organization for Values in Education (LOVE), complained to the Howell school board about the sexual content of four books in the Howell (Michigan) High School curriculum: *Black Boy*, by Richard Wright; SLAUGHTERHOUSE-FIVE, by Kurt

Vonnegut; THE BLUEST EYE, by Toni Morrison; and *The Freedom Writers Diary*, by Erin Gruell. Their challenge demanded that the books be removed from the curriculum; a LOVE spokesperson compared the books to *Penthouse* and *Playboy* magazines, asserting that they "contain similarly graphic materials in written form [and] are equally inappropriate." *The Bluest Eye* was described as a "graphic child rape book." Letters were also sent to the offices of the U.S attorney, state attorney general, and Livingston County prosecutor, requesting opinions about whether the books violate laws on obscenity and distribution of materials that are harmful to minors. The federal and state offices forwarded the request to the FBI which is a routine procedure with such complaints.

On February 12, the school board voted 5-2 to reject LOVE's complaint. They will continue to be used in AP classes. The district superintendent explained, "We should also be very careful about dismissing literary works because they test our own belief system or challenge our values." David Morse, the county prosecutor, concluded that the books are legal on two grounds: 1) Since the school board has approved use of these books, the teachers and administrators have complied with school codes and are exempted from criminal prosecution; 2) To qualify as obscene, a book must be found to appeal only to readers' prurient interest in sex and have no literary or educational merit.

". . . it is clear that the explicit passages [in the books] illustrated a larger literary, artistic or political message and were not included solely to appeal to the prurient interest of minors." Michigan attorney general Mike Cox and U.S. attorney Stephen Murphy concurred with Morse and indicated in mid-March that they would not prosecute.

FURTHER READING

"ASTA Release." *Anaheim Secondary Teachers Association* (September 27, 1978, and November 15, 1979).

Attacks on Freedom to Learn: 1980–1983, 1994–1995, and 1995–1996. New York: People For the American Way, New York Regional Offices, November 1983 and Washington, D.C.: People For the American Way, 1995 and 1996.

Gayle, Addison. *Richard Wright: Ordeal of a Native Son.* Garden City, N.Y.: Anchor Press/Doubleday, 1980.

Graham, Maryemma, and Jerry W. Ward, Jr. "*Black Boy (American Hunger):* Freedom to Remember." In *Censored Books: Critical Viewpoints,* edited by Nicholas J. Karolides, Lee Burress, and Jack Kean, 109–116. Metuchen, N.J.: Scarecrow Press, 1993.

Hurwitz, Leon. *Historical Dictionary of Censorship in the United States.* Westport, Conn.: Greenwood Press, 1985.

Jenkinson, Edward B. *Censors in the Classroom: The Mind Benders.* Carbondale: Southern Illinois University Press, 1979.

Newsletter on Intellectual Freedom 24 (1975): 104, 120; 25 (1976): 34, 61–62, 85–86, 115; 26 (1977): 45; 27 (1978): 57; 28 (1979): 6, 141–145; 31 (1982): 12–13, 166, 197; and 36 (1987): 225.

North, William D. "Pico and the Challenge to Books in Schools." *Newsletter on Intellectual Freedom* 31 (1982): 195, 221–225.

Rich, R. Bruce. "The Supreme Court's Decision in Island Trees." *Newsletter on Intellectual Freedom* 31 (1982): 149, 173–186.

SIECUS. "FBI, State Deem Books Legal after Obscenity Complaints." March 2007. Available online. URL: http://www.familiesaretalking.org/index.cfm?fuseaction=feature.showFeature&featureID=1069. Accessed September 17, 2010.

Simoneau, Duke. "Book Controversy Flares in Nashua." *New Hampshire Sunday News,* March 5, 1978, pp. 1, 18.

Weathersby, Dorothy T. *Censorship of Literature Textbooks in Tennessee: A Study of the Commission, Publishers, Teachers, and Textbooks.* Ed.D. diss., University of Tennessee, 1975.

Webb, Constance. *Richard Wright: A Biography.* New York: Putnam, 1968.

BLOODS: AN ORAL HISTORY OF THE VIETNAM WAR BY BLACK VETERANS

Author: Wallace Terry
Original date and place of publication: 1984, United States
Publisher: Random House
Literary form: Personal narratives

SUMMARY

Twenty veterans, representing all four major service units, tell their backgrounds and experiences in *Bloods.* They reveal their attitudes and expectations as well as their postwar reactions. They range in rank from private first class to sergeant major among the 15 enlisted men and first lieutenant (U.S. Marine Corps) to lieutenant commander (U.S. Navy) and colonel (U.S. Air Force) among the officers. Their specialties and assignments also vary: combat tasks—rifleman, reconnaissance patrolman, platoon leader, engineer, radio wireman, paratrooper, and pilot—and noncombat tasks—hospital corpsman, interpreter, combat photographer, armorer, and radarman. This variety provides multiple perspectives of the Vietnam scene, as do the attitudes of the men themselves.

Several of these men had enlisted in the service to escape poverty and the limitations of dead-end jobs and to have careers. In parallel motivation, others had traveled the ROTC or service academy routes to the dignity and opportunity of being an "officer and a gentleman." Others joined because they had failed in or been unable to continue college or to "see what the war was all about" or because of intense desire to fly. One of them had been an antiwar activist, had evaded the draft, had been caught by the FBI, and had chosen, finally, war over jail.

This negative perception of the war when the men entered the service was at one extreme of a continuum. At the other extreme—not limited to the officers—were attitudes whose identified purposes aligned with stated United States government policy: "I thought communism was spreading, and as an American citizen, it was my part to do as much as I could to defeat the Communist from coming here. Whatever America states is correct was the tradition I was brought up in"; "the people in South Vietnam wanna be free to make their own decisions, to have a democratic government. And the Commies were trying to take over. . . . when the commander in chief says time to go, we head out." Some of these personnel express disillusionment with the purposes of the war while in Vietnam.

War situations and events are expressed, some more extensively and horrifically than others. Such differences are factors of the situations and locations and the personalities or psychologies of the individual men. Captain Anderson provides a dispassionate, tactical approach and an overarching motivation to protect his men and achieve his assigned mission. Describing his first operation (when he was a second lieutenant), to locate and rescue an ambushed platoon, he identifies his procedures and his emotions: "I can't remember wondering if I was ever gonna get out of this. I just did not have time to think about it. I was just too busy directing fire to be scared." The squad of specialist 4 Kirkland, a recoilless rifleman, is ambushed. Machine-gun fire pins them down; grenades (fired from grenade launchers captured from a previously ambushed squad) are dropping around them. Two of the men get shot, and the fire team leader, who had been brave and ruthless in previous firefights, loses courage and is unable to fire or move. Before they are rescued, eight are seriously wounded, and the fire team leader has an emotional breakdown. In another example, with a month of service in Vietnam left, Sergeant Daniels, radio wireman, is sent on a mission. Despite a minesweeper ahead, the vehicle he is in hits a mine. First blown up into the air, his leg is pinned by an armored vehicle track, and his body is burned from exploded gasoline. "I had three-degree burns everywhere. The skin was just hangin' off my left arm. My right arm was burned completely to the bone. My face was all burnt up. It was white." Other memories, too, describe scenes of sudden attacks; arms, legs, heads blown off; and men dying in pain. The focus is on the human misery and loss.

Brutalities of another sort are exposed. While the narrators for the most part abhorred such practices, they observed American soldiers collecting ears or fingers of dead Viet Cong as trophies or severing their genitals. Others threw tear-gas grenades or explosive grenades into crowds, or they shot or drove into people on the road. One "game," called Guts, was played in retaliation for the downing of an observation plane and capturing of its pilot. A prisoner was tied naked to a tree while the men took turns mutilating or beating him. Rapes and even gang rapes of young girls are evidenced. In contrast, comparable to the individuals who rejected such behavior for themselves, Lt. Anderson's platoon did not pillage villages or molest people; the platoon.

would set up our medics to treat the children and the people. We would tend to scars, wounds, whatever. Give them aspirin and soap. We'd give the kids gum, cookies, C-rations. If we wanted to eat off the land, we would buy a chicken or buy a pig. . . . this was probably the first army in the history of the world that did not take what it wanted.

The acts of the North Vietnamese are also documented: wrapping explosives around women and children and using them as bait; castrating captured American bodies; tying Americans to trees or torturing them by mutilation (an officer is cited as representing the Guts episode as a method of retaliation for these). The most extreme situation described is the live American discovered staked to the ground: beaten and mutilated, the skin of his chest had been peeled to his waist; maggots and flies were eating the exposed flesh; he had been left to die. Additionally, two of the narrators have been prisoners. They report beatings and torture, starvation diets, and insufficient medical care.

Race relations are a significant issue threaded through the narratives. There was ready consciousness of race and frequent mention of the denigration of black personnel: racist language, menial assignments, "the overwhelming majority of the blacks in the lowest level of jobs," those that are most dangerous. Other examples: the Marine on leave who is jailed by MPs who insist he is an impostor: "There ain't no damn nigger Marines," a captain exclaims; and the initial reluctance of white soldiers to accept the authority and ability of a black officer.

Despite these frictions, resulting at times in fighting and rioting, there is also recognition of respect for each other in the field, of the necessity to trust and depend on each other. There are examples of life-saving helpfulness, lasting friendships between whites and blacks and genuine bereavement when a companion dies. There is a suggestion of surprise that friendship and understanding, of commonality, is also evident. Two telling points are made by the two black prisoners of war who suffered propaganda intended to cause them to turn away from the United States because of its racist history. Both resisted. Colonel Cherry recognizes that he owes his life to a white prison mate, a southerner, who saves his life, feeding him, tending his wounds, providing for him. Captain McDaniel, while acknowledging that "black people have problems in the United States" and "some people do not live up to the ideals our country stands for" and that "black people are kind of behind the power curtain," states, "we have as much claim to this country as any white man. America is the black man's best hope."

Most of these men experienced distress or post-traumatic stress disorder upon their return to their homes: sleep disturbances and dreams; nightmares of combat or being left behind in Vietnam; erratic, hostile behavior; and unexplained rages. Depression was exacerbated by a sense of rejection: The environment was hostile to the returning veterans, their purposes and activities questioned; jobs were unavailable; and there was insufficient help for and understanding of the plight of disabled veterans. When the war ended in what they perceived as defeat, they were angry, feeling it had been a waste of time, that somehow the leadership had failed and deceived them. "The killing, the marauding, the atrocities destroyed human values. They prepared us . . . to annihilate whatever enemy we came upon . . . a thousand and one ways to destroy a human being," one man says. "Not to say that I was involved in both incidents (rapes and murders), but I had turned my back, which made me just as guilty as everyone else. . . . I had learned not to care. And I didn't care." Several closing statements are particularly revealing.

"I really feel used. I feel manipulated. I feel violated."

"I think we were the last generation to believe, you know, in the honor of war. There is no honor in war."

"I don't walk around blind anymore. If another war breaks out and they want me to go, I'd rather die. I'll fight anyone here in America. But if they come and get me to send to another country, I'm going to have my gun ready for them."

"And now I read where the people in Vietnam still havin' the same problems. . . . Well what the hell they sent us over there for? I read the Americans lost. It was nothin'. Nothin'. . . . All I did was lost part of my body. And that's the end of me."

CENSORSHIP HISTORY

A censorship issue was initiated when Dan McIntyre, the principal of West Hernando Middle School in Spring Hill, Florida, removed *Bloods: An Oral History of the Vietnam War by Black Veterans* (along with an issue of *People* magazine) from the library in 1986. He claimed it was too violent for young readers; he acted on a complaint from a teacher who saw a student with a copy. McIntyre indicated that he had "an unequivocable right to monitor the [library] collection. . . ." Librarian Susan Beach Vaughn and the Hernando Classroom Teachers Association filed a grievance in November 1986, claiming that established procedures for considering book complaints had not been followed, that McIntyre had acted arbitrarily.

The Hernando County school board voted on February 3, 1987, to uphold McIntyre, who convinced them that he should be permitted to bypass the review procedures. Board members said that *Bloods* presented a moral danger to students. The school board's attorney, Joe Johnson, had argued that the review policy did not apply to principals; rather it was intended for persons outside the school system. He is quoted in the *Newsletter on Intellectual Freedom* as adding that "you cannot allow segments of society to control your library" by claiming First Amendment rights, which, he charged, are sometimes "prostituted." He also indicated the book's "harsh words" were unnecessary. Counterarguments were offered by parents, one of whom pointed out that "language inappropriate to the classroom is germane to such a bitter and emotional narrative"; by a teacher union representative, the chair of the Florida Library Association Freedom Committee, who referred to the board's ruling as "totalitarian"; and by an ACLU representative.

When Vaughn received her annual evaluation in April 1987, she filed a second grievance, claiming McIntyre had violated her contract by using the censorship dispute as part of her evaluation. This led to the complaint being submitted for binding arbitration. The American Arbitration Association's representative, Perry Zirkel, ruled on September 10, 1987, in Vaughn's favor, ordering that "the disputed materials shall be returned immediately to the shelves."

In addition, however, the arbitrator, who found the review policy flawed and recommended its reconsideration, indicated that books could be removed from school libraries and media centers by the superintendent. Thus, 40 minutes after *Bloods* was returned to the library shelf, it was removed as ordered by School Superintendent James K. Austin. In response to a review request filed by a representative of the Hernando teachers' union, the five-member Media Advisory Committee was convened to review the book. (A committee was also established to consider the existing policy and to make recommendations.) The advisory committee, composed of two teachers, a guidance counselor, and two parents, recommended that *Bloods* be removed from the middle school library and placed in the high school library.

FURTHER READING

"Arbitrator's Decision: Restore *Bloods* to Shelf." *School Library Journal* 34 (October 1987): 14.

Connor, Collins. "Panel Finds Book on Vietnam Too Graphic for Middle School." *St. Petersburg Times*, October 2, 1987, pp. 1, 10.

———. "Teachers' Union Official Seeks Review of Banned Reading." *St. Petersburg Times*, September 23, 1987, [n.p.].

Daniel, Elizabeth. "Publication Fight Takes New Turn." *Tampa Tribune*, September 25, 1987, pp. 1, 3.

Manak, Evelyn H. "Books Pulled Off Shelves Again." *Hernando Free Press*, September 16, 1987, pp. 1, 12.

———. "Librarian Not Surprised Books Were Removed." *Sun Journal*, September 16, 1987, pp. 1, 12.

"Spring Hill, Florida." *Newsletter on Intellectual Freedom* 36 (1987): 85–86, 173–174; 37 (1988): 9.

Varney, Mark Nesbit. "A.C.L.U. Watching School Censorship." *West Hernando News*, September 30, 1987, pp. 1A, 3A.

———. "Librarian Beats School Board." *West Hernando News*, September 16, 1987, pp. 1A, 3A.

BORN ON THE FOURTH OF JULY

Author: Ron Kovic
Original date and place of publication: 1976, United States
Publisher: McGraw-Hill Company
Literary form: Autobiography

SUMMARY

"Ron Kovic's personal tract is perhaps the most singularly powerful vision of the war experience among the memoirs." This tribute within *Walking Point*, a critical examination of the most important novels and memoirs written by Americans about the Vietnam War, expresses the power of *Born on the Fourth of July*. Additionally, the *New York Times* book reviewer, C. B. D. Bryan, identifies it as "the most personal and honest testament published thus far by any young man who fought in the Vietnam War."

Much of the text of *Born on the Fourth of July* is postwar, that is, when the war was over for Sergeant Ron Kovic. On the first page he is wounded and trapped in a sand pit, unable to move his legs. The terror, the screams of pain, the curses of fear and rage are reenacted against a foreground of his agonized plea for life. A few pages reveal the searing anguish.

Surrounded by other men, their screams and thrashings, Kovic is airlifted to an emergency hospital where the second phase of his ordeal begins. He feels nothing below his chest, nor has he any sensation, yet he welcomes the morphine to escape the screams, to enter his dream of being in his backyard again. When he is awake, he is alert to the events around him: the activity to revive a pilot whose heart has stopped, amidst the laughing and bantering of the doctor and corpsman about the Green Bay Packers; a general marching down the aisle, mechanically delivering the same speech to each man, awarding a Purple Heart, but only barely glancing at him. Subsequently, at hospitals in the United States, his images are of being taken to the shower where he can watch his legs shrinking, the muscle tone disappearing; of the enema routine, the men lined up on frames like so many carcasses; the filthy wards. During this time, Kovic still believed in the war, in winning.

The narrative, midbook, shifts to the past, to Kovic's childhood and adolescence. A natural athlete, he was always moving. He loved baseball—playing, watching the Yankees, hero-worshipping Mickey Mantle. His other heroes, John Wayne and Audie Murphy, and his deep sense of patriotism emerged out of war movies. Being a "Yankee Doodle boy," having been born on the Fourth of July, seemed to energize these feelings. The scene of the raising of the flag on Iwo Jima with the Marines' hymn as background music caused him to cry. Afterwards, he and his friends play at war games. In high school, he was a wrestling champion. He wanted to be a hero, to be admired. After graduation, imbued with heroic-patriotic fervor, he joined the Marines.

Estrangement from his traditional patriotic stance evolves slowly. Perhaps it is the discomfort and loneliness he feels as grand marshal of the parade honoring Vietnam War veterans. There are no cheers, no feet stomping, no streamers of paper and confetti—only stares. There is no hugging, except after the speeches when his childhood friend reaches him and they hug each other and cry. Perhaps it is his bitterness and loss, the bouts of self-pity and anger: He grieves about his immobility and is particularly depressed about the premature end of his sex life.

The Kent State demonstration is a turning point. Then, after participating in the anti-Cambodian invasion rally in Washington, he joins the Vietnam Veterans Against the War (VVAW), where he finds companionship and understanding. He identifies with their mission to tell the truth about the war. To further their cause, he gives speeches and begins attending rallies. Two crescendo events highlight this period. The first: During a picketing demonstration in front of Nixon's Los Angeles campaign headquarters, he is dumped out of his wheelchair by an undercover agent, kicked, and beaten. His medals are torn off. He is handcuffed, dragged, and jailed. He is cursed because he identifies himself as a "Vietnam veteran against the war." The second: The Last Patrol, a caravan of young men, drives across country to create an antiwar presence at the 1972 Republican National Convention. Though barred from entering, then clubbed and arrested, the veterans persist. Kovic manages to get inside and wheel himself down the aisle toward the stage. Amid the commotion, he attempts to call attention to the VVAW position; he manages to gain the attention of CBS's Roger Mudd, who interviews him over national television. Subsequently, he and two others in wheelchairs, holding "Stop the War" signs, break into President Nixon's acceptance speech, shouting, "Stop the bombing, stop the bombing." Secret Service men grab their wheelchairs and pull them out of the hall. En route, a man spits in Kovic's face and calls him a traitor. He responds screaming to a newsman: "I served two tours in Vietnam. I gave three-quarters of my body for America. And what do I get? Spit in the face!"

A rerun of the Vietnam scene concludes the novel, returning the reader to the war. Kovic reveals that in the heat of battle, he had accidentally shot one of his men, a corporal. He tried to think of a way out of admitting he has done it; he even, at first, reported that the shot had occurred when the squad was retreating. Unable to live with this deception, he reported what he believes he had done. Nothing happened on the military level, but Kovic recognizes that everything for him has changed:

> All his life [Kovic] wanted to be a winner. . . . But now it all seemed different. All the hopes about being the best marine, winning all those medals. They all seemed crushed now, they were gone forever. Like the man he had just killed with one shot, all those things had disappeared and he knew, he was certain, they would never come back again.

He continues to be haunted by the event, the memory darkening his days and shadowing his sleep.

Weeks later, Kovic and a lieutenant led a patrol, heading toward a village, where, they were told, the enemy was waiting. They fired into the village, then later discover their grievous error:

> "We just shot a bunch of kids!" The floor of the small hut was covered with them, screaming and thrashing their arms back and forth, lying in pools of blood, crying wildly, screaming again and again. They were shot in the face, in the chest, in the legs, moaning and crying.

The men were overcome with horror, remorse and grief. Kovic was numbed. His heroism-oriented mindset has begun to change, as evidenced by his surreal responses to a brutal artillery attack, his depression, his inability to cry for all his friends who died in the barrage. A slow-motion reprise of the book's opening sequence brings the reader back to Kovic's personal horror: "All I could feel was the worthlessness of dying right here in this place at this moment for nothing."

CENSORSHIP HISTORY

Born on the Fourth of July, as reported in Lee Burress's 1982 national survey, was censored in Maryland. A parent objected to the book as un-American, finding fault also with its language and its display of sex. Upon review of the complaint, the book was placed on a closed shelf.

FURTHER READING

Bryan, C. B. D. "Growing Up the Hard Way." *New York Times Book Review*, August 15, 1976, p. 1.

Burress, Lee. *The Battle of the Books: Literary Censorship in the Public Schools, 1950–1985.* Metuchen, N.J.: Scarecrow Press, 1989.

Myers, Thomas. *Walking Point: American Narratives of Vietnam.* New York: Oxford University Press, 1988.

BOSS: RICHARD J. DALEY OF CHICAGO

Author: Mike Royko
Original date and place of publication: 1971, United States
Publisher: E. P. Dutton and Co.
Literary form: Biography

SUMMARY

While a brief chapter is devoted to Richard J. Daley's origins and youth, *Boss* essentially is a political biography that focuses on his rise through the office-holding stepping-stones to the power of the mayoralty and on his tenure in that office. Also expressed is the sociopolitical history of Chicago during this period with emphasis on turning-point events that affected Daley's career and Chicago.

Shadowing Mayor Daley in his daily routine, we meet a seemingly simple man who lives in an unprepossessing brick bungalow in the "inner city," avoids haute-cuisine restaurants, and rejects fine art for his office in order to maintain a down-to-earth profile. His routine includes daily Mass. He is loyal to friends and, encompassing cronyism, supportive of loyal party workers whom he keeps employed. His behavior, however, expresses racism. He is smooth in public and with petitioners, but when provoked vents his anger loudly and offensively. He exerts his power both subtly and dynamically, controlling the city council by dominating the aldermen of his party—he is also the local Democratic Party chairman—and the ward bosses through patronage, by careful screening of appointees and candidates for office. Their loyalty to him is primary. He seems to respond to adulation; he does not accept criticism.

Daley's origins give evidence of sources for these attributes. The Chicago of his youth was composed of blue-collar, ethnic neighborhoods, each self-sufficient and nationalist-oriented. They hated each other and bullied those from other ethnic locales who crossed into their territory.

Upward mobility for Daley in Chicago politics was incremental. It was dependent on his connections in the organization, his opportunism and machinations, his patience and a certain degree of luck. On the political scene, he started as a precinct captain of a ward organization and then as personal secretary of the ward leader, an alderman, in conjunction with his first City Hall job as a clerk in the city council. While working in City Hall, he attended DePaul University's School of Law, attaining a degree in 1934. Favorable elections moved him into other jobs, broadening his experiences; several convenient deaths—and the clever manipulation of the Chicago political machine—gained him his first elective office, the state house of representatives. Two years later, another death brought him to the state senate. After serving as a member of the Cook County Democratic Central Committee, he was elected its chairman, aided again by a death. (The author, in this instance, uses the language "somebody got killed . . . in an auto accident" with regard to the death of an announced countercandidate for the chairmanship.) Subsequently, Daley was ostensibly "drafted" to run for the mayoralty.

An associate—later a political antagonist—of those days describes his recipe for success while serving in state-level offices:

> . . . He rarely said anything on the Senate floor. He was quiet, humble and respectful of everyone, and he developed a reputation for being good on revenue matters, but that was about all. . . . Most of the time he kept to himself, stayed in his hotel room, and worked hard. In Springfield you could tell real

fast which men were there for girls, games, and graft. He wasn't. I'll tell you how he made it. He made it through sheer luck and by attaching himself to one guy after another and then stepping over them. His ward committeeman in those days was Babe Connelly. Babe was always pushing Daley out front. He sent him to Springfield, pushed him for better jobs. Then, when Daley got a chance, he squeezed Connelly out.

During this period, seeming in opposition to his manipulativeness and in contrast to many of his peers, Daley's moral code began to take shape: "Thou shalt not steal, but thou shalt not blow the whistle on anybody who does."

Patronage, based on cronyism, and corruption were rampant in Chicago's governmental operations both before and during Daley's tenure. Job rewards were given to the politically faithful, sometimes with no work to be done, sometimes with no apparent training or skill for the job. Higher-ranking party officials, most holding elective posts, got more lucrative plums: a slice of the city's insurance on public properties, judgeships, retainers for real estate ventures. The system of rewards was also solidly nepotistic: Sons, brothers, cousins, in-laws, and friends reaped the benefits of relationships. Daley's explanation for the patronage and the control of the nominee selection process: "The party permits ordinary people to get ahead. Without the party, I couldn't be mayor. The rich guys can get elected on their money, but somebody like me, an ordinary person, needs a party. Without the party, only the rich would be elected." This statement winks at election fraud, that is, the buying and bullying of people for votes. It also belies the fact that contracts for city projects were awarded in accordance with contributions to the party, and that party members became rich because of their connections.

In contrast to the above implication of promoting the cause of the working class, Daley's administration concentrated on projects that in effect enriched the empowered, projects that would improve his image. Downtown buildings, expressways, the O'Hare Airport, a convention hall on the lakefront (despite the opposition of conservationists)—these projects enriched the business community, the banks and real estate developers. Neighborhoods, especially those of the blacks (the nomenclature used in this book), were allowed to deteriorate. Indeed, an Italian neighborhood, colorful and in the process of renovation, was destroyed to become the site of the University of Illinois campus; having heard Daley's promise of urban renewal to help restore and stabilize the community, the residents felt betrayed.

Scandals emerged during Daley's second term. A litany of corruption is detailed. Health inspectors were taking bribes; in the traffic court "an entire department did nothing but fix tickets"; the police at every level expected and accepted graft. The police also routinely brutalized some of the citizens, particularly blacks. Honest policemen were isolated. The scandals included ticket fixing in the traffic court and a burglary ring made up of Chicago policemen.

Daley denied the existence of segregation, claiming in 1963 that "there are no ghettos in Chicago," but it was in effect condoned. Efforts to integrate were literally beaten back by residents, supported by the ward organizations. Personally and politically, blacks were exploited. However, in Daley's third term, the black silence ended. Picketers came out to demand better schools; schools were boycotted. When the picketers, led by the activist comedian Dick Gregory, marched in Daley's home neighborhood, they were greeted by jeers, eggs, tomatoes, and rocks. The police arrested the peaceful picketers rather than the disorderly neighborhood crowd in order to maintain peace. A subsequent accident ignited a riot. The situation came to a head when Martin Luther King, Jr., brought his movement to Chicago, with little acknowledged effect on the whites, until there were further riots and daily marches in neighborhoods instead of downtown. A "summit conference" brought forth an agreement for open housing, but once the crisis passed, the agreement was just "a goal to be reached."

One highlight of Daley's tenure as mayor was a disaster: the 1968 nominating convention of the Democratic Party. Daley wanted to present the glory of *his* Chicago; he wanted to extend his power-wielding status. But the city's situation had began to unravel after King's April 4 death: Scores of buildings in black wards (those run by whites) burned immediately after; later that month an unprovocative peace march sponsored by the Chicago Peace Council was hassled and attacked by riot police. The mostly white, middle- and upper-class war protesters were beaten and arrested.

These were preludes to the convention events during which the police were "subjected to . . . allegedly intolerable abuse."

> Instead the city forced the confrontation and the police became the aggressors, striking out at militant and middle-roaders alike, involving thousands of people in the violence, and making the dominant event of the convention a battle over a few acres of grassland. The police made their first sweep through the park, moving from the east toward the streets, shedding whatever discipline they had shown earlier in the day. They beat people beyond the point of subduing them. They chased them down and left them bleeding.

Reporters, passersby, clergymen, young and old, males and females—all were victims. Daley denied what was happening, even blaming the reporters. When the worst of the beatings were being perpetrated, he sat inside the convention hall in his delegate's chair. During his nomination of Senator McGovern, Senator Abraham Ribicoff was critical of "the Gestapo in the streets of Chicago," generating a verbal assault from Daley and intense feelings in the hall. Afterward, he watched a replay on television and saw what had been evidenced to the world. No longer able to deny the event, he developed a strategy, an explanation that the police were protecting the three leading candidates from a reported assassination attempt. He provided no proof.

CENSORSHIP HISTORY

Censorship of *Boss* was almost immediate. Officials of Chicago's National Tea Company in September 1971 imposed a ban that lasted for three days. In his column on September 17, Mike Royko reported that the National Tea Company's ban was effected by a complaint from Eleanor Daley, the mayor's wife, to a store manager; she "wanted the books out of the store." The manager called the company's downtown headquarters; in "10 minutes" the books were off the racks. A directive to all stores was issued the next day. Harry B. Smith, the company's Chicago division vice president, indicated the ban resulted from customers' requests. The ban's revocation several days later resulted from the opposite, a large number of requests for the book. Chicago's three airports also banned the book. This ban was also revoked at the O'Hare Airport within days, though the other two did not reshelve the book.

In Ridgefield, Connecticut, *Boss* had been approved by the administration for use in a high school elective course on American politics. However, on April 11, 1972, the Ridgefield Board of Education on a close vote, ordered it removed from the class reading list. The chairwoman, Lodi Kysor, whose vote broke the tie, noted that she "didn't think the book was very good and it wouldn't have improved the curriculum." A board member, Leo F. Carroll, argued that *Boss* "slandered" the Chicago police and, in reference to the passages that identified members of the police taking part in a burglary operation, he objected to "any book that didn't tell the truth." A third member, Joseph Negreen, charged that the book "downgraded the police departments and the political structure of this country." He continued, "It plays right into the hands of the Communists and those liberal segments who border on Communism." On April 19, the Ridgefield board reversed its decision and sanctioned the use of *Boss*. The rehearing was called because, according to the chair, the first vote had created misunderstanding.

A similar challenge occurred in February 1983 in Hannibal, New York, where *Boss* was assigned reading in the "Literature of Politics" English class at Hannibal High School and had been since 1975. William and Barbara Younis complained that *Boss* was "detrimental to students and contributed to social decay because it contains rough language." In April, the book, which had been used without protest since 1975, was supported for continued use in a report issued by the local school board.

FURTHER READING

"Connecticut School Bans Book on Mayor Daley." *New York Times*, April 12, 1972, p. 36.
"Daley Denies Wife Induced Stores to Ban *Boss*." *New York Times*, September 2, 1971, p. 23.

"Ridgefield Board Reverses Its Decision to Ban *Boss.*" *New York Times*, April 20, 1972, p. 23.

Royko, Mike. "Now, About That Book . . ." *Chicago Daily News*, September 17, 1971, p. 3.

Shaffer, Terry. "Food Chain Lifts Book Ban." *Chicago Daily News*, September 19, 1971, p. 4.

BURGER'S DAUGHTER

Author: Nadine Gordimer
Original dates and places of publication: 1979, Great Britain; 1979, United States
Publishers: Jonathan Cape; Viking Press
Literary form: Novel

SUMMARY

Lionel Burger is not the center-stage character in *Burger's Daughter*. Yet the novel revolves around him as the life of his daughter, Rosa, emanates from and seems dominated by him. Lionel, a white Afrikaner from a wealthy family, is well reputed as a doctor, but has gained notoriety as a leader of the South African Communist Party and through his activities against the government's system of apartheid. He and his second wife, Cathy, have established a household that welcomes black Africans in an atmosphere of equality, a household in which social consciousness and responsibility are givens. Both parents constantly face the threat of arrest; indeed, Lionel dies of illness in prison during the third year of his life sentence, and Cathy dies of multiple sclerosis, her health damaged by imprisonment. The immediate sociopolitical context of these events is the South Africa of the March 1960 Sharpeville massacre in Rosa's childhood and the June 1976 Soweto school riots in her adulthood.

Despite the powerful presence of Lionel in the lives of this novel's characters, it is Rosa's story. Her early years are punctuated by activities that mark her parents' philosophy and expectations. Indeed, the story opens with Rosa, age 14, waiting outside a prison with a quilt and hot water bottle to deliver to her mother, who had been picked up by the police the night before and is being detained. But that act is not as revealing as the fact that she has secreted a note, seemingly innocuous in its message should it be discovered, inside the bottle cap to convey to her mother the status of her father. A few years later, at age 17, she takes on the pretense of being engaged to a political prisoner, a known associate of her father, to obtain permission to visit him in prison. At these monthly visits, she communicates information to him in the guise of a love letter and receives messages in return about the political prisoners through his vocal nuances and body language.

Rosa's early memories reveal her parents' activities and household. The evening of the Sharpeville massacre, African National Congress (ANC) leaders, Pan-African Congress people, lawyers, and others gather at their house, talking through the night about the changed political situation. At the opposite extreme, celebratory events—a successful boycott or march, a leader's release from prison, or Lionel found not guilty of a charge—also bring gatherings of the anti-apartheid faithful, white and black, to the house. Vivid in her memory is Boasie, a black child Rosa's age, the son of an ANC organizer, who is cared for by her family while his father travels on ANC business. She recurrently recalls their learning to swim together, fighting for "the anchorage of wet hair on Lionel Burger's warm breast in the cold swimming pool." They are separated once when both of Rosa's parents are arrested together; she does not see him again until many years later in London, a meeting that is emotionally traumatic for her.

In her recollections of her adolescent and young adult past, Rosa also reveals a note of resentment against the claim of familial relationship that enforces upon her certain situations—standing outside the prison, waiting for her mother and attending her father's trial for 217 days, both in the public eye. She expresses anger at her parents for their expectations of her playacting role as fiancée to the prisoner (for whom she really has tender feelings). After her mother's and then her father's death, the note of resentment swells at the expectations of the faithful that she will continue their activities, their social commitment. She muses:

> Even animals have the instinct to turn from suffering. The sense to run away. Perhaps it was an illness not to be able to live one's life . . . with justice defined in terms of respect for property, innocence defended in their children's privileges, love in their procreation, and care only for each other. A sickness not to be able to ignore that condition of a healthy, ordinary life: other people's suffering.

The suffering referred to is that of the black populace. This suffering is not actually visited, except in the connotations of shootings, protests and imprisonment, the oppression of pass laws and curfews. Instead, attention is given to raids that net one or another or both parents for periods of incarceration (the last leading to Lionel's trial and conviction to a life sentence) as well as others of the party. Cathy Burger and others are banned from certain occupations, from free movement around the country, even banned from house arrest, and banned from associations with particular people. There is a consciousness, too, of surveillance: The authorities' knowledge of Rosa's domiciles, her lovers, her movements, her contacts—her need to account for every visit and visitor just in case there is an interrogation.

The reader knows that the authorities are aware of her visits a year later to Pretoria; who she visits, the dates and frequency. Her purpose is to obtain a passport to leave the country (for she is forbidden access to a passport through normal channels), because, as she says, "I'd like to see Europe." After a year, Rosa is granted a passport (with understandings of where she is not to travel and with whom she is not to associate) and departs from South Africa, expecting to be stopped even as she is walking across the tarmac toward the plane. She isn't stopped, but "Surveillance watched her go in."

Book II chronicles Rosa's escape to France, first very briefly to Paris and then to the south of France to be with Lionel's first wife, whom she has never met. Katya (actually Colette), an aspiring ballerina, had been disciplined by the party for her "inactivity" and her "bourgeois tendencies to put [her] private life first." Rosa is overcome by the luminous landscape, its voluptuousness; the "pleasure of scents, sights and sounds exciting only in themselves, associated with nothing and nobody." She responds to a life lived for itself, without social mission and surveillance. Soon she has a lover; upon her impending departure for London he arranges for a rendez-vous in London.

The sojourn in London does not evolve as anticipated. Her lover delayed by illness, Rosa spends relaxed hours wandering about London, chatting with people, taking a French class. She begins to think about meeting the people she had planned to avoid and does so. She goes to a gathering with other Africans in attendance, including South African revolutionaries. When she is recognized, she is introduced within the context of a speech about revolutionary heroes, particularly Lionel Burger.

Boasie is there. He seems guarded. Later that night, however, he tele-phones, but instead of reestablishing their childhood relationship, he rejects her, her memories, and her father. He is bitter that Lionel should be enno-bled as heroic, while his own father, also a victim of the struggle, is forgot-ten, that whites should be credited and blacks neglected. Rosa is angered, her thoughts and emotions in turmoil.

Rosa returns to South Africa and to a job as a physiotherapist in a Johannesburg hospital. She is on duty in 1976 when the Soweto school riot victims fill the wards, after the police fire machine guns against the students' stones. A student rebellion ensues against the separate system of education; most never return to school after June 1976.

In October 1977 many people are detained, arrested, or banned; many organizations are banned as is the only black newspaper. Most of the banned people are black. Among the few whites is Rosa Burger, who is detained without charges. She is, however, subject to charges of collusion in a "con-spiracy to further the aims of communism and/or the African National Congress. The charges would allege incitement and aiding and abetting of the students' and school children's revolt." One piece of evidence that will be identified in the indictment against her is her attendance at a leftist "rally" in London.

CENSORSHIP HISTORY

On July 5, 1979, *Burger's Daughter* was banned by the Republic of South Africa on the grounds that it "endangers the safety of the state" and that it depicts "whites as baddies, blacks as goodies." Further, it was deemed a "political novel" whose theme is black militancy and one that as a whole was harmful to relations between sections of population. The novel was also judged to be "indecent." The author was accused of using her central character "as a pad from which to launch a blistering and full-scale attack on the Republic of South Africa (and) its government's racial policies." The publications committee cited six categories of violation of the Publications Act of 1974.

In early October, however, the censoring committee was overruled by the Publications Appeal Board. The board's ruling was made on the advice of a committee of literary experts and an expert on security measures, and despite "crudities and profanity, derogatory references to whites and a distorted picture of the political situation in South Africa."

> The state security expert found there was no threat to the state from the novel. The literary experts concluded that the original censorship committee, in banning the book, stood "convicted of bias, prejudice, and literary incompetence. It has not read accurately, it has severely distorted by quoting extensively out of context, it has not considered the work as a literary work deserves to be considered, and it has directly, and by implication, smeared the authoress [sic]."

This turnabout resulted from a change of strategy by the Directorate of Publications, which administered the censorship system in South Africa. The 1974 Publications and Entertainments Act permitted appeals of censorship decisions made by committees appointed by the Directorate; the right to appeal was granted to the Directorate itself, to persons with financial interest and to the body that had originally submitted the text for censorship consideration. The change referred to above was that the Directorate itself appealed the decision of its own committee. *Burger's Daughter* was the first banned text so appealed and the first to be reinstated. However, as Gordimer herself stated, ". . . the censorship laws remain the same." Two previous novels, *World of Strangers* and *The Late Bourgeois World*, were banned for about a decade; the bans were lifted.

Ironically, in 1980, Gordimer was awarded the CNA Prize, one of South Africa's highest literary awards, for *Burger's Daughter*. She also was awarded the Nobel Prize in literature in 1991.

FURTHER READING

Gordimer, Nadine. *The Essential Gesture: Writing, Politics and Places.* New York: Alfred A. Knopf, 1988.
Index on Censorship 6 (November/December 1979): 69; 2 (April 1980): 73.

"Latest Gordimer Novel Banned in South Africa." *New York Times*, September 7, 1979, p. 8.

"South Africa Bans Two Novels." *Newsletter on Intellectual Freedom* 28 (1979): 147.

"South Africa Lifts Ban on Gordimer Novel." *New York Times*, October 7, 1979, p. 79.

"South Africans Cancel Ban on Gordimer Book." *New York Times*, October 5, 1979, p. 6.

BURY MY HEART AT WOUNDED KNEE

Author: Dee Brown
Original date and place of publication: 1970, United States
Publisher: Holt, Rinehart and Winston
Literary form: Nonfiction

SUMMARY

Bury My Heart at Wounded Knee: An Indian History of the American West represents the voices of American Indians. In his introduction, Dee Brown writes, "Out of these sources of almost forgotten oral history, I have tried to fashion a narrative of the conquest of the American West as the victims experienced it, using their words whenever possible." These sources included first-person statements by American Indians at treaty councils, authentic accounts written by Indians, and newspaper interviews. This history contrasts with the great myths of the American West in which the "Indian was the dark menace."

The text is composed of 19 chapters. Eighteen of these recount episodes of the western history between 1860 and 1890, the period of "greatest concentration of recorded experience and observation." Revealed are not merely dates and places of battles, leaders, and troop movements, but also attitudes, concerns, and emotions of the participants. The focus, as the subtitle shows, is on the Indian perspective.

Chapter 1, "Their Manners Are Decorous and Praiseworthy," sets the stage for the text by encompassing in broad strokes the four centuries from 1492 to 1890. Its title is the second clause of Columbus's description of the Tainos on the island now called San Salvador, ". . . and though it is true that they are naked, yet their manners are decorous and praise-worthy." Columbus also wrote that the people should be "made to work, sow and do all that is necessary to *adopt our ways.*"

The broad strokes include the destruction of the New England tribes—the Pemaquid, Wampanoag, and Narragansett—who were virtually exterminated in a war of an Indian confederacy led by King Philip (Metacom of the Wampanoag) against the arrogant colonists who took their land; the defeat of the Five Nations of the Iroquois who "strove in vain for peace" and to save their political independence; the defeat also of the tribes united by

Pontiac of the Ottawa in the Great Lakes region and, a generation later, of the confederacy of midwestern and southern tribes formed by Tecumseh of the Shawnee, both of whom attempted to protect their lands from invasion.

Treaties were made and broken. The southern Indians—Cherokee, Chickasaw, Choctaw, Creek, and Seminole—had been promised their tribal lands forever, but in 1829 Andrew Jackson recommended to Congress "the propriety of setting apart an ample district west of the Mississippi . . . to be guaranteed to the Indian tribes, as long as they shall occupy it." This became law; Congress passed an act that established the Mississippi River as the boundary between white and Indian territories. This act of Congress was broken before it could be put into effect by settlers pushing into Wisconsin and Iowa. Together these laws caused the forced removal of the southern tribes to Indian Territory—the infamous "trail of tears"—along with surviving elements of many tribes from the North. Despite these enacted laws, the United States marched through Indian Territory to "war with the white men [the Spanish] who had conquered the Indians of Mexico," subsequently taking possession of this vast expanse of territory, despite its being west of the "permanent Indian frontier."

"War Comes to the Cheyenne," chapter 4, details events of the infamous Sand Creek Massacre. In 1851, six of the 44 chiefs of the Southern Cheyenne tribe signed a treaty that permitted the establishment of roads and military forts across their territory. They did not relinquish any claims or rights to their lands. In the 1860s, incursions into their territory increased, the number of Bluecoat soldiers multiplying.

War tensions were escalated by Colonel John M. Chivington, commander of the Colorado volunteers, and John Evans, governor of Colorado Territory. While Black Kettle was saying, "I want to be friendly and peaceable and keep my tribe so. I am not able to fight the whites. I want to live in peace," Chivington was stating that he was not authorized to make peace and that he was on the warpath. He had ordered his lieutenant in a preceding skirmish to "kill Cheyenne whenever and wherever found." Governor Evans, blaming the Cheyenne for the Bluecoats' attacks on them, indicated that "the great Father is angry and will certainly hunt them out and punish them"; he told friendly Indians to go to the safety of Fort Lyon. Two months later, he issued a proclamation authorizing all citizens of Colorado to pursue and kill hostile Indians.

The Cheyenne and Arapaho gained the respect and confidence of Major Edward W. Wynkoop, the commanding officer of Fort Lyon, who wrote, "I felt myself in the presence of superior beings; and these were the representatives of a race that I heretofore looked upon without exception as being cruel, treacherous and bloodthirsty without feeling or affection for friend or kindred." The Cheyenne thereafter moved to a camp at Sand Creek about 40 miles from Fort Lyon. Wynkoop, however, was relieved of his command because of his friendly dealings with the Indians. His replacement, Major Scott J. Anthony, an officer of Chivington's Colorado Volunteers, pretended friendliness as he offered reassurances to the Cheyenne of their protected status, but he plotted their destruction.

In early December 1864, the cavalry columns of Chivington's Colorado regiment, with more than 700 men supported by four 12-pound mountain howitzers, attacked the Sand Creek encampment. Three officers, Captain Silas Soule and Lieutenants Joseph Cramer and James Connor, protested the attack as dishonorable but were forced to accompany the expedition. Chivington cried angrily, "Damn any man who sympathizes with Indians. I have come to kill Indians, and believe it is right and honorable to use any means under God's heaven to kill Indians." There was no night watch at the encampment; the Cheyenne believed they were safe. Most of the men were several miles away hunting buffalo. The attack came at about sunrise with only the drumming of hooves as warning.

Robert Bent, who was forced to ride with the troops as a guide, reported the event:

> I saw the American flag waving and heard Black Kettle tell the Indians to stand around the flag, and there they were huddled—men, women, and children. . . . When the troops fired, the Indians ran, some of the men into their lodges, probably to get their arms. . . . I think there were six hundred Indians in all. I think there were thirty-five braves and some old men, about sixty in all. . . . There seemed to be indiscriminate slaughter of men, women, and children. There were some thirty or forty squaws collected in a hole for protection; they sent out a little girl about six years old with a white flag on a stick; she had not proceeded but a few steps when she was shot and killed. All the squaws in that hold were afterwards killed, and four or five bucks outside. The squaws offered no resistance. Every one I saw dead was scalped. I saw one squaw cut open with an unborn child, as I thought, lying by her side. Captain Soule afterwards told me that such was the fact. I saw the body of White Antelope with the privates cut off, and I heard a soldier say he was going to make a tobacco pouch out of them. I saw one squaw whose privates had been cut out. . . .

The result of this massacre was the death of 105 Indian women and children and 28 men, including several chiefs, among them White Antelope and One Eye; Chivington reported between 400 and 500 dead. Black Kettle escaped southward with about 400 Cheyenne.

Later Black Kettle and Arapaho chief Little Raven were sought out by United States officials (some of whom were calling for an investigation of Evans and Chivington) to formulate a new treaty. Though it was resisted, the treaty was eventually signed. They agreed to "perpetual peace" and "to relinquish all claims and rights" to their lands, the territory of Colorado.

Chapter 15, "Standing Bear Becomes a Person," tells the story of the Ponca. In 1804, Meriwether Lewis and William Clark met the Ponca, a peaceful tribe living on the west bank of the Missouri River in the area of what today is Nebraska. They then numbered 200 to 300 individuals, having been decimated by a smallpox epidemic. In 1850, numbering about 1,000, they were still peaceful, growing corn and vegetables and raising horses. In 1858, they were guaranteed by U.S. government officials, in exchange for giving up some of their territory, protection of their persons and property and a permanent home. However, in a bureaucratic blunder in the 1868 treaty with the Sioux, their land was ceded to the Sioux. The Ponca's protests were ignored.

In 1876, after the defeat of Custer and despite their noninvolvement in that battle and their never having warred against the United States, a decision was made to exile the Ponca to the Indian Territory "with the consent of said band." That consent was never given. Indeed, the Ponca adamantly rejected the proposal; the chiefs, having been tricked by a United States Indian inspector into going to evaluate the proposed lands, were even more resistant to the move when they realized the barren, rocky prospects. The inspector then refused to return them to their own territory, causing them to walk the almost 500 miles. Their resistance was of no avail; the tribe was forced at gunpoint to move to the Indian Territory. This removal was supported and ordered by Secretary of the Interior Carl Schurz and General-in-Chief of the U.S. Army William Tecumseh Sherman. By the time they reached the reservation on July 9, having been driven like a herd of ponies, many had died of sickness resulting from exposure. Agent E. A. Howard recommended to his superiors that they be returned to a northern region before they "become poisoned with the malaria of the climate." By the end of their first year almost one-fourth of them had died.

In 1878, the Ponca, having been moved to a new reservation on the Arkansas River, again suffered sickness and death. One of these was Chief Standing Bear's son. Fulfilling a promise to his son, Standing Bear led a burial party of 66 members of his clan back toward their home territory. They reached the Omaha reservation before they were found. There, under orders from Schurz, they were arrested by General George Crook and brought to Fort Omaha.

Crook, however, was "appalled by the pitiable condition of the Indians." Promising help to Standing Bear to get his orders countermanded, he enlisted the help of the press, specifically an Omaha newspaper editor, Thomas Henry Tibbles. Tibbles spread the Ponca's story across the city, state, and country. Two lawyers volunteered their services: young John L. Webster of Omaha and Andrew Poppleton, chief attorney of the Union Pacific Railroad. What emerged as a civil rights case, *Standing Bear v. Crook*, was heard before Judge Elmer S. Dundy.

Dundy issued a writ of habeas corpus upon General Crook—with Crook's tacit consent—to show cause. Crook presented his military orders; the district attorney for the United States argued that the Ponca had no right to the writ of habeas corpus because Indians were "not persons within the meaning of the law." The Ponca's attorneys responded during the trial that Indians were as much "persons" as any white, and that Standing Bear and others had the right to "separate themselves from their tribes and live under protection of United States laws like any other citizens" and "could avail themselves of the rights of freedom guaranteed by the Constitution." The United States attorney's position was that these Indians were subject to the rules and regulations that the government had made for tribal Indians.

Standing Bear was permitted to speak for his people:

> I am now with the soldiers and officers. I want to go back to my old place north. Oh, my brothers, the Almighty looks down on me, and knows what I am, and hears my words. May the Almighty send a good spirit to brood over you, my brothers, to move you to help me. If a white man had land, and someone should swindle him, that man would try to get it back, and you would not blame him. Look on me. Take pity on me, and help me to save the lives of the women and children. My brothers, a power, which I cannot resist, crowds me down to the ground. I need help. I have done.

Judge Dundy ruled in favor of Standing Bear and his clan that an Indian is a "person within the meaning of the habeas corpus act," that "the right of expatriation was a natural, inherent, and inalienable right of the Indian as well as the white race," and that in times of peace no authority existed, civil or military, for transporting Indians from one section of the country to another without their consent or to confine them against their will.

> I have never been called upon to hear or decide a case that appealed so strongly to my sympathy. The Poncas are amongst the most peaceable and friendly of all the Indian tribes. . . . If they could be removed to the Indian Territory by force, and kept there in the same way, I can see no good reason why they might not be taken and kept by force in the penitentiary at Lincoln . . . or any other place which the commander of the forces might, in his judgment, see proper to designate. I cannot think that any such arbitrary authority exists in this country.

The 530 Ponca in the Indian Territory were barred from joining Standing Bear's group in Nebraska. Bureaucrats and politicians in Washington recognized the threat to the reservation system if they were allowed to do so; agents and others who were making fortunes on supplies to Indians also objected. General Sherman decreed: "The release under writ of *habeas corpus* of the Poncas in Nebraska does not apply to any other than that specific case."

CENSORSHIP HISTORY

In 1974, a Wild Rose, Wisconsin, district administrator banned *Bury My Heart at Wounded Knee* from use in the schools. Not having read the book, but having heard a radio review, he found the book's viewpoint objectionable, saying that it was "slanted." An English teacher with whom the administrator discussed the book, argued that it was not "slanted." In deciding to ban the book, the administrator said, "If there's a possibility that something might be controversial, then why not eliminate it." The *Wisconsin Censorship Dateline*, a survey of censorship challenges of the period, identifies "un-American" as the reason for the challenge.

FURTHER READING

Heath, Susan. *Wisconsin Censorship Dateline*. Unpublished survey, 1983.
"Wisconsin Schools Badgered by Censors." *Newsletter on Intellectual Freedom* 23 (1974): 145.

BUS STOP (*CHEZHAN*)

Author: Gao Xingjian
Original dates and places of publication: 1983, People's Republic of China; 1998, United States
Publishers: *Shiyue* (literary quarterly); M. E. Sharpe (in anthology)
Literary form: Drama

SUMMARY

Subtitled *A Lyrical Comedy on Life in One Act*, *Bus Stop*, an experimental absurdist drama (referred to as Western modernism by Chinese critics), is set in the countryside. Six strangers assemble individually at a bus stop, apparently isolated from a community, joining the Silent Man who is already waiting, en route to a nearby city. They are identified but not named—Gramps, Young Woman, Hotheaded Youth, Spectacles, Mother, Master Worker. Director Ma, a party functionary, the section or division chief of a state-run store, also arrives to await the bus. Their missions seem urgent to themselves: Gramps, 60-some years old, has challenged a chess champion to a match; Young Woman, aged 28, has a blind-date rendezvous, perhaps her final opportunity to meet the right man; Spectacles, 30, plans to take the college entrance examination, later claiming this is his last opportunity; and Master Worker, 45, is relocating to the town to teach apprentices his craft so that the skills will not be squandered in the country. Mother, 40, will spend the weekend with her child and her husband, who lives in town because of his work assignment. The 19-year-old Hotheaded Youth wants to stroll in town and have a yogurt, and Director Ma, 50, has been invited by "someone with connections" to have a meal and drinks.

There is essentially little action in the drama: at the onset some jostling for position in the line, principally by the Youth; at midpoint, Silent Man abruptly and without comment leaves, heading for the city; and at the conclusion after a few false starts, steps are taken by the group to walk to the city. There is also the passage of time—10 years, if Spectacles's electric watch is to be believed, along with the evidence of two strands of white hair on Young Woman's head. Many buses have passed them by.

The real "movement" of the drama is in the relationships among the members of the group. Initially, quarrelsomeness and distance pervade. The angry complaints of Gramps aimed at the pushy, "obnoxious" Hotheaded Youth erupt into a near fistfight with Spectacles. The atmosphere of distance, however, gradually erodes—snatches of conversation about chess, about why parents with a child are, in effect, forced to live separately, and aspects in the operation of a "commercial unit." The realization of the passage of time—and that Silent Man has already left—begins to bring them together—emotionally and physically. At long last they decide to walk to town, helping one another, realizing at that moment that the bus stop had been abolished, thus explaining why none of the buses had stopped. They had waited for nothing.

Within the fragments of dialogue are embedded statements that express dissatisfaction with services and policies. Early on, when the bus does not arrive and when it passes by them, questions about "serving the customer" are raised, and Gramps responds, "On the contrary, the passengers have to serve them! If there's no one waiting at the bus stop how can they show off how vital they are?"

When Spectacles asks Mother why she does not get a job in town so that she can live with her husband and child, she responds, "Who doesn't want a work assignment in town, but you have to have a way to get to it," a reference to the 1980s system of government-assigned employment under which a desirable town work assignment, difficult to obtain, would frequently have the effect of separating a couple. She explains, "I have a child. . . . You know what the level of education is like in the schools on the outskirts of town. Hardly anybody from there can pass the college entrance exams!" Spectacles's concern about his last opportunity to take the college entrance exams, which require knowledge of a foreign language, and his not having studied a foreign language, echoes this concern.

Personal issues are also expressed. The Young Woman admits to being jealous of other, more privileged women and to her despair of her young man not waiting for her: "Never again. No one will ever wait for me again!" Mother mourns not being able to care for her husband and son, who need her. Hotheaded Youth, softened, also reveals parallel feelings: When Gramps suggests that he ought to apply himself to a craft, he admits, "There's no one to take me on. What's the use. . . ." After Master Worker agrees to take him on as an apprentice, his manner and attitude markedly change.

A ribbon of thought, of dismay, trails through the script. Spectacles says (furiously) to the Youth: "You don't understand what it is to suffer, so you're apathetic. Life has left us behind. The world has forgotten us. Your life is trickling away before your eyes." Gramps states: "I've waited a lifetime, waiting like this, and waiting. I've gotten old waiting." Young Woman observes: "Your whole life is wasted like this. To waste time like this, will we keep on wasting it forever?" Youth remarks: "Mister, we've been waiting for nothing. We've been cheated by the bus company." This implication that people should actively take charge of their lives rather than wasting their lives in passive waiting is solidified by character indecision about leaving the bus stop. At last, however, as a community, helping and caring for one another, they take to the road.

CENSORSHIP HISTORY

The play, titled *Chezhan* in Mandarin, was staged as a "rehearsal" by the Beijing People's Art Theatre, China's foremost theater company at the time, to which Gao Xingjian had been assigned. It was banned after 10 or 13 performances (reports differ). The play provoked controversy between two critical camps, those who found it creative and who approved its antipassivity message and those who argued that the "play contained a basic questioning if not a fundamental negation of the organization of contemporary Chinese society, a condescending attitude toward the deluded 'pitiable multitude,' and an elitist and individualistic impulse embodied in the 'silent man' walking alone to the city," as noted by University of Colorado professor Haiping Yan. A senior party member asserted that *Bus Stop* was "the most pernicious work since the establishment of the People's Republic." The "Anti-Spiritual Pollution Movement" under way at the time, targeted Gao, accusing him of being antisocialist. He was barred from publication for one year.

Earlier, Gao had attracted negative attention with his 1981 published booklet "A Preliminary Exploration into the Techniques of Modern Fiction," which, too radical for promoting decadent modernist ideas of the capitalist West, was condemned as a serious challenge to the party line. His experiential play known in English as "Signal Alarm" (1982) achieved positive audience response; it dramatized social issues of youth unemployment and juvenile delinquency. Nevertheless, its breakthrough aspects of staging aroused vehement sentiments about modernism and realism in theater. It was also banned in 1983.

Subsequently, facing rumors of further punishment—a labor camp in Quighai to "receive training"—Gao self-exiled himself to the mountains of southwestern China, walking over a 10-month period along the Yangtze River to get from its source to the coast. Returning to Beijing, he was permitted to publish, including the fictionalized memoir *Wild Man*, the play *The Other Shore*, and the novel *Soul Mountain*, but he left China in 1987, settling in France. The publication of the play FUGITIVES (*Taowang*), which takes place against the background of the massacre on the Square of Heavenly Peace (Tiananmen Square) in 1989 led to his being declared persona non grata by China. All of his works were banned. Beijing also denounced the awarding of the Nobel Prize in literature (2000) to Gao, diminishing the merits of *Soul Mountain* and accusing the Nobel committee of being politically motivated. The Chinese press maintained a near blackout of the Nobel news. Gao's books are not available in bookstores in China.

Gao, now a citizen of France, has been awarded the Chevalier de l'Ordre des Artes et des Lettres, 1992; Prix Communaunté francaise de Belgique,

1994, for *Le somnambule* (The sleepwalker); and Prix du Nouvel au Chinois, 1997, for *Soul Mountain.*

FURTHER READING

Gao Xingjian. *The Bus Stop: A Lyrical Comedy on Life in One Act.* Translaed by Kimberly Besio. In *Theater and Society: An Anthology of Contemporary Chinese Drama.* Edited by Haiping Yan. Armonk, N.Y.: M. E. Sharpe, 1998.
Yan Haiping, ed. *Theater and Society: An Anthology of Contemporary Chinese Drama.* Armonk, N.Y.: M. E. Sharpe, 1998.

BY WAY OF DECEPTION: THE MAKING AND UNMAKING OF A MOSSAD OFFICER

Authors: Victor Ostrovsky and Claire Hoy
Original dates and places of publication: 1990, England; 1990, United States
Publishers: Bloomsbury; St. Martin's Press
Literary form: Nonfiction

SUMMARY

In his foreword to this exposé of the Mossad, Israel's intelligence agency, Victor Ostrovsky reveals how his point of faith as a Zionist that "the state of Israel was incapable of misconduct" is challenged by his four-year experience inside the Mossad. This experience led to disillusionment, which in turn led to this revelation.

> But it was the twisted ideals and self-centered pragmatism that I encountered inside the Mossad, coupled with this so-called team's greed, lust and total lack of respect for human life, that motivated me to tell this story.
> It is out of love for Israel as a free and just country that I am laying my life on the line by so doing, facing up to those who took it upon themselves to turn the Zionist dream into the present-day nightmare.

The prologue immerses the reader in an extended sting operation. The Mossad's purpose and methods are revealed through this detailed account of "Operation Sphinx." Mossad's purpose ultimately was to destroy Iraq's nuclear complex; immediately, its purpose was to establish the stages of development of the Iraqi project and to ascertain its design of the "nuclear research center" being developed in France. The operation required agents tracking and luring an Iraqi scientist employee, first to gain his confidence, then to seduce him into revealing information. The tracking included "bugging" the employee's apartment to learn personal data, spying on and tracking him, and initiating acquaintance. The lures were money and sex. Once he was hooked, the Iraqi employee was compromised by becoming involved in a fake business deal and then being suckered into supplying details of the plans of the nuclear plant under the cover of a fraudulent scheme to sell nuclear power plants to Third World countries. The result was the destruction by the Israelis of the reactor cores prior to their shipment from France to Iraq. This particular dupe escaped to Iraq, but others died: another scientist involved in the project, who "would have had the blood of Israel's children on his hands if he'd completed [the] project," and a prostitute, a sometime employee of Mossad, who had visited the scientist before his death and talked to the police of her suspicions afterward. These killings are described in the context of this assertion: "The Mossad doesn't execute people unless they have blood on their hands."

The first eight chapters provide extensive information revealing how Ostrovsky was tested and trained. The tests and schooling established and developed his abilities to conduct undercover operations, tasks that required deception, quick thinking, imagination, and self-control; they also measured and monitored his emotional reliability and his political loyalty. A flaw in these traits, a questioning of the system, put Ostrovsky in conflict with some of the leaders. This came to a head in the final exercise of his training in 1986. As a consequence, he quit and then, anticipating reprisals, escaped from Israel to the United States and, eventually, Canada.

A significant aspect of these pages is the revelation of attitudes and behaviors, both of the hierarchy of the Mossad and of the Israeli government. The motto of the Mossad, "By way of deception, thou shalt do war," is all the more revealing when understood in the context of a comment made by the head of the training department for operational security: "We do most of our work in foreign countries. For us, everything is enemy or target. Nothing is friendly. I mean nothing." Another attitude "engraved in our minds" was that "we were to do what was good for us and screw everybody else, because they wouldn't be helping us." In an extension to this comment, Ostrovsky cites an Israeli saying that those who were not helping the Jews during World War II were in effect against them. These included those with overt hostile behavior as well as those who did nothing, that is, those who "ignored" the plight of the Jews. He reveals his aforementioned flaw when he comments:

> Yet I don't remember anybody in Israel going out to demonstrate when all those people were being murdered in Cambodia. So why expect everybody to get involved just for us? Does the fact that Jews have suffered give us the right to inflict pain and misery on others?

Situations are revealed that disclose the double-dealing activities of the Israeli government; these express a philosophical orientation parallel to that of the Mossad. The Israelis were selling at high cost reserve fuel tank pilons through a third country to Saudi Arabia. When Saudi Arabia attempted to buy them directly from the United States at lower cost, an objection was raised by the Israelis, who lobbied against the sales because it would give the Saudis capability to attack them. In a similar fashion, Israel secretly sold between 20 and 30 U.S.-made Skyhawk fighters to Indonesia, despite its armaments agreement with the United States, which forbade resale of the Skyhawks without approval. In addition, the Israelis were training two opposing factions from Sri Lanka at the same time, a special forces group representing the Sinhalese majority and a group of Tamil guerrillas who were bitter enemies of the Sinhalese.

Later chapters reinforce attitudes and behaviors already identified in the text: the uneven partnership of the Mossad with similar agencies, for example, the Mossad received information but told nothing; the sale of arms to Iran in conflict with the policy of the United States, its benefactor; the Mossad's clandestine operations in New York and Washington, despite its active denial, including the bugging of U.S. ambassador to the United Nations Andrew Young's conversations with Kuwaiti ambassador Abdalla Yaccoub Bishara; the theft of research material from U.S. aircraft-manufacturing firms, leading to a successful contract bid by an Israeli firm; and the world-wide allegiance of *sayanim*, non-Israeli Jews living abroad who actively help the Mossad in many different roles.

The mendacity of Mossad is further illustrated in its many efforts to defeat peace negotiations between the Palestine Liberation Organization and Israel; the unwillingness of its head, Nahum Admony, to give Americans in Beirut known, detailed information about the imminent truck-bomb attack that killed 241 U.S. Marines; and Admony's refusal to release information to CIA officials concerning the whereabouts of William Buckley, though Prime Minister Shimon Peres had instructed him to do so. In relation to the Beirut truck bombing, the author comments:

> For me, it was the first time I had received a major rebuke from my Mossad superior, liaison officer Amy Yaar. I said at the time that the American soldiers killed in Beirut would be on our minds longer than our own casualties because they'd come in with good faith, to help us get out of this mess we'd created. I was told: "Just shut up. You're talking out of your league. We're giving the Americans much more than they're giving us." They always said that, but it's not true. So much of Israeli equipment was American, and the Mossad owed them a lot.

The closing chapter reveals Israel's involvement in the Iran-contra affair through Peres's "advisor on terrorism," Amiram Nir, who was in contact with Lieutenant Colonel Oliver North and Vice President George H. W. Bush, providing a front and a physical base for the operation.

Ostrovsky's "Epilogue" recounts a litany of post-1986 incidents that had negative psychological and political repercussions for Israel. He cites statements of political leaders of the United States who reflect disenchantment and withdrawal of support. The contrasting statements, of Israeli right-wing spokespersons, rabbis who encourage hate and violence, are also noted.

> The intifada and resultant breakdown of moral order and humanity are a direct result of the kind of megalomania that characterizes the operation of the Mossad. That's where it all begins. This feeling that you can do anything you want to whomever you want for as long as you want because you have the power. . . . This is what happens after years and years of secrecy; of "we're right, let's be right, no matter what"; of keeping the officials deliberately misinformed; of justifying violence and inhumanity through deceit, or, as the Mossad logo says: "by way of deception."

CENSORSHIP HISTORY

The attempt to ban *By Way of Deception* was short-lived; it did, however, create a first. The challenges occurred in Canada and, days later, the United States. The government of Israel initiated the challenges through lawsuits seeking to block publication. The Israelis won a court order in Toronto on September 7, 1990, that blocked publication until a September 17 hearing. Under the ban, Canadian news media could not publish details of the book. Comparably, state supreme court justice Michael J. Dontzin of New York issued a temporary restraining order on September 12, 1990, at 1:00 A.M. that ordered St. Martin's Press to stop publication and distribution of the book pending a hearing. (About 17,000 copies had already been shipped to bookstores.) Israel's request was based on its claim that the book "would disseminate extremely confidential information and that this information could endanger the lives of various people in the employ of the State of Israel and would be detrimental to the State of Israel."

Justice Dontzin's restraining order was termed an aberration by a leading First Amendment lawyer who noted that this was the first time any foreign state had sought and obtained a prior restraint against the publication of a book.

St. Martin's Press appealed the restraining order. On September 13, the appellate division of the New York State Supreme Court overturned Justice Dontzin's ruling by unanimous agreement of the four justices. They found the Israeli claims of endangered lives "groundless" and that the "heavy presumption against a prior restraint on publication" had not been overcome. Allusion was made to the Pentagon Papers case (see UNITED STATES–VIETNAM RELATIONS, 1945–1967). Following this ruling on September 17, the Israeli government withdrew its lawsuit in Canada.

The attempt to ban *By Way of Deception* had the effect of accelerating sales of the book.

FURTHER READING

"Canada Blocks Book by Former Israeli Agent." *New York Times*, September 10, 1990, p. A16.

Cohen, Roger. "Ban on Mossad Book Is Overturned." *New York Times*, September 14, 1990, p. C29.

——. "Judge Halts Publication of Book by Ex-Israeli Intelligence Officer." *New York Times*, September 13, 1990, p. A1.

"Prior Restraint." *Newsletter on Intellectual Freedom* 39 (1990): 219.

CANCER WARD

Author: Aleksandr Solzhenitsyn
Dates and places of original publication: 1968, Great Britain; 1969, United States
Publishers: Bodley Head; Farrar, Straus and Giroux
Literary form: Novel

SUMMARY

Cancer Ward is essentially a cast of characters, ward mates in the mid-1950s for about two months in a Central Asian USSR hospital. The comings and goings of the patients and doctors are the action of the novel; movement is generally within the hospital from the ward to a treatment room and to the outside world upon being discharged, either because death is inevitable (it helps statistics) or because the cancer is in remission. Only occasionally are there visitors.

The overcrowded hospital is perceived as a prison as expressed through the attitude of the patients and the confinement itself. The patients feel trapped and victimized, dispirited by their isolation and confinement as well as their disease. Pavel Nikolayevich Rusanov, a self-important minor official, first enters the ward with a sense of doom; feeling depersonalized, he loses his assertive authoritativeness and willpower. Another patient, Oleg Filimonovich Kastoglotov, establishes the prison analogy in a letter in which he identifies himself as a prisoner, referring to the bars on the first floor windows and being pulled in for talks with officials, processing, and the searches that are conducted. "They take away personal belongings, so we have to hide them and fight for our right to go out and exercise."

This alienation is encouraged by a medical principle practiced by the doctors: "The patient must never be frightened, he must be encouraged. . . ." This attitude seems to be translated into a kind of noncommunication in which the patients are told little about their condition—"generally speaking, we don't have to tell our patients what's wrong with them . . ."; and next to nothing about their treatment or its potential effects. Patients discharged to die at home are not told they are to face death, their discharge certificate written in incomprehensible Latin. Kostoglotov argues vehemently that patients have the right to know of both their condition and its prognosis; also he claims the right to refuse treatment. His argument is rejected by the doctors.

The ward patients represent a range of Soviet citizens, an array of regional origins, conditions of life and age. Russian patients include Rusanov, a middle-aged career secret-service bureaucrat who is used to an upscale lifestyle; Kostoglotov, exiled to an Asian province for political reasons (Solzhenitsyn himself served eight years as a political prisoner after criticizing Joseph Stalin in letters to a friend); 16-year-old Dyomka who anxiously continues to study for his examinations; Vadim, 26 years old, a young geologist dedicated to his work, an intellectual engrossed in proving his theory that radioactive water is an indication of ore deposits; and "Yefrem" Podduyev, an aging construction engineer who has led a sensuous, irresponsible life. The other patients are working-class Asians: a collective farm watchman, a middle-aged shepherd, a young tractor driver, a concentration camp guard. The revealed backgrounds and beliefs of these men, chiefly the contrasting characters, Rusanov and Kostoglotov, offer substantive glimpses of Soviet social and political culture, the nature and extent of purges, the dislocation of individuals and groups, and the excesses of nationalism.

Rusanov, initially affronted by the prospect of being in a ward rather than a private room, further feels demeaned by his undesired companions and worse still by the humiliation of having to lie between the Russian exile on one side and the shriveled-up old Uzbek on the other. The men of the ward do not acknowledge his status; indeed, Kostoglotov taunts him. Rusanov, dedicated to the Communist Party and the regime, is given to claiming precedence and attention over others, to threatening to report individuals to officials for antiregime sentiments or perceived incompetence. During discussions or ward arguments, he sternly and pointedly adheres to the party line. He is upset when on Stalin's birth date the newspaper does not have a portrait, a black border, or an article about the nation's grief of his death.

Rusanov is portrayed, however, as a hypocrite. At the outset he affirms ". . . distinctions have to be made . . ." between himself and others in the ward; later, when in an argument an antagonist recalls the Revolution's beginning tenet, "No official should receive a salary higher than the average pay of a good worker," Rusanov thinks, "Imagine paying the health service director and the floor-scrubber the same rate!"

There is a malevolent side to Rusanov's character. His propensity for reporting political "errors" has its experiential history. His climb up the political-economic ladder was effected initially by his writing a letter denouncing a friend with whom he and his wife shared an apartment (they wanted the apartment for themselves); the friend was exiled. The climb up came on the backs of many other people whose "guilt he had also helped to establish . . . more boldly and openly as time went on." These individuals had been too outspoken in their criticisms.

Two events catapult Rusanov from self-satisfaction to shivering fear: the information that his "friend" has been rehabilitated—"what *right* have they to let these people out now? Have they no pity? How dare they cause such traumas"; and the report that the whole membership of the Supreme Court of the Soviet Union had been changed. "Who'd look after the state and Party cadre now?" Who would protect him? (These events were precursors of the liquidation of the labor camp and exile system.)

Kostoglotov is the counterpoint, Rusanov's antagonist in personal-historical terms as well as in the immediate situation. Articulate, independent, assertive, he is comparable to Rusanov's victims. After army service during the war, he was a member of a group of students who, besides dancing, drinking and flirting, talked politics and aired dissatisfactions. "And sometimes we talked about . . . about *him!*" Charged and convicted, he served first a seven-year labor camp sentence—"anyone who got less than eight years had done nothing, the accusations were based on thin air"; and then, because a group was involved, exile "in perpetuity." These experiences have not cowed Kostoglotov; though perhaps careful, he asserts his intelligence to question rules in the hospital and on the outside and to take issue with human behavior and philosophy. For example, he rejects out of hand Rusanov's assumption of precedence and privilege in the ward, denounces the concept of "social origins" as a factor of behavior, and condemns the greed of individuals (Rusanov) who put their pensions above the love of their country.

Four young people appear on the stage of the novel as well, the aforementioned Dyomka and Vadim, and two of Rusanov's children, Aviette and Yuri, the latter pair for individual cameo appearances. Vadim, a practical realist, on the surface has accepted his fate—a very short life—and seems also to have accepted philosophical-political underpinnings of Soviet society. He is more concerned with practical matters. Dyomka, interested in studying literature and history, expresses an evolving mind; he does not reflect certainties. Indeed, it is his question about the "need for sincerity in literature" that propels Aviette toward a fiery denunciation:

"Listen, my boy," she announced in powerful, ringing tones, as though speaking from a platform. "Sincerity can't be the chief criterion for judging a book. If an author expresses incorrect ideas or alien attitudes, the fact that he's sincere about them merely increases the harm the work does. Sincerity becomes *harmful.* Subjective sincerity can militate against a truthful presentation of life. That's a dialectical point."

Aviette, ambitious and dogmatic, is her father's daughter. She blames the returning prisoners, the rehabilitated, for signing the trumped-up confessions in the first place; anyway, "it can't mean the man was completely innocent! He must have done *something,* however trivial." She berates officials for causing reconsideration of the cases by bringing in the accuser for a confrontation. Yet these people "were doing a job of work for society." She proceeds to support her father and others like him, for they were motivated by the best intentions toward society. Their responsibility for the imprisonment of many thousands of innocent people escapes her.

Yuri, however, troubles his father. Rusanov judges him to be soft, gullible, easily endangered. A representative of the law, Yuri takes his defense attorney's position seriously, and actually defends his clients against harsh sentences. He suspends the five-year sentence of a truck driver who abandoned his truck when stranded by a snowstorm; the driver had been accused because of the loss of a case of macaroni while he was gone. Rusanov is appalled by his son's actions, seeing the driver guilty and deserving of the sentence (an instance of his hypocrisy).

Several doctors face examination. Three who have meaningful roles face close scrutiny: Dr. Ludmilla Afansyevna Dontsova, the chief radiologist; her radiotherapist intern, Dr. Vera Kornilyevna Gangart; and the chief surgeon, Lev Leonidovich. Each is accorded respect. They are dedicated, knowledgeable, expert, and hardworking. Each evinces compassion and concern for his or her patients. However, other members of the staff are incompetent. Three surgeons cannot be trusted to operate. The nurses are similarly divided. The incompetents cannot be fired, one because he is a token "native."

The novel's ending is bittersweet. Vadim is heartened when special medication finally arrives, but the outcome is fraught with doubt. Dyomka's leg is surgically removed to prevent the spread of cancer. Dr. Dontsova herself is diagnosed as having cancer, quite possibly the effect of radiation exposure. Her emerging understanding that excess radiation from X-ray therapy may itself be dangerous comes too late. Rusanov is discharged; he believes he is cured, but the prognosis is not favorable. Kostoglotov is also discharged, though his condition is uncertain. The closing chapters are virtually his panegyric to freedom as he experiences the sights, sounds, and tastes of life outside of confinement. However, at the zoo he is given pause when it occurs to him that the animals have lost their sense of freedom, that they will not be able to cope with freedom. He eagerly boards the train to return to his exile in order to join his friends, the old doctor, and his wife.

CENSORSHIP HISTORY

Solzhenitsyn's works were barred from publication in the Soviet Union after Nikita Khrushchev lost power in 1964; previously under the Khrushchev regime, ONE DAY IN THE LIFE OF IVAN DENISOVICH had been approved for publication. J. M. Coetzee cites Dina Spechler's analysis of "permitted dissent" in the USSR from the death of Stalin in 1953 to 1970. Given the twists and turns of Soviet political life, Khrushchev, reacting to the "nagging resistance from the Party and bureaucracy, used *Novy mir* [which first published *One Day in the Life of Ivan Denisovich* in 1962] as a vehicle to 'expose and dramatize problems and reveal facts that demonstrated . . . the necessity of the changes he proposed.' "

In 1965, according to Solzhenitsyn's letter to the Fourth Congress of Soviet Writers, dated May 16, 1967, the state security authorities confiscated his novel *The First Circle*, thus preventing its publication. It was " 'published' in an unnatural 'restricted' edition for reading by an unidentified select circle" without the author's permission and knowledge. Other literary papers dating back 15 to 20 years were also removed. Solzhenitsyn also identifies a three-year "irresponsible campaign of slander" conducted against him.

The political situation took another turn in 1967 when *Cancer Ward* was thwarted from publication in the Soviet Union, rejected either in its entirety or as chapters by magazine and book publishers. The first part had been approved for publication by the Moscow writers' organization. Solzhenitsyn implies in his May 16, 1967, letter to the Fourth Congress of Soviet Writers that these rejections resulted from censorship policies and the slandering of his reputation, which caused him to appear to be an enemy of the state. Then, after Part I was accepted for publication in the January 1968 issue of *Novy mir*, the Soviet Union's best literary periodical, *Cancer Ward* was specifically banned by Konstantin Fedin, the head of the Soviet Writers' Union. This occurred four months after a meeting of the Secretariat of the Union of Writers on September 22, 1967, when Solzhenitsyn was accused of writing a symbolic novel. It was, during this time, circulating widely within the USSR in typescript.

A footnote in Valery Chalidze's *To Defend These Rights* reveals that Solzhenitsyn was expelled from the Soviet Writers' Union in 1969 for "ideological dissent." Such expulsion, labeled an administrative persecution, is "almost tantamount to dismissal from work."

Solzhenitsyn was awarded the Nobel Prize in literature in 1970, but he declined to go to Stockholm to receive the award for fear that he would not be readmitted to the USSR. The ban on his works continued in the Soviet Union, despite this prestigious award. Moreover, in February 1974, Solzhenitsyn was arrested and charged with treason; he was stripped of his Soviet citizenship and was deported, that is, exiled from his country in KGB (Committee for State Security) handcuffs. A Russian-language edition of the first volume of THE GULAG ARCHIPELAGO had been published in September 1973, the American edition having been delayed for six months. The underlying reason for the 1974 action against him was Solzhenitsyn's rejection of then-current Russian orthodoxy, specifically, his statement in this latest book that "the abuses of justice under Stalin were the direct consequences of the personality of the dictator."

Still in 1988, a senior Soviet leader, Vadim Medvedev, a member of the politburo responsible for ideology, ruled against publication in the Soviet Union of leading works by Solzhenitsyn, accusing him of "anti-social, anti-Soviet views"; he singled out *The Gulag Archipelago* trilogy and *Lenin in Zurich*. A growing number of intellectuals had hoped that the new glasnost policies would lead to publication of Solzhenitsyn's works, and the Soviet Union of Cinema Workers had urged their publication. In October 1988, *Novy Mir* announced its intention to publish *Cancer Ward* and *The First Circle*, a project initiated in 1989. Also in this year the Secretariat of the Board of Union Writers revoked its 1969 decision to expel Solzhenitsyn from this organization. The Soviet Union was collapsing; General Secretary Mikhail S. Gorbachev restored Solzhenitsyn's full citizenship on August 15, 1990. Solzhenitsyn returned to Russia in 1994, after 20 years of exile.

Elsewhere in the world, in November 1989, the *Denver Intermountain Jewish News* reported that a number of books had been confiscated from those sent to Palestinian security prisoners at the Ketziot detention camp in the Israeli Negev. *Cancer Ward* was among them, along with such texts as *Hamlet* by Shakespeare, *The Sea Wolf* by Jack London, and *Lord of the Rings* by J. R. R. Tolkien. They were deemed to be unsuitable reading matter by the camp security officer.

Upon its publication in the West, *Cancer Ward* received favorable reviews. The *Saturday Review*'s critic Maurice Friedberg identified Solzhenitsyn as "the greatest living Russian writer" and *Cancer Ward* as "his best work to date."

Under the heading "index of banned books," the *Encyclopedia of Censorship* identifies both *Cancer Ward* and *The First Circle* as among the "most often" censored books.

FURTHER READING

Blake, Patricia. "A Diseased Body Politic." *New York Times Book Review*, October 27, 1968, VII 2.

Burg, David, and George Feifer. *Solzhenitsyn*. New York: Stein and Day, 1972.

Chalidze, Valery. *To Defend These Rights: Human Rights and the Soviet Union*. New York: Random House, 1974.

Coetzee, J. M. "Censorship and Polemic: The Solzhenitsyn Affair." *Pretexts* 2 (Summer 1990): 3–22.

Green, Jonathon, and Nicholas J. Karolides, reviser. *The Encyclopedia of Censorship, New Edition*. New York: Facts On File, 2005.

Hosking, Geoffrey. *The First Socialist Society: A History of the Soviet Union from Within*. Cambridge, Mass.: Harvard University Press, 1985.

Newsletter on Intellectual Freedom 38 (1989): 4; 39 (1990): 51.

Saunders, George. *Samizdat: Voices of the Soviet Opposition*. New York: Monad Press, 1974.

Wilson, Raymond J., III. "The Misreading of Solzhenitsyn's *Cancer Ward*: Narrative and Interpretive Strategies in the Context of Censorship." *Journal of Narrative Technique* (Spring 1989): 175–96.

CAT'S CRADLE

Author: Kurt Vonnegut, Jr.
Original date and place of publication: 1963, United States
Publisher: Holt, Rinehart and Winston
Literary form: Novel

SUMMARY

Cat's Cradle, identified by critics as science fiction, is written as a memoir of its narrator, an informal rendering of events and people that lead to the destruction of the world. The narrator, John, is a ringside observer and participant—perhaps, victim. John introduces himself in the opening of the novel. "Call me Jonah," he writes, at once recalling Herman Melville's "Call me Ishmael" in *Moby-Dick* and foreshadowing disaster with its biblical undertone.

John reveals the origin of his present situation. A journalist, he had begun to collect material for a book to be titled *The Day the World Ended.* It was to feature accounts of what famous Americans had done on August 6, 1945, the day the first atomic bomb was dropped on Hiroshima. The book was never completed. However, he does initiate it by writing to Newt Hoenikker, the youngest child of physicist Dr. Felix Hoenikker, "one of the so-called 'fathers' of the first atomic bomb"; and he also contacts Hoenikker's other children, colleagues, and acquaintances; the physicist himself is deceased.

The action of the novel follows John in his sporadic, seemingly accidental research. He encounters a couple of classmates of Hoenikker's children in a bar; he interviews Hoenikker's supervisor, Dr. Asa Breed, vice president in charge of the research laboratory of the General Forge and Foundry Company and, in a tombstone salesroom, Marvin Breed, Asa's brother, who is an admirer of Emily (Mrs. Felix) Hoenikker.

In their interview, Asa Breed identifies Hoenikker as "a force of nature no mortal could possibly control" and a pure scientist, one who works on what fascinates him in search of knowledge, "the most valuable commodity on earth." Breed illustrates Hoenikker's personality and mind with his response to a Marine general's urging to discover a way to freeze mud. In "his playful way" he suggests that there "might be a single grain of something—even a microscopic grain—that could make infinite expanses of muck, marsh, swamp, creeks, pools, quicksand and mire as solid. . . ."

Though Breed insists otherwise, our narrator reveals, as he later ascertains, that Hoenikker's "last gift for mankind" was his creation of "ice-nine." His curiosity piqued, without telling anyone, he discovered a new way for water to freeze, a new arrangement of the atoms, with a melting point of 114.4 degrees Fahrenheit. A seed of ice-nine dropped into any body of water would freeze it entirely, traveling to its origins and far reaches. Having created it, he had taken it with him to his Cape Cod cottage, where he was celebrating Christmas with his family. After showing them his invention, he had died, probably its first victim. They had divided the chip of ice-nine amongst themselves.

The plot turns aside from John's book research to his account of the Caribbean island of San Lorenzo. He has been sent there to research a magazine feature about Julian Castle, an American sugar millionaire and former playboy who has founded, in the manner of Dr. Albert Schweitzer, a free hospital in the jungle. On board the plane to San Lorenzo he meets Newton Hoenikker, a midget, and Angela Hoenikker Conners, a "giantess," as well as the newly appointed American ambassador to San Lorenzo and his wife. The Hoenikkers are en route to attend the wedding of their average-sized brother Frank, who had disappeared on the day of their father's funeral. Frank is identified as the minister of science and progress of the Republic of San Lorenzo; a major general, he is, in effect, the chief aide of its dictator, "Papa" Monzano.

San Lorenzo is a geographical and political-historical case in point. Its landscape is rocky and desolate, as "unproductive as an equal area in the Sahara or the Polar Icecap"; all of its arable land is controlled by Castle Sugar. Its people are disease ridden and destitute; it had "as dense a population as could be found anywhere, India and China not excluded." The island's history is that of one subjugation after another. First claimed for Spain by Hernando Cortes, successive claimants were France, Denmark, Holland, England, Spain (again), escaped African slaves, Castle Sugar, and then, in 1922, Lionel Boyd-Johnson and Earl McCabe, respectively an educated wandering "Negro" from Tobago and an idealistic marine deserter. The two had a dream: to create a utopia. The dream failed.

Boyd-Johnson, pronounced Bokonon in the island's dialect, invented a religion to replace the priests who had been thrown out. As it became evident that government and economic reforms could not possibly raise the people's lives out of misery, Bokononism became "the instrument of hope. Truth was the enemy of the people, because the truth was so terrible, so Bokonon made it his business to provide the people with better and better lies." To make the people's religious life more vibrant, he asked McCabe to outlaw him and his religion. Thus, McCabe became the tyrant and Bokonon (Boyd-Johnson) the saint, each suffering the "agony" of the "terrible price." McCabe never caught Bokonon, nor had his successor, Monzano, each understanding that "without the holy man to war against, he himself would become meaningless."

Despite its being outlawed, the San Lorenzians are adherents of Bokononism (indeed, John becomes one); they practice a "ritual of awareness" enacted by two individuals pressing the soles of their feet together. *The Books of Bokonon* provide pithy statements, used by John to establish a tenet and to make a point. For example, Bokonon is quoted as stating, more universally, that "all religions, including Bokononism, are nothing but lies."

The plot action picks up its pace in San Lorenzo. When they arrive, during his welcoming speech to the American ambassador and his wife, the dictator, "Papa" Monzano, collapses; recognizing imminent death, before he is rushed to a hospital, he appoints Frank to be the next president. However, he does not die immediately. Frank, unwilling to be president because of his own basic public inadequacy, offers the job to John, along with the option to marry Mona, the adopted daughter of the dictator; she is dazzlingly beautiful and serene, and she loves everyone. John, enchanted by her—she is an ideal—accepts.

The plan is to announce John's elevation to the presidency on the next day, which is the holiday honoring the Hundred Martyrs to Democracy.

Just before the ceremony, unable to withstand the pain of his cancer, "Papa" commits suicide by swallowing a sliver of ice-nine and becoming a block of ice. His physician, who out of medical curiosity touches the frost on Monzano's lips and then touches his own lips, also dies instantly. Frank decides that the only way to stop the cycle is to place the bodies on a funeral pyre as a conclusion to the planned ceremonial events.

The ceremony proceeds. However, one of the air force planes participating in a target-shooting display, trailing smoke and out of control, crashes into the castle, causing its walls to collapse. "Papa" is thrown clear, his body flying into the water, "and all the sea was *ice-nine*. The moist earth was a blue-white pearl."

Two characters in the novel speak on behalf of science. Breed, in a commencement address, states, as recalled years later by one of the students, "The trouble with the world was that people were still superstitious instead of scientific. He said if everyone would study science more, there wouldn't be all the trouble there was." And "Papa" Monzano, when appointing Frank to succeed to the presidency, does so in the name of science: "Science—you have science. Science is the strongest thing there is." The antithetical statement is made by the physician, who agrees to conduct the Bokononist last rites for the dying Monzano: "I am a very bad scientist. I will do anything to make a human being feel better, even if it's unscientific. No scientist worthy of the name could say such a thing."

Hoenikker, the represented pure scientist, in this context dominates the novel. He is defined by his sons as uninterested in people, undemonstrative and distant. Marvin Breed wonders if Hoenikker "wasn't born dead. I never met a man who was less interested in the living. . . . how the hell innocent is a man who helps make a thing like the atomic bomb." Asa Breed identifies Hoenikker's ways as "playful" and asserts that "the main thing with [him] was truth." His research, it appears, is disconnected from consequence, its effects on humanity. On the day when the bomb was first successfully tested at Alamogordo, a scientist remarked to Hoenikker, "Science has now known sin," to which the Nobel Laureate in physics responded, "What is sin?"

The title of *The Fourteenth Book of Bokonon* is "What Can a Thoughtful Man Hope for Mankind on Earth, Given the Experience of the Past Million Years?" The text of the book consists of one word: "Nothing."

CENSORSHIP HISTORY

The censorship controversy in Strongsville, Ohio, began in June 1972 when the members of the school board refused to approve the use of Joseph Heller's CATCH-22 and Kurt Vonnegut's *God Bless You, Mr. Rosewater* for use in high school English classes. Then, in August, *Cat's Cradle* and *Catch-22* were removed from the school libraries. Board members objected to the language and the content.

On behalf of five students, the American Civil Liberties Union (ACLU) field suit against the board of education's actions to ban the books. The suit is identified as *Minarcini v. Strongsville City School District*. In presenting its case in October 1973 before Judge Robert B. Krupansky of the U.S. District Court for the Northern District of Ohio (Sixth Circuit), the Strongsville Board of Education argued that only a school board had the right to determine the books to be used in schools, stating that its members were elected to represent the people who pay for education. An attempt to abridge that right would be unconstitutional. The ACLU argued in response that the board's ban of *Cat's Cradle*, *God Bless You, Mr. Rosewater*, and *Catch-22* was unconstitutional because it was a violation of students' First and Fourteenth Amendment rights.

The U.S. District Court judge dismissed the complaint on the basis of a ruling in 1972 of the U.S. District Court for the Eastern District of New York (Second Circuit), which was affirmed by the district's court of appeals. This case emanated from a Queens, New York, school district in which the school board ordered the limited availability to parents of *DOWN THESE MEAN STREETS* by Piri Thomas. The court found no constitutional issue in the removal of books from a library. A factor that apparently influenced the court's ruling was the availability of the novel in community bookstores.

However, the Sixth Circuit's court of appeals in 1976 overturned the Second Circuit court's ruling. It asserted: "A library is a storehouse of knowledge. When created for a public school it is an important privilege created by the state for the benefit of the student. . . . That privilege is not subject to being withdrawn." While acknowledging the school board's general authority to select books for classrooms and school libraries and the "winnowing" of library collections, the court indicated that removal of a book from the library required a legally defensible and constitutionally valid reason. In this case there were no such reasons, the school board members having reacted to Vonnegut and Heller's language and views of life. Specifically, "once having created such a privilege for the benefit of its students [i.e., providing a library and acquiring a particular novel] . . . neither body could place conditions on the use of the library related solely to the social or political tastes of school board members."

The court reinforced this decision by rejecting the argument that a book's availability at "alternative" sites was acceptable and by giving emphasis to the educational function of the school library:

[A] public school library is also a valuable adjunct to classroom discussion. If one of the English teachers considered Joseph Heller's *Catch-22* to be one of the more important modern American novels (as, indeed, at least one did), we assume that no one would dispute that the First Amendment's protection of academic freedom would protect both his right to say so in class and his students' right to hear him and find and read the book. Obviously, the students' success in this last endeavor would be greatly hindered by the fact that the book sought had been removed from the school library. The removal of books from a school library is a much more serious burden on freedom of classroom discussion than the [prohibition on the wearing of black arm bands found unconstitutional in the *Tinker* case].

In his discussion of this case, Robert M. O'Neil (in *Classrooms in the Crossfire*) signals the importance of a content-based versus a content-neutral reason for removing a book (i.e., censorship). He also points to the U.S. Supreme Court's "emerging doctrine," explicitly recognized in the interim between the two cases: the "First Amendment right to receive information and ideas." Thus, "freedom of speech necessarily protects the right to receive"; this protection has developed to include readers' and listeners' rights. By the time the Strongsville case was heard, O'Neil explains, "a new constitutional basis for the students' claim existed, and could be invoked with a conviction that would have been unwarranted four years earlier."

Julia Bradley advances this position. She acknowledged the application of the "right to receive information doctrine" and that the "court held that the board could not condition the privilege of library use on the social and political tastes of board members, but must operate using criteria which are 'neutral in First Amendment terms.'" She compares the "easy" *Minarcini* case with the "more complex" Island Trees case. The Strongsville school board in the former did not explain the reasons for its ban; this "lack of an educational rationale for the decision virtually compelled the court's conclusion of arbitrariness." By providing reasons for the removal of books from its schools' libraries, the Island Trees school board required a consideration of those reasons.

Another challenge to *Cat's Cradle* occurred in 1982 in Merrimack, New Hampshire. A parent, Robert Duarte, requested that four novels, *Cat's Cradle*, ORDINARY PEOPLE by Judith Guest, ONE FLEW OVER THE CUCKOO'S NEST by Ken Kesey, and *The Other* by Thomas Tryon, be removed from the required reading list of a high school elective contemporary literature course, one of 10 choices. He also requested that his son be excused from the course. He complained that *Ordinary People* was obscene and depressing.

The Merrimack school board by a 4-1 vote rejected the request. Its chair, Carolyn Disco, commented, "These four books are acceptable and fine choices for a course of this type. . . . We're trying to represent the entire community. What may upset some people will be acceptable to others. [Students] do have the option of taking another class." A compromise of sorts emerged when Arthur "Pete" Gagnon, a planning board member, requested that the novels be made optional reading with "notification to parents that some of the material could contain offensive matter." The latter suggestion was apparently accepted; appropriate courses would be "flagged" in the succeeding year's course description catalog.

FURTHER READING

Averback, Ronna. "Authors Defend Books in Ban Suit." *Strongville News Sun*, June 27, 1974, p. 1.

Boyle, Maureen. "Board Nixes Book Ban, Sets Warnings Instead." *Union Leader*, June 23, 1982, p. 6.

Bradley, Julia Turnquist. " 'Censoring the School Library;' Do Students Have the Right to Read?" *Connecticut Law Review* 10 (Spring 1978): 747–74.

Haight, Anne Lyon, and Chandler B. Grannis. *Banned Books: 387 B.C. to 1978 A.D.* New York: R. R. Bowker, 1978.

Kinsey, Linda. "Books Still Ire, But Okayed." *County Line Magazine* (June 12, 1974): 1.

Newsletter on Intellectual Freedom 24 (1975): 6; 28 (1979): 85; 31 (1982): 170.

O'Neil, Robert. *Classrooms in the Crossfire: The Rights and Interests of Students, Parents, Teachers, Administrators, Librarians and the Community.* Bloomington: Indiana University Press, 1981.

THE CHINA LOBBY IN AMERICAN POLITICS

Author: Ross Y. Koen
Original date and place of publication: 1960, United States
Publisher: Macmillan Publishing Company
Literary form: Nonfiction

SUMMARY

Two striking declarations anticipate the purpose of *The China Lobby in American Politics:* the accusation in 1951 by Senator Wayne Morse that the China lobby was "conducting a violent campaign against American policies in China, chiefly by charging that the State Department, and especially its Far Eastern Division, is a nest of Reds controlled by Communists and fellow travelers"; and Marquis Childs's statement in the *Washington Post* in 1952 that "It would be hard to find any parallel in diplomatic history for the agents and diplomatic representatives of a foreign power exerting such pressures—Nationalist China has used the techniques of direct intervention on a scale rarely, if ever, seen." Ross Y. Koen's purpose in this book is "to examine the nature of these techniques of intervention and to isolate and analyze the 'campaign against American policies in China.'"

The first section, "The American Perspective on the Far East," provides critical background on the attitudes held by Americans toward China and how these attitudes influenced their inclination to accept an "extreme explanation" of postwar events in the Far East. Among the early influences cited are past trade and investment experiences with China; missionary activities; and the official Open Door policy, intended to control the actions of foreign powers, that is "to . . . preserve Chinese territorial and administrative entity . . . and safeguard for the world the principles of equal and impartial trade. . . ." Neither the United States government nor the American people recognized the ineffectiveness of the Open Door policy, leading, according to Koen, to the belief that "words and ideals were sufficient to control events in China."

During World War II, a confusion of views was circulated in the United States. One view held that the Chinese were valiant people fighting against great odds to preserve their independence and to establish democracy. Generalissimo Chiang Kai-shek was portrayed as an enlightened, valuable anti-Communist ally. A contrasting, negative view presented Chiang as being autocratic, without support of the people, ruler of the corrupt Kuomintang (KMT) party and a failure in carrying out necessary agricultural and economic reforms. Another view held that the Chinese Communist regime was the least corrupt and the most benevolent and democratic, having accomplished social, political, and economic reforms. These disparate views, particularly the first two, became the core of the pro-Chiang and anti-Chiang factions that emerged.

Of the policy alternatives available to the United States, the one chosen represented a cautious approach: economic assistance, technical aid, and military support in an effort to develop a compromise between the two Chinese factions and an end to the civil war. Underlying this choice was the understanding that the American people would not support massive intervention in China. However, at the crux of the events and with the ensuing issues discussed in this book is the recognition that "when it developed that their refusal to intervene was accompanied by the creation of a government unfavorable to the United States, Americans were equally unprepared to accept that result."

Thus, there was a need and a "predisposition" for the American people to accept an extreme explanation of events in China. This explanation was that the defeat of the Nationalist Chinese government was the fault of the United States and that it resulted from the "betrayal and sellout of China perpetuated by Far Eastern experts, Foreign Service officers, and State Department officials." In Koen's view, the China lobby was instrumental in achieving this effect.

What was the China lobby? What were its purposes and methods, the issues it exploited? The term *lobby*, not here used in the standard way, includes agents of the Chinese Nationalist government. This "inner core" group also included Americans "whose personal interests [like those of the Chinese] were immediately dependent upon a continuation of American aid to Chiang," including those with official positions that were contingent upon Chiang's government remaining in power and those with financial interests. A second category consisted of "a kaleidoscopic array of affiliates who were increasingly allied to the Chiang regime in their sympathies." These individuals or groups supported Chiang for political or ideological reasons or assumptions regarding American security and concern about the spread of communism.

The foremost foreign relations goal of Chiang and his government was to regain the sympathy and the support of the United States, and to convince Americans that a strong and friendly Nationalist China was essential to American security. In concert with these purposes, the initial purpose of the China lobby was to obtain foreign aid for China during World War II, during the ensuing civil war between the Nationalists and Communists, and after the Communist victory. The second major goal, of increasing importance after this victory, was to prevent United States recognition of the Communist government.

Propaganda organs were primary mechanisms used to achieve the purposes of the lobby. They included a political party, two Chinese-language newspapers, a central news agency, and other outlets. These outlets promoted the Chinese Nationalist point of view through articles and reports. In addition, business firms owned by the Nationalist government of China promoted trade. Their agents, Americans who were required to register as foreign agents, acted to combat Communist propaganda and to promote the Nationalist cause through "public relations" activities (e.g., "conversations" with the media, published articles, various contacts with legislators, and analysis of American public opinion).

Two examples illustrate the tactics. First, the Yalta Agreement of 1945 was labeled the "Yalta betrayal"; Roosevelt and Churchill were charged with having "completely succumbed to all Stalin's demands" and "sacrificed to Soviet imperialism the vital rights of China" as well as some of its territory. The American pro-Chiang analyst Alfred Kohlberg, for example, "declared that the President had 'bought' Stalin's aid in the Pacific war out of pique with Chiang Kai-shek." A lead editorial in *The China Monthly* indicated that Roosevelt and Churchill "were playing the part of traitors," an epithet that was frequently repeated. Second, the Amerasia affair, revealed in June 1945, involved leakage of information from government agencies to the editor of the magazine *Amerasia;* he had been identified as a Communist before congressional committees. Despite three separate investigations concluding otherwise and four of the six suspects being cleared, lobby spokespeople continued to refer to the case as espionage, the leaked information as top secret, and the suspects as "the presence of Soviet agents in the State Department." Again, the word *treason* was used in reference to the government's handling of the case.

Other factors include the resignation of Ambassador (to China) Patrick J. Hurley in November 1945; the failure of George C. Marshall's mission to China in 1946 and 1947, after which the United States was accused of betraying China by forcing the Chiang government into a coalition with the Communists; the spy ring revelations of ex-Communists and the conviction of Alger Hiss; and the war in Korea. By means of semantically loaded labeling, careful selection of and omission of data, misrepresenting data, constant attacks, and innuendo, the China lobby agencies sought to affect public opinion and congressional actions.

Incrementally, the China lobby viewpoint was accepted in the United States. Those who had been neutral or silent became active supporters and joined the original lobbyists. Such support was evident in the tendency to support requests for aid to Chiang's Kuomintang regime in China and Formosa, the use of and reference to the views and materials of China lobby propagandists; and the adoption of the China lobby's tactics and techniques when criticizing American policy and those who made it.

Two events helped to escalate this acceptance pattern: publication in *Life* magazine on October 13, 1947, of William C. Bullitt's "Report on China"; this "report" was not based on direct contact with the events but upon interviews with Chinese in Nanjing (Nanking); and Senator Joseph R. McCarthy's public accusation in 1950 that he had a list of 205 employees in the State Department "who have been named as active members of the Communist Party and members of a spy ring. . . ." (McCarthy's charges were found to be a "fraud and a hoax.")

The remainder of Koen's text expresses the effects of acceptance of the China lobby position on private specialists, scholarly organizations and foundations, and governmental specialists, primarily Department of State personnel. The task of the lobby was to discredit the prevailing skepticism of Chiang's future by asserting the specialists had Communist sympathies and/ or membership, thus undermining also the organizations with which they were allied and casting a significant shadow on Department of State policies and procedures. The case of Owen Lattimore, an esteemed scholar with extraordinary expertise, is highlighted. The campaign against him lasted for four years, and it led to a perjury indictment that was ultimately dismissed. However, the result was to substantially thwart Lattimore's research, undermine his reputation (as well as that of his associates), and diminish the position of neutral or anti-Chiang groups.

The "tragic results" go beyond destroyed reputations of individual specialists and agencies; beyond the subverting of objectivity and intellectual honesty; beyond, too, the turning of the congressional investigation from "a forum of inquiry into a weapon of slander, intimidation, and deception." The myths created by the China lobby, adopted as the official view of the Republican Party and accepted by many Democrats, led to the adoption of an "official policy which prohibited all direct contact by Americans—private or governmental—with mainland China. In Koen's view, this disallowing of communication with China as well as necessary research resulted in a significant gap of information, forcing the United States to "depend on the distortions, the falsehoods, and the self-serving propaganda of the Formosa regime." If peaceful relations with China are to be achieved, "unyielding hostility to China" must be reversed; this would require Congress to repudiate its past actions and work toward a major reexamination of the American position.

CENSORSHIP HISTORY

The China Lobby in American Politics was first published in 1960 by Macmillan. However, more than 4,000 copies were destroyed before the book was released, and the publisher attempted to recall those already distributed to reviewers and libraries. A few books were not returned, escaping destruction, and were placed in rare book rooms of libraries. (According to Richard C. Kagan in his introduction to the text, "Many . . . were stolen from libraries by right wing groups. . . .")

Ross Y. Koen indicates, as reported in a 1974 article in the *New York Times*, that he had been commissioned to write the book in 1958 and that his manuscript had been accepted after being reviewed by China specialists and Macmillan lawyers. About 7,500 copies were printed and bound and scheduled for release in March 1960. However, about two weeks before publication the Chinese Nationalist embassy took offense with sentences in the preface and threatened a libel suit.

> There is, for example, evidence that some Chinese have engaged in the illegal smuggling of narcotics into the United States with the full knowledge and connivance of members of the Chinese Nationalist Government. The evidence indicates that several prominent Americans have participated in and profited from these transactions.

Koen notes that he agreed to "modify his language," and Macmillan agreed to issue a "revised" book. Subsequently, Koen was asked to make "further changes of substance"; he declined. Copies of the book were destroyed by the publisher.

Richard C. Kagan's introduction asserts, "Working through the State Department, the Central Intelligence Agency, and the Federal Bureau of Narcotics, the KMT [Kuomintang] prevented the book from being published." Koen agrees with this assertion, but both he and Kagan rely on "considerable" circumstantial rather than documentary evidence in making this statement.

In 1968, Koen obtained the rights to his text with the provision that he could not mention Macmillan's name in reprinting the book or describe in writing the details of its suppression. According to Koen, "a few modest changes" were made in the Harper and Row 1974 edition with his approval, but the original offending passage was retained.

Commenting on the reissue, James C. Thompson, Jr., curator of the Nieman Foundation and member of the East Asian Research Center at Harvard, said, "The book is a highly important account of a central aspect of our China relationship."

FURTHER READING

"Ideas and Trends: Education, Religion, Privacy." *New York Times*, December 15, 1974, sec. 4, p. 7.

Kagan, Richard C. "Introduction." In *The China Lobby in American Politics*, by Ross Y. Koen. New York: Harper and Row, 1974.

Whitman, Alden. "Suppressed China Book Sees the Light Again." *New York Times*, December 10, 1974, p. 55.

THE CIA AND THE CULT OF INTELLIGENCE

Authors: Victor Marchetti and John D. Marks
Original date and place of publication: 1974, United States
Publisher: Alfred A. Knopf
Literary form: Nonfiction

SUMMARY

The CIA and the Cult of Intelligence provides both a broad and detailed view of the Central Intelligence Agency within the context of the "intelligence community." The authors set the stage for their revelations about the CIA and their attitudes toward it in their first sentence: "There exists in our nation today a powerful and dangerous secret cult—the cult of intelligence." This idea is extended by their expressing that its "clandestine professionals" and its "patrons and protectors" are a "secret fraternity of the American political aristocracy." The initial statements of purpose of the CIA are no less revealing:

> The purpose of the cult is to further the foreign policies of the U.S. government by covert and usually illegal means, while at the same time containing the spread of its avowed enemy, communism. Traditionally, the cult's hope has been to foster a world order in which America would reign supreme, the unchallenged international leader. Today, however, that dream stands tarnished by time and frequent failures. Thus, the cult's objectives are now less grandiose, but no less disturbing. It seeks largely to advance America's self-appointed role as the dominant arbiter of social, economic, and political change in the awakening regions of Asia, Africa, and Latin America. . . . to maintain a self-serving stability . . . using whatever clandestine methods are available.

The official size (16,500 personnel) and cost ($750 million budget) are understated. The personnel figure does not include mercenaries, agents, consultants, or employees of proprietaries—altogether tens of thousands—who are under contract to the CIA. The budget figure is also deceptive, being supplemented by the earnings of those proprietaries that are money-making enterprises and annual contributions from the Pentagon amounting to hundreds of millions of dollars.

> Fully aware of these additional sources of revenue, the CIA's chief of planning and programming reverently observed a few years ago that the director does not

operate a mere *multimillion*-dollar agency but actually runs a *multibillion*-dollar conglomerate—with virtually no outside oversight.

In terms of financial assets, the CIA is not only more affluent than its official annual budget reflects, it is one of the few federal agencies that have no shortage of funds. In fact, the CIA has more money to spend than it needs.

In addition to the director's office and staff, the CIA is organized into four functional directorates. The largest of these with about 6,000 professionals and clericals is the Directorate of Operations, also known as Clandestine Services. The activities of this directorate include liaison, espionage, counterespionage, and various forms of covert action; that is, interventions (paramilitary operations, subsidizing political parties, labor unions, and others) in the internal affairs of other countries. Among its 15 worldwide geographic area units is the "Domestic Operations Division," which conducts "mysterious clandestine activities" in the United States. A second directorate is that of Management and Services, which is the CIA's administrative and housekeeping section with over 5,000 career employees. The two smaller units are the Directorate of Intelligence and the Science and Technology Directorate, with 3,500 and 1,300 employees respectively. The former has two basic functions: to produce finished intelligence reports from the analysis of information and to operate several services for the benefit of the intelligence community, such as its computerized biographical library and its photographic information center. The latter conducts basic research and development of technical espionage systems, handles the electronic data-processing work, and operates spy satellites and intelligence analysis in highly technical fields.

The intelligence community is made up of 10 different components of the federal government concerned with the collection and/or analysis of foreign intelligence. Among these, in addition to the CIA, are the three armed services, three cabinet departments, and three agencies. These range in size from the smallest, the Treasury Department, with 300 personnel and an annual budget of $10 million, to the largest, Air Force Intelligence, with 56,000 personnel and an annual budget of $27 billion. The total personnel count and annual budgets for the intelligence community add up to 153,250 and $6.228 billion. The CIA makes up less than 15 percent of these totals, 16,500 and $750 million, plus the director's special contingency fund.

An issue raised in the discussion of the intelligence community is that of redundancy—duplication in the collection effort with parallel duplication of expenditure: "[T]wo or more agencies often spending great amounts of money to amass essentially the same data, and that much of the information was useless for anything other than low-level intelligence analysis." The analyses of several study groups, cited by Marchetti and Marks, are relatively uniform in their criticism and recommendations for reform; these have been ignored or buried. Factors operating against change are "tribalism," especially in the military intelligence agencies, where personnel loyalty is toward the parent service; and the unmanageable size and unwillingness of agencies to cut programs. With regard to Congress, the authors state, "The fear on Capitol Hill of violating the sacred mystique of 'national security' prevented any effective corrective action."

The strategies and tactics used by the CIA are explored in the four central chapters of the book. Special operations, "the crudest, most direct form of covert action," primarily uses activities of a paramilitary or warlike nature. Differentiated from the "CIA professional," the paramilitary operator is a "gangster who deals in force, in terror, in violence." The CIA also finances "proprietary corporations," ostensibly private businesses or institutions—front organizations for missions—to carry out clandestine activities, usually covert action operations.

Psychological warfare techniques range from the benign—straight news or orchestra tours or rock music—to the devious. (The explanatory paragraph is censored in the text.) "Against a closed-society target, simply supplying information and news that the government wishes to keep from its people can have a significant effect. If, in addition, some clever disinformation can be inserted, then so much the better." False information—lies—is used to breed unrest or resistance in the targeted country. These deceptions met with some success in China and South Vietnam, for example. Another effect was the misleading of other CIA China analysts as well as those of the State and Defense Departments. Also, unwitting scholars and news reporters who accepted the disinformation at face value published articles based upon the phony data, some of which were never corrected.

Espionage and counterespionage in the traditional sense are not especially successful methods for the CIA. Technical espionage systems have become more important sources of information for foreign intelligence. Additionally, in the context of espionage, the authors reveal the CIA's domestic operations despite its being forbidden to exercise any "police, subpoena, law-enforcement powers, or internal security functions."

The clandestine mentality, the dominant force of the CIA, "thrives on secrecy and deception" and promotes covert-action operations. This mentality separates "personal morality and conduct from actions, no matter how debased, which are taken in the name of the United States government and, more specifically, the Central Intelligence Agency." The CIA's sense of its "immunity to law and morals" is expressed in an ends-justifies-the-means mentality; thus, William Colby, CIA director in the 1970s, can "devise and direct terror tactics; secret wars, and the like, all in the name of democracy." Another specific example of "confused morality" is the Watergate break-in.

Within the CIA, similar activities are undertaken with the consent of "competent authority." The Watergate conspirators, assured that "national security" was at stake, did not question the legality or the morality of their methods; nor do most CIA operators. Hundreds if not thousands of CIA men have participated in similar operations, usually—but not always—in foreign countries; all such operations are executed in the name of "national security." The clandestine mentality not only allows it; it veritably *wills* it.

These activities and the accompanying mentality breed secrecy and deception not limited to the CIA operators. Official lying, called "plausible denial," seems ubiquitous up the ranks to the president. Other government agencies and officials, Congress, and the public are told lies by omission or denial.

In the words of former CIA director Richard Helms, the CIA "make[s] no foreign policy; the White House must approve its main programs." The authors, however, argue that the CIA does have a "profound determinative effect on the formulation and carrying out of American foreign policy. The very existence of the CIA as an instrument for secret intervention in other countries' internal affairs changes the way the nation's highest leaders look at the world." Presidents seem to fall victim to the secrecy of CIA operations, which allow swift actions and interventions that "if conducted openly, would brand the United States as an outlaw nation." Marchetti and Marks cite other policy effects: "blackmail" and other diplomatic responses to provocations when an operation goes wrong; the use of intelligence reports, sometimes one-sided, favoring the bias of the director, to achieve an aim. Former assistant CIA director for research Herbert Scoville, Jr., is quoted as stating to the Foreign Relations Committee in 1972: ". . . the history of the past twenty years is dotted with example after example of intelligence being misused to promote within the Congress the programs of individual organizations or even the administration as a whole."

The authors' basic thesis is that the CIA is in need of being controlled. They argue that unfortunately the oversight committees are ineffective. For example, the 40 Committee, an interdepartmental panel of the executive branch responsible for overseeing the CIA high-risk covert-action operations, is "loaded in favor of the CIA"; among its membership are the director of Central Intelligence, the chairman of the Joint Chiefs of Staff, the undersecretary of state for political affairs, the deputy secretary of defense, and the assistant to the president for national security affairs. It is "relatively ineffective in monitoring the CIA's covert operations and is totally in the dark on espionage operations." Congress has, over the early years, abrogated its surveillance responsibilities. This situation began to change in 1971 as a result of indignation over the CIA's "36,000 man 'secret' army" in Laos as well as the Watergate disclosures in 1973.

Marchetti and Marks conclude that it is time for the "United States to stand openly behind its actions overseas, to lead by example rather than manipulation." They provide a democratic and moral stance in their closing paragraph:

> The mechanisms used to intervene overseas ignore and undermine American constitutional processes and pose a threat to the democratic system at home. The United States is surely strong enough as a nation to be able to climb out

of the gutter and conduct its foreign policy in accordance with the ideals that the country was founded upon.

CENSORSHIP HISTORY

As it presently exists, therefore, the manuscript of *The CIA and the Cult of Intelligence* demonstrates with remarkable clarity the actual workings of the CIA's "classification" system. In this edition, passages the CIA originally ordered excised—and then reluctantly permitted to be reinstated—are printed in **boldface type.** Firm deletions, including the 140-plus passages cleared but still tied up in litigation, are indicated by blank spaces preceded and followed by parenthesis: **(DELETED).** The spaces correspond to the actual length of the cuts.

This "Publisher's Note" reveals the status of the censorship challenge against *The CIA and the Cult of Intelligence* in 1974. The original number of deletions required by the CIA were 339 passages; all but 168 were reinstated. The litigation continued into mid-1975.

Victor Marchetti's right to publish a book or articles related to intelligence activities, sources, methods, or information was first challenged on April 17, 1972, when a federal judge, acting at the request of the Department of Justice, issued a restraining order. Judge Albert V. Bryan, Jr., of the Federal District Court for the Eastern District of Virginia, issued, in effect, the first official censorship order served on an American writer by a United States court. In contrast to the Pentagon Papers case (see UNITED STATES–VIETNAM RELATIONS, 1945–1967) in which the materials were classified documents, Marchetti's proposed text would be an original work. On April 26, a three-judge panel of the United States Court of Appeals for the Fourth Circuit declined to invalidate the temporary restraining order.

The trial before Judge Bryan took place on May 15; it resulted in a permanent injunction against Marchetti. Again, the court of appeals upheld the lower court's ruling. The three judges unanimously ruled, however, that Marchetti would not be deprived of his right to speak and write about the CIA; the limitation of the injunction applied to the disclosure of "classified information obtained by him during the course of his employment which is not already in the public domain." The court also indicated that the secrecy agreement signed by Marchetti when accepting CIA employment did not violate his First Amendment rights of free speech. The court added that Marchetti could seek judicial review of any CIA disapproval of a manuscript.

In December 1972, the Supreme Court refused to hear the case. The American Civil Liberties Union (ACLU) defense had anticipated that the Supreme Court's 1971 decision against the government's "prior restraint" in the Pentagon Papers case would support its case. In contrast, the Marchetti situation was perceived as a "contract action" rather than a disclosure-of-injurious-information situation.

Having submitted the completed manuscript for review on August 27, 1973, according to the terms of the judicial order, Marchetti received notification in mid-September from the CIA that 100 pages of allegedly classified material would be excised from the 530-page text. The material was described as dangerous and "would have blown us out of the water in a lot of places—identities, operations, things like that."

On October 15, after Marchetti had already proven that some of the material censored had been acquired after his departure from the CIA or was already in the public domain, the CIA released 114 items of the original 339 excisions. Subsequently, additional items were released bringing the number of deletions to 168. These included, for example, mention of the well-known fact that the CIA supported efforts to overthrow the Sukarno government in Indonesia in 1950; a paragraph about a program to send propaganda-carrying balloons from Taiwan over mainland China; references to Air America as a "CIA-owned airline"; and some statements that were embarrassing to the administration and to the CIA.

On October 30, the authors and their publisher, Alfred A. Knopf, Inc., filed a suit "to enjoin the Government from deleting roughly 10 percent of the book's material and to halt all interference with its publication." The brief cited the government's violation of the First and Fifth Amendments by prohibiting the plaintiffs from submitting an uncensored version of the manuscript to the publisher; this constituted a "forbidden prior restraint upon freedom of the press" in that publication of the excised material would not "surely result in direct, immediate and irreparable injury to the nation or its people."

Federal Judge Albert V. Bryan on December 21 first ordered the government to provide data to justify its deletions, which it considered classified. In early January, he rejected a plea of CIA director Colby that the material was "highly classified" and its release to the court's "security experts" and the plaintiffs' lawyers would "lead to serious harm to the national defense interest."

The trial over the government right to delete sections of the text was convened in the U.S. District Court on February 28, 1974, and lasted two-and-a-half days. Judge Bryan's decision was issued on March 29. He essentially rejected the government's claim of injury to the national defense as evidenced by finding that only 26 of the 168 deletions had been classified while Marchetti had been an employee of the agency and thus subject to deletion. Of the 168 items still being contested, 140 items and parts of two others did not meet the burden-of-proof standard to which the government must be held, according to Judge Bryan. First Amendment guarantees protected the authors against the "whim" of a government official. However, in accordance with his earlier 1972 decision, which was approved by the court of appeals, he supported the government's right to review the manuscript prior to its publication. During the trial Judge Bryan had refused to hear testimony on First Amendment issues; he had ruled that Marchetti was governed by a "secrecy" contract he had signed prior to joining the CIA. Both sides planned to appeal.

The Court of Appeals of the Fourth Circuit, having heard arguments on June 3, 1974, reversed the decision of the lower court in its February 7 ruling. Judge Bryan's burden-of-proof requirements of the government were "far too stringent." Writing for the three-judge panel, Judge Clement F. Haynesworth, Jr., upheld the government's need for secrecy and maintained the binding effect of the signed secrecy agreement. "There is a presumption of regularity in the performance by a public official of his public duty." To censor a particular item, the CIA did not have to prove that the item was the focus of a secret classification. Rather, "the government was required to show no more than that each deletion disclosed information which was required to be classified in any degree and which was contained in a document bearing a classification stamp." Further, "[i]f secret matters become public in other ways, Marchetti and Marks still cannot talk about them—unless the CIA approves." The judge's ruling did not mention the Supreme Court's 1971 contrasting decision in the Pentagon Papers case.

The Supreme Court on May 27, with only Justice William Douglas dissenting, declined to review the ruling against Marchetti and Marks and their publisher. The effect was to concur with the appellate court's decision. In such a decision not to review a case, the judges are not required to provide an opinion.

In 1980 a new lawsuit filed under the Freedom of Information Act by Morton Halperin, director of national security studies, sought the release of all censored passages in *The CIA and the Cult of Intelligence*. In August, in response to the suit, the government agreed to permit the printing of 25 passages previously banned, either entirely or in part, conceding that there was no security objection. Among these was a statement made by Henry Kissinger, then assistant to the president for national security affairs, at a meeting in the White House on June 27, 1972, of the 40 Committee, which directed CIA covert actions, to consider the situation in Chile under the leadership of Salvador Allende: "I don't see why we need to stand by and watch a country go Communist due to the irresponsibility of its own people. Another sentence about Kissinger had had two words omitted, as bracketed below: "Henry Kissinger talked about the kind of general posture the United States could maintain toward the [white regimes] and outlined the specific policies open to the President." This followed another partially banned sentence: "There were sharp disagreements within the government how hard a line the United States should take with the [white-minority regimes of South Africa, Rhodesia and the Portuguese colonies in Africa]." The bracketed words were released.

FURTHER READING

"CIA Will Give Data to Enjoin Ex-Agent." *New York Times*, April 27, 1972, p. 7.

Crewdson, John M. "CIA Will Seek to Excise Parts of Book by Ex-Aide." *New York Times*, September 12, 1973, p. 18.

Gent, George. "Knopf Sues Over CIA Censoring of Book." *New York Times*, October 31, 1973, p. 36.

Green, Jonathon, and Nicholas J. Karolides, reviser. *The Encyclopedia of Censorship, New Edition.* New York: Facts On File, 2005.

Haight, Anne Lyon, and Chandler B. Grannis. *Banned Books: 387 B.C. to 1978 A.D.* 4th ed. New York: R. R. Bowker, 1978.

Hurwitz, Leon. *Historical Dictionary of Censorship in the United States.* Westport, Conn.: Greenwood Press, 1985.

Ledbetter, Les. "Appeals Court Supports CIA in Blocking Article by Ex-Aide." *New York Times*, September 18, 1972, p. 23.

Lewis, Anthony. "And a Threat to That Freedom: A Court of Appeals Decision on Prior Restraint." *New York Times*, February 16, 1974, p. 16.

———. "Don't Look Now. . . ." *New York Times*, January 10, 1974, p. 37.

———. "The Mind of the Censor." *New York Times*, April 7, 1980, p. A19.

———. "Security and Freedom." *New York Times*, May 22, 1974, p. 39.

Newsletter on Intellectual Freedom 23 (1974): 69–70; 24 (1975): 69, 85.

Oelsner, Lesley. "CIA Head Loses Appeal to Judge." *New York Times*, January 11, 1974, p. 29.

———. "Judge Backs Publishing of CIA Book." *New York Times*, April 2, 1974, p. 12.

———. "Judge Orders Data in Suit to Justify Deletions in Book on CIA." *New York Times*, December 22, 1973, p. 22.

Pace, Eric. "Cuts That CIA Sought in Book Touch on Official Slips." *New York Times*, April 15, 1974, p. 24.

Rosenbaum, David E. "Judge Bars Book by Ex-CIA Agent." *New York Times*, April 19, 1972, p. 19.

Weaver, Warren, Jr. "Justices Let Stand Censorship Order over a CIA Book." *New York Times*, May 28, 1974, p. 1.

Wicker, Tom. "The CIA and Free Speech." *New York Times*, March 18, 1974, p. 37.

CITIES OF SALT (MUDUN AL-MILH)

Author: Abdul Rahman Munif
Original dates and places of publication: 1984, Lebanon; 1987, United States and Canada
Publishers: The Arab Institute for Research and Publishing; Random House
Literary form: Novel

SUMMARY

Cities of Salt is set in a Middle Eastern sultanate (fictitious but identifiable as the kingdom of Saudi Arabia), spotlighting initially an imaginary oasis town, Wadi al-Uyoun, and subsequently Harran, an imaginary seaside village. The focus of the plot is oil, the politics of oil, and its impact on these communities, their residents, and the environment.

Wadi-al Uyoun: an outpouring of green amid the harsh, obdurate desert, as if it had burst from within the earth or fallen from the sky. It was nothing like its surroundings, or rather had no connection with them, dazzling you with curiosity and wonder: how had water and greenery burst out in a place like this? But the wonder vanished gradually, giving way to a mysterious respect and contemplation. It was one of those rare cases of nature expressing its genius and willfulness, in defiance of any explanation.

Whatever its origin, an ordinary place to its inhabitants, it was to the caravans that traveled through it "a salvation from death in the treacherous, accursed desert," an unforgettable beacon for their journey, an "earthly paradise" when they arrived. The traditional Bedouin society, which made its home there, seems not to have changed over the decades—perhaps centuries—living their lives in remote naïveté, getting news from the caravan personnel and from their traveling sons. These do not reveal upon their return the geography and culture of the world beyond, perhaps Damascus. In this context, certainly, the industrial progress of the world is foreign to them.

The lives of the residents of Wadi al-Uyoun are pacific, unruffled by caravan events and travelers, welcoming and assisting them. They trust their traditions and are devoted to their God and His prophet, Mohammed; they seem unchanging. The arrival of three foreigners and two marsh Arabs, who speak Arabic, is disruptive, causing Miteb al-Hathal, one of the leaders, to become both confused and depressed—and full of fear: He does not know what they want and cannot find out. In contrast, Ibn Rashed, another leader, welcomes them, in concert apparently with the local emir.

Miteb's intuitive premonitions of disaster are eventually confirmed. The foreigners, identified as Americans, without revealing to anyone their purpose, except perhaps Ibn Rashed and the local emir, eventually took action.

> For anyone who remembers those long-ago days, when a place called Wadi al-Uyoun used to exist, and a man named Miteb al-Hathal, and a brook, and trees, and a community of people used to exist, the three things that still break his heart in recalling those days are the tractors which attacked the orchards like ravenous wolves, tearing up the trees and throwing them to the earth one after another and leveled all the orchards between the brook and the fields. After destroying the first grove of trees, the tractors turned to the next with the same bestial voracity and uprooted them. The trees shook violently and groaned before falling, cried for help, wailed, panicked, called out in helpless pain and then fell entreatingly to the ground, as if trying to snuggle into the earth to grow and spring forth alive again.

The environmental destruction continued until everything was gone. Miteb disappears into the darkness. His family, as are others, is forced to disperse. Compensation for the land is promised, but Miteb's family receives none, presumably because his objections to the anticipated destruction had been overt. The "emir's men had begun to regard Miteb's family with special spite and suspicion."

Dispirited and disillusioned, Miteb al-Hathal's family "felt the departure from Wadi al-Uyoun like a hard, unexpected punch. From the first night in Ujra they had an overpowering feeling that they were totally alone and that they would not be able to begin a new life." The most significantly affected member of the family is Wadha, Miteb's wife, who was once a strong woman, competent and efficient, a woman of power, seemingly unruffled in times of stress; she, finding the places they traveled through unnatural, hostile, and cruel, shrinks inside herself. Fawaz, the eldest at home, but still young son, "knew that night, that what had happened was not just a loss of a place called Wadi al-Uyoun, nor any loss that any man could describe or grow accustomed to." He realized it was a breaking off, like death, that nothing and no one could heal.

The focus of the narrative shifts to the venue of Harran, a community located on the sea, also doomed to physical and cultural disaster. It had been chosen by company men, Americans, for their headquarters and for their port. Its demolition follows the pattern experienced by Wadi al-Uyoun, Harran being reduced to rubble by machines, the residents forced to relocate, tents and money being distributed to them. Another area was allocated to the workers, again tents. The American section was constructed first:

> The nucleus of a large and well-ordered city had appeared and sped toward completion: hard streets, some wide and others narrow, all perfectly straight, rolled smooth by the accursed heavy machines and coated with a gleaming black substance. Houses like the geese who flew over Wadi al-Uyoun in winter, small houses and others so tall and huge that no one could imagine who would inhabit them. Many swimming pools, on several scattered sites, near them houses made of straw and palm branches, and a long street linking the northeastern hill to the sea.

American Harran became, in effect, an air-conditioned "gated community," surrounded by fences, its gate guarded—off-limits to the Arabs, unless invited.

Workers came by ship and by land, riding on camels. Among these is Fawaz, who had left his family to search for his father but en route was induced by Ibn Rashed to join the workforce. The workers, arriving from the desert, are unnerved by the expanse of water; at once amazed and anxious, "lost in a whirlpool of thought and bewilderment. . . . They felt afflicted by total paralysis; in this isolated place . . . they were only a band of men besieged, not knowing what to do or what their lives would be like in days to come."

Soon, the men became aware of the Americans' contempt and ridicule. "The Americans gazed at them with a neutral curiosity when Naim gave them instructions, but this neutrality turned to amazement when they saw the Arabs carrying the lumber and steel posts from one place to another, and then the amazement turned to hilarity as they pointed at the workers bumping into the crates and falling down. The loud peals of laughter and pointing fingers made the men nervous and bitter and they made more mistakes." After a day's work, "they wanted to get to their tents as quickly as possible, to fling themselves to the ground, to flee in sleep from the imbecile manners and mocking smiles and sneers that pursued them every moment of the day."

The work itself was arduous, the blazing sun parching their throats, labor—hard and constant—leading to exhaustion. Their negative state of mind is further affected by their new living conditions—the metal roofing "not only radiated heat but also shed melted leaden death from the earliest hours of daylight until late at night—in contrast to those of the Americans, who, they perceived, thought of them as animals. Rage bordering on despair encompasses their state of mind.

"They regarded Ibn Rashed with hatred and contempt—and their self-hatred increased for they had chosen to come here. They were possessed by an urge to leave, to destroy things and to kill Ibn Rashed, who had embroiled them in this predicament in the first place."

During the construction of the seaport, Mizban—loved and respected by the workers—drowns; his brother, Hajem, falls into a state of shock, "looking bewilderedly into people's faces, smiling his imbecilic smile." There was "silent unrest" among the workers. Months later when Hajem returns with his uncle—he had been mysteriously taken to his original home under the auspices of Ibn Rashed—to claim compensation, the Americans' response is bureaucratic:

> The question of cash compensation for Mizban's death was still very complicated, because the company's legal department judged that "the company is neither responsible nor liable, since the transfer of the workers to the company's responsibility was not effected until after the disease." The compensation due Hajem would, it was promised, be paid "within the coming few days, on condition that law and order prevail."

This response was painful evidence to the Arab workers of how inhumanely the Americans viewed them.

Against this backdrop of increasing discontent, much to the consternation of the original inhabitants, Harran grows exponentially—waves of foreigners followed by merchants and professionals. Their croplands are threatened, their pasture partly appropriated. In addition, the activity, the clamor, the constant construction, and modern improvements destroy the world—their lives as they know it.

Three emirs are introduced in the novel, the last one playing a major role. The first, the emir of the Wadi al-Uyoun area, approves the oil-drilling project; his orientation is toward the "oceans of blessings under this soil"— "oceans of oil, oceans of gold." He is angered and vindictive when challenged by Mited al-Hathal, considering him a troublemaker, denying his arguments, rejecting the lifestyle of the status quo. The second, the emir of Harran, Ghafel al-Suweyd, was a prince unlike others—in effect, an absentee emir.

"He bothered no one and wanted no one to bother him. Very few people had seen him, and even fewer had known him from close up. He liked neither his position of authority nor Harran itself, not even the desert. He memorized poetry, recited and sometimes sang it. He would go to the remotest corner of the desert to hear an ode, to see its author and hear it from a reliable narrator." When the Americans came, he packed his tents and left.

The new emir, Khaled al-Mishari, is introduced as a "combination of sternness and menace"—that "he ordered executions for the slightest of crimes and would take pity on no one." When asked to "include the people of Harran among his concerns, for they had no one but god and himself," he repeats his moral stance, adding, "Truth is truth, and natives come before strangers." Yet, he seems readily distracted by hunting, demonstrating he is an excellent marksman.

This emir's inexperience with the modern world becomes gradually evident. Unfamiliar with boat travel, he is hesitant to do so, expressing fear. Having never seen or heard a radio, he is startled and shocked. "The emir crept nearer, as a child who knows what fire is creeps nearer to it. . . . When the box emitted loud music he started and drew his hand away, and when the music rose to fill the tent he retreated slightly and looked into the men's silent faces." He responds in the same way to the telescope and the telephone, experimenting with them, seemingly endlessly, distractedly. The emir also focuses on the construction of the emirate building, the emir's residence, approving the plans devised by the Americans without understanding them.

Contrary to his supposed concern for the people, Emir Khaled seems to shrug off their problems. With regard to the compensation of Hajem as an outcome of his brother's drowning death, he responds to Ibn Rashed's plea for help, speaking wearily, "Pull your thorns with your own hands"; he does attempt to mediate, but it seems half-hearted, indicating to Rashed, "I will not intercede. You know the company better than I do—go and borrow money from them, or from the Devil." During the crisis between the company and the workers, Khaled does not understand the explanation of the problem and is further "astonished" to view the workers through his telescope in "a state of total anarchy"; indeed, in the heat of the crisis, the "emir talked about the wonderful device [the telephone] all evening. . . ." He seems indecisive and irresolute.

The tension, between the Arab workers and the company builds through the novel, causing the simmering discontent to boil. Increased accusations against the Americans reflect their frustration and fears of their lives and livelihood: the loss of their jobs; increased prices of goods, significantly depleting their salaries and savings; and the promise of permanent housing that would include their families, promises the Americans never honored.

Two catalysts ignited the fuse of their anger: The cruel treatment of Mufaddi al-Jeddan, a traditional herbalist physician and "odd-job man"— people friendly and generally respected—the abuse leading to his death, his "murder." A recently formed military, seemingly under the patronage of the emir, is attributed with the death, notably Johar, its leader. The second catalyst was the dismissal of 23 workers without prelude or warning; they were "no longer needed." Their shocked reaction spread to others who then did not go back to work, despite threats, in support of their "brothers." Their anger spilled over to encompass the emir:

> And the emir, was he their emir, there to defend and protect them, or was he the Americans' emir? He had been a different man when he first came to Harran. He used to stroll through the market and invite townsfolk to his house to drink coffee, but he changed abruptly when Hassan Rezaie and others started bringing him gifts—he was enthralled by those gadgets and left all of his responsibilities to Johar.

The strikers demonstrate—marching through the streets, joined by townspeople, and chanting. Johar and his men drive around menacingly, showing a presence. The workers have two demands: "the reinstatement of the workers who'd been fired and an inquiry to find Mufaddi's murderer." The workers claim they have rights. The company responds that it will not comply with the workers' demands but promises to study the matter on condition that the workers return to work immediately. There is a stalemate and tension. But the workers refuse to be "persuaded or provoked" to violence.

Yet, violence occurs. Johar acts, ordering his solders to open fire. A few Arabs are wounded; fury is unleashed. "Within moments the people became like a flame, or a tempestuous wind. They feared nothing and cared for no consequences. Johar, who was still shouting 'Fire . . . fire!' could not believe his eyes. The people were charging, a human flood, swarming forward like locusts; he could not believe that his armed soldiers were retreating and beginning to flee." The wounded are rescued, and the workers withdraw.

During this tempest, the emir is "suddenly ill." His reaction to the gunfire is deeply emotional. The next day, the emir, his bodyguards, staff, and family leave. At noon the emirate issued a short statement: "His Highness Emir Khaled departed Harran this morning for medical treatment. Before leaving, His Highness ordered the reinstatement of all workers to the company, and the company has acceded to his wishes. His Highness also ordered the formation of a committee to study and identify the responsibility for the recent events."

CENSORSHIP HISTORY

Abdul Rahman Munif had a history of political activism. When in Iraq studying law, as a member of the emerging Arab Ba'ath political party, he joined the protests against the signing of the Baghdad Pact. This cost him his residence and education in Baghdad; he was expelled from Iraq in 1955. His political activities continued to cause him problems: having criticized the Saudi regime in 1963, his Saudi nationality was revoked.

His novel *Cities of Salt*, the first part of a quintet informed by his knowledge of oil economics, depicts the history of the Arab world during the oil era and expresses the theory that, in his words, the Arabs were "the subjects of injustice, deprivation and oppression." Also, he indicates that official history has falsified Arab experience, particularly that of ordinary people. His novel expresses the consequences of Western influence on Arab culture.

Cities of Salt was banned in Saudi Arabia. Munif's passport was withdrawn. The Saudi Arabia Ministry of Culture and Information is a strict censor on work submitted for publication. Texts that criticize monarchies, even fictional ones, are apt to be rejected; they might be interpreted as critical of the Saud royal family. According to the reporter Scott Wilson, the royal family, reacting to "intense pressure from the kingdom's conservative Sunni clergy, is most concerned about appearing to give its imprimatur to potentially controversial fiction." Yet if such texts are published out of the country, as many are—*Cities of Salt*, for example—they may be permitted entry by custom agents. "Through the compromise, the Saud royal family is making a concession to a smaller but also influential segment of society: a highly educated, westernized elite now demanding more freedoms."

FURTHER READING

Allen, Roger. *The Arabic Novel: An Historical and Critical Introduction*. Syracuse, N.Y.: Syracuse University Press, 1982.
Jiad, Abdul-Hadi. "Obituary: Abdul Rahman Munif." *Guardian*, February 5, 2004.
Liukkonen, Petri, and Ari Pesonen. "Abdelrahman Munif (1933–2004). *Books and Writers*. Helsinki, Finland: Kuusankosken kaupunginkirjasto (2008).
Serafin, Steven R., ed. *Encyclopedia of World Literature in the 20th Century*. Vol. 5. Farmington Hills, Mich.: St. James Press, 1998, pp. 433–444.
Wilson, Scott. "Disapproval Still Hangs over Saudi Writers." *Washington Post*, March 16, 2005.

CITIZEN TOM PAINE

Author: Howard Fast
Original date and place of publication: 1943, United States
Publisher: Duell, Sloane and Pearce
Literary form: Fictional biography

SUMMARY

These are the times that try men's souls. The summer soldier and the sunshine patriot will, in this crisis, shrink from the service of their country; but he that stands it now, deserves the love and thanks of man and woman. Tyranny, like hell, is not easily conquered. . . .

I call not upon a few, but upon all: not on this state or that state, but on every state: up and help us; lay your shoulder to the wheel; better have too much force than too little, when so great an object is at stake. Let it be told to the future world, that in the depth of winter when nothing but hope and virtue could survive, that the city and the country, alarmed at one common danger, came forth to meet and repulse it. . . .

Thomas Paine wrote these ringing words at a point of crisis during the Revolutionary War. There were to be others. It was his first *Crisis* paper. The army under the command of George Washington was reeling from defeat after defeat—New York, White Plains, Fort Washington, and Fort Lee and across New Jersey. The troops were in despair, and many were deserting. The intent of *Crisis I* was to reenliven support for the army and to encourage the spirits of the troops. The first victory—at Trenton with the Christmas Day, 1776, attack on an encampment of German mercenaries— came soon after it was first circulated.

Paine had been in America only since the autumn of 1774, having come to Philadelphia from England. In England he had led a tortured life. Dissatisfied with his status as a staymaker's apprentice under his father's hard hand, rebellious, dreaming of more from life, he ran away. London was not a welcoming city. He had groveled in the muck, drinking heavily, eating meagerly. He had worked. He had married and lost his beloved wife to a "festering fever" and probably poor nutrition.

Arriving in Philadelphia with a letter from Ben Franklin, he had found work as a tutor of children but lost those positions because of his drinking. He found his beginnings as the editor of the *Pennsylvania Magazine*, which earned him recognition and conversation with Philadelphia's notables, including the delegates to the Continental Congress. Upon the event of the Battle of Lexington on April 19, 1775, Paine was immersed in the heating up of the tensions of war, and also the divisiveness and doubts about the status of the colonies.

Through these days, Paine's political credo was refined, his political position established: Rights: "I think there are no such things. I think that by right of birth all things belong to all men. You can take away rights, but you can't give what belongs to all. . . . It's not reform for men to claim what is theirs." War: "Of all ways to hold man in contempt and make a beast of him, war is the worst. There is nothing on earth I hate more than war." Revolution: "All the way. . . . Independence." Paine's *Common Sense*, which was published in January 1776, gained him fame—or infamy. He was at once a grand, even worshiped hero, molding public opinion for a just cause, and a dangerous firebrand. (It sold 150,000 copies in 1776, altogether a half-million copies, about one for every six people in the land.)

In the ensuing years, he followed the army on and off. While with the troops he offered succor to the wounded and the weak, encouragement to the despairing. Recognizing him as one of them, they listened to his words.

The officers credited him with keeping the "American cause from dissolving in thin air." Washington respected him and valued his help. The *Crisis* papers grew out of these conditions.

Away from the army he wrote and spoke, apparently not carefully. Being absolutely committed himself, he found cause to rebuke others; he spoke vehemently against those who undermined Washington or suggested he be removed. He continued his attacks on privilege, on slavery, and on economic injustices; thus he made enemies among those in high places, though he also had friends in Jefferson, Washington, and others. As secretary for the Office of Foreign Affairs, he uncovered profiteering individuals making fortunes on the backs of the soldiers; Paine also suspected an underlying effort to undermine democratic principles in favor of aristocratic ones, casting Gouverneur Morris of New York, among others, in this negative light.

As the war drew to a close, Paine continued to write *Crisis* papers passionately, while increasing his consumption of liquor. He was often not well, frequently drunk. He began to feel purposeless: "His trade was revolution, and now he was without a trade." When Washington came to Philadelphia, triumphant but haggard, he extolled Paine:

> My dear Paine, no one of us will ever forget your value. . . . Even Morris recognizes what you have done. On two fronts, the home front and the fighting front, it was Paine who kept the cause together—I tell you that with the deepest conviction, my good friend—

Washington's words helped, but they were momentary. At age 46, Paine was lonely and tired and ragged.

The portrait of the emerging United States given in this book is a mixed one. On the one hand, "a way of life, a way for children to smile, some freedom, some liberty, and hope for the future, men with rights, decent courts, decent laws. Men not afraid of poverty and women not afraid of childbirth," and the evident freedom and prosperity. On the other hand, the sordidness of a slave sale—exhibiting the frightened, shivering slave girl and the arrogant slave auctioneer who "prided himself on the fact that when he sold a pregnant Negress, she was pregnant by him." The contrast emerges in the revolutionary settings as well: the valiant, loyal soldiers who stayed with Washington through defeats, freezing winters, insufficient supplies, and hard times versus the deserters, the profiteers, and those who barred their doors and windows to the soldiers in need of sustenance.

After the war Paine went to France, taking with him an iron bridge model he had designed, and then to England. There, in response to an attack in the House of Commons by Edmund Burke on the French Revolution that "man, as man, had no rights," Paine wrote *The Rights of Man*. It was labeled treasonous; it advocated political democracy and denied the rights of monarchy.

> Toleration is not the *opposite* of Intolerance, but is the *counterfeit* of it. Both are despotisms. The one assumes to itself the right of withholding Liberty of Conscience, and the other of granting it. . . . But Toleration may be viewed in a much stronger light. Man worships not himself, but his Maker; and the liberty of conscience which he claims is not for the service of himself, but of his God. . . . Who then art thou, vain dust and ashes! by whatever name thou art called, whether a King, a Bishop, a Church, or a State, a Parliament, or anything else, that obtrudest thine insignificance between the soul of man and its maker?

This in addition to becoming party to a group of underground revolutionary cells forced him from England and the threat of the gallows. As he waited to board the Channel boat, a crown gathered and screamed, "Paine, Paine, damned be his name!"

In France, the welcome was different. He was idolized upon his arrival in Calais with shouts of "Vive Paine," a file of soldiers with fife and drum and a request to represent the city as a deputy in the National Assembly. In the assembly, gestures of "honor, even of worship, and then soaring acclaim" greeted him. The adulation was not to last. As the wheels of the revolution turned, the leftist Jacobins gained power, and Paine, who had voted with the rightist Girondins, lost favor. He thought of leaving France but didn't know where to go. These were times of desperation, destruction, and drunkenness.

Paine had not been able to write. Then, he heard a deputy scream to the convention: "God is dethroned, and Christianity, corrupt as a priest, is banished from earth! Henceforth, reason shall rule, pure reason, incorruptible reason!" Paine had found his thesis; over the next months he wrote *The Age of Reason*, his treatise on religion.

> I believe one God, and no more; and I hope for happiness beyond this life. I believe [in] the equality of man; and I believe that religious duties consist in doing justice, loving mercy, and endeavoring to make our fellow creatures happy. . . . All national institutions of churches, whether Jewish, Christian or Turkish, appear to me no other than human inventions, set up to terrify and enslave mankind, and monopolize power and profit.

Shortly after finishing the manuscript in December 1793, he was charged with conspiring against the republic. En route to the Luxembourg, which housed prisoners headed for the guillotine, he delivered the manuscript to a friend for safekeeping. At first he expected an early release, then the intervention of the American ambassador, Gouverneur Morris; Morris, however, had not forgotten the judgment against him in Philadelphia in which Paine had been a key figure. Morris took no action, but Paine did not die either from the guillotine or from a severe fever. The intervention of the new ambassador, James Monroe, and a change in the revolutionary leadership brought about his release in November 1794, 10 months after he had been imprisoned.

He returned to the United States in 1802 and visited his friend President Jefferson, hoping for a government appointment; he was disappointed. Paine was too controversial to an administration already charged with being atheistic. He had enemies; a bitter public letter to Washington, whom he blamed for not interceding in his behalf when he was imprisoned and waiting for the guillotine, had made him more enemies. Publication of *The Age of Reason* had defamed him.

His last years were unhappy ones. He was ridiculed and slandered as an atheist, pursued and beaten in the streets, shot at with murderous intent. His property was invaded. He was not allowed to vote. Only his old soldier friends stood by him. After he died at age 72 in 1809, his grave was desecrated, and his bones were taken to England, where they disappeared after a permit to exhibit them was refused.

Paine emerges from these pages as an extraordinary human being, idealistic, dedicated, and unswerving, courageously outspoken but often unwise. He was generous and kind spirited, but also rough mannered, too often unkempt and given to drunkenness. He fervently believed in democracy, promoted the brotherhood of man and envisioned a federation of nations. In a sense, he was a man without a country; as he said to Napoleon Bonaparte: "Ask the people of three nations whether Paine spoke other than for humanity."

CENSORSHIP HISTORY

The "wave of censorship" that affected the nation in the 1940s extended to the public schools. The New York State Board of Superintendents in 1947 voted to recommend the removal of *Citizen Tom Paine* from all school libraries. According to John Tebbel's account in *A History of Book Publishing in the United States*, the "board did not object to Howard Fast's politics—he was then associate editor of *New Masses*—but to scattered passages in his book that it said were 'too purple to be read by children.' " The emerging controversy divided authors.

The Authors League Committee on Censorship protested the ban; its spokesperson, Marc Connelly, demanded that "the bigotry behind its condemnation be investigated in the interest of public welfare." Other objections to the banning were issued by the American Civil Liberties Union and the Association of Teachers of Social Studies. The latter asserted that the selection of reading materials in the schools "is properly a part of the educational process to be entrusted entirely to teachers." Altogether representatives of 11 organizations condemned the banning of the novel during the Board of Education's deliberations. However, the American Writers Association issued a statement that identified Fast as a "leading Communist" and urged the board not to yield to "Communist demands." The Board of Education voted 6-1 to bar the book from school libraries.

Accused by the House Un-American Activities Committee of writing Communist propaganda, Fast was blacklisted by the Federal Bureau of Investigation in the 1950s. Subsequently, publishers would not handle his work in the United States, notably *Spartacus* and *Sylvia*, although he published the former himself; *Sylvia* and others were released under a pseudonym, E. V. Cunningham.

In 1953, the same year Fast was awarded the Stalin Peace Prize for "strengthening peace between peoples," the United States withdrew *Citizen Tom Paine* from U.S. Information Agency libraries overseas.

FURTHER READING

Fein, Esther B. "Book Notes." *New York Times*, September 23, 1992, p. C20.
Haight, Anne Lyon, and Chandler B. Grannis. *Banned Books: 387 B.C. to 1978 A.D.* 4th ed. New York: R. R. Bowker, 1978.
Tebbel, John. *A History of Book Publishing in the United States*, Vol. 4. New York: R. R. Bowker, 1981.

THE COMMERCIAL RESTRAINTS OF IRELAND CONSIDERED

Author: John Hely-Hutchinson
Original date and place of publication: 1779, Ireland
Publisher: M. H. Gill and Son (1888 edition)
Literary form: Nonfiction

SUMMARY

Originally published anonymously, *The Commercial Restraints of Ireland Considered* was presented as a series of letters addressed to the lord lieutenant of Ireland, Lord Buckinghamshire. Its focus was the commercial distress of Ireland with a review of the chief causes of this distress.

The problem and purpose are stated directly: "Ireland teems with every circumstance of national poverty"; to identify "some permanent cause for such disastrous effects," Hely-Hutchinson provides a basic accounting of the economic privations: reduced value on land produce, rent reductions, farm failures, insufficient merchant sales, high unemployment, and annihilated public and private credit. The country itself is close to bankruptcy and unable to pay its bills; its debt is rising. Given Ireland's natural resources, climate, and intelligent people, a "permanent cause" for such "often experienced extremes of poverty" must be identified.

A comparison of periods of prosperity and benefits to the years of distress establishes the first line of argument. The factors operating in the former instance were encouragements to increase trade and manufacturing, and the removal of restraints on exports and imports. In contrast, the latter situations were brought about by prohibiting export of woolens from Ireland and discouraging manufacturing. These factors are illustrated for each period of the 17th and 18th centuries.

As his discussion moves into the middle of the 18th century, Hely-Hutchinson provides a litany of details about the nation's debt and the people's poverty. In doing so, he reiterates the effect of the prohibitions but advances other factors that increased Ireland's debt, notably the requirement to help defray Britain's expenses:

> . . . the expenses of the late war, the heavy peace establishment in the year 1763, the increase of that establishment in the year 1769, the sums paid from 1759 to forces out of the kingdom, the great increase of pensions and other additional charges on the civil establishment . . .

Placing these burdens on Ireland in part resulted from a mistaken opinion of Ireland's wealth and the ability of its resources to sustain deeper expenditures. This opinion is reversed by Hely-Hutchinson, who provides evidence of Ireland's economic frailty.

The author finds opportunities to expose the cycle of poverty, particularly with reference to farmers and laborers, the lowest classes, identified as constituting a large segment of the Irish population. If the manufacturers have insufficient employment, they cannot purchase the produce of the land. Nor can the farmers then make purchases of goods. In addition, the scarcity of corn and the failure of the potato crop created conditions of famine.

Having provided an expanded view of these issues, Hely-Hutchinson spotlights a particular feature—the prohibition of wool manufacture and the offered "compensation," the manufacture of linen. The quotations, from the Act of 1699, the *Lord's Journals*, and other data, provide evidence of England's strongly selfish interest in protecting its industry without full consideration of the consequences to Ireland and England. The author argues that England prevents Ireland from being prosperous by discouraging Ireland from working with her own materials and exporting her manufactures to other nations, by causing Ireland to export her workable raw materials and to buy what she is capable of manufacturing and selling to others. These prohibitions "must necessarily tend to reduce [Ireland] weakness and poverty." In practice, England has suffered from its policy. As a result of the prohibition, Irish woolen manufacturers were forced to relocate to France, Spain, and Germany; wool from Ireland and England is sold on the Continent. The result: French woolen manufacture has much improved, and France is now underselling England.

The substitution of linen manufacture, the "compensation" for the loss of woolen manufacture, was ill conceived. It assumed that the industry was in place or could replace the woolen industry. Woolen manufacture had been the staple and the principal trade commodity. Further, the declaration of the [House of] Lords of England "that they shall be *always* ready to give [linen manufacture] their *utmost* assistance" was belied by the restrictions to the linen trade and bounties placed on imported flax seed. The nature of these restrictions is counter to the necessity of a "commercial country to cultivate every considerable manufacture of which she has or can get a premium." A commercial country cannot subsist on one manufacture; such a concentration will have the effect of constraining other commercial activities and causing numerous classes of people to become deprived.

Bringing his arguments toward closure, Hely-Hutchinson provides two contrasts to lead to a central point: He contrasts the nature and restrictions of the colonies to Ireland, and he contrasts the language and intention of acts of Parliament affecting commercial relationships. Applying the policy of restrictions of manufacture to the colonies made some sense, given the differences in climate, crops, and industry. (He points out in a later passage that the policy backfired, for the colonies eventually refused to be held to such constraints. England needs to recognize and adapt to changes in the world commercial environment.) Ireland, however, is unjustly treated as equivalent to the colonies though its location, climate, growth, and productions are the same as in England. The language and intent of the pre-1663 statutes bear this out in the context of recognizing Ireland to be in the same trading relationship; that is, when restrictions were made to trade with foreign countries, Ireland and Wales were excepted, these being as much "favored and protected" as England. There is conveyed in the early acts a sense of unity and equality among partners in contrast to later language, which gives Ireland a subordinate status. This early policy (toward the colonies and Ireland) "was liberal, just and equal; it opened the resources and cultivated the strength of every part of the empire." Clearly, the 1699 prohibitions, still in existence, are neither reasonable nor just.

A final plea is for need and profit in the context of changed human and commercial circumstances. The population of Ireland more than doubled since 1698, to "not less in this kingdom than 2,500,000 loyal and affectionate subjects to his Majesty" in 1799. What might have been sufficient employment and the means of supplying subsistence for 1 million people is insufficient for the present population. Great Britain itself will suffer loss of trade and revenues through its perseverance of the restrictive policy. Irish manufacturers will immigrate to America and will establish competitive manufactures there. Also, revenues to England from Ireland will diminish: An economically healthy Ireland is a source of wealth to England both in remittances and in the consumption of goods; a poor and underpopulated Ireland is an expense and burden to England.

The center of Hely-Hutchinson's concluding point, pulling together several isolated ideas, is the concept of family. The closing passages are directly addressed to this "elder," "respected" sister, pleading the case of common parentage and strength in unity.

> Our increased force, and the full exertions of our strength, will be the most effectual means of resisting the combination formed against you by foreign enemies and distant subjects, and of giving new lustre to our crowns, and happiness and contentment to our people.

CENSORSHIP HISTORY

When *The Commercial Restraints of Ireland Considered* was published, it was known to be the work of the provost of Trinity College, John Hely-Hutchinson, despite its author being anonymous. It received two quite different receptions. Because its doctrines were regarded as seditious, it was ordered burned by the common hangman, perhaps the last work so condemned. In contrast, the advocates of free trade praised it considerably; it also in effect "pardoned" Hely-Hutchinson's reputation among Irish patriots "for his [previous] subserviency to the Court."

According to the "Introduction" to the 1888 volume, the text "was burned by the Common Hangman so effectually . . . that the libraries of all three branches of the legislature could not produce a copy." The 1888 edition was reproduced from a copy obtained from the Trinity College Library.

FURTHER READING

Carroll, W. G. Introduction to *The Commercial Restraints of Ireland*, by John Hely-Hutchinson. Dublin, Ireland: M. H. Gill and Son, 1888.
Haight, Anne Lyon, and Chandler B. Grannis. *Banned Books: 387 B.C. to 1978 A.D.* 4th ed. New York: R. R. Bowker, 1978.

COMPARATIVE POLITICS TODAY: A WORLD VIEW

General editor: Gabriel A. Almond
Original date and place of publication: 1974, United States
Publisher: Little, Brown and Company
Literary form: Textbook

SUMMARY

This introduction to the political institutions, processes, and policies of modern nations provides a conceptual framework with which to compare and evaluate these political features. Issues confronting modern nations are then identified and illustrated comparatively with 10 nations, selected in part for their diversity.

A key concept upon which this text is developed is *system;* it conveys an "ecological concept implying an organization interacting with an environment, influencing it and being influenced by it." Societies use political systems to establish and carry out their goals with regard to human and environmental resources and needs. Political *structures* or institutions conduct the necessary *functions* of the political system. These activities in turn help the system establish and enforce its policies. We are forewarned early in the text that what we anticipate for the performance of political functions by the structures of a national political system may not be, upon analysis, what is real.

In the chapters focusing on issues, the United States is one of the 10 countries featured for comparison. The 10 are chosen to represent industrial and preindustrial nations, democracies, and authoritarian states, as well as other social variations. A primary issue is the *economic status* of nations in relation to physical size and population and such features as natural resources and levels of economic and social development. These features must be considered interactively and comparatively to reflect a nation's status. Thus, one chart identifies the United States as having the strongest per capita gross national product in 1972 of the 10 selected nations, almost double that of runner-up France and not quite triple that of fourth-place Soviet Union. However, the United States (5.3 percent) is behind the Soviet Union (7.3 percent) and Egypt (5.4 percent) in the percentage of the gross national product expended for education, even though the United States does have the highest dollar value, per capita expenditure. In the discussion of a related issue, economic equality within nations, the United States ranks second, after Britain, in the equality of income distribution, based on 1972 data. On another chart, however, Tanzania, the Soviet Union, and China are estimated to have a more equal distribution of income than the United States.

Another problem area discussed is *political conflict and instability* within nations during the 1950–66 period. The United States has the highest incidence of riots and antigovernment demonstrations, 45 and 147, respectively, in contrast to the Soviet Union, five and three, and second-place India, 85 and 25. Most of the incidents in the United States were related to racial segregation; the Vietnam War unrest during the 1965–72 period increased these figures. A complementary issue is that of *political variation.* In this regard the United States heads the list as being most open for opportunities of political opposition, followed by Great Britain and Japan. Last in this group of 10 nations is China, preceded by the Soviet Union (1971 data). Another chart offers parallel information that these two nations offer their citizens the least opportunities to compete for public office and to influence public policy (1971 data).

Political processes are defined, described, and analyzed in five chapters. Distinctions among countries are illustrated, the range of these being broadened beyond the original 10. The presentation of the first process, *political socialization and political culture,* informs the reader about the "processes through which political attitudes and patterns of behavior are acquired" and about the agents of political socialization: the family, school, peer groups, occupation, mass media, and direct political contacts. Political socialization may be transmitted directly or indirectly. The attempts in post-World War II West Germany of both the occupation forces of the Allies and the German government to alter political values and behavior, that is, to support democratic political structures, were resisted by many Germans. School civics courses, another direct method, also were relatively unsuccessful. Informal socialization seems to have more positive results. In some respects, the attempts of the Cuban revolutionary government to create a new political culture, a revolutionary, Communist "new Cuban man," for example, who participates in public life, have also been resisted. Commitment seems more a matter of revolutionary control and media communication than public values and beliefs. The regime's focus is on youth, however; they are engaged in weeks of rural work experience and study, a setting of equality and service. This, along with the required participation by adults, seems to be effecting a breakdown of the values of materialism, strong family ties, and hierarchy, the values of the upper and middle classes.

The two more formal aspects of political processes—political parties/party systems and policy making/implementation—are compared. The contrast of legislative models is representative:

When we compare assemblies on the basis of their importance as political and policy-making agencies, the United States Senate and House of Representatives, which play a very important role in the formulation and enactment of legislation, are at one extreme; the other extreme is represented by the Supreme Soviet in the U.S.S.R., which meets infrequently and does little more than listen to statements from Soviet political leaders and legitimize legislative decisions already made elsewhere.

Six nations are selected for in-depth "Country Studies," chosen to represent variant political systems—democracies and authoritarian states—and levels of development—industrial and preindustrial. They are England, France, the USSR, China, Mexico, and Tanzania. The censorship challenge to this text concerned the presentation of the "Soviet Union and Communist world" in contrast to the United States.

According to the text, the Soviet Union as we knew it in the mid-20th century was forged out of the power struggle within the Communist Party. Stalin asserted control: "His ruthless dictatorship drastically limited participation in decision making and established a rigid censorship and a terrorist political force, thus creating a pattern of rule that has lasted, in modified form, up to the present." In this context the Soviet political system is described as "one of the most stable in the world," a stability that perhaps is "more apparent than real."

The formal institutions of government are controlled by the "monolithic" Communist Party of the Soviet Union (CPSU); the Council of Ministers, comparable to the cabinet of parliamentary democracies, is essentially also so controlled because of overlapping membership with the executive organs of the party.

The CPSU, however, is not a "party" in the sense of being one of several organizations competing for state power. It is the only legitimate, functioning political organization in the U.S.S.R. It guides, controls, integrates, and coordinates the activities of all governmental, economic, social, and cultural agencies in the land. The CPSU recruits, trains, and supplies executive personnel for all governmental and other social organizations, gives them guidance, systematically checks up on how its directions are carried out, and mobilizes citizens for "mass participation" in carrying out party policy.

In addition to its authority over policy-making leaders and institutions, the CPSU coordinates and controls the governmental and bureaucratic structures that implement its policies. Two important and telling characteristics of the bureaucracy are its "vast scope and pervasive influence on the daily life of the citizen" and, in contrast to nations of the West, the "practice of investing even minor governmental acts with ideological sacredness."

Law enforcement and the courts also fall within the scope of CPSU control. Judges, for example, are expected to be influenced by the doctrine of "socialist legal consciousness," which requires them essentially to be guided by party policy when deciding which statute to apply to a case. While the Soviet constitution states that "judges are independent and subject only to law," almost all judges are CPSU members and, thus, subject to party discipline. The Soviet courts have a parental or educational role in society, that is a "socializing instrument" to "teach the transgressor the error of his ways" and point to him the path he must follow if, after his sentence, he is to be an "honest," public-spirited Soviet citizen. The judges follow party policy in this teaching role as well as in determining how severely crimes are to be punished.

Soviet social structure is evidently not classless. There are the "power elite," the top levels of party and state bureaucracy, the military, and the security police; and the "prestige elite," the leaders of the scientific and cultural intelligentsia (those who earn their livings through mental activity). The power elite is at the top; the scientists and artists, suspect because some of them oppose political orthodoxy and insist on exerting the creative process freely, are kept under surveillance and control. Communist Party members at any level are more influential than nonmembers. While workers are identified as the leading class of Soviet society, they are not rewarded comparably with the elite classes. The collective farm peasantry are the most poorly represented group. Unlike the workers with their trade unions, they have no organizational support.

Political communication is also controlled by the CPSU, whose purposes are to reform the citizen and to reinforce official versions of the truth.

In both the United States and the Soviet Union, access to communication channels is easiest for groups and individuals of high status. And in both, the cards are stacked against information or opinions thought by elite groups to be subversive. Obviously, however, the range of permissible disclosure and advocacy is vastly broader in the United States and other Western democracies.

In the Soviet Union all information agencies are supervised by party functionaries. Newspapers are published by the party and its organs, and directives from the CPSU's propaganda section are issued to state and public organizations, such as, respectively, the State Commission on Radio and Television and the Union of Soviet Writers. Another instrument for communicating the party's message and for enlisting support is organized "oral agitation." This method serves a particularly important function in areas of low literacy. In the late 1960s an underground literature began to be circulated, some of it emanating from civil rights activists.

From today's vantage point, the concluding segment of the text, "The Soviet Future: Alternative Paths of Development," provides an historically intriguing prediction: "The most probably foreseeable future for the Soviet Union appears to be a continuation of the present system." This is supported by the recognition of the CPSU's control of Soviet life, the "strong sense of political community, supportive of the status quo," and the party's accomplishments in consolidating the social revolution and industrializing the country. Two possibilities of change emerge: that the top leadership will be influenced by pragmatic, managerial types among them and that increased pressures and demands of writers, scientists, and others will have an effect.

CENSORSHIP HISTORY

The challenge to *Comparative Politics Today: A World View* came on January 11, 1988, during a school board meeting in the Albemarle County School District. The text was being considered as a social studies textbook for an advanced placement class, "American Government and Comparative Politics." The challenger, Ed Bauer, a recent unsuccessful candidate for county office, argued: "This textbook . . . presents a Marxist distortion of the Soviet Union and the Communist world that is dangerous to our national security. The book is promoting Marxist economic dogma instead of the American free enterprise system."

To support his claim, Bauer objected to charts comparing income distribution and referred to a passage that reported that "wealth was distributed more equally in the Soviet Union and China than in the United States and other western democracies." He also asserted that the book "advocate[s] continued communist control in Cuba." Bauer quoted this passage from the book:

"Cuban political socialization has sought the creation of a 'new Cuban man' who is revolutionary and a Communist whose qualities include attachment to the values of cooperation, political equality, hard work, self-improvement, obedience and incorruptibility."

He asserted that the text's authors were "saying it was a good idea to maintain the communist controls in Cuba in order to continue their political socialization process." A further objection was that Soviet military involvement in Afghanistan, Nicaragua, and other places was ignored in the book.

One of the board members also raised objections. William Finley cited passages questioning whether direct participatory democracy is possible today and statements that equality exists in the Soviet Union. The passage that indicated that guidelines have been blurred in modern times also disturbed him. He asked, "Is the Constitution blurred?"

The text was defended by Mark Tate, the social studies coordinator for the Albemarle school district. He indicated that the sentences were "taken out of context. . . . If you look at one or two sentences, you don't get a flavor of what the book is really about. You have to look at the way the whole thing is written."

The board members voted to approve the book, four in favor, two opposed.

FURTHER READING

Finn, Elaine. "Communist Passages Spark Debate Over Textbook." *Daily Progress*, January 12, 1988, pp. A1, 12.
"Interest Healthy—Up to a Point." *Daily Progress*, January 17, 1988, p. C2.
Newsletter on Intellectual Freedom 37 (1988): 105.

THE CORPSE WALKER: REAL-LIFE STORIES, CHINA FROM THE BOTTOM UP

Author: Liao Yiwu
Original date and place of publication: 2008, United States
Publisher: Pantheon Books
Literary form: Oral History

SUMMARY

Real-Life Stories, China from the Bottom Up, the subtitle of *The Corpse Walker*, is more revealing of the subject of this collection of interviews. Liao Yiwu has interviewed 27 individuals, ranging in age from the 30s to the 100s and including a broad range of professions: a Professional Mourner, a Leper, an Abbot, a Retired Official, a Former Landowner, a Tiananmen Father, a Composer, a Yi District Chief's Wife, a Former Red Guard, and a Migrant Worker. They share a commonality: They all are from the bottom level of Chinese society, although some of them were well-to-do officials or businessmen or working farmers-landowners prior to the defeat of the Nationalist government of Chang Kai-shek in 1949. Others were ordinary, often outcast, Chinese who reaped no benefits from the revolution.

Among the most compelling of those interviewed were those accused of being landowners, of having exploited the poor. Among these was the Buddhist Abbot (age 103 at the time of the interview). The monks abided by the vow of poverty, and none ever claimed ownership of the properties of the temple. Yet, during the land reform movement, a team of government officials and peasant activists set up a tribunal inside the temple to "dispense justice," calling him "a rich temple owner." He recalled the event:

> My captors dragged me onto the stage, stripped me of my *kasaya*, and forced me to stand in front of a large crowd of villagers, with my arms pulled up behind my back in the jet-plane position. One by one, peasant activists stood up to share with the crowd about my "crimes." I was accused of accumulating wealth without engaging in physical labor, and spreading feudalistic and religious ideas that poisoned people's minds.

Subsequently, public beating occurred during which the abbot was slapped, kicked, and hung from the ceiling. By the end of the land reform movement, the local government seized all the Buddhist treasures and confiscated hundreds of hectares of pristine forest and farmland from the temple.

During the Great Leap Forward, launched by Chairman Mao in 1958, the temple was stripped of all its metal: incense burners, metal collection boxes, bells, the metal edges of wooden incense tables, the four bronze statues on the four corners of the temple roofs, and a pair of royal cast-iron cauldrons, a gift from Emperor Yongle in the Ming dynasty. These were melted. Hundreds of trees were chopped down to fuel the furnaces, stripping mountains bare.

The Former Landlord (age 89 when he was interviewed) suffered comparable treatment in 1950. His grandfather had purchased the property; his father had died of exhaustion from overwork. The land reform work team branded him an "evil landowner." His view of himself, being well versed in Confucianism, was that he was kind to others and had never harmed anyone or harbored any ill feelings.

> However, my fellow villagers, who used to be polite and respectful, had suddenly changed, as if they had all donned different facial masks. At the "speak bitterness meetings," two of my hired farmers accused me of exploiting them by forcing them to work in the cold winter days and randomly deducting their pay. I didn't agree with their accusations because I was working along with them in the field.

The Former Landlord's land titles, land leasing, and property rental agreements were annulled and everything he owned was confiscated. He remarked: "Of course, the world around me suddenly changed: rich people ended up suffering and the poor became masters. It was hard to accept at first."

The Former Landlord described the "speak bitterness" meetings:

The militiamen beat me up pretty badly. I was in my forties then. Years of hard labor, such as carrying heavy sacks of salt on my back, made me pretty strong. . . . But as time went by, my back started to go because the militiamen forced me to bend down very deeply. I never complained or disobeyed. At the end of the Land Reform movement, the leader of the work team came to talk with me. He complimented me for being cooperative with the government. I was all smiles and bowed to him. In my heart, I felt as if someone had been stabbing me with a blunt knife.

Because some relations had been local officials during the Nationalist Chang Kai-shek government, the family of the former Yi District Chief suffered more torment. The district chief's wife was interviewed (age 84); she detailed the events in 1952, when she was 31 years old, after the land reform work team arrested her husband and brother. She was forced to witness their execution—rifles to their chests—and the cutting out of their tongues. When she screamed against this desecration, she was hit on her head with the butt of a rifle and knocked unconscious.

After the execution, the Yi District Chief's wife was locked up for more than 40 days. "Whenever there was a public speak bitterness meeting, the militiamen would drag me out in front of the podium, with hands tied behind my back and my head down. I had to carry a big cardboard sign on my neck. The cardboard sign said 'Wife of the Evil Landlord.' I would be asked to confess the crimes of my husband." All of her property was confiscated. While she was in detention, her youngest child, age two, died. Her two eldest sons, who had been caring for the children, were accused of crimes; the eldest hid in the mountains, the second, accused by a neighbor of writing anti-land reform slogans on a latrine wall, was sentenced to seven years in jail. The others begged for food or searched in the fields and trash cans.

The 1958–61 famine, "treated as a 'state secret'"— an estimated 30 million people starved to death—is mentioned by many of those interviewed. The Illegal Border Crosser remarked, "You probably would say that people were desperate to leave China in 1962 because of the famine." Rejecting the official government explanation of "three years of natural disasters," the Retired Official identified the extreme policies of Chairman Mao as the cause of the disaster. In the 1950s, for example, Chairman Mao said that sparrows ate seeds and should be eliminated; a nationwide campaign essentially accomplished this goal in two years. "Little did we know that killing sparrows would disrupt the delicate balance of nature." Sparrows ate crops, but they also ate bugs, which flourished and brought disasters to many areas after the sparrows were gone.

The Great Leap Forward, the intention of which was to make China self-reliant and independent from the Soviet Union and to transform it into an industrialized country, was identified as a significant cause. The Retired

Official, who headed a government work team at a rural region and who witnessed the devastating impact of the famine, reports that commune leaders followed Party instructions and ordered that peasants use the new "reasonable density" method: "Furrows were plowed very deep. Rice or wheat seedlings were planted very densely. The Party claimed that the method could increase the grain output ten times." This method didn't work. Many plants died and surviving ones did not pollinate. Nationwide displays of "agricultural miracles" were deceptions.

Then the Party switched focus from agriculture to steel production. Several results: All the peasants turned from farming to building and fueling brickyard furnaces—cutting down trees, neglecting harvesting; all metal objects—pots and pans, included—were collected for smelting; commune kitchens were set up. Early inspection of the communal dining rooms by the Retired Official suggests deception as to the quality and quantity of food to impress the inspectors, proven so by fall 1960 when the scarcity of food was evident. "In many places, commune leaders had turned over the grain that peasants saved over the years to meet [government grain] quotas. Peasants were left with little food for winter."

The Mortician (age 71 when interviewed) corroborates not only the number of famine-caused deaths—"in the second half of 1960, we were so overwhelmed here that I had to work overtime," but also the desperation of the people. In 1961:

> . . . food shortages got worse. As more bodies poured in, I didn't even have time to do any makeup. In that year, thousands of people roamed the mountain like locusts, desperately searching for things that were edible—tree bark, grass roots, wild vegetables, even bugs. Unfortunately, all the mountaintops had been deforested to feed the furnaces for iron and steel production. There wasn't much available for people to eat.

Both the Retired Official and the Mortician revealed the emergence of cannibalism: "As people became more and more desperate, they turned to their fellow human beings." A peasant was discovered secretly boiling the meat of his three-year old daughter; he explained that two children had died of starvation and they had no food for this daughter who was stunted; he sacrificed her for the rest of the family. After being lashed 50 times, the peasant was released.

> [The villagers] took it as a sign of approval from the government and more families began to follow suit. Since boys were traditionally favored over girls, young girls were targeted. Some families ruthlessly murdered and ate their own daughters. Others would exchange their children with neighbors. Since a child could only last them for a couple of days, some, including Mo Erwa [the originally discovered cannibal], began to kidnap children from other villages. Booby traps, which were used for wolves, were employed to capture kids.

The Mortician reported further that when the reclaimed bodies were brought back from the mountains, they "were mostly dismembered. The flesh around the thighs, the shoulders, the backs, and the buttocks was all gone."

The Great Proletarian Cultural Revolution, launched by Chairman Mao in 1966, deliberately engaged the support of college and high school students to, according to the Former Red Guard, give impetus to the Communist revolution rather than focusing on developing China's economy. Thus, students were mobilized and radicalized in defense of Chairman Mao. Their targets were government officials at several levels, hierarchal leaders, such as principals and teachers, former landlords. They were publicly discredited and beaten in the manner of the "speak bitterness" meetings. The Former Red Guard asserted: "Ordinary folks turned around en masse and began to target those in power"; "In those last days, it was very common to see students beat their teachers to death. So, if an accused capitalist was tortured to death, nobody cared"; "In those days, many of the Public Security Bureaus were paralyzed. Nobody was in charge. Nobody dared to question the case [of the six-month torture and ultimate death of a once honored high school principal]. If they had they would have been accused of siding with the enemy. It was a lawless society. The words of Chairman Mao were the ultimate law of the land."

The Former Red Guard expressed his rationale for these activities:

I was born into a family of blue-collar workers. The Cultural Revolution offered me the opportunity to finally trample on those elite. It was glorious. I couldn't get enough of it. My youth, my dream, and my passion were all associated with the Cultural Revolution. The most exciting moment in those days was to see Chairman Mao in person, when he greeted millions of Red Guards in Beijing's Tiananmen Square.

His current responses parallel these: He does not have the same euphoric feelings, but cherishes the memories. "I will never forget them. We were so pure and innocent. . . . We were fighting for our beliefs. We were defending Chairman Mao and the Communist revolution. Anyone who obstructed the revolution deserved to be punished."

Among the more sensitive interviews was that of the Tiananmen Father who lost his elder son, Guofeng, at the massacre on June 4, 1989. This working class family was generationally quite poor, the father constantly hungry as a youngster and undereducated. Both parents worked. Guofeng excelled in school, the top of his high school class, and got the highest score of the township in the college entrance exams. He became the family's great hope for a change in their fortunes.

Guofeng became active politically, joining the students' pro-democracy movement. His parents became anxious:

My generation went through many political campaigns. We've seen them all. One minute, the Party seems to relax its political control. Once you let down your guard, they come out to get you. They've played this trick for years. The Communist leaders change their face like the April weather. I guess living with the fear of persecution made us jaded and overcautious.

Their fears were warranted: The student demonstrations initially identified as a patriotic movement were later called a riot—a counterrevolutionary riot. The troops were ordered to crack down on the student protestors. After warning the protesters to leave by 6:00 A.M. and permitting those who had negotiated safe passage to depart, the armed personnel carriers rolled up the road, firing on the crowds ahead and to the sides. Hundreds were killed, among them Guofeng. The devastated parents traveled to Beijing to bring their son's body home, but the Party Central Committee had ordered that all victims be cremated immediately. The parents, in response to their pleading, were allowed to take a picture of their son "on the condition that I keep those pictures confidential. [The Party secretary] made me promise not to use the pictures to tarnish the image of our government."

The family suffered further injuries: the death of the younger brother, a debilitating head concussion of the mother, and kidney cancer of the father. The family situation rolled downhill.

It's been sixteen years since the June 4 massacre happened. Sooner or later, justice will be done. We probably won't live long enough to see the day. Whatever happens, we can't let the Communist Party get away with the bloody debt owed to families like mine.

The above interviews were selected for their political orientation in keeping with this volume's focus. Other interviews relate traditions, rites, and roles, some of which are disappearing or have been declared illegal. Some of these are the Corpse Walker, the Professional Mourner, the Human Trafficker, and the Falon Gong Practitioner. Alas, the Migrant Worker is not disappearing.

CENSORSHIP HISTORY

In summer 2009, Liao Yiwu wrote: "I didn't witness the killings in Tiananmen Square. I was home in Fuling, a small mountain town well known for its pickled and shredded turnips. When I heard the news, I was outraged. I composed an epic poem, 'Massacre,' to commemorate the government's brutality against its people. With the help of a visiting Canadian friend, I made a tape, chanting my poem into an old toothless tape recorder."

Liao circulated the tape. (It was also smuggled out of China by sympathetic Western literary contacts.) He was arrested while making a movie about Tiananmen Square. Charged with organizing a large-scale counterrevolutionary group (later in 1992, changed to "engaging in individual counterrevolutionary activities"), he was sentenced to four years in prison. During his imprisonment, he was severely tortured; he twice tried to commit suicide. Liao's writings are officially banned in China, and he is frequently harassed. His works are circulated underground, however, and pirated versions can be found in some Chinese bookstores.

Liao has been denied travel opportunities outside of China, most recently in 2010 for a literary festival in Cologne; in 2009, he was prevented from attending a Berlin event affiliated with the Frankfurt Book Fair, at which China was designated the honored guest. All together, there have been 13 such travel denials.

Peter Gourevich's observation in the "Foreword" of *The Corpse Walker* is apt in the context of these censorial challenges:

> Liao is at once an unflinching observer and recorder, a shoe-leather reporter and an artful storyteller, an oral historian and deft mimic, a folklorist and satirist. Above all, he is a medium for whole muzzled swathes of Chinese society that the Party would like to pretend do not exist: hustlers and drifters, outlaws and street performers, the officially renegade and the physically handicapped, those who deal with human waste and with the wasting of humans, artists and shamans, crooks, even cannibals—and every one of them speaks more honestly than the official chronicles of Chinese life that are put out by the state in the name of "the people."

FURTHER READING

Kristof, Nicholas D. "Tiananmen Square." *New York Times,* June 11, 2010.
Liao Yiwu. "Nineteen Days." *Paris Review* 189 (Summer 2009). Available online. URL: www.theparisreview.org/letters-essays/5929/nineteen-days-liao-yiwu. Accessed January 24, 2011.
Wines, Michael. "For 13th Time, Critic of China Is Barred from Travel Abroad." *New York Times,* March 3, 2010, p. A4.

CRY AMANDLA!

Author: June Goodwin
Original date and place of publication: 1984, United States
Publisher: Africana Publishing Company/Holmes and Meier
Literary form: Nonfiction

SUMMARY

The subject of *Cry Amandla!* is South Africa, but the focus is "South African Women and the Question of Power." Across all African languages, *Amandla* signifies power, accompanied by a highly raised fist. Following several introductory chapters providing background, the book is primarily composed of interviews with an array of women, black and white, representing a broad spectrum of social attitudes and political opinions. The author's reactions to these are often expressed.

At the heart of South Africa's political and social life is apartheid, the "most codified and elaborate blueprint ever devised for human relationships. It covers every facet of life." Expressing "separateness," apartheid was developed by the Afrikaners (descendants of the Boers, the original Dutch settlers) to establish their own political, economic, and social agenda; it divided the races and defined controls placed on the native black people. The system of apartheid is divided into grand and petty aspects, the former being the master plan for maintaining white minority rule, the latter being the laws of prejudice.

The grand design established areas where blacks may live—the bantustans, or homelands—and where whites live. The "homelands for twenty-one million blacks comprise only 13 percent of the land surface of South Africa. The remaining 87 percent of the land is controlled by the 4.6 million whites." There are also temporary black townships, which fringe white areas where blacks who provide services to whites may live. "Temporary" refers to the fact that blacks are identified as citizens of the tribal homelands (even if they have lived their entire lives outside), and they cannot own this land; if land is needed to expand or develop a white area, the blacks are evicted, and their structures are razed. The petty features of apartheid represent restrictions covering the gamut of possible joint activities: entering a store from the same door; using the same toilet facilities; performing on stage together; going to the same school, unless with special dispensation to a white private school; and having sexual relations.

Laws directed toward blacks violate basic canons of criminal justice: They permit detention and interrogation in isolation and witness detention for 180 days. Further, they exclude the rights of habeas corpus, for arrested persons to be informed of the causes of their arrests and to be visited by lawyers. Inhuman and degrading treatment is permitted.

In 1978, under apartheid, there were "261 people detained under security laws, 50 people banned, 149 people shot and killed by on-duty police, over 100 prisoners awaiting trial who died in police custody, 403 people wounded by police gunfire, 76 political trials, and people hanged, one every fourth day." The Banning Act permits the imposition of extended house arrest and/or limited movement and association; for example, a banned person may be allowed to speak with only one person at a time, but not with another banned person. A white woman, a friend of Nelson Mandela and other leaders of the African National Congress (ANC), was under house arrest for 20 years; from 1953 to 1984, more than 1,400 people were banned for five-year durations. Pass laws, or "influx control," also limit travel of blacks or ensure that they stay in particular areas. Censorship of newspapers, books, and photographs is another tool of the government.

The Afrikaner women interviewed are not all of a kind politically: Four are conservative with some variation in attitude but supporting apartheid;

one is liberal, very much opposed to apartheid. A basic status and belief system joins the four of them. They are privileged, economically and socially, living in upscale suburbs. They are Christians, members of the Dutch Reformed Church. They are fearful of communism, which they connect with the blacks' freedom movement. They are fearful of blacks and of their coming to power in South Africa.

The wife of a minister, Gabrielle Malan, ties her apartheid position to Christian doctrine and God's plans: "We have the sense that God plans everything. Nothing happens without his willing it. There is a certain task for us in this country and until it is completed, we just have to stay here." God's way of averting human conflict is to divide people into groups. Thus, "I see this whole policy of separate development as an excellent policy." A more adaptive Afrikaner, Freda Van Rooyen, heads an organization, Kontak, whose intent is to change the image of Afrikaners through social-cultural contacts. In a four-way conversation with the author and two of her Kontak members, two of them, despite their adaptive outlook, clearly separate themselves from blacks in their "development" in relation to civilization and in their ability to interpret and be logical. They perceive separation as normal: "Very naturally people are against mixing. Black people are as scared as we are because it has been proven it [mixed marriages] seldom works." The most liberal of the three, who believes she has rejected apartheid, nevertheless admits to the necessity of "influx control," the pass laws: "You cannot just open the portals of the cities and sit back and watch people stream in."

One Afrikaner, anonymous in the text, expresses deep despair over the effects of government policies on the blacks. She feels guilt and powerlessness. Her social work with the noneducated, nonliterate blacks made her aware of the realities of their situations and the "Catch-22 legalisms that form the web of apartheid," as well as injustices toward them and corruption among Afrikaner officials. "They're people, they're people like you and me. Officials won't concede they are making enemies of people in our country. It's their country, too. We can't regiment people's lives like that. It's impossible."

The liberal group in South Africa, essentially descendants of the English, are portrayed as somewhat more diverse and oriented toward the blacks, but are nevertheless viewed critically to a large extent in this book. Helen Suzman, a member of the Progressive Federal Party (PFP), has been a representative in South Africa's Parliament since 1953. She has been honored by the United Nations for her defense of human rights. However, although she is able to claim, "The minutes record my vote against every bit of oppressive legislation this country ever introduced," and despite her consistent efforts against repressive functions of the police and the Natal Code, which makes all black women permanent minors, Suzman is criticized because she is said not to believe in a complete overhaul of the system. The PFP opposes universal suffrage, which would place blacks in power, opting for "power-sharing with blacks" instead.

Among the other liberal women is Sheena Duncan, leader of the Black Sash, a group of women whose activities include protesting apartheid in public marches, providing assistance to blacks in "advice offices," and otherwise peaceably and legally trying to educate about the "desecration of human rights" by government policies. Mary Benson was put under house arrest in 1965 and then exiled in 1966. Her books, representing an accepting racial attitude and historical truths about the black protest movement, have been banned in South Africa. Benson maintained friendships with Nelson Mandela and Bram Fischer, leader of the South African Communist Party, who was considered a traitor to his Afrikaner heritage because of his opposition to the government's antiblack policies.

Black women are represented by three who are servants in white households and two who actively resist the system but in quite different ways. These at once suggest contrasts and a certain unanimity. These three domestic servants, aged 34 to 41, live in the homes of their employers; their families live at some distance in a homeland or on a farm. They complain about separation from their families and apartheid's effect on their relationships. They recognize that their color separates them, prevents closeness. "You can't be friends. You can't eat with them; you can't touch their food. You can't touch their dishes. You must have your own dishes. Separate." They understand that they are essentially "unwanted" persons who are needed for their strength.

Some political attitudes are evident, as are apprehensions. They recognize that freedom is the goal and that they have to fight for it. But they fear that should the whites leave South Africa, the black factions or tribes will fight against each other. "Then who's going to help us?" asks Tiny. "I don't think so; I don't think they must leave," says Eunice; Rosalyn adds, "We must live together because if we live without them, we will fight." Yet, they are not innocent of the current climate of terror, the killing and harassment of their leaders and danger to themselves: "I mean to say, it's not good to talk about [Nelson Mandela]. If you do, it means you know something. They'll take you to tell them more. So we must be careful. You must turn stupid."

The differences between Kitty Duma and Thenjiwe (Thenjie) Mtintso are not their humanity or their ultimate objectives, but rather their backgrounds, their economic conditions, and their strategies. While Kitty has had contacts with whites throughout her life and is employed with whites in the office of a California-based evangelist organization, Thenjie has had substantive conversations with only three whites. Thenjie acts to confront the system, while Kitty resists it in less overt ways. She is outspoken (to the author) about double standards and white racism.

It's a hard road we're walking, very hard. How can they possibly be Christians and do the things they do? How can they believe in Jesus when they discriminate the way they do?

Apartheid affects everything . . . everything, everything. You've always got to restrain yourself. If I want to go to Cape Town with you, I have to think . . . the police there . . . are they active or what? Just the whole thing. I'm not worried about parks or cinemas. It's this undermining of one's brain because of the color of your skin. That is what bugs me, because you find it all over.

Before switching allegiance to the African National Congress, Thenjie was a leader in the Black Consciousness Movement advocating overt struggle for freedom—blacks depending on blacks. As a black nationalist she rejects working with whites: "It is always the same, with whitey up there and black down here." She argues for the withdrawal of financial investments from South Africa because they support the government.

The text essentially concludes with a revelation of Thenjie's mistreatment while imprisoned. She had been imprisoned five times in a two-year period, once for four and a half months and once for 10 months. She was never charged. The details of her first detention include being assaulted; being required to stand for three days in a room without any exception, not even to use toilet facilities; being subjected to insults, interrogation, and beatings and a near-strangulation-suffocation procedure with a wet towel; and being placed in a cell dirtied with excrement, lice, and flies.

Just anywhere. It is called assault with intent. The first time this guy just claps [hits] me. A rather tough guy. I weighed about forty-six kilograms [101 pounds]. So when they clap you, they clap you. They punch you, you fall; they kick you; they lift you up.

When interrogation became more serious, their assault was systematic. They made me stand next to the wall and the man next to me just hit my head on the wall like a ball, a tennis ball. *N-kgoon, n-kgoon, n-kgoon.* I had been wearing a beret. They removed it so bare head hit bare wall. At the end of three hours, my head, I could feel it growing.

After her release, unaccountably, Thenjie was restricted to her mother's home in Soweto. When, however, she was charged with violating her banning order, thus subject to imprisonment for several years, she fled secretly with her young son to Lesotho, a black-ruled country whose boundaries were surrounded by white-ruled South Africa.

CENSORSHIP HISTORY

Cry Amandla! South African Women and the Question of Power was banned in August 1984 by the Directorate of Publications in Cape Town, South Africa. The directorate did not give a specific reason but indicated that "it will be an offense to import or distribute" the book.

FURTHER READING

"Cape Town, South Africa." *Newsletter on Intellectual Freedom* 22 (1984): 197.
"South Africa Bans Book by American Journalist." *New York Times*, September 19, 1984, p. 24.

DAS KAPITAL

Author: Karl Marx
Original dates and places of publication: 1867 (Volume I), 1885 (Volume II), 1894 (Volume III), Germany; 1880 (extracts) and 1886, United States
Publishers: O. Meissner; F. A. Sorge (extracts) and Humboldt
Literary form: Nonfiction

SUMMARY

Karl Marx's *Das Kapital* (*Capital*) has been called the bible of communism by some, while others argue that it is more a critique of capitalism than a promulgation of Marx's beliefs in and about communism. A massive three-volume study, it is today often abridged into a single volume. In the books, Marx examines the nature and flaws of capitalism. Marx, who died in 1883, completed only Volume I in his lifetime; his partner and fellow socialist, Friedrich Engels, using Marx's extensive notes, completed and published the other volumes.

Marx roots his examples mostly in the economy of England in the 1860s; his monetary theory is the gold standard. His view of business is of rather small family firms, although he does anticipate the rise of larger conglomerations. The conditions for workers were hard; the businesses, in their competition with one another, had to hold down costs in an effort to sell what the market would bear. One of the easiest ways of holding down costs was to hold the price paid for labor as low as possible while still attracting competent workers.

Any effort to summarize the work will, of necessity, perhaps oversimplify certain aspects. It should also be noted that Marx himself completed only the first of the three volumes and that much of the "meat" of *Das Kapital* can be found in this volume. As Engels's influence on the volumes increases, the literary style becomes increasingly turgid.

Marx begins Volume I by examining the idea of the commodity as some tangible thing that can be exchanged for other commodities; according to Marx, all commodities have a "use-value," which means that they satisfy a desire or need, either directly or indirectly. The "exchange-value" of a commodity may differ from the "use-value," in that the exchange-value is what the commodity is worth to other commodity traders, while the use-value is what the commodity is worth to the user. He applies similar analysis to the value of labor. "Useful labor" produces use-value, while "abstract labor" is the actual expenditure of time and effort. Neither commodities nor labor have fixed value, but will vary according to others within the market system. Value in the market exists only relative to what someone else will pay for the commodity or the labor. Moreover, the market cannot exist without recognizing that one person has a right to exchange a commodity with another. In barter societies, the exchange will simply be one item for another; in modern capitalist society, the medium of exchange is money circulating throughout the economy.

Capitalism would be pointless if, in exchanging commodities and money, the capitalist got back only as much money as he had at the beginning of the exchange. The goal is to create "surplus value" for oneself. The source of that surplus value is "labor-power," the selling of the worker's labor. Capitalists will always attempt to get more value from the laborer than they will actually pay. Thus, the amount of time that the worker must put in to equal his pay is "necessary labor," while the capitalist makes his profit off the worker's "surplus labor." While the England of his day had rejected slavery and feudalism, Marx chastises society for long and arduous working conditions, running factories around the clock, and the reluctance of capitalists to allow for a shorter workday. It is to the benefit of all capitalists to pay less for the labor-power and to receive more surplus labor; this keeps the wages of all workers low, as the capitalists do not have to compete as much in offering better compensation to labor.

In the development of capitalism, workers become more and more specialized, and the capitalist attempts to find ways to have machines do a larger share of the work in an effort to reduce the cost of labor. Wages cannot really represent the value of labor, because that would leave the capitalist with no surplus-value. Wages do rise as capitalism advances, but they always represent less than the workers' total value.

The surplus-value is transformed into "expanded reproduction," or an increase in the ability to produce commodities. As capital is accumulated, there is greater centralization of that capital. This is so because larger companies will have lower costs and can therefore sell at lower prices than smaller companies, even as they turn their surplus-value into ever greater expanded reproduction and increase their competitive advantage. As businesses go under, an "industrial reserve army" of workers begins to form. These unemployed further help to hold down the wages of workers, as there is always someone ready to replace the worker at a lower wage. The workers are forced into overwork while the unemployed are in forced idleness.

Volumes II and III were put together by Engels, as they had been unfinished at the time of Marx's death. They therefore tend to repeat themselves more than the first volume. The main ideas in the second volume include a discussion of the "spheres of production and exchange," the intertwining of capitalist interests (for example, the workers are paid by one capitalist and buy the commodities of other capitalists), and the vulnerability of the system because of this interdependence. By its nature, Marx argues, capitalism will have cycles that will vary due to the turnover of capital. Large-scale investments, for example, set up the possibility of economic downturns by rapidly pushing up prices and wages.

The bulk of the rest of the second volume finds Marx disputing with other economists over the nature of capital accumulation and attempting to find numerical formulas to support his views. In essence, his point is that capitalism promotes hoarding, a part of the process of accumulating capital and increasing production.

Volume III takes up the issue of how surplus-value tends to be divided: profit, rent, and interest. "Profit" is the result of subtracting the cost of production from the selling price; the excess is the profit. The cost of production itself is a combination of the cost of the materials, the wages paid to workers, and the cost of production itself. The "rate of profit" is the ratio of the profit obtained to the capital needed to produce the commodity. To obtain a good rate of profit, the capitalist will always try to hold down the cost of production, including the wages paid to workers. When capitalists own the means of production, prices are based largely on cost of production; if workers were to control the means of production, Marx asserts that price would be based on value. He rejects the notions of supply and demand as explanations for prices.

When he moves to the subject of interest, Marx maintains that interest is created as a division of profit and exists because of the need to borrow to accumulate capital. Money made from interest is not the same as "profit of enterprise," or money made from producing commodities. The existing system of banks and credit also does much to encourage centralization of capital; the system itself is exploitative without adding any real productive economic good to the society.

Das Kapital ends with a discussion of rent; rent can be divided into "ground rent," which is payment to an owner for use of agricultural land, water, and other such resources, and "differential rent," which arises when equal amounts of capital investment in land yield different returns due to some natural condition. These kinds of rent differ from the feudal system's "labor-rent," which is the paying off of debts for use of land through the use of labor directly (or the paying of a share of the harvest). These final sections of the book are generally filled with mathematical formulas and are less cogent than early sections. This is understandable when one realizes that they were put together by Engels almost 30 years after Marx first jotted notes on the issues discussed.

CENSORSHIP HISTORY

As noted in the *Encyclopedia of Censorship*, "It is impossible to itemize every country in which Marxist works are prohibited." Marx's writings in their entirety were on the Roman Index of some 600 books that devout members of the faith were generally prohibited from reading. Not only has Marx's *Das Kapital* met with opposition in the nominally capitalist societies, but even countries that identify themselves as "Marxist" have often seen fit to restrict access to his works.

Marx himself was certainly persecuted in his own lifetime. The man who declared, "I am not a Marxist," was exiled from his native Germany in 1843 and expelled from France in 1845. While eventually acquitted, he was put on trial on the charge of treason in Prussia in 1849. He lived the remainder of his life in England, although he never held a steady job, usually lived in poverty, and suffered from poor health.

In 1877, Scribner, Armstrong and Company rejected publishing a translation of *Das Kapital*, largely because of the conservative views of Blair Scribner himself. Also in 1877, the American Fred Perkins published *Best Reading*, a guide for librarians. Among the thousands of titles he suggested that librarians stock, there is no mention of Balzac, Rousseau, Voltaire, or Marx.

A book on Marx was banned in Russia in 1894; the same year *Das Kapital* was forbidden to be reprinted. However, the Russian censor finally allowed the third volume of *Das Kapital* to be printed in 1897 because he decided that no one would be able to understand it anyway. The writings of Marx in their entirety were prohibited in China in 1929. Under the Nazi regime, books by Marx were burned as being contrary to the spirit of German nationalism.

In 1940, Robert Wood, the state secretary of the Communist Party of Oklahoma and a bookstore owner, was among six defendants found guilty of acts dangerous to national security; a book burning at the City Stadium of Oklahoma City included *Das Kapital*, among other books. Wood's conviction was eventually overturned in 1945 by the state court of appeals.

During the McCarthy era, groups such as the Sons of the American Revolution in Montclair, New Jersey, demanded that books of a corrupting nature carry warning labels. Sexual books might use one color for their labels, while Communist writings, such as *Das Kapital*, would use another. The American Library Association refused to comply in this instance, arguing that the labels were a form of censorship. Efforts at labeling or restricting access also took place at several Catholic universities. The entire period saw not only the "witch hunts" of the House Un-American Activities Committee but also smaller purges of both people and books throughout American society.

In the early 1960s, a bookstore owner in Kansas City, Kansas, received threats from the John Birch Society over stocking *Das Kapital*. Even efforts to support the right to read were less than unequivocally supportive. In 1965, the Los Angeles Public Library created an exhibit on banned books. The library argued, somewhat contradictorily, that books such as *Das Kapital* "have a place in public libraries, although the ideas they contain should be repulsive to all Americans."

During World War II, 1939–45, identical indexes of forbidden literature were applied by the Nazis in all occupied countries as well as in Germany's allied countries: Denmark, Norway, France, Luxembourg, Belgium, the Netherlands, Lithuania, Latvia, Estonia, Belarus, Poland, Yugoslavia, Greece, and of course, Germany.

Censorship occurred in countries that felt particular threats by communism. In South Africa, during the apartheid period, the African National Congress (ANC) was supported by the South African Communist Party. Thus, under the Customs and Excise Act No. 55 of 1955 and Publication Act 42 of 1974, Marx's texts were included on the Index of Objectionable Literature. *Das Kapital* and the MANIFESTO OF THE COMMUNIST PARTY were removed from the list in September 1991, the ANC and the South African Communist Party having been unbanned in February 1990.

In South Korea, where communism is illegal, a publisher released an edition of *Das Kapital* in 1987. The Ministry of Culture and Information, which maintained a list of books estimated to contain 600 to 1,000 titles at that time, sued the publisher in court, charging a violation of South Korea's National Security Law.

Marx also faced censorship in marxist nations. East Germany rewrote or expurgated all of Marx's writings in 1953. On November 13, 1959, Erich Ollenhauer, the chair of the German Social Democratic Party, stated that "the demand that the political programs of Karl Marx and Friedrich Engels be made the basis of a Social Democratic program is so un-Marxist as to be unthinkable." The Soviet Union began fairly heavy editing of Marx's writings in the 1960s, often altering works to more fully support the positions held by the Communist Party.

In almost all instances, comments referring to *Das Kapital* also apply to the *Manifesto of the Communist Party*.

FURTHER READING

Balmuth, Daniel. *Censorship in Russia, 1865–1905*. Washington, D.C.: University Press of America, 1979.

Geller, Evelyn. *Forbidden Books in American Public Libraries, 1876–1939*. Westport, Conn.: Greenwood Press, 1984.

Green, Jonathon, and Nicholas J. Karolides, reviser. *The Encyclopedia of Censorship, New Edition*. New York: Facts On File, 2005.

Haight, Anne Lyon, and Chandler B. Grannis. *Book Banning 387 B.C. to 1978 A.D.* 4th ed. New York: R. R. Bowker, 1978.

Tebbel, John. *A History of Book Publishing in the United States*. New York: R. R. Bowker, 1975.

—Mitchell Fay
University of Wisconsin–River Falls
Updated by Nicholas J. Karolides

DAUGHTER OF EARTH

Author: Agnes Smedley
Original date and place of publication: 1929, United States
Publisher: Coward-McCann
Literary form: Novel

SUMMARY

This "largely autobiographical book" is the first-person narrative of the life of Marie Rogers from her first memories of early childhood on a Missouri farm to the time of her estranged departure from the United States at about age 30. The time represented begins in the early 1890s and closes in the post–World War I period.

Unsuccessful and bored with farming, Marie's father's wanderlust takes over. The family begins a series of moves, following his schemes and dreams, and beginning, too, a series of disasters. Though there are some hopeful times, more often, despite long and hard work, the father's enterprises fail. At times he is a victim of natural disasters; more often he is victimized by unscrupulous men or his own ignorance and mistakes. Occasionally, he deserts the family, leaving them destitute.

Deprivation is a constant. Hope and hard work are followed by disappointment and despair. Marie's mother tries operating a boardinghouse, then boards her husband's workers; at last she becomes a washerwoman. She ages quickly and dies young. Upon the failure of his enterprises, Marie's father turns to alcohol, anger, and abusive behavior. The older children are forced to work; Marie's first "formal" job, at about age 13, is after school as a "kitchen help" to a family.

Schooling is erratic. Marie, however, is an eager and able learner, except for arithmetic. She learns, beyond school, lessons that are to drive her later life: the distinction between the rich and the poor; the haughty superiority and often thoughtless cruelty of the rich; the greed and inhumanity of bosses, specifically owners and managers of the mines; the lower status of women and, particularly, their humiliation and loss of rights and worth in marriage. Indeed, the physical, emotional, and economic abuse that she witnesses toward her mother and other women causes her to reject marriage, except under her conditions of equality. By this time she also has learned to distrust and confront her father, protecting her mother and her younger siblings. She makes peace with her mother, becoming her friend and support until her early death.

She learns the value of independence and education. Her goal is to gain the latter to achieve the former. And she gradually does. Her formal studies are invariably interrupted by her obligations to care for her siblings and by needing to work to support herself while going to school and college. At two significant times she sacrifices her responsibility to her siblings to maintain her goals, decisions that haunt her with feelings of guilt in later years.

This human rights issue is interwoven in the story, emerging from contrasting images of humiliation and empowerment of women. They are disadvantaged in marriage, where they become dependent vassals to their husbands and lose their right to be. When living apart from her husband, she thinks, "I knew that I was a woman not yet broken in to slavery." In business, women held inferior positions and faced the threat of sexual abuse. In public affairs they were not afforded equality of voice and status. Marie devotes herself to this "cause" and asserts her intelligence and her physical being to make a place for herself and to change attitudes toward the status of women.

From her childhood, Marie is made cognizant of the chasm between herself and her school peers (though not in the ability to learn), between her family and those she works for, between workers and management. She feels her isolation and her rejection. She knows how her own mother and father have given all their strength and lost. When the workers strike for higher wages, safer conditions, and just treatment, she recognizes how they are broken by hunger to give in.

> Over Tercio brooded the same atmosphere as in Delagua—smoldering discontent and hatred. Here were the same complaints about the weigh boss, the hours, wages, insufficient props and other precautions against falls, the high prices and dishonesty of the Company store, the payment of script instead of American money. The miners dragged themselves to the holes in the mountain-side each morning, and, black with coal smut, dragged themselves home at night. Their children—boys of ten onward—worked around the mines until they were strong enough to become miners themselves. . . . Hatred and hunger walked hand in hand through all the camps. There was no food except in the Company store and the store could not give credit. . . . Then after weeks of bitter struggle and hunger, the strike came to an end. Nagging women and crying children helped send the men back to the mines, defeated.

While a university student, her outrage at the treatment of working men, socialists, and members of Industrial Workers of the World (IWW), who are protesting for free speech, draws her into this movement. As she matures and experiences, so does her animosity toward the United States—the government and the powerful men who rule it. If it were invaded by a foreign, armed power, she would work for its freedom, but not "just to put it in the hands of a few rich men or groups who would make the rest of us work for them and live in poverty." These ideas lead her to value the Russian Revolution as a means of birthing "a new world order," a breakdown of the unjust capitalist system.

In her view, the government of the United States is implicated in the deprivation of the people. Her bitterness is evident in her opposition to United States involvement in World War I and her younger brother's decision to join the army to escape his poverty-stricken conditions. "Dan was only eighteen. Now he was offering his life for a country that could not feed or educate him. And so I hated the city about me, hated the wealth that rested upon the bodies of working men." She sees wealth around her in New York and is embittered.

Critical attitudes emerge from her involvement in India's movement for freedom from England's colonial yoke. She is arrested and held in jail (illegally, as it turns out) for conspiracy against the government because of this involvement. She is accused of being a German spy, of having seditious tendencies. She suffers days of questioning, threats, and mistreatment. Her cell is cold and damp, the toilet leaks onto the floor, and she is denied food and drink. Before being indicted, she is asked to help her country. She thinks of her mother and the women of her class and denies that she is part of the country of these officials: "*You* are not my country!" she says. "I have done nothing wrong. . . . you are indicting me because I help men who are trying to get their freedom—as America once got its freedom!"

Marie, sentenced to jail in the Tombs, expresses through this experience and her observations the injustice of American society. Aside from her false arrest, her own mistreatment and conviction, she provides evidence of bias. Among her examples, an upper-class college girl charged with grand larceny for stealing $1,500 worth of goods is released without trial after two days; a poor young "Negro" girl who had stolen a pair of green stockings is sentenced to the workhouse; abandoned unwed mothers are sentenced to three years of incarceration for stealing to feed and care for their infant children.

Marie recognizes that another America exists, an America of which she feels a part. Her "instinctive appeal to principles, traditions and ideas of the American people" expresses how "native [she was to her] soil." She sees her life—and her religion—in working to help people achieve freedom and rise from economic oppression.

CENSORSHIP HISTORY

Agnes Smedley had a history of confrontations with United States law agencies. Though the details of the event vary from those in her autobiographical novel, her biographers, Janice and Stephen MacKinnon, reveal that Smedley was indeed arrested in 1918, jailed, and indicted under the Espionage Act for attempting to stir up rebellion against British rule in India, thereby abetting the German enemy, and representing herself as a diplomat; she was also charged with distributing birth control information, a violation of a local ordinance.

A more direct relationship to the censoring of *Daughter of Earth* can be found in the attacks on Smedley in Congress and by the military. Reacting to Smedley's newspaper accounts of racism in the South, Representative John S. Gibson of Georgia complained in a 1944 *Congressional Record* of her connection with international communism, her portrayal of the "glory of the Communist Party and its great cause . . . the great benefits received from the Communist revolutions." Later in 1944, J. Edgar Hoover, director of the FBI, requested that Smedley be placed on the Censorship Watch List and that "all communications to, from, or regarding her be forwarded to the Bureau." In "close contact with the anti-communist right in Congress . . . the point of [Hoover's] investigation was to find evidence of Smedley's ties to the Soviet Union . . . as an agent, a spy, or both." Her situation was not helped by her being presumed a Communist by Whittaker Chambers, an assumption that became "fact."

Despite having no concrete evidence that Smedley was a Soviet agent, by 1946 the FBI was convinced of her guilt. A late 1946 study described her as "an important fanatical Soviet propagandist," despite articles in which she had criticized some Soviet policies. When no evidence of illegal activities was found after three years of surveillance and mail censorship, the Albany division deleted her name in 1947 from the Key Figure List and requested the bureau to do the same.

Increasingly, however, Smedley was attacked in the press (notably, by Alfred Kohlberg and Freda Utley, spokespersons for the China lobby; Drew Pearson, a nationally syndicated columnist; and Henry Luce's publications). Smedley was often heckled at her public addresses. Citing Kohlberg's accusations that she was a traitor, local residents protested one scheduled appearance. Fewer editors, too, were accepting her articles.

In 1949, the army released a report that had emerged from General Douglas MacArthur's headquarters in Japan, written by his chief of intelligence, General Charles A. Willoughby, describing a Soviet spy ring in Japan. Agnes Smedley was accused of being a spy and an agent of the Soviet government. Within a day of Smedley's public denial, the army apologized and retracted its charges. The repercussive effects were tighter, more evident surveillance by the FBI. Also, Smedley, in effect, was blacklisted by editors. Further, Smedley "recognized that she was irrevocably labeled in the public eye as a pro-Soviet fellow traveler and suspected Communist spy." According to MacKinnon and MacKinnon in their biography of Smedley,

> One of the last entries in Smedley's F.B.I. file—dated October 11, 1954—was a military intelligence report of an interview with an American soldier who had been taken prisoner by the Chinese during the Korean War; the soldier, it said, had been made to read portions of *Daughter of Earth* in an attempt to "educate" him about the evils of the capitalist system. This conveyed perfectly the extreme right's image of Smedley: she was the disloyal American whose willingness to show the weaknesses of the American system made her a tool the Communists could use in undermining the United States.

In 1950, after she left for England in hopes of getting a permit to reenter China, Agnes Smedley died. The House Un-American Activities Committee had planned to recall her to the United States for further questioning. Her travail did not end, however. In 1951, the United States Information

Agency removed her books from its shelves. Libraries in the United States followed suit. Except for *Daughter of Earth*, which has been reissued, her texts are not readily available today.

FURTHER READING

Chapman, Ralph. "Agnes Smedley Denies Charge of Acting as Spy for Soviets." *New York Herald Tribune*, February 11, 1949, n.p.

Hoffman, Nancy. "A Journey into Knowing: Agnes Smedley's *Daughter of Earth.*" In *Tradition and Talents of Women*, edited by Florence Howe, 171–82. Urbana: University of Illinois Press.

Johnson, Chalmers. *An Instance of Treason: Ozaki Hotsumi and the Sorge Spy Ring.* Stanford, Calif.: Stanford University Press, 1964.

Knapp, Shelley Lyn. *Quoting Revolution: A Study of Agnes Smedley's Attempt to Express a Revolutionary China to the West.* M.A. thesis. University of Washington, 1987.

Lauter, Paul. "Afterword." In *Daughter of Earth*, by Agnes Smedley. New York: Feminist Press, 1973.

MacKinnon, Janice, and Stephen MacKinnon. *Agnes Smedley: The Life and Times of an American Radical.* Berkeley: University of California Press, 1988.

Selden, Mark. "Agnes Smedley, American Radical." *Monthly Review* 40 (October 1988): 32.

Smedley, Agnes. *Battle Hymn of China.* New York: Alfred A. Knopf, 1943.

Warmbold, Carolyn Nizza. *Women of the Mosquito Press: Louise Bryant, Agnes Smedley, and Margaret Randall as Narrative Guerrillas.* Ph.D. diss. University of Texas at Austin, 1990.

THE DAY THEY CAME TO ARREST THE BOOK

Author: Nat Hentoff
Original date and place of publication: 1982, United States
Publisher: Delacorte
Literary form: Novel

SUMMARY

Though it is decidedly fiction, in some respects *The Day They Came to Arrest the Book* reads like nonfiction. It seems like a case study of censorship. Nat Hentoff has supplied all the necessary ingredients: a controversial book—Mark Twain's *The Adventures of Huckleberry Finn*—incensed parents, African Americans, and others; an unctuous, deceptive principal; a beleaguered teacher and an assertive librarian; well-spoken advocates on either side of the debate, an American Civil Liberties Union (ACLU) lawyer and a representative of the Citizen's League for the Preservation of American Values; a review committee and school board hearings; and national TV coverage.

The plot begins to simmer almost immediately. Barney, the incoming school newspaper editor, discovers on the first day of school that the librarian has resigned under shadowed circumstances. In the library, Deirdre Fitzgerald, the new librarian, gets an insinuating earful from Nora Baines, the history teacher. That afternoon over coffee, Baines reveals all: The principal, Mr. Moore, is a closet censor, concurring without contest to any book complaint, circumventing the school's procedures, which require a review committee hearing.

Against this backdrop, the focal censorship issue emerges. Nora Baines assigns *Adventures of Huckleberry Finn* in conjunction with Alexis de Tocqueville's *Democracy in America* in her 19th-century American history course. An African-American student complains to his father about the abundant use of the word *nigger* in the text and other expressions of inhumanity. This, of course, leads to a confrontation with the principal, Mr. Moore. The father, Carl McLean, insists,

> Let me lay it right on the line, Mr. Moore. I do not want my son, or any other black child to have to hear in a classroom, day after day, "nigger," "nigger," "nigger." It's demeaning and degrading and if you will excuse me, stupid on the part of whoever selected that book. I believe I have made myself clear, and I expect the book will be pulled out of the course. Immediately!

Further, he adds,

> And it has to be eliminated not only from the curriculum. That book cannot be allowed to remain in the school library for any child who may come upon it.

Baines vehemently declines to accede to the principal's pressure to withdraw the book as a required assignment, insisting on her part that a formal complaint be filed and that a review committee be formed. Mr. Moore is not accustomed to such recalcitrance. Much to his irritation, young Deirdre Fitzgerald also rejects his proposition that the book be removed from library circulation. She reminds him, "according to the school's procedures, a book is presumed innocent until proven guilty."

Midway in the story, Hentoff inserts a debate on the topic "Is Individual Freedom Getting Out of Hand?" as part of an American problems class. The antagonists, an ACLU lawyer and the Citizens' League for the Preservation of American Values representative, provide for the readers cogent arguments on either side, against which, presumably, the events of censorship challenge may be interpreted.

This issue is escalated at the review committee's hearing. The challengers are well represented, including, in addition to African Americans who cite racism and "psychic injury to our children," feminists who claim *Huckleberry Finn* is sexist, its female characters portrayed as sentimental and foolish, as subservient to men. A third group, Parents for Moral Schools, finds offensive the references to Huck and Jim being naked on the raft, inferred as expressing a homosexual relationship, as well as Huck's lying and stealing, his disrespect toward religion, and his poor use of grammar.

The defenders of the book rely principally on arguments of freedom under the First Amendment to read and discuss controversial thoughts. They argue against legitimizing the power of censorship, giving anyone the power to decide what books are right for others to read: "It never is just one book, once you give out the power to go after books." Additional points underscore the moral sense of the text in its totality and the humane morality of Huck Finn in his efforts to save Jim from slavery, even if it means going against the social norms and religious persuasions of the day.

After the review committee votes 4-3 in favor of removing the book from the curriculum and limiting library access to it, the former librarian decides to reveal to Barney the past events, Moore's "sneaky censorship," that led to her resignation. Mr. Moore's attempt to censor the story fails. Its publication heats up the local controversy and garners national publicity, including a broad array of television coverage. On a national talk show, Kate Roth, an outspoken student with feminist ideals, argues:

> Freedom is a seductive word, and it can be a dangerous word. In the name of freedom of thought, should schools be allowed to put poison in children's minds by making them prejudiced[?] . . . if [schools] are supposed to teach what is right, then, of course, they *must* have the authority to say that certain books are wrong and harmful and cannot be allowed in the classrooms and the library.

Deirdre Fitzgerald responds,

> Oh, of course, freedom can be dangerous. It is dangerous. But the alternative is worse, far worse. Look at all the countries around the world where the people are told by their governments what they can say and what they can read, and what they can't. All the countries where people are afraid that their very inner thoughts might become known and get them into terrible trouble.

Eventually, the school board votes to reverse the decision of the review committee, upholding the use of the book in the curriculum and the library. Mr. Moore is reprimanded; the school board president considers the expiration date of Moore's contract. Moore, however, is not disturbed. He contemplates the probable results of the next school board election, which he believes will vindicate him.

CENSORSHIP HISTORY

The assignment in 1990 of *The Day They Came to Arrest the Book* to seventh-grade American history classes in Burley Middle School, Albemarle County, Virginia, caused the parents of two students to challenge its use. The Albemarle County school board reviewed their request.

The parents' objections focused on two central issues: the approach to teaching the First Amendment and the challenges to authority. The parents charged that the book, which was used as a supplementary text in the study of the First Amendment, "backs into the First Amendment. Students should study the basics about the First Amendment and then study issues surrounding it." Further, the book was seen as offering "an inflammatory challenge to authoritarian roles. The principal in the book is a sneaky book killer, and a teacher is obsessed beyond the point of reason with the First Amendment." The parents argued that the book challenged parental authority.

Other parents spoke in favor of the teacher's approach to the First Amendment, asserting that it motivated students to learn. Support was stated for the educators' training and experience in choosing appropriate materials.

The Albemarle County school board voted to retain *The Day They Came to Arrest the Book* as a supplementary text. The novel was used to teach about the First Amendment in 1990; however, the teacher used another unit in 1991.

FURTHER READING

Hentoff, Nat. *The First Freedom: The Tumultuous History of Free Speech in America.* New York: Delacorte Press, 1980.
Newsletter on Intellectual Freedom 40 (1991): 18.
"Officer, Arrest That Book." *Washington Post*, October 7, 1995, p. A29.
Standbury, Beth. "Parents Air Concerns over Books." *Charlottesville Progress*, October 15, 1990, pp. B1, 2.
———. "Parents Seek Removal of Supplementary Books." *Charlottesville Progress*, September 26, 1990, pp. A1, 12.
Zimorski, Thomas (formerly principal of Burley Middle School). Telephone conversation. December 1994.

DECENT INTERVAL

Author: Frank Snepp
Original dates and places of publication: 1977, Canada; 1977, United States
Publishers: Random House of Canada; Random House
Literary form: Nonfiction

SUMMARY

An Insider's Account of Saigon's Indecent End Told by the CIA's Chief Strategy Analyst in Vietnam, this extended subtitle reveals Frank Snepp's purpose in *Decent Interval.* A large measure of his disclosure exposes aspects of strategy and battlefield encounters of both North Vietnam and South Vietnam forces. He also recounts the thinking and activities of the men who shaped these strategies. A significant focus interwoven in these accounts is the making of American policy, its operation, and the chief actors in Saigon and Washington. The title's "decent interval" refers to the accusation of critics against the assistant to the president for national security affairs, Henry Kissinger, with reference to the January 1973 cease-fire agreement: "that he had never meant for the agreement to work anyway, but was merely trying through its convolutions and vagaries to assure a 'decent interval' between the American withdrawal and a final fight to the death between the two Vietnamese sides."

The author, too, is a player, as the subtitle reveals. In the text, he identifies his activities and attitudes; however, he is the on-the-spot observer and documenter, his "spot" being one of the upper floors of the United States Embassy in Saigon where the CIA had its central operation. The time period for the core of the book is from October 1972 through April 30, 1975, the date when the last evacuation helicopter pulled off.

By October 1972, American troops had largely been withdrawn from Vietnam. "Vietnamization," that is, the transfer of responsibility for managing and protecting the country to the South Vietnamese, had become the basis of United States policy. Despite this policy, the United States, through its ambassador and CIA station chief who had "manipulated and penetrated" South Vietnam president Thieu's government, was still controlling the situation.

On January 28, 1973, a cease-fire agreement went into effect. Signed in Paris for the United States by Secretary of State William Rogers, it had been negotiated by Henry Kissinger, starting in early 1969. The treaty was significantly flawed. Both political and military issues were unresolved. The problem of who would rule South Vietnam was ignored, though it did provide for a process of political evolution. Technical aspects vital to the cease-fire's enforcement were also omitted: nondesignation of control of disputed territory; an imprecise date for enacting such control; nonestablishment of "legal" limitations for providing additional supplies; and reinforcement for communist troops in South Vietnam. The postwar strategy of "equilibrium," which was to lead to a stalemate and a live-and-let-live attitude on both sides, was thrown off balance from the start. "At no point did [Kissinger] seriously consider the alternative of promoting a genuine coalition arrangement. To have done so would have meant abandoning the ideal of a non-Communist South Vietnam to which he and Nixon remained committed."

Overshadowing these flaws were those of the process itself. Both Kissinger and Nixon had "continued to bombard [President] Thieu with threats and promises in a relentless effort to bring him to heel." After Thieu reluctantly agreed, Kissinger neglected to inform him of changes in the document effected subsequently. During the negotiations, Kissinger made secret commitments to both combatants: continued U.S. support to South Vietnam; suspension of U.S. reconnaissance flights over North Vietnam; and withdrawal of all American technicians within a year. If either commitment had become known to the opposite combatant, or to the American people, each might have withdrawn support and questioned Kissinger's diplomacy.

As the events unfold from the maneuvering to establish a cease-fire to the final collapse of South Vietnam and the American evacuation, three individuals are portrayed in a negative light. As suggested by the discussion of the cease-fire accord, Kissinger, who was elevated to the position of secretary of state in 1973, is the first of these. Two particular traits are expressed: his "penchant for the virtuoso performance," a determination to do everything himself, which led him to fail to delegate oversight responsibilities of Vietnam activities; and his "addiction to secrecy." He was not candid or honest with Thieu and other South Vietnam officials, nor did he reveal to Congress the commitments he had made (which required congressional approval). He is shown to be impatient with CIA assessments that do not support his position and direction; in later months, against evidence to the contrary, he maintained a position that a negotiated truce with the intervention of the Soviet Union or China could be achieved. Accusing his critics of being self-serving, he is identified as being "so inflexible on so many issues—or so intolerant of debate." These attributes and this perceived goal caused significant delays in activating the evacuation procedures, leading to the chaos of the final days and the failure in meeting "moral" obligations to those Vietnamese who had worked with United States officials.

Five months after the cease-fire in June 1973, Graham Martin became Kissinger's hand-picked ambassador to Saigon. His personality and character traits combined with his perceptions and beliefs are defined as counterproductive to the operation of the embassy and handicaps to the final mission: evacuation. Supremely confident in himself, he was conscious of his status and demanded the rights and respect of hierarchy; he was sensitive to any slight and held a grudge against any "insubordination," transferring those who questioned his opinions or judgments. He used deception with Congress and the press to further his political purposes. Fervently anticommunist, he sought additional aid to bolster the Thieu government and army while hiding their faults and weaknesses, so as to convince Congress of the worthiness of such action. Believing in the probability of a negotiated peace, along with Kissinger, he assiduously discounted increasingly persuasive evidence that questioned this view.

Thomas Polgar, the CIA section chief, Snepp's immediate superior, is also identified as falling victim to the belief that additional aid would save South Vietnam and that a negotiated peace was imminent. He, too, was blindsided, so that he put aside evidence that did not support his position. Despite his strong anticommunist beliefs, Hungarian-born Polgar was successfully duped by the Hungarian delegation to the International Commission of Control and Supervision; the communist group received information from him ostensibly in its role as intermediary with the North Vietnamese, while supplying him with false information that fed his false expectations.

The thrust of most of Snepp's book is the final offensive, in its several stages, of the North Vietnamese forces from mid-December 1974 through April 1975 and the retreat and eventual defeat of the South

Vietnamese armies. In conjunction, he offers extensive details of the evacuation experiences of the Americans and their associated South Vietnamese personnel.

Two significant images are revealed. The North Vietnamese leadership carefully planned the military offensive, establishing details and options. Data gleaned from the memoirs of General Van Tien Dung, who commanded the North Vietnam army, indicate frequent and precise consultations and reassessments so as to adapt strategies to the dynamic situation. In contrast, the South Vietnamese leadership, though anticipating an attack, was in a reactive mode. Planning was global; decisions were delayed, partly because the leaders were operating under a "borrowed vision" (i.e., dependence on Americans), partly because there was limited coordination, and the choices threatened their egos and their status. Decisions seemed not to be based on analysis of the ability to accomplish selected strategies. The military situation was also handicapped by contradictory shifts in strategy in midstream. The South Vietnamese army's defeat was further encouraged by several ineffective, corrupt commanders.

Fearing that Saigon would be surrounded and isolated with his major divisions on the outlying boundaries, Thieu issued a belated order for them to withdraw to new positions. Given the conditions identified above, the result was havoc. When Dung recognized what was happening, he moved expeditiously to take advantage of the situation. Two armies were cut off; another was surrounded while attempting to defend two northeastern coastal cities. The evacuation of these cities in the area north of Saigon, especially Danang, was chaotic and in some respects disastrous. This "unraveling" occurred during March 1975.

The "ides of March," however, did not sufficiently forewarn Saigon. Anticipating that the serious situation would at last convince Congress to agree to the aid requested and that negotiations would take place to forestall the attack, Ambassador Martin stonewalled necessary arrangements for evacuation of the city. Though the war around Saigon heated up in early April, even Washington officials did not resolve their position to exert pressure on Martin to expedite the evacuation until mid-April. Martin, who had thwarted efforts to plan the evacuation, stalled further, essentially effecting the panic and chaos that resulted.

Snepp's heroes are the men who worked around these delaying orders and exerted their energies and imagination to establish an evacuation plan and to put it into motion. Among others, he applauds General Homer Smith and Colonel Bill Legro, the DAO (Defense Attache's Office) intelligence chief, and Legro's staff. Heroes also are the many men who put their energies and lives on the line to initiate (sometimes against orders) and operate the evacuation process, including officials of the embassy and other staff personnel. Praised also are the fixed-wing and, subsequently, the helo-lift pilots who flew in and out continuously under heavy pressure and the marines on the ground who were the last Americans to evacuate.

The book poses a pair of interlocking issues that evolve from these events. Kissinger establishes a political-moral view: He was convinced that the United States had to show some support for South Vietnam "as a surety for American prestige abroad"; he argued that if the United States did not, other nations, Israel, for example, would doubt U.S. consistency. He is quoted in a press conference: "There is also a moral question for the United States, a question of whether when an ally with whom it has been associated for ten years wishes to defend itself, it is the United States that should make the decision for it by withholding supplies."

A second issue is expressed time and again in the text: What was the responsibility of the United States to safeguard South Vietnamese who had worked closely with the embassy, the CIA, and other agencies? Many, including Snepp, felt a deep moral obligation to evacuate these associates and friends—"our people"—to save them from certain abuse at the hands of the Communists. Others were unconcerned; their personnel were left to fend for themselves when the Americans departed. Still others, like Polgar, caught up in false expectations, placed their local collaborators in jeopardy by waiting too long. Indeed, this was the "real" disaster referred to earlier. While the near disaster was averted when the Americans were evacuated, many of these South Vietnamese personnel were left behind because the evacuation procedure was delayed by both Saigon and Washington officials. Time ran out.

CENSORSHIP HISTORY

In a postscript to his basic text, Snepp reveals the "cover-up and the cosmeticizing of events" by the administrations; he specifically identifies Kissinger, Polgar, and Martin in this regard. He is directed to "fill out an affidavit which in effect attributed the breakdown of the evacuation to 'local enemy action.'" He refused to sign it. Having been denied an opportunity to prepare a "damage assessment," criticized for presenting a "full-fledged commentary on what had taken place," and realizing that the agency's precensorship would contravene his intention of revealing what had actually happened in Vietnam, Snepp made a critical decision:

> Because of its continued assaults on my integrity, and its reluctance to deal candidly with the Vietnam issue. . . . I also resolved not to submit my manuscript to the agency for clearance and censorship, as all former employees-turned-author are required to do. In my view, if the CIA could officially leak to the press to whitewash its role in Vietnam, it had forfeited the right to censor me in the name of security or national interest.

The preparations to publish *Decent Interval* were conducted in an atmosphere of secrecy; it was issued in November 1977.

In February 1978, the U.S. Department of Justice filed a civil suit in federal district court against Snepp, asserting a breach of contract, that is, the agreement signed by all CIA employees to "not . . . publish . . . any information or material relating to the agency, its activities or intelligence activities generally, either during or after the term of employment . . . without specific prior approval by the agency." A concurrent factor is the requirement of nondisclosure of any classified information related to the agency. The U.S. Justice Department sought an injunction requiring prepublication review of future writing and damages, that is, a constructive trust—the confiscation of all royalties from the sale of the book. Snepp, in response, filed papers that the suit violated his First Amendment rights, a case of "prior restraint on protected speech."

During the trial, government lawyers argued that trust and confidence in the CIA had been undermined by Snepp's publishing without permission. Further, in response to Snepp's claim that there was no violation of security, the government claimed that it, not the individual, had the right to decide whether there was such a violation. Snepp's claim of nonviolation of security was not contested.

U.S. District Court (Eastern Division of Virginia) judge Owen R. Lewis in June 1978 found that Snepp had "willfully, deliberately and surreptitiously" breached his position of trust with the CIA and the secrecy agreement. Publication of his book had "caused the United States irreparable harm and loss." He enjoined future breaches of this secrecy agreement and imposed a constructive trust on Snepp's royalties (estimated as $60,000 by Robert L. Bernstein, president of Random House). Thus, the contract factor superseded the issue of revelation of classified information, emphasizing the agency's prepublication right to review.

The Fourth Circuit Court of Appeals (Judges Harrison L. Winter, J. Dickson Phillips, and Walter Hoffman) in March 1979 concurred with the findings of the district court with regard to the breach of contract and the CIA's prepublication right to review; it upheld the injunction against future violations of this obligation. However, the appellate court rejected the constructive trust, asserting that the confiscation of all of Snepp's royalties was improper punishment. Such damages would have been proper only if he had disclosed classified information. "In other words, the court thought that Snepp's fiduciary obligation extended only to preserving the confidentiality of classified material."

The U.S. Supreme Court in February 1980, having been asked by Snepp to review the ruling of the U.S. Court of Appeals that upheld the validity of the CIA contract, responded to the case with an unsigned opinion; it did not formally grant a review or hear arguments. The restraints on CIA employees were upheld: The secrecy agreement is a judicially enforceable contract that applies to classified and unclassified information. Snepp "deliberately and surreptitiously violated his obligation to submit all materials for prepublication review"; a former agent cannot rely on his own judgment about what information is detrimental against the "broader understanding [of the CIA] of what may expose classified information and confidential sources. . . ." Further, it reversed the court of appeals and upheld the district court with regard to the constructive trust of all of Snepp's royalties.

The dissenting opinion written by Justice John Paul Stevens (concurred in by Justices William J. Brennan, Jr., and Thurgood Marshall) argued that the purpose of the secrecy agreement was "not to give the CIA power to censor its employees' critical speech, but rather to ensure that classified, nonpublic information is not disclosed. . . ." Further he argued that granting to the government a constructive trust over Snepp's profits was "unprecedented and drastic relief." Justice Stevens noted that the rule of law the Court announced with this ruling was not supported by statute, by the contract, or by the common law.

> The Court has not persuaded me that a rule of reason analysis should not be applied to Snepp's covenant to submit to prepublication review. Like an ordinary employer, the CIA has a vital interest in protecting certain types of information; at the same time, the CIA employee has a countervailing interest in preserving a wide range of work opportunities (including work as an author) and in protecting his First Amendment rights. The public interest lies in a proper accommodation that will preserve the intelligence mission of the Agency while not abridging the free flow of unclassified information. When the Government seeks to enforce a harsh restriction on the employee's freedom, despite its admission that the interest the agreement was designed to protect—the confidentiality of classified information—has not been compromised, an equity court might well be persuaded that the case is not one in which the covenant should be enforced.

This case was the first to make it illegal for an American intelligence official to publish any information, secret or otherwise, that had been gleaned from official sources. Further, while upholding the more draconian of the earlier rulings, that of the U.S. District Court—a lifetime gag order and confiscation of earnings—the Court had in effect lowered the standard of prior restraint in all First Amendment cases. Its ruling in the UNITED STATES–VIETNAM RELATIONS, 1945–1967 ("Pentagon Papers") case of 1971, the controlling precedent, had effectively barred prior restraint, excepting concrete demonstration of a real and immediate threat of irreparable harm to national security. In effect, the new standard permitted constraint if a publication imperiled the "appearance" of reliable government official secrecy.

Subsequent to the ruling of the Supreme Court, Snepp petitioned for a rehearing so that arguments could be presented. This appeal was denied in April 1980. On August 21, 1980, Anthony Lewis reported that Snepp had paid a fine of $116,658.15 to the government—all that he had earned. He still owed $24,000, which he had promised to pay as soon as he could borrow it.

On March 3, 1980, not quite a month after the Supreme Court's decision against Frank Snepp, the Justice Department sued John R. Stockwell for the profits obtained from his book, *In Search of Enemies: A CIA Story*. Its text accuses the CIA of lying to Congress and the public about its covert military activities in Angola in 1975–76. Stockwell, a former CIA employee, had been chief of the agency's task force in Angola. The book was published in 1978.

Given the Supreme Court judgment against Snepp, on July 25 Stockwell agreed to pay any profits from future sales. The government allowed Stockwell to keep past earnings of about $40,000, which he had already spent. Stockwell, who did not admit to violating his secrecy agreement, agreed to submit future manuscripts for prepublication review by the CIA.

The CIA also targeted Philip Agee by seeking profits from two of his books, *Dirty Work: The CIA in Western Europe* and *Dirty Work II: The CIA in Africa*. (Agee's INSIDE THE COMPANY: CIA DIARY was not included in this suit.) The Justice Department in mid-February attempted to halt the publication of *Dirty Work II* before realizing it was already for sale in several Washington, D.C., bookstores.

FURTHER READING

Carmody, Dierdre. "Ex-Aide Challenges CIA's Secrecy Suit." *New York Times*, March 9, 1978, p. 19.

Eder, Richard. "Why Decisions in Snepp Case Disturbs Publishers." *New York Times*, March 11, 1980, sec. 3, p. 5.

"Ex-CIA Agent and U.S. Settle Suit over Profits from Book." *New York Times*, June 28, 1980, p. 14.

Green, Jonathon, and Nicholas J. Karolides, reviser. *The Encyclopedia of Censorship, New Edition*. New York: Facts On File, 2005.

"High Court Backs CIA in Curb on Articles Its Employees Write." *New York Times*, February 20, 1980, p. 1.

"High Court Ends Snepp's Fight to Keep Royalties." *Publishers Weekly* 217 (April 25, 1980): 18, 23.

Hurwitz, Leon. *Historical Dictionary of Censorship in the United States*. Westport, Conn.: Greenwood Press, 1985.

"Judge Rules Snepp Violated Contract and Must Forfeit Profits on Book." *New York Times*, July 8, 1978, p. 8.

Kaplan, Steven H. "The CIA Responds to Its Black Sheep: Censorship and Passport Revocation—The Cases of Philip Agee." *Connecticut Law Review* 13 (Winter 1981): 317–96.

Lewis, Anthony. "The Price of Secrets." *New York Times*, August 21, 1980, p. A27.

Morro, Anthony. "Judge Says He Thinks Ex-Official of CIA Violated Secrecy Pact." *New York Times*, June 22, 1978, p. 12.

———. "Reporters' Notebook: Alarums and Explosions at Ex-Agent's Trial." *New York Times*, June 23, 1978, p. 8.

———. "Trial Over CIA Book Raises Rights Issues." *New York Times*, June 19, 1978, p. 15.

———. "Turner, Testifying in Snepp Case, Says Book by Ex-Agent Has Hurt CIA." *New York Times*, June 21, 1978, p. 15.

Newsletter on Intellectual Freedom 27 (1978): 67, 100, 124; 28 (1979): 81, 110; 29 (1980): 48, 53–54.

Oliver, Malcolm. "Appeals Court Upholds CIA Secrecy Pact in Snepp Case." *Publishers Weekly* 215 (April 2, 1979): 24, 26.

Snepp, Frank. *Irreparable Harm: A Firsthand Account of How One Agent Took on the CIA in an Epic Battle over Free Speech.* New York: Random House, 1999.

———. "On CIA Secrecy, News Leaks and Censorship." *New York Times*, March 3, 1978, p. 25.

———. "Postscript." *Decent Interval.* New York: Random House, 1977.

"Stockwell Settles with CIA to Keep Profits from Book." *Publishers Weekly*, July 11, 1980, 16, 18.

"Third Ex-CIA Agent Sued by U.S. for Profits." *New York Times*, March 4, 1980, p. 13.

Weaver, Warren, Jr. "Justice Department to Sue Author of CIA Book." *New York Times*, February 15, 1978, p. 21.

DID SIX MILLION REALLY DIE?
THE TRUTH AT LAST

Author: Richard Harwood
Original date and place of publication: 1974, United Kingdom
Publisher: Historical Review Press
Literary form: Nonfiction

SUMMARY

Richard Harwood's central purpose in *Did Six Million Really Die? The Truth at Last* is to reveal that the claim that 6 million Jews were exterminated by the Nazi Germans is "the most colossal piece of fiction and the most successful of deceptions." In this context, Harwood (a pseudonym of Richard Verrall, a British neo-Nazi writer) asserts that the Jewish people themselves have benefited: "Every conceivable race and nationality had its share of suffering in the Second World War, but none has so successfully elaborated it and turned it to such great advantage."

A second significant assertion stated in Harwood's introduction is that any form of nationalism—the existence of the nation-state—is discouraged by reactions to the question.

> Thus the accusation of the Six Million is not only used to undermine the principle of nationhood and national pride, but it threatens the survival of the Race itself. It is wielded over the heads of the populace. . . . Many countries of the Anglo-Saxon world, notably Britain and America, are today facing the gravest dangers in their history, the danger posed by the alien races in their midst. Unless something is done in Britain to halt the immigration and assimilation of Africans and Asians into our country, we are faced in the near future, quite apart from the bloodshed of racial conflict, with the biological alteration and destruction of the British people as they have existed here since

the coming of the Saxons. In short, we are threatened with the irrecoverable loss of our European culture and racial heritage.

German National Socialist policy toward the Jews is explained. Identifying Jewish persons among the leadership of revolutionary movements in Germany as being "disproportionately prominent," including Karl Marx himself, the Nazi solution to the problem was to legislate against them, depriving them of their influence, and to encourage their emigration—not their extermination. "Never at any time had the Nazi leadership even contemplated a policy of genocide towards them." Prewar detention was "used for . . . political opponents and subversives—principally liberals, Social Democrats and Communists of all kinds, of whom a proportion were Jews."

Among the emigration plans were the establishment of Madagascar as a national homeland for the Jews, a main plank of the Nazi Party platform before 1933; immigration to Palestine under the Schacht Plan of 1938; and immigration to other European nations. "By 1939, the consistent efforts of the German government to secure the departure of Jews from the Reich had resulted in the emigration of 400,000 German Jews from a total population of about 600,000, and an additional 480,000 emigrants from Austria and Czechoslovakia, which constituted almost their entire Jewish populations." The Madagascar Plan as a "final solution" continued after the onset of World War II, serious negotiations with the French being conducted in 1940 after the defeat of France. In the context of this discussion, Harwood asserts that "the term 'Final Solution' meant only the emigration of Jews, and also that transportation to the eastern ghettos and concentration camps such as Auschwitz constituted nothing but an alternative plan of evacuation," the latter destinations replacing Madagascar.

The situation of the Jews in Germany changed significantly after the war began in response to the September 5, 1939, declaration of war issued by Chaim Weizmann, the principal Zionist leader, on behalf of the world's Jews. This authorized, with "ample basis under international law," the internment of the Jewish population in Germany "as a hostile force." Two purposes are identified: to prevent unrest and subversion for reasons of military security and, later, to use Jewish detainees for labor in the war effort. The latter is used as an argument against intended genocide—"a senseless waste of manpower, time and energy while prosecuting a war of survival on two fronts." The industrial plants and factories at Bergen-Belsen and Auschwitz are cited as examples.

Throughout the text, Jewish population figures are identified and questioned to prove that "reliable statistics . . . especially those relating to emigration are sufficient to show that not a fraction of six million Jews could be exterminated." Harwood cites the *Chambers Encyclopedia*'s "total number of Jews living in pre-war Europe [as] 6,500,000." Then he tallies the prewar emigration numbers from all countries, those who fled to the Soviet Union after 1939, and those living in neutral countries, totaling approximately

3.45 million. Thus, "around 3 million Jews in German-occupied Europe is as accurate as the available emigration statistics will allow." He argues that the majority of the 2.1 million Russian Jews and an additional 260,000 in the Baltic states were evacuated eastward as German armies approached, and that according to one source, the president of the American Jewish Council for Russian Relief, "two million Jews were thus saved." Another source, the Jewish journalist David Bergelson, confirms this estimate by indicating that 80 percent of these Jews had been rescued, and Philip Friedman in *Their Brother's Keeper* (1957) indicates "at least a million." Jews survived in the very crucible of Nazi hell, writes Harwood, "while, subsequently, the official figure of the Jewish Joint Distribution Committee is 1,559,600."

Another focus is on the exterminations themselves. Harwood describes the first accusations by Polish Jew Rafael Lemkin in his book *Axis Rule in Occupied Europe* (1943) as "fantastic exaggerations." The testimony of Dr. Wilhelm Hoettl, a "highly dubious person," is discredited, his "proof" being something that Adolf Eichmann had "told him." Harwood argues the absence of evidence: "the fantastic and quite groundless assumption throughout is that transportation to the East, supervised by Eichmann's department, actually meant immediate extermination in ovens on arrival." Documentary evidence, he asserts, is lacking in William Shirer's "generally wild and irresponsible book" *The Rise and Fall of the Third Reich*, as well as in Roger Manvell and Heinrich Frankl's *The Incomparable Crime* (1960). The former states the order "apparently was never committed to paper—at least no copy of it has yet been unearthed. It was probably given verbally to Göring, Himmler, and Heydrich, who passed it down . . ."; the latter refers to "secret discussion." The minutes of the Wannsee Conference, January 20, 1942, where the final details of the plan to exterminate the Jews were supposed to have been made, in the words of Manvell and Frankl, "are shrouded in the form of officialdom that cloaks the real significance of the words and terminology that is used."

Harwood also rejects the "confessions" at the Nuremberg Trials as having been secured by torture. He refers to the officers of the elite guard unit SS Leibstandarte Adolf Hitler, who "were flogged until they were soaked in blood, after which their sexual organs were trampled on as they lay on the ground," and to the "notorious" Malmedy Trials of private soldiers, who were "hoisted in the air and beaten until they signed the confessions demanded of them." The confessions of SS captain Dieter Wisliceny, Gestapo chief in Slovakia, and SS general Otto Ohlendorf, chief of the Security Service, who commanded the Einsazgruppe D in the Ukraine, also were obtained by torture; the former was "reduced to a nervous wreck" and became addicted to uncontrollable fits of sobbing for hours on end prior to his execution. The testimony of SS general Erich von dem Bach-Zelewski and other former German officers is termed "spurious" and "fraudulent"; Bach-Zelewski, threatened with execution because of his suppression of the revolt by Polish partisans at Warsaw, August 1944, was "cooperative" on the assurance of leniency.

The case of Auschwitz is projected in two ways: denying the wholesale gassing of Jews and providing favorable statements about life conditions. These overlap in the account given by Theis Christopherson in "The Auschwitz Legends: An Account of His Experiences."

> I was in Auschwitz from January 1944 to December 1944 [to research the production of synthetic rubber]. After the war I heard about the mass murders which were supposedly perpetrated by the S.S. against the Jewish prisoners, and I was perfectly astonished. Despite all the evidence of witnesses, all the newspaper reports and radio broadcasts I still do not believe today in these horrible deeds. . . . I never observed the slightest evidence of mass gassings. Moreover, the odour [sic] of burning flesh that is often said to have hung over the camp is a downright falsehood . . . the smell of molten iron was naturally not pleasant.

While a detailed summary is not given, Harwood notes that Christopherson provides "facts about camp routine and the daily life of prisoners totally at variance with the allegations of propaganda." Harwood further discounts the myths created by the "blending fragments of truth with the most grotesque of fantasies and impostures," as in Olga Lengel's "absurd" *Five Chimneys* (24,000 corpses handled every day); Commandant Rudolf Höss's "catalogue of wild exaggerations" testimony, "a mindless monotone as he stared blankly into space" (16,000 people a day); and Gerald Reitlinger's estimates in *The S.S.: Alibi of a Nation* of 6,000 a day, which would total more than 5 million by October 1944.

> The exterminations at Auschwitz are alleged to have occurred between March 1942 and October 1944; the figure of half of six million, therefore, would mean the extermination and disposal of about 9,400 people per month for thirty-two months—for over two and a half years. This kind of thing is so ludicrous that it scarcely needs refuting.

An alternative scenario is provided by two documents. Harwood refers to Margaret Buber (*Under Two Dictators*, 1950), who provides a contrasting image. Having experienced two years of brutal and primitive conditions—squalor, disorder, and starvation—in a Russian prison,

> she found Ravensbrück to be clean, civilized and well administrated. Regular baths and clean linen seemed a luxury after her earlier experiences, and her first meal of white bread, sausage, sweet porridge and dried fruit . . . She observed, too, that the barracks . . . were remarkably spacious compared to the crowded mud hut of the Soviet camp. In the final months of 1945, she experienced the progressive decline of camp conditions, the causes of which we shall examine later.

The second document was a report of the International Committee of the Red Cross (ICRC), indicating, Harwood reports, that working inmates received "a daily ration even throughout 1943 and 1944 of not less than 2,750 calories." The internees were under regular medical care and could receive parcels of food, clothing, and pharmaceutical supplies from the Special Relief division of the Red Cross. The testimony of other individuals, including SS judge Dr. Konrad Morgan of the Reich Criminal Police Office, Communist leader Ernst Ruff, Polish underground leader Jan Piechowiak, and Dachau food service worker Berta Schirotschin, is noted in support of these claims.

The decline of camp conditions in 1945—the "unavoidable chaos"—is attributed to the saturated bombing by the Allies, effectively paralyzing the transport and communication system of the Reich; starvation resulted from interrupted food deliveries. Overcrowding resulted from prisoners being evacuated eastward before the advance of Russian troops; as a consequence, a "ferocious" typhus epidemic broke out in March 1945, leading to the "death camp" reputation of the Belsen camp. It is "these conditions that are represented in the photographs of emaciated human beings and heaps of corpses which the propagandists delight in showing, claiming, that they are victims of extermination."

Also included in this text are segments on the Warsaw Ghetto, Treblinka Fabrications, Best Seller Hoax (*The Diary of Anne Frank*), Death Camps Behind the Iron Curtain, and Fake Photographs. One of the concluding segments, "The Truth at Last: The Work of Paul Rassinier," a French historian, who has "expose[d] the dishonest and reckless distortions concerning the fate of the Jews by a careful statistical analysis." Because Rassinier had "experienced life" in the German concentration camps, he is acknowledged as a credible researcher. The final pages reject the "enormous fraud" of the "six million falsehood, and reiterate emigration as the final solution."

CENSORSHIP HISTORY

Ernst Zündel, a German émigré to Canada and a successful graphic artist, dedicated himself to redeeming the reputation of his fellow Germans by publishing works through his Samisdat Publishing House and by distributing books, leaflets, newsletters, and audio- and videocassettes. Among these was a 1980 reprint edition of *Did Six Million Really Die?* Canadian law bars the import of materials considered seditious, treasonable, immoral, or indecent; so-called hate crime is included in these categories. Zündel was charged under S.181 of Canada's Criminal Code with "publishing false news"—the 1892 statute law forbids publication of statements known to be false or likely to cause injury or mischief to the public interest—and was tried in 1985 for publishing a booklet that denies official accounts of Nazis exterminating Jews in wartime prison camps. He was found guilty in 1985 and sentenced to

15 months' imprisonment, but the Ontario provincial appeals court reversed the verdict, ruling the district court judge had given improper instructions to the jury and had improperly excluded defense evidence.

Zündel was retried in 1988. At the outset of this trial, Judge Ronald Thomas took judicial notice, recognizing that the Holocaust is historical fact. Zündel was again found guilty; Judge Thomas described him as a hatemonger and a threat to Toronto's ethnic harmony, sentencing him to a nine-month jail term. Zündel appealed his conviction to the Supreme Court of Canada arguing that S.181 infringed upon freedom of expression guaranteed under 5.2(b) of the Canadian Charter of Rights and Freedom. Ruling in 1992 (*R. v. Zündel*), the Supreme Court in a 4-3 decision held that section 181 of the Criminal Code was indeed unconstitutional as a violation of the right of freedom of expression guarantees. The code requires the expression to be nonviolent; the court found *Did Six Million Really Die?* to be nonviolent. Thus, Zündel was acquitted.

Zündel's legal problems did not end with this verdict. Within days, the leaders of the Canadian Jews accused him of hate propaganda under Canada's hate law. However, on March 5, 1993, Ontario Provincial Police announced Zündel could not and would not be charged with incitement or race hatred. However, Canada's Human Rights Tribunal heard a case against him starting in 1997; it ruled in January 2002 that Zündel's Web site violated its prohibition against hateful speech—it "viciously targeted Jews on the basis of their religious and cultural associations"—and ordered the site to be shut down. It noted that its decision proves a "symbolic value in the public denunciation" of Zündel's Holocaust-denial views as well as educational and deterrent benefits.

Having spent two years in custody in Canada because he was considered a security threat, Zündel was extradited from Canada to Germany in 2005 to face trial for inciting racial hatred and Holocaust denial. The yearlong trial was stopped in November 2005 for three months; the judge complained that Zündel's defense lawyers "were deliberately and unnecessarily trying to prolong it." Indeed, one lawyer was subsequently excluded from the trial because she signed her correspondence to Zündel with "Heil Hitler."

Zündel was found guilty on 14 counts "for inciting racial hatred and denying that the Nazis murdered six million Jews." He received the maximum sentence of five years in prison. The judge, Werich Meinerzhagen, identifying Zündel as a "dangerous agitator, a rabble-rouser and haranguer" and an admirer of Adolf Hitler," asserted that he was ordering the harshest sentence because the state had "the right and the duty to protest the basic principles of the law." Zündel's supporters portrayed him as a "peaceful advocate of the right to free speech who was being denied that right."

Publishing or distributing neo-Nazi or Holocaust-denial literature, including *Did Six Million Really Die?* is illegal in Germany. Zündel was convicted during a 1991 visit to Germany for inciting racial hatred and ordered to pay a fine equivalent to $9,000. Zündel created a Holocaust-denial Web site, access to which was available on three Internet providers in Germany. In 1996 incitement charges against these providers was considered, leading Deutsche Telekon's online service, Germany's largest provider, to block its 1 million subscribers from gaining access to the server in California where Zündel had posted his tracts. (This block prevented access to more than 1,500 other sites on that part of the network.) CompuServe has not blocked the server. It is unclear how such laws can be enforced in cyberspace.

Did Six Million Really Die? itself has been criticized as to its accuracy. Chief among its critics, Deborah E. Lipstadt, in *Denying the Holocaust: The Growing Assault on Truth and Memory*, asserts that Harwood has revised history to "transform the Nazis into supporters of emigration." She claims that the immigration of Jews to Madagascar was never included in the Nazi Party platform prior to 1933, and was not mentioned until the late 1930s. She also specifies that the Nazi slogan was *Jude Verrecke*, or "perish Judah," not "emigrate Judah," as Harwood states. Furthermore, she argues that emigration was vigorously applied to push the Jews out of Germany, but the intent was not "benign" but "diabolical"—to sow seeds of anti-Semitism abroad.

Lipstadt quotes the full text of *Chambers's Encyclopedia* regarding the total prewar Jewish population of Europe to reveal Harwood's misuse of statistics and data.

> On the continent of Europe *apart from Russia*, whose western provinces also suffered terribly, only a handful of numerically unimportant communities in neutral countries escaped and of the 6,500,000 Jews who *lived in the Nazi-dominated lands in 1939*, barely 1,500,000 remained alive when the war ended six years later.

Chambers specifies the year 1939 and excludes the Jewish population in the Soviet Union and non-occupied countries. In addition, Lipstadt points out that

> Errors of omission occur in the account of Margaret Buber in *Under Two Dictators:* Buber explicitly describes conditions that had broken down long before 1945. She made specific reference to executions, starvation, and terrible conditions that existed prior to the Allied raids of 1945. In addition to relating how inmates died as a result of being "beaten, starved, or frozen to death in the punishment cells," she made specific references to gas chambers and executions. Referring to the crematorium in the camp, she wrote the "SS men were fond of telling us that the only way we should ever leave Ravensbrück would be 'up the chimney.' "

Lipstadt insists that this flaw applies as well to the ICRC report, which makes note that Nazi-rule Jews had been transformed into "outcasts condemned by rigid racial legislation to suffer tyranny, prosecution, and systematic extermination." The ICRC was not permitted to intervene in their behalf.

FURTHER READING

Connoly, Kate. "Holocaust Denial Writer Jailed for Five Years." *Guardian* (International), February 16, 2007, p. 21.
Lipstadt, Deborah E. *Denying the Holocaust: The Growing Assault on Truth and Memory.* New York: Free Press, 1993.

DOCTOR ZHIVAGO

Author: Boris Pasternak
Original dates and places of publication: 1957, Italy; 1958, United States
Publishers: Giangiacomo Feltrinelli Editore; Pantheon Books
Literary form: Novel

SUMMARY

Doctor Zhivago spans the life of its title character until his death before age 40. It spans also a vital period in Russia's history from just after the turn of the 20th century, through the 1917 revolution, the civil war, and up to the terror of the 1930s. An epilogue set during World War II (after Zhivago's death) affords a glimpse of the future as well as closure to the past.

Yurii Andreievich Zhivago is orphaned at a young age. His father, a rich industrialist who abandoned the family even before the early death of his mother, has squandered the family fortune. Yurii is brought up in the home of a cultured, intellectual family in Moscow. He studies to become a physician, earning esteem as a diagnostician, and marries Tonia, the daughter of his "adoptive" parents. A child is born, but their lives are sundered with Zhivago's induction into the military during World War I.

During this military service, Zhivago meets Lara—Larisa Feodorovna Antipova (née Guishar), the daughter of a Russianized, widowed Frenchwoman. He had encountered her twice during adolescence. Trained as a nurse, she is searching for her husband, Pasha—Pavel Pavlovich Antipov—who is rumored to have been injured or slain in battle. Lara carries with her the weight of a past bereavement—the loss of her innocence and purity, having been seduced during adolescence by the lecher Komarovsky, her mother's lover. Yurii and Lara gradually become friends before she departs for her home in Yuriatin in the Ural region and he to his family in Moscow.

"Big news! Street fighting in Petersburg! The Petersburg garrison has joined the insurgents! The revolution!"

This announcement closes part one of the text and ushers in dramatic changes in the lives of the protagonists and of Russia.

Upon his return, Yurii finds Moscow disordered and depressed. Fuel and firewood are scarce. Maintaining subsistence is challenging and enervating.

Yurii attempts to reestablish his medical practice and his social circle, but he finds himself feeling alienated from associates and friends. He begins to recognize the dangers to the family in the new political environment because of their past status.

After a brutal winter, Tonia and her father, with the help of Yurii's half brother, Evgraf, convince Yurii they must escape Moscow to Varykino, Tonia's grandfather's estate, a dangerous choice because it identifies them with its past. The long train ride in a freight car is itself dangerous; they must endure frequent searches. Along the way within sight of Yuriatin, Zhivago briefly meets the infamous Strelnikov, the fanatic officer of the Red Army. (He is in reality Lara's missing husband, who has taken the rumors of his death as an opportunity to change his identity.)

The Zhivagos' life at Varykino takes on an aura of peace and obscurity. Yurii's sense of peace, however, is broken by two events: his love affair with Lara, upon whom he chances in the Yuriatin library—he is tormented by this egregious betrayal of Tonia, whom he also loves; and his being conscripted at gunpoint by the Red partisans, the Forest Brotherhood, to replace their slain surgeon. This imprisonment lasts over a year before he is able to escape on his fourth attempt.

After a six-week walk, Yurii, black with grime, emaciated and weak, arrives in Yuriatin to find Lara. He learns his family has returned to Moscow and, later, that they have been exiled from Russia. However, because she is the wife of Strelnikov, he and Lara are not safe. They disappear to Varykino. Their paths separate when she escapes to a Pacific province, expecting him to follow. He stays behind, deceiving her for her safety, determined to go to Moscow. Before he leaves, Strelnikov arrives, seeking his wife and a hideout. The next day, anticipating capture, he shoots himself.

In Moscow again, Yurii seems unable to commit himself to either his work or his writing. Even his efforts to obtain an exit permit seem half-hearted. He deteriorates physically and intellectually. At last, with the help of his half brother, Evgraf, he takes initial steps toward revitalizing himself. He dies, however, of a heart attack, en route to a new hospital position.

Among those gathered for the wake is Lara. She has come to Moscow on an urgent mission—apparently to locate her and Yurii's lost child; for memory's sake she had come to visit her husband's student apartment, the very one in which Yurii had last lived. After the funeral, she stays to help Evgraf with Zhivago's papers—and then disappears.

> One day Larisa Feodorovna went out and did not come back. She must have been arrested in the street at that time. She vanished without a trace and probably died somewhere, forgotten as a nameless number on a list that afterwards got mislaid, in one of the innumerable mixed or women's concentration camps in the north.

Within this plot, Pasternak introduces an array of characters from all walks of life and portrays their life situations. He provides vignettes of personal and sociopolitical events to evoke the historical and human landscape. In the prewar, prerevolutionary period, the prosperity and charm of upper-class life is contrasted with that of the working class—musical evenings and a Christmas party of dancing, feasting, and card playing in opposition to an angry railroad strike and Cossack dragoons attacking and massacring a group of peaceful demonstrators.

In contrast to the Varykino interlude, a creative haven of happiness found in family, the rewards of work and the beauty of nature, there is the surrounding devastation—the shelled and burned villages viewed from the train, caught between the crossfire of the White and Red armies or destroyed because of uprisings. The peasants live in misery, their lives disrupted, their sons taken as soldiers.

Yurii's initial response to the revolution anticipates the "promises of a new order" as it had been expressed in the idealized revolutionary thought of 1905 and 1912–14; he had been cognizant of the oppression in czarist Russia. Subsequently, he is provoked by less familiar ideas growing out of the reality of a savage and ruthless war and the upheaval of the "soldiers revolution led by those professional revolutionaries, the Bolsheviks." While en route to Moscow, a train companion, a revolutionary, counters Zhivago's suggestion that the country must return to "relative peace and order" before embarking on "dangerous experiments":

> "That's naive. . . . What you call disorder is just as normal a state of things as the order you're so keen about. All this destruction—it's a natural and preliminary stage of a broad creative plan. Society has not yet disintegrated sufficiently. It must fall to pieces completely, then a genuinely revolutionary government will put the pieces together and build on completely new foundations."

Zhivago resists this siren song; as the train approaches Moscow, to him the war and the revolution seem empty and meaningless while his home, intact and dear, is meaningful.

Episodes of the revolution in progress provide glimpses beyond the surface devastation and deprivation and cast a shadow over the occasional political rhetoric of revolutionaries. A village is gratuitously shelled from an armored train because it is adjacent to another that had refused to adhere to the party line. Another is raided and burned to the ground for withholding food from the army, food supplies needed by the villagers. The second stage of the revolution is characterized as one of suspicion and intrigue—informers acting on hatred and envy, ready to destroy individuals in the "name of higher revolutionary justice."

Yurii, too often outspoken for his own safety, expresses his antagonism:

> "But, first, the idea of social betterment as it is understood since the October revolution doesn't fill me with enthusiasm. Second, it is so far from being

put into practice, and the mere talk about it has cost such a sea of blood, that I'm not sure that the end justifies the means. And last—and this is the main thing—when I hear people speak of reshaping life it makes me lose my self-control and I fall into despair."

In another passage, he questions marxism and its leaders:

"Marxism a science? . . . Marxism is too uncertain of its ground to be a science. Sciences are more balanced, more objective. I don't know a movement more self-centered and further removed from the facts than Marxism. Everyone is worried only about proving himself in practical matters, and as for the men in power, they are so anxious to establish the myth of their infallibility that they do their utmost to ignore the truth. Politics doesn't appeal to me. I don't like people who don't care about the truth."

At the height of his energy and power, Yurii dreams of living his life wholly and individually, "living by the sweat of [his] brow." He responds to "man's eternal longing to go back to the land." He embraces the beauty around him and loves to experience and express. He wants his freedom expanded, not diminished; he struggles to protect his privacy and the personal basis of his life. Zhivago maintains these values, although his lust for life and his life ebb away.

The epilogue, set during World War II in 1943, features two of Zhivago's childhood friends. They have been in Soviet penal camps but are now officers in the army. They mull over their past, the atrocities they have experienced. One of them comments on an important aspect of the Soviet system:

"I think that collectivization was an erroneous and unsuccessful measure and it was impossible to admit the error. To conceal the failure people had to be cured, by every means of terrorism, of the habit of thinking and judging for themselves, and forced to see what didn't exist, to assert the very opposite of what their eyes told them. This accounts for the unexampled cruelty of the Yezhov period, the promulgation of a constitution that was never meant to be applied, and the introduction of elections that violated the very principle of free choice. And when the war broke out, its real horrors, its real dangers, its menace of real death were a blessing compared with the inhuman reign of the lie, and they brought relief because they broke the spell of the dead letter."

CENSORSHIP HISTORY

After the death of Stalin, during the Khrushchev period when the Kremlin eased its censorship policy in 1953, Boris Pasternak began writing *Doctor Zhivago*. He had been silent during the Stalinist period, which had "muted creative individualism and exacted conformity to party dictates from all writers." Upon submitting it to the State Publishing House and receiving a positive reaction, the author sent a copy to Giangiacomo Feltrinelli Editore, a publisher in Italy. Subsequently, the State Publishing House had second thoughts and condemned the book; its "cumulative effect casts doubt on the validity of the Bolshevik Revolution which it depicts as if it were the great crime in Russian history." Pasternak was required to request the book's return from the Italian publisher for "revisions." The publisher refused.

When Pasternak was awarded the Nobel Prize in literature in 1958, he was forced to refuse the award: "[I]n view of the meaning given to this honor in the community in which I belong, I should abstain from the undeserved prize that has been awarded me."

The Soviet Union denounced the award—and the Swedish judges—as a "purely political act hostile to our country and aimed at intensifying the cold war" and as a "hostile political act for recognizing a work withheld from Russian readers which was counter-revolutionary and slanderous." The award had "nothing in common with an impartial assessment of the literary merits of Pasternak's work." Further, Pasternak was expelled from the Soviet Union of Authors and deprived of the title "Soviet writer."

In 1986, reflecting more open policies under Mikhail Gorbachev, issues of censorship and bureaucratic interference in literature were debated at the Eighth Soviet Congress of Writers. A reform-oriented slate was elected to the leadership position of the Writers' Union. Its chief announced that the state publishing agency was considering the publication of *Doctor Zhivago*. It was published at last in 1988. In February 2004, publishers in Russia announced that the entire 11-volume set of Pasternak's writings would be published; two volumes were already available, including poems written between 1912 and 1959, the nine others being anticipated by February 2005. Nevertheless, *Doctor Zhivago* remains controversial with regard to its status as a school reading—whether it should be optional rather than required. The Education Ministry's recent ruling is that dissident writers be optional reading in schools.

In the United States in 1964, a Larchmont, New York, bookstore owner revealed that a man who identified himself as a member of the John Birch Society had telephoned to protest the great number of "subversive" books on the shelves. The titles identified were *Doctor Zhivago*, INSIDE RUSSIA TODAY by John Gunther, and DAS KAPITAL by Karl Marx; he also mentioned a book by Nabokov and a Russian-English dictionary. He threatened that if these and other "un-American" books were not removed from view, the society would organize a boycott of the bookstore. The editor of the *Newsletter on Intellectual Freedom* advised the bookseller, "Don't take any guff from a self-appointed censor." Presumably, the bookstore owner did not.

FURTHER READING

Chalidze, Valery. *To Defend These Rights: Human Rights and the Soviet Union.* New York: Random House, 1974.

Conquest, Robert. *The Pasternak Affair: Courage of Genius.* Philadelphia: J. B. Lippincott, 1962.

Haight, Anne Lyon, and Chandler B. Grannis. *Banned Books: 387 B.C. to 1978 A.D.* 4th ed. New York: R. R. Bowker, 1978.

Newsletter on Intellectual Freedom 13 (1964): 81; 35 (1986): 196–97; 36 (1987): 72.

Payne, Robert. *The Three Worlds of Boris Pasternak.* Bloomington: Indiana University Press, 1961.

Rowland, Mary F., and Paul Rowland. *Pasternak's Doctor Zhivago.* Carbondale: Southern Illinois University Press, 1967.

Salisbury, Harrison E. "Triumph of Boris Pasternak." *Saturday Review* 41 (November 8, 1958): 22.

Simmons, Ernest J. "Russia from Within." *Atlantic Monthly* 202 (September 1958): 67–68, 72.

THE DRAPIER'S LETTERS

Author: Jonathan Swift
Original dates and place of publication: 1723–1724, Ireland
Publisher: John Harding
Literary form: Nonfiction

SUMMARY

The full title of the collected volume of Swift's seven letters is *The Drapier's Letters to the People of Ireland against receiving Wood's Halfpence.* The seven letters written by an author identified as M. B. Drapier but signed simply M. B. were published separately; the author notes in the first letter that he has a "pretty good Shop of Irish Stuffs and Silks."

The letters react to the controversy created by the king of England's granting of a patent on July 12, 1722, to William Wood, authorizing him to "coin during the next fourteen years 360 tons of copper, which at the rate of 30d. to the pound weight of pure copper made the total value of the currency thus authorized 100,800 pounds." Granted in London, there was no consultation with the Irish parliament; initial protests, including the unanimous protest of both houses of parliament of Ireland, were ignored. Subsequent letters, a negative pamphlet, and further official and constitutional protests heated up the controversy, at which time Swift's pseudonymous letters intervened.

The tone and direction are set in the first letter, printed in March 1723 and addressed to the "Shop-Keepers, Tradesmen, Farmers, and Common-People of Ireland." Drapier/Swift issues a call for resistance: "I do most earnestly exhort you as *Men*, as *Christians*, as *Parents*, and as *Lovers of your Country*" to reject the half-pence issued by Mr. Wood, "*a mean ordinary Man, a Hard-Ware Dealer.*" Simply, the people of Ireland should not accept the coins in exchange for goods or services or, if forced to, they are urged to ask 10 times more so as to obtain payment equal to the goods or services.

A central argument is their value. The metal of the coins is debased; a brazier evaluating the worth of the metal would not give more than a penny for a shilling of Wood's coins. In contrast, an estimate of the value of comparable English coins would not lose more than a penny in a shilling. Because the coins are so debased, they will be easily counterfeited, thus allowing the kingdom to be flooded. Drapier/Swift predicts economic disaster since the money available to the people will be worthless.

Basic law of England is cited to support the resistance: Refusal "to accept the KING's Coin made of *Lawful Metal*" is punishable by imprisonment. Since Lawful Metal is defined as silver and gold coined by the king, refusal to accept Wood's coins, the *"Filthy Trash,"* is not treasonous. In the subsequent letter, Drapier/Swift reacts with considerable umbrage at a phrase in Wood's proposal to prevent objections to his coins: *"that no Person be OBLIGED to receive more than Five pence Half-penny at one payment."* Even the king of England does not prescribe how many brass coins a person is obliged to take; his patent does not authorize such an obligation, nor does the law establish such power.

The controversy about the coinage caused Wood to have a number of them assayed. In the second letter, dated August 4, 1724, Drapier/Swift disqualifies the assay as "impudent and insupportable." He asserts that Wood could easily have coined a dozen pieces of good metal to have these tested as representative samples, but they were indeed not representative. This assay is referred to as fraudulent.

In letter three, dated August 25, 1724, Drapier/Swift directs his correspondence to the nobility and gentry of the Kingdom of Ireland, seeking to gain their attention and support. While some arguments are repeated, as is the urging of the tactic of the coin's rejection, a political position is established herein. He reflects on the abridgment of freedom, since Ireland's parliament and its chief officers were not consulted about the proposed patent and the unanimous objection of both houses of parliament was ignored. The discrepancy of treatment of the Irish in contrast to the English is expressed. "Are [the people of Ireland] not Subjects of the same King? Does not the same *Sun* shine on them? And have they not the same *God* for their Protector? Am I a *Free-Man* in *England*, and do I become a *Slave* in six Hours by crossing the *Channel?"*

In this political context Drapier/Swift questions the declaration that Ireland is in "great want of Copper Money." He casts doubt on the witnesses identified to prove this need and asserts that the Irish nation, its parliament, privy council, and people are the appropriate judges of need. These have declared to the contrary.

Considerable agitation against Wood's coin was evident in late August and September 1724 in the form of petitions, declarations, and popular demonstrations. The former were made by individuals, by corporations of tradesmen, and by cities and towns. In this excited state of public opinion. Drapier/Swift's fourth letter was printed in October 1724, concurrent with the arrival of Lord Carteret, newly appointed as lord lieutenant. (The content of this letter is the immediate cause of action against the printer, John Harding, and of a proclamation offering 300 pounds to discover the author.)

Condemned are the assertions that the dispute of the *"King's Preroga-tive"* indicates the Irish are *"grown Ripe for Rebellion, and ready to shake off the Dependency of* Ireland *upon the Crown* of England." Drapier/Swift argues that the power of the king to give a coining patent is not questioned; the Irish are asserting that *"nobody is obliged to take [the coins]."* He also questions the language and implications of the word "dependence," that Ireland is a "Depending Kingdom . . . that the People of Ireland is in some State of Slavery or Dependence different from those of England." He cites a statute made under Henry VIII to the effect that whoever is the king of England and his successors is also king of Ireland and that the two kingdoms shall be "forever knit together under one King." This is not a dependency relation-ship. He notes, however, that his allegiance is to the "King my Sovereign, and on the Laws of my own Country," denoting that should a pretender come to the throne in England, he would fight to keep him from becoming king of Ireland.

A personal comment in the letter leads to a potential affront. Drapier/ Swift offers compliments to the character and accomplishments of Lord Carteret. These are followed by a litany of corrupt practices used by his predecessors to manage or delude. These include expectations of service supported by threats, lures of promises and conviviality, indications of favors upon compliance, and false reports of invasion to create a need for unity.

The next two letters, addressed to Lord Viscount Molesworth, dated December 14, 1724, and published December 31, 1724, and Lord Chancellor Middleton, dated October 26, 1724, reiterate and support the positions taken earlier. Their tone is of defense against the proclamation; they attempt to establish the virtue and honest intentions of the author, while strengthen-ing his arguments. The Middleton letter was not published until 1735, after Swift apparently was advised against it because he had signed his own ini-tials. The last letter, addressed to both Houses of Parliament, was to have been issued on September 7, 1725, but on August 31 Swift received news of Wood's surrender of his patent; he stopped publication.

CENSORSHIP HISTORY

Censorship of Drapier/Swift's letters was initiated by Lord Carteret, the newly appointed lordlieutenant of Ireland. He may have taken umbrage at the com-pliments in the context of satirically veiled expressions of corruption; he may also have recognized an undercurrent of bitterness toward England within the context of the controversy of Wood's coin that might "encourage the dangerous notion of independency." He proposed to the Privy Council that the printer be prosecuted and a proclamation be issued offering a reward for information about its author. The Privy Council did not accept this proposal against the entire letter, but only against "several seditious and slanderous paragraphs."

Having been apparently forewarned, Swift deferred the publication of his *Letter to the Lord Chancellor Middleton*. Although he did not stand trial, the printer, John Harding, was apprehended and imprisoned, as was his wife, Sarah. Swift wrote on November 11, 1724, and distributed *Seasonable Advice*, a letter addressed primarily to the grand jury, outlining the charges and providing arguments against the charges. Carteret deemed it "scandalous and seditious"; these libels were brought before the grand jury by the attorney and solicitor general, but the grand jury would not make a charge either of the whole or of particular passages. Because of the uproar occasioned by *Seasonable Advice* and the grand jury proceedings, the cases against other seditious libels, among them the Harding case, were dropped. No jury would have found him guilty. (Harding printed the *Letter to Lord Viscount Molesworth* in December 1724; he died in April 1725.)

FURTHER READING

Davis, Herbert. "Introduction." In *The Drapier's Letters to the People of Ireland against Receiving Wood's Halfpence*, by Jonathan Swift. Oxford: Clarendon Press, 1935.

A DRY WHITE SEASON

Author: André Brink
Original dates and places of publication: 1979, Great Britain; 1980, United States
Publisher: W. H. Allen and Co.; William Morrow and Company
Literary form: Novel

SUMMARY

The central text of *A Dry White Season* is preceded by a "Foreword" and concluded by an "Epilogue." In these a narrator introduces himself and reveals his relationship to Ben Du Toit, the protagonist. They had been college roommates but not close friends; Ben had been reserved and quiet, somewhat of a loner, studious, and, as evidenced on one occasion, dedicated to principle and honor. They had had but infrequent correspondence and one visit over a 30-year period. Then came the urgent phone call, the hurried meeting, steeped in mystery and paranoia, and the request to receive his papers. Two weeks later, Ben Du Toit was dead, the victim of an accident, a hit-and-run driver. His story, encompassing a few months more than a year, is drawn from these papers.

South Africa is seething with disquiet, an undercurrent of agitation that will lead to the Soweto riots. The repressive tactics of the police, the killings, beat down the blacks, feeding their hatred and rebellious spirit. Jonathan Ngubene, 17-year-old son of Gordon and Emily, disappeared during the riots.

His parents could not find him among either the dead or the wounded. Weeks later, he is reported to have died of natural causes while in detention, though it is also reported that he never was in detention, a contradiction, too, of the information that he had been seen in the hospital, his head swathed in bandages.

These events are a prelude. The action truly begins with the death of Gordon Ngubene while in detention. Dissatisfied with the evident deception of the Security Police, Gordon had insisted on tracing leads to discover the truth about his son's death. "How can I have peace again if I do not know how he died and where they buried him?" This does not come to pass, however, for the day after he obtains crucial signed statements from two witnesses, he, too, is imprisoned for questioning by the Special Branch. Weeks later, he is found dead in his cell, reportedly having committed suicide by hanging himself with strips of blanket.

Ben Du Toit had become involved from the beginning. Gordon, who worked as a janitor in the school where Ben taught history and geography, had come to him for help in locating Jonathan. As a white, Ben could get answers. Now, Emily repeats the plea when Gordon is first detained. Ben is certain it is a mistake, that Gordon will be released. He is reasonable; he is hopeful. (To such a statement, a black character responds, "You're white. Hope comes easy to you. You're used to it.") He believes that justice will be served. He is wrong.

He agrees to help, thereby initiating the year-long travail down the road to failure, fear, and destruction. He sees a lawyer; he interviews Colonel Viljoen of the Security Police (Special Branch)—with two of his officers in attendance—to praise Gordon's character and assert his innocence. He arranges for a court order and a hearing on the basis of leaked information and evidence of Gordon's mistreatment. To no avail.

After Gordon's death, driven by his innate humanity and by his failed assumption that even blacks can obtain justice, Ben struggles with the codes of his Afrikaner-white life, codes that are interwoven with the constraints of his Christian church. Viewing Gordon's body and the evident falsifying and censoring of evidence at the inquest of Gordon's death convince Ben of the actions he must take. What follows is the search for witnesses, for bits of evidence and, not entirely unexpectedly, a consciousness of surveillance of his activities. Surveillance gradually becomes more overt—obviously opened mail, harassing nighttime phone calls, graffiti painted on his house, shots through windows, and bombs by mail. His home is searched by the Special Branch officially and subsequently burglarized in an attempt to find the evidence he is amassing and in an effort to convict him. The final overt act against him is the "accident" that kills him.

The Special Branch appears to be ubiquitous. Its men are characterized as supremely confident of the right of their position and actions: safeguarding the nation—the party—against a Communist threat and a black menace. Their tactics range from veiled threats to overt brutality. Ben recognizes that all the persons who respond and supply information, even the least bit, are subject to reprisal: disappearance, banishment, jail, detention.

Ben's involvement affects incrementally his family and professional relationships. His wife, initially astonished and appalled by occasional black "visitors" at the door, becomes increasingly hostile and hysterical. At his school, Ben becomes a pariah, except for one young member of the staff, and eventually is forced to resign. Comments of his family members and friends reveal the social fabric, the attitudes of Afrikaners. A particularly vibrant set of responses resound from a photograph taken after the inquest's verdict when a distraught Emily, unable to speak, "simply threw her arms round [Ben's] neck and started sobbing on his chest. Her great weight caused him to stagger back and in order to keep his balance he put his arms round her." It was published on the front page of the Sunday paper over the caption, "The face of grief." By the end of the year his wife, Susan, has left him. Suzanne, his daughter, with whom he had frequently quarreled over their clashing values, pretends a change of mind. Falling victim to her feigned understanding of his drive, he reveals the hiding place of his documents to her. Within days it is ransacked.

Stanley Makhaya, a black undercover worker, Ben's go-between with Emily and others of the black community, asks the question, what about the children? Several vignettes—beyond the Soweto riots—amplify the image of the minds and emotions of black children. Robert, Jonathan's younger brother, rejects Ben and his offer of help because Ben is white. " 'Go to hell! First you kill him, now you want to help.' He stood swaying like a snake ready to strike, overcome by all the hopeless, melodramatic rage of his 16 years." In another instance, a desperate Ben drives into Soweto alone to seek Stanley. In Soweto, he is beaten by a group of black youths; managing to get into his car, he is barely able to complete his escape under the bombardment of rocks.

Ben's own teenage son provides a comparable but alternative expression. The only family member to speak for his father's defense with regard to the infamous photograph, Johan fights a gang that taunts him about his father's being a "nigger lover." A subsequent conversation with Ben reveals Johan's intensity of feeling.

> Johan spoke with difficulty because of his swollen mouth, but he was too angry to be quiet: "I tried to reason with them, but they wouldn't listen. They don't even know what you're trying to do."
>
> "You sure *you* know?" [Ben] had to ask him, however hard it was.
>
> He turned his head so that his only good eye could look squarely at me. "Yes, I know," he said impetuously. "And only if you stop doing it I'll have reason to be ashamed of you."

Johan and Robert and the other black children have lost their innocence at a young age. In his fifties, Ben faces his innocence directly for the first time. Responding to Stanley's question, "Why bother about Gordon?" he reveals:

> "Because I knew him. And because—" He didn't know how to put it; but he didn't want to avoid it either. Lowering his glass, he looked into Stanley's eyes. "I don't think I ever really *knew* before. Or if I did, it didn't seem to directly concern me. It was—well, like the dark side of the moon. Even if one acknowledged its existence it wasn't really necessary to live with it." A brief moment, the suggestion of a smile. "Now people have landed there."

Though he is told he has a choice—to ask questions or to accept that "such things happen"—Ben believes he has none: " . . . once in one's life, just once, one should have enough faith in something to risk everything for it. . . . All I know is that it won't be worthwhile having a soul left if I allow this injustice to stand." Toward the end, after the beating by the black youths, Ben recognizes that he cannot choose not to intervene, for such inaction would be denial and a mockery of his principles. Yet, he also recognizes the right, indeed the need, of blacks to reject him and his efforts. Their need is to "discover for themselves their integrity and affirm their own dignity." His rationalization for his actions is the possibility of bridging the gulf between the races. He acknowledges at the end a philosophy professor's earlier words, whose repetition suggests thematic significance: "There are only two kinds of madness one should guard against, Ben. One is the belief that we can do everything. The other is the belief that we can do nothing."

CENSORSHIP HISTORY

On September 14, 1979, South African censors banned *A Dry White Season*, branding its author a "malicious writer." Prior to its being banned, André Brink had attempted to circumvent the censors by having his book sent directly to subscribers without submitting it for review. About 3,000 copies had already been mailed before this date.

Soon after the Publications Appeal Board had "reinstated" Nadine Gordimer's novel BURGER'S DAUGHTER in October 1979, it also "reinstated" *A Dry White Season*.

Brink's book *Looking on Darkness* has also been banned, and in August 1979 *Rumours of Rain* was declared by censors to be "offensive but not undesireable." In this case, the censorship board had delayed action on the book for six months before releasing its decision.

FURTHER READING

Gordimer, Nadine. "The Unkillable Word." *The Essential Gesture: Writing, Politics & Places.* London: Jonathan Cape, 1988.
Newsletter on Intellectual Freedom 28 (1979): 147.
"South Africa Bans Novel by Popular Africaner." *New York Times*, September 15, 1979, p. 4.

DU PONT: BEHIND THE NYLON CURTAIN

Author: Gerard Colby Zilg
Original date and place of publication: 1974, United States
Publisher: Prentice-Hall
Literary form: Biographical nonfiction

SUMMARY

Written with "the conviction that biography cannot stand outside history," *Du Pont: Behind the Nylon Curtain* represents the DuPont family over several generations set against significant historical and economic events. Before starting at the beginning in France during the French Revolution and the United States at the turn of the 19th century, the author introduces the readers to the Du Ponts from two angles: their wealth and the impact of their power.

Irénée du Pont, Jr., director of DuPont Company (and others), drives from his 70-room mansion on his 1,000-acre estate past several other DuPont estates; he passes buildings displaying the names and businesses controlled by members of the family. "The Du Ponts own the state of Delaware. They control its state and local government; its major newspapers, radio and TV stations, university and colleges, and its largest banks and industries, with four exceptions. . . ." The 50 DuPonts who make up the family's powerful inner core (of the 250-member inner circle of about 1,600 living members) "control over $150 billion worth of assets, greater than the annual Gross National Product of most nations. They own controlling interests in over 120 multimillion dollar corporations and banks, including some of the world's largest, to say nothing of their 170-year-old pet project, E. I. duPont de Nemours & Co." DuPont influence is also evident in Washington in both houses of Congress as well as in other positions of government in the past and present. Their wealth and power used to their own advantage have not been advantageous to Americans and to the United States.

With this power, "The Armorers of the Republic," as they like to call themselves, have helped drive America into world war, sabotaged world disarmament conferences, built deadly arsenals of atomic weapons and nerve gas, flirted with Nazis, and according to charges brought before a congressional committee, once were even implicated in an attempt to overthrow the United States government—at the same time managing to avoid paying their share of taxes.

Zilg's text expresses the interaction of wealth and power as well as the corruption of power to achieve wealth.

The DuPonts by the end of World War I were more infamously known as the "Merchants of Death." Within two years after landing in Newport, Rhode Island, on January 1, 1800, Eleuthère Irénée du Pont had initiated the gunpowder mill upon which the family's fortunes were spawned. Markets were readily available in an expanding United States; by 1811 the DuPont Company was the largest producer of gunpowder in the United States and charged the highest prices. The War of 1812, subsequent skirmishes and wars, explorations, and enterprises further enhanced DuPont's growth and profits. During the Civil War, the U.S. government purchased over $2.3 million worth of cannon and musket powder. World War I generated for them over $1 billion in gross income.

These profits were not made without cost to workers and to moral scruples. Employees worked long hours under dangerous conditions. Explosions resulting in their deaths were common. (Most often the reigning DuPont denied culpability, blaming workers' carelessness rather than faulty equipment or standards.) Increased rates of production fatigued workers and further endangered their lives. Their compensation was not commensurate with their efforts or with the DuPonts' profits. During the Spanish-American War, for example, with workers being paid 18 cents an hour, DuPont delivered 2.2 million pounds of powder at 33 cents a pound at a cost of only 8 cents a pound to produce. "That was a 320 percent profit, extortion in anyone's book." Comparably, during World War I, in 1915, the DuPonts lowered their price to 97 cents per pound (from one dollar) for smokeless powder, which cost only 31 cents a pound to produce. That year DuPont's net earnings reached an all-time high of $57.4 million.

Details of such profits and palatial living standards are juxtaposed with war's devastation—deaths and mutilations, working conditions, and workers' salaries. Relative to World War I, the DuPont Company held more than 100 war contracts, involving 85 percent of its business in the slaughter.

> Du Pont "soldiers" on the home front didn't have it much easier than their brothers overseas. While a dozen Du Ponts enjoyed an annual income of over $1 million during the war, workers at DuPont plants were paid only $1 an hour. With the depression and starvation of 1914 still fresh in their minds, 100,000 men, women, and even children swarmed into the plants, willing to risk violent death, injury, or chemical poisoning for that precious one dollar. Sixty thousand of them were housed in shanty barracks, dorms, boarding houses, or Du Pont-built "hotels." Working conditions were even worse. In Du Pont's Deepwater, New Jersey, plant across the river from Wilmington, workers died from poisonous fumes of the lethal benzol series, their bodies turning a steel blue. At the Penns Grove, New Jersey, plant workers were called "canaries"; picric acid had actually dyed their skins yellow. Picric acid poisons the mucous membranes of the respiratory tract, attacks the intestinal tract, and destroys the kidneys and nerve centers.

In the mid-1930s, concerted attempts were taken to cover up deaths and other physical and emotional effects occurring at the complex of poison gas plants at Deepwater, New Jersey, publicly identified as "dye works."

The label "merchants of death" grew out of these immediate situations piled onto the century-long activities of amassing profits from the misery of wars. A companion factor was the DuPonts' activities to foster wars, for example, by promoting with other industrialists the United States entry into World War I through the "infamous" National Security League.

> For two years before the declaration of war, the League, aiming to draw America into the conflict, published vicious attacks on congressmen who opposed entering the slaughter. When German submarine warfare threatened Du Pont munitions shipments, the League demanded that America defend her right to "freedom of the seas" and the right to sell military aid to Germany's enemy.

After the war, they promoted conflicts with sales of gunpowder and other munitions to European countries. This included secret rearming of Germany, despite the treaty forbidding it, and smuggling arms to Manchurian warlords in violation of an imposed embargo.

Wealth asserted and gained power: pressuring railroads for rebates for shipping business; buying up smaller powder firms after undercutting prices to bring them to their knees; bribes and payoffs to competitors' agents for inside information to effect buyouts; campaign contributions; buying votes; bribing congressmen and senators; threatening President William Taft; and using public relations propaganda and media control. Essentially, these tactics worked. With each accomplishment, power became more manifest, thus less easy to resist.

Similar power pressures are evidenced in DuPont's decision to diversify into chemicals and automobiles, including pressuring the British government for German patents and "buying" the government's alien property custodian, who sold hundreds of secret German patents confiscated from German firms to DuPont. An invitation to Pierre du Pont, who owned 2,000 shares of General Motors common stock, to assume the chairmanship of General Motors as a neutral arbiter between the GM corporation and its bankers led to the conquest of GM.

Political involvement was not new to the DuPonts in the 20th century, having been evident in behind-the-scenes maneuvers and contributions, at the national level primarily to the Republican Party ($2,980,755 from 1904 to 1972 as compared to $167,200 donated to the Democratic Party). Generally those involvements were in relation to the needs of their industry (e.g., to gain protective tariffs) or attempts to withstand constraints such as taxes. Political activities became more overt during President Franklin D. Roosevelt's New Deal in opposition to such issues as unionization, which had been successfully resisted by the DuPonts; disclosure of financial information for new stock issues; regulation of the securities market with the creation of the Securities and Exchange Commission; abandonment of a balanced budget, that is, deficit spending to assist citizens through publicly financed work projects; and rejection of the sales tax in favor of higher taxes on large incomes and inheritances.

Zilg includes an extended litany of frauds and immoral behavior, including high-level tax evasions and land taxes exemptions, using the loophole of classifying their estates as farm land; thus a normal assessment of $64,500 was reduced to $1,100. Another ruse is some 30 to 35 (as of 1963–67) tax-free foundations that are granted exemption from inheritance and income taxes. There are examples, too, of court cases centered on taxes with suggestions of collusion in their adjudication, often leading to results favorable to the DuPonts.

Among this litany of negatives is an occasional positive note. During the depression, for example, Pierre du Pont "initiated no direct reform on [his] own with regard to assistance to the unemployed." Alfred du Pont, then living in Florida, used his personal fortune to gather unemployed men and put them to work in public places. For two years, he paid them a daily "survival" wage of $1.25, totaling $400 a day. He wrote, "They [the Republicans] are not willing to obligate the government to take care of those out of employment, when it is patently their duty to do so." He was considered the family rebel.

The final chapter exposes a decline in the DuPonts' overt power as well as in the income level of the DuPont Company in conjunction with a resurgence of criticism. The government's successful General Motors antitrust case against them was a significant event in this regard as were the effects of inflation and competition. DuPont family focus on the DuPont Company had diminished; family holdings have diversified. More than 100 multimillion-dollar companies in which the DuPonts have a controlling interest are listed, along with many others in which they hold minority blocks of stock "important enough to exercise some measure of control." Sixteen pages of the book identify the influential DuPonts in the major cities around the United States and indicate their activities.

CENSORSHIP HISTORY

The author's accusation of censorship grew out of alleged pressure by DuPont Company executives on the Fortune Book Club. The Book-of-the Month Club had optioned *Du Pont: Behind the Nylon Curtain* to the Fortune Book Club, which it owns, for $5,000. However, after Harold G. Brown, a DuPont Company public relations spokesperson, called F. Harry Brown, executive vice president of the Book-of-the-Month Club, to indicate that his company considered the book "scurrilous and unfair" and "actionable," the book club canceled its plans to carry the book. The DuPont executive denied that the phone call was a threat. The Book-of-the-Month Club official denied that the phone call had influenced its action; he said he had subsequently read the book and, finding it "unpleasant," advised against it.

As a result, the publisher, Prentice-Hall, reduced its planned 15,000-copy first printing to 10,000. It also cut the advertising budget from $15,000 to $5,500.

Gerard Colby Zilg filed suit against both his publishers and DuPont, charging they had conspired to suppress his book. He claimed that his financial prospects were damaged because Prentice-Hall had been intimidated by the DuPont organization and had refused to hold a press conference to exploit the controversial nature of his text. He asked for $350,000 in compensation and $1 million in punitive damages for breach of contract.

In April 1982, U.S. District Court judge Charles L. Brieant cleared DuPont of any wrongdoing, saying there was "no evidence that Du Pont attempted to 'suppress' the book." He did, however, fine Prentice-Hall, ruling the publisher had breached its contract by "not printing enough copies, failing to advertise it, and letting it go out of print." He awarded Zilg only $24,250, the amount the judge felt Zilg had lost.

This ruling was unanimously reversed in September 1983 by the three-judge panel of the U.S. Court of Appeals for the Second Circuit. The decision, written by Judge Ralph K. Winter, affirmed the publisher's right to determine the size of the press run and its advertising budget; its obligation according to the decision, was to be "fair and reasonable" in promoting its books.

In 1984, *Du Pont Dynasty: Behind the Nylon Curtain* was reissued by Lyle Stuart, an independent publisher. An extended version, it seems also to be under boycott.

FURTHER READING

"Author Loses Court Ruling." *New York Times*, April 22, 1982, p. 30.
Berry, John F. "Du Pont Book Contract Breach Ruled by Judge." *Washington Post*, July 24, 1982, p. D9.
"Club Withdraws Book on Du Ponts." *New York Times*, January 21, 1975, p. 30.
McDowell, Edwin. "Publishing: Reversal of Ruling Troubles Authors." *New York Times*, September 16, 1983, sec. 3, p. 24.
Newsletter on Intellectual Freedom 29 (1980): 41; 31 (1982): 136–137; 32 (1983): 192–93.

FAIL-SAFE

Authors: Eugene Burdick and Harvey Wheeler
Original date and place of publication: 1962, United States
Publisher: McGraw-Hill Book Company
Literary form: Novel

SUMMARY

Now the world was living on two levels. There was an overt public level and a covert secret level. On the overt level the world's business proceeded serenely, innocently, and in its normal fashion: men worked, died, loved, and rested in their accustomed ways. But alongside this normal world, and ignored by it, the covert world went about its huge task of bringing two war plans to readiness. At that moment the covert, counter-poised world of war was in a waiting stage;

its war dance had come to a high level of preparation and then stood arrested, held in a miraculous balance, a marvelous intricate suspension brought about by suspicions, intentions, information, and lack of information.

This covert action has been initiated by an "accident": A small condenser in a Fail-Safe Activating Mechanism has blown. It is undetected by the two men whose task it is to monitor the functioning of the machine. The machine itself does not give any indication of malfunctioning as it is expected to do. The Fail-Safe Activating Mechanism is generally considered infallible by the United States military establishment.

The plot of *Fail-Safe* is straightforward. During a "routine" follow-up operation to identify the nature and purpose of an unidentified flying object on an intercontinental radar screen, after friendly clearance has been given, one group of six Vindicator Bombers, which had been sent to intercept the UFO, does not get the message to return. The blown condenser has flawed the system. Each bomber loaded with 20-megaton bombs crosses the Fail-Safe point and heads for Moscow at a speed of 1,500 miles per hour. They are on an attack course, "flying on orders . . . received by mechanical transmission."

The "accident," that is, the flight of the Vindicators beyond their Fail-Safe point, is discovered in the Omaha War Room instantaneously, but the military staff there cannot detect the cause—is it a flawed system or a madman? The assumption is made of the former cause—thus, a mistake, an "accident." Efforts to communicate with the pilots to recall them and of fighter planes shooting them down also fail.

All efforts having failed, the president of the United States (portrayed to resemble John F. Kennedy) telephones Premier Khrushchev to reveal the urgent situation, to detail the accident, to plead the nonhostile intentions of the United States. Khrushchev believes enough from the evidence not to order immediate retaliation, but he orders a war alert; he assumes Soviet planes will destroy the six Vindicators. This does not fully happen, even with the help of the Omaha War Room. As two Vindicators fly through the Soviet defenses, as the hours, then minutes tick away, with all key personnel listening, the president offers his last proof of American nonaggressive intentions: He will order a like number of bombs dropped on New York City moments after any Vindicator achieves its mission. Khrushchev feels obliged to accept the eye-for-eye destruction to prevent the retaliation of the people. The plot concludes with the bombs dropped on New York City, and the pilot, whose family is there as is the president's wife (dedicating a museum), commits suicide.

The issue of military appropriations and military preparedness emerges early in the story, introduced by Congressman Raskob of New York City. His criticism of military preparedness collides with the committed purposefulness of the Omaha War Room personnel, exemplified by General Bogan. His criticism is also measured against the spectacular display of the machinery and system for detecting and identifying presumed-to-be-hostile flying objects invading United States territory. The display includes the fighter planes sent to intercept the Vindicator bombers. Through the tension, the system works beautifully, the military appearing vindicated, until the condenser blows and the Fail-Safe mechanism fails. The assumption of the system's infallibility hovers over the ensuing events.

Centering the conflicts of the book is the antiwar/prowar debate. The prowar debate is sustained by historical-psychological arguments of its necessary existence; the antiwar position is charged by the foreknowledge of absolute devastation. The chief antagonists are Dr. Walter Groteschele and Brigadier General Warren A. Black. Groteschele argues probability and, thus, preparedness, a first-strike mentality: "The best armed, . . . the best bomb shelters, the best retaliatory capacity, the strongest defense, would have an ancient and classical advantage." Human error is discounted because of the elaborate checks and devices to prevent flaws in the mechanical system. Images of a thermonuclear first strike against the United States and the resultant surrender are used to encourage responses favorable to his position. General Black knows the reality of destruction. He urges against spending billions to develop a "military posture," recognizing the inevitable escalation on both sides. "The thing of piling bombs on bombs and missiles on missiles when we both have a capacity to overkill *after* surviving a first strike is just silly." His position is emphasized by the doomsday predictions of the world's annihilation in a nuclear war and the anticipated effects of retaliation strikes.

The stark potential of these arguments is brought home in the emergency consultations that follow the Vindicators' attack mission. Both the president, operating from the White House bomb shelter, and Premier Khrushchev, evacuated from Moscow, are cognizant of the ramifications. Some members of their staff exhibit trained "automatic" responses. Each is physically and emotionally unable to disengage his embedded responses and reacts without control. The issue is crystallized by Khrushchev in the final moments before the bombs are dropped on the two cities: "Yes, we both trusted these systems too much. You can never trust any system, Mr. President, whether it is made of computers, or of people. . . ."

Several ironies are expressed in the last chapters of the novel. The safeguards of both the American and the Soviet systems each act to ensure the success of the accidental attack mission. General Bogan, working with his counterpart Soviet general in a final human effort to mutually outwit the system and destroy the bombers, realizes how professionally alike they are. When their attempt fails, they address each other as "comrade" and "my friend." The final irony is that it is General Black who pilots the aircraft ready to destroy New York City—and himself. His final words to his copilots: "You are accomplices and I would be dishonest with you if I said otherwise. But the ultimate act is mine. I think it is worth it, for it is a chance, the only chance, for peace."

CENSORSHIP HISTORY

In 1963 Lee A. Burress, Jr., under the auspices of the Wisconsin Council of Teachers of English, conducted a survey of censorship challenges in the state. *Fail-Safe* was identified as having been challenged by a public school librarian. The objection: "undermines Americans' confidence in their defense system." While the specific result of this challenge is not identified, in his discussion of books "objected to on ideological grounds," he refers to books being "quietly removed," apparently to avoid controversy.

FURTHER READING

Burress, Lee A., Jr. *The Battle of the Books: Literary Censorship in Public Schools 1950–1985.* Metuchen, N.J.: Scarecrow Press, 1989.

———. "The Pressure of Censorship on Wisconsin Public Schools." *Wisconsin English Journal* 6 (October 1963): 6–28.

FIELDS OF FIRE

Author: James Webb
Original date and place of publication: 1978, United States
Publisher: Prentice-Hall
Literary form: Novel

SUMMARY

The two central protagonists of James Webb's *Fields of Fire*, Snake and Hodges, are introduced in the first chapters before they go to Vietnam, in 1968 and 1969 respectively. Snake, an urban, street-smart, natural fighter, is at odds with his world. Responding to a news photo and headline, "Marines Retake Citadel at Hue," he enlists, seemingly in reaction to his downhill situation; he discovers he has found his place.

> It was nothing as magical as discovering some secret part that had lain dormant, but rather that his energies had finally found their outlet. He had always fought, and now it was right to fight. He had never been coddled, and now it was weakness to have been coddled. And there was that hard core, the nucleus of ferocity which sustained him, and which no one else could dent. He could not be broken.

E. Lee Hodges, from rural Tennessee, culturally a man of quite different stamp, responds to family history: "a continuum, a litany. Pride. Courage. Fear. An inherited right to violence." Having for 15 years heard stories of his grandfather and father in wars, he is ingrained with the idea that "it was the fight that mattered, not the cause." Going to Vietnam was a natural outcome, an "issue of honor."

Vietnam and the Vietnam War, setting and event, are at the base of action and imagery. Lt. Hodges's third platoon of a Marine company is featured; he, Snake, and several others of his men are spotlighted, revealing their attitudes and their behaviors. Except for a brief prologue and a set of epilogues, the novel's plot represents the activities of the platoon over an eight-month period and the impact of the war on the platoon's personnel. These and the landscape they endure are, presumably, a microcosm of the United States military's experiences in Vietnam.

The platoon is not stable in its specific location; however, they operate in Quang Nam province at a fictional base, An Hoa. There is no "front" backed by a traditional rear base; there is little security that they are safely behind the lines. Rather, there is a sense of the area being surrounded; there is significant, constant infiltration of Viet Cong. The company moves from one location to another within the An Hoa Basin, sometimes on specific missions to ferret out and destroy a suspected enemy activity, sometimes, it seems, to maintain a presence and retain control. The platoon's operations encompass these offensive-defensive measures as well as activities defending their perimeter.

The combat episodes are intensely violent, with harrowing details. The men's fears are of the unexpected—the ambush, the savagery of weapons and the deceptiveness of the landscape and people. They also fear the incompetence of some officers and others among their own ranks. Ambushes occur both on the trail and in the relative safety of the perimeter. The numerous examples of sudden deaths or agonized bodies punctuate the pages:

> Big Mac reached over and lifted the ammo box, to show it to Cat Man. He straightened, the lid of the ammo box in hand, and—disappeared. At one moment he was stooping, grinning caustically to Cat Man, and in the next there was a violent rending of the earth, a belch of smoke and dust that sprayed half the platoon, the equivalent of a large artillery round impacting underneath him as the pressure-release detonator set off the booby trap. He did a full flip in the air. His rifle spun into the distance, a black baton. He landed where he had stood grinning to them only a half-second before, but now he was a scorched, decapitated ash heap that reminded them all of how very close they stayed to death, even on a boring day.
>
> Pieces of Big Mac pattered on the leaves and grass for several seconds, like gentle rain.

The platoon's personnel, racially integrated, are individualized. They range from the fearful Flaky, who ducks out of danger, absenting himself when needed, to Snake, who "seemed driven by a need to dominate this weed-filled existence that the others were merely submitting to." The focal members of Snake's squad (he provides the nicknames) include Cat Man, gentle and cautiously alert to details; Bagger, dependable but frustrated and given to complaining or worrying about his wife and child; good-natured Cannonball, shy and sensitive; Phony, whose innocent eyes and smile mark a basic amorality; and Senator (Goodrich), a Harvard dropout, an intellectual who is fraught with moral doubts and fears. This community of men, highly interdependent, fiercely loyal to each other (excepting Goodrich), is gradually decimated.

The countryside and its inhabitants are ravaged. Hillsides are "chewed and devoured," fields "porous with bomb and mortar craters," and treelines "torn out by bombs." Village life is totally disrupted: houses burned, livestock killed, and fields ruined.

> Far into one paddy a helicopter hovered in the rain, soaking a rice seedbed with aviation fuel that had been rigged to shower down in the rotorwash. In a few days the seedbed would be dead. The helicopter, remembered Hodges, was a part of Operation Rice Denial. If We Kill Off All The Rice, the logic ran, There Won't Be Any To Give To The Enemy. If The Enemy Doesn't Have Rice, It Will Have To Quit Fighting.

Hodges understands the rationale but reacts with concern that the villagers will starve. The villagers are dispersed and destitute. The expressed images are dualistic: prematurely aged women and dirty, numbed, scarred children; eyes of cold hatred toward the marines in contested territory.

Other features of the U.S. military operation come under scrutiny. The life and hazards of the infantry, the "grunts," are contrasted with those of the noncombatant officers and noncommissioned officers. Some officers design tactics that put the lives of the men in jeopardy, seemingly unwilling to acknowledge this factor. A colonel and first lieutenant who ordered and enforced from their underground command bunker a dangerous perimeter lookout post outside the barbed wire encirclement, which led to the deaths of three men of Snake's squad, are each awarded a Silver Star. There is corruption too. The sergeant major steals the beer and soda ration of the field troops and sells it for his own profit. The district chief in charge of the Vietnam resettlement village claims he has 500 people in the camp though he has but 200, then lines his own pockets from the sale of the extra 300 food rations.

The moral center of the novel, however, evolves from Goodrich's attempt to evade participation in killing and his alienation from his comrades. His behavior leads to the bitter ironies of the plot's denouement as well as his own change of perspective. Imbued with the war's immorality, he hesitates and withdraws from action. Sometimes he shoots above the heads of escaping Viet Cong, convinced that their civilian garb is real, disregarding "evidence" to the contrary. Immobilized by terror and self-regard, he doesn't help a comrade who is bleeding to death, despite the man's pleas for help. (This break in the marine code of honor to help a fellow soldier alienates him from his comrades.) The plight and misery of the civilians, especially the children, affects him. He finds nothing but tragedy and horror emerging from the firefights.

In this context he views his squad members as villains, murderers of women and children. Indeed, he officially accuses Snake and several others of atrocities when they undertake retribution for the execution deaths of Baby Cakes and Ogre by shooting two suspected Viet Cong who are disguised as civilians. It is in this context, too, on a fatal observation-post mission, disobeying Snake's instructions, lured by a smiling little girl, that Goodrich victimizes Snake, Bagger, Cannonball, Hodges, and himself. Several good men die; Goodrich loses a leg.

The novel's conclusion is embellished with irony. Snake gives his life to save Goodrich, who had failed to try to save another and who had been a detriment to the platoon's safety. Other examples emerge in the epilogues. Snake's mother, reflecting sadly on her son's death, is comforted by the ennobling of her son. She doesn't know that the anticipated and deserved Medal of Honor will never come; Goodrich's well-written accusation has caused it to be canceled. Hodges's young son, born to a beloved Japanese woman of Okinawa, is distressed by taunts of his peers about his forgetful father, who had abandoned him and his mother. His feelings are assuaged by his mother's words that Hodges had been a brave warrior, unafraid to fight for his country. The boy "with hushed determination and a fierceness" vows, "Then I too will be a warrior." Neither he nor his mother knows that Hodges has come to a different realization before his death:

> Hodges scratched his head, climbing the hill. I hate it. It's terrible. It's destructive. Nobody gives a rat's ass whether any of us live or die. They've sold us out back in the World. It makes me cry every time somebody gets screwed up. The damn civilians are all VC. It's so stupid any more I can't believe it.

The major irony, the moral evolution of the story, is Goodrich's changed perspective. Back at Harvard, he is haunted by images of Snake, Baby Cakes, and Hodges, by the pleas of his bleeding buddy. He recognizes the flaw in those, including himself, who criticized and even condemned the soldiers without considering their motivations and without understanding their experiences under fire. Having lived through Vietnam, he has the "standing" to evaluate them and the war's meaning. In the novel's concluding episode, an anti-Cambodia invasion rally, Goodrich repudiates the antiwar protesters for their nonsupport of the soldiers.

CENSORSHIP HISTORY

Fields of Fire, identified as "one of the best novels of the Vietnam War," was challenged in Fort Mill, South Carolina, in the fall of 1987. Jim Newman's efforts to have the book removed from the Fort Mill High School library were initiated when his 14-year-old son, a ninth grader, checked it out of the library. Newman objected to the strong language in the book, episodes of sexually explicit dialogue, and definite profanity. "I don't consider it an uplifting book," he said. Further, he claimed his objections were not based on religious beliefs. "This is strictly a decency issue." He said that it was hypocritical that the school would allow students to read a book that included descriptions of behavior not allowed in school.

After the complaint was aired with the high school principal and media specialist, according to district policy, an eight-member committee was appointed to review the questioned text. The committee, consisting of the high school principal, the media specialist, two English teachers, and four parents, recommended on a vote of 6-1 to keep the book on the library shelves.

Following policy in April 1988, Newman appealed the decision to the school board; he presented a petition signed by 55 parents requesting the book's removal. The next month, after having an opportunity to read *Fields of Fire*, board members voted to reject the request to ban the novel. They did, however, decide to consider setting up a "restricted" shelf for "controversial" books that would require parental permission before a student could check them out.

FURTHER READING

Buie, Lisa. "Attempt to Have Book Banned Makes National Group's Report." [Rock Hill] *Herald*, September 1, 1988, p. 2A.

———. "Fort Mill School Won't Ban Book." [Rock Hill] *Herald*, May 6, 1988, pp. 1, 14.

———. "Parents Want Book Removed from School." [Rock Hill] *Herald*, April 27, 1988, pp. 1, 19.

"Do Not Ban This Book." *Fort Mill Times*, May 4, 1980, p. 2.

Newsletter on Intellectual Freedom 37 (1988): 122, 178–179.

Palm, Edward F. "James Webb's *Fields of Fire:* The Melting-Pot Platoon Revisited." *Critique: Studies in Modern Fiction* 24 (1983): 105–118.

"Parent Wants Vietnam Book Removed from High School Library." *Fort Mill Times*, April 27, 1988, pp. 1, 3.

Puhr, Kathleen M. "Four Fictional Faces of the Vietnam War." *Modern Fiction Studies* 30 (1984): 99–117.

"Restricted List FMHS Library?" *Fort Mill Times*, May 11, 1988, pp. 1, 3.

THE FRAGILE FLAG

Author: Jane Langton
Original date and place of publication: 1984, United States
Publisher: Harper and Row
Literary form: Fable (in narrative form)

SUMMARY

Two visions of the flag introduce *The Fragile Flag*, one penned by James R. Toby, president of the United States, the other by Georgie Hall, a fourth grader from Concord, Massachusetts. The statements read, respectively: "The flag of our nation stands for a strong defense in a dangerous world. . . ." and "The flag means American people being friends with all other people. . . ."

Nine-year-old Georgie Hall gets an instant lesson on the hazards of nuclear warfare upon her parents' return from Washington, D.C., after their unsuccessful attempt to petition against President James R. Toby's proposed Peace Missile. That afternoon the family watches the president deliver a speech inviting the youngsters in the United States to enter a "What the Flag of My Country Means to Me" essay contest; a winner from each state will be invited for a day in Washington. Afterward, Georgie gets a lesson in the American flag: A contrast is evident between the one displayed by the president, its stars glittering with gold sequins, and the faded, possibly historical, flag that her father retrieves from the attic.

This awesome flag has a mysterious quality. The stars seem to draw a viewer into them, magically, creating a vision. The sensation is not merely startling, but breathtaking. When Georgie is enveloped by the mystery, she sees herself floating amidst the Milky Way; a second time she sees the Concord Minutemen defending the town against the British—and, then, a sudden flash of light, a roaring explosion, and a vision of Concord in ashes, gray flakes lifting from and swirling to the ground.

Georgie decides to enter the contest and write a letter that will cause the president to understand and stop the building of the Peace Missile. But she gets sick and misses the deadline. So, she determines to walk to Washington to deliver it: She will not be dissuaded. She does agree, however, to be accompanied by her stepcousins, Eddy, age 12, and Eleanor, age 15.

So begins what comes to be called the Children's Crusade. The trio is initially joined by Georgie's best friend, Frieda, a born organizer-leader, and Robert Toby, the self-effacing grandson of the president for whom Eleanor has romantic inclinations. Georgie's father charts their course: from Concord to Walpole, then Route 1, the Boston Post Road, all the way to Washington: 450 to 500 miles.

On the second day, three miles from Route 1, they are joined by Cissie from Eddy's class and her 14-month brother, who is in a stroller. One week into their journey, beyond Providence, Rhode Island, they are joined by another school group from Concord, which arrives by school bus, bringing their number to 64. After New Haven, en route to Bridgeport, Connecticut, after three days of rain, after arguments and irritation and a near mishap, after a discouraging vote by most of the group to quit, they are revitalized by a massive collection of 1,000 kids who have walked from Hartford, Poughkeepsie, Buffalo, and other nearby cities or bused from far away Illinois, Indiana, Kentucky, Tennessee, and Missouri. They gain more recruits along the way. By the time they reach Baltimore, they number 4,000 and are joined there by still another 4,000. When they enter Washington, D.C., they number 14,000 strong. Indeed, the world of children is on the move. Kids are marching on Paris, London, Amsterdam, Bonn, and New Delhi—and even, if rumor has it straight, on Moscow.

The route has not been easy. After the countryish atmosphere of the Massachusetts state highway, Route 1 is disappointingly ugly—billboard dominated, littered and heavily trafficked. Early on, the group encounters a motorcycle gang, who harass them and attempt to steal their backpacks. But eventually, as a result of newspaper coverage and then local and national television coverage, they come under the protection of first the Rhode Island State Police and thereafter other state police groups. In addition, in town after town, they enjoy the hospitality of church groups, school groups and community groups who graciously feed, house, and support them. These result from, first, newspaper coverage and, then, local and national television coverage. Their trek is applauded and marveled at; their goals are disseminated.

Meanwhile, the state winners of the president's contest, one by one, make their appearance and read their letters. They write of the beauties of their states (the letters have been carefully screened), but only the first two are allowed to speak their postscripts: " 'Please, Mr. President, I hope you change your mind about the Peace Missile' "; " ' . . . flag stands for being friendly to other people. You know, like it says in the Bible. . . . So maybe we shouldn't put that missile up there in outer space, right?' " In contrast to the children's visions, the president's sense of the flag is presented: faces of Marines, firm and controlled; devoted generals; the Statue of Liberty, guarding the shore against enemies; the brave fleet of nuclear submarines patrolling the waters; tight squadrons of fighter planes thundering overhead; the new missile, ready to attack, to annihilate, to win.

The innocent insistence of the children is counterpointed against adult thinking and dishonorable behavior that includes attempts to undermine the Children's Crusade, even to steal the "fragile flag." A capsule of the adult arguments includes the difficulties of arranging discussions with the Soviets, the complexities of bargaining if you were behind in the armament race and the need to catch up or be ahead. But it is clear the president is becoming uncertain. He remembers Bible lessons of his childhood and is haunted by one memorized verse: "Verily I say unto you, except ye turn, and become as little children, ye shall in no wise enter the Kingdom. . . ."

> The only deterrent to global war is military strength. When this powerful new weapon is launched to orbit the earth, we will at last achieve real superiority in the arms race with the Soviet Union.
> —James R. Toby, President of the United States

> Stop, stop, stop. . . .
> —Georgie Hall, Grade 4

The fable concludes happily. Robert, who has traveled along, a silent witness, and, indeed, absented himself from any public media encounters, secretly leaves the group after they arrive in Maryland. The initial members feel betrayed. But Robert's spirit is in the "right" place. He goes to Washington ostensibly to visit his grandfather but actually to discover the government's plans against the children. He is able to circumvent the plans to steal the flag and to bar actual contact with the president. He leads Georgie to the president, presenting her as that day's contest winner; she reads her letter, a plea on behalf of the green earth and a world without nuclear weapons. The president falls under the magic spell of the flag and sees a vision of waves and vessels and children; he also sees a vision of massive destruction. He changes his mind.

CENSORSHIP HISTORY

In late October 1986, Susan Cameron, a sixth-grade teacher from the Maple Grove Elementary School in Golden (Jefferson County), Colorado, requested that *The Fragile Flag* be banned from all Jefferson County school libraries. The teacher expressed the concerns that the book portrayed the United States government as "shallow" and "manipulative" and "lacking in intelligence and responsibility." Further, it "does nothing to promote children's respect for adults in authority." It portrayed parents and government officials, she added, as being "shallow, manipulative, scheming and lacking in responsibility." The story "amounts to thinly disguised anti-nuclear propaganda at best, designed to appeal to boys and girls who won't find much in their school libraries to balance this view." The book was not required reading.

Jane Langton, the author, welcomed the challenge to her novel. "I wrote it as a patriotic novel and it's being called unpatriotic. . . . The little children in the book don't understand things like strategic defenses. They try to make it understood to the administration, with this magical flag, that these things will kill us all."

A November 24 public hearing had been set before a school district curriculum subcommittee to review the challenge (along with that of another book). It planned to make its recommendation to school superintendent John Peper within a couple of weeks. The school superintendent is empowered to make the final decision on whether the books remain on library shelves. In the interim, members of Citizens to Revitalize Education planned to campaign to keep the book in circulation. However, on October 31, the teacher withdrew her request. She indicated that the extensive and unexpected media attention had "made it impossible for me to pursue the challenge process" and that it would interfere with her working effectively with her students.

FURTHER READING

Graf, Thomas. "Jeffco Teacher Withdraws Challenge." *Denver Post*, November 1, 1986, p. 6B.
———. "Teacher, Citizen Challenge 2 Jeffco Children's Books." *Denver Post*, October 30, 1986, p. B1.

Knox, Don. "More Books Challenged in Jeffco School District." *Rocky Mountain News*, October 30, 1986, p. 41.
Newsletter on Intellectual Freedom 35 (1987): 29, 49.

THE FUGITIVE (*PERBURUAN*)

Author: Pramoedya Ananta Toer
Original dates and places of publication: 1950, Indonesia; 1990, United States
Publishers: Balai Pustaka Publishing; William Morrow and Company
Literary form: Novel

SUMMARY

Disguised as a beggar and living among beggars, Hardo is drawn out of his refuge to secretly visit Ningsih, his fiancée, at her home during the festivities celebrating her brother's circumcision. The celebratory scene is at odds with Hardo's condition and urgent self-denial as well as with the political condition of Java. The yoke of the Japanese occupation is heavy on the shoulders of the Javanese, their oppression and the concomitant loss of freedom insufferable to Hardo and his companion rebels.

Raden Hardo, we learn, had been a platoon leader in the Indonesian volunteer army. He and others had allied themselves with the Japanese military in order to force the Dutch colonialists out of Indonesia. Since his ultimate goal was independence for Indonesia, he became dissatisfied with the Japanese and, along with two other platoon leaders, Dipo and Karmin, conspired against them. The nationalist rebellion failed, however, when Karmin withdrew his support at the last moment for unspecified reasons. In the intervening six months, Hardo and Dipo have been fugitives, their capture and death by beheading seemingly imminent.

Now, on the eve of the Japanese surrender to the Allies, Hardo has been recognized, first by Ningsih's brother, Ramli, who idolizes him, and then by her mother, who came out to chase him away. Furthermore, he is followed by Ningsih's father, recently appointed village chief by the Japanese, who confirms the identification but is unable to convince Hardo to return with him to his home.

Hardo finds haven in a hut, seemingly isolated in a cornfield. Shortly, its owner, an old man, arrives, out of breath and fearful, for he is being chased by the police. It is Hardo's father. In the ensuing conversation, the old man reveals how he has come to this sorry state; he was fired from his position as district head of Karangjati, which includes the city of Blora. He has suffered the loss of his wife and his son—and then his selfhood and his job. Both he and his wife grieved upon hearing the news of their son's involvement in a rebellion against the Japanese, the failure of the rebellion and the search-to-kill order against him. The district head had been ordered to mobilize the search party; his wife, though ill, had been forced to accompany the search party. Devastated, weak, in pain, and filled with fear, she had died. This loss and the rumors of his son's death had taken away life's meaning; the father had escaped from his visions and empty life into gambling, losing his home and possessions. Now he is pursued by the police.

During this exchange, Hardo attempts to keep his identity secret, denying the old man's suspicions and pleas of acknowledgment. (Perhaps Hardo, in addition to protecting himself, is protecting his father in the event he is questioned and tortured.) The suspicions are not allayed and are indeed confirmed when Hardo talks in his sleep, providing evidence of his identity. Shortly thereafter, a patrol searching for Hardo arrives, but is finally put off by the father's denials of knowledge of his son's whereabouts. A Japanese officer, accompanied by the current district head and an Indonesian soldier, also fails to get information, though he strikes the old man down. It is revealed that Ningsih's father has betrayed Hardo.

That night Hardo rejoins the company of beggars, which includes his friend and coconspirator, Dipo. They debate their perilous situation: Dipo is critical of Hardo's "sentimentality" because he cannot control his feelings about his fiancée; he has forgotten his oath as a soldier and endangered himself and their cause. Dipo expresses a militaristic sense of behavior that rejects emotions and consideration of human frailty. These contrasting ideals are reflected in their argument about Karmin: Hardo would consider Karmin's reason for his actions and his human fallibility, and even defend him; Dipo would summarily decapitate him. During their discussion, another conspirator reports that Japan has surrendered to the Allies. But in Java, Japan is still in power and at that moment calling out the patrols. The conspirators disappear into the elephant grass.

The Japanese are determined to find Hardo and his companions. When they cannot find them among the beggars, they detain the village chief, Ningsih's father, and imprison Hardo's father. The village chief is brought before the Japanese officer, the district head, and the platoon commander, Karmin. He is questioned, threatened, and brutalized by the Japanese; he finally implicates his own daughter, Ningsih, to protect himself from further beatings.

Karmin's role is clarified in this and subsequent scenes. Aware that he has failed his friends for personal reasons, inaction rather than betrayal, he has been working for the past months to protect Hardo's personal and political interests. He has undermined the Japanese by making sure that the conspirators escape the raids, though this is becoming increasingly difficult. He goes to Ningsih's home to forewarn her. When the Japanese officer arrives, she, too, is threatened, but she is steadfast. At this moment of tension, almost simultaneously an uproar of voices broadcasts Japan's surrender and a patrol arrives with Hardo and Dipo in custody.

In the ensuing melee, among a riotous crowd of Indonesians, Karmin attacks the officer, who has taken out his gun and begun firing. During their fight, Dipo removes the officer's sword, presses its point into his back and attempts to decapitate him. At the crowd's urging that Karmin is a traitor, Dipo turns on him; Karmin bows his head, accepting the accusation and sentence. With a word, Hardo intervenes; he also dispels the crowd when Karmin places himself in its hands. "Hardo offered his scabby hand and Karmin took it in his own. They walked together toward the door, but there they were halted by the sight of the village chief bent over his daughter, Ningsih." A stray bullet from the Japanese officer's gun has found its victim.

The characters personify the political core of *The Fugitive*. The Japanese officer reveals the oppression and ruthlessness of that nation's occupation forces: threats, beatings and beheadings. The village chief and Ningsih are held hostage until Hardo is found and are subject to decapitation in his stead. These actions reflect an arrogance seen in the response to Ningsih's daring to ask why her father is being detained:

> "Silence!" the officer repeated. "Indonesians may not ask questions! You are Indonesian so you say nothing!" His fluency rapidly faded. "When Indonesians with Japanese . . . with Japanese, you understand? No telling stories. You remember that." The man's eyes bulged as he spoke. "Indonesians no good. Indonesians must learn to keep their mouths shut. You understand? Do you understand?"

Indonesian independence suffers from the words and behavior of Indonesians themselves. Ningsih's father's ready betrayal of Hardo expresses this demoralization. His act is dramatized by its evident self-serving nature. He admits to Karmin that he betrays Hardo for Ningsih's sake; he cannot see her marrying a beggar. Materialistic and status-oriented—he sells teak on the black market—he cannot countenance such a union. At critical moments, he thinks of himself, not merely his physical safety, but also of money dealings. When arrested, he complains about people who owe him money; during the concluding drama, when Japan's surrender is announced and Hardo has been captured, he reaches for his daughter and says: "It was for you . . . it was all for you that I did it." He loosens his hold to stand beside her. "I'm free, Ningsih! And you're free too. I saw him. And we're rich, Ningsih! We're rich."

Hardo is the heroic ideal, in contrast to Dipo, who lacks compassion, and Karmin, who is derailed from action at a crucial juncture. Hardo acts and argues for freedom from oppression. In response to his father's wearied comment that "there's no such thing as a free man" and that freedom from oppression is "rubbish," Hardo asserts:

No, the fact is no one is completely sane. And there's no such thing as complete freedom. There's nothing that's one hundred percent in this world. That's just a dream in a dreamer's mind. . . . All the same, we have to try to free ourselves from our present bonds and to climb upward, even if it means that we will be bound again. Freedom is upward, not downward!

In the responses of these characters to their situations and in their interrelationships, Pramoedya exposes the variance and complexity of human values and aspirations. In the irony of his conclusion, he expresses the terror, injustice, and sorrow of the human condition. In expressing one day in the life of this fugitive, he spotlights the oppressive force of the occupying army and the energy and the persistence to gain independence.

Pramoedya's Buru tetralogy—THIS EARTH OF MANKIND, CHILD OF ALL NATIONS, *Footsteps*, and *House of Glass*—is also the object of censorship. Spanning 20 years, beginning in the 1890s, the novels are set in Java during the colonial rule of the Netherlands. "Colonial rule" signals a recognition of two factions: the rulers and the ruled. There is also the division of the Native peoples, those hierarchically operating in conjunction with the colonials, and the underclass outsiders. The cultures of these groups, their interactions, and the tensions among them, are revealed through the situations and difficulties that beset the two central characters, Minke and Nyai Ontosoroh, also identified as Sanikem, her birth name.

CENSORSHIP HISTORY

The works of Pramoedya Ananta Toer (1925–2006) have been banned in Indonesia, his native country. He was imprisoned for political reasons for 14 years and on house or city (Jakarta) arrest for an additional 20 years—from 1979 to 1999. Pramoedya wrote *The Fugitive* in 1949 while he was imprisoned by the Dutch from 1947 to 1950 for his role in Indonesia's anticolonial revolutions; he had been a member of the revolutionary underground and had printed and distributed revolutionary pamphlets. He wrote the book secretly when he was not doing forced labor and at night beneath his concrete bedstead. The text was smuggled out of the prison by a Dutch professor. With the success of the revolution in 1949, *The Fugitive*, published in 1950, was acclaimed and then banned; it contained elements of class conflict and was perceived as a potential threat to society.

See *This Earth of Mankind* for further discussion of censorship of Pramoedya's works.

FURTHER READING

Bald, Margaret. "For Indonesia's Rulers, the Fiction Hurts." *Toward Freedom* (August–September 1992): 17–18.
Charle, Suzanne. "Prisoner without a Cell." *The Nation*, February 3, 1992, 134–135.

Crosette, Barbara. "Banned in Jakarta." *New York Times Book Review*, January 19, 1992, p. 24.
Jones, Sidney. *Injustice, Persecution, Eviction: A Human Rights Update on Indonesia and East Timor.* New York: Asia Watch, 1990.
McDonald, Hamish. *Suharto's Indonesia.* Blackburn, Victoria, Australia: Dominion Press/Fontana Books, 1980.
Scott, Margaret. "Waging War with Words." *Far Eastern Economic Review* (August 9, 1962): 26–30.
Tickell, Paul. "Righting History." *Inside Indonesia* (May 1986): 29–30.

FUGITIVES (*TAOWANG*)

Author: Gao Xingjian
Original dates and places of publication: 1992, France; 1993, United States
Publishers: French edition (*La fuite*), Emile Lansman; English edition, University of Chicago Press
Literary form: Drama

SUMMARY

Fugitives (also published in English in 2007 as *Escape*) takes place in the capital of an unnamed country that is experiencing a violent and apparently successful suppression—the noise of tanks and machine gun fire are mentioned—of a people's revolt. The immediate setting is a room in a dilapidated warehouse-like building.

The young man enters the room first; he has been running. Surveying the room quickly, he signals to the young woman. They are in a panic; she, hysterical with fear, her fear recurring again and again during the drama. She is blood spattered; he, brain splattered. He attempts to calm her by holding her, but it becomes evident that they are strangers to each other. Soon, a middle-aged man slips into the room. He has been warned to escape from his home—his life is endangered—and "even home isn't safe." It becomes clear that each of them is an involved participant in the revolt—the young man as a leader of sorts, the young woman as the one who broadcast most of the statements and protests against martial law, and the middle-aged man as a spontaneous speaker.

The tension of the dialog among these communicants pits the ideals and purposes of the young man, principally—"The people's struggle for democracy and freedom" and "the People's struggle for freedom will triumph sooner or later, even if it means spilling blood" against the recognized reality, the bitter pessimism of the middle-aged man. Even in the anguish of defeat, the young man cries, "You mean all this blood was shed in vain? History, history will remember this day! This blood-drenched day! [Yelling] This victorious day—." The other man responds: "History? The one you write or the one I write? Or theirs? History is a mire, a rubbish heap of waste paper."

After preliminary observations about house-to-house searches and the square being surrounded by tanks and "already [having] a blacklist of people they want to arrest," the nature of the state and attitudes toward it are indicated in such comments as:

They've got everything from wiretaps to videotapes. Who wrote what, who said what, its all in their computers. They can arrest whomever they want anytime they choose. And you've only got the one life.

Even the elderly and the children they'd surrounded were slaughtered? D'you know what slaughtered means? Even at midnight people were milling about the square, just like some national holiday. Who could have dreamt it?

. . . In all likelihood they've got the confession written out already, and all they need is some young fellow to go through the motions for the TV cameras.

That's a real insult to human dignity. . . . But what they insult is more than human dignity. They can take what you like to call the People and turn them all into mincemeat, and all *in the name* of the People too!

What do you mean by country? Whose country? Has the country acted responsibly towards you or me? Why should I be responsible for the country? I'm just responsible for myself.

The action seems stagnant while the three wait for dawn, the moment when escape seems possible, their emotions wildly ebbing and flowing, the young man increasingly despondent, the young woman enacting a fantasy. The youth goes outside to investigate. Shots are heard. The woman, hysterical, assumes he's dead. In response to the older man's consolation, his embrace, she responds with sexual desire. The scene ends with intimacy.

The quite short second act shifts its orientation from the revolt to the characters. While despair and fear haunt them—or perhaps because of these emotions—the characters alternately offer tenderness or acrimony toward each other. Before the young man returns, the couple's sense of gratitude toward each other shifts to recriminations about who has caused the presumed death. Upon his return, finding her naked, the youth is stunned, disillusioned, claiming that he loves her.

Between moments of sympathy and passion and repudiation, the young woman acknowledges her independence of action—"If I want to do it with somebody, I'll do it, but it's me who decides!"—and her rejection of and disassociation from men—"Leave me alone, leave me alone! I don't want anybody, just get the hell out of it, you don't deserve a woman's love, you men just don't deserve it!" Her accusations of men are sweeping: " . . . deep down you're all the same, you think ill of women, in fact, you're the ones who are filthy, you're only happy when you're defiling women but what you're really defiling is yourselves," and "But are you capable of the kind of affection women are? You just think about possessing, grasping, have you ever thought of giving anything to a woman?" This mix of activities and talk leads to a tussle among the three of them and then separation. The act ends with the heavy knocking at the door.

Bam, bam bam!
  Bam, bam!
  Bam, bam, bam, bam, bam!
  Like the rattle of a machine gun. The three remain motionless sitting in sewage which looks like blood.

CENSORSHIP HISTORY

Fugitives, titled *Taowang* in Mandarin, was written a few months after the massacre on the Square of Heavenly Peace (Tiananmen Square) in 1989. This led to Gao Xingjian being declared persona non grata by China. All of his works were banned. Beijing also denounced the awarding of the Nobel Prize in literature (2000) to Gao, accusing the Nobel committee of being politically motivated, and diminished the merits of Gao's novel *Soul Mountain.* The Chinese press maintained a near blackout of the Nobel award. Gao's books are not available in bookstores in China. Earlier in his career Gao's play BUS STOP was banned, leading to his being placed under surveillance. For more on the censorship of Gao's works, see *Bus Stop.*

Gao is now a citizen of France, having lived there since 1987 as a political refugee.

FURTHER READING

"Fugitives: A Modern Tragedy in Two Acts." Trans. by Gregory Lee. In *Chinese Writing in Exile,* edited by Gregory Lee, 89–137. Chicago: Center for East Asian Studies, 1993.

Yan, Haiping, ed. *Theater and Society: An Anthology of Contemporary Chinese Drama.* Armonk, N.Y.: M. E. Sharpe, 1998.

GIRLS OF RIYADH

Author: Rajaa Alsanea
Original dates and places of publication: 2005, Lebanon; 2007, United States
Publisher: Dar al Saqi (Arabic); Penguin (English)
Literary form: Novel

SUMMARY

Girls of Riyadh tells the story of a shillah, or clique, of four upper-class young women in Saudi Arabia: Gamrah, Sadeem, Lamees, Michelle. The story mostly focuses on their struggles to find true love and maintain romantic relationships within the rigid, oppressive, and repressive Saudi society. The novel also features the ups and downs of the intimate friendship shared by the four women, as they help each other understand and navigate their lives in Saudi Arabia. Sadeem's neighbor, Um Nuwayyir, provides her home for the women to meet with each other and occasionally with their love interests.

Girls of Riyadh is structured as a series of e-mails sent to a subscriber group. A first-person narrator, identifying herself as a friend to the four main characters, introduces each chapter (which is then narrated in the third person). In these introductions, she responds to readers and critics of her e-mails (both playfully and seriously) and addresses the growing popularity and scandal of her e-mails. She offers criticism of Saudi society and Saudi men but maintains optimism about love. She makes clear in these introductions that the desires, experiences, and perspectives of herself and the four women she writes about are not exceptional but typical of women in Saudi society.

Because of restrictive rules and social customs regarding interaction between the sexes, cell phones become the key means to maintain relationships. Single men frequently try to give their phone number to any single woman, and long-term romantic relationships are regularly maintained through late-night phone calls and frequent text messages:

> for so many [. . .] lovers in the country, the telephone was the only outlet, practically, for them to express the love that brought them together. The telephone lines in Saudi Arabia are surely thicker and more abundant than elsewhere, since they must bear the heavy weight of all the whispered croonings lovers have to exchange and all their sighs and moans and kisses that they cannot, in the real world, enact—or that they do not want to enact due to the restrictions of custom and religion, that some of them truly respect and value.

It is difficult for a single man and single woman to be physically together in Riyadh; in some cases, it is a thrill for the women when their beloved men are able to drive in a car near them. Even acknowledging Valentine's Day is forbidden: "The Religious Police banned anything that might remotely suggest a celebration of the holiday of love [. . .] Love was treated like an unwelcome visitor in our region."

The story begins with Gamrah's wedding to Rashid, a man who treats Gamrah poorly and shows little personal or sexual interest in her. Gamrah lives with Rashid in America, where she feels increasingly isolated and miserable. She discovers that Rashid is having an affair with a woman named Kari, and later learns that Kari was Rashid's long-time girlfriend, but that his family disapproved and forced Rashid into marriage with Gamrah. Against Rashid's wishes, Gamrah does not take birth control and becomes pregnant; when Rashid learns about the pregnancy, he becomes enraged and sends her back to her family in Saudi Arabia, eventually divorcing her. Gamrah has a son, but Rashid never takes any part in his life. In Saudi Arabia, Gamrah struggles to find her place: as a divorced woman with a child, she feels restrained, rarely leaving her family home and despairing of ever finding another husband. She does find joy and fulfillment raising her son.

Sadeem meets a man named Waleed, and the two have a happy relationship that leads to an engagement. However, between the signing of the marriage contract and the actual wedding ceremony, Sadeem initiates a sexual encounter with Waleed. Afterward, Waleed avoids contact with Sadeem, eventually sending her divorce papers. Heartbroken, Sadeem goes to live temporarily in London, where she meets Firas, "a diplomat and a politician, widely connected and respected." Sadeem falls deeply in love with Firas, and while they maintain a long, passionate relationship (mostly through phone conversations), Firas avoids official commitment and hints that marriage will not be possible. Eventually, shortly after Sadeem's father dies, Firas becomes engaged to another woman, leaving Sadeem heartbroken once again, and she moves to Khobar to live with family. After the engagement, they again pick up their relationship, but five days later Sadeem, frustrated, breaks up with Firas, "finally cured of her love addiction' . . . los[ing] her respect for all men." In Khobar, Sadeem becomes a party planner, aspiring ultimately to plan weddings. She becomes a successful businesswoman, enlisting Um Nuwayyir and Gamrah to plan parties in Riyadh and planning for the possibility of Lamees running parties in Jeddah and Michelle in Dubai. Sadeem is pursued by her cousin Tariq, and while he offers love and security, Sadeem does feel love for Tariq. However, after Firas calls Sadeem offering to make her his second wife, Sadeem angrily hangs up and agrees to marry Tariq. The book is somewhat ambiguous: Sadeem has given up on passionate love, but she seems to have a happy relationship with Tariq.

Michelle is the most liberated of the four women; she spent her early life in America (her mother is American), and she "loathed Saudi society and its severe traditions." She often incisively and angrily criticizes the conservative Saudi society; for example, "She was well aware that genuine love had no outlet or avenue of expression in this country. Any fledgling love relationship, no matter how innocent or pure, was sure to be seen as suspect and therefore repressed." She falls in love with Faisal, but because Faisal's mother does not approve of their relationship, he breaks up with her rather than defy his family. Michelle becomes even more bitter about the rigid traditions and social customs of Saudi society. She attends school in America, but when she grows close to her American cousin, her parents force her to move back to Saudi Arabia. They eventually move to Dubai, where Michelle works her way up as a successful television producer. Michelle achieves "the best closure ever" when she appears at Faisal's wedding, forcing him to see her before she walks out laughing. But she knows "behind their smiles, many of those brides and grooms were concealing their own sad and yearning hearts because they had been kept from choosing their life's partner." While she ends the novel railing against Saudi society and the lack of courage in men, she holds hope for love: "I will never sell myself short and I can never be satisfied with crumbs."

Lamees attends college training to become a doctor. In college, Lamees develops a close friendship with a Shiite woman, Fatima, becoming interested in her religious beliefs and practices. Fatima introduces Lamees to her brother Ali. Lamees and Ali meet together at a café, where they are arrested by Al-Hai' ah, the religious police (a single man and woman together in public is enough cause for arrest), and though they are released after questioning, this ends her friendship with Fatima and relationship with Ali: "If Lamees had been allowed to continue seeing him, and more important if he hadn't been Shiite, she might actually have fallen in love with him." Eventually, Lamees goes to train at a hospital in Jeddah, where she meets Nizar, another medical student. In the end, she is the most romantically satisfied of the women: she marries Nizar, a man whom she loves and who treats her with caring, respect, and love. She is "the only one who had fulfilled the dream they all had, the dream of marrying the first love of their lives."

The novel ends with the narrator's bitter critique mingled with idealistic hope that characterizes most of the book:

> As for love, it still might always struggle to come out into the light of day in Saudi Arabia. You can sense that in the sighs of bored men sitting alone at cafes, in the shining eyes of veiled women walking down the streets, in the phone lines that spring to life after midnight, and in the heartbroken songs and poems, too numerous to count, written by the victims of love unsanctioned by family, by tradition, by the city: Riyadh.

CENSORSHIP HISTORY

According to James Adams,

> After completing her manuscript, Alsanea decided not to submit it to the Ministry of Information—a normal prepublication caution in Saudi society. Instead, she sought out a publisher in Beirut. " 'In Saudi,' she explained, 'you're supposed to take your draft to the ministry and they kind of censor it for you or tell you it's horrible and unpublishable, or they take out some lines and then say it's okay for publication. Well, I didn't want to have to go through that stuff.' "

Indeed, the novel was banned in Saudi Arabia, according to Claudia Roth Pierpont, "apparently for suggesting that upper-class Saudi girls might wish to escape their luxurious designer cages." Harry De Quetteville notes,

"In the kingdom where women are banned from driving and alcohol is forbidden, the behind-the-wheel exploits of her Dom Perignon-quaffing heroines have not been 'approved' for publication by the Ministry of Information." The initial banning only provoked interest: De Quetteville and Bruce Ward point out that copies of the book were selling in Saudi Arabia for hundreds of dollars. Fatema Ahmed writes that the book was "quickly withdrawn from bookshops and the ministry of information placed it for a while on its lengthy list of banned books," but that "Photocopies of *Girls of Riyadh* subsequently changed hands for up to $500." The BBC reports that Saudi customers often traveled to Bahrain, where they could purchase the book.

Eventually the book was approved for sale in Saudi Arabia, but that did not end problems. James Adams notes that the many e-mails Alsanea received included death threats, and that

> In February, 2006, her Lebanese publisher "brought in hundreds of copies to sell" at the Riyadh International Book Fair. Unfortunately, Sunni fundamentalists blasted the book as blasphemous and seditious and proceeded to buy up all available copies. Even now, [the novel is hard] to find in stores in Saudi Arabia.

According to Arabnews.com, in 2006 two Saudi men filed a lawsuit in the Court of Grievances against Rajaa Alsanea and "the Ministry of Information for giving the author permission to distribute the novel":

> The two Saudis had asked the court to withdraw the ministry's permission that allowed the author to distribute her book in the Kingdom through various bookstores. They also requested that all airports and seaports in the Kingdom ban the book's entry from abroad. They further said that the author be punished according to the laws of the land. In addition, they alleged that the Ministry of Information violated the laws of publication and distribution in Saudi Arabia by allowing the book to be sold at the International Book Exhibition held in Riyadh several months ago. According to the lawsuit, the book is "an outrage to the norms of Saudi society. It encourages vice and also portrays the Kingdom's female community as women who do not cover their faces and who appear publicly in an immodest way."

The Court of Grievances rejected the lawsuit.

FURTHER READING

Adams, James. Review of *Sex and the City*. *Globe Review*, May 29, 2010.

Ahmed, Fatema. "Velvet Lives: Fatema Ahmed Goes Searching for Romance in Saudi Arabia." *Guardian Review*, July 14, 2007, p. 16.

De Quetteville, Harry. "Sex and the Saudi Kingdom a Hot Seller: Banned Novel Lifts the Veil on Conservative Society." *National Post*, February 8, 2006, p. A2.

McWatt, Jennifer. "Saudis Flock to Bahrain to Buy Book Banned by Riyadh." *BBC Worldwide Monitoring* (January 31, 2006).

Pierpont, Claudia Roth. "Found in Translation: The Contemporary Arabic Novel." *New Yorker*, January 18, 2010, pp. 74–80.

Qusti, Raid. "Court Rejects Case against Rajaa Al-Sanea." *Arab News* (October 9, 2006). Available online. URL: http://archive.arabnews.com/?page=1&section= 0&article=87886&d=9&m=10&y=2006. Accessed January 24, 2011.

Ward, Bruce. "Carving out Their Own Way: Novel Has Ignited a Debate about Women in Saudi Arabia." *Montreal Gazette* (August 11, 2007): p. J4.

—Joseph K. M. Fischer
University of Wisconsin-River Falls

THE GRAPES OF WRATH

Author: John Steinbeck
Original date and place of publication: 1939, United States
Publisher: Viking Press
Literary form: Novel

SUMMARY

Set during the Great Depression in Oklahoma and California—the dust bowl and the verdant promised land—and the long road in between, *The Grapes of Wrath* expresses the travail of the Joad family in their journey to find a place for themselves. The dust claimed the land and destroyed their crops year after year; the people living on it are stranded. Hope, generated by handbills proclaiming job opportunities in California and emblazoned by images of verdant and fruited lands, lures the divested westward.

The Joad family is one of thousands of the dispossessed. They take to the road in a decrepit car turned into a truck, with a precariously low supply of money. They number 12, in addition to Casy, a former preacher, who joins them. Chief among them are Ma and Pa; Tom, just released on parole from prison, where he'd served time for murdering a man who had knifed him; 16-year-old Al, who is a capable driver and mechanic; and Rose of Sharon, who is pregnant.

The journey from Oklahoma is hazardous. Reminiscent of pioneer west-bound travelers, they face problems of supplies and water, transportation, and challenging landscape. Not unexpectedly, the car breaks down; tires give out. Al's alertness and skill, with help from Tom, salvage these exigent situations before disaster strikes. Their meager savings dwindle—gas, car repairs, food—so diet and health suffer. However, the Joads do make it.

Unfortunately, Grandpa Joad dies at the first encampment, and his wife, in a state of emotional collapse and physical exhaustion, dies while crossing the desert. The eldest son, Noah, decides to leave the family when they arrive in Needles, California; he is captivated by its river. Rose of Sharon's husband abandons her and the family when he realizes he will not have easy access to a job and personal advancement that he had expected. At the end of the novel, Rose of Sharon delivers a stillborn, apparently malnourished baby.

The promise of California proves to be barren. Before the journey, Ma Joad had said apprehensively, "I hope things is all right in California," and there are forewarnings along the way from returning emigrants that the handbill advertisements are a false lure, that the land is pretty but unavailable. There are two deceits: the jobs and the welcome. The handbills have lured thousands of workers for relatively few seasonal jobs. The Joads learn the script quickly. Out of food and money, they accept the first available work, picking peaches for five cents a box. They're ushered into the ranch area by police on motorcycles through throngs of striking men. They, too, had been offered five cents a box.

> "Lookie, Tom," [Casy] said at last. "We come to work, there. They says it's gonna be fi'cents. They was a hell of a lot of us. We got there an' they says they're payin' two an' a half cents. A fella can't even eat on that, an' if he got kids—So we says we won't take it. So they druv us off. An' all the cops in the worl' come down on us. Now they're payin' you five. When they bust this here strike—ya think they'll pay five? . . . We tried to camp together, an' they druv us like pigs. Scattered us. Beat the hell outa fellas . . . We can't las' much longer. Some people ain't et for two days. . . ."

The Joads and others hired with them are paid as promised, but as soon as the strike is broken, the wage is reduced to two and a half cents a box.

The living conditions add to the migrants' misery and dehumanization. Instead of the neat white house that Ma Joad and Rose of Sharon dream of, they find "Hooverville" (a reference to President Hoover's failed aid program) camps, a collection of some 40 tents and shacks: "The rag town lay close to water; and the houses were tents, and weed-thatched enclosures, paper houses, a great junk pile." These are scattered randomly, some neatly maintained, others surrounded by the debris of travel. Sanitary facilities do not exist, nor are there hot water and any other amenities.

The rare alternative is Weedpatch, the camp established by the government. Limited in the number of families it can house, it is a cooperative enterprise, operated and maintained by its residents, who establish its rules of order, conduct, and cleanliness through elected committees. The camp provides sanitary facilities—toilets, showers, and sinks, clothes-washing basins, and other amenities such as wood for fires. Equally meaningful to the Joads, who find space in the camp for a time, are the community relationships and support, the sense of being treated as human beings, the unity and mutual protectiveness.

The government camp is perceived by the landowners as a "red threat" (a reflection of the fear of socialism) to the status quo they wish to maintain. When Tom Joad asks about the availability of hot water at the peach ranch camp, he is treated contemptuously. A guard remarks,

> "Hot water, for Christ's sake. Be wantin' tubs next." He stared glumly after the four Joads.

... "It's them gov'ment camps," he said. "I bet that fella been in a gov'ment camp. We ain't gonna have no peace till we wipe them camps out. They'll be wantin' clean sheets, first thing we know."

While the Joads are at the government camp, the local landowners and police indeed attempt to instigate a fight within the campgrounds to give them an excuse to send in a riot squad to destroy it.

The physical miseries are compounded by the attitude reflected in the hiring policies and the actions taken by police. The migrants are bullied and beaten, charged and jailed as vagrants for any resistance, even verbal. One "vagrant," who complains about the dishonest promises of pay rates, is labeled a "red": "He's talkin' red, agitating trouble." Other migrants are warned: "You fellas don't want to listen to these goddamn reds. Troublemakers. . . ." Hooverville communities are burned as well for such small infractions. The people themselves are judged by their surface condition: their poverty and hunger, their grime and tatters. They are condescendingly called "Okies": "Well, Okie use'ta mean you was from Oklahoma. Now it means you're a dirty son-of-a bitch. Okie means you're scum. Don't mean nother itself, it's the way they say it."

Two interlocking strands reveal aspects of the political-philosophic under-pinnings of the novel. One strand signals the destruction of the family farm and the farmer; the second focuses on the tractor and other machinery that displace men and their animals, making them extraneous.

The family farm and farmer are victims of owners and banks, of companies with extensive acreage. In Oklahoma, when crops fail again and again, the owners, the Company, the Bank moved in. Eventually, the farmer is forced from the land. But the owners go one step further: "One man on a tractor can take the place of twelve or fourteen families." The tractor destroys the concept of the family farm and the farm itself: Keeping "the line straight," it drives through the dooryard, turns over buildings, tramples fences. The novel frequently refers to the farmers being "tractored off."

In California, the operation is essentially the same. The great owners and companies dominate: They control the land. The small landowner is pressured into line by the Farmers Association run by the Bank, which "owns most of this valley, and it's got paper on everything it don't own." They set the low wages and the cutthroat policies. Since this isn't enough to satiate their greed, a great owner buys a cannery, then sells the fruit to the cannery at a low price and the canned goods to consumers at a high price, ensuring a profit. The little farmer is squeezed out of business.

In direct contrast, the sharing ethic is evidenced among the migrants. From the outset when the Joads graciously welcome Casy as a travel companion despite the overcrowded vehicle, to the closing scene when Rose of Sharon readily nurses the starving man discovered in the barn, there is consistent expression of the need to help and to accept help without becoming a burden. Ma crystallizes the ethic and the contrast: "I'm learnin' one thing good. . . . Learnin' it all a time, ever' day. If you're in trouble or hurt or need—go to poor people. They're the only ones that'll help—the only ones."

Two opposing forces converge to climax the action and issues of the novel. The men, hungering for work until they are hired to pick peaches or cotton, wonder how they'll manage when all the picking seasons are over. "Fella had a team of horses, had to use 'em to plow an' cultivate an' mow, wouldn' think a turnin' 'em out to starve when they wasn't workin.'" The deprivation and desperation of the migrants brings them together; they begin to unite to create a solid front, culminating in a spontaneous strike. The owners, feeling the status quo threatened by the "reds" and needing to maintain control against a perceived insurrection, develop a counterforce of the police and citizens. The latter themselves feel threatened in their status and livelihood.

The clash of forces at the strike leads to Casy's death—he's the strike leader—and Tom's becoming a wanted man for battering Casy's murderer. While in hiding, Tom determines his future role: to take on Casy's mission, to unite his people, to help them to achieve their goal—"to live decent and bring up their kids decent."

> "I been thinkin' a hell of a lot, thinkin' about our people livin' like pigs, an' the good rich lan' layin' fallow, or maybe one fella with a million acres, while a hundred thousan' good farmers is starvin'. An' I been wonderin' if all our folks got together an' yelled, like them fellas yelled, only a few of 'em at the Hooper ranch—"

In the concluding chapters, the Joads, having helped Tom escape, are trapped by a flood, unable to leave their boxcar "home" because Rose of Sharon is delivering her stillborn child. When the birthing is over and the floodwaters have receded slightly, the three remaining adults carry Rose of Sharon and the two children through the chest-deep waters to higher ground where they find refuge in a barn. It is occupied, they discover, by a boy and his starving father; he had given all the food to his son. The Joads have found a temporary haven. Like their pioneer forebears, however, they have not found the promised land of opportunity.

CENSORSHIP HISTORY

The Grapes of Wrath faced censorship challenges just months after it was published (April 1939). National, regional, and state surveys attest to this, as well as to the novel's rating among the "most frequently" challenged books. Lee Burress in his five national surveys of librarians or schoolteachers/administrators reports multiple cases: 1966—five challenges (tied for fourth most frequently); 1973—four (tied for third); 1977—eight (second place); 1982—six (tied for sixth); 1988—two challenges. In Burress's master list of the 22 most frequently challenged books in American high schools 1965–81, *The Grapes of Wrath* placed second; on a comparable list for 1965–82, the novel was in fourth place. Surveys conducted by James Davis in Ohio (1982) and Kenneth Donelson in Arizona (1967) also identify challenges, as do those of Georgia (1982, 1984), North Carolina (1983), Minnesota (1991), and People For the American Way (1992). (Other titles reported by Burress among the top 25 most censored and included in this volume are 1984, SLAUGHTERHOUSE-FIVE, and JOHNNY GOT HIS GUN.)

Specifically documented attacks on the novel in its first year occurred in widely separated parts of the country: Kansas City, Kansas, where the board of education on August 18, 1939, voted 4-2 to order copies of the novel removed from the 20 public libraries for reasons of indecency, obscenity, abhorrence of the portrayal of women, and for "portray[ing] life in such a bestial way"; Buffalo, New York, where Alexander Galt, head librarian of the city libraries, barred it from being purchased because of its "vulgar words"; Kern County, California, where the county board of supervisors, voting 4-1 on August 21, 1939, "requested that the use, possession, and circulation of [the novel] be banned from the county's libraries and schools"; East St. Louis, Illinois, where five of nine library board members voted unanimously on November 15, 1939, to have three copies of the book burned on the courtyard steps (within a week, by a 6-2 vote, the board rescinded its burning order in response to the "national commotion it had aroused"; it placed the three copies on the "Adults Only" shelf); Greene County, Ohio, where in late November the library board members voted 4-3 to ban the novel as "unsuitable" for circulation among its patrons; and the USS *Tennessee*, where the chaplain removed it from the ship's library.

These challenges occurred as *The Grapes of Wrath* was becoming a best seller: 360,000 copies were in print, including a new printing of 50,000. The East St. Louis burning order occurred in 1939 during the week the novel had its largest sales order to date, 11,340 copies. A record 430,000 copies were sold by the end of the year. The East St. Louis librarian indicated that the waiting list for the novel was the largest of any book in recent years; a Greene County librarian noted that her library's five copies had been on reserve since it came out, the waiting list of 62 names in November stretching to March; there were 50 men on the waiting list of the USS *Tennessee*. In Kern County, with 60 copies in circulation at the time of the ban, 112 persons were on the several waiting lists.

Kern County, California

Of these challenges, the Kern County, California, event was the most organized in its opposition. Kern County is in the center of the agricultural region featured in *The Grapes of Wrath*. Though there had not been any registered complaints at the local libraries nor any articles or editorials debating the merits of the book, the board of supervisors—which also had not previously discussed the issue—passed the banning resolution proposed by Supervisor Stanley Abel on August 21, 1939. It read in part: "*The Grapes of Wrath* has offended our citizenry by falsely implying that many of our fine people are a low, ignorant, profane and blasphemous type living in a vicious, filthy manner." Another section objected to Steinbeck's choosing to ignore the education, recreation, hospitalization, welfare and relief services made available by Kern County. In addition to the banning of the book from the county libraries and schools, the resolution requested that Twentieth Century–Fox Film Corporation not complete its motion picture adaptation that was then in production. County librarian Gretchen Knief wrote immediately to Supervisor Abel. An excerpt follows:

> If that book is banned today, what book will be banned tomorrow? And what group will want a book banned the day after that? It's such a vicious and dangerous thing to begin and may in the end lead to exactly the same thing we see in Europe today.
> Besides, banning books is so utterly hopeless and futile. Ideas don't die because a book is forbidden reading. If Steinbeck has written truth, that truth will survive. If he is merely being sensational and lascivious, if all the "little words" are really no more than fly specks on a large painting, then the book will soon go the way of all other modern novels and be forgotten.

The offended citizens appear to have been the Associated Farmers of Kern County. Led by its president, Wofford B. Camp, a prominent rancher, it had sent a telegram of praise to Kansas City. Camp called Steinbeck's novel "propaganda of the vilest sort" and claimed, "We are defending our farm workers as well as ourselves when we take action against that book." Camp and two other men "ceremoniously burned" a copy of the book; a photograph of this act appeared in *Look* magazine.

The Associated Farmers group also organized a statewide action plan to suppress the book, to "remove the 'smear' to the good name of Kern, the state of California and agriculture." They urged all organizations in the San Joaquin Valley to approve a measure comparable to that of Kern County. Camp declared:

> We are angry, not because we were attacked but because we were attacked by a book obscene in the extreme sense of the word and because our workers with whom we have lived and worked for years are pictured as the lowest type of human life when we know that is not true.
> You can't argue with a book like that, it is too filthy for you to go over the various parts and point out the vile propaganda it contains. Americans have a right to say what they please but they do not have the right to attack a community in such words that any red-blooded American man would refuse to allow his daughter to read them.

Established in 1933 through the joint efforts of the California Farm Bureau Federation and the state Chamber of Commerce with the financial backing of the Canners League and large landholders, the Associated Farmers' original purpose was to organize local citizen committees to pass anti-picketing regulations so as to derail farm workers' strikes and unionizing activities; strike breaking efforts were a second phase of the organization's purposes.

During the ensuing week the battle lines were drawn. Supported, perhaps, by a series of articles and editorials that had appeared early in August in the *Bakersfield Californian*, which noted the irreconcilability between Steinbeck's fiction and the facts of assistance to migrants, adherents argued for even stronger action than a ban. Pro-America, a national women's organization, which was meeting in San Francisco, denounced the book as a "lie promoting class hatred" and indicated that the "farmworkers of California are better paid and better housed than agriculture workers anywhere else in the world."

Denunciations of the banning by the American Civil Liberties Union (ACLU) were joined by protests of several local unions—Oil Workers Union, Hod Carriers Union, Butchers Union, and the Brotherhood of Engineers—and the Workers Alliance, an organization of relief recipients, as well as library clients. The debate centered on the abridgement of constitutional rights; it also included discussion of the ethics of the supervisors' action and their "hidden motivation," that is, the influence of the Associated Farmers of Kern County.

Editorials and articles in newspapers throughout the Central Valley were highly critical of the censorship. In response to the endorsement of the banning by Pro-America, the *Selma Irrigator* editorialized about the politics of special interest groups:

> As for the meeting in San Francisco at which Mr. Steinbeck's book was denounced, wasn't it significant that the men and women who have read the book but don't want others to read it assembled in one of San Francisco's most luxurious hotels far from the San Joaquin cotton fields.

John Raymond Locke of the *Dinuba Sentinel* wrote:

> It is absolutely foolish to try and deny the conditions pictured, whether of the Dust Bowl West or of our own California. Here in our own state most of the pioneers have been "run off" the land they brought into bearing. Look over files of the *Sentinel* for the past 20 years and see the hundreds that have been foreclosed.

The board of supervisors meeting on August 28 was crowded. Pickets carried banners urging the rescinding of the ban in front of the courthouse meeting room. The discussion was heated and lasted an entire day. R. W. Henderson of the ACLU argued that book censorship "could lead to partisan coloration of the library's contents"; Reverend Edgar J. Evans, in reaction to a supervisor's claim, after citing selected passages, that the "book was lewd," questioned whether it was language that was objected to, suggesting that instead it was "the exposure of a sociological condition." Supervisor Stanley Abel, the resolution's sponsor, admitted that the local Chamber of Commerce secretary had written the resolution. He pursued the morality issue for the most part, but at one point claimed that he was trying to bring national attention to the migrant workers in hopes of improving their lot. Despite the efforts of antiban partisans, the vote to rescind failed on a 2-2 vote, the chairperson being absent on vacation.

Some attempts to have the ban lifted were made at the following meetings of the board, but no action was taken until January 27, 1941, when such a vote did succeed. The books were returned to the Kern County library shelves. In the November 1940 election, Stanley Abel had been defeated. It was not until 1972, however, that the teaching of the book was permitted in Kern High School District at East Bakersfield High School. The official policy was at last overturned in July 2002; a resolution was adopted by the Kern County Supervisors officially rescinding the ban and praising Steinbeck for chronicling "the courage and humanity of common Americans during the Depression."

1970s

In April 1972, in Herman, New York, a petition from 100 residents, led by Rev. Barber, argued for the removal from the library and curriculum of books "containing profanity or descriptions of a sexual nature which arouse sexual desire" or those with "references and dialog that condone immorality or references that promote disrespect or defiance of parental or other constituted authority." Among the 10 books identified were three by Steinbeck—*The Grapes of Wrath*, OF MICE AND MEN and *In Dubious Battle*—as well as THE CATCHER IN THE RYE by J. D. Salinger and TO KILL A MOCKINGBIRD by Harper Lee. Three committees were established, one to reevaluate the named books and one each to evaluate the high school and elementary school collections. In Richlands, Virginia, representatives of 17 churches complained in February 1973 about *The Grapes of Wrath* being in the Richland High School library; they characterized it as "pornographic, filthy, and dirty." In Buncombe, North Carolina, two challenges were issued, the first in the fall of 1973, the second in February 1981. The complaints: passages were objectionable to parents; the book was morally [in]decent to the community. The books in both cases were *The Grapes of Wrath*, *The Catcher in the Rye*, and ANDERSONVILLE by MacKinlay Kantor; Steinbeck's OF MICE AND MEN, Eldridge Cleaver's SOUL ON ICE, and Gordon Parks's *The Learning Tree* were also included the first time. The board of education rejected the resolution, reaffirming its "Policies for Selection," in both instances. In Scituate, Rhode Island, in June 1975, after they had been denied their request to censor *The Grapes of Wrath* (and *Of Mice and Men*, *The Catcher in the Rye*, LORD OF THE FLIES by William Golding, THE ART OF LOVING by Erich Fromm, and *Listen to the Silence* by David Elliott) a group of ministers and other citizens protested by distributing leaflets with excerpts that would have "caused the devil to blush." Farmville, North Carolina, in 1977 established written guidelines for the classroom and library use of books like *The Grapes of Wrath*, *The Catcher in the Rye*, and *Of Mice and Men*. They were placed on restricted shelves, available only with written parental permission.

THE GRAPES OF WRATH

Kanawha, Iowa

The challenge to *The Grapes of Wrath* in Kanawha on February 11, 1980, emerged as a language issue. Marvin E. Stupka, the vice president of the bank and father of a 10th grader, read the first 11 pages of the novel assigned to his son's English class and "became incensed with the book's language." He concluded after reading "scattered portions" that the book is "profane, vulgar and obscene" because "it takes the Lord's name in vain dozens of times" and features a preacher who is an immoral hypocrite. He and others complained to superintendent Leroy Scharnhorst, who ordered the books collected and stored until the school board could decide the issue. At its February 11 meeting, the board voted 5-0 to permanently remove the books from two sophomore English classes. Teachers could not require it but might recommend it to their students; copies of the novel would remain in the school library.

While none of the parents told school officials they objected to the novel's message, school board president Wayne Rietema commented that the United States was "going pell mell downhill" morally and the Kanawha community had a chance to act and reverse that trend by banning the book from the classes. "This is the backbone of America—the small town." He added, "We do not intend to become a censoring committee," but he urged nevertheless that the board act to control the book. The attempt of one reporter to interview residents of Kanawha found them reluctant to be quoted, some out of fear of reprisals. However, letters and commentary in the Des Moines *Register* were entirely critical of the school board's action. One predictable result was that *The Grapes of Wrath* became a bestseller in surrounding communities' bookstores and libraries; the Kanawha Public Library borrowed a dozen copies to supplement its own single volume so as to meet reader demand.

In his discussion/analysis of the censoring of *The Grapes of Wrath*, Lee Burress points to the coincidence that in this instance a banker in Iowa should attack the novel for its language, ignoring the Jeffersonian agrarianism that permeates the book and Steinbeck's "charge that capital [of banks] is used to buy big tractors and drive the farmers off the land." He further notes:

> It is an interesting coincidence that approximately at the same time the book was removed from use in the English class at Kanawha, the Sioux City Diocese of the Roman Catholic Church issued a report concerning land ownership patterns in Iowa after two years of study. The report stated that in the 14 north-western counties of Iowa, 77% of the land was owned by absentee owners.

Vernon, New York

Censorship of seven books from reading lists for junior and senior high students was demanded by Rev. Carl Hodley in February 1980. He labeled them "filthy, trashy sex novels." In addition to *The Grapes of Wrath*, his list included *Of Mice and Men* and THE RED PONY by John Steinbeck, *A SEPARATE PEACE* by John Knowles, *It's Not the End of the World* by Judy Blume, *To Kill a Mockingbird* by Harper Lee, and *A FAREWELL TO ARMS* by Ernest Hemingway. The Vernon-Verona-Sherill school district refused to adhere to his request.

Buncombe County, North Carolina
The Grapes of Wrath was among the books challenged by a group led by several fundamentalist ministers. This censorship history is detailed in the discussion of *Andersonville*.

Richford, Vermont
In early fall 1981, five parents, led by Claire Doe, complaining *The Grapes of Wrath* contained immoral and offensive material, requested the book be banned from the high school library and dropped from the junior year American literature class. Objections centered on the image of the former minister, who describes how he used to "take advantage" of young women when he was a preacher, and on "the Lord's name being taken in vain." Doe, whose 16-year-old son was in the class, said that it was a good book for adults but not for children.

Following the school district's procedures, superintendent Forest Farnum appointed a nine-member committee, made up of teachers, parents, and church leaders, to study the book. Its chairperson, Edward Wilkins, an elementary school principal from a neighboring town, advised the members to consider historical value, literary merit, and religious symbolism. The committee heard the objections of Doe's group and reactions of some 25 parents who supported the book. The committee recommended to the school board that Steinbeck's novel be retained for classroom and library use without restrictions. The school board concurred. Carroll Hull, principal of Richford High School, said,

> "The decision reaffirms our right to require what we feel is necessary for a child's education. . . . In some cases, we allow students an alternative if the parents object to the material. But some works, like *The Grapes of Wrath*, we consider essential."

Barry Steinhardt, executive director of the ACLU in Vermont, had indicated that legal action would be taken if the book was banned.

Anniston, Alabama
In fall 1982, a group of about 50 ministers together with church members, representing the Moral Majority, a fundamentalist conservative faction, targeted seven school library books, including *The Grapes of Wrath*, for removal. They labeled the books "ungodly" and "obscene" and circulated petitions to be presented to the Calhoun County Board of Education on October 18.

They also planned to ask permission to form a church-assigned committee to review books on the library shelves as well as new selections. The other books were *Doris Day: Her Own Story*, Steinbeck's *EAST OF EDEN*, J. D. Salinger's *The Catcher in the Rye*, Anthony Burgess's *A CLOCKWORK ORANGE*, Barbara Beasley Murphy's *No Place to Run*, and Frances Hanckel and John Cunningham's *The Way of Love*.

Before the school board met to hear the request, two principals ordered the removal of books. Principal Grover Whaley, of Alexandria High School, caused Steinbeck's books to be withdrawn because of some language in *Of Mice and Men* he found to be vulgar and profane; he had not been contacted by the ministers but had talked with one parent who disapproved of the book. He had received a few telephone calls protesting his action. Principal Wayne Wigley removed *Doris Day: Her Own Story* from the Pleasant Valley High School library upon a parent's complaint.

On a unanimous vote on November 16, the board of education returned all of the books to the library shelves but on a restricted basis. A 10-person committee consisting of Calhoun County superintendent Dan Henderson and school representatives so recommended after being advised by the board's counsel, H. R. Burnham, that comparable attempts to censor school library books around the country had failed in the courts. The ministers' request to screen library books was also rejected. Alternatively, a five-person committee to include a school administrator, teacher, librarian, and two parents was to be appointed at each county school to select and screen books, undertaking the function of the school's librarians.

Burlington, North Carolina
"The book is full of filth. My son is being raised in a Christian home and this book takes the Lord's name in vain and has all kinds of profanity in it," complained Robert Wagner in March 1986. Though not formalized, his complaint about his son's 11th-grade literature class reading led to the assignment of an alternative text.

Carthage, North Carolina
A similar but formalized complaint about the use of the book in an 11th-grade class at Pinecrest High School by Marie Mofield on August 5, 1986, led the Moore County school system to appoint a study committee to evaluate whether *The Grapes of Wrath* should be required reading or banned per her request. The committee, led by Peggy Olney, the head librarian, met with Mofield, who subsequently withdrew her banning request, being satisfied that her 11th-grade child would not be required to read it.

Greenville, South Carolina
The purpose for the January 29, 1991, petition signed by 864 people and submitted to the Greenville County school board was the removal of five books from the approved reading list. The basis: They used the name of God

and Jesus in a "vain and profane manner along with inappropriate sexual references." The school district's materials review committee had already approved the books' retention on the reading list; however, the instruction committee of the school board voted to conduct its own review. In addition to *The Grapes of Wrath*, the books objected to were *Second Heaven* by Judith Guest, MY BROTHER SAM IS DEAD by James L. Collier and Christopher Collier, *The Water Is Wide* by Pat Conroy, and EAST OF EDEN by John Steinbeck.

The argument was joined at a second board meeting with 13 speakers supporting the books, asserting, "It is vital that along with American pride, we have humility and show all aspects of American life"; and one speaker favoring the ban because "Under the definitions you have given tonight, we would have to approve *Playboy* and *Hustler*, too." At a third meeting on April 9, the school board affirmed by a 4-2 vote the district policy that allowed administration-appointed panels to review books about which parents raise concerns. The p olicy also authorized the parental option of refusing to have their children read a given book. A proposal from a school board trustee to provide reading lists with potentially offensive books identified was labeled as censorship by Pat Scales, a librarian:

> "[I]f the district does that, it might as well remove the books. Labeling books in any way is censorship. I do in my heart believe parents should be able to select reading material for their children. But our calling attention to [the fact the book may offend some] relieves them of that responsibility."

Union City, Tennessee

A somewhat more complex controversy emerged from Bobby Pegg's December 1993 objection to his daughter's 11th-grade advanced placement (AP) English class assignment of *The Grapes of Wrath*. His formal request of the Union City school board was for an alternative selection for his daughter without penalty to her grade. His claim: "Reading this book is against my daughter's religious beliefs." His request led to parental voices of support for the class and the book as well as parental opposition to the book; the latter individuals called for the book's being "outlawed and banned," citing "offensive and vulgar material" and language as being inappropriate for high school students. An eight-member ad hoc review committee denied Pegg's basic request for an alternative book assignment; the school board heard his appeal on January 10, 1994. The committee reviewed the book on specific criteria, including its appropriateness, content, and authenticity. Pegg had itemized the number of offensive passages: God's name taken in vain—129 times; vulgar language—264 times; and references to sex—31 times. After a two-hour debate the school board voted unanimously in support of the committee's recommendation of maintaining the reading list for the AP English class, which was not a required class. In opposition to the "moral consciousness of the student" and alternative-selection arguments, proponents of the book argued for the maintenance of standards of the AP national course requirements and resisting exceptions, reasoning that one would potentially lead to many. A selected spokesperson, Glenda Candle, said:

> There were books that could be deemed offensive by spokesmen for any number of religious, political, sexual and racial agenda. But does that capacity to offend mean these books should be ignored for their ultimate value and thus removed from the list of required reading? . . . I must respectfully suggest that if she wishes to continue as a student in the AP English program, she should be required to complete the work as assigned by her teacher.

Puyallup, Washington

After a series of racially charged incidents in 1999, a suit filed in U.S. District Court in 2000 by 36 students and 23 parents against the Puyallup School District accused the district of tolerating a racially hostile environment, citing assaults on minority students and racist graffiti and slurs. In addition, the group also complained of racial slurs in exams and in class discussion of several offending texts, identified as *The Grapes of Wrath*, THE *ADVENTURES OF HUCKLEBERRY FINN*, and *To Kill a Mockingbird*. Each text is similar in that it contains dialogue that refers to blacks with a particularly degrading slur, as alleged; however, each text also makes a powerful statement against racism, classism, and intolerance. The suit was settled in September 2002 before the scheduled trial: The school district agreed to pay $7.5 million and to make administrative and curricular changes, including the establishment of an office of diversity affairs, to encourage racial diversity.

International

By order of the Propaganda Administration, *The Grapes of Wrath* was banned in Germany in 1942–43. It was banned in Ireland in 1953. In Turkey, on February 21, 1973, 11 publishers and eight booksellers went on trial on charges of publishing, possessing, or selling books in violation of an order of the Istanbul martial law command. The charges: spreading propaganda unfavorable to the state.

The Film

The filming of *The Grapes of Wrath* was protested on the grounds that "it would be inflammatory and widely censored." Many conservatives, including most of Twentieth Century–Fox's board of directors, thought it was unsuitable for the screen—it was radical and subversive. The California Chamber of Commerce condemned the project, and the Agricultural Council of California, whose chairman, C. C. Teague, was also an official of the Associated Farmers of California, conducted a campaign in rural newspapers against the filming. Despite a clause in Steinbeck's contract with Twentieth Century–Fox that the film would "fairly and reasonably retain the main action and social intent," the final product, as Robert Morsberger points out, softens Steinbeck's "harsh criticism, generalizes the oppressors . . . leaves out the dialogue about reds, deletes the novel's tragic ending, reverses the sequences of the benevolent government camp and the vicious Hooper ranch, and ends with an upbeat note, leaving the impression that everything will be 'awright' and that nothing needs to be done."

Steinbeck was awarded the Nobel Prize in literature in 1962.

FURTHER READING

"Anniston Coalition Targets 'Obscenity.'" *Tuscaloosa News*, October 9, 1982, [n.p.].

Bixler, Paul. "Book Banned by Greene County Libraries, Is Offered to Public by Antioch College." *Steinbeck Newsletter* (Winter 1993): 10–11.

Bowden, Kevin. "Community Split on Steinbeck Novel." *Union City Daily Messenger*, December 13, 1993, pp. 1, 2.

———. "Request For Alternate Book Denied." *Union City Daily Messenger*, January 11, 1995, pp. 1, 2.

Burress, Lee. "*The Grapes of Wrath:* Preserving Its Place in the Curriculum." In *Censored Books: Critical Viewpoints*, edited by Nicholas J. Karolides, Lee Burress, and John M. Kean, 278–287. Metuchen, N.J.: Scarecrow Press, 1993.

Cowperthwait, Richard, and Alan Abbey. "Richford Parents Fermenting Over *Grapes of Wrath.*" *Burlington Free Press*, November 11, 1981, pp. 1–2B.

"Fifty Years of Wrath." *Newsletter on Intellectual Freedom* 38 (1989): 121–123.

Gehrke, Donna. "Kanawha Bans Classic Book from Classes." *Des Moines Register*, February 12, 1980, p. 1A.

———. "School Board May Ban *Grapes of Wrath.*" *Des Moines Register*, February 10, 1980, p. 1B.

Hollobaugh, Dix. "The Wrath of Kanawha." *Des Moines Sunday Register*, February 24, 1980, pp. 1A, 5A.

Jarvis, Richard. "Let Parents See Reading Lists, Trustee to Urge." *Greenville Piedmont*, April 10, 1991, p. 3.

Kappel, Tim. "Trampling Out the Vineyards—Kern County's Ban on *The Grapes of Wrath.*" *California History* (Fall 1982): 210–221.

Karolides, Nicholas J., and Lee Burress, eds. *Celebrating Censored Books.* Racine: Wisconsin Council of Teachers of English, 1985.

"K. C. Libraries Ban *Grapes of Wrath.*" *Bakersfield Californian*, August 18, 1939, [n.p.].

May, Lucy. "Group Wants Five Books Off Schools List." *Greenville News*, January 30, 1991, p. 1C.

———. "Proposal to Ban Some Books Draws Crowds to Board Meeting." *Greenville News*, March 13, 1991, p. 2.

———. "School Board Affirms Policy Allowing Panel to OK Books." *Greenville News*, April 10, 1991, p. 2.

McVicar, D. Morgan. "Disputed Books Go to Reserve Shelves." *Anniston Star*, November 17, 1982, pp. 1, 5A.

Morsberger, Robert E. "Steinbeck and Censorship." Available online. URL: http://www.csupomona.edu/~jis/2003/Morsberger.pdf. Downloaded August 23, 2004.

Mutter, John. "*Grapes of Wrath* Survives Banning Attempt in Vermont Town." *Publishers Weekly*, December 11, 1981, 9.

Newsletter on Intellectual Freedom 21 (1972): 103–04; 22 (1973): 88, 146; 24 (1975): 139; 30 (1981): 74; 31 (1982): 18, 58, 59–60; 32 (1983): 7, 37; 35 (1986): 210; and 36 (1987): 32–33.

Rintoul, William T. "The Banning of *The Grapes of Wrath.*" *California Crossroads* (January 1963): 4–6.

———. "The Banning of *The Grapes of Wrath.*" *California Crossroads* (February 1963): 26–28.

Roos, Jonathan. "Kanawha's Ban Turns Novel into Best-Seller." *Des Moines Register,* March 6, 1980, pp. 1A, 4A.

"Support of *Grapes* Ban Is Urged by Farmers Group." *Bakersfield Californian,* August 22, 1939, [n.p.].

Tebbel, John. *A History of Book Publishing in the United States.* Vol. 3. New York: R. R. Bowker, 1978.

Veon, R. J. Kern County Clerk and Clerk of the Board. Letter to Gretchen D. Knief, County Librarian. January 27, 1941.

THE GULAG ARCHIPELAGO 1918–1956

Author: Aleksandr Solzhenitsyn
Original dates and places of publication: 1973–1974, France; 1974 (Volume I), 1975 (Volume II), 1978 (Volume III), United States
Publishers: YMCA Press; Harper and Row
Literary form: Nonfiction

SUMMARY

Aleksandr Solzhenitsyn's purpose in his three volumes of *The Gulag Archipelago 1918–1956: An Experiment in Literary Investigation* is to document and reveal a great holocaust in the Soviet Union—exceeding that of Germany against the Jews and others during World War II. Tens of millions of Soviet citizens were imprisoned, savagely mistreated, and often murdered by their own government. The "archipelago" of the title refers to the forced-labor camps, "thousands of islands" scattered across the country geographically "from the Bering Strait almost to the Bosporus" but "in the psychological sense, fused into a continent—an almost invisible, almost imperceptible country inhabited by the zek people [prisoners]." "Gulag," an acronym, designates the Soviet penal system. Solzhenitsyn uses the background of his own prison experiences from 1945 to 1953; these are supplemented with reports by memoirs of and letters by 227 other eyewitnesses.

An early chapter in Volume I, "The History of Our Sewage Disposal System," establishes the origins and continuity of government repression from 1917 to 1956, in effect rejecting the Soviet government's acknowledged purges during Stalin's regime as being limited in time and scope. The text otherwise provides an internal structure from scenes of arrest to confinement and interrogation, then to first cell. Subsequently, the reader travels cross-country with the prisoner to the "ports," the prisons of the archipelago. The destinations are forced labor camps. Each chapter is illustrated with the experiences of individual prisoners, thus providing verifying detail. Another quartet of chapters expresses the shift in the Soviet government's laws and "justice"—attitudes and procedures, including the initial rejection of capital punishment to its massive, seemingly capricious utilization.

A significant assertion is that the arrests and imprisonments did not begin and end with the three biggest "waves" of repression. Of these the acknowledged purges in 1937 and 1938 of "people of position, people with a Party past, educated people" were not the main wave, nor were they accurately represented. Assurances that the arrests were chiefly of communist leaders are not supported by the fact that about 90 percent of the "millions arrested" were outside this circle. "The real law underlying the arrests of those years was *the assignment of quotas* . . . to every city, every district, every military unit. . . ." Before this, the wave of 1929 and 1930 "drove a mere fifteen million peasants, maybe more, out into the taiga and the tundra" and afterward the wave of 1944 to 1946 "dumped whole *nations* down the sewer pipes, not to mention millions and millions of others who . . . had been prisoners of war, or carried off to Germany and subsequently repatriated."

The chronology of purges begins with V. I. Lenin's edict in late 1917 and connects with those of Stalin, who refined and enlarged Lenin's tactics. Arrests encompassed a broad segment of the populace: tens of thousands of hostages; peasants revolting against the taking of their harvests without compensation; students for "criticism of the system"; religious practitioners and believers who were "arrested uninterruptedly"; workers who had not met quotas; and nationalist groups in Central Asia. Soviet soldiers who had been prisoners of war were also arrested and sent to labor camps, even those who had escaped and joined the resistance forces.

> It would appear that during the one thousand one hundred years of Russia's existence as a state there have been, ah, how many foul and terrible deeds! But among them was there ever so multimillioned foul a deed as this: to betray one's own soldiers and proclaim them traitors?

The presumption was that the soldiers had become traitors or had "acquired a very harmful spirit living freely among Europeans."

The Criminal Code of 1926, specifically Article 58, defined the crimes against the state. Operative for many years, the code's basic tenet was that any action—or any absence of action—directed toward the weakening of state power was considered to be counterrevolutionary. Along with armed rebellion, espionage and suspicion of espionage or unproven espionage, the list of criminal activities included subversion of industry, transport, and trade; propaganda or agitation containing an appeal, including face-to-face conversation between friends and spouses, private letters, and preparation of literary materials; failure to make a denunciation of any action and conscious failure to carry out defined duties or intentionally careless execution of them.

The charges against victims were unanswerable. Indeed, "interrogations under Article 58 were *almost never* undertaken to elicit the truth" but rather to induce a confession to an alleged crime or to draw the individual into statements that could be interpreted as self-incriminating. The burden of proof of innocence was upon the victims, who were given little opportunity to provide proof, nor were they apprised of their rights. Interrogation by torture was practiced:

> . . . that prisoners would have their skulls squeezed within iron rings; that a human being would be lowered into an acid bath; that they would be trussed up naked to be bitten by ants and bedbugs; that a ramrod heated over a primus stove would be thrust up their anal canal (the "secret brand"); that a man's genitals would be slowly crushed beneath the toe of a jackboot; and that, in the luckiest possible circumstances, prisoners would be tortured by being kept from sleeping for a week, by thirst, and by being beaten to a bloody pulp. . . .

Psychological torture was also employed, including interrogations at night, foul language, intimidation accompanied by false promises, threatening harm to loved ones, and being placed in a box without being informed of charges. "The more fantastic the charges were, the more ferocious the interrogation had to be in order to force the required confession."

Once condemned, the prisoners' miseries continued on the transport railroad cars, cattle cars, or barges. Subjected to severely overcrowded and underventilated conditions, at extreme temperatures and with insufficient food, they were brutalized by both the common criminals with whom they traveled and the guards.

A pervasive theme in *Gulag Archipelago I* is of corruption not merely of top officials but also of men and women at all levels of officialdom, who had been corrupted by power and, often, a justifiable fear that if they acted otherwise they would become victims. At base, Solzhenitsyn maintains that the destruction of millions of innocent people is derived from the Bolshevik revolution and the Soviet political system.

The author provides ironic counterpoints, such as the comparison of the Soviet and czarist practices. For example, during a 30-year period of revolutionary agitation and terrorism from 1876 to 1904, executions were rare—17 people a year for the whole country. In contrast, during the 1937–38 wave, a half-million political prisoners and almost a half-million thieves were executed in a year and a half; another source cited for the period identifies the execution figure as 1.7 million. Another counterpoint: The direct victims in the Soviet Union number between 15 and 25 million people; those of Nazi Germany number between 10 and 12 million.

The brutality of life and death in the "destructive-labor camps," or slave labor camps, is the focus of Volume II. During Stalin's reign, 10 to 15 million men, women, and children over age 12 were imprisoned in these "extermination factories" in any one year. Solzhenitsyn distinguishes between the prisons where a human being is able to confront "his grief face to face . . . to find space within himself for it" and the slave labor camps where survival, often at the expense of others, demanded every energy. The lives of the imprisoned consisted of "work, work, work; of starvation, cold, and cunning." Solzhenitsyn provides a brief capsule enumerating the range and types of work and expressing its exhausting, debilitating effects: back-breaking, hand-wearing labor with picks and shovels on the earth, in mines and quarries, in brickyards, tunnels, and on farms (favored for the food to be grabbed from the ground) and lumberjack work in the forests. The workday in the summer was "sometimes sixteen hours long." The hours were shortened during the winter, but workers were "chased out" to work in cold lower than 60 degrees below zero in order to "prove it was possible to fulfill" quotas.

> And how did they feed them in return? They poured water into a pot, and the best one might expect was that they would drop unscrubbed small potatoes into it, but otherwise black cabbage, beet tops, all kinds of trash. Or else vetch or bran, they didn't begrudge these.

In several chapters Solzhenitsyn scrutinizes the relationship between the penal system—the Gulag—and the Soviet economy "when the plan for superindustrialization was rejected in favor of the plan for supersupersuperindustrialization . . . with the massive public works of the First Five-Year Plan. . . ." Slave labor allowed Stalin to industrialize the nation cheaply. The laborers were expendable: The victims were sent to isolated regions and worked brutally without concern for their well-being and safety to construct railroads, canals, highways, hydroelectric stations, and nine cities. The laborers were not paid: "[F]orced labor should be set up in such a way that the prisoner should not earn anything from his work but that the state should derive economic profit from it." This system was termed "correction through labor."

The system did not work; corruption and thievery were rampant. Construction materials were stolen; machinery was damaged. The prisoners were not dutiful workers, nor did their weakened condition make for efficient and effective work.

As in Volume I, examples of individuals caught in the mesh provide details to reveal the extent of villainy. A particularly emotional chapter details the fate of children who are bereft as a result of the war or the imprisonment of their parents. They are swept up and sent away to be mistreated in colonies or workhouses. From the age of 12 they can be sentenced under the Criminal Code and end up in the Archipelago. "In 1927 prisoners aged sixteen (they didn't count the younger ones) to twenty-four represented 48 percent of all prisoners."

Solzhenitsyn enumerates and explains the "traits of *free* life," which were determined by the everpresent threat of the Archipelago: constant fear—of arrest, purges, inspections, dismissal from work, deprivation of residence permit, expulsion or exile; servitude; secrecy and mistrust; universal ignorance; squealing; betrayal as a form of existence; corruption; the lie as a form of existence; and cruelty.

Volume III turns away from the brutality and suffering of slave labor to focus on resistance within the camps. In Part V, *"Katorga"* (hard labor), Solzhenitsyn recounts the attempted escapes by individuals and small groups. An extended pair of chapters explores the reactions and behaviors of "a *committed* escaper," one who "never for a minute doubts that a man cannot live behind bars." The exploits of this individual, who does successfully escape but is recaptured because he refuses to kill innocent people, and the plans and procedures of others attest to the energy and determination of those who had not resigned themselves.

Particularly in the Special Camps, which had been established to separate the "socially irredeemable" political prisoners from the others, did the idea of rebellion begin to take shape and spread. Avengers emerged from the formed comradeships to murder informers. Though only a relatively few got the knife, the result was extensive: Informers stopped informing, and the air was "cleansed of suspicion." Insurrections occurred with varying degrees of success; military power was used to quell the major revolts. In May 1954, the prisoners of Kengir gained control of the camp for 40 days. Without any outside support, having been encircled by troops and deceived by an announcement that their demands had been accepted, the prisoners were crushed, literally (by tanks) and politically. More than 700 were killed.

Exile or banishment—the Soviet euphemism was "deportation"—was another instrument of power borrowed from the czars. The "export of undesirables" started shortly after the revolution; in 1929 a system of exile to remote localities in conjunction with forced labor was developed. The exile system grew steadily in capacity and importance in the World War II and postwar years, particularly from the "liberated" (occupied) territories and the western republics. The crimes for which a citizen was punished by exile or banishment included "belonging to a criminal nationality [including both whole nations and, as in the case of the Baltics, special categories of citizens]; a previous term of imprisonment in the camps [prisoners were 'released into exile' in perpetuity]; and residence in a criminal environment." All these deportations, "even without the exiled peasants, exceeded many times over the figure of 500,000 exiles which was all that Tsarist Russia, the prison house of nations, could muster in the whole course of the nineteenth century."

With Stalin's death there came a political thaw and some reprieve for the prisoners. Indeed, many were released. However, Solzhenitsyn points out that in the 40 pre-Khrushchev years, release meant "the space between two arrests." Even when the prisoner was rehabilitated, after being found to be falsely accused, the villains escaped judgment and punishment. Equally profound is the recognition that the camps, approved by the party, continued to exist; there are "still millions inside, and just as before, many of them are helpless victims of perverted justice: swept in simply to keep the system operating and well fed."

Solzhenitsyn specifically reveals his own error, the degree to which he had been deceived. He had let himself be persuaded by the state's authorization to publish *One Day in the Life of Ivan Denisovich* and by the "complacent mainland" that the relaxation was real. He writes, "But I (even I) succumbed and I do not deserve forgiveness."

CENSORSHIP HISTORY

Solzhenitsyn's works were barred from publication in the Soviet Union after Nikita Khrushchev lost power in 1964; previously under the Khrushchev regime, *One Day in the Life of Ivan Denisovich* had been approved for publication. J. M. Coetzee cites Dina Spechler's analysis of "permitted dissent" in the USSR from the death of Stalin in 1953 to 1970. Given the twists and turns of Soviet political life, Khrushchev, reacting to the "nagging resistance from the Party and bureaucracy, used *Novy Mir* [which first published *One Day in the Life of Ivan Denisovich* in 1962] as a vehicle to 'expose and dramatize problems and reveal facts that demonstrated . . . the necessity of the changes he proposed.'"

In February 1974, Aleksandr Solzhenitsyn was arrested and charged with treason; he lost his Soviet citizenship and was deported, that is, exiled from Russia. A Russian-language edition of *Gulag Archipelago I* had been published in Paris in September 1973. The American edition, which should have appeared immediately after the Russian, was delayed for six months, a delay to which the author attributes his arrest and exile, according to his memoir, *The Oak and the Calf.* He believes that "if all America had been reading *Gulag* by the New Year," the Soviets would have been hesitant to move against him.

The events leading to the publication significantly reflect the text. It had been completed in June 1968; a microfilm of the manuscript had been secretly and at great peril sent to the West, but the author had postponed its publication. The decision to publish was forced upon him in August 1973 when a Leningrad woman to whom Solzhenitsyn had entrusted the manuscript revealed the hiding place of a copy after having been terrorized through five sleepless days of interrogation by the KGB. (Released after the manuscript was located, she hanged herself.) The author understood that he had no alternative but to authorize publication immediately: The book contained the names of several hundred people who had provided him with information.

The underlying reason for the action against Solzhenitsyn with the publication of this volume was the rejection of the then-current Russian orthodoxy, that is, that "the abuses of justice under Stalinism were the direct consequence of the personality of the dictator." His data insist that the tyranny began with Lenin and continued under Nikita Khrushchev.

In contradiction of the United Nations (UN) Universal Declaration of Human Rights, which binds members to uphold the dissemination of ideas and information "through any media and regardless of frontiers," *Gulag Archipelago* was removed from two Swiss bookshops operating on United Nations premises. It was reported that the removal was instigated by the Soviet Union. Secretary-General Kurt Waldheim, at a July 1974 press conference, indicated a policy of giving "guidance" to the bookshops, that is, as indicated by Geneva director-general Vittorio Winspeare-Guicciardi, telling them it was their "duty" to avoid "publications *à caractère outrageant pour un Etat Membre*" (publications of an insulting character for a Member Nation). The press conference was held in response to the protest of the books' removal by more than 250 UN employees.

In addition to his works being barred from publication after 1964 (a collection of his short stories was published in 1963), Solzhenitsyn faced increasing criticism and overt harassment from authorities. In 1970, having been awarded the Nobel Prize in literature, he declined to go to Stockholm for fear that he would not be readmitted to the Soviet Union. During his exile, *Novy Mir* attempted to publish *The Gulag Archipelago*, but publishing was blocked by order from the Central Committee, particularly Vadim Medvedev, the Communist Party's chief of ideology. However, President Mikhail S. Gorbachev authorized the publication of extracts in 1989. On August 15, 1990, Gorbachev issued a decree restoring full citizenship to Solzhenitsyn and 22 other exiled dissident artists and intellectuals. In 1994, Solzhenitsyn returned to Russia.

An about-face was revealed on September 9, 2009, when Russia's Education Ministry announced that excerpts of the *Gulag Archipelago* have been added to the curriculum for high school students. The rationale behind the decision: the "vital historical and cultural heritage on the course of 20th century domestic history" contained in Solzhenitsyn's work.

Aleksandr Solzhenitsyn died in 2008.

FURTHER READING

Blake, Patricia. *"The Gulag Archipelago." New York Times Book Review*, October 26, 1975, pp. 1, 18–21.

Burg, David, and George Feifer. *Solzhenitsyn*. New York: Stein and Day, 1972.

Chalidze, Valery. *To Defend These Rights: Human Rights and the Soviet Union*. New York: Random House, 1974.

Coetzee, J. M. "Censorship and Polemic: The Solzhenitsyn Affair." *Pretexts* 2 (Summer 1990): 3–26.

Conquest, Robert. "Evaluation of an Exile." *Saturday Review*, April 20, 1974, 22–24, 30.

"Gulag at the UN." *Newsletter on Intellectual Freedom* 23 (1974): 162.

Kramer, Hilton. "The Soviet Terror Continued." *New York Times Book Review*, June 18, 1978, pp. 1, 28–29.

Rubenstein, Joshua. *"The Gulag Archipelago."* *The New Republic*, June 22, 1974, 21–22.
"Russia Makes Gulag History Required Reading." *Boston Globe* (September 10, 2009).
Available online. URL: http://www.Boston.com/news/world9sep2009. Accessed
June 14, 2010.
Solzhenitsyn, Aleksandr. *The Oak and the Calf.* New York: Harper and Row, 1980.
Steiner, George. "The Forests of the Night." *New Yorker,* June 16, 1974, 78–87.

GULLIVER'S TRAVELS

Author: Jonathan Swift
Original dates and places of publication: 1726, England; 1808 (Volume I),
1809 (Volume II), United States
Publishers: Benjamin Motte; Mathew Carey
Literary form: Fiction

SUMMARY

While studying mathematics and physics at Emanuel College in Cambridge,
Lemuel Gulliver also devotes much time to the study of navigation. His appren-
ticeship to Mr. James Bates, a London surgeon, leads into an occupation
as a ship's surgeon during his first experience on the sea. After six years of
this, however, he grows weary, and so he spends the next three years close
to his family in Redriff. He returns to the sea on May 4, 1699, again as ship's
surgeon, after receiving a lucrative offer from Captain William Pritchard.

The first of four voyages encounters a violent storm that destroys his
vessel, and Gulliver is washed ashore on an unknown island. Alone and
exhausted, he falls into a deep sleep. Upon awakening, he realizes that he is
bound to the ground with ropes and stakes from head to toe. After unsuccessfully trying to wrest free, he watches as tiny people, the Lilliputians,
who are no more than six inches high, await with arrows and spears, ready
to strike at him if he tries to break away. Deciding to keep a passive course,
Gulliver allows the tiny people to feed him and transport him to a special
dwelling. Gulliver is chained by one ankle in a dwelling no larger than a
small room, allowing him limited mobility. The emperor dispatches troops,
tailors, civilians, and all able bodies to perform tasks for the one they call
"Man Mountain." They guard him, clothe him, feed him, and search his
pockets. Gradually, as Gulliver gains their trust by behaving in a civilized
way, the Cabinet concedes to repeated requests for granting him liberty,
but only after he swears to them twice: once in his own fashion and again
according to Lilliputian custom.

One condition of his liberty states that he "shall be our ally against our
enemies in the Island of Blefuscu . . ." The emperor suggests to Gulliver
that he ought to wade across the channel and capture the Blefuscudian fleet.
He does this with little effort and is awarded the highest-ranking label of

honor: Nardac. This action, however, does not sit all too well with Gulliver's conscience; he proclaims that he will from now on be at least amiable to the Blefuscudians. Meanwhile, dissension rises among higher-ranking officials who become concerned that Gulliver may be more of a liability than an asset, primarily due to the staggering cost of feeding him, which has taken a toll on Lilliputian resources. Lord High Treasurer Flimnap, Admiral Skyris Bolgolan (Gulliver's mortal enemy since his arrival), and other jealous council members draw up articles with the intent of having Gulliver banished from the island. Their claims include various misdeeds: the incident when Gulliver saved the flame-engulfed palace by urinating upon it, Gulliver's unwillingness to totally destroy and enslave the Blefuscudians after capturing their fleet, and his befriending of the Blefuscudian emperor out of pity.

Gulliver realizes that he has no choice but to flee Lilliput. He is fortunate to find a human-size longboat aimlessly floating in the bay. Courting the Blefuscudian emperor for aid, Gulliver receives a sail and victuals for a journey home, which he begins on September 24. Three days later, he is picked up by a wayward ship, the *Adventure*, captained by John Nicholas of Liverpool.

Gulliver's second voyage takes him to the land of Brobdingnag, where everything but he is incredibly large, which makes Gulliver realize how the Lilliputians must have felt in their encounter. His third voyage takes him to the lands of the Laputans and the Balnibarbians, rival factions that have the former being light-years ahead of the latter in terms of technology, thus holding the upper hand in terms of rule and class domination. Gulliver returns to Redriff on April 10, 1710.

Gulliver departs on his fourth voyage from Redriff on September 7, 1710, this time as the captain of the *Adventure*. Supposedly a peaceful trade voyage, the crew turns rogue and commits mutiny. Gulliver is abandoned in a longboat, once again alone at sea. He comes upon an island and notices many sets of prints in the sand, mostly of horses. He encounters a beast-like creature he knows is not human, yet he cannot help noticing striking similarities, the greatest being its ability to walk upright rather than on all fours. Feeling threatened, Gulliver strikes the creature aside the face. This action only serves to attract many more, who corner Gulliver back to a tree and release excrement upon him until a bay horse arrives; then a dapple gray appears, causing the raucous beasts to flee. Gulliver soon learns that these are not horses but a species known as Houyhnhnms (pronounced winams) that take him to their village.

After being led through three long narrow buildings occupied by more Houyhnhnms, the gray takes Gulliver to another building where three Yahoos, the creatures Gulliver first encountered, are tied up at their necks and madly clawing away at the remains of animal flesh. The largest Yahoo is retrieved by a bay Houyhnhnm and made to stand by Gulliver for comparison's sake. Then, after a hearty meal, Gulliver is given a stable and sleeps deeply in his hay bed. Five months pass and Gulliver has been able to explain fully his origin and species to the gray Houyhnhnm, the leader and his master, in such a way as to not offend, for Gulliver thought that they might find the horse's role in his society unfavorable. But his master insists on knowing all aspects of how horses are treated, and Gulliver obliges him. He also explains how he came to the land of the Houyhnhnms, which perplexes his master because Houyhnhnms cannot comprehend the many vices of the pirates who were under the employ of Gulliver and why they behaved the way they did in causing mutiny. Gulliver then explains war, politics, and taxes, which further confuses his master, who cannot understand how Yahoos with the ability to reason (which is the classification he bestows upon Gulliver and all humans) and so worthy of virtue could demote themselves to a level of savagery and unwarranted chaos in order to make progress. Gulliver comes to realize that perhaps humans are no more than Yahoos; he becomes ashamed of his origins and vows to spend the rest of his days with the wise and noble Houyhnhnms.

One day Gulliver's master imparts news that Gulliver must leave the Houyhnhnms because he is, by their definition, a Yahoo, albeit a reasonable one, who could cause strife among the Houyhnhnms due to his ability to reason and use logic, unlike the real Yahoos. Gulliver is devastated, but he willingly departs for home in a handmade vessel on February 15, 1714.

The longing for the Houyhnhnms is reflected in Gulliver's behavior upon returning to Redriff in December of 1714. So disgusted is he with his similarity to and relations with "human Yahoos" (i.e., his family), he will not converse with them or others, instead choosing to spend the majority of his time caring for and admiring two recently purchased horses.

CENSORSHIP HISTORY

Swift is a master of allegory, with much critical acclaim for his works. This point is pivotal when focusing on the censorship of *Gulliver's Travels* because allegory, according to Donald Thomas, is used as a tool to disguise libel. In *A Long Time Burning: The History of Literary Censorship in England* Thomas states that "the allusions of the allegory might be so abstruse as to prevent not only prosecution but even straightforward interpretation." An argument may be derived from any of the symbolism employed by Swift. For instance, there is no way to be totally sure if Swift intends the Lilliputians and Blefuscudians to represent the English Protestants and the French Catholics. It is unknown which religious practice Swift is mocking when he discusses the reason why the Blefuscudians were exiled for not breaking their eggs on the small end. And whether there is a connection between the high heels and low heels and the Tories and Whigs is uncertain. Many who have studied and analyzed *Gulliver's Travels* contend that Swift intended these relationships, but the author never revealed that was the case.

Published in 1726, *Gulliver's Travels* was, according to Anne Lyon Haight in *Banned Books: 387 B.C. to 1978 A.D.*, "denounced on all sides as wicked and obscene." This possibly stems from two viewpoints. First, Swift, in many instances, portrays Gulliver as a human being whose virtues and merits do not measure up to the species he encounters. In his first voyage to Lilliput, he is consistently preoccupied with fighting rather than maintaining the passive course that ultimately gains him his freedom. This is shown when he partakes of the first meal offered by the Lilliputians: "I confess I was often tempted, while they were passing backwards and forwards on my body, to seize forty or fifty of the first that came in my reach, and dash them against the ground."

The second viewpoint is highlighted by T. O. Wedel in his essay "On the Philosophical Background of *Gulliver's Travels.*" Wedel explains that around the time *Gulliver's Travels* was published there had been a shift in the view of man from that of a sinful and evil creature to one of being a creation of God, whose image should be upheld and revered, neither of which connects with Swift's portrayal of Gulliver, who is ultimately shunned and exiled wherever he goes. Wedel states: "The year of our Lord 1726, when Gulliver appeared, was in no mood to put a proper value upon a work which spoke of *homo sapiens* as 'the most pernicious race of odious little vermin that nature ever suffered to crawl upon the surface of the earth.' " He further explains that, "if Swift had written *Gulliver's Travels* a few generations earlier, he would have given little cause for complaint. . . . For the transition from the seventeenth century to the eighteenth was experiencing a revolution in ethical thought."

In the introduction of his *Twentieth Century Interpretations of Gulliver's Travels,* Frank Brady supports Wedel's viewpoints about how, "in the Houyhnhnms [Swift] satirized the increasingly popular optimistic concept of human nature exemplified in deism." These observations show that Gulliver is not what the public wanted to see in an epic hero; rather, he is a man whose guilt surfaces all too quickly when he is forced to look at himself and see prevalent shortcomings in the comparison to the race of beings with whom he is associating.

In *The Mind and Art of Jonathan Swift,* Ricardo Quintana says that the mood of the times and reaction to the book were mixed; everyone was reading it, with "Swift's grave verisimilitude (being) highly relished." While this statement somewhat contradicts Haight's statement, Quintana adds that there were also those in higher positions who didn't appreciate the satirical jabs. Certain upstanding ladies said it was "an insult on Providence depreciating the works of the Creator." According to Swift, the Irish archbishop "said that book was full of improbable lies, and for his part, he hardly believed a word of it." Evidence would suggest that censorship of *Gulliver's Travels* was sporadic and not on a massive scale; rather, those whom Swift wrote about seem to be the ones who found offense with his words and ideas.

With the turn of the 19th century, a change of taste ushered in an intense prudishness that replaced general acceptance of most literature as suitable for younger reading. While the early editions of *Gulliver's Travels*—about 60 were published between 1726 and 1800 and 150 more between 1800 and 1900—were complete, more than half of the 19th-century editions were bowdlerized. Editors either removed the ribald features or tried generally to prepare texts suitable for young readers. Swift seemed to insist on unflattering descriptions of the Yahoos (the bodies of the males are hairy all over but bald on their buttocks "except about the anus"; the females' sagging breasts "often reached almost to the ground"), and he also depicts the Lilliputian army marching 24 abreast between Gulliver's legs, the young officers glancing up to view his genitals through his ragged breeches. For a general audience the considerable number of expurgations range from the scholarly version done by the vice president of the Royal Irish Academy in 1862 to the haphazard one supervised by Harriet Beecher Stowe in 1873. She is quoted in Noel Perrin's *Dr. Bowdler's Legacy* as stating, "Swift's genius commands our admiration, but his works should never be introduced into the home-circle save in such revised and clearly edited editions as this one."

Of the five common types of expurgations, four apply to young readers, two to children, two to adolescents. (The last is for general readers.) One version for children includes only two voyages—to Lilliput and Brobdingnag, drastically abridged (for example, the Lilliputian officers keep their eyes down). Thus, the Yahoos are eliminated altogether. Other versions for children include only the bland segments of Swift's tale. For adolescents there are bowdlerized school textbooks, originating in Victorian England, and 20th-century illustrated editions. The most bowdlerized of these remove all references to the torso of the human body and its activities—urinating on burning palaces, or, a Brobdingnagian mother nursing a baby, for example. Also the Houyhnhnms limiting the number of their foals was excluded, as was the mention of the English medical practice of giving laxatives. Overall, the purpose of these Victorian bowdlerizations was to maintain humanity on pedestals, by removing aspects of humans' animal nature. It was, as critic Noel Perrin says, "a reflection of moral progress in real world. People in the eighteenth century, and earlier, did not take offense at coarse passages because they were coarse themselves. They all talked like characters in Sterne and Fielding anyway, so how could they find it wrong in a book?"

The first French edition, 1727, is bowdlerized; its editor, the Abbé Desfontaines, explained that a complete version "would have revolted the good taste which reigns in France." The two 18th-century editions in the United States were not expurgated; there were two brief abridgments.

FURTHER READING

Brady, Frank, ed. *Twentieth Century Interpretations of Gulliver's Travels.* Englewood Cliffs, N.J.: Prentice-Hall, 1968.
Haight, Anne Lyon, and Chandler B. Grannis. *Banned Books: 387 B.C. to 1978 A.D.* 4th ed. New York: R. R. Bowker, 1978.

Quintana, Ricardo. *The Mind and Art of Jonathan Swift.* London: Oxford University Press, 1936.

Perrin, Noel. *Dr. Bowdler's Legacy: A History of Expurgated Books in England and America.* New York: Atheneum, 1969.

Thomas, Donald. *A Long Time Burning: The History of Literary Censorship in England.* New York: Frederick A. Praeger, 1969.

Wedel, T. O. "On the Philosophical Background of *Gulliver's Travels.*" *Studies in Philology* 23 (1926): n.p.

—Eric P. Schmidt

HANDBOOK FOR CONSCIENTIOUS OBJECTORS

Editor: Robert A. Seeley
Original date and place of publication: 1952, United States
Publisher: Central Committee for Conscientious Objectors
Literary form: Nonfiction

SUMMARY

The primary need for the *Handbook for Conscientious Objectors* has been to give information on conscientious objection (CO) and about war and how war affects individuals. Beyond information about the draft law and how to make a CO claim, apparently the orientation of the earlier editions, the 1981 edition responds to the need for discussion of war resistance as a moral problem. The author's feeling is that "a book like this one should help people to take the stands which they can take—even if they do not fit under the narrow provisions of the draft law."

The draft and the military are the first focus of attention. The recruitment of 400,000 new soldiers every year to maintain troop strength results from the departure from the military of tens of thousands of troops each year. The overall size of the armed forces is much larger than the military "defense" of the United States mainland needs. The size is determined in part by the "doctrine of deterrence"—having so many weapons that opponents will be deterred from attacking—and geopolitical obligations. The draft is used when voluntary recruitments for the armed forces fall short, as well as for expanding the military when a war makes such expansion necessary.

As part of this section, the structure of the existing Selective Service System is explained in conjunction with its operation. Included are registration procedures and the workings of the lottery, leading to induction orders. This sets the stage for discussion of how to apply for a new classification—deferment or exemption, a CO claim. The procedures are identified, along with the 17 classifications, including 1-A-0: Conscientious objector to combatant military duty, available for induction as a noncombatant only ("judgment classification"); 1-0: Conscientious objector to combatant and noncombatant military duty, available for civilian alternative service ("judgment classification"); and 1-W: Conscientious objector performing alternative service ("administrative classification"). The individual's rights for appeal and the process of appeal are explained.

Resistance to military service may be initiated at the registration stage. "The Military Selective Service Act requires male U.S. citizens to register for the draft when the President orders them to do so." Individuals have six choices: They may refuse to register, telling the Selective Service and others, or they may refuse to register and tell no one. They may register for the draft under protest or as a conscientious objector. They may register and file a CO application later or make a CO statement at the time of registration verification. Explanations are qualified with cautionary notes; for example, the first two violate the draft law and potentially lead to prosecution. (Punishment for prosecution could be five years in federal prison or up to a $10,000 fine or both.) "[Y]ou shouldn't decide not to register because you don't think you'll be caught. Always think first about the worst that could happen, and whether you could face it, before you break the law." Foremost advice is that individuals must live with their decisions so they must decide for themselves and must do so early enough to avail themselves of every option.

Conscientious objection under the law is defined. The Supreme Court has defined it as based on religious training and belief and objection to *all* wars. This basic definition has been qualified to recognize that the religious belief must be "sincere and meaningful" and that it "occupies a place in the life of its possessor parallel to that filled by [an] orthodox belief in God"; it need not be based on a traditional religion, but may be moral, or philosophical, or a mixture of these with religion. These beliefs must be "deeply held."

Current law does not grant CO status to "selective objectors," those who would fight in some wars or under some conditions but not in others—for example, objecting to fighting in the Vietnam War, but being willing to defend the United States against direct attack. An underlying position that has operated in these situations is the so-called just war theory: "Beginning with St. Augustine (A.D. 354–430), the Just War Theory tried to set up standards for deciding which wars were right and which wrong." Many theologians now identify seven standards. Generally, in addition to the war being "openly and legally declared by a legal government," the war must be a last resort, fought to "redress rights actually violated or for defense against unjust demands backed by threat of force." Also, soldiers must distinguish between armies and civilians and avoid killing the latter on purpose.

The *Handbook* also provides information about federal court jurisdiction and procedures and the kinds of defenses that COs have used in court. There are four possible courses of action: to plead not guilty, to stand mute, to plead guilty, and to plead nolo-contendere or "I do not contest the charge."

In Part III, "Thinking About War Resistance," Seeley steps away from representing draft law and related issues and instead expresses his own ideas about war and resistance. War is defined as "armed conflict between two or more countries or between rival military forces within one country" with or without a formal declaration of war. Guerrilla warfare is appropriately named "war" while the cold war is merely a form of geopolitics. Modern warfare is often termed "total war" because it is not limited to small armies fighting on distant battlefields. Increasingly since the American Civil War, wars have involved attacks on an enemy's civilian populations and industries, the latter being largely engaged in war supplies production. Nuclear wars and other modern wars use weapons that broaden the scope and impact of military strategies.

The causes and costs of war are directly discussed with frequent examples throughout. Referred to as causal ideas are the beliefs of some anthropologists in a "killer instinct" in humans; the Marxist contention that capitalistic countries must continually expand their markets and their control of other countries' resources; people's misunderstandings or lack of knowledge of each other, and nations acting "like a law unto [themselves] in foreign affairs." A more immediate cause, potentially, is the arms race: Tensions between countries are increased; a readiness to fight is created. "The arms race may be called defense or a 'necessary response to imperialist aggression,' or whatever. In fact it is a preparation for war. Types of weapons, size of armies, placement of troops, etc., are determined mainly by plans for future wars." However, an opposing explanation is offered:

> The causes of any particular war are many, and it's hard to know which is most important. And the causes of war itself—the explanation of why people fight—may not even include the arms race. It may be that people make weapons because they're willing to fight—not that people are willing to fight because they make weapons.

The costs of war emerge in the statistics of casualties—soldiers and civilians as well as the destruction of cities and regions.

> Wars have always been deadly. In the seventeenth century, eight million people died in Germany alone during the Thirty Years War (1618–1648). The American Civil War killed 529,000 on both sides; World War I, ten million; World War II, 38 million. . . . But worst of all for the world of today were the deaths of 100,000 in one brief moment at Hiroshima.

These statistics and data do not, however, reveal the horrors of war—the atrocities committed upon individuals, the miseries inflicted upon communities, the destruction of crops and property, and the damage to the environment.

Throughout the text, the author asks thought-generating questions so readers might consider their reactions and beliefs. Here are two examples:

Think about others. There's nothing wrong or unusual about being concerned with your family. How would your resistance affect them? If you're married, how would it affect your marriage? Your children? Do you think it's worth the risk? Many do; others don't. Neither position is "wrong."

Can you be personally responsible for the results of policies that you disagree with and didn't make? What is your responsibility?

Augmenting these in the "Appendices" are three pages of "Questions Asked COs," provided both to provoke thought and to help the individual prepare for the necessary personal appearance before the draft board.

CENSORSHIP HISTORY

A unanimous vote of 5-0 in March 1982 by the school board of the Coleman, Wisconsin, Area School District in effect censored *A Handbook for Conscientious Objectors* edited by Robert A. Seeley. The book was placed on restricted access in the Coleman High School Library. The reason behind the action: alleged political overtones. School Board President David Rakowski clarified the restriction: "If a student needs the books for reference or resource material, he is free to check them out." (The other book restricted at the same time was WORDS OF CONSCIENCE: RELIGIOUS STATEMENTS ON CONSCIENTIOUS OBJECTION edited by Shawn Perry.) Apparently in support of the restriction, the school librarian, Arlene Valenti, stated, "Though the freedom to read is everyone's right, a young mind is very impressionable, and so it becomes important for educators to guard against misleading ideas and writing. [The material] has a number of procedures showing the reader numbers of ways to beat the draft."

Donna Meyer, a concerned mother of two teenaged sons, had initiated the request for the books. She had reacted to the fact that the school permitted military recruiters to speak with the students but did not permit expression of the other side of the issue. She argued that informed decisions by students about future choices should be based on balanced information.

A telephone conversation in April 1996 with an assistant to the current librarian of Coleman High School revealed, after she checked the restricted shelves, that the two books were not in the library; they had been withdrawn "a few years ago" because they were "out of date."

The issue of "equal access" raised by Meyer has become a significant First Amendment concern. The controversy has centered on the pervasive military presence in schools: military men in uniform routinely walk down the halls, post materials/recruiting literature in the school library and guidance office, and often distribute funded "magazines" that promote military service. The Central Committee for Conscientious Objectors, publisher of *A Handbook for Conscientious Objectors*, and allied organizations have attempted to ensure a balanced picture of military life and outcomes.

The balanced-picture position offers arguments to counter some of the military's claims. They include discussion of the ethics and horrors of war, information about the realities of military training, and information regarding the application of military training to military jobs rather than civilian jobs. Also included are revelations about misleading advertising about the GI Bill: Fewer than half of all GIs have received benefits at all, yet all enlistees must pay a nonrefundable fee of $1,200. The advertised economic benefits are also countered: On average, veterans earn less than nonveterans and, in recent years, are two to five times more likely to be homeless.

Typically, these organizations have been denied equal access to the students by school administrators. The standard argument of rejection is: The military has always recruited here; you're just an interest group; we have no obligation to let you in.

Federal district and appellate courts have upheld the Equal Access Act's applicability in the "nonpublic forum" of the public school. In such nonpublic forums, access to information may be limited as long as the regulations are reasonable and not a "facade for viewpoint-based discrimination." However, once a controversial issue is allowed to be raised and one viewpoint is permitted access, thus creating a "limited public forum," then equal access must be available to the opposing viewpoints.

Such a situation occurred at the Grossmont Union High School District in San Diego in 1986. Military recruitment advertisements were accepted in the school newspaper; counter-recruiting materials were rejected. In San Diego, in *Committee Against Registration and the Draft (CARD) v. Governing Board of Grossman Union High School District* (1986) the 9th Circuit Court of Appeals ruled:

> The Board cannot allow the presentation of one side of an issue, but prohibit the presentation of the other side. . . . Here, the Board permitted mixed political and commercial speech advocating military service, but attempted to bar the same type of speech opposing such service. Accordingly, the Board violated the First Amendment.

It further added: "It has long been recognized that the subject of military service is controversial." When schools create a forum for the proponents of the military, they must, under the First and Fourteenth Amendments, provide equal access for those with opposing points of view.

In a parallel case in Atlanta a year later, *Scearcey v. Crim*, the 11th Circuit Court of Appeals ruled that a school may not prevent a peace group from presenting information on peace-oriented careers and educational opportunities when access has been given to the military to provide such information; they may also distribute information on the military as a career.

FURTHER READING

"Coleman, Wisconsin." *Newsletter on Intellectual Freedom* 31 (July 1982): 126.
Diener, Sam. Central Committee for Conscientious Objectors. Telephone interview.
June 27, 1996.
Feldman, James. "The Right to Present Alternatives." Unpublished article.

THE HOAX OF THE TWENTIETH CENTURY

Author: Arthur R. Butz
Original date and place of publication: 1975, Great Britain
Publisher: Historical Review Press
Literary form: Nonfiction

SUMMARY

The "hoax" of the title of *The Hoax of the Twentieth Century* refers to Germany's "murderous outburst during World War II," specifically to features of the Holocaust. Arthur R. Butz in his foreword establishes his position in response to potential questions about his qualifications: "If a 'scholar,' regardless of his specialty, perceives that scholarship is acquiescing, from whatever motivation, in a monstrous lie, then it is his duty to expose the lie, whatever his qualifications." Butz defines his purpose with reference to specific features: "The subject of this book is the question of whether or not the Germans attempted to exterminate the European Jews. We are not concerned with considering in any detail the general question of alleged brutalities of all sorts or with presenting a complete picture of the functioning of German camps." Further, "The thesis of this book is that the story of Jewish extermination in World War II is a propaganda hoax."

Questions are raised about the "war crimes trials," which were "precedent shattering in their scope and in the explicitness of the victorious powers' claims to some sort of legal jurisdiction in respect of laws or understandings which did not exist at the time they were allegedly broken by the Axis powers." This "disregard of European honor conventions which had been respected for centuries" was further compounded by judicial prejudgment: The judges had previous to the trials talked about the obvious guilt of the defendants.

A basic argument disputes the claim that 6 million Jews were exterminated. The statistics of the demographics of Jewish population in the world are attacked. "The 1948 *World Almanac* (p. 249) also gives the American Jewish Committee estimate for 1938 [sic], 15,688,259, while the 1949 *World Almanac* (p. 204) reports new figures from the American Jewish Committee which were developed in 1947–1948: 16,643,120 in 1939 and 11,226,600 in 1947." This last figure is immediately countered by citing military expert Hanson Baldwin's 1948 *New York Times* article data of 15 to 18 million world Jewish population. This contention of erroneous population figures is furthered by questioning United States Jewish population statistics given by the Jewish Statistical Bureau, identified as a subsidiary of either the American Jewish Conference or the Synagogue of America: 1,770,647 in 1937 and 5.3 million in 1959. The author proposes two conservative estimates of Jewish population growth in the United States, both of which approximate a figure of 1 million to 1.5 million in excess of that of the Jewish Statistical Bureau's figure.

> Moreover, in the demographic argument for a five or six million drop in world Jewish population, the sources and authorities for the figures used are Communist and Jewish and thus, by the nature of the problem we are examining, must be considered essentially useless. In addition, the post-war figures for the United States are demonstrably too low by a significant amount.

To counter the "extermination mythology" as an explanation for any drop in Jewish population, Butz builds a case for deportations and deaths resulting from disease and starvation. Before the war, the "German Government had used all means to encourage the emigration of Jews from Germany and most German Jews had left before the outbreak of the war." The difficulty of arranging for other countries to take the Jews was solved by the German army's easterly movement. A resettlement program got under way in autumn 1941 to move European Jews, most of whom were within the German sphere of influence, to the East. It was only partially carried out.

> . . . of course, nowhere near six million Jews were involved. Excluding Polish and Rumanian Jews, perhaps 750,000 Jews were resettled, primarily in the Ukraine, White Russia and Latvia. Not all Polish Jews fell under German domination. Apart from those who managed to flee before or after the German occupation, several hundred thousand or perhaps a million Jews had been deported from Poland by the Russians in 1940 and had been dispersed in the Soviet Union. For the most part, the Polish Jews who came into German hands were crowded into ghettoes in eastern Poland (1939 boundaries).
>
> What happened to all of these people can be established only in a very general way, because all of the territory that the Jews had been resettled onto became Soviet territory after the war, and because the victorious powers engaged in considerable suppression of the data. However, there is sufficient evidence to permit us to see approximately what happened. Although it is very likely that a fair number perished in the disorderly and chaotic conditions that accompanied the German retreats, it is established that a large number of Jews, predominantly of pre-war Polish nationality, were absorbed into the Soviet Union, and the remainder of the Jews who had been uprooted ultimately resettled in Palestine, the U.S., Europe and elsewhere.

Disease, specifically typhus, plagued the German concentration camps since early in the war. A typhus epidemic at the Belsen camp, for example, is cited as the major cause of deaths, resulting from a "total loss of control" at the end of the war, not a "deliberate policy." Butz suggests that scenes of "a large number of unburied bodies" were repeated in other German camps for the same reasons. The epidemic caught the Auschwitz authorities with inadequate crematory facilities. ("It was German policy to cremate the bodies of camp inmates who died.") Epidemics were also "common in the ghettos," according to German attribution, because of a "lack of discipline on the part of the Jews."

Among the many types of German camps, only 13 were "concentration camps" and only six were "alleged" to be "extermination camps." Only two camps, Auschwitz and Lublin, fit into both of these categories. The number of inmates in the entire German concentration camp system was "224,000 in August 1943 and 524,000 a year later."

Butz focuses on Auschwitz because of its notoriety. Actually a collection of neighboring camps, it was a huge industrial operation, including a hydrogenation plant and a Buna synthetic rubber plant, employing both free and prison labor. Birkenau was an important satellite camp with the largest number of deportees and prisoners. Typical inmate strengths for these two camps were 20,000 and 35,000 respectively (30 to 60 percent women), making it the largest complex of camps in the German system. Besides discussing the operation and labor functions of these camps, Butz examines the claim that at Birkenau "a program of mass killings of Jews via gas chamber was in operation, the Jews having been transported to Auschwitz primarily for this purpose."

In discrediting the "extermination legend," Butz disputes the data by pointing to "inconsistencies and implausibilities." Among these are the inconsistencies of the figures of the exterminated, ranging from 750,000 to 7 million. Colonel Rudolf Höss, commandant of Auschwitz from May 1940 to late 1943, admits in his affidavit to 2.5 million victims, which Butz discredits. Butz also rejects the existence of gas chambers for extermination purposes, asserting they were used for disinfecting clothing in order to destroy all lice, which were carriers of typhus. The gas chambers allegedly disguised as showers were indeed showers: "all 'survivor literature', sincere or inventive, . . . report the same basic procedure involved in entering a German camp: disrobe, shave hair, shower, dress in new clothes or in old clothes after disinfection." Höss refers to this procedure as an attempt to fool the victims. In contrast, Butz states:

> In any case Birkenau was, in a very real sense, a "death camp"; dead, dying and sick people were sent there and, after the crematoria were built, the dead were disposed of in them. If one is to claim an "extermination camp" when there is none, what better choice is there but a "death camp"?

To substantiate his claims about the exaggerated figures of Jewish deaths, Butz demonstrates in detail the insufficient numbers of crematoria to accommodate the alleged numbers of bodies.

The text is not limited to discourse about the events and situation at Auschwitz. Information about other camps is also included for supporting detail. An entire chapter focuses on the Hungarian Jews, that is, the alleged deportation of approximately 400,000 persons by rail to Birkenau, where they were killed. Further discussion of the trials focuses on the defendants with an analysis of their responses in relation to their anticipation of the trials' purpose and outcome.

A consistent assertion within the text relates to the origins and promotion of the hoax: Zionist Jews are the source of the propaganda. "The claims of exterminations of Jews have their origin not in Allied intelligence information but in the operations of the World Jewish Congress . . . ." Butz traces the 6 million figure to Rabbi Israel Goldstein's December 13, 1942, declaration, printed in the *New York Times*, that there were "authenticated reports" of 2 million Jews slain "and plans for the total extermination of all Jews" by the Nazis. By December 20, 1942, a second figure of 5 million "in danger of extermination" had been added to the original number. Several pages of excerpts of stories from the *New York Times*, from June 14, 1942, to April 25, 1943, each story expressing the tyranny of the Nazis against the Jews, are presented to support the allegation of a propaganda buildup. Subsequently, the World Jewish Congress supplied the figure of 5,721,800 "missing" Jews to the International Military Tribunal at Nuremberg.

The Americans and British adopted these atrocities as the "propaganda basis for their war," then fed the fire with additional data and enraged reactions. Butz points to individuals of considerable rank in the American government who mobilized energy and attitudes in this regard. He particularly cites the influence of Secretary of the Treasury Henry Morgenthau, Jr. (in conflict with U.S. Department of State leaders), who interfered in foreign policy as part of his "long crusade against Germany." He is linked with Zionist causes; his name and department are joined in the text with the World Jewish Congress and its leader, Rabbi Stephen S. Wise. One accomplishment of this group was to convince President Franklin D. Roosevelt to establish the War Refugee Board, "an instrument of Wise and other Zionists," which subsequently issued its "most consequential propaganda achievement," a booklet, *German Extermination Camps: Auschwitz and Birkenau*. The booklet is identified as the "formal birth of the 'official' thesis of extermination via gas chamber at Auschwitz."

> Of course the WRB report failed to change the opinions of the State Department people who had scoffed at the extermination propaganda from the very beginning. In private with [Josiah] DuBois, they were blunt in their opinion of the WRB report: "Stuff like this has been coming from Bern ever since 1942. . . . Don't forget, this is a Jew telling about the Jews." . . . "This is just a campaign by that Jew Morgenthau and his Jewish assistants."

CENSORSHIP HISTORY

Challenges to *The Hoax of the Twentieth Century* have taken several forms. One of these occurred in November 1984 at the California Library Association (CLA) convention and earlier, in 1983, at the Torrance City Library, California. The two incidents are parallel and interrelated; both involve David McCalden, director (in 1985) of Truth Missions and former director of the Institute for Historical Review, identified with Holocaust revisionism.

McCalden was denied access to exhibit space in 1983 during the Torrance City Library's Banned Book Week event. Its librarian, James Buckley, indicated that McCalden's intent was to display books that "presented one-sided views by obscure authors." In addition to *The Hoax*, other titles included ANNE FRANK: THE DIARY OF A YOUNG GIRL and DID SIX MILLION REALLY DIE? THE TRUTH AT LAST by Richard Harwood. The chair of the Southern California Coalition for Intellectual Freedom, Jeffrey Selth, a librarian at the University of California, Riverside, suggested the CLA annual convention as an alternative venue for McCalden's exhibit. Selth felt that McCalden had been unfairly treated.

In late spring, CLA's executive director, Stefan Moses, himself a Jewish refugee from the Nazis, approved McCalden's application both for exhibit space and for a meeting room to offer discussion about revisionist history to include "an overview . . . of the severe censorship and intellectual terrorism which inhibits any objective, open discussion of this controversial topic." When, in September 1984, several council members discovered this potential forum under CLA's auspices, the protests began. One ex officio council member, "as a matter of conscience," informed the American Jewish Committee. Feeling pressured by the "threat" of organized Jewish demonstrations and the ruination of CLA's and his own "good name," Moses canceled McCalden's contract. When McCalden indicated he would sue for breach of contract, the contract was reinstated. On November 13, Moses said, "I just keep thinking of the same quote over and over again . . . 'I may not agree with what you say, but I'll defend with my life your right to say it,' and the fact is, whether you agree with him or not, as a publisher, McCalden has rights."

On November 16, however, Moses and CLA "caved in" under pressure to "strenuous objections" from California assembly Speaker Willie Brown, Los Angeles mayor Tom Bradley, and the Los Angeles City Council. The city council voted unanimously to direct the Los Angeles Public Library to withdraw from CLA if the contract was not rescinded. A Los Angeles Police Department official's stated concern for Moses's safety at the hands of members of a militant Jewish organization added to the pressure on Moses along with the threatened demonstration and boycott of the conference.

The contract's cancellation was disavowed by Bernard Krussman, the president of CLA (who is Jewish), and Carol Sobel, associate director of the ACLU of Southern California, respectively on intellectual freedom and free speech grounds.

Another challenge removed the book itself from the University of Calgary (Canada) library by the Royal Canadian Mounted Police customs and excise division on August 8, 1984. Canada had banned the book (and did the same for *Did Six Million Really Die?*) under a Canadian law that barred import of materials considered seditious, treasonable, immoral, or indecent; so-called hate crime is included in these categories. The inclusion of *The Hoax of the Twentieth Century* on the barred list resulted from a complaint by B'nai B'rith against its distribution. The University of Calgary library had purchased *The Hoax* before its import was barred under the law. The then director of libraries at Calgary, Alan MacDonald, and the Library Association of Alberta condemned the seizure. MacDonald noted the "responsibility of the university . . . to make available all materials of an intellectual nature regardless of their viewpoints." The League of Human Rights of B'nai B'rith national chair David Matas agreed that it is inappropriate to take books from university libraries because they are not "really a source of propaganda and hatred if it means the propaganda could be refuted."

Supported by President Norman Wagner, the university decided to fight the seizure. A comprehensive brief was filed against the action of the customs department. According to Tom Eadie, current director of libraries, and MacDonald, the two copies of *The Hoax of the Twentieth Century* were returned to the library on September 17, 1984. The "technicality" that the books had been purchased prior to the law barring importation was the rationale for the return.

MacDonald has identified two other events in Canada. In January 1995, a copy of *The Hoax of the Twentieth Century* was seized from the rural Didsbury public library. It was shredded on the same day. The book is on the list of books whose importation into Canada is illegal; possession of the book is legal. In 1983, James Keegstra was dismissed from his teaching position because he had introduced Holocaust-denial materials in his curriculum, including the use of this book. After an extended trial over a period of years, Keegstra lost his case.

Protests on the campus of Northwestern University where Arthur R. Butz is a faculty member brought the third challenge. One incident occurred in January 1977. A controversy on the campus and in the community was sparked by a news report in *The Daily Northwestern*, the student newspaper, which revealed the existence of the book and expressed the nature of its contents. Petitions signed by faculty members and students were circulated to, in effect, censure the author. The petitions warned that the book gave "academic legitimacy to anti-Semitic propaganda" and criticized the administration for not "expressing any personal outrage over the book's allegations." Both the university president and the provost responded by noting that Butz had the right of any private citizen to publish what he chose.

A comparable incident at Northwestern University in 1994 caused the cancellation of a "fireside on Holocaust revisionism," a scheduled presentation by Butz. The Public Affairs Residential College (PARC), through its student academic chair, Dan Prosterman, had invited Butz to speak. In the ensuing emotional debate about the upcoming event among the dormitory residents, some advocated Butz's right to speak, while others, feeling personally offended, objected to providing a forum. The fireside speech was specifically canceled after the vice president for student affairs, Peggy Barr, informed the residents that they would be required to pay for security for the event, a fee of $1,500 for 11 security officers. When an anticipated source for this money was denied, the cancellation became inevitable. Despite the cancellation, about 120 demonstrators rallied against Holocaust revisionism. Other students—Prosterman and some PARC residents—expressed being "extremely upset" because the university administration had not been "up front" about the use of funds and had acted so late. Professor Charles Thompson, PARC's master, was quoted as saying that the financial qualification was part of Northwestern University's "campaign of intimidation" against Butz's presenting his views. Butz himself said that "this was the closest" he had gotten to doing so.

Another academic freedom–free speech controversy developed during the fall semester of 1996 when Sheldon Epstein, a part-time lecturer at Northwestern University's School of Engineering, discovered that Butz had created a home page on Northwestern's Web site. Epstein criticized Butz's home page and the university's role in a classroom lecture, in a course on engineering design and entrepreneurship; it was deemed an "inappropriate" topic by the dean of the School of Engineering, Jerome Cohen, who warned Epstein. Epstein maintained that his course included a "segment on ethics and social responsibility in engineering"; he gave his students a research assignment on the Holocaust. These actions led to Epstein's contract not being renewed. Cohen argued that if Epstein were allowed to continue, then Butz could demand the right to espouse his views in class; he added, "This is an engineering school, not a political battleground." Northwestern University president Henry Bienen cited the university's policy of open access to the Internet for any purpose that is not illegal as rooted in traditional principles of free speech and academic freedom. Should he "draw the line" on Butz's access to the university's Web site, what, he pondered, would be next? In a statement on the Web, Northwestern called Butz's views a "contemptible insult" to the Nazis' victims and their families, but "we cannot take action based on the content of what Mr. Butz says regarding the Holocaust without undermining the vital principle of intellectual freedom that our policy serves to protect."

In a telephone interview in March 1996, Butz revealed that the German translation of his book is X-rated, that is, not suitable for use in Germany. Restrictions are so heavy that they amount to censorship: The book cannot be displayed or advertised; mail order purchases are severely constrained.

In 2001, a patron of the Capilano branch of the North Vancouver District Public Library requested that the library's copy of the book be removed on the grounds that it could cause hatred toward Jewish people. When the request was denied, he appealed the decision at a library board meeting. The board voted to retain the book in the collection.

FURTHER READING

"Calgary, Canada." *Newsletter on Intellectual Freedom* 34 (1985): 15–16.
"CLA Cancels 'Holocaust Hoax' Publisher." *Newsletter on Intellectual Freedom* 34 (1985): 1, 30–31.
Eadie, Tom. Director of Libraries, University of Calgary. Telephone interview. February 12, 1997.
"Index Index." *Index on Censorship* 14 (1985): 48.
King, Seth S. "Professor Causes Furor by Saying Nazis Slaying of Jews Is a Myth." *New York Times*, January 28, 1977, p. 10.
Landy, Heather. "Protestors Condemn Butz, Holocaust Revisionism." *Daily Northwestern*, May 10, 1994, p. 4.
MacDonald, Alan. Director of Information Services, University of Calgary. Telephone interview. February 11, 1997.
McRae, Lorie. "Seized Book Is Back." *Feliciter* (October 30, 1984): 1.
"Northwestern Is Thrust into Debate over Academic Freedom." *Minneapolis Star Tribune*, January 10, 1997, p. A9.
Schwendener, P. "The Holocaust Didn't Happen." *Reader* 12 (February 1983): 8–14.
"Seizing Anti-Semitic Book Wrong—Jews." *Edmonton Journal*, September 14, 1984, p. B3.
Stadtmiller, Amanda. "PARC Cancels Controversial Fireside after NU Intervention." *Daily Northwestern*, May 10, 1994, p. 4.
Winer, Todd. "Tangled Web: NU Professor and the Holocaust." *Chicago Jewish News* (October 25–31, 1996): n.p.
Witteles, Ron. "PARC Bureaucrats: 'We Know What's Best for You.'" *Northwestern Chronicle*, May 13, 1994, p. 1.

I AM THE CHEESE

Author: Robert Cormier
Original date and place of publication: 1977, United States
Publisher: Pantheon Books
Literary form: Novel

SUMMARY

Two disparate alternating components—a narrative adventure and a series of transcripts of taped interviews—provide the structure and build the plot and ideas of *I Am the Cheese*. Adam Farmer, in the first, is journeying on his old-fashioned bicycle from Monument, Massachusetts, to Rutterberg, Vermont, to visit his father in the hospital. It is an adventure with a purpose, but Adam is afraid. The taped interviews between Adam and Brint, identified as a psychiatrist, an identity that is doubted by Adam and made suspect in the text, reveal an attempt to help Adam regain his memory; these tapes are supported by third-person narrative accounts of past events that fill in the memory blanks. These two components gradually intertwine, the tension mounting, the clues and bits of evidence fitting together to reveal what has happened and is happening to Adam Farmer.

Adam Farmer is really Paul Delmonte. He does not know this, however, until he is 14 when his father tells him the truth (the reader does not learn this until midway through the book). When Adam/Paul was young, his father, an energetic investigative reporter, had uncovered documents in the Albany, New York, state house that were damaging, indeed irrevocably ruinous, to both state and federal officials. The evident corruption involved links of government to criminal syndicates. After testifying in Washington in strict secrecy, under promises of protected identity, he returned home to resume his life. Two attempts on his life change that.

A "Mr. Grey" enters their lives. An agent of the U.S. Department of Re-Identification—a precursor of the Witness Re-Establishment Program—he provides the Delmontes with new identities and histories, new situations, even a newspaper article about their deaths by automobile accident. He causes them to be relocated to begin life anew. Mr. Grey remains in their lives, visiting their home once or twice a month for private conversations with David (Delmonte) Farmer in a sealed basement room.

But that is the past. In the present, Adam is on his bicycle pedaling toward Rutterberg, Vermont. He is fearful because it is his nature to be so, he says, but this is a striking foreshadowing. Remembering his father's singing, Adam tries to mimic his joyous rendering of "The Farmer in the Dell" to give himself courage. He is, however, terrified, first by a dog that tears after him and, subsequently, by three men in a lunchroom. Although they threaten him, he manages to escape from them temporarily. They follow him in a car, mockingly passing him, returning and passing him again and again, closer and closer until they knock him over the side into a gully. Adam is rescued and taken as far as Hookset, Vermont. There his bicycle is stolen by Junior Varney, but Adam is able to reclaim it after a tussle.

Two other incidents provide clues of wonder and suspense. Adam tries to telephone his best friend, Amy Hertz. But after calling the familiar number twice, he is told by a stranger who answers that he has had the number for three years. The information operator tells him there is no Hertz listing in Monument, Massachusetts. When Adam reaches Belton Falls, he goes to the Rest-A-While Motel, where he and his parents had happily stayed the year before, only to discover it is closed. The gas station attendant across the street tells him it has been closed for "two or three years . . . at least."

At last arriving at the hospital in Rutterberg, Adam is greeted by a doctor who walks with him. They pass Whipper, Dobbie, and Lewis, the three troublemakers from the lunchroom; he hears the growl of a ferocious dog and watches for the lurking Junior Varney. Adam is taken to his own room, where he sings "The Farmer in the Dell." He doesn't respond to the name Paul, nor does he recall his other name. But he knows who he is; "I am the cheese," he says. He stands alone.

The interviews are also in the present, conducted in a confinement facility. The interviews peel away the shrouds, sheet by sheet, from Adam's memory. These conversations help Adam remember the past, starting from an earliest memory of a stealthy trip when he was four, moving through the first clues to his first questions and suspicions, leading to the revelations about the changed identity and situation of his family. Adam also raises doubts about where he is—it does not seem like a hospital to him—and who Brint really is. Brint seems something more or other than a psychiatrist; his questions seem to reach beyond a search for Adam's personal life, but rather to a search for certain specifics, secrets. He seems at times "a predator, an enemy." Despite his constantly drugged condition, Adam suspects Brint and resists his inquiries, maintaining a slight degree of self-protective will.

Mr. Grey, always dressed in gray, is an important figure of the past. He does not merely protect the Delmontes by reestablishing them. He watches over them and maintains surveillance over them. He determines the options at every stage; he controls the family's movements and life. It is his "emergency" call that sets the stage for the demise of the family.

Mr. Grey had called, saying that their identities may have been discovered, that they had to leave town for a few days so that his men could check for any suspicious developments. The Farmers take this enforced holiday, staying the first night at the Rest-A-While Motel, enjoying each other and their escape. The next day, David Farmer notices a car following them. When they stop and get out of their car to admire a distant view and stretch their legs, a car hurtles toward them and crashes into them.

Adam remembers. In slow motion he remembers himself flying through the air, twisting and trembling. He remembers seeing his mother die instantly. He remembers a voice saying that his father, hurt, had run away but that "They'll get him—they never miss." He remembers the men coming toward him, looming over him: "Grey pants. Him. Hearing his voice again: 'Move fast. Remove her. The boy—check him. He may be useful. Fast now, fast.'"

The novel concludes with the annual report, filed presumably by Brint. It summarizes the third annual questioning of Subject A, Adam Farmer, establishing that he "discloses no awareness of data provided Department 1-R by Witness #599-6" (David Delmonte). It indicates that these results are consistent with the two previous interrogations and that "Inducement of medication . . . plus pre-knowledge interrogation failed to bring forth suspected knowledge. . . ."; also, it notes that "deep withdrawal" occurs when these topics are approached and "complete withdrawal accompanies recapitulation of termination of Witness #599-6 and affiliate (spouse)."

The report includes three advisories: 1) that the policy, which does not allow termination procedures by Department 1-R, be eliminated; 2) that the suspension of Personnel #2222 (Mr. Grey) be discontinued, granting him full reinstatement (the suspension had resulted from suspected complicity of Mr. Grey in the termination of Witness #599-6; the evidence of his contacting the Adversaries and revealing the location of the witness was only circumstantial); 3) that Subject A's confinement be continued, since he is "final linkage between Witness #599-6 and File Data 865-01," until "termination procedures are approved" pending revision of policy, or his "condition be sustained" until he "obliterates."

The closing paragraph of the novel is identical to the opening paragraph: Adam is on the bicycle, pedaling, pedaling.

CENSORSHIP HISTORY

The challenge in Panama City, Florida, against *I Am the Cheese* (winner of three awards—best young adult book by *Newsweek*, the *New York Times*, and the *School Library Journal*—and critical acclaim) was initiated by a formal complaint in April 1986 (which also included *About David* by Susan Beth Pfeffer). It eventually resulted in a federal court case (*Farrel v. Hall*) that was adjudicated on July 18, 1988; the situation was not finally resolved for another three years.

A preliminary pair of letters preceded the formal complaint. Marion Collins, grandmother of a student at Mowat Junior High School, complained by letter in fall 1985 to Leonard Hall, superintendent of the Bay County School District; she objected to vulgar language and advocacy of humanism and behaviorism. Hall immediately ordered Mowat's principal, Joel Creel, to ban the book. In follow-up letters to Hall and Creel, Collins further complained that the book was still in use.

The formal complainant was Claudia Shumaker, Collins's daughter and mother of a seventh grader in ReLeah Hawks's accelerated English class. Her complaint was filed upon the suggestion of Superintendent Hall after Hawks, anticipating the Shumaker complaint, had informed parents of her intent to teach *I Am the Cheese* and to offer an alternative text to students whose parents objected; she had received 88 favorable permission slips and only four declinations. Shumaker wanted the book banned altogether, noting her daughter would be ostracized.

Both *I Am the Cheese* and *About David* were withdrawn immediately from classroom use, pending consideration of the district review committee. That committee in a month's time recommended the reinstatement of *I Am the Cheese*. (It did not act on *About David* because it was not scheduled for classroom use.) However, Superintendent Hall did not act on the recommendation, thus effectively preventing Hawks and other teachers from using it in their classrooms.

Thereupon, the controversy heated up. Claudia Shumaker had protested that *I Am the Cheese*'s theme is "morbid and depressing," its language "crude and vulgar" and the "sexual descriptions and suggestions are extremely inappropriate." The offending words were *hell*, *shit*, *fart*, and *goddam*; the sexual descriptions included a scene of teens kissing, a description of breasts as "large" and "wonderful," and a reference to a supermarket display of Kotex.

Her father, Charles E. Collins, who had served on the Bay County school board from 1954 to 1970, in a May 22, 1986, letter mailed to all the parents of Mowat students, protested in addition the novel's "subversive theme . . . which makes the 'government agents' out to be devious and 'hit teams' that killed the boy's parents, and now must kill the boy because he knows too much about the government's activities." In the letter and in an advertisement in the *Panama City News Herald*, he asked for telephone calls and mail-in coupons. M. Berry, M.D., in a letter to the editor, complained that the novel "slyly casts doubt on the U.S. government, parental authority and the medical profession."

The teachers called a public meeting on May 27, inviting students, teachers, and parents to discuss the issue. On that morning, Hall instructed the teachers not to discuss the First Amendment or the book controversy with their students; he also ordered them to tell the students not to attend the meeting and that their exclusion was the teachers' idea. About 300 parents attended the meeting; approximately two-thirds of them indicated support for the teachers and the English program.

Hall, on June 5, rejected the review committee's recommendation and ruled against use of *I Am the Cheese*. He argued that the book had never been officially adopted by the school board. In a later statement, however, he expressed a negative reaction to an idea he inferred from the novel: "You know what happens at the end? The mother and father are exterminated by the United States government. What does that tell you? I mean do you ever trust government again?" He said further that students should not be taught that a government agency might be corrupt and untrustworthy.

Beyond rejecting *I Am the Cheese* because the school board had not approved it, Hall added that any other materials that had not been approved, except state-approved textbooks, would also have to be approved by a five-step procedure: 1) the teachers would submit a detailed rationale for each book to be included in the curriculum and the classroom library; 2) the principal would either reject the rationale or send it to the county instructional staff; 3) the staff would either reject it or send it to the superintendent; 4) the superintendent would either reject it or send it to the school board; and 5) the board would make the final decision. Rejection at any stage would terminate the procedure; teachers would not be allowed to appeal. An additional procedure allowed citizens who objected to an approved book to appeal its inclusion; a procedure for a citizen to appeal a decision to reject a book was not included. This had the effect of eliminating classroom libraries and most classroom novels. Further, if a book was approved and then challenged, it would be withdrawn until judged by a series of review boards.

The proposed policy was debated at an extended school board meeting in August 1986. Parents and teachers who opposed Hall's proposed policy "protested that it was ham-fistedly authoritarian and heavily biased toward excluding, rather than including, material." Of the 25 citizens attending the meeting, 17 spoke against the proposal. Collins, however, submitted a stack of antiobscenity petitions, containing by his account 9,000 signatures. (An enterprising television journalist, Cindy Hill, discovered in the fall that there were actually only 3,549 signatures.) The school board voted to approve Hall's policy, changing it only to add a one-year grace period for books that had been taught in 1985–86. This still denied teachers and students access to *I Am the Cheese* and *About David*.

Gloria T. Pipkin, chair of the English department, filed a request to teach *I Am the Cheese* to her advanced eighth-grade English class. Creel, having consulted Hall, rejected her request. Pipkin revised the rationale and sent it to Hall, who responded that the principal's rejection terminated the procedure. Pipkin then asked to be placed on the school board agenda; the chair at first attempted to prevent her from speaking, reminding her that "as a Mowat employee, she was subject to Creel's authority." Granted the right to speak, Pipkin asserted, "Make no mistake about it, *I Am the Cheese* has been banned in the Bay County school system because the ideas it contains are offensive to a few: no ruse can obscure that fact." Her request that the board go on record to restore the book to the classroom was ignored.

As the time arrived for the receipt of a rationale for teaching non-state-approved books, Hall added another step to the review process; he required senior high school teachers to categorize their books: Category I—no vulgar, obscene, or sexually explicit material; Category II—very limited vulgarity and no sexually explicit or obscene material; Category III—quite a bit of vulgarity or obscene and/or sexually explicit material.

When the review procedure was completed, Hall had eliminated 64 classics from Bay County classrooms. They included the following:

"Banned" from Bay High School: *A Farewell to Arms* by Ernest Hemingway; *The Great Gatsby* by F. Scott Fitzgerald; *Intruder in the Dust* by William Faulkner; *Lost Horizon* by James Hilton; *Oedipus Rex* by Sophocles; *The Red Badge of Courage* by Stephen Crane; *A Separate Peace* by John Knowles; *Shane* by Jack Schaefer; and *Three Comedies of American Life* by Joseph Mersand. "Banned" from Mosley High School: *Adventures in English Literature; After the First Death* by Robert Cormier; *Alas, Babylon* by Pat Frank; *Animal Farm* by George Orwell; *Arrangement in Literature; The Autobiography of Benjamin Franklin* by Benjamin Franklin; *Best Short Stories; Brave New World* by Aldous Huxley; *The Call of the Wild* by Jack London; *The Canterbury Tales* by Geoffrey Chaucer; *The Crucible* by Arthur Miller; *Death Be Not Proud* by John Gunther; *Deathwatch* by Robb White; *Desire Under the Elms, The Emperors Jones*, and *Long Day's Journey Into Night* by Eugene O'Neill; *Exploring Life Through Literature; Fahrenheit 451* by Ray Bradbury; *The Fixer* by Bernard Malamud; *Ghosts* [sic] and *Miss Julie* by August Strindberg; *The Glass Menagerie* by Tennessee Williams; *Great Expectations* by Charles Dickens; *The Great Gatsby* by F. Scott Fitzgerald; *Growing Up; Hamlet, King Lear, The Merchant of Venice*, and *Twelfth Night* by William Shakespeare; *Hippolytus* by Euripides; *In Cold Blood* by Truman Capote; *The Inferno* by Dante (Ciardi translation); *The Little*

Foxes by Lillian Hellman; *Lord of the Flies* by William Golding; *Major British Writers* (shorter edition); *The Man Who Came to Dinner* by George S. Kaufman and Moss Hart; *The Mayor of Casterbridge* by Thomas Hardy; *McTeague* by Frank Norris; *Mister Roberts* by Thomas Heggen; *Oedipus the King: The Oedipus Plays of Sophocles; Of Mice and Men* and *The Pearl* by John Steinbeck; *The Old Man and the Sea* by Ernest Hemingway; *On Baile's Strand* by W. B. Yeats; *The Outsiders* by S. E. Hinton; *Player Piano* by Kurt Vonnegut; *The Prince and the Pauper* by Mark Twain; *Prometheus Unbound* by Percy Bysshe Shelley; *Tale Blazer Library: A Raisin in the Sun* by Lorraine Hansberry; *The Red Badge of Courage* by Stephen Crane; *A Separate Peace* by John Knowles; *To Kill a Mockingbird* by Harper Lee; *Watership Down* by Richard Adams; *Winterset* by Maxwell Anderson; and *Wuthering Heights* by Emily Brontë.

These exclusions engendered public protest and ridicule, including resolutions from the Chamber of Commerce. A letter of protest, signed by almost 2,000 county residents, was submitted to the school board on May 13. Hundreds of high school students wearing black armbands packed the boardroom in protest.

On May 12, 1987, a suit was filed by 44 Bay County parents, teachers, and students against Hall, Creel, and the school board. The suit, labeled *Farrell* (after a student, Jennifer Farrell, whose name headed the list of plaintiffs) *v. Hall*, went forward despite the school board's reactive effort to revise the review policy by permitting the inclusion of books used in 1986–87 that were recommended by the school principal. This "revision," while reinstating the 64 titles, maintained the Hall policy and the banning of *I Am the Cheese, About David,* and *Never Cry Wolf,* which had been barred in the interim. (The offense: one phrase shouted by a dogsled driver to his barking dogs—"FURCHRSAKE-STOPYOUGODAMNSONSABITCHES!")

The plaintiffs' case asked that *I Am the Cheese* and other young adult novels be restored to the curriculum; further, it asserted that the review policy denied students their First Amendment rights to receive information and be educated according to their parents' wishes and denied teachers their rights of free speech and academic freedom as well as placing an undue burden upon them in the preparation of rationales for every book taught and placed in their classroom libraries. At the core, the plaintiffs argued that Hall had acted counter to the First Amendment by using his position as superintendent of schools to reject books whose ideas violated his religious or political beliefs rather than because of their language. The defendants argued that the revised policy answered the plaintiffs' complaints and that the courts should not interfere in educational matters.

On July 18, 1988, Judge Roger Vinson of the U.S. District Court for the Northern District of Florida gave neither side a clear victory. He denied motions to dismiss the case. On behalf of the plaintiffs he noted in reference to Hall:

[He] accepts as true . . . [that his] actions were motivated by his personal beliefs which form the basis for his conservative educational policy. Hall believes that his duty as superintendent is to restore Christian values to the Bay County school system. He thinks that one vulgarity in a work of literature is sufficient reason to keep the book from the Bay County school curriculum. Hall's opposition to *I Am the Cheese* arises solely from his personal opposition to the ideas expressed in the book. He believes that it is improper to question the trustworthiness of the government. Thus, students should not be presented with such ideas.

With regard to the accusation that books had been removed because of disagreement with the ideas they contained, he ruled:

Local school officials may establish and implement the curriculum to transmit community values, a task which requires decisions based on the social and ethical values of the school officials. . . . On the other hand, the discretion of state and local school authorities must be exercised in a manner that comports with the First Amendment. Local school officials may not suppress ideas simply because they disagree with those ideas so as to create a "pall of orthodoxy" in the classroom.

Thus, he supported the claims about the removal of *I Am the Cheese* and other works in order to suppress their ideas.

However, Judge Vinson did not support the plaintiffs' complaint relating to language; he asserted that rejecting books because of one vulgar word is within the school board's authority. So, too, the review policy was acceptable to the court because school boards have the right to approve books by whatever process they choose. The significant factor in this context is that board *decisions* may be challenged if deemed illegal or arbitrary. This applies also to books selected for school and classroom libraries.

Judge Vinson also ruled that federal courts, when First Amendment issues are involved, are obligated to intervene in educational matters.

The case was eventually settled out of court, after Hall decided not to run for reelection. Upon the request of his successor, Jack Simonon, to be given time to try to resolve the situation, a 60-day suspension of the trial was granted. The suspension lasted three years, during which time the People For the American Way organization negotiated on behalf of the teachers with the school board attorney to achieve a book review policy that was acceptable to all. Key features of this policy included time limits set for each stage of the review procedure; detailed procedures for handling challenges for existing materials; procedures established for the appeal of negative decisions; and provisions made to inform parents whose children would be affected by any complaint against a book so they could support or oppose the complaint.

Two additional challenges are recorded by the *Newsletter for Intellectual Freedom,* one in Cornwall, New York, in October 1984, and one in Evergreen, Colorado, in November 1993. In the former, Mrs. Oliver F. Schreiber objected to the contents of two of Robert Cormier's books: *I Am the Cheese* and *THE CHOCOLATE WAR*; her complaint described the books as humanistic and destructive of religious and moral beliefs and of national spirit. No action was taken on this complaint since, according to superintendent R. Lancaster Crowley, Schreiber's son was not required to read the novel and had been excused from class discussion.

The second incident was more complicated. Principal Larry Fayer removed 42 books from the Wilmot Elementary School Media Center after 10 parents objected to foul language and violence in six titles; *I Am the Cheese* was among them. The removal was appealed by librarian Theresa March. During the review procedure, Fayer agreed to display the books for parental inspection and to return to the shelves all those that were not challenged. Thirty-one of them met this criterion, including *I Am the Cheese*. When the challengers of the remaining 11 discovered that their complaints would become public information, the challenges were withdrawn, and those books, too, were reshelved.

FURTHER READING

Carlson, Peter. "A Chilling Case of Censorship." *Washington Post Magazine*, January 4, 1987, 10–17, 40–41.

Collins, Charles E. Letter to Parents, Mowat Middle School, Panama City, Florida. May 22, 1986.

Collins, Marion. Letter to Joel Creel, Principal, Mowat Middle School, Panama City, Florida. February 3, 1986.

DelFattore, Joan. *What Johnny Shouldn't Read: Textbook Censorship in America.* New Haven, Conn.: Yale University Press, 1992.

Foerstal, Herbert N. *Banned in the U.S.A.: A Reference Guide to Book Censorship in Schools and Public Libraries.* Westport, Conn.: Greenwood Press, 1994.

Gallo, Donald R. "Reality and Responsibility: The Continuing Controversy Over Robert Cormier's Books for Young Adults." In *The VOYA Reader,* edited by Dorothy M. Broderick, 153–160. Metuchen, N.J.: Scarecrow Press, 1990.

Linn, Jennifer. "Censorship Fight Has Just Begun." *Panama City News-Herald*, May 15, 1987, pp. 1A, 2A.

———. "Lawsuit Filed Against Hall, School Board." *Panama City News-Herald*, May 13, 1987, pp. 1A, 2A.

———. "Leonard Hall Bans 64 Books." *Panama City News-Herald*, May 8, 1987, pp. 1A, 2A.

May, Greg. "Hall Challenged: City Protests Categories." *Panama City News-Herald* (May 13, 1987): pp. 1B, 7B.

Newsletter on Intellectual Freedom 34 (1985): 45; 35 (1986): 209–10; 36 (1987): 52, 126–28, 168–69, 224; and 43 (1994): 97.

"One Arbitrary Policy Doesn't Justify Another." *Panama City News-Herald*, May 13, 1987, p. 6A.

Peyser, Andrea. "Battles over Book-Bans Getting Dirty." *Tampa Tribune*, May 17, 1987, pp. 1B, 10B.

Pipkin, Gloria. "Confessions of an Accused Pornographer." *Arizona English Bulletin* (1994): 14–18.

INSIDE RUSSIA TODAY

Author: John Gunther
Original date and place of publication: 1958, United States
Publisher: Harper and Brothers
Literary form: Nonfiction

SUMMARY

With John Gunther we step inside Russia in 1957 during the Nikita Khrushchev period. His tour geographically begins in Moscow but also visits Leningrad and Kiev; he travels into the countryside and far afield into the Black Sea and Caucasus regions as well as several of the soviet republics of central Asia. His observations encompass politics and political leaders; government and party; images of the people and their lives; economics; the armed forces; science and education; writers and the arts.

In keeping with Gunther's self-identification as a "writer of good will," one of the dominant impressions of *Inside Russia Today* is of a balanced view, moderation, and objectivity in showing positive as well as negative features, in addition to giving glimpses of so many facets of the Soviet Union. This is evident in the frequent expression of contrasting impressions as well as contradictions.

"De-Stalinization" is immediately evident as shown by Gunther's ease in entering the USSR, in contrast to the past: "the passport examination at Riga was extremely cursory" and "no examination of luggage takes place at all." Yet areas of the country are closed to visitors; the Baltic States and the "most notorious of the old forced labor camps" are disparate examples. As a "minor instance," it is notable that, unlike other world capitals where Americans and other Westerners are scattered around the cities, the total population of about 150 Americans is limited to several residence locations in Moscow.

Gunther reveals that the Soviet Union is still a closed society with regard to communication. There is no access to a free press. "Western newspapers are not allowed in, and news coverage in the Soviet press is, to put it mildly, slanted and inadequate. Certain fields in particular are rigorously screened." Secrecy and closedness are identified as "traditional Russian characteristics and censorship is an old, old story." A related factor is surveillance of both visitors and citizens. Examples include the hotel desk clerk's awareness of a minor question that Gunther asked of the pilot, an official tourist driver's knowing the destination of a visiting European philosopher when it has only been discussed privately with his wife in their hotel room, and the careful guarding of members of the diplomatic corps and the vigilant observation of eminent visitors.

The government structure is described as pyramidal, that is, "political authority derives from the local soviets, which exist in every rural area or town, and which represent workers or peasants in a particular cell, factory, or collective farm. . . . Power flows upward and each higher body is elected directly by the people . . . until the Supreme Soviet is reached." Ninety percent of entitled voters do vote. However, elections are not free in the sense of Western democracies. "All candidates are nominated by the local Communist party or allied organization, and opposition, once the nominations have been made, is unknown." Membership in the party is purposefully kept small so as to concentrate power. Many Russian citizens who are loyal Communists are not members.

The deputies to the Supreme Soviet do not freely debate; they simply give reports. However, since de-Stalinization, a "democratization" is evident in the "very lively talk . . . including criticism" as deputies describe their local problems. The system of indoctrination of the whole population, which begins in childhood, acts to support the conformity and to discourage open criticism. *Agitprop*, the agitation and propaganda agency of the party, disseminates the party line extraordinarily successfully. "We should, however, point out again that conformity is not merely imposed from the top, but as a result of forty years of indoctrination, rises from below. People obey not merely out of fear, but because they think in uniform terms."

Two features of history are drawn: the contemporary—since 1953, and the past—the rise of the czars and the subjugation of the people. Out of the past, Gunther makes a case for absolutism and cruelty. He also establishes the steady accretion of the class structure.

> The main thing to say is that, as reign followed reign, the major characteristics of the Russian scene as we knew it later became fixed. Steadily—to mention just one example—the gap widened between rulers and people, between the privileged and nonprivileged, between a fantastically rich and ornate upper class and a peasantry downtrodden, miserable, and unspeakably poor. Serfdom, the cancer of the old Russia, became as time went on a force debasing the entire moral structure of the community.

More immediately pertinent are the events surrounding Khrushchev's ascendancy after Stalin's death, particularly the manipulation used to gain power in 1958. Georgi Malenkov, Stalin's successor, was dismissed; Lavrenty Beria, Stalin's police chief, was executed; and V. M. Molotov, Stalin's foreign minister, was expelled. In his February 1956 speech to the Twentieth Party Congress, Khrushchev repudiated the Stalinist cult of personality and condemned Stalin for the excesses of moral and physical brutality against individuals and groups.

Subsequently, changes occurred within the Soviet Union. The administration of justice was reformed, most of the labor camps for political prisoners have been broken up, the power of the secret police was modified, the civil liberties of citizens broadened, and overt terror ended. Gunther notes that there is still "plenty of terror," an estimated 30 percent of prisoners not yet released and one-third of all labor camps still operating.

The reforms that have occurred so far are perfectly genuine, if limited, but this does not mean that Khrushchev is a liberal or a democrat. The system is still the same in principle, and is still a tyrannical dictatorship; the motive for de-Stalinization has not been merely humanitarian, but lies in the desire to create a more efficient, modern state.

Comparisons with the United States abound throughout Gunther's text. Some of these are implied, for example, access to communication and the democracy of government. Soviet education is more demanding—"The Soviet child must absorb in ten years much more than an American child gets in the equivalent 12 under the American system"; they are particularly advanced in the sciences and mathematics. Curricula are uniform throughout the country and every subject is obligatory, except in choice of foreign language. Education is universal, and illiteracy has been virtually wiped out; more than 100 million people have been taught to read and write since the beginning of the Soviet regime. However, the "people do not have the right of fundamental inquiry. Immense areas of the world's knowledge are cut off from the Russian people, and they are fed lies incessantly."

Comparisons of industry, transportation, power production, and agriculture are favorable to the United States. Planning, however, focusing the nation's energies on a master plan, is a source of internal strength; it can be allied to its "mobilization potential" for instant change of action.

And what hasn't the Soviet Union got? "Freedom. Therefore the whole Soviet structure is built on quicksand. . . ."

Gunther shows that two seemingly opposing attitudes toward the United States existed. The attitude directed toward the government, its leaders, and its capitalistic system, is negative; however, the American people are "all right, but are victimized by 'reactionary' capitalists and 'monopolists.' " The Soviet regime considers the United States an "enemy" and identifies it as imperialistic. Soviet people parrot this language, their attitudes supported by reports in the press.

Soviet ignorance about America and Americans was "formidable." They do not believe, for example, that college attendance is not limited to rich males, that travel is unrestricted without passports, that varieties of food are available, that there is a comprehensive social security system and that President Eisenhower's father was a railroad worker. They question the extent of freedom. This lack of information is frequently evident in the eager questioning by ordinary folks and professionals, once some personal level of contact is established, about all facets of life in America.

The people of the Soviet Union on the whole emerge with a quite positive image. In happenstance meetings in airplanes and the like, we meet kind, gracious, and generous folk. They are tough and proud and also puritanistic; discipline and self-sacrifice are key traits. Perhaps an outcome of these traits is the pride in their plainness and poverty expressed by some. "They like hardship. That mildewed suit is a badge of honor, because it proves virtue and sacrifice." (The majority of the people in Moscow lived very poorly by our standards.) Accompanying these traits is a certain defensiveness and touchiness, an unwillingness to admit that life and goods might be better elsewhere, a strong desire to be acknowledged and appreciated.

In the final two chapters, Gunther looks to the future in light of then current Soviet goals and behavior. "The Russians want peace, but they are still gambling for the world." These basic conceptions of Russian policy are represented in the official position that war is not inevitable, but vigilance is necessary to counteract any force against the regime and in the expanding of influence and dominance around the world: the Middle East, Asia, the European satellites. Soviet and United States foreign polices are alike: Each is willing to "do anything possible" to weaken the other. The Soviets stir up "ferment," while the United States exerts pressure through "containment" and propaganda for the liberalization of the satellites.

Gunther is critical of both sides—of American behavior in arrogantly flying surveillance missions over Soviet territory and dropping propaganda material by satellite and the Russians' use of "brazen and blackfaced lies without a tremor" to take advantage of situations. He opts for coexistence. Having pointed out that democracies have coexisted with dictatorships in the past, he insists we try.

> Whether we like it or not it is our duty . . . to know the full nature of our adversaries, comprehend frankly their massive power, and if possible, live side by side with them peaceably even if difficulties largely of Russian making appear to be insuperable. This is strictly to American self-interest.

CENSORSHIP HISTORY

In the summer of 1964, a member of the John Birch Society entered the Anderson Bookshop in Larchmont, New York, and, after browsing, called attention to a great many "subversive" books on the shelves. He identified *Inside Russia Today* along with Marx's DAS KAPITAL, Pasternak's DR. ZHIVAGO, and a book on Lenin by Robert Payne. He threatened that the John Birch Society would organize a boycott of the bookstore if these and any other "un-American" books were not removed from view. The editor of the *Newsletter on Intellectual Freedom* advised the bookseller, "Don't take any guff from a self-appointed censor." Presumably, the bookseller did not.

In Glenwood, Iowa, on December 1970, about 50 parents attended a school board meeting, seeking explanation of a series of censorship incidents. A total of nine books including *Inside Russia Today* were removed from library shelves over the spring and fall periods at the decision of the board. Board president Richard Owen acknowledged that he could remember only one complaint; however, some community members contended that the board had been pressured by the local John Birch Society, identified as probably the most active Birch group in Iowa.

Orval Jensen, principal of the high school, revealed in a telephone interview in 1996 that he had come upon a school board member in the high school library removing books from the shelves. He told Jensen that he had become irate when his daughter had brought one of them home, and he wanted them removed from the library. Jensen had indicated the need for a review of the books before they could be summarily removed. Jensen also reported that the high school librarian, Jo Bayer, had become quite angry about the censorship challenge. This was corroborated in 1996 by Leanna Scarnulis, the president of the local PTA in 1970, who added that Bayer had found the situation "intolerable" and had been a leader in activating the community to oppose the books' removal.

As two of the school board members, Alex Christiansen and Duane Sell, recalled the board's deliberations in 1996, the censoring controversy centered on objections to the language and sexual features of J. D. Salinger's *THE CATCHER IN THE RYE.*

The board members discussed forming a committee to "review" library books about which there had been complaints or criticism. A motion was carried to the effect that "any controversial books from the high school library now in the possession of school board members shall be turned over to the review committee, when such committee is formed." Subsequent minutes do not report the appointment of this committee, though its formation was identified in the *Glenwood Opinion Tribune.* Curiously, Richard Owen, then the president of the school board, in 1996 claimed that the issue "was discussed at one board meeting and that was the end of it." He insisted that the books had not been removed or placed on restricted shelves.

The review committee, appointed on January 8, 1970, consisted of Orval Jensen, high school principal; Jo Bayer, high school librarian; a high school English teacher; and seven local residents. After discussing the books, the committee voted them "in" or "out" of the library. A report of the committee's decision/recommendation or the school board's reaction to it was not found among the minutes of the board. However, three involved persons— Jensen (who indicated uncertainty), Leanna Scarnulis, and Ed Scarnulis (who was elected to the school board subsequently)—established the following: *The Catcher in the Rye* by J. D. Salinger and *Who's Afraid of Virginia Woolf* by Edward Albee—removed (all agreed); *Inside Russia Today* by John Gunther, *Looking Backward* by Edward Bellamy, *The Liberal Hour* by John Kenneth Galbraith, *BLACK LIKE ME* by John H. Griffin, and *Black Power* by Stokely Carmichael—removed (two agreed, the third could not specifically remember). None of the three could remember the vote of Irving Wallace's *The Prize* or the ninth book (which also was not identified in the newspaper account).

The controversy over these books spilled over into this integrated community—population 500. A chief thorn in its midst was the John Birch Society, whose attitudes toward library materials had affected some of the school board members, much to the consternation of the community. The issue was brought to a head in the succeeding school board election; Ed

Scarnulis, according to him a relative newcomer to the community, was seated by a significant margin in a record voter turnout. One result: The banned books were returned to the library shelves.

Another aspect of censorship in Glenwood concerned the North Central Association of Colleges and Secondary Schools (NCA) report, which had threatened loss of membership because of certain administrative procedures and "censorship of books and materials." Parts of the NCA report critical of the school system were alleged to be suppressed.

In *Inside: The Biography of John Gunther*, Ken Cuthbertson reports that *Inside Russia Today* was not sold in shops in the Soviet Union, and there was no Russian translation. It was being sold, however, on the black market in Moscow.

FURTHER READING

"Controversy at Glenwood over Censorship of Books." *Newsletter in Intellectual Freedom* 19 (1970): 30.

Cuthbertson, Ken. *Inside: The Biography of John Gunther.* Chicago: Bonus Books, 1992.

"Don't Take Any Guff from a Self-Appointed Censor." *Newsletter on Intellectual Freedom* 13 (1964): 81.

Jensen, Orval O. High school principal. Telephone interview. August 1996.

Krutz, Robert. "Controversy at Glenwood over Censorship of Books." *Des Moines Register,* December 5, 1969, n.p.

"Large Attendance at School Board Meeting" *Glenwood Opinion Tribune,* December 10, 1969, n.p.

"Minutes." Board of Directors of the Glenwood Community School District. December 4, 1969.

Owen, Richard, Alex Christiansen, and Duane Sell. 1970 school board members. Telephone interviews. July 1996.

Scarnulis, Ed, and Leanna Scarnulis. Review committee members. Telephone interviews. August 1996.

"School Board Selects Committee to Review Library Books." *Glenwood Opinion Tribune,* January 14, 1970, p. 1.

INSIDE THE COMPANY: CIA DIARY

Author: Philip Agee
Original dates and places of publication: 1975, Great Britain; 1975, United States
Publishers: Penguin; Stonehill Publishing Company
Literary form: Nonfiction

SUMMARY

Philip Agee's CIA diary begins in April 1956 in his last college term at Notre Dame University, South Bend, Indiana, and concludes in May 1975 in London.

It centers on his 12-year career as a CIA operations officer, under the cover of Foreign Service appointment chiefly in Quito, Ecuador, and Montevideo, Uruguay, followed by a stint in Mexico City in a tangential capacity. His CIA career ended in early 1969 when, disillusioned, he resigned. The 1970–75 period when Agee determined to write this book is compressed into the final 40 pages.

Agee entered the training program to become a member of "the company," the CIA. He signed secrecy agreements whose "wording makes it permanent, eternal and universal about everything I learn in the company." The preparation included two years of military training, graduating as an air force second lieutenant. He studied, in particular, communism and Soviet foreign policy, the National Security Act, the CIA structure and intelligence techniques. These techniques included foreign intelligence (to obtain information on the capabilities and intentions of foreign governments, especially enemy and unfriendly governments), counterintelligence (to protect CIA operations from detection by the opposition), and paramilitary and psychological features (actions—"never attributable to the CIA or to the U.S. government, but rather to some other person or organizations [which] nearly always mean intervention in the affairs of another country with whom the U.S. enjoys normal diplomatic relations").

> Psychological warfare includes propaganda (also known simply as "media"), work in youth and student organizations, work in labor organizations (trade unions, etc.), work in professional and cultural groups and in political parties. Paramilitary operations include infiltration into denied areas, sabotage, economic warfare, personal harassment, air and maritime support, weaponry, training and support for small armies.

Ecuador in late 1960 through 1963, the period of Agee's assignment, was a country of extreme injustices and acute poverty, due to the country's land tenure system. It stringently divided the population into the wealthy 1 percent and the poor 66 percent; the rest were economically and socially marginalized Indians and mixed-blood individuals. Against this situation, the CIA's priorities were to collect intelligence about Communist and other political organizations hostile to the United States; to collect intelligence about the Ecuadorean government and dissident political groups and,

> Through propaganda and psychological warfare operations: (1) disseminate information and opinion designed to counteract anti-U.S. or pro-communist propaganda; (2) neutralize communist or extreme-leftist influence in principal mass organizations or assist in establishing or maintaining alternative organizations under non-communist leadership.

The CIA station's efforts during his tenure, according to Agee, focused on bringing about a break in diplomatic relations between Ecuador and

Cuba and getting the government to take action against the local Communist and related movements.

In the process of representing the nature and extent of CIA involvement in Ecuador, Agee identifies each operation in the three categories listed above and how they were accomplished. He identifies the agents, their cryptonyms and their affiliations. For example, "[O]ur operation against the Communist Party of Ecuador [PCE] . . . consists of two agents who are members of PCE and close associates of the principal PCE leader in the sierra." Such agents are paid operatives; their willingness to accept bribes and to carry out the CIA's work is identified as a reflection of the dire economic and turbulent political situation.

The tactics used in Ecuador by the CIA span the gamut from the recognizably traditional "collection" of information—tapping telephones and bugging rooms—to the more heinous "action" operations. The Cuban embassy's telephone was tapped, as were telephones of individual leaders or their associates. "Alert" notices were prepared and distributed, calling attention to the Communist threat; comparably, propaganda materials were fed to sympathetic correspondents and agents for newspaper publication. Demonstrations were instigated through agents; these were financed by the CIA, though they were organized by anticommunist organizations. The CIA also financed the expansion of a militant action organization as well as political campaigns to defeat undesirable officeholders or to elect agents. Propaganda, often with veiled or direct misinformation, was circulated in every possible medium. The success of the mission rather than accuracy or truth was the barometer of victory.

Two significant cases of duplicity occurred in mid-1963, surrounding the activities of José María Roura, who had gone to Communist China presumably to get payments to finance armed action, and Antonio Flores Benítez, a member of the same guerrilla group, who had gone to Cuba. The government official acting as the contact agent/informant was Juan Sevilla, the minister of the treasury. When Roura returned carrying $25,000 in cash, Agee suggested to Sevilla that he start a story that false documents and compromising papers were also found in his possession. The sensation of this story forced the government's hand against Roura: "Now he'll have to stand trial on the basis of the 'documents' and the money. We'll have plenty of time to fabricate appropriate documents."

In the Flores case, Agee and another agent developed a plan to plant incriminating documents on him upon his return. Sevilla again was the agent/official monitoring the situation. The concealed report was inserted in a tube of toothpaste, which was dropped into Flores's suitcase. When the authenticity of the discovered document was questioned, the CIA station chief called the minister of government (internal security) to insist it was authentic; Agee acted to leak the document to the press. He reported in his diary: "[T]he sensation is immense."

Uruguay, from March 1964 to August 1966, provided a quite different political and social scene from Ecuador, being an "integrated society organized around a modern, benevolent welfare state." However, the country had fallen on hard economic times leading to political and social unrest. Despite this seemingly different context, the purposes and practices of the CIA Montevideo station followed the pattern of the Quito station.

Another note emerges more strongly in this section: Agee's developing consciousness of error in American policy and of the continued deprivation of the poor. Revealed is the CIA's involvement in undermining governments in South America.

1 April 1964: Our campaign against [President Goulart of Brazil] took much the same line as the ones against communist infiltration in the Velasco and Arosemena governments two or three years ago in Ecuador . . . the Rio station and its larger bases were financing the mass urban demonstrations against the Goulart government. . . . Goulart's fall is without doubt largely due to the careful planning and consistent propaganda campaigns dating at least back to the 1962 election operation.

15 May 1964: The Santiago station has a really big operation going to keep Salvador Allende from being elected President. He was almost elected at the last elections in 1958, and this time nobody's taking any chances.

18 December 1964: A new victory for the station at Georgetown, British Guiana, in its efforts to throw out the leftist-nationalist Prime Minister and professed Marxist, Cheddi Jagan. . . . The victory is largely due to CIA operations over the past five years to strengthen the anti-Jagan trade unions.

4 June 1965: . . . the Dominican invasion that we're trying to promote. Holman was Chief of the Caribbean branch in headquarters at the time and was deeply involved in planning the assassination of Trujillo, which was done by Cuban exiles from Miami using weapons we sent through the diplomatic pouch.

It is the last incident, however, which seems to be the catalyst for turning Agee away from his automatic acceptance of U.S. government policy and his "sense of identification with the work and people of the CIA. . . ."

4 June 1965: Why is it that the invasion seems so unjustifiable to me? It can't be that I'm against intervention as such, because everything I do is in one way or another intervention in the affairs of other countries. Partly, I suppose, it's the immense scale of this invasion that shocks. On the other hand, full-scale military invasion is the logical final step when all the other tools of counter-insurgency fail.

The Dominican invasion started me thinking about what we are really doing here in Latin America. On the one hand the spread of the Cuban revolution has been stopped and the counter-insurgency programmes are successful in most places. Communist subversion at least is being controlled. But the other side, the positive side of reforming the injustices that make communism attractive, just isn't making progress.

In the concluding chapter, after an interval in Washington, D.C., and Mexico City (where in late 1968 he submits his resignation, effective early 1969), Agee recounts briefly the evolution of this book and the CIA harassment he experienced during the 1972–73 years. Agee also summarizes outcomes in Ecuador, Uruguay, Brazil, and Mexico, illustrating the negative effects on their economic-social situations, that is, the widening gap between rich and poor.

In an interview with Richard Eder in 1974, Agee stated that his central purpose for writing *Inside the Company: CIA Diary* was to establish the destructiveness of American influence around the world: "[B]y beating down anything to the left, we just reinforce the status quo, the hold of the oligarchy on the great mass of people."

CENSORSHIP HISTORY

The censorship challenge to *Inside the Company: CIA Diary* began before it was published. It surfaced overtly in January 1972 in Paris, where Agee had gone to write the book. He was visited by an "old friend from the CIA" who was attempting to ascertain what Agee was up to; he then officially warned him. Thereafter began the surveillance, which continued for years: cars and people following him, his telephone conversations monitored, his parents and his estranged wife queried. He was befriended by two Americans, one claiming to be a freelance journalist, the other claiming to be a student at the University of Geneva. Erroneously, Agee dropped his guard and accepted their help and money. An incident in October 1972 aroused his suspicions; he discovered a transmitter inside the typewriter they had lent him that had helped the CIA track him.

In Britain, Agee, revising the first draft of *Inside the Company*, was apprised of another tactic against him. In July 1974, stories appeared in the *New York Times* about a CIA agent who was "said to give secrets to the Russians in 1972," and on an Associated Press release, about "an unnamed former CIA officer who told everything he knew to the KGB." The officer was described as "drunken and despondent . . . disgruntled"; subsequently a *Washington Post* article, dismissing the story as "nonsense," named Agee as the suspected officer. Agee, presuming it was a CIA plant, denied the allegations as "complete fabrication," part of an "effort to discredit his book in advance." In subsequent *New York Times* articles referring to this event, Agee was mentioned. This was one of many subsequent stories. In documents received some years later through the Freedom of Information Act, Agee was able to identify parallel language between CIA materials and newspaper articles. A sample spinoff article from *Newsweek*'s "Periscope" follows:

> The Spy Who Came in for a Drink. That drunken CIA agent who blabbed to a Russian KGB man revealed far more than simply the use of a Washington, D.C., public relations firm as cover for some operatives. He gave his KGB friend names of a whole string of legitimate private companies in North and South America performing an identical function. The list compromised an uncounted number of agents. The man, who later tried unsuccessfully to peddle the story as a book in Europe, is still under CIA surveillance.

Comparably, in 1976, upon the murder of Richard S. Welch, the chief of the Athens station, Agee's name again surfaced. Welch had been identified as an agent in *Counter Spy*, a publication of the Organizing Committee for a Fifth Estate, whose intent was to uncover CIA agents. Agee, listed as an unpaid adviser to the group—indeed, he had been active in promoting such publications—was blamed for the identification of Welch. He denied this accusation. Agee also filed a $4 million lawsuit against Barbara Bush, who included this information in the hardback edition of her autobiography, *Barbara Bush: A Memoir:* "This gentle Greek scholar's [Welch's] cover has been blown . . . by a traitorous, tell-all book written by former CIA agent Philip Agee." The subsequent paperback edition omitted mention of Agee.

The Justice Department filed a brief on February 5, 1976, in federal district court in an attempt to prevent Agee from publishing *Dirty Works II: The CIA in Africa.* The book's announced purpose was to expose hundreds of CIA employees in Africa. However, on February 15, this suit was withdrawn, despite the book's not having had prepublication review by the CIA, because it was already being sold in Washington bookstores.

A consequence of Agee's activities—speeches, travel, and publications— and, perhaps, of pressure from the United States government (denied by both the United States and Great Britain) was Great Britain's decision to revoke Agee's residency permit. He was accused of threatening British security and of maintaining contacts with unidentified foreign agents. Initiated in November 1976, Agee was finally deported on June 3, 1977, after a series of legally narrow hearings and rejection of appeals. (A postscript: Philip Agee was allowed to return to Great Britain in 1995, 18 years after being deported. Agee in a newspaper interview indicated that he had no idea why the home secretary had allowed him to return.)

Agee went to the Netherlands, one of two countries listed as willing to receive him, but by the end of March 1978, he lost his fight to maintain residency there. Action to cancel his temporary residency had been taken in December 1977 on the grounds that he was a danger to public order and national security. Some months earlier he had gone to France; when he was discovered there, he was expelled and "barred from entering and residing in France because of past activities and the consequences of present activities to relations France maintains." A similar attempt by Agee to enter West Germany in December 1977 ended with a like expulsion. However, after a period of residency in Switzerland, he did manage, at first secretly, with the help of a marriage, to establish residency in Germany.

His return to the United States was barred by his fear of prosecution. His lawyers had long sought clarification of his status, but the Justice Department had demurred, pending determination of whether his book had violated espionage laws by publishing classified materials. In March 1977, having found no grounds, the Justice Department indicated it would not prosecute but could not guarantee that it wouldn't do so in the future if additional evidence was discovered.

Forces came to a head in 1980. On December 23, 1979, Secretary of State Cyrus Vance revoked Philip Agee's passport on national security grounds, a decision triggered apparently by Agee's proposal that CIA files on Iran be exchanged for the hostages in the United States embassy in Iran. The grounds: Agee's activities "are causing or are likely to cause serious damage to the national security or foreign policy of the United States"; "it is his stated intention to go about disrupting the intelligence activities of the United States" and "Agee's statements about the CIA intensified anti-American feelings and increased the likelihood of attacks on Embassies."

Agee filed suit in the federal district court to force the State Department to restore his passport, claiming that without due process of law the government was penalizing and suppressing criticism of the United States government's policies and practices.

On January 28, 1980, Federal District Court judge Gerhard A. Gesell ruled in favor of Agee (*Agee v. Vance*) and ordered his passport returned. Gesell noted that Congress never authorized such a sweeping regulation. On June 27, 1980, the United States Court of Appeals for the District of Columbia affirmed on a 2-1 vote (*Agee v. Muskie*) that the government may revoke a passport during war or emergency condition but not based on reports that he was invited to Iran to participate in the trial of the American hostages.

The Supreme Court on June 29, 1981, reversed these rulings (*Haig, Secretary of State v. Agee*) with a 7-2 vote, arguing that while Congress had not explicitly authorized the policy in the 1926 Passport Act, it had in effect allowed the executive branch discretion in regulating foreign travel; since the secretary of state was empowered to deny a passport application for a certain reason, a passport may be revoked for the same reason. The Court differentiated between beliefs that taken in isolation are protected and actions that are not protected by the Constitution, that is, conduct jeopardizing national security. The passport revocation would restrict Agee's freedom of movement; it would not affect his freedom of speech. The dissenting justices, William J. Brennan, Jr., and Thurgood Marshall, argued the distinction between administrative *practice* and *policy*, claiming the Court had confused the two and that a consistent practice had not been demonstrated; a "standard of consistent practice" had been a guideline adhered to in previous cases that were referred to in the majority opinion.

Despite the specific references to Agee in Chief Justice Warren Burger's opinion, the statutory issue centered on whether the State Department had the power to issue the passport regulation. The Court thus ruled that the executive branch had broad legal and constitutional authority to revoke passports on national security grounds. Agee's attempt in 1990 to get his U.S. passport back was unsuccessful.

Several other court cases were concurrent with the passport suit. In October 1979, Agee filed a Freedom of Information Act (FOIA) suit through which he sought documents from the CIA, the National Security Agency, and the State and Justice Departments. Prior to his doing so, as a resident of West Germany, he was out of reach of legal action against him; this suit gave the government the right to intervene in Agee's suit. An outcome was a countersuit: The Justice Department sought a court order, or injunction, to require Agee to submit all of his writings to the CIA for prepublication review. Federal District Court judge Gerhard A. Gesell ruled on April 1, 1980, that the Justice Department could proceed in its suit to attempt to confiscate Agee's profits from two books: *Dirty Works I* and *Dirty Works II*, about CIA activities in Europe and Africa; and to obtain an injunction enforcing the CIA's prepublication clearance of future writings. (The Supreme Court had ruled on this issue against Frank Snepp in February 1980—see DECENT INTERVAL.)

In October 1980, Judge Gesell rejected the Justice Department's request. Agee's lawyers had provided evidence that the CIA had only selectively enforced its policy that required former employees to submit to prepublication clearance. Gesell, however, warned that Agee would be cited for contempt if he did not clear future writings emerging from his CIA employment period. With regard to Agee's FOIA, Gesell ruled on July 20, 1981, in favor of the CIA: The CIA had acted properly in refusing to release copies of 8,175 documents on national security grounds. (It had agreed to release portions of 524 documents.)

Despite the CIA's threat to block publication of *Inside the Company: CIA Diary* in the United States, legal action was never taken. Perhaps the reason for this is parallel to that mentioned in articles about possible prosecution of Philip Agee himself if he returned to the United States: Prosecution might require the government to introduce even more sensitive material into evidence.

Agee returned to the United States for the first time in June 1987, after a lapse of 16 years, entering via Canada. "I wore sneakers and a Cincinnati Reds baseball cap when we drove across the border, and nobody asked me for a passport." Subsequently, he had reentered the United States many times without being arrested and was allowed to return to Britain under the Major government.

FURTHER READING

Agee, Philip. *On the Run.* Secaucus, N.J.: Lyle Stuart Inc., 1987.
"Agee Passport Ordered Restored." *New York Times,* January 29, 1980, p. 14.
Cambell, Duncan. "G2: The Spy Who Stayed out in the Cold." *Guardian* (London), January 10, 2007; p. 14.
"CIA Whistleblower Returns to UK." *Guardian,* November 3, 1995, p. I8.
"Court Backs Philip Agee in Dispute over Passport." *New York Times,* June 28, 1980, p. 6.
"Covers for CIA Are Big Problem." *New York Times,* January 16, 1976, p. 5.
Eder, Richard. "The Disillusion of a CIA Man: 12 Years from Agent to Radical." *New York Times,* July 12, 1974, p. 4.
"Ex-Agent Is Permitted to Profit from Books Not Cleared by CIA." *New York Times,* October 3, 1980, p. 16.
"Ex-CIA Man Denies He Gave Information." *New York Times,* July 11, 1974, p. 9.
"France Expels Agee as an Undesirable." *New York Times,* August 19, 1977, p. 10.
Green, Jonathon, and Nicholas J. Karolides, reviser. *The Encyclopedia of Censorship. New Edition.* New York: Facts On File, 2005.
Greenhouse, Linda. "Ex-CIA Agent Loses Appeal on Passport." *New York Times,* June 30, 1981, pp. 1, B8, B9 (excerpts from court opinion).
"Judge Backs Refusal by CIA to Provide Data to an Ex-Agent." *New York Times,* July 21, 1981, p. 11.
"Judge Rules That U.S. Can Continue Suit for Agee Book Profits." *New York Times,* April 3, 1980, sec. 2, p. 9.
Kaplan, Steven B. "The CIA Responds to Its Black Sheep: Censorship and Passport Revocation—The Cases of Philip Agee." *Connecticut Law Review* 13 (Winter 1981): 317–96.
Kilborn, Peter T. "Agee Sees Long Legal Fight over Britain's Ouster Order." *New York Times,* January 29, 1977, p. 8.
———. "Another American Told to Quit Britain." *New York Times,* November 18, 1976, p. 11.
Pear, Robert. "Plea by Ex-CIA Agent to Restore Passport Is Denied." *New York Times,* January 1, 1980, p. 6.
"U.S. Seeking to Block Former Agent's Book about CIA in Africa." *New York Times,* February 6, 1980, p. 17.

IN THE SPIRIT OF CRAZY HORSE

Author: Peter Matthiessen
Original date and place of publication: 1983, United States
Publisher: Viking Press
Literary form: Nonfiction

SUMMARY

Prefatory comment: As the censorship history will detail, two major libel suits against the author and publisher challenged *In the Spirit of Crazy Horse.* The plaintiffs in these suits, William Janklow, then governor of South Dakota, and Special Agent David Price of the Federal Bureau of Investigation (FBI), will be given some prominence in this summary to provide a context for the cases.

While spotlighting the tensions and events of the 1970s on the Sioux reservations in South Dakota, *In the Spirit of Crazy Horse* provides in Book I a brief history of the Sioux nation from 1835 to 1965 as well as the origins (1968) and growth of the American Indian Movement (AIM). Four major issues emerge from the text: the loss and despoiling of Indian lands; the quest for sovereignty; FBI and BIA (Bureau of Indian Affairs) interference and brutality on the reservations; and the severe schism and distrust within the Sioux nation. These issues are represented through two major confrontations—Wounded Knee in 1973 and the Oglala shoot-out on June 26, 1975—as well as the subsequent manhunt for witnesses and fugitives, particularly Leonard Peltier, and their trials.

One of the major treaties of the Midwest region, the Fort Laramie Treaty of 1868, is at the heart of the claims of the Sioux (also designated Lakota) nation, which includes the Teton tribes from the western plains of North and South Dakota; and the Dakota, Santee, and Yankton tribes from the prairies of Minnesota and eastern North and South Dakota. This treaty guaranteed

> absolute and undisturbed use of the Great Sioux Reservation. . . . No persons . . . shall ever be permitted to pass over, settle upon, or reside in territory described in this article, or without consent of the Indians pass through the same. . . . No treaty for the cession of any portion or part of the reservation herein described . . . shall be of any validity or force . . . unless executed and signed by at least three-fourths of all the adult male Indians, occupying or interested in the same.

The lands so guaranteed, which included the sacred Black Hills area, were gradually taken away. As early as 1876, the Black Hills were invaded by miners seeking gold; they were supported by government troops. The forced sale of this sacred area along with 22.8 million acres of surrounding territory followed. The resident tribes were resettled elsewhere on the reservation lands, but were "forbidden to trespass on the 40 million acres of unceded land that was supposedly still a part of the Great Sioux Reservation." During President Benjamin Harrison's administration in 1889, the original reservation tract was dismantled, and the seven reservations that exist today were established.

In subsequent years, a series of "reforms," some of them well intentioned, further reduced the Indian lands: The General Allotment Act of 1887 broke down the Indians' communal attitude toward land by parceling it out; the Indian Claims Commission of 1946 in effect eliminated existing and potential land claims by monetary compensation; the termination legislation enacted in the 1930s, by relocating Indians off the reservations and giving them "independence" from tribal dependent status, made Indian reservation lands available to whites. Further, the BIA's land-tenure rules required that each family's allocation of land be equally divided among heirs, which created parcels too small to support a family.

A particular example illustrates the landmass lost:

> By 1942, nearly 1 million of the 2,722,000 acres assigned to Pine Ridge when the reservation was created in 1889 had passed into other hands, and by the 1970s, over 90 percent of reservation lands were owned or leased by white people or people with a low percentage of Indian blood, not because these people were more able but because the dispossessed traditionals had no money or means to work their land.

In recent years, the forests already having been stripped off and other minerals removed, the push to gain access to the uranium and coal fields on reservation lands had further threatened the reservations. However, resistance of the tribes had also mounted, accompanied by attempts to reclaim the lost lands.

The issue of sovereignty of Indian nations and the revalidation of Indian treaties are concomitant with the land claims. Two statements illustrate the opposing viewpoints. In the first, Judge Warren Urbom, a trial judge in some of the Wounded Knee cases, who dismissed 32 cases before trial, noted that, despite the "ugly history" and the "treaties pocked by duplicity," the Lakota claims to sovereignty were "squarely in opposition" to law and Supreme Court rulings, as developed in "an unbroken line." Judge Urbom pointed out that treaties were placed "by the Constitution of the United States on no higher plane than an Act of Congress, so if a self-executing treaty and an Act of Congress be in conflict, the more recent governs." In summary, he said, "the law is that native American tribes do not have complete sovereignty, have no external sovereignty, and have only as much internal sovereignty as has not been relinquished by them by treaty or explicitly taken by act of the U.S. Congress." The second statement is from Darrelle Dean (Dino) Butler's opening remarks at his trial for the murder of the two FBI agents at Oglala:

> We are members of a sovereign nation. We live under our own laws, tribal and natural. We recognize and respect our own traditional and elected leaders. The treaties that were made between Indian nations and the United States government state that we have the right to live according to our own laws on the land given to us in the treaties. That the laws of the United States government shall not interfere with the laws of our nations.

The conflict of these views of sovereignty is expressed in the behavior of United States official personnel, who presumed a proprietary status, and the reactions of the members of the Sioux nation. The overt conflict surfaces in the Wounded Knee episode, reported in Book I, and resurfaces in the Oglala shoot-out, detailed in Book II.

FBI and BIA agent intervention in reservation affairs is highlighted in the Wounded Knee and Oglala episodes, but it does not begin or end there. The agents of these bureaus are portrayed as vehemently antagonistic to AIM leaders and activities and, along with police, are frequently identified with injustice, harassment, and brutality. These range from intimidating and beating Indians, notably suspects or potential witnesses, to invasion of private property, presumably in search of suspects:

> Under cross-examination by the defense, [Wilford] "Wish" Draper [a young Navaho visitor] acknowledged without hesitation that he had lied to the grand jury in January and also as a prosecution witness in this trial; that when he had been apprehended in Arizona in January, he had been thrown against a car, then handcuffed and strapped for three hours in a chair while being threatened with a first-degree murder charge, until he finally agreed to supply useful testimony about the killings; that before the trial, he had told the defense attorneys that Peltier, Robideau, and Butler were all in camp when the shooting started; . . . and that most of his damning testimony on this subject was based on instruction from the FBI agents at the time of the grand-jury hearing, and also by Assistant U.S. Attorney Robert Sikma.
>
> That morning of September 5, an air-land-and-river operation had descended at daybreak on the Crow Dog and Running properties, in a massive racketing of helicopters that swept in over the dawn trees. More than fifty FBI agents in combat dress, with four large helicopters, military vehicles, trucks, vans, cars, and even rubber boats—presumably to prevent aquatic escapes down the narrow creek called the Little White River—surrounded the houses and tents, shouting, "This is the FBI! Come out with your hands up!" No one was given time to dress—Crow Dog himself was marched out naked—and even the small frightened children were lined up against walls as the agents ransacked and all but wrecked every house, tent, cabin, and car on both properties.

At the conclusion of the Dennis Banks–Russell Means conspiracy trial, federal judge Alfred Nichols severely criticized the FBI for its manipulation and unethical behavior. He had at first seemed sympathetic to the government's case and had indicated he had "revered" the FBI.

The FBI was also accused of fomenting discord among Indian factions on the reservations and promoting violence. Dino Butler, an AIM leader, is quoted as saying:

> The stories that go out from the reservations look like Indian versus Indian—you know, Dick Wilson and his goons versus the American Indian Movement. But we know different. The Federal Bureau of Investigation, the CIA, and the BIA, and all these different organizations working for the government—they are the ones causing all the trouble. They give Dick Wilson and his goons money. . . . When AIM gathers, the FBI buys ammunition and booze and stuff for these goons so that they will start drinking. That's how they get their courage.

Dick Wilson, the tribal chairman, and his "goon squad" (an acronym for Guardians of the Oglala Nation), identified in the book as Wilson's private police force, represent one faction. As accused by Butler, they are depicted as drunkenly brutal and repressive, holding the "traditionals" hostage, in effect. Outrageously corrupt, they milk the tribal coffers for their own benefit. The AIM organization is perceived as their enemy; thus, Wilson and his men are in league with the FBI, apparently to protect their privileges. The antagonism is decidedly bloody. These combined negative forces are evident in the Wounded Knee and Oglala incidents.

Judge Nichols was not the only judicial officer who started out with an anti-Indian bias, but not all changed their attitudes. Another legal officer, the attorney general of South Dakota during the Oglala episode, William Janklow, is quoted as having said, "The only way to deal with Indian problems in South Dakota is to put a gun to the AIM leaders' heads and pull the trigger." Janklow had taken his first job after law school as head of the legal services program on the reservation; he was serving effectively. In 1967, however, a 15-year-old girl accused Janklow of raping her. (He was her legal guardian.) "The hospital records included evidence, suggesting that an attack had occurred." Janklow was not prosecuted at the time after the FBI "smoothed over" the incident. In September 1974, during the Banks-Means trial, the charges resurfaced. "The would-be Attorney General refused to answer his summons, the BIA refused to deliver the subpoenaed file, and the FBI refused to cooperate in any way. Nevertheless, Janklow was charged by Judge Mario Gonzales with 'assault with intent to commit rape, and carnal knowledge of a female under 16.'" Janklow denied the charges and refused to appear in court; the charges were rejected repeatedly by the FBI, and the government did its best to thwart the investigation. In March 1975, the victim died as a result of a hit-and-run accident on a deserted road.

The siege at Wounded Knee began as a gesture of protest against injustices and the presence of federal officers on the reservation. The Oglala Sioux Civil Rights Organization (OSCRO) allied itself with AIM; on February 28, 1973, several hundred men, women, and children drove in caravan to Wounded Knee and took over the community. They issued a public statement demanding hearings on their treaty and an investigation of the BIA. Wounded Knee was surrounded the next day by an armed force consisting of the FBI, the U.S. Marshal Service, and the BIA police, supported by Dick Wilson's men. On May 9, after several attempts to negotiate and after exchanged gunfire that led to the death of a young Indian male, it was over. "The few Indians still left in the settlement submitted themselves to arrest by the U.S. government."

The Wounded Knee trials, particularly that of Dennis Banks and Russell Means, from January to September 1974, gained widespread notoriety. The prosecution, "dismissing past wrongs as irrelevant to this case, portrayed the two leaders as common criminals who had invaded, terrorized and looted a helpless community." At the end of this eight-and-a-half-week trial, the prosecution produced a surprise witness, former AIM member Louis Moves Camp, who "filled in every gap in the prosecution's case." Moves Camp had been assigned to FBI agent David Price, who, with his partner, had met daily with him from August 5 through August 10 and then had accompanied him from August 13 to 16, the day of his testimony. Moves Camp's testimony and the role played by Price were significantly questioned.

> More serious than Louis Moves Camp's lies was the all but inescapable conclusion that Agent Price and perhaps Agent Williams had knowingly prepared this man to give false testimony; or, at the very least, they had found his story so convenient that they had not bothered to find out if it was true.

There was a further assertion that Price was implicated in an "alleged cover-up of a disputed rape" committed by Moves Camp in River Falls, Wisconsin, on August 14. One of the Indians' legal aides is quoted as recalling: "Price can be friendly when he feels like it, and he can look you in the face and lie and know you know he's lying—and *still* not show a damned thing in his eyes."

Both Banks and Means were acquitted; others had charges dismissed, while a few received minor sentences for related charges. Of the leaders, only Crow Dog served any jail time—a few months—on charges directly related to Wounded Knee.

A little more than two years later, on June 26, 1975, the shoot-out at Oglala, specifically the Jumping Bull property, occurred. The firing erupted suddenly, catching the Indians off guard. Two special agents who had driven onto the property were wounded in the firefight, one seriously; subsequently, they were killed by shots at close range. One young Indian was also killed when a bullet struck him in the forehead. Federal reinforcements had arrived seemingly, to the Indians, almost immediately and set up roadblocks. Nevertheless, all but one—the dead Indian—had managed to escape.

What followed was a massive "reservation murders" investigation into the deaths of the two officers; the shooting death of the Indian was not considered. Public statements, printed in major newspapers, by FBI spokesmen and South Dakota attorney general William Janklow (who was subsequently reprimanded by Governor Richard Kniep for his inflammatory statements) that the agents' bodies had been "riddled with bullets" and that their cars had also been "riddled by machine-gun bullets" turned public opinion against AIM. (Each agent had actually been struck three times.) Outraged FBI officers "ransacked . . . house[s] without a warrant," harassed, coerced and bribed witnesses and, in the words of the U.S. Civil Rights Commission, overreacted so that the investigation took on "aspects of a vendetta . . . a full-scale military-type invasion." Special Agent David Price is identified as a member of some of these groups.

The activities of the fugitive Indians are also followed, from one camp or hideaway house to another. Some who had not been on the Jumping Bull property that fateful morning were pursued as AIM members. One of them,

Anna Mae Aquash, died in a strange, questionable, hit-and-run accident. Eventually, four individuals were indicted on two counts of first-degree murder: James Theodore Eagle, Darrelle Dean Butler, Robert Eugene Robideau, and Leonard Peltier. Initially, Peltier was not in custody; he was later located in Canada, extradited to the United States with falsified documents, and tried separately.

The trial of Butler and Robideau was transferred from Rapid City, South Dakota, to Cedar Rapids, Iowa, based on the successful argument of anti-Indian prejudice. The trial opened on June 7, 1976, and concluded on July 16, 1976, with their acquittal on all counts. In addition to the significant testimony of a prosecution witness to defense cross-examination (quoted above relative to FBI manipulation of witnesses), the following argument to the court by a defense attorney regarding David Price's testimony was revealed:

> Mr. William Kunstler: We want to show this man fabricated testimony. That he has suborned perjury with witnesses in Indian trials involving A.I.M. people before. That he was the principal agent that produced witnesses they don't dare use now, produced witnesses that were to be used in this trial. John Stewart, Myrtle Poor Bear, Marvin Bragg, who was one they didn't produce on the stand, and that this man is notorious for producing fabricated evidence. They have put a witness like [James] Harper [a white man who had shared a cell with Dino Butler] on the stand and we are permitted to show, I think, under the rules of evidence that this is the way they prepare and work on witnesses, that they deliberately suborn perjury and use perjurious witnesses.

The case against James Theodore Eagle was abandoned as a result of the Cedar Rapids decision, but that of Leonard Peltier was pursued in Fargo, North Dakota. It ended on April 18, 1977, when the jury brought in a verdict of guilty on two counts of murder in the first degree. (The author comments that had Peltier been tried in Cedar Rapids, "it seems almost certain that he would have been acquitted" since there was "no good evidence that his actions had differed in a meaningful way. . . .")

Book III details Peltier's escape from prison, his recapture, and life in federal penitentiaries. Two chapters—one significantly titled "Forked Tongues"—investigate and analyze the evidence against Peltier. A third chapter, which includes a telephone interview with Special Agent David Price, investigates the situation of a potential prosecution witness, Myrtle Lulu Poor Bear, whom Price had been implicated in manipulating. There are also chapters on the "real enemy" of the Indians, that is, "the corporate state," that "coalition of industry and government that was seeking to exploit the last large Indian reservations in the West"; and on the attempt of the Indians in April 1981 to reassert their ownership of the Black Hills, the sacred Paha Sapa, by occupying sections of it.

CENSORSHIP HISTORY

The author and publisher of *In the Spirit of Crazy Horse* faced two libel suits two months after the book was published in 1983. The first plaintiff was William J. Janklow, then governor of South Dakota; the second was David Price, an FBI special agent. Peter Matthiessen, in his epilogue in the second edition, which came out after the trial, indicates that he assumed that the "FBI itself had sponsored [Price's] suit in order to lend some sort of credibility to the suit by Janklow" because Price himself "had assured me in our lengthy interview that he never made a move without the approval of his superiors, and since an FBI agent's salary could never pay for the very expensive attorneys he retained." There were altogether eight court decisions in eight years of litigation.

In April 1983, Governor Janklow called bookstores in Rapid City and Sioux Falls (he indicated he was attempting to call all bookstores in South Dakota) asking them to remove *In the Spirit of Crazy Horse* from their shelves because it was libelous and contained passages critical of him: "Nobody has the right to print lies and injure me or my family." While Janklow indicated he was acting as a private citizen, three of the booksellers reported that he had called from his office; one call was made by his secretary. Some stores removed the books; others did not. The disclosure of the governor's actions caused the sales of the book to increase.

Janklow filed a suit on May 19, 1983, asking $24 million in damages, against Viking Press, Peter Matthiessen and three bookstores. Janklow alleged that the book portrayed him as "morally decadent, a drunkard," "a racist and bigot," and "an antagonist of the environment." He claimed that Matthiessen's recounting of historical charges that he had raped a teenage Indian girl in 1967 and accusations against him by the American Indian Movement were "prepared either with a reckless disregard for truth or with actual malice for plaintiff." The defendants had edited all references to him and disregarded contrary evidence "in order to present a false and defamatory picture." His suit said that three federal investigations had determined that the rape charges were unfounded.

An attempt by the defendants for a change of venue from a state court in South Dakota to a federal court was denied on September 2, 1983, by U.S. District Court judge John B. Jones. The defendants had argued that Janklow had deliberately included the booksellers in his suit so that the case would be heard in the state courts. There was a presumption of bias in Janklow's favor at the state level.

On February 6, 1984, the booksellers' attorneys filed a joint memorandum asking Judge Gene Paul Kean of the Circuit Court of the Second Judicial Circuit in Sioux Falls to dismiss the case. The attorneys argued that courts had never required booksellers to investigate the accuracy of the books they sell. Further, a ruling to prove that the identified passages were

indeed libelous had not been made, nor had it been shown that the booksellers knew of the libel.

In support of the booksellers, the Freedom to Read Foundation on February 23 filed an amicus curiae brief in which they argued that if Janklow's

> contention were to be accepted, every bookseller, librarian, and other passive
> distributor of information would be confronted with a Hobson's choice: they
> would either have to review every potentially controversial book for factual
> accuracy and be prepared to defend such review in court, or accept at face
> value every claim made by a disgruntled reader who alleges that a particular
> work defames him and suppress all further distribution until such time, if ever,
> that the claim is resolved.
>
> It requires no prescience to recognize which choice must and will be made.
> Booksellers and librarians simply do not have the resources to undertake an
> in-depth review of every publication they are asked to distribute. . . . [there-
> fore] the only way in which booksellers, librarians and other passive distribu-
> tors of literary materials could minimize their risk of litigation and liability
> under plaintiff's theory would be to categorically reject for distribution all
> works which address public controversy. . . .
>
> Plaintiff's theory of bookseller liability is not only insupportable under
> the First Amendment but also unconscionable in a society founded on the
> rule of law. . . . The hazard of self-censorship can be avoided only by equating
> "responsibility" with "authority." The remedy for libel must rest against the
> person responsible for it and by whose authority it was published. . . . To hold
> defendant booksellers proper defendants in this case would thus render their
> defense of First Amendment rights the very source of their liability for libel.
>
> A society which permits its legal process to become an instrument of coer-
> cion cannot long preserve the rule of law. And, as Justice Brandeis noted, silence
> coerced by law is the argument of force in its worst form. The defense of plain-
> tiff's name does not require the "argument of force" he demands. The remedy
> for libel does not require the right to close the marketplace of ideas at will.

The booksellers were successful in their motion to have the suit against
them dismissed. On June 25, 1986, Judge Kean granted the defendants'
motion. Having noted the author's reputation as neither a sensationalist nor
a scandalous writer and the like reputation of the publisher, he stated:

> The calling up of booksellers and book distributors and expressing a view that
> something in the book may be false is not adequate. . . . If anyone who felt that
> he was libeled in written material could stop distribution in such fashion it
> would have a "chilling" effect on book distributors and book publishers.

Janklow did not appeal this decision.

Meanwhile, on July 13, 1984, Judge Kean issued an opinion granting
Viking and Matthiessen's motion to dismiss Janklow's entire case. He found
Matthiessen's reporting of the historical charges to be fair, balanced, and

protected as "neutral reportage." (This is an "evolving First Amendment doctrine that affords protection to reporting of charges.") Judge Kean stated further: "To force a writer to determine the responsibility of an organization or an original speaker at the risk of substantial liability would undoubtedly have a chilling effect on the dissemination of information." He also said that Matthiessen had the right to criticize Janklow in the book, which dealt with a longstanding public controversy.

Janklow's appeal of Judge Kean's decision was upheld on December 11, 1985, when the Supreme Court of South Dakota reversed the dismissal. It refused to adopt the principle of neutral reportage in South Dakota since the U.S. Supreme Court had not yet adopted the neutral reportage privilege. It remanded the case for summary judgment, requiring Judge Kean to rule on whether there was any evidence of wrongdoing by Viking and Matthiessen.

The Circuit Court of the Second Judicial Circuit in Sioux Falls again dismissed Janklow's case on June 2, 1989. Judge Kean ruled that "By no means are the statements concerning Janklow . . . a reckless publication about a public official. Defendants have provided evidence to support the statements in a lengthy affidavit by Matthiessen, accompanied by several exhibits totaling over 1,200 pages." Janklow's appeal to the South Dakota Supreme Court was rejected in a 4-1 decision, the majority citing First Amendment requirements.

This suit was formally ended in late October 1990 when Janklow allowed the 90-day deadline for appeal to the U.S. Supreme Court to lapse.

FBI special agent David Price filed his complaint of libel in January 1984 in state court in Rapid City, South Dakota, asking damages of $25 million. Price contended that he had been defamed by Matthiessen's charges that he and other FBI agents had engaged in illegal conduct in the events leading up to a gunfight between FBI agents and a few members of AIM living on the Pine Ridge Reservation. Specifically, he objected to allegations "that agents induced witnesses to commit perjury, and obstructed justice in the Peltier case . . . ; that they were racist and killers; and that they were 'corrupt and vicious' in their treatment of Indians on the reservation." He tried to impugn Matthiessen's sources by declaring that the AIM members among them had been convicted of criminal acts resulting from the Wounded Knee episode. Price also questioned the book's conclusion that Peltier's conviction had been a miscarriage of justice resulting from FBI misconduct.

In February 1985, South Dakota State Circuit Court judge Merton B. Tice, Jr., ruled that FBI agent Price's case against Viking Press and Matthiessen was not appropriate to South Dakota jurisdiction because Viking did not do enough business in South Dakota to establish the necessary "contact"; thus, if Price was harmed, it was not in South Dakota.

At the federal level, Judge Diana Murphy of the U.S. Federal District Court in Minneapolis in late January 1986 dismissed three of four counts in Price's suit. A significant rejection was Price's allegation of "group libel," that is, passages critical of the FBI had thereby defamed him personally. Judge Murphy's dismissal indicated that under these circumstances "the context of publication [must raise] a reasonable presumption of personal allusion." With regard to the remaining claims, Judge Murphy allowed Price two years of investigation. Thereafter, on January 13, 1988, she granted a motion for summary judgment and dismissal of the remaining claims. Judge Murphy upheld the right of an author "to publish an entirely one-sided view of people and events." Further, she noted that statements alleged by Price as defamatory were opinion and entitled to constitutional protection. With regard to factual statements about Price, the judge did not find that many were false; she also ruled that minor factual errors were not motivated by malice or negligence.

"The book deals with historical events, but does so from a very pointed perspective. The book's tone and style suggests the statements in question are opinion"; it seeks to persuade readers of the justice of a cause. She wrote, "The conduct of [FBI] agents in exerting their Federal authority is a matter of legitimate public interest" and noted that many statements of opinion were criticisms of government: "*In the Spirit of Crazy Horse* concerns speech about government officials, and it is this form of speech which the framers of the Bill of Rights were most anxious to protect. Criticism of government is entitled maximum protection of the First Amendment." She also pointed out that "Viking recognized that responsible publishing companies owe some duty to the public to undertake difficult but important works."

Price appealed the federal district court ruling. The unanimous decision of the U.S. Court of Appeals for the Eighth Circuit on August 7, 1989, granted summary judgment to Viking and Matthiessen, affirming all of Judge Murphy's rulings. The court, in effect, ruled that the challenged statements were constitutionally protected either as opinion or as "neutral reportage" in which the author transmits the views of others. Judge Gerald Heaney, writing for the three-judge panel, cited a 1964 precedent, *The New York Times v. Sullivan* decision of the Supreme Court. He wrote:

> The motivating factor in the Court's analysis was protection for criticism of public officials and speech regarding issues of political concern. The *New York Times* standard was constructed in light of three truths about public speech. First, false statements would necessarily occur in the course of a vigorous public debate. Second, absent protection for even false statements, destructive self-censorship would result. *Third, the legal standards for defamation must protect defendants from the self-censorship imposed by threats of litigation.* The Court felt that debate on matters of public concern "should be uninhibited, robust, and wide-open . . . [though] it may well include vehement, caustic, and sometimes unpleasantly sharp attacks on government and public officials. [Emphasis added by Martin Garbus, defense attorney for Viking Press and Matthiessen.]

While Price had relied on the previously accepted law that repeating a false accusation, even against a government official, could be libelous, Matthiessen had argued that some of the accusations he had printed were true and that reporting the historical fact that an accusation had been made was necessary to show the Indians' views. Further, the distinction between responsible critics and those whom Price labeled as leftists, that is, "good" and "bad" sources, was not accepted.

In conclusion, Judge Heaney reiterated Judge Murphy's sense that even if a government official could be injured by critical reports, to suppress them would unduly inhibit debate on issues of public significance:

> Sometimes it is difficult to write about controversial events without getting into some controversy along the way. In this setting, we have decided that the Constitution requires more speech rather than less. Our decision is an anomaly in a time when tort analysis increasingly focuses on whether there was an injury, for in debating this case we have searched diligently for fault and ignored certain injury. But there is a larger injury to be considered, the damage done to every American when a book is pulled from a shelf, as in this case, or when an idea is not circulated.
>
> In its entirety, *Crazy Horse* focuses more on public institutions and social forces than it does on any public official. The sentiments it expresses are debatable. We favor letting the debate continue.

Price made two separate applications to the U.S. Supreme Court to reverse the appellate court ruling. In his appeal for review, Price argued that the appeals court had created an "insurmountable hurdle" for plaintiffs in libel cases. "Any author with even a modicum of cleverness can publish purposely false allegations of criminal wrongdoing . . . or include clever and meaningless qualifiers to his defamatory allegations . . . he is absolutely protected by the opinion doctrine." In both instances, the Supreme Court refused to hear the appeal, thus leaving intact the appeals court ruling. The latter Supreme Court rejection occurred in January 1990.

Except for the initial printing of 35,000 copies, *In the Spirit of Crazy Horse* had been unavailable since the first lawsuit was filed in 1983. It was republished in 1991.

FURTHER READING

"Court Dismisses Janklow Suit against Viking and Matthiessen." *Publishers Weekly*, June 16, 1989, 14.

"Crazy Horse Suit Ends; Viking to Publish New Edition in 1991." *Publishers Weekly*, November 9, 1990, 12.

Fields, Howard. "High Court Rejects Libel Appeal against Viking." *Publishers Weekly*, January 26, 1990, 310, 312.

Garbus, Martin. Afterword to *In the Spirit of Crazy Horse*, by Peter Matthiessen. New York: Viking Press, 1991, 589–96.

Greenhouse, Linda. "Reviving Affirmative Action Issue, Court Will Decide." *New York Times,* January 9, 1990, pp. A1, 18.

"Libel Suit Against Viking Dismissed." *New York Times,* June 21, 1984, sec. 3, pp. 17.

Mitgang, Herbert. "Crazy Horse Author Is Upheld in Libel Case." *New York Times,* January 16, 1988, II 5.

Newsletter on Intellectual Freedom 32 (1983): 112; 33 (1984): 18, 75–76, 116, 148; 34 (1985) 34; 35 (1986): 52, 91; 37 (1988): 99; and 40 (1991): 55.

"South Dakota Governor Calls Stores to Ask Book's Removal." *New York Times,* May 1, 1983, p. I32.

"Viking and Matthiessen Prevail in Libel Suit." *Publishers Weekly,* January 29, 1988, 314.

"Viking, Matthiessen Win in Price Libel Suit." *Publishers Weekly,* September 1, 1989, 8.

AN INTRODUCTION TO PROBLEMS OF AMERICAN CULTURE

Author: Harold O. Rugg
Original date and place of publication: 1931, United States
Publisher: Ginn and Company
Literary form: Nonfiction

SUMMARY

Harold Rugg's *An Introduction to Problems of American Culture* was designed to introduce high school students to "the economic, political, and social problems of American culture." As part of a series of textbooks by Rugg, its aim was to integrate the various social science subjects of history, geography, and civics; Rugg's method of discussing these subjects is through the frequent use of dramatic episodes, stories, and political cartoons; the interrelating of topics; and the employment of a critical attitude that invites students to question their preconceived notions of American life. The series was developed through experimental versions used in secondary schools and was widely distributed, selling more than 5.5 million copies.

Rugg begins by examining America as a nation of widely different communities. He contrasts the wealth of white-collar workers and executives with the hard lives of those who work in unskilled labor; he introduces the problems of American families: increasing divorce, shrinking family sizes, the drifting away from tightly knit family units. He also pays attention to the need for greater economic planning, explaining that it is false that "those who don't want to work are not trying hard enough." Instead, Rugg blames industrialists for a lack of foresight and a rush to use machines to replace human workers.

While other textbooks of the age were almost uniformly positive in their portrayal of American democracy, Rugg maintains that it is difficult for America to truly be a nation "of the people, by the people, and for the people." Instead, the incredible growth in the sizes of communities and the resultant corruption mean that America has many failed promises that serve only to add to the vicious circle by creating a sense of apathy and helplessness among the electorate. This helplessness is also seen in attitudes toward crime. One political cartoon included in the book shows a blindfolded policeman reaching out to apprehend the "small offender" while "Gunman," "Professional Killer," "Crime Syndicate," and other underworld figures laugh in the background. Rugg blames public apathy (including refusal to testify in court and jury dodging), corruption among judges and police, the power of gangs, and the irresponsibility of "yellow journalism."

On each issue, *An Introduction to Problems of American Culture* examines a variety of viewpoints. The problems of immigrant crowding in cities is contrasted with the desire to find a new life in America; the rise of American arts and letters is set against the fads of sport and radio programs. While jobs are seen as important, it is also shown that those who perform those jobs are often not given the justice they deserve; in part, Rugg blames the desire for making profit too rapidly at the expense of consumers, workers, and the environment.

Rugg also challenges students to think for themselves. His questions for discussion do not simply ask readers to recite back a summary of what the previous chapter has covered. Some examples of his provocative queries include

- Does the growth of organizations increase the breakdown of American homes?
- Can political machines be beaten?
- How can a poor man own a house?
- Should all citizens have an equal opportunity to speak over the radio, regardless of their political, economic, or social beliefs?
- Does the guarantee of rights in the Constitution really protect the individual?
- Is it possible to arouse in voters a keen interest in exercising their right to vote and thereby take an active part in government?

Rugg provides few direct answers himself. The general tone of the book truly is one that introduces problems in American culture and what some may suggest are solutions, but it is left to the individual reader to determine what those solutions might be.

CENSORSHIP HISTORY

Those engaged in business were generally not great fans of *An Introduction to Problems of American Culture*. They saw the book as an attack on the American way of life and particularly on their business practices. In 1939,

B. C. Forbes, the editor of *Forbes* magazine, tried to get the textbook removed from the schools of Englewood, New Jersey. An El Paso, Colorado, council that claimed to represent 40 different patriotic groups also asked their local school board to ban the book. At the same time, the Advertising Federation of America contended that Rugg had falsely claimed that advertising tried to manipulate consumers and sometimes deceived; the federation maintained that advertising was generally truthful and that it actually reduced prices by encouraging mass production. The federation also attacked Rugg personally, according to author John Tebbel.

In the winter of 1940, delegates at the Daughters of the American Revolution demanded that Rugg's book be repressed; of particular concern was his apparent endorsement of a "cooperative commonwealth." Meanwhile, the Georgia state legislature tried to have several textbooks, including *An Introduction to Problems of American Culture*, removed from public schools; this move, however, failed to gain enough legislature support for its adherents to take action. The September issue of *American Legion Magazine* contained an article by O. K. Armstrong titled "Treason in the Schools," which included Rugg's book, among others, on a blacklist of "subversive books." The article was later released as a pamphlet by the advertising department of the magazine. Not long after, *An Introduction to Problems of American Culture* was removed from schools in Binghamton, New York.

Also in 1940, the National Association of Manufacturers commissioned a conservative academic, Ralph W. Robey, to examine textbooks used in American classrooms. In 1941, Robey issued the results of his study of over 500 books; he maintained that many of them were un-American in tone, with "an out-and-out leftist slant" that denigrated America and capitalism. Worse still, books such as Rugg's encouraged students to adopt "a critical attitude" toward the issues raised by the book. While publishers and scholars rallied around Rugg, conservative publications defended Robey and his charges; some of Robey's supporters even went so far as to suggest that social studies be removed from high school curricula. Where the controversy would have gone is impossible to say; the signing of the Smith Act of 1940 essentially created an "omnibus gag bill," a law designed to quell any discussion of issues in such a way as deemed vaguely unpatriotic, while the entry of the United States into World War II shifted attention away from the subject.

FURTHER READING

Sproule, J. Michael. "Whose Ethics in the Classroom? An Historical Survey." *Communication Monographs* (October 1987): 317–326.

Tebbel, J. *A History of Book Publishing in the United States: The Great Change*, Vol. 4. New York: R. R. Bowker, 1987.

—Mitchell Fay
University of Wisconsin–River Falls

THE INVISIBLE GOVERNMENT

Authors: David Wise and Thomas B. Ross
Original date and place of publication: 1964, United States
Publisher: Random House
Literary form: Nonfiction

SUMMARY

The "Invisible Government" is defined as that "loose, amorphous grouping of individuals and agencies drawn from many parts of the visible government." Although the Central Intelligence Agency (CIA) is at the heart of the Invisible Government, it was made up in 1964 of nine additional agencies— "the intelligence community"—and other units, agencies, and individuals that on the surface appear to be part of the visible government. Seemingly private business firms and institutions are also part of it. The purposes of the Invisible Government are to gather intelligence, conduct espionage, and plan and execute secret operations all over the globe.

The thesis of *The Invisible Government* is certainly cautionary, perhaps foreboding. Citing the words of the Declaration of Independence that the United States government is based on the "consent of the governed," the authors point out that, in the demanding situations of the mid-20th century, "the nation's leaders have increasingly come to feel that certain decisions must be made by them alone without popular consent, and in secret, if the nation is to survive." The authors question the compatibility of this secret government with the American system and to what extent the secret government is necessary to preserve this system.

Essentially, the book provides two vantage points from which to view the CIA. The first spotlights a selection of CIA operations so as to reveal purposes, methods and outcomes. The second compactly represents the structure and workings of the agency itself.

The debacle of the Bay of Pigs in 1961 is depicted in considerable detail. The military maneuvers and troop deployments, the cover missions, the actions and outcomes are conveyed in conjunction with the consultations and machinations that take place far from the battlefield. The military action, which began on April 15, emerged from President Dwight Eisenhower's decision, ordered in March 1960, to "take measures to help these people [Cuban exiles] organize and to help train them and equip them," a mission that President John Kennedy inherited.

Intriguing as the military events may be to postmortem strategy analysts, the focus here is on CIA involvement. Once Eisenhower had authorized the secret training and arming of the Cuban rebels, the CIA swung into action. By April, it was arranging for a secret training site in Guatemala, followed by the construction of a secret airstrip, barracks, and other facilities. The CIA organized and conducted training of the exile groups in Guatemala and the United States and supplied financial support, millions of dollars, for the revolutionary *frente* (later, the Cuban Revolutionary Council). On the propaganda front, it fed "information" and prepared releases throughout the events to a *frente*-hired public relations man. It also attempted unsuccessfully to develop an effective underground guerrilla movement in Cuba, including the delivery of weapons.

As for the invasion itself and the "cover" operations used to create the illusion that the rebels were operating from bases inside Cuba, the CIA was significantly involved in planning the strategies and scenarios. During the invasion and military action, the CIA was on site at the embarkation points and in Washington, monitoring the situation, reacting to events, and reconsidering strategies. At the crisis stage, the CIA deputy director for plans, Richard M. Bissell, who was in charge of the Bay of Pigs operation, urged the use of U.S. air power to support the Cuban rebel forces; Kennedy resisted in keeping with a pledge that both he and Eisenhower had made that no U.S. forces would be used. A compromise flight of navy jets to protect the Cuban-flown bombers was authorized. Unbeknown to the Washington group, several pilots salaried by the CIA volunteered to fly these bombers to replace the weary Cubans; two of these, that is, four Americans, were shot down.

United States government involvement in this effort to overthrow Fidel Castro's regime is evident. Both Kennedy and Eisenhower subsequently made admissions to this effect. At the time, however, one denial of involvement followed another, even at the United Nations: of knowledge of the training being conducted in Guatemala; of awareness of the invasion; of responsibility for the invasion. However, the CIA presence in Guatemala—the training operation—was acknowledged by local gossip and reported in the *New York Times* and the *Miami Herald*. Furthermore, since the "cover" scenarios were rather readily unmasked, leading to open questioning of the U.S. position, the result was a serious undercutting of the U.S. world reputation.

In May 1958, during a rebellion against Indonesian president Sukarno, an American piloting a B-26 bomber, which had just completed a bombing and strafing run, was shot down and captured. Echoing President Eisenhower's earlier denial of charges that the United States was supporting the rebellion—"Our policy is one of careful neutrality and proper deportment all the way through so as not to be taking sides where it is none of our business"—Ambassador Howard P. Jones identified the pilot as "a paid soldier of fortune." He was, in fact, flying for the CIA, which was secretly supporting the rebels.

In Guatemala on June 18, 1954, a United States/CIA "coup against the Communist-dominated regime of President Jacobo Arbenz Guzman" began; it ended in his being deposed on June 27. "By late 1953 Eisenhower had reached his decision: Arbenz must go. To implement this decision, he turned to the CIA and [CIA director] Allen Dulles. A plan was evolved." It included the assignment of a cooperative ambassador; selecting a leader for the coup and helping him set up a headquarters in Honduras; training of the rebel forces and assigning the CIA's air force to support the rebels. The Guatemalan government's charges against the United States were denied.

Other less fully explored examples illustrate similar circumstances of the CIA's "secret" intrusion into the affairs of foreign countries. The CIA plotted the overthrow of the government of Iran in 1953. It supported, from 1949 to at least 1952, 12,000 Nationalist Chinese troops who had escaped from China to Burma, despite the Burmese government's efforts to evict them; the American ambassador received assurances from his superiors that the CIA was not involved. In Vietnam, prior to the 1961 military buildup, the CIA had organized the Vietnamese Special Forces, at a cost of $3 million a year, and the training of the Montagnard mountain tribesmen as scouts and border guards, at a cost of $4.5 million. They were involved also in Laos, Korea, Costa Rica, and other nations.

The outcomes of these undercover activities included public resentment against the CIA, and therefore the United States, complicating United States relations with these countries; and negation of the American image. Needed political and economic reforms were not carried out. For example, reforms in Guatemala were stalemated:

> And so, a decade after the CIA's liberation of Guatemala from Communism in 1954, the lot of Guatemalans was about the same. The *finca* owners prospered. The 2,000,000 Indians, still largely illiterate, toiled on for wages still ridiculously low. . . . And another military junta was in the saddle.
>
> As is so often the case, the Invisible Government had moved in, accomplished its task, and moved on. The yoke of Communism had been thrown off but in its place there remained the yoke of poverty and an indifferent oligarchy. The abysmal conditions that led to Arbenz in the first place were as apparent as ever.

Historical background of the CIA is provided—from its simple origins during World War II to its maturation in the 1960s. Its initial duties, explained in five short paragraphs, did not include special operations until 1948; the guidelines for these specified "that the operations be secret and that they be plausibly deniable by the government."

The chapter entitled "The Inner Workings" identifies and defines the agency's four divisions as of 1963: Intelligence (gathers information and "produces" intelligence), Plans (controls all foreign special operations), Research (provides expert assessment of foreign advances in science, technology, and atomic weapons), and Support (maintains charge of equipment, logistics, security, and communications). The CIA, created to deal exclusively with foreign intelligence, operated in 1963 in 20 United States cities, in addition to its headquarters in Langley, Virginia, outside Washington,

D.C. Its officials claimed that these offices were needed to collect foreign intelligence domestically, principally from travelers and business firms with foreign operations. The CIA also financed refugee activities and political activities of ethnic groups from a $100 million fund, which was part of the budget of the intelligence establishment.

Throughout their text but focused in their concluding chapter, the authors point to and reflect on the dangers emanating from the 1963 "dimensions" of the "intelligence apparatus." Central to these dangers is the conflict between America's democratic institutions and the clandestine government: The Invisible Government "operated outside the normal checks and balances, [thus] posed a potential threat to the very system it was designed to protect." In foreign countries, the U.S. ambassador is designated as the "in-charge" official; yet, CIA officials and agents are shown to operate independently, at times circumventing official policy. The Invisible Government has achieved a "quasi-independent status and a power of its own" with many of its important decisions seemingly "delegated to the Special Group, a small and shadowy directorate nowhere specifically provided for by law."

The authors assert the necessity of establishing control: "Most important, the public, the President and the Congress must support steps to control the intelligence establishment, to place checks on its power and to make it truly accountable, particularly in the area of special operations." Their recommendation is a joint committee of both houses of Congress along with reappraisal of activities abroad and at home. Specifically, they also question the government's misleading of the American people in order to protect secret operations and its righteous public declarations that turn out to be lies. Along with President Harry Truman, they lament the damage to national prestige.

CENSORSHIP HISTORY

A spokesperson from Random House, publisher of *The Invisible Government*, confirmed that John McCone, director of the Central Intelligence Agency, and Lt. General Marshall S. Carter, deputy director, had personally communicated with the publisher in an apparent effort to suppress or alter the book. The incident was reported on June 8, 1964; the book was scheduled to be issued later in the month.

While their complaints about the content were "for the most part on rather general grounds," there were also claims of errors in the text. The publisher reported having asked twice for a list of any errors, but these had not been submitted. The complaints of the two CIA officials referred to the book's being harmful to "national security" but did not allege that the text was in violation of any security classification of information.

Ben Bagdikian repeats the report of newspaper columnist Marquis Childs of the *St. Louis Post Dispatch* that the authors committed 112 breaches of security, uncovered 26 CIA agents, and exposed four important CIA operations. A Washington, D.C., newspaper also reported that the CIA officials complained about the disclosure of CIA agents' names. The Random House spokesperson, however, denied these allegations: "We named no CIA agents that had not previously been named in public someplace else—in newspapers, printed transcripts of hearings, court records." It was indicated further that dozens of names had been voluntarily withheld so as not to reveal names not previously on the public record, though an enemy would probably not have any more trouble learning these names than the authors.

Look magazine had planned to publish excerpts from the book. A spokesperson indicated that the agency had approached them and asked for changes to be made, "Things they considered to be inaccuracies. We made some changes but do not consider that they were significant."

FURTHER READING

Bagdikian, Ben H. "Working in Secret." *New York Times Book Review*, June 28, 1964, pp. 3, 20.
Bailey, Charles W. "Publisher Says CIA Tried to Censor Book." *Minneapolis Morning Tribune*, June 9, 1964, p. 35.
"CIA Concerned over Book." *Newsletter on Intellectual Freedom* 13 (1964): 48.
Marchetti, Victor, and John D. Marks. *The CIA and the Cult of Intelligence.* New York: Alfred A. Knopf, 1974.

IT CAN'T HAPPEN HERE

Author: Sinclair Lewis
Original date and place of publication: 1935, United States
Publisher: Doubleday, Doran and Company
Literary form: Novel

SUMMARY

The "it" in the title, *It Can't Happen Here*, refers to fascism. More exactly, it represents the overthrow of the American republic by a duly elected president and the institution of a totalitarian regime. The book begins in 1936. The country is swinging into its presidential-nominating activities. The primary setting is the rural community of Fort Beulah, Vermont.

Doremus Jessup, central protagonist and moral-political conscience of the novel, is the still vital but aging and relatively prosperous editor of the Fort Beulah *Daily Informer.* His son is a lawyer in Boston; his elder daughter, herself a community leader, is married to a competent doctor; and his younger daughter, a feminist and aspiring architect, is in her last year of high school. Jessup is politically liberal, intellectually honest, and probing; locally he is considered "a pretty smart fella but kind of a cynic."

In the early pages of the novel, the reader is introduced to the issues and conservative opinions of the day, which are anathema to Jessup, the first group spoken by General H. Y. Edgeways, USA (ret.), and the last two by acquaintances: 1) the defense budget—to "defend our shores against all the alien gangs of international racketeers that call themselves 'governments' "; 2) unions, war, and communism—"I do abhor war, yet there are worse things. . . . a state of so-called peace in which labor organizations are riddled, as by plague germs, with insane notions out of anarchist Red Russia"; 3) pacifism—"a sickeningly big percentage of students were blatant pacifists"; 4) prejudice—"we ought to keep all these foreigners out of the country, and what I mean, the Kikes just as much as the Wops and Hunkies and Chinks"; and 5) the poor and relief—"these are serious times—maybe twenty-eight million on relief, and beginning to get ugly—thinking they've got a vested right now to be supported."

The reader is also introduced to Senator Berzelius "Buzz" Windrip, a self-promoting and outrageously deceitful political chameleon and opportunist. As a candidate for the Democratic nomination, he steamrolls the convention and defeats Franklin D. Roosevelt after many ballots to win the nomination. His campaign proclamation, "The Fifteen Points of Victory for the Forgotten Men," includes these excerpts:

(1) All finance in the country, including banking, insurance, stocks and bonds and mortgages, shall be under the absolute control of a Federal Central Bank, owned by the government and conducted by a Board. . . . [which] shall consider the nationalization and government-ownership, for the Profit of the Whole People, of all mines, oilfields, water power, public utilities, transportation, and communication.

(2) The President shall appoint a commission, equally divided between manual workers, employers, and representatives of the Public, to determine which Labor Unions are qualified to represent the Workers. . . .

(4) We shall guarantee to all persons absolute freedom of religious worship, provided, however, that no atheist, agnostic, believer in Black Magic, nor any Jew who shall refuse to swear allegiance to the New Testament, nor any person of any faith who refuses to take the Pledge to the Flag, shall be permitted to hold any public office or to practice as a teacher. . . .

(5) Annual net income per person shall be limited to $500,000. No accumulated fortune may at any one time exceed $3,000,000 per person. . . .

(7) Our armaments and the size of our military and naval establishments shall be consistently enlarged until they shall equal, but—since this country has no desire for foreign conquest of any kind—not surpass, in every branch of the forces of defense, the martial strength of any other single country or empire in the world. . . .

(10) All Negroes shall be prohibited from voting, holding public office, practicing law, medicine, or teaching in any class above the grade of grammar

school, and they shall be taxed 100 percent of all sums in excess of $10,000 per family per year. . . .

(12) All women now employed shall, . . . except in such peculiarly feminine spheres of activity as nursing and beauty parlors, be assisted to return to their incomparably sacred duties as home-makers and as mothers. . . .

(13) Any person advocating Communism, Socialism, or Anarchism, advocating refusal to enlist in case of war, or advocating alliance with Russia . . . shall be subject to trial for high treason. . . .

(15) Congress shall, immediately upon our inauguration, initiate amendments to the Constitution providing (a) that the President shall have the authority to institute and execute all necessary measures for the conduct of the government during this critical epoch; (b) that Congress shall serve only in an advisory capacity, . . . (c) that the Supreme Court shall immediately have removed from its jurisdiction the power to negate, . . . any or all acts of the President, his duly appointed aides, or Congress.

Windrip is elected; his pledge of several thousand dollars a year to every person in the country as part of his redistribution-of-wealth promise effectively brings in the vote. Among his first acts is a special message to Congress demanding the instant passage of a bill giving him complete control of legislation and execution as well as removing from the Supreme Court all capability of blocking his actions. When this demand is rejected, Windrip proclaims a state of martial law; he also acts immediately to arm the Minute Men (initially organized as unpaid volunteers to march in parades but increasingly encouraged and licensed to model the Nazi blackshirts), who then arrest and jail congressmen who resist. Despite riots around the country and in Washington, D.C., "bloodily put down by the Minute Men," the president maintains his power.

Predictably, the situation worsens. Political parties are abolished; only the corporate or corporative state (nicknamed the "Corpo" and its agents, the "Corpos") exists. The states and their governments are also abolished, replaced by provinces subdivided into districts; their officials are appointed. Unemployed workers are sent to labor camps with their families; work is found for them at a dollar a day on state projects and in private industry. And concentration camps are established to commemorate Windrip's birthday.

> The kind-hearted government was fed-up, and the country was informed that, from this day, on, any person who by word or act sought to harm or discredit the State, would be executed or interned. Inasmuch as the prisons were already too full, both for these slanderous criminals and for the persons whom the kind-hearted State had to guard by "protective arrest," there were immediately to be opened, all over the country, concentration camps.

The lives of the Jessup family change dramatically when Doremus drops his wait-and-see stance and writes an editorial condemning the tyranny of the Windrip administration. The next morning, the newspaper office is mobbed; Jessup is arrested, jailed, mistreated, and summarily tried for "criminal libel and conveying secret information to alien forces and high treason and homicidal incitement to violence." He is released on parole so he can train the former school superintendent, now a Corpo, to run the newspaper. At the moment of sentencing, his son-in-law doctor, outraged, forces himself into the courtroom and protests disrespectfully. The judge orders the doctor shot; within moments he is dead.

Fear settles like heavy fog around the Jessups and the country as they watch changes enacted and freedoms sharply eclipsed. Secret news of individuals and groups bullied and slaughtered by terrorists begins to circulate. After an attempt to escape to Canada fails, Doremus becomes involved in the New Underground (NU), a partisan activity headquartered in Canada. His underground station, which receives news of Corpo activities and tyrannies, prints and distributes leaflets as part of an attempt to undermine the Corpo administration and prepare citizens for revolt. The cell, however, is discovered, and its members are sent to concentration camps. There they are repeatedly beaten and brutalized. Eventually, after he has all but given up hope, Doremus escapes with the help of a bribed guard. He is transported to Canada, where he joins the New Underground movement.

Meanwhile back in Washington, D.C., President Windrip has isolated himself, having become increasingly fearful of both shadows and reality. And well he should be. After two years in office, about the time Jessup is helped to escape from the concentration camp, Windrip is deposed and exiled by his longtime, loyal right-hand man whom he had appointed secretary of state. This coup d'état shocks the idealists among the Corpos and the Minute Men, as do the flippant governmental style and Romanesque White House parties of the new president. Soon the secretary of war marches into the White House with selected storm troops, assassinates the president, and declares himself to that office. The nation's situation worsens.

In 1939, the United States declares war on Mexico, seemingly to distract Americans from the misery and deprivation at home. At the same time, a popular rebellion against the Corpo regime rises up in the United States, initially in the north-central and northwestern areas with large patches elsewhere in the country joining. At this time, too, Doremus Jessup returns to the United States via Minnesota as a new underground leader, in charge of some 60 other agents.

Comparison to the events and affairs of Nazi Germany is not left to reader imagination; the author provides references to these affairs as well as admiring comments from Windrip and other Corpos. A less direct comment near the conclusion suggests Lewis's deeper concern about the state of the American mind and psyche in relation to the rising concern about the politics of Europe.

But there the revolt halted, because in America, which had so warmly praised itself for its "widespread popular free education," there had been so very little education, widespread, popular, free, or anything else, that most people did not know what they wanted—indeed knew about so few things to want at all.

CENSORSHIP HISTORY

Despite a "bureaucratic" disclaimer from Dr. Frank L. Tolman, head of the New York Library Extension Service, that the service since 1930 did not have the right to approve or disapprove books for school libraries, its library commission had "suggested eliminating some books not as closely connected with the curriculum as others." According to Tolman, the commission had responded to requests from school librarians for assistance. *It Can't Happen Here* was one of those eliminated. John Tebbel reports that the New York *World-Telegram* headline read, "School Bars Lewis' Book Also Broun's— Others Kept Off Library Shelves by State Disapproval." (The Heywood Broun book referred to is *Thunder over the Bronx*; Robert Graves's *I, Claudius* was also listed.)

Tebbel focuses attention on the 1936 proposed film version of *It Can't Happen Here:* "The American Civil Liberties Union reported that . . . in Hollywood, *It Can't Happen Here* was having as difficult a time in its movie version as the book had endured, and for the same reasons—the authoritarian belief that authoritarianism could not happen in America." The controversy emerged when Metro-Goldwyn-Mayer (MGM), which had acquired the rights to the novel, announced that production had been postponed indefinitely; according to Louis B. Mayer, cost was the factor. Sinclair Lewis, however, citing a telegram from his agent with official information, indicated that the studio's action resulted from Will H. Hays's forbidding the production on the grounds of "fear of international politics and fear of boycotts abroad." Lewis argued further that Hays would "probably base the suppression on the ground that the film industry is opposed to using the motion pictures for controversial politics." (Hays administered the Motion Picture Production Code, commonly referred to as the Hays office.) Lewis also attributed Hays's action to domestic political concerns: uncertainty of how the election would develop and not wanting to offend the Republicans. The director of the Production Code Administration, Joseph I. Breen, Hays's assistant, attacked *It Can't Happen Here* as too "anti-fascist."

Though Hays and his spokespersons denied the order to ban the film, Sidney Howard, who wrote the screen adaptation, produced a memorandum from Breen that suggested the elimination of sections of the script because they were "so inflammatory in nature and so filled with dangerous material." Howard noted that Hays didn't "ban" the film; he "just talked the producers out of it."

Doubleday, the novel's publisher, entered the fray with an advertisement in the *New York Times,* charging censorship and asserting "It *is* happening here." The controversy doubled the sale of the book.

In 1937, upon the translation of the book into German, it was banned in Germany. In 1954, all of Sinclair Lewis's books were banned in East Berlin.

FURTHER READING

"Berlin and Rome Hail Ban on Lewis Film." *New York Times*, February 17, 1936, p. 21.

Green, Jonathon, and Nicholas J. Karolides, reviser. *The Encyclopedia of Censorship, New Edition.* New York: Facts On File, 2005.

"It Can't Happen Here Storm Continues Unabated." *Publishers Weekly*, March 14, 1936, 1, 174.

Haight, Anne Lyon, and Chandler B. Grannis. *Banned Books: 387 B.C. to 1978 A.D.* 4th ed. New York: R. R. Bowker, 1978.

"Hollywood Tempest Breaks on *It Can't Happen Here." Publishers Weekly*, February 22, 1936, 900.

"Lewis Says Hays Bans Film of Book." *New York Times*, February 16, 1936, pp. 1, 35.

"Reich Bans *It Can't Happen Here." New York Times*, January 31, 1937, p. 26.

"Sidney Howard Backs Lewis in Film Row." *New York Times*, February 23, 1936, p. 3.

Tanner, Stephen L. "Sinclair Lewis and Fascism." *Studies of the Novel* 22 (Spring 1990): 57–66.

Tebbel, John. *A History of Book Publishing in the United States.* Vol. 3. New York: R. R. Bowker, 1978.

JOHNNY GOT HIS GUN

Author: Dalton Trumbo
Original date and place of publication: 1939, United States
Publisher: J. B. Lippincott
Literary form: Novel

SUMMARY

Johnny Got His Gun is divided into Book I, "The Dead" and Book II, "The Living." "The Dead" is structured with chapters alternating from present to past as the protagonist, Joe Bonham, attempts to come to grips with what has happened to him. "The Living" concentrates on the present, though there are occasional reflections of the past. The novel is written in first person, an extended monologue—the mind, memories, and hallucinations of the protagonist.

> He was the nearest thing to a dead man on earth. He was a dead man with a mind that could still think. He knew all the answers that the dead knew and couldn't think about. He could speak for the dead because he was one of them.

These thoughts toward the close of Book I reflect Joe's realization and attitude. He has come far from the dull confusion and semiconsciousness of the first chapter. He begins to realize that he has been badly hurt and that he is deaf, but he is alive and in a hospital. In subsequent chapters, he realizes that he has lost one arm and then the other and then both legs. At last, he knows he has no mouth nor tongue nor nose and that he is blind.

The trauma and terror of these discoveries are like a bad dream; at times, Joe thinks he is dreaming or does not know when he is awake and when he is asleep. The nightmares shake him but being awake shakes him too.

The balancing chapters, Joe's recollections of the past, reveal Joe's *every-man* background—the normality of his life and love of his family; the buoyant adolescence and emerging manhood. His memories encompass the everyday: his mother's wordless singing while canning or making jelly; the smell and taste of freshly cooked hamburgers; camping-fishing holidays with his father; kissing and loving his sweetheart. By the close of Book I, Joe has established his sensibility and his stability of character. As his memories unravel and clarify, he establishes his sanity.

An antiwar element materializes in Book I. It is introduced in Chapter 2— "He lay and thought oh Joe Joe this is no place for you. This was no war for you. This thing wasn't any of your business. What do you care about making the world safe for democracy?" In Chapter 10 an extended stream-of-consciousness essay denounces fighting for empty words: freedom, liberty, honor, death before dishonor. The dead renounce these, for they died "yearning for the face of a friend . . . moaning and sighing for life." Joe knows for he is "the nearest thing to a dead man on earth."

In Book II, Joe tries to maintain control of his memory and gain cognizance and control of his environment. He works his mind, starting with recollections of numbers, quotations, and books; he tries to establish time, the passage of time. During a quite poignant moment, Joe solves this problem when he realizes he has identified the coming of dawn and opens up his memory bank of sunrise. He marks time, counting the days into years.

He works also on space and the message of vibrations until he can tell who is with him and what is being done. He is at first bewildered by a group of visitors in the fourth year of his hospitalization and then intensely angered when he realizes that he has been awarded a medal. His anger leads him to recall his use of a wireless set years before; he initiates efforts to communicate by tapping the Morse code "SOS" on his pillow.

Months later, a young substitute nurse recognizes the code, and Joe's attempt to communicate. His joy at being acknowledged a live man with a mind is a "new wild frantic happiness." When he answers her question, "What do you want?" the answer is, "What you ask is against regulations."

What did he want? He wants, of course, his life back—his senses, his limbs. He asks to be let out, to be released from the hospital "prison." He longs for air, sensations on his skin, to be among people. His mind runs ahead of his tapping, revealing his desire to make an exhibit of himself to show ordinary people—parents, schoolchildren—and legislators: "Here is war."

The text concludes in emotional antiwar rhetoric.

CENSORSHIP HISTORY

Dalton Trumbo's acclaimed World War I novel—it won the American Booksellers Award in 1940 as the "most original novel of the year"—is one of the finest by an American in the 1930s. *Johnny Got His Gun* was his statement against the war, against the United States getting involved in a European war. However, during World War II, Trumbo deferred his doubts, shifting from the antiwar attitudes to "militant support for the war effort."

In his 1959 introduction to *Johnny Got His Gun*, Trumbo recounts the book's "weird political history." "Written in 1938 when pacifism was anathema to the American left and most of the center, it went to the printers in the spring of 1939 and was published on September third—ten days after the Nazi-Soviet pact, two days after the start of World War II." Subsequently, serial rights were sold to *The Daily Worker* of New York City, becoming for months a rallying point for the left.

During World War II, after the book went out of print, Trumbo himself resisted requests to have it reprinted; his publishers agreed. These requests came from the extreme American right, which wanted a negotiated peace and which perceived the novel, according to Bruce Cook, to be "useful as propaganda . . . as the Axis fortunes began to fall" because of the antiwar message. "Anti-Semitic and native Fascist groups put on a big push for an early peace, demanding that Hitler be offered a conditional peace." Individuals of these persuasions claimed that Jews, communists, and international bankers had suppressed the novel. Trumbo was distressed that his book was being so used by these groups.

The army initiated a program, during World War II, of distributing books to soldiers overseas. From 1941 to 1943, 3 million books were shipped. Subsequently, the army invited the Council on Books in Wartime, an organization formed by the publishing industry to assist the war effort, to help in this program. In the next three years, 1,080 separate titles, more than 122 million books, were made available to servicemen.

There was an underlying censorship stance involved in the book selection. Prior to 1943, magazines and newspapers of Axis propaganda were rejected. In addition, three books were banned by the Special Services Division, two of them "by direction from higher authority." One of these was *Johnny Got His Gun*, presumably because of its pacifist message.

Johnny Got His Gun has been challenged and/or censored in schools: in the Midwest (1973) for vulgarity of incidents and language; in Michigan (1977) for too much profanity, too gruesome of details of a human being, expressing unpatriotic and anti-American ideas and sexual passages; in Wisconsin (1977) for too much profanity; in Texas (1977) as unpatriotic and anti-American; in Colorado (1977) for the description of the main character after he had been maimed in the war; in California (1977) for the language and for several passages describing sexual encounters; in Wisconsin (1982) as antiwar; in Vermont and Illinois (1982) as too violent.

Trumbo was also a successful screenwriter. Talented and prolific, he was nominated for and had won Academy Awards. In 1947, Trumbo was black-listed as one of the Hollywood Ten. He had joined the Communist Party in 1943 (he left the party in 1948) when the United States and the Soviet Union were allies, and he had been active representing his views. As such, he was an obvious recipient of a subpoena to appear before the House Committee on Un-American Activities in Washington, D.C., on October 23, 1947. The hearings focused on the "Communist Infiltration of the Motion Picture Industry": The presumption was that communist dogma and propaganda had been written into film scripts. The Hollywood Ten perceived the essential question to be one of freedom of speech.

Dubbed "unfriendly witnesses" because of their refusal to answer the committee's questions about membership in the Screenwriters Guild and the Communist Party, they, upon the committee's unanimous vote to seek indictments for contempt of Congress, were found guilty of contempt of the House of Representatives in a 346-17 vote. All 10 individuals served prison terms; Trumbo, sentenced to a year, served 10 months, starting on June 7, 1950.

Despite disclaimers that they would do anything so un-American, the motion picture industry prepared in November 1947 the notorious Waldorf Agreement which, in effect, declared the Hollywood Ten and others like them to be "no longer employable in the motion picture industry." The Hollywood Ten did bring suit on their contracts, but on November 14, 1949, the Supreme Court turned down their petition and refused to hear the case. Trumbo refers to this situation as a domestic manifestation of the cold war that was then developing: "We are against the Soviet Union in our foreign policy abroad, and we are against anything partaking of socialism or communism in our internal affairs. This quality of opposition has become the keystone of our national existence."

Before and after his imprisonment, Trumbo wrote for the movie black market under pseudonyms or under the cover of other screenwriters' names. In 1957, he won the Oscar for the Best Motion Picture Story for *The Brave One* under his pseudonym Robert Rich; this award "marked the beginning of the end of the black list," according to Cook, which by this time affected any writers implicated in the anticommunist witch-hunt. Cook quotes Trumbo as remarking that because there were so many screenwriters working in the movie black market under false or borrowed names, "no record of credits between 1947 and 1960 can be considered even remotely accurate." Cook also credits Trumbo with the dissolution of the blacklist in 1960: It was "a coordinated and deliberate personal campaign in the media . . . a crusade, a vendetta."

FURTHER READING

Cook, Bruce. *Dalton Trumbo.* New York: Charles Scribner's Sons, 1977.

DeMuth, James. *"Johnny Got His Gun:* A Depression Era Classic." In *Censored Books: Critical Viewpoints,* edited by Nicholas J. Karolides, Lee Burress, and John M. Kean, 331–337. Metuchen, N.J.: Scarecrow Press, 1993.

Jamieson, John. *Books for the Army: The Army Library Service in the Second World War.* New York: Columbia University Press, 1950.

Leary, William M., Jr. "Books, Soldiers and Censorship during the Second World War." *American Quarterly* 20 (1968): 237–245.

Trumbo, Dalton. "Introduction." In *Johnny Got His Gun.* New York: Bantam Books, 1983.

THE JOKE (ŽERT)

Author: Milan Kundera

Original dates and places of publication (definitive version): 1992, United States (Kundera's approved text); 1967, Czechoslovakia (rejected by Kundera)

Publisher: HarperCollins; Československý spisovatel

Literary form: Novel

SUMMARY

The Joke is narrated with four voices—Ludvik Jahn, the central protagonist; Helena Zemanek, the woman whom Ludvik uses for his sexual-revenge against his enemy, Pavel Zemanek, a Communist youth leader, who condemned Ludvik in college; Jaroslav, his childhood best friend, in Moravia; and Kostka, a physician and professor acquaintance from his university days. The story is not told in chronological sequence. It opens and closes in Moravia in the present. In most of the intervening chapters, the narrative returns to the past in the 1950s Stalinist period. The temporal distance between then and the present is 15 years.

By his own admission, the joke significantly changes and ruins Ludvik's life, but it also causes remarkable changes in his character. Ludvik, a university student, had been recognized for his competence as a student and had achieved some status in the Party's League of University Students. The joke was written on a postcard to Mařketa, a college friend whom he was courting: "Optimism is the opium of the people! A healthy atmosphere stinks of stupidity! Long live Trotsky!" Mařketa was attending a two-week Party training school "to fortify her zeal with concrete knowledge of the strategy and tactics of the revolutionary movement." Ludvik's joke responds to her enthusiastic message to him about the training course; his intention was to suggest his worldly detachment, to poke fun at her sincerity by taking on an attitude of cynical nonchalance. This "silly joke" as Ludvik refers to it was the catalyst of the major disaster.

Charges are brought against Ludvik, and he is summoned to the District Party Secretariat. Questioned at length, not at all sympathetically by three students he knew well, his responses resulted in a failed interview; he was relieved of his post in the Student Union. The case was turned over to the Party Organization at the university's Natural Sciences Division, the Party chairman of which was his good friend Pavel Zemanek. But the sympathy Ludvik may have anticipated in that relationship was also dashed. After being called before various committees and commissions, he was at last summoned to the plenary meeting in the lecture hall of the Natural Sciences Division, "at which Zemanek delivered the opening address on me and my errors (effective, brilliant, unforgettable), recommending . . . that I be expelled from the Party." Ludvik offered a self-critical statement to no avail. No one spoke on his behalf. Everyone voted to approve his expulsion from the Party and from the university.

During the period of Ludvik's being investigated, Marketa contacts him to explain what had happened. As part of the conversation she asserts:

> "I'm not apologizing," she protested, "and I'm not ashamed of giving them the card. That's not what I meant at all. You're a Party member, and the Party has a right to know exactly who you are and what you think." She had been shocked by what I had written, she told me. After all, everybody knew that Trotsky was the archenemy of everything we stood for, everything we were fighting for.

No longer in a deferred status as a student, Ludvik is conscripted into the army. After training, perceived as a "Trotskyite and imperialist—an enemy of the revolution," he is assigned to work in the mines, digging coal. He is attached to the penal battalion, the disinherited. They were depersonalized, Ludvik gradually losing his sense of self-esteem, of being above the others. The harsh, underground work conditions of constant drudgery unify them all, as does the attitude that they are unworthy of any consideration, conveyed by the commandant and the guards. Ludvik even found moments of pleasure after their escapades in town when on a pass. On one occasion, alone on a pass, he met Lucie, whom he follows into a cinema. Lucie becomes his escape mechanism, his liberator. They begin seeing each other when he's on leave, taking long platonic walks, though she is timid and tentative. Once when he reads some poems to her she weeps. She becomes the light of his life, an unexpected bonus to him; he comes to believe he loves her. He tries to make love with her twice; when he becomes physically insistent, she pushes him away and literally runs away. Her disappearance shocks him. Later in the book, in Kostka's section we learn that she had been repeatedly gang-raped when she was 16, that trauma being the apparent cause of her resistance—and her escape.

Ludvik's affair with Helena (in the present) is driven by lust and revenge—and consummated by pretense. Helena loves the Party, is dedicated to its principles; when a married colleague had an affair with a girl in another department and was accused of breaking his vow to end the affair—"having deliberately deceived and misled it," she proposed that he be expelled from the Party. Yet, she admits that she is cheating on her husband, Pavel Zemanek. However, she excuses herself because she is looking for love. She and her husband, are out of love, Pavel having told her "we didn't marry for love, we married out of Party discipline."

Helena first meets Ludvik at his office to interview him for a radio broadcast about his research institute. He diverts her, deliberately charms her; he suggests that she needs "to devote more time to the joys of life" and invites her to drive with him to the countryside the next day—and thereafter to meet in his hometown, she to report on the annual Ride of the Kings celebration. He plans to seduce her, not because he loves her or lusts for her body but to avenge himself against her husband, whom he has never forgiven. Pretentious and callous, he uses her body cruelly, pretending passion. His malevolent plan works; she interprets his intensity as love. He determines to leave for Prague—"I had nothing more to do here: my deceitful mission to my hometown was over." The finale of the experience, revealed in the concluding section, causes him to recognize that his plan had failed. Pavel had not been cuckolded; he has another woman, a student, young and vibrant, on his arm, having already separated from Helena.

The last section of the novel visits the Ride of Kings, and it brings together the old friends, Jaroslav, whom earlier he had consciously ignored, and Ludvik. Jaroslav, recalling the presence and honoring of the King ritual in the past, when as a youth he enacted the king, becomes despondent. His entire life, passing before him, seems a failure—a midlife crisis against the backdrop of his becoming aware that his son, this year's chosen king, has actually managed to avoid the performance. Realizing his wife's conspiracy with their son, Jaroslav loses control of himself; he systematically breaks his wife's favorite dishes and furniture. Disillusioned, he picks up his violin and leaves; he is scheduled to perform with his folk-music ensemble as part of the celebration.

Ludvik, contemplating his life's bondage to vengeance, is equally despondent. "When it is postponed, vengeance is transformed into something deceptive, into a personal religion, into a myth that recedes day by day from the people involved, who remain the same in the myth though in reality they long ago became different people." He realizes that "the blow that I still owe [Pavel] can be neither revived nor reconstructed, it is definitely lost."

On his way to the bus station, Ludvik, finding the despairing Jaroslav lying on a field adjacent to the path with his violin case, asks if he might sit in with the band. They had both been members in their youth.

... for at that moment I was filled with a sorrowful love; love for this world I had abandoned years ago, for this world, distant and ancient, in which horsemen ride around a village with a masked king, in which people walk around in white frilled shirts and sing songs; ... all day long that love had been quietly growing in me, and now it had burst out almost tearfully; I loved that ancient world and begged it to offer me sanctuary and to save me.

The folk songs at the band's concert are memory replenishing and emotionally satisfying, the playing intense and inspiring to the players. During the concert, the audience had been, however, changed from elderly people, warmly respondent to the music, to a swaggering loud crowd of young people. The band played for itself. Then, Jaroslav, sweat running down his brow, suddenly stops playing—a heart attack.

Kundera identifies *The Joke* as a love story, despite the overshadowing of these emotions by the social and political imperatives of the time and place of its setting, that is, the Stalinist repression. Ludvik's love, innocent and dreamlike, for Lucie is continuous, though it is never consummated—or even acknowledged. And when she resists, his love intentions turning into lust, she rejects him: the love resides in Ludvik's memory. His relationship with Mařketa is reminiscent of adolescent behavior, his insecurity and inexperience being covered by a masquerade of bravura. The Helena episode reflects lust accompanied by revenge rather than desire. Alternative situations: Pavel commits adultery, apparently frequently; Helena follows suit, searching for love—these behaviors despite the then Party policy opposing such activity.

On the surface a soap opera plot with excessive behavior of the characters, the novel at its core is an exploration of human character. The search for love—a true honest relationship—is fraught with self-inflicted delusions and misunderstandings. The attempt to achieve love suffers from both incapacity and misconstrued definition of love-lust. The role of power as a practice and an outcome of love-lust situations is examined: the male overpowering the female object of his love, the use of sexuality as a power contrivance of revenge; the female's resistance and despair of such manipulation. In contrast, the final scenes reveal a homecoming through musical memory and friendship.

CENSORSHIP HISTORY

The Joke (Žert) was published in 1967 on the eve of Prague Spring during the period of de-Stalinization that followed the 20th Party Congress of 1956; some criticisms of society, carefully controlled, were permitted. Before this approval in Prague, Communist censors had attempted to reject publication of Kundera's manuscript: He had rejected all the changes that they had wanted to impose, and the novel had finally been allowed to appear as it had been written. In 1968, however, after the invasion of

Czechoslovakia, Kundera's books were removed from libraries, confiscated from bookshops, and banned from legal publication; also, his plays were banned from theaters. In 1969, Kundera was fired from his teaching position, and the entire Hungarian edition of *The Joke* was destroyed before it reached bookstores in 1968. It was published in Poland in 1970 and in three languages in Yugoslavia. All other Eastern European countries banned *The Joke*.

In his "Author's Note," of the "Definitive Version" of *The Joke* (fully revised by the author), published in 1992, Kundera asserts another type of censorship: the translations were both inadequate and incomplete. The first version, published in London by MacDonald in 1969, translated by David Hamblyn and Oliver Stallybrass, was "entirely reconstructed, having been divided into a different number of parts." Some chapters were shortened or omitted. The second edition, also 1969, was published in the United States by Coward-McCann. Based on the Hamlyn-Stallybrass translation, the original sequence was maintained, but the "entire text was systematically curtailed." Kundera's telegrams of protest were not answered. He accused "The American publisher was ready to show his sympathy for censored authors in Communist countries, but only on the condition that they submit to his own commercial censorship."

Kundera's letter of protest to the first edition in the *Times Literary Supplement*, however, resulted in a revised, complete edition, in Britain without deletions and with the chapters in their original sequence (Penguin Books, 1970). The author, upon scrutiny of the text, was not satisfied: the "translation was still very free" and his punctuation had not been adhered to, notably Helena's monologue in Part II in which the paragraphs of "one long 'infinite' sentence . . . had been broken up into many very short sentences."

A fourth edition published by Harper & Row (1982) was translated by Michael Henry Heim, who had achieved Kundera's trust, given his approved rendering of Kundera's 1980 novel *The Book of Laughter and Forgetting*. Because of this assurance the manuscript of the new translation was not carefully perused. Years later, another edition was proposed. Kunder's reading of the fourth edition led to a "word-for-word translation of my original in English or in French, wherever I thought it necessary." Thus, along with segments of Heim's version and that of Hamlyn-Stallybrass, the fifth version took shape.

FURTHER READING

Books and Writers. "Milan Kundera." Available online. URL: http://www.kirjasto.sci.fi/kundera.htm. Accessed September 21, 2010.
Misurella, Fred. *Milan Kundera: Public Events, Private Affairs*. Columbia: University of South Carolina Press, 1993.
Porter, Robert. *Milan Kundera: A Voice from Central Europe*. Aaarhus, Denmark: Arcona, 1981.

A JOURNEY FROM ST. PETERSBURG TO MOSCOW

Author: Aleksandr Nikolaevich Radishchev
Original dates and places of publication: 1790, Russia; 1958, United States
Publishers: Alexandr Radishchev; Harvard University Press
Literary form: Nonfiction

SUMMARY

With the publication of *A Journey from St. Petersburg to Moscow,* Aleksandr Radishchev achieved, in the eyes of generations of Russians to follow, the historic role of the first to speak out against the enslavement of the serfs. It was a self-identified role, for he writes in *Liberty: An Ode,* "He who was born here under the yoke of tyranny and bore gilded fetters was the first to proclaim Liberty to us."

Written between the years 1780 and 1790, Radishchev's *Journey* takes us across a Russian countryside where serfs, 95 percent of the population, are enslaved by tyrannical noblemen landlords in a system validated by an egocentric sovereign class and enforced by the military. More than an abolitionist tract, the book attacks the entire societal structure: the class-biased judicial system, the unjust laws, the slave-based agricultural system, the practice of selling peasants to the military service to support unnecessary conquest, the power-driven clergy, the history of censorship of ideas and opinions, and the culpability of a lineage of rulers who presided over the evolution of the status quo, making decisions based more on vanity than benefit for the entire population. He holds the sovereign responsible for changing the system, being the only party in an autocracy with the power to do so.

Radishchev strongly warns the perpetrators of peasant slavery that, if conditions continue in this corrupt, unjust way, a peasant uprising is inevitable and even justified: "Death and fiery desolation will be the meed for our harshness and inhumanity. . . . Peril is already hovering over our heads." He refers to the actual recent rebellion led by Emel'yan Pugachev in 1773 during which the peasants "in their ignorance" could think of no other way to free themselves of their shackles except by killing their masters. In describing a group of peasants who slay their abusive master, he exonerates their action because they were driven to it by cruelty and because "natural law" overrides the Russian law based on servitude for the economic gain of the nobility.

He also attacks serfdom from an economic standpoint, claiming it decreases both production and population. Because man is naturally motivated by self-interest, the serf cultivates his master's land lazily and does not care if it goes to waste. But on the field given him for his family's meager sustenance, "Nothing distracts him from his work. The savagery of the weather he overcomes bravely; the hours intended for rest he spends at work; he shuns pleasure even on the days set aside for it. . . . Thus his field will give him an abundant harvest; while all the fruits of the work done on the proprietor's demesne will die or bear no future harvest." Inadequate harvests further result in low population growth: "Where there is nothing to eat, there will soon be no eaters. . . . But this is not the only thing in slavery that interferes with abundant life. To insufficiency of food and clothing they have added work to the point of exhaustion. Add to this the spurns of arrogance and the abuse of power . . . and you see with horror the pernicious effects of slavery, which differs from victory and conquest only by not allowing what victory cuts down to be born anew."

Further, he appeals to the morality of his fellow nobles: "Shall we not be brave enough to overcome our prejudices, to suppress our selfishness, to free our brothers from the bonds of slavery, and to re-establish the natural equality of all?" As equals, he claims, men enact and agree to abide by laws only such as they are for their own good—since slavery in no way benefits the slave, he has no reasonable obligation to uphold such a law. He appeals also to the conscience of the sovereign, careful to avoid specifying a particular monarch, suggesting that the ruler *could* be just and fair if she could just remove the "cataracts of vanity" from her eyes and see "Truth" through her egotistical fog.

This portrayal of the blindly vain ruler is an example of how the characters in the book are used to buttress Radishchev's abolitionist message and to demonstrate the pervasiveness of corruption within Russian society. Landed gentry are portrayed as autocratic rulers who treat the peasants who work their land as slaves, not human beings but as mere tools to their own aggrandizement. They have no qualms against breaking up peasant families by auctioning off peasants who have loyally worked their master's land, even risked their lives for their master. The gentry class and city folk are corrupt, greedy, lascivious, and lazy. Peasants are impeccably honest, hard-working, loyal people of pure morals. But should a young peasant seek to buy his freedom by working in the city (which apparently was allowed by some masters) the mere association with city "dandies" could corrupt his morals. Similarly, entering the military before one's morals are formed teaches youths contempt for honest men who scorn underhanded methods.

Radishchev exposes corruption in the court system—graft, payoffs, promotions based on servility to superiors. The judicial laws themselves are unjust, the severity of punishment being based on the class and financial status of the accused. For example, once a merchant achieves a certain amount of capital worth, he is exempt from corporal punishment, regardless of his crime. Landowners are given judicial power over their own peasants and allowed to punish them in any manner short of killing them—although, Radishchev points out, there is no regulation against killing them *slowly* by overwork and starvation.

The clergy, too, are criticized for being part of the system, maintaining the status quo in order to protect their own power. They stand in the way of enlightenment and liberation by accommodating the nobility, thus enabling the oppressors to persecute people whose views are not precisely orthodox, as defined by the empowered class to which they belong. Throughout history the clergy aimed to keep the masses ignorant, fearing that the dissemination of general knowledge might challenge their powerful influence and control. Learning was to be considered divine and untouchable and, at certain times and places in history, those who tried to translate the biblical texts into vernacular languages were subject to excommunication. Radishchev quotes author Johann Beckman whose works provided him with factual data on censorship: "Priests have always been the inventors of fetters [burdening] the human mind . . . lest it should soar to greatness and freedom."

Though Radishchev prophesizes that the inequities and corruptness of the existing societal system will inevitably lead to a grand-scale serf rebellion, he does not *advocate* a violent rebellion, but rather appeals to his peers to enact legal reforms, which he discusses extensively. In the laws of nature, he explains, enslavement is a crime. Because society is blinded with greed, however, it enslaves the farmer who feeds it. Those who work the land (and thus have the natural right to it) are not only completely excluded from owning it, but see their very sustenance—the fruits of their own labor—controlled by their landlords. He outlines a scheme for abolishing slavery gradually. *Domestic* serfs would be freed outright, while every peasant would be given the following rights: the right to marry without his master's approval, the right to own the plot he cultivates and to not be arbitrarily deprived of it, the right of citizenship, the right of trial by a jury of the peasant's own peers with no arbitrary punishment without due process of law, the right to buy land, and the right to obtain freedom by paying his master a fixed sum. Virtue, Radishchev says, is the highest human action and should not be impeded by *anything*, including customs, civil law, ecclesiastical law, or sovereign command.

A lengthy essay is devoted to the destructiveness of censorship, which is anathema to enlightenment and improvement. Writers, unable to think for themselves, become "babies" and slaves to the establishment. Quoting Johann G. von Herder, German poet and philosopher, Radishchev stresses that "Any inquisition is harmful to the realm of learning; it makes the air stifling and smothers the breath. A book that has to pass through ten censorships before it sees the light of day is no longer a book, but a creature of the Holy Inquisition, very often a mutilated unfortunate, beaten with rods, gagged, and always a slave." Not only is censorship destructive, it is ineffectual. "What is prohibited is coveted." But let the public be the judge of an author's work and "stupidity will find a thousand censors. The most vigilant police cannot check worthless ideas as well as a disgusted public."

Furthermore, censorship is a symptom of an unjust government. "In prohibiting freedom of the press, timid governments are not afraid of blasphemy but of criticism of themselves." Freedom of thought, he elaborates, is terrifying only to a corrupt, hypocritical government that fears its mask will be torn off and its true character laid bare. As Radishchev's quote from Herder further points out, a state that is confidently grounded in its principles is not fearful of "any pasquinade of an overwrought writer; all the more readily, then it will grant freedom of thought and of writing through which truth will ultimately be victorious. Only tyrants are suspicious; only secret evildoers are fearful." But as Radishchev says, "Let the government be honest and its leaders free from hypocrisy; then all the spittle and vomit will return their stench upon him who has belched them forth; but the truth will always remain pure and immaculate. . . . Let the government proceed on its appointed path; then it will not be troubled by the empty sound of calumny . . . but woe to it if in its lust for power it offends against truth. Then even a thought shakes its foundations; a word of truth will destroy it; a manly act will scatter it to the winds."

Herder's criticism of governments is notable: "All monopolies of thought are harmful. . . . The ruler of a state must be almost without any favorite opinion of his own in order that he may be able to embrace, tolerate, refine, and direct toward the general welfare the opinions of everyone in his state: hence great rulers are so rare."

The Russian government, Radishchev notes, allows anyone to operate a printing press, but the Department of Public Morals inspects and censors what it finds objectionable in what is printed. "A single stupid official in the Department of Public Morals may do the greatest harm to enlightenment and may for years hold back the progress of reason."

"O ye who introduce censorship . . . ," he concludes, "burn with shame."

CENSORSHIP HISTORY

The censorship of Radishchev's *A Journey from St. Petersburg to Moscow* must be understood within the historical context of the time the book was written—between 1780 and 1790. During the 18th century, the laws had become increasingly grim for the peasant. In 1722, Peter the Great established the Table of Ranks for the military, court, and civil services. Of the 14 ranks, the upper eight could own serfs and were exempt from the per-capita tax collected exclusively from the peasants by their landlords. To facilitate this taxation and to have a ready source of men for the military, Peter the Great decreed that no serf could leave his master's estate without his written consent. Though Peter's intent in tying the serf to the landed gentry was to enable the gentry to better serve the sovereign, after Peter's death, the tables of power began to turn—the gentry gradually freed themselves from obligation of service to the state, but kept and even increased their powers over the serfs for their own benefit. With the peasants deprived of citizenship, the nobility alone had the power to "vote in" the emperor, and by the time of Catherine II the Great's rule, the gentry were powerful enough to have the empress "in the palm of their hand." Empress Anna, in 1736, gave the gentry the power to punish their serfs in any way seen fit except death, and in 1765, Catherine II made it legal for the landlords to demand *all* their serfs' time to work the manorial land with no provision for them to work their own plots. Pleas to the courts were pointless for serfs since judges were all gentry—usually the landlord judged his own serfs.

In 1773, Emel'yan Pugachev, pretending to be Peter III, instigated a rebellion that found many followers among the peasants, burning down manorial houses and killing the occupants. Though he was stopped and executed, the rebellion shook the society. The journey upon which Radishchev based his book was a trip he made to visit his parents in 1775 through towns ravaged by Pugachev. Because Radishchev's father, who was among the landed gentry, was enlightened and generous, his peasants had hidden or disguised the family members to save them from the massacre.

If memories of the Pugachev Rebellion were not enough to alarm Catherine II while she read Radishchev's book, then the fact that it was published in 1790 after the onset of the French Revolution compelled her to write the following: "The purpose of this book is clear on every page: its author, infected and full of the French madness, is trying in every possible way to break down respect for authority and for the authorities, to stir up in the people indignation against their superiors and against the government."

Despite being in the throes of two wars while governing Russia, Catherine was captivated (or incited) enough to write 10 pages of commentary on the book. A well-educated woman and a writer herself, she notes that the author is obviously well read. She even notes some inconsistencies in the author's own thesis: "[H]e points out the evil inclinations of a man of low estate, whereas, according to his system (the present French system), all estates are established equal in the name of man and his so-called rights."

In her notes she writes, "The author is a complete deist. . . . It is evident throughout this whole book that [he] has little respect for the Christian teaching and that he has adopted, instead, certain ideas which are not in conformity with the Christian and civil law." Repeatedly she discredits the author in her notes. For example, in reference to his "rules for the conduct of life," she writes, "These prove that the author is a true egotist and more concerned about himself than about anything else." Later she comments that the author "has imagination enough and loves to disseminate hypochondriac and gloomy thoughts." Of Radishchev's writing on the ruling class, she writes, "The author does not love monarchs, and wherever he can vilify love and respect for monarchs, he does so with rare audacity and greedy relish." In response to Radishchev's cry of "What right did [the czar] have to take Novgorod for himself?" Catherine writes, "Answer: the old right of sovereignty and the law of Novgorod and of all Russia and of the whole world, which punishes rebels, and apostates from the Church. But the question is raised here only to deny monarchical [sic] rights."

Further, she notes that "in the guise of a discussion of prosody," the author includes an ode "most clearly, manifestly revolutionary, in which Czars are threatened with the block. Cromwell's example is cited and praised. These pages are of criminal intent."

At the end of Radishchev's book he includes the stamp "With the permission of the Department of Public Morals" although after they censored out large portions of the book, he re-included them and printed the whole text on his own press. Catherine writes that "it is a deceitful and contemptible act to add anything to a book after the permission has been signed. It must be determined how many copies were published and where they are."

Although Radishchev published the book anonymously on his own press, Catherine keenly discovered his identity from various clues. For instance, Radishchev describes the breadth of his own scholarly education in enough detail that Catherine suspects him to be one of the two men she herself had sent as youths to Leipzig to study. "I think that information was picked up in Leipzig, hence the suspicion falls on Messrs. Radishchev and Chelishchev, the more so since they are said to have established a printing press in their house." Further, she notes the author's thorough knowledge of the mercantile industry, pointing toward the man she herself had appointed to be director of the custom house in St. Petersburg.

Catherine immediately issued orders for the book to be confiscated from sale and the whole edition destroyed. Radishchev was quickly arrested and condemned to death; this sentence was later commuted to an exile in Siberia, a location 3,300 miles from St. Petersburg, the capital. After almost six years in exile, Catherine having died, her successor Paul I issued orders for many in disfavor during his mother's reign to be released; Radishchev was permitted to return to his estate in 1797. He was not, however, restored either in his civil rights or his rank of gentleman. Alexander I, the next czar, granted him a full pardon in 1801. But his health having deteriorated, suffering from a "mental disease," Radishchev committed suicide by drinking poison on September 12, 1802.

FURTHER READING

Catherine the Great. *The Empress Catherine II's Notes on the Journey*. In *A Journey from St. Petersburg to Moscow*, edited by Roderick Page Thaler, 239–249. Cambridge, Mass.: Harvard University Press, 1958.

Thaler, Roderick Page. Introduction to *A Journey from St. Petersburg to Moscow*, by Aleksandr Radishchev. Cambridge, Mass.: Harvard University Press, 1958.

—Alexis Karolides

JULIE OF THE WOLVES

Author: Jean Craighead George
Original date and place of publication: 1972, New York
Publisher: Harper and Row
Literary form: Adolescent fiction

SUMMARY

Miyax lives where few people could put themselves and expect to survive. Yet her heritage, lineage, and will serve her well as she fights to stay alive in the Alaskan tundra with no food, no weapon for defense, and no human companionship.

Miyax, or Julie, as she is called by the Gussak (whites), is the young daughter of Kapugen, a wise and well-respected Eskimo hunter, and a mother she barely knew. Kapugen is devastated when his wife dies, but he takes over Miyax's upbringing, showing her the ways of the wilderness in which they live. It is here where Kapugen feels most at ease, and he finds great satisfaction being able to teach Miyax about the ways of the land. Summers at the seal camp with Mekoryuk (their people) are fondly remembered and appreciated by Miyax. These end abruptly when Kapugen's aunt Martha comes to take Miyax into her custody to enroll her in school and marry her to Daniel (a marriage which had been arranged since birth, a common practice with most Mekoryuk). Though distraught, Miyax is also curious about her new lifestyle. Kapugen is shaken by the abrupt loss of the bond that had developed with Miyax; he leaves the seal camp, never to be seen again.

When Miyax meets her new husband, Daniel, she immediately gathers that he is mentally challenged. Fortunately, Nusan, Daniel's mother, explains to Miyax that her primary role need not be as wife, but rather to help with the household chores. Comfortably adjusting to her new lifestyle, Miyax makes friends, learns to read and write, does chores, and corresponds with Amy, her new pen pal whom she meets through Pearl, a villager. These changes help Miyax cope with her new lifestyle, but an unwelcome element that has surfaced is the drinking and the emotional and verbal abuse from Naka, Nusan's husband. Then Daniel attempts to rape Miyax:

"They're laughing at me. That's what's wrong. They say, 'Ha, ha. Dumb Daniel. He's got a wife and he can't mate her. Ha.' "
He pulled her to her feet and pressed his lips against her mouth. She pulled away.
"They're laughing," he repeated, and tore her dress from her shoulder. She clutched it and pulled away. Daniel grew angry. He tripped her and followed her to the floor. His lips curled back and his tongue touched her mouth. Crushing her with her body, he twisted her down onto the floor. He was as frightened as she.
The room spun and grew blurry. Daniel cursed, kicked violently, and lay still. Suddenly he got to his feet and ran out of the house. "Tomorrow, tomorrow I can, can, can, ha ha," he bleated piteously.

Miyax suddenly packs and heads toward San Francisco. On the journey, hungry, tired, and many miles from any kind of human civilization, Miyax finds herself in a predicament that challenges her to call forth all of Kapugen's teachings (now five years past) in order to survive. Besides battling these elements, she must also deal with a pack of wolves that have migrated into her proximity. Miyax realizes that alone she cannot live off the land; she remembers Kapugen telling her that he once called upon a wolfpack in order to live:

The very life in her body, its spark and warmth, depended upon these wolves for survival. One year [Kapugen] had camped near a wolf den on a hunt. When a month passed and her father had seen no game, he told the leader of the wolves that he was hungry and needed food. The next night the wolf called him from far away and her father went to him and found a freshly killed caribou. Unfortunately, Miyax's father never explained to her how he had told the wolf of his needs.

Patiently, Miyax begins a vigil of watching the wolves, picking up their every mannerism, behavior, and action. She also names them: Amoroq, the mighty black leader; Silver, his mate; Nails, another male; Jelly, the misfit male often shunned by the others; and the pups, Kapu, Zip, Zing, and Zat. They cautiously grow used to her, eventually accept her as a nonthreatening member, and allow her to share in the kill. Miyax has conquered the barrier that separates human from beast by gaining the pack's trust and respect. Now upbeat and rejuvenated, she gladly continues her journey toward civilization and her friend Amy, and away from the life on the tundra.

Miyax's journey climaxes as she reaches the outposts of human civilization. Steel barrel markers she now regularly sees signal the not-distant coast and her final stop where she will be freed from her lonely status. Her path is abruptly altered, though, when a plane containing poaching "hunters," who are looking for an easy shot, strike Amoroq dead with rifle fire. Kapu, the heir to Amoroq's throne, is also injured in the assault. Miyax realizes that without a strong leader, the pack will die. She decides that her role now must be to nurse Kapu back to health and provide for the pack until he is able to do so, just as they did for her. Amy and San Francisco will have to wait.

Having regained his strength and established himself as leader, Kapu is once again able to provide for the pack without Miyax's aid. She has repaid her gratitude and, in the process, has decided to remain in the wilderness, where her soul is embedded with Amoroq's. The "hunters" who stole her friend's life are a clear reminder that she has changed too much to fit in with her human counterparts. She is a wolf at heart, as is evidenced by her song:

Amoroq, wolf, my friend,
You are my adopted father.
My feet shall run because of you.
My heart shall beat because of you.
And I shall love because of you.

One day Miyax encounters a hunter—the first human she has actually seen face-to-face for quite some time. It is Atik, an Englishman, who invites Miyax to meet his wife, Uma, and child, Sorqaq. Through conversation, Miyax discovers that Kangik, the village in which Atik lived after his grandfather died, was tutored by a wise and highly respected man named Kapugen, who had surfaced there some time beforehand. Bewildered with joy and curiosity, Miyax wonders how her father is. Has he changed? Will he remember her? Can he explain his disappearance? These questions become answers, which serve to help stabilize the recent difficulties in Miyax's life.

CENSORSHIP HISTORY

Parents from the city of Mexico, Missouri, specifically cite reasons of political censorship as their primary concern with *Julie of the Wolves*. Complains citing "socialist, communist, evolutionary and anti-family themes," as well as nonconforming religious themes, were launched against the book in June 1982. These arguments were not supported with specific details from the book, but rather with vague generalizations. The book was reviewed by the school board and retained. This mirrors statistics provided by *The Missouri Censorship Survey*, conducted by the Missouri Coalition Against Censorship, which showed that in school districts where written complaint policies were established, only 2 percent of books challenged were removed; in contrast, a 35 percent removal rate resulted in districts where policies were not established.

A sixth-grade classroom in Littleton, Colorado, was the venue of 1994 for a challenge against *Julie of the Wolves*, which deemed the content of the book inappropriate for those students in the sixth grade and lower. Parents claimed that the issues of alcoholism, abuse, and divorce would be "better suited for older students." The school board, after reviewing the text, voted to keep it on the shelf. As one member put it simply: "It is important people see the other side of life."

A case from Chandler, Arizona, in 1994 concerned the use of the text by Julie Hardy to instruct third through fifth graders in an Antarctic studies unit. At issue was not the content of the book in terms of its accurate portrayal of the Eskimo lifestyle, but rather one scene in particular where Miyax is sexually assaulted by her young husband, who feels peer pressure to consummate the marriage. Although the teacher had previewed the book, this scene escaped her notice. Parents felt it alone was enough to deem the book inappropriate. The principal felt that the book might be appropriate for fifth graders "with explanation," but not for younger ages. The book was voluntarily pulled off the shelves pending a principal's meeting, whose outcome is unknown.

Palmdale School District in Southern California was another site where the questionable scene of rape and sexual assault came to the forefront. In December 1995, parents requested the book be removed due to the nature of the scene. Prior to the challenge, however, the book received rigorous attention before it was ever shelved in the school. It was reviewed by no less than three professional and local review boards, including the English Language Arts Curriculum Committee and the PSD Library Review Committee. As the book came under fire, the review committee cited merit in a study of two cultures (American and Eskimo), Miyax's problem-solving ability and the present values of respect, responsibility, and persistence. The Palmdale Materials Reevaluations Committee, after listening to the objection and reviewing the text, decided that compliance was met with the adopting procedures for the library, and that the book was more appropriate and age-protected for grade seven.

The so-identified rape scene was objected to in Cromwell, New York (1980), and in the New Brighton Area School District, Pennsylvania (1996), where it was described as a "graphic marital rape scene," and in Ramona, California (1996). In New Brighton, the challenge was successful in that the book was removed from the curriculum but retained in the library. In Ramona, the challenger's daughter was given an alternative assignment. The district created a community task force that in January 1998 issued a publication, identifying books that would be "required" and those that would be optional "recommended." *Julie of the Wolves* was placed in the latter category, followed by an asterisk, designating books that "may contain material of concern to some individuals." In 2003–04, in accordance with California state standards a new core literature list was promulgated; *Julie of the Wolves* was recommended for grades 6 through 8 rather than required.

FURTHER READING

"Libraries." *Newsletter on Intellectual Freedom* 31 (November 1982): 215.
"Parents Request Removal of Books." *Antelope Valley Press*, December 19, 1995, p. A1.
"Schools." *Newsletter on Intellectual Freedom* 31 (1982); 156; 38 (1989): 186; and 43 (1994): 9.
"Two Books Likely to Stay in LPS Libraries Despite Challenge." *Littleton Sentinel*, June 29, 1989, n.p.

—Eric P. Schmidt

THE JUNGLE

Author: Upton Sinclair
Original dates and place of publication: 1905 and 1906, United States
Publishers: Robert Bentley, Inc., and Doubleday, Page
Literary form: Fiction

SUMMARY

Upton Sinclair's 1946 introduction to *The Jungle* clearly illuminates the author's purpose for writing the novel. As a young man of 26 years, Sinclair spent seven weeks observing the daily lives of individuals who worked in the meat packing industry in Chicago's Packingtown. Being from the South, an area torn by the Civil War, he hated poverty and its effects on humans. While in Chicago, he witnessed these effects firsthand. "The worst of which was the ignorance of the victims themselves. With the exception of a very small minority, they had no idea that they had the right to a better way of life. It was moral, spiritual and physical degradation, a 'jungle' in which humans lived barely above the level of animals." Sinclair continues his introduction by lauding the benefits of socialism. He clearly states his desire to turn the reader toward socialist viewpoints.

The novel begins with the wedding of Jurgis Rudkus and his 16-year-old bride, Ona Lukoszaite. Six months earlier, the couple had traveled to America from Lithuania to make a better life for themselves. Accompanying them were Teta Elzbieta, Ona's stepmother; Marija, Ona's cousin; Jonas, Elzbieta's brother; Dede Antanas, Jurgis's father; and five of Elzbieta's children.

Although they can speak English only well enough to say "Chicago," the family travels from New York to their final destination. A friend who has supposedly made his fortune in Chicago agrees to help the men find jobs, and he gives the family a tour of the stockyards and packing plant. They are overwhelmed by the machinelike efficiencies of the packing plant but appalled by the inhumanity of the process. Their guide informs the family that the big packing plants combined "employed thirty thousand men; it supported directly two hundred and fifty thousand people in its neighborhood, and indirectly it supported half a million. It sent its products to every country in the civilized world, and it furnished the food for no less than thirty million people." Jurgis, Ona, and the others are thrilled at the opportunity to become integral parts of this empire.

Each family member who seeks employment, with the exception of old Antanas, finds work immediately. After much consideration and budgetary planning, the family decides to move out of their boardinghouse and purchase a home from one of the many fliers they see around Packingtown. This is their first pitfall due to their lack of proficiency with the English language and their belief in the integrity of those in whom they put their faith.

Soon after purchasing the house, sold to the family as a new construction, they learn that it is actually 15 years old and has been owned by at least four other families. The builders spent less than $500 for its construction and sold the house to the family for $1,500. "Cheap as the houses were, they were sold with the idea that the people who bought them would not be able to pay for them. When they failed—if it were only by a single month—they would lose the house and all that they had paid on it, and then the company would sell it over again." They also learn that the $12-a-month house payment does not include interest on the loan, which equals an additional $7 per month. This new dilemma forces Ona to find a job sewing hams, for which she pays a forelady $10. Fourteen-year-old Stanislovas lies about his age and finds work earning five cents per hour.

In the ensuing 18 months, the family faces many financial, physical, and psychological hardships. Shabby construction causes the house to be nearly as cold inside as the weather is outside. The conditions on the job are horrific, especially for Jurgis, who is working on the unheated killing floor at the packing plant.

> On the killing beds you were apt to be covered with blood, and it would freeze solid; if you leaned against a pillar, you would freeze to that, and if you put your hand upon the blade of your knife, you would run a chance of leaving your skin on it. The men would tie up their feet in newspapers and old sacks, and these would be soaked in blood and frozen, . . . and so on, until by nighttime a man would be walking on great lumps the size of the feet of an elephant.

The situation continues to deteriorate: Members of the family lose their jobs at frequent intervals; they find out in January that they must buy insurance and pay taxes on the house; Ona is forced, at risk of losing her job, to return to work immediately after giving birth to their first child, thus jeopardizing her health; Jurgis injures his ankle and continues to work, resulting in further damage and the need to be on unpaid bed rest for two months; Jonas never returns home from work one Saturday; and two of the children must quit school to sell newspapers.

In late April, finally allowed to return to work, Jurgis begins seeking employment. Two months later, he is hired at the fertilizer plant, the most hideous of all jobs.

> Working in his shirt sleeves, and with the thermometer at over a hundred, the phosphates soaked in through every pore of Jurgis' skin, and in five minutes he had a headache, and in fifteen was almost dazed. The blood was pounding in his brain like an engine's throbbing; there was a frightful pain in the top of his skull, and he could hardly control his hands. Still, with the memory of his four months siege behind him, he fought on in a frenzy of determination; and half an hour later he began to vomit—he vomited until it seemed as if his innards must be torn into shreds.

After one week at the plant, he is finally able to eat, "and though his head never stopped aching, it ceased to be so bad that he could not work." To ease his physical and mental pain, Jurgis begins to drink alcohol.

After learning that Ona has been forced to prostitute herself to her boss, Connor, Jurgis rushes to the packing plant to find him. In an uncontrollable rage, he beats Connor until stopped by half a dozen men. Jurgis is sentenced to one month in jail. During his confinement, the family's situation collapses. The adults and Stanislovas lose their jobs. They cannot pay the rent and interest on the house. They cannot afford coal and food. Jurgis's feelings of helplessness are worsened following his release. The bank forecloses on the house; Ona and her unborn child die; Jurgis is blacklisted in the packing plants; and his son drowns in the street. After escaping to the life of a tramp, he eventually returns to Chicago, finds a job digging tunnels, but is injured when he is hit by an engine and loaded car. He is unable to work. During a 14-day cold spell, he nearly freezes and starves to death.

Life seems unbearable to Jurgis until he connects with Jack Duane, a professional safecracker whom he met in jail. Duane introduces Jurgis to Chicago's criminal world. Through this criminal association, Jurgis gradually loses his integrity. He participates in a fraudulent payroll scam, becomes involved in shady election politics and works as a "scab" foreman in the packing plants during a strike. Without realizing it, he has become as corrupt as the men who preceded him. This all ends when Jurgis is forced to leave Packingtown because he attacks Connor again.

While searching for a job, Jurgis is reunited with Marija. Much to his dismay, she has become a drug-addicted prostitute. That evening, he stops to rest at a meeting hall and hears the Socialist Party message for the first time. The speaker illustrates the anguish and toil of the working men, women, and children of Chicago. He denounces the extravagance, greed, and luxury that befall the undeserving "masters" of this society.

Jurgis feels reborn after he hears the orator at the meeting hall.

> He had never been so stirred in his life—it was a miracle that had been wrought in him. He could not think at all, he was stunned; yet he knew that in the mighty upheaval that had taken place in his soul, a new man had been born. He had been torn out of the jaws of destruction, he had been delivered from the thraldom of despair; the whole world had changed for him—he was free, he was free! Even if he were to suffer as he had before,. . . . He would no longer be the sport of circumstances, he would be a man, with a will and a purpose; he would have something to fight for, something to die for, if need be!

Subsequently, Jurgis learns about socialism, reunites with Elzbieta and the family, and finds a job as a hotel porter in a small hotel owned by a member of the Socialist Party.

Throughout the rest of the novel, Jurgis finds more peace and security than he has had since arriving in America. "His outward life was commonplace and uninteresting; he was just a hotel porter . . . but meantime, in the realm of thought, his life was a perpetual adventure. There was so much to know—so many wonders to be discovered."

Although the Socialists do not win the presidential election that year, their numbers come in higher than ever before. An orator upon the platform reminds the party faithful of the great success they have achieved in just four years, and he encourages them to continue the work. He says of Chicago's outraged working men, "We shall organize them, we shall drill them, we shall marshal them for the victory! We shall bear down the opposition, we shall sweep it before us—and Chicago will be ours! Chicago will be ours! CHICAGO WILL BE OURS!"

CENSORSHIP HISTORY

Immediately after publication, *The Jungle* created extreme controversy. President Theodore Roosevelt, astonished by what he read in the novel, asked Sinclair to come to Washington and give his personal account of the living and working conditions of the laborers and the illegal and unethical use of condemned animals. Later, the president sent his own commissioners, Charles P. Neill and James B. Reynolds, to investigate Packingtown.

During the time of the investigation, as cited in the editor's note preceding Sinclair's article in the May 1906 issue of *Everybody's*, J. Ogden Armour, owner of one packing plant, denied allegations regarding conditions in an article in the *Saturday Evening Post*: "In Armour and Companies business not one atom of any condemned animal or carcass finds its way, directly or indirectly, from any source, into any food product or food ingredient." Sinclair directly rebuffed Armour's statements in his article: "I know that . . . Mr. Armour willfully and deliberately states what he absolutely and positively knows to be falsehoods." Sinclair cited specific examples of the atrocities in Packingtown. He also supplied statements from well-known citizens who supported his position.

President Roosevelt's inspectors found that Sinclair's statements were, if anything, "less startling than the reality." The report was that the inspectors "happened to discover nothing but filth, disease, intolerable stenches and a worse than bestial disregard of elementary decency." The president prepared a message to Congress and "within an hour, both packers and packing house senators were tumbling over each other" to pass a law regarding government inspection at the packing houses if the president would withhold his message to Congress, which would substantiate Sinclair's story. This ended the attempts to discredit *The Jungle*.

In the 1920s, the Carnegie Corporation began to focus on better library services and education and establishing the library as the "community intelligence center." The libraries were affected by an increase in campaigns for moral legislation at all levels of government. The new literature of the times was challenging the old morality. John Sumner, head of the New York Society for the Suppression of Vice, successfully passed a bill through the New York State Assembly in 1923 that allowed a book to be judged obscene on the basis of a single passage. Two months later, after a handful of critics spoke out against it, the bill was defeated in the state senate. The question raised across the country was, "Should the librarian be a censor?"

In 1924, the American Library Association testified against the New York State censorship bill. However, local librarians were encouraged by special interest groups to continue censoring. In this context, Geller notes that Upton Sinclair's novels were banned by the Lisbon, Ohio, trustees and librarian. A Belleville, Illinois, library trustee and union leader lashed out at this censorship. "Prohibition, Blue Laws, antievolution, library censorship— for goodness sake what's coming next?"

As part of his anticommunism campaign, in 1953, Senator Joe McCarthy led an investigation of the Overseas Library Program to bring about the removal of controversial books. His investigation led to a change in policy: to reject books by "controversial persons, Communists, fellow travelers, etc." The House Un-American Activities Committee, which McCarthy chaired, listened to testimony regarding many well-known Americans. A list, published in 1953, named those who had been mentioned unfavorably throughout the hearings. Directives indicated that their works "should be withdrawn from U.S. libraries overseas, and that they should not be the subjects or authors of feature articles or broadcasts distributed or broadcast overseas." Upton Sinclair was on the list. (See MANIFESTO OF THE COMMUNIST PARTY for more details.)

Nazi censorship began escalating in 1933 with a large-scale burning of books by Jewish authors at the University of Berlin. Students in Nazi Germany used torches to burn any book that was deemed to "act subversively on our future or strike at the root of German thought, the German home and the driving forces of our people." Due to his strong socialistic viewpoints, which are evident throughout his novels, Upton Sinclair was one of the authors whose books were frequently burned, *The Jungle* being among them. The practice of book burning continued until World War II.

Yugoslavia banned all of Sinclair's works from its public libraries in 1929. Fifty years after its initial publication, the novel was banned in East Germany because it was deemed in opposition to Communist viewpoints. South Korea banned the novel in 1985.

A rare discovery in 1980 of the original manuscript and Sinclair correspondence by a young man hired to clean out the cellar of a farm in Girard, Kansas, resulted in the uncovering of prepublication excisions in contrast to the initial serialized (seven months, beginning on February 25, 1905) version in *The Appeal* and three issues of *One Hoss Philosophy*, a quarterly journal, from which one section was omitted by Sinclair. Professor Gene De Gruson, curator of rare books at Pittsburg (Kansas) State University, ascertained that the Doubleday, Page edition had been excised by almost a third. De Gruson in his introduction to the 1988 complete edition writes, "Despite his protestations that he wished the novel published as he had written it, revision was drastic." Most of the deletions pertained to socialism and the workings of the Socialist Party, paragraphs critical of the press, and derogatory comments about "big business," self-made men, and captains of industry. Also omitted was his criticism of marriage and one section in which a woman, refused permission to take off work to have her baby, gives birth and places it on the cart; it is last seen just as it is about to go inside the sausage machine. Paragraphs emphasizing the malpractice of the meatpacking industry were added.

FURTHER READING

Doyle, Robert P. *Banned Books: 1994 Resource Guide*. Chicago, Ill.: American Library Association, 1994.

Geller, Evelyn. *Forbidden Books in American Public Libraries: 1876–1939*. Westport, Conn.: Greenwood Press, 1984.

Green, Jonathon, and Nicholas J. Karolides, reviser. *The Encyclopedia of Censorship, The New Edition*. New York: Facts On File, 2005.

Haight, Anne Lyon, and Chandler B. Grannis. *Banned Books: 387 B.C. to 1978 A.D.* 4th ed. New York: R. R. Bowker, 1978.

"*The Jungle* Vindicated." *Bookman* (July 1906): 481–485.

Sinclair, Upton. "The Condemned-Meat Industry: A Reply to Mr. J. Ogden Armour." *Everybody's* (May 1906): 608–616.

———. "Is *The Jungle* True?" *Independent*, May 17, 1906, n.p.

"A Special *New Republic* Report on Book Burning: Who Are the Book Burners? What Happened in San Antonio, St. Cloud and Boston? Senate Transcript—McCarthy vs. Conant." *New Republic*, June 29, 1953, 7–9.

—Laurie Pap
Updated by Nicholas J. Karolides

KEEPING FAITH: MEMOIRS OF A PRESIDENT

Author: Jimmy Carter
Original date and places of publication: 1982, United States and Canada
Publisher: Bantam Books
Literary form: Autobiography

SUMMARY

Jimmy Carter's autobiography encompasses his White House years, from January 20, 1977, from his inauguration as 39th president of the United States and his nontraditional walk with his wife, Rosalyn, down the 1.2 mile parade route from the U.S. Capitol to the White House, to the final days of negotiation for release of the American embassy hostages in Iran. The day of their release to freedom, January 20, 1981, was the last day of Carter's presidency; their actual departure from Iran came after Carter's successor, Ronald Reagan, had taken the oath of office.

After several chapters in which Carter introduces the reader to his administrative team, to his organizational structure, and to his leadership style, both in the executive branch and in relation to Congress, he focuses on major issues: energy, human rights, the Panama Canal, China, the nuclear threat, Israel and the Middle East, Iran and the hostages, and Afghanistan. Revelations of and negotiations with the Soviet Union occur principally in the context of the nuclear issue and the Afghanistan crisis.

The energy effort was declared to be "the moral equivalent of war." Carter perceived the nation moving toward disaster in its energy consumption and its dependence on foreign oil supplies. He foresaw the need for a comprehensive program

> that would encourage conservation, more fuel production in the United States, and the long-range development of alternate forms of energy which could begin to replace oil and natural gas in future years. These goals were complicated by the need to protect our environment, to insure equity of economic opportunity among the different regions of our country, and to balance the growing struggle between American consumers and oil producers.

The administration's efforts, initiated in 1977, were not fully accomplished until 1980. Public support had to be aroused and sustained. Members of Congress, influenced by the energy industry lobby and acting on other consumer priorities, could not readily agree. However, year by year pieces of legislation were enacted. In the lame-duck legislative session after Carter's defeat in his bid for a second term, the Superfund legislation to clean up toxic wastes and the bill to protect more than 150 million acres of land in Alaska were passed by Congress and signed into law.

In the Carter administration, human rights was a constant concern on both the national and international scenes. He cites flaws in the recent past: lies told to the American people, the CIA's (Central Intelligence Agency) role in plotting murder, and other situations. His announced goal was "That this country set a standard within the community of nations of courage, compassion, integrity, and dedication to basic human rights and freedoms." He acted to promote this goal: at home—by applauding and "searching for ways to root out the vestiges of discrimination against our own citizens"; abroad—by public exposure of persecutions, as in the case of Andrei Sakharov, the distinguished scientist and dissident who had been detained by the Soviet Union; by negotiating with the Soviet Union for prisoner exchanges; by pursuing more liberal emigration policies in the Soviet Union; by asserting to the shah of Iran (and others) the need for just treatment of dissident groups and the easing of "strict police policies; by condemning as brutal and outrageous the Soviet invasion of Afghanistan and declaring it to be direct aggression by the Soviet armed forces against a freedom-loving people, whose leaders had been struggling to retain a modicum of independence from their huge neighbor." He also condemned in like terms the treatment of the American embassy hostages by their captors in Iran.

> It will always be impossible to measure how much was accomplished by our nation's policy when the units of measurement are not inches or pounds or dollars. The lifting of the human spirit, the revival of hope, the absence of fear, the release from prison, the end of torture, the reunion of a family, the newfound sense of human dignity—these are difficult to quantify, but I am certain that many people were able to experience them because the United States of America let it be known that we stood for freedom and justice for all people.

In significant measure, the Panama Canal treaties issue is couched in human rights terms—the reassertion of Panama's sovereignty over the Canal Zone, which it had in effect lost (though not in a strict reading of the 1903 treaty) in a historical power play. Following the efforts of President Lyndon Johnson, Richard Nixon, and Gerald Ford, who had in turn negotiated with Panama for a new treaty (but not President Reagan, who repudiated their efforts), Carter took up this cause in earnest. Intense negotiations with the Panamanians over a seven-month period led to the signing ceremonies. Equally intense, often acrimonious, negotiation with Congress over this period and the months following led to ratification of the treaties in March 1978 by the Senate, but not until September 1979 did the House of Representatives pass the laws implementing the treaties.

The nuclear "Shadow Over the Earth," the unbelievable destruction represented by the multitudes of tactical weapons that could "kill tens of millions—perhaps a hundred million—people on each side," was another major problem upon which the Carter administration focused. Carter perceived his "most difficult and important task" to negotiate a SALT II

Treaty to include not only the *limitation* of arms but also their *reduction*. Preliminary proposals (which were rejected) were presented to the Soviets in March 1977; a SALT II Treaty was signed in June 1979 by President Jimmy Carter and General Secretary Leonid Brezhnev. The years between were marked by disputes, accusations, defensive postures, and tediously slow progress—and reversals by Brezhnev of private assurances. Despite its provisions, as generalized by Carter in his speech to a joint session of Congress,

> SALT II is the most detailed, far-reaching, comprehensive treaty in the history of arms control. . . . The SALT II treaty reduces the danger of nuclear war. For the first time, it places equal ceilings on the strategic arsenals of both sides, ending a previous numerical imbalance in favor of the Soviet Union. SALT II preserves our options to build the forces we need to maintain that strategic balance. The treaty enhances our own ability to monitor what the Soviet Union is doing, and it leads directly to the next step in more effectively controlling nuclear weapons.

The SALT II Treaty was not ratified. Vociferous opposition by some members of Congress; Soviet troops in Cuba; the treaty's rejection by Republican presidential nominee, Ronald Reagan; and the Soviet aggression against Afghanistan made ratification impossible.

Considerable time and energy were consumed by the Middle East peace effort that led to a treaty between antagonists of long duration, Egypt and Israel. President Carter nourished and brokered the treaty, which included the prevention of Soviet intervention in the area, as well as attention to the human rights plight of the Palestinians. Conversations were initiated early in 1977; negotiations escalated as the year progressed, moving into high gear for the 13-day Camp David summit. President Anwar Sadat of Egypt is presented as flexible on many aspects of the negotiations but absolutely fixed on the Sinai land-ownership issue and the removal of the Israeli settlers. In contrast, Prime Minister Menachem Begin of Israel appears to be rigid and uncompromising, more than his own deputy negotiators; commitments are not fully honored. The day-by-day presentation of the Camp David summit reveals the political and linguistic maneuvering, the intensity of feelings and effort, the all-too-frequent sense of failure and, yet, the determination that led eventually to success. While there was still appreciable work to be done, the Camp David accords were signed at the White House on September 17, 1978.

Carter's accomplishments were overshadowed in his final year in office by the takeover of the American embassy in Iran on November 4, 1979, by some 3,000 Islamic militants who, against the efforts of the prime minister, refused to release the 50 or 60 Americans. Carter identifies the subsequent year as the "most difficult period of my life. The safety and well-being of the American hostages became a constant concern for me, no matter what other duties I was performing as President." Actions taken by the government included expelling Iranian students; forbidding Iranian demonstrations on federal property; discontinuance of Iranian oil purchases; freezing of Iranian gold and cash held in American banks; resisting the militants' demand that the shah be returned to Iran; assisting the Canadian embassy personnel in a successful cloak-and-dagger effort to develop an escape plan for six American diplomats who had found refuge there; attempting a rescue of the hostages—without success; as well as ongoing direct and indirect diplomatic exercises.

In the last month, indeed the last days, after the defeat of Carter at the polls on the anniversary of the embassy invasion, an Algerian delegation, acting in behalf of the United States, broke through Iranian resistance. The negotiated release was based on the exchange of the hostages for the frozen Iranian assets. The final two-day countdown included transfer of the funds with, perhaps to be expected, legal, political, and financial problems and monitoring of the departure of two planes from Teheran with the hostages abroad. This was delayed, but accomplished at 12:33 and 12:42 P.M. on the day Carter stepped down from office. Carter wrote, responding to the notification by Secret Service radios, "I was overwhelmed with happiness—but because of the hostages' freedom, not mine."

CENSORSHIP HISTORY

The Fourth Moscow International Book Fair, a biennial event, was held in September 1983. Few American publishers participated. According to John Macrae, III, vice president and editor-in-chief of Holt, Rinehart and Winston and chair of the Association of American Publishers' International Freedom to Publish Committee in a letter published in the *New York Times Book Review*, publishers objected to the propagandistic nature of the book fair. He also asserted that most leading Soviet writers who had been present at past fairs were then in prison or had been forced to immigrate to the West. In another venue, Macrae said, "As literary publishers our presence in Moscow at a time when leading Soviet writers are in prison or in exile would dishonor our writers and ourselves. . . . We are obliged to call attention to the hypocrisy behind a book fair that asks us to be silent and forget."

Several prominent American publishers had withdrawn from participation because of objections to the exhibition rules announced by officials; books were prohibited if they "progandize war and racial or ethnic exclusivity"; "insult another country participating in the book fair"; and were written "by renegades who have made a profession of slandering our life." The American publishers considered these rules censorship.

The Moscow International Book Fair did experience direct censorship. The organizers of the American Jewish publishers' exhibit reported that

49 of their titles had been seized by Soviet officials as "anti Soviet." Among these were Carter's *Keeping Faith: Memoirs of a President,* MY NAME IS ASHER LEV by Chaim Potok, MY PEOPLE: THE STORY OF THE JEWS by Abba Eban, *Tsar Nicholas and the Jews* by Michael Stanislawski, *The Many Faces of Anti-Semitism* by Rose Feitelson, *Understanding Israel: A Social Studies Approach* by Amos Elon, and *The History of Israel* by Howard Sachar, as well as 15 books in Russian on Jewish holidays.

Other exhibitors, including the Israeli and American Protestant Church-owned publishers association, reported that only a few of their books were barred. It was conjectured that the American Jewish publishers' books were seized as a demonstration of Soviet displeasure with their organizers who openly fraternized with the Soviet Jews who visited their exhibit, and who distributed large numbers of Russian-language catalogs with a detachable Hebrew-Russian alphabet and extensive information on Jewish holidays and traditions. The Soviets believed that the intention of these publishers was to introduce Russians to a literature largely denied them in their country rather than to seek the sale of rights of their books in the Soviet Union.

FURTHER READING

"Exiled Writers Differ with U.S. Publishers." *Publishers Weekly,* September 22, 1983, 14–15.

Hartzell, Richard. "Eye on Publishing." *Wilson Library Bulletin* 58 (1983): 200.

Macrae, John, III. Letter: "The Moscow Book Fair." *New York Times Book Review,* September 4, 1983, p. 30.

"Moscow, USSR." *Newsletter on Intellectual Freedom* 32 (1983): 201.

Reuter, Madalynne. "Fourth Moscow Book Fair: Controversy as Usual." *Publishers Weekly,* September 23, 1983, 14.

Schmemann, Serge. "Moscow Bars 49 Books of U.S. Jewish Group." *New York Times,* September 12, 1983, p. A9.

KISS OF THE SPIDER WOMAN (*EL BESO DE LA MUJER ARAÑA*)

Author: Manuel Puig
Original dates and places of publication: 1976, Spain; 1979, United States and Canada
Publisher: Seix Barral; Alfred A. Knopf
Literary form: Novel

SUMMARY

Molina and Valentín, sharing a cell in the penitentiary of the city of Buenos Aires, are an unlikely pair. And not solely in temperament. Molina is a homosexual accused of child molestation; he wants to be a woman. Valentín is a political prisoner, "dedicated to political struggles, or, you know, political action," the purpose of which is social revolution. He refers to himself as a marxist. A further difference in that Molina is uneducated, a window dresser, not intrested in books, and Valentín, college educated, pursues knowledge, often commenting on texts he is studying.

Nevertheless, this unlikely pair gets along. Molina "entertains" Valentín by recounting the plots of movies, six in total throughout the novel; some are actual films and some are inventions. The movies give them something to talk about, calming them down, diminishing their defensiveness, and permitting escape from their confinement. Their conversations are self-revealing.

The films are mainstream, rather than sophisticated art films, categorized perhaps as romantic adventures, with the exception of *Cat People*, a classic horror film. They are melodramatic, using exotic landscapes. And gimmicky—they feature voodoo and zombies for example. The women, with whom Molina identifies, are often victims of their situation, the man in her life, or herself; their suffering is horrific, as in the case of the cursed panther woman, or noble, represented by the actress in the Nazi films, or the chanteuse, who having rejected her wealthy magnate for the reporter, stoops to prostitution to support her lover. The heterosexual relationships are perceived as shallow or troubled, sometimes forced.

Midway through the novel we are privy to documents of the Ministry of the Interior of the Argentine Republic, which identify the backgrounds and prison behavior of the two inmates. Also, it is evident that both are transferred to Pavilion D, cell 7, on the same date. We are also privy to an interview of the warden of the penitentiary with Molina on the pretext of his having a visitor. He is offered an early pardon if he can get Valentín to reveal vital information about his political accomplices. (It is unclear whether this offer was made at the time of the transfer to cell 7 or later.)

The warden also reveals that Valentín's food is "prepared" (read "poisoned") so that he becomes ill, the purpose being to weaken him. Molina eats from this plate the first time and subsequently suffers from stomach cramps, pains, and extreme diarrhea. Valentín, who eats this prepared food again and again, is indeed sickened and weakened, losing control of his bowels. Out of need and compassion—and an emerging affection—Molina cares for Valentín during these crises, washing his body and both his clothes and the sheets. He advises—no, urges—Valentín not to eat the prison food, providing food, ostensibly gifted by his mother as in the past but provided this time by the warden. Gradually, Molina gains his cellmate's confidence. Further, while they are feasting, Molina reveals he's being nice to Valentín "because I want to win your friendship, and, why not say it? . . . your affection." Further, he differentiates himself from other "faggots," the "kind who fall in love with one another. But as for my friends and myself, we're a hundred percent female. We don't go in for those little games—that's strictly for homos. We're normal women; we sleep with men." The plan works so well that Valentín's resistance erodes, and he reveals features of his personal life and psyche. He seems to have regained a life force, revealing his memories of a woman he has loved.

Molina reveals that he is being considered for parole and, if so, that he will be removed from cell 7—part of the warden's enticement-for-information plan. Molina, however, having come to love Valentín, revises the objective to gain information about the political accomplices in order to insure parole. He cries and admits to being scared, not only of whether the release expectation will be fulfilled, but also of separation from his friend. This confession leads to a comforting massage which, in turn, leads to a sexual seduction.

Molina does get his early parole despite his having refused information from Valentín—probably another artifice of the warden—and has one last night in cell 7 and a final sexual experience. And a kiss. Valentín response to Molina's "I'm not the panther woman," is "It's true, you're not the panther woman. . . . You, you're the spider woman, that traps men in her web!"

The novel concludes with a transcript—a report on Luis Alberto Molina, prisoner 3.018, paroled on the 9th, placed under surveillance by CISL in conjunction with wiretap unit of TISL. It contains a meticulously detailed report of Molina's activity and phone calls. The conclusion: After a brief phone call, subsequent to dialing three times, Molina traveled by bus and subway; just after he was picked up by Central Bureau for interrogation, he was shot from a passing vehicle. He dies. Has he sacrificed his life consciously?

Meanwhile Valentín has been tortured. A medical intern, against regulations, gives him morphine, commenting on the "unbelievable" injuries and the burns on his groin. He is in a semiconscious state, dreaming of and talking to Marta, the woman he had loved before he got involved in subversive politics.

Homosexuality is expressed in two ways in *Kiss of the Spider Woman*. First, the plot itself in an honest and natural way portrays a love affair between two men without shame or apology. Second, a series of eight extended footnotes offers theories and clarifications to create understandings. Theorists and researchers are quoted to explore possible causes, to review controversies, to explain and deny misconceptions and stereotypes. Altogether, these footnotes are significant in educating the reader.

CENSORSHIP HISTORY

Between 1930 and 1983, Argentina experienced 31 military coups. Denial of civil liberties and censorship of newspapers and broadcasting media were the rule. Systematic repression became government policy under the military junta that overthrew the Perón government, ruling from 1976 to 1983. When released in July 1976, *Kiss of the Spider Woman* was immediately banned.

The novel was responding in part to the brutality of this military regime: Citizens were tortured and killed; thousands who were suspected of subversion "disappeared," including educated young people. Valentín in this novel represents this last group. According to Jonathan Tittler, Puig wanted "to discredit the Argentine military in the eyes of the rest of Latin America." Also in 1977 at the International Book Fair in Buenos Aires, *Kiss of the Spider Woman* was included on a distinguished list of books that could not be imported, displayed, or sold. While political subversion is a significant theme in *Kiss of the Spider Woman*, so, too, is homosexuality, a taboo subject at the time. Its positive expression in this novel would have been a factor in the novel being suppressed.

The suppression was lifted upon the election of President Raúl Alfonsín (1983–89), who returned the Argentine government to more liberal principles.

Other novels written by Puig also faced censorship. Completed in 1965, *La traición de Rita Hayworth* (*Betrayed by Rita Hayworth*) was hampered by censorship problems but was eventually published in 1968. The first edition of *Fattaccio a Buenos Aires* (*The Buenos Aires Affair*) was confiscated by censorship agencies as soon as it was released in 1973. Shortly thereafter, Puig was threatened by Alinza Anticommunista Argentina (AAA) and forced to leave the country.

FURTHER READING

Balderston, Daniel, and Francine Masiello, eds. *Approaches to Teaching Puig's* Kiss of the Spider Woman. New York: Modern Language Association of America, 2007.

Green, Jonathon, and Nicholas J. Karolides, reviser. "Argentina." In *Encyclopedia of Censorship, New Edition*. New York: Facts On File, 2005.

Levine, Suzanne Jill. *Manuel Puig and the Spider Woman: His Life and Fictions*. New York: Farrar, Strauss and Giroux, 2000.

Tittler, Jonathan. *Manuel Puig*. New York: Twayne, 1993.

THE LAND AND PEOPLE OF CUBA

Author: Victoria Ortiz
Original date and place of publication: 1973, United States
Original publisher: J. B. Lippincott Company
Literary form: Nonfiction

SUMMARY

The overview of *The Land and People of Cuba* reveals the history of the Caribbean island from its "discovery" by Christopher Columbus to the 20th century. The history of the early centuries traces the Spanish conquest and rule; the 19th century features revolutions and attempts to gain independence, finally achieved in 1898. Revolutions continued in the 20th century, revolutions from the oppression and corruption of Cuban dictators, leading eventually to the victory of Fidel Castro Ruz. Concluding historical episodes focus on the Bay of Pigs invasion by the United States in 1961 and the subsequent missile crisis.

The chief inhabitants of Cuba in 1492 were the Arawak Tainos. The Tainos were essentially peaceable people, managing to avoid war. Thus, they initially welcomed the Spaniards who, in turn, treated them brutally, leading to genocide.

> The genocide did not stop with the establishment of Spanish settlements. Indian lands were expropriated, native labor enslaved, resisters beaten and tortured, and women raped. . . . [D]uring a period of three or four months . . . thousands of children die[d] of starvation, because their parents had been forced to work in the mines and they had no one to feed them. The record of Spanish atrocities includes such acts as hunting Indians as if they were animals, testing the sharpness of swords by beheading Indians, and feeding Indians to dogs.

The Indians, who were forced to work for the Spaniards in their mines and fields, died off by about 1559.

The enslavement of Africans followed with the arrival of the first large group of 300 in 1524. Living and working under inhumane conditions, their lives comparable to the slaves in the United States, the Cuban slaves had a few advantages. They were allowed to own and sell property, as well as to accumulate capital; and they could purchase their freedom. Also, they were allowed to marry; children born of a slave and a colonial were automatically free.

Slave revolts, big and small, were "countless," the first occurring as early as 1533 at the Jobabo mines. As their situation worsened with the increased numbers of slaves, so did the uprisings. In an attempt to control the problem, the Spanish Crown passed a law in 1789 regulating the treatment of slaves on the island, providing standards for food and clothing, for punishment, and for work. This law was rarely observed. Major uprisings occurred in 1812 and in 1844. In the latter case, "thousands of people—slaves and freedmen, Creoles and mulattoes, Cubans and foreigners—were arrested and tortured. The blacks and mulattoes were especially mistreated. . . ." Slavery was abolished in Cuba in 1886. However, the same social structure continued for many years.

The next stage was independence. The heroes—José Julián Martí y Pérez, Antonio Maceo y Grajales, Carlos Manuel de Céspedes—and their efforts are extolled. The 10 years' war (1868–78) was lost by the rebels, but their planning and preparation continued, particularly in New York. Secret support was given to the rebels by members of the United States government, but Martí warned against accepting too much aid; he feared that the economic interests that motivated official support would lead the United States to take over the role of the ejected Spanish rulers. This prediction was prophetic.

The United States entered Cuba's Second War of Independence, which began in 1895. Responding to the urging of the American consul in Cuba to protect American lives and property, it dispatched the USS *Maine* to Cuba. A mysterious explosion, the cause of which has never been established, "provided the United States with just the right opportunity for entering the war." And despite its public disclaimer of "any disposition or intention to exercise sovereignty, jurisdiction or control over [the] island" and its determination "to leave the government and control of the island to its people," it acted in opposite fashion. American diplomats signed the Treaty of Paris; American military personnel appointed men who had remained loyal to Spain as officials to administer the island. The Cuban constitution was drafted in Washington; it was accepted by the elected Cuban constituent assembly "for fear that further resistance would lead to greater U.S. control."

The first 60 years of Cuban independence were marked by three interlocking features: economic dominance by the United States; ruthless repression of the people and corruption by government officials; and increased resistance to both the Cuban government and the American presence. The economic-political situation assured profits to American business interests, "uninterrupted prosperity for wealthy Cubans," and "grinding and deadening poverty for the mass of Cuban workers and peasants." These conditions in conjunction with officials' selfish greed and extreme brutality—torture and execution of thousands of people—fomented resistance leading to rebellion. Fulgencio Batista, the last of the dictator presidents, is given one of the author's "prize" awards "for pure despotism" and cruelty. However, "he enjoyed great American support."

The first major blow against Batista occurred in July 1953. Though it was unsuccessful, it launched Fidel Castro Ruz's direct involvement in the armed struggle and formed the guerrilla movement that was successful in January 1959. In this effort, Castro was joined in leadership by Ernesto (Che) Guevara de la Serna. (Castro is identified as an energetic, brilliant lawyer; Guevara, as a capable medical doctor.)

From the outset, opposition in the United States to the Castro regime was evident. This mindset was exacerbated by the nationalization of 36 sugar mills and refineries and over 300 other companies, many of which had been American-owned; by the treaties with the Soviet Union and China; and by Castro's declaration that the Cuban government was socialist in nature. A major confrontation was instigated and planned by the United States: the Bay of Pigs invasion, April 15–19, 1961. A few details of the invasion, participants, and outcome are given: the CIA involvement and its attempt to create an illusion of a Cuban military outbreak; the denials of

U.S. involvement at the United Nations by Ambassador Adlai Stevenson; the secret authorization by President John F. Kennedy; and the complete defeat of the invaders by Cuban government forces—"a miserable failure for the exiles [the invasion forces] and a tremendous embarrassment to the United States government." The Cuban government also rounded up and jailed all known counterrevolutionaries—thousands, including 2,500 CIA agents, in order "to [take] out of action all those who might have responded favorably to the invasion. . . ."

The second major confrontation, the Soviet missile crisis, developed on October 16, 1962, when the missiles were discovered and identified, and lasted until October 27 after "President Kennedy [agreed] to [Premier Nikita] Khrushchev's terms, much against the advice of the Joint Chiefs of Staff, and . . . the Russians agreed to remove the missiles." The terms: The missiles would be removed if the United States would guarantee that it would not participate in another attack on Cuba. In contrast to President Kennedy's position, held also by Attorney General Robert Kennedy and Secretary of Defense Robert McNamara, several United States government members recommended air strikes and land attacks against Cuba in order to destroy the missiles and expel the Castro government.

The final chapters of *The Land and People of Cuba* are a paean to progress. With the confiscated wealth of Batista and other high officials, the Castro government, whose officials are described as "meticulously honest," initiated essential programs: agrarian reform, public works, housing, health programs, social security, and education. The economy was rebuilt.

> When rents were reduced by 50 percent in 1959 and subsequently to 10 percent of the tenant's salary (with many people now paying no rent at all), when water and public telephones were provided at no cost, when health and education services became available free (almost immediately after the revolution), and when wages and salaries for the mass of people were raised, the demand for consumer goods became tremendous. With so many essentials provided free of charge, and with more money being paid them, the average Cubans were able finally to buy things they had never before owned.

A family, descendants from generations of peasants, is spotlighted; its progress from extreme poverty and malnutrition and disease to relative prosperity and health, with education for the children and the adults, illustrates the social changes that have occurred. Also, the progress of women is particularly noted. In conjunction with these changes, there had been attention to and growth of the arts: Cuban literature, popular and classical music, art, ballet, and cinematography.

With regard to a concluding question about the survival of the Cuban socialist government, the author responds positively. There is "every reason to believe" that the Cuban people will continue to support it with "energy and enthusiasm." Life is better for them. The fact of improved lifestyle is effectively "balanced" against certain realities: "some control of the Press"; freedom of speech is denied to "those who openly express hostility to the regime"; and the "Castro promised" elections of 1959 "have never been held."

> Socialist Cuba, then, seems to be here to stay. If Cuba is allowed to pursue its national destiny without interference by other countries, if helped and advised when it requests assistance but left to make its own decisions, there is no reason to believe that the present system will change radically.

CENSORSHIP HISTORY

Principal James Davis of the Rockaway Junior High School, Miami, Florida, in 1974 removed six copies of the reference book, *The Land and People of Cuba*, from the school library. He ruled that the book was anti-American propaganda favoring the pro-Castro viewpoint. Part of a widely used *Portraits of Nations* series, the book was also rejected by Dade County's public libraries.

Davis's specific censorial comments included these charges: "At every opportunity it portrays Castro as the benefactor and savior of Cuba"; "It is anti-American throughout." He cited a passage which shows President Kennedy "backing down on the Cuban missile crisis." Davis also objected to passages in which the United States was criticized by revealing that American business interests historically have exploited Cuba's people and natural resources, following early Spanish settlers and landowners. Also referenced was a passage in the epilogue in which the author defends the absence of national elections because the life of Cubans has so improved with regard to health care, free education, regular salaries, and the availability of an array of cultural and leisure-time activities.

Another reason for the book's being banned, according to Davis, was its "poor taste." "It's not that I'm for banning or burning anything of this nature. I just feel you have to consider Dade County and its people. Fifty percent of the children in this school have Cuban parents." (The *Miami Herald* reported an "about 41 percent" figure.) In this regard the book was criticized especially for its portrayal of the early Cuban refugees as "people who had been either directly involved in the Bastista regime . . . or who had been active in the more corrupt aspects of Cuban life—prostitution, gambling, abortion racket, drug traffic." Also cited is the author's contention that many refugees have regretted leaving Cuba: "they have heard from relatives that things are not as bad as they feared, that in fact in many ways things are a great deal better in Cuba than they thought."

Principal Davis's action was, in effect, supported by library consultant Madeline Paeto, who "reacted to the anti-American sentiment in it"; she urged school librarians to review the book. Richard White, the director of program development for the Dade school system, went a step further: "I have asked the librarian to check out other books in this extensive series, especially those about the Iron Curtain countries, to see if these materials should be used in a restricted sense here." Davis observed that *The Land and People of Cuba* may reappear on library shelves in a collection devoted to propaganda.

Authors League of America president Jerome Weidman responded to the censorship in a letter to Davis:

> While individual parents may prohibit their children from reading books, they have no right to dictate which books other parents' children may read. Yet by capitulating to the demands of some parents and removing Miss Ortiz' book from the library, your school has effectively given them that power of censorship. In so doing, it has violated the First Amendment rights of other students to read the book if they choose; it has violated the author's freedom of expression; and it has besmirched the basic principles of academic freedom.

The *School Library Journal* in its review noted that the author, Victoria Ortiz, "makes a clear statement against foreign intervention" in Cuban affairs.

FURTHER READING

Feigenbaum, Lynn. "S. Dade School Bans Book on Cuba." *Miami News*, March 28, 1974, p. 5A.
Kronholz, June. "School Drops 'Anti-American' Book." *Miami Herald*, March 29, 1974, p. 1B.
"Miami, Florida." *Newsletter on Intellectual Freedom* 23 (1974): 79.

LAND OF THE FREE: A HISTORY OF THE UNITED STATES

Authors: John W. Caughey, John Hope Franklin, and Ernest R. May
Original date and place of publication: 1965, United States
Publisher: Benziger Brothers
Literary form: Textbook

SUMMARY

The opening inscription by Adlai E. Stevenson and a series of contrasting features about the United States set the tone and direction of *Land of the Free*, a social studies textbook.

> When an American says that he loves his country, he means not only that he loves the New England hills, the prairies glistening in the sun, the wide and rising plains, the great mountains, and the sea. He means that he loves an inner air, an inner light in which freedom lives and in which a man can draw the breath of self-respect.

The contrasts are seen in the political and the environmental realms. Excerpts from the Constitution's high aims and Abraham Lincoln's Gettysburg Address—"government of the people, by the people, and for the people"—"are arrayed against American practice [that] has not always measured up to the ideal of 'government of the people'": the initial limitation of the right to vote to men of property; not granting this right to women until 1920 and even later to Indians; denying slaves voting rights and barring or discouraging them from voting for more than 100 years after slavery's end.

The United States, symbol of freedom, boldly represents itself in terms of "liberty and justice for all"; these are guaranteed by the Bill of Rights. But "promises of equal rights have not always been kept—or, worse yet, have been kept for some Americans but not for others." Cited are discrimination in the job market for African Americans as well as in access to housing and education.

The beauty of the American landscape and the rich resources of the land are extolled. These features are contrasted with examples of waste and damage from the pioneers who destroyed timber stands to later overuse of resources and the sprawl of housing, industry and highways. Mounting pollution ranges from "cities . . . in danger of being buried under their own trash and garbage" to the spoiling of the earth and sea with chemicals and other wastes.

The text begins with a standard unit, "Earliest America," that discusses explorations and their background, provides a 14-page glimpse of the "first Americans" and describes the first colonies. The glimpse of the first Americans is superficial, but differentiation is made among broadly grouped tribes of the regions of the country. One page is devoted to the plight of the Indians: "These first Americans were the first to have their lands taken from them, the first to be segregated, the last to get the vote, and the last to share in the rewards of the American system." Justification by the settlers for the first of these actions is that the "Indians were a barrier to progress and should be eliminated by force or negotiation."

The developmental stage of the English colonies leading to the founding of a nation represents expansionist actions: land takeover (English kings, claiming title, exercised their prerogative to grant lands from sea to sea); increased trade, agriculture, and industry; and wars among the European powers until the English gained control. The population was diversified; it included enslaved Africans as well as people from non-English origins. Emerging tensions are evident: the banishment of Anne Hutchinson and Roger William from the Massachusetts Bay Colony for religious heresy and political criticism; the quarrel about freedom of the press; protest against slavery. Tensions also developed between the colonists and England, resulting in large measure from taxation without representation, which led to the impulse for independence and war, followed by the Declaration of Independence. That the Americans were divided among themselves is carefully noted. "Some were patriots, some were loyalists, some were undecided. With the changing fortunes of war, many shifted from one camp to another."

During the war and after victory the leaders of the states did not come to an easy solution in the establishment of a union. In framing the Constitution, compromise was the key to resolution, particularly in the nature of representation in the houses of Congress and the powers of the central government over the states.

The first decades of the new nation were developmental and precedent setting in establishing principles and practice. An important principle emerged from the "revolution of 1800" when Thomas Jefferson was elected. Instead of leading a political overthrow, Jefferson acted to calm the populace and the politicians; he appealed to all Americans: "Let us then, fellow citizens, unite with one heart and one mind. We are all Republicans, we are all Federalists." In the succeeding years, however, sectional rivalries were prominent: The slavery issue separated the South; although an 1807 law ended the slave trade, slaves were still smuggled into the South. The status of slavery in the western territories as they achieved statehood increased sectional rancor.

Two great issues of the 19th century were westward expansion and the Civil War. Westward expansion represented the territorial growth and political definition of the nation as now known. It also represented a rise of democracy in government: The new states granted suffrage to every white male adult and some eastern states followed suit. However, westward expansion also meant annexing land: by purchase—Louisiana from France; by conquest; by persuading Indians to release land for settlement; by making and breaking treaties—some settlers ignored them; and by removing all Indians from the area east of the Mississippi through treaty and enforced requirement. Most of the estimated 100,000 Indians living east of the Mississippi River were moved out.

In discussing the tragedy of the Civil War, the authors illustrate slavery's inhumanity and effects.

> Constantly watched and subject to complete control by the master, a slave was never allowed to forget that he was a slave. . . . Most of the slaves endured what they had to. If they loafed on the job, it was often a form of protest. Slaves pretended to be ill and unable to work. Sometimes they destroyed tools or other property or damaged the crops. A few slaves were so desperate that they cut off their own hands or committed suicide.

Abolitionists, passionate and unequivocal, demanded immediate emancipation. Slave owners defended slavery as necessary to their operations and to keep the South prosperous.

> Glancing through history, the southern apologist for slavery found other arguments. Every progressive society, he argued, was built on slavery. The Egyptians had slaves; the Greeks held slaves; the Romans held slaves. "In all

social systems," the governor of Sousth Carolina said, "there must be a class . . . to perform the drudgery of life." With Negroes as slaves, he said, the southern whites had the leisure to become more cultivated.

After President Abraham Lincoln's Proclamation of Emancipation, the end of the bloody war, and the murder of the president, the freed slaves found their problems had just begun. Unprepared for freedom and for citizenship, without employment and education, they were easily abused. Every former Confederate state enacted a Black Code that treated the freedmen unjustly. The codes denied the rights to vote and to an education and instituted segregation. The Ku Klux Klan "terrified, tortured and often killed Negroes and their white sympathizers."

In contrast, partly in response to the actions of the former Confederate states, Congress acted to thwart these actions. They imposed reforms, the formula being "less forgiveness to Confederate leaders and more participation by the freedmen." During this period the Thirteenth, Fourteenth, and Fifteenth Amendments to the Constitution were ratified. These ended slavery and granted citizenship to Negroes, guaranteeing due process of law, equal protection of law, and the right to vote. After 1877, however, the southern states enacted a battery of Jim Crow laws that separated the races by treating "Negroes" as inferior.

In the discussion of succeeding decades the authors take three major tacks: the developmental progress of the United States; the social and political problems and issues, often outgrowths of progress; and the attempts to achieve reform and broader humanity. The first of these encompasses major inventions and industrialization, the transcontinental railroad, mining bonanzas of the far West, and the industrial revolution. Cities with skyscrapers developed as business and industrial centers, offering new opportunities for leisure and learning. Later advances in science became triumphs with achievements in space and medicine. At the turn of the century, the United States "acquired an empire," an extension of expansionist urges. Alaska was purchased from Russia; additional territory was taken through war with Spain and then annexation. In the 20th century, the United States became a world power.

While industrialization resulted in progress, especially for millionaires concerned with profits, it also resulted in crowded cities whose residential districts near town centers were stifling and unhealthy and created a "runaway problem of crime." Laborers' working conditions were mean; their long hours were filled with drudgery, their lives destitute. The waves of emigrants from Asia and from eastern and southern Europe faced hardships and language problems, but also unfair treatment and intolerance. Indians were gathered on reservations: "One purpose was to teach them to farm, thereby releasing most of the hunting area on which they had lived." Intolerance and violence against "Negroes" accelerated. During World War II, "Americans of Japanese ancestry . . . were treated as one great security risk, which they were not. With no questions asked, and no allowance for positive evidence of loyalty, they were hustled off to detention camps. . . . they were deprived of protections that the Constitution otherwise would have given them against arrest, detention, forced removal, and implication of lack of loyalty. They also had the embarrassment of being put where they could do little for the war effort."

Reform efforts were manifested in the workplace, in the community, in business, and in government. Labor unions were formed; strikes yielded successes and failures. As labor unions grew in strength and gained higher wages, fewer hours, and better working conditions, employers organized against them, hiring strikebreakers and using publicity and the courts to defeat them. A resurgence of union power in the 1930s helped to ensure prosperity for millions of workers. Muckraking newspapers, social activists like Jane Addams and progressive governors like Robert La Follette of Wisconsin acted to ease the conditions of the poor; laws were enacted to control child labor. At the federal level, such laws also controlled women's labor as well as abuses of "big business," drug manufacturers, and monopolies and trusts. A conservation program was launched. Attacks on corruption in government ranged from the eradication of the spoils system, replaced by a professional civil service, to the ratification of the Seventeenth Amendment, which provided for the popular election of senators.

The closing pages of the text juxtapose "Panic about Security" in response to the fear of communism with the civil rights movement for "Equal Rights and Fair Treatment." The former alludes to loyalty oaths, widespread suspicion, and the terrorizing of the State Department and many persons in government by Senator Joseph R. McCarthy. The latter expresses the denunciation of segregation in 1954 by the Supreme Court and the expansion of the civil rights movement from schools to buses, restaurants, and voting rights. Strong support for these civil rights measures was won among whites and blacks in all parts of the country.

> The drive also drew savage resistance from local police, the White Citizens Council, the Ku Klux Klan; and mobs and assassins. Seeing the Negroes set upon with police dogs, fire hoses, cattle prods, gas, whips, and clubs roused the nation. So did the bombing of Negro homes and churches and the assassination of literally dozens of persons, white and black, who were working for civil rights.

The demonstrations led to the Civil Rights Act of 1964 and the Voting Act of 1965.

CENSORSHIP HISTORY

The challenges to *Land of the Free* were multi-staged, coming from varied sources. The first occurred at the state level, from California's state assembly and the superintendent of public instruction, Max Rafferty. The controversy apparently began in May 1966 when Assemblyman John L. E. Collier identified the book as "very distasteful, slanted and objectionable" and said he would attempt to block appropriation of the text. Joining Collier in objecting to the text were Assemblyman Charles Conrad and state senator John G. Schmitz. The text was criticized for stressing a one-world government, quoting accused communists, portraying the United States as a bully, distorting history, and putting American forefathers in a bad light. The Textbook Study League, Inc., formerly the National Anti-Communist League of America, charged that the book exercised "thought control" rather than providing information.

Of particular notoriety was a criticism by Rafferty that the text is "slanted in the direction of civil rights," a judgment based on a critique of the text prepared by his "longtime advisor, Emery Stoops, a professor of educational administration at the University of Southern California." In contrast, Assemblyman Collier is cited as having said that the book is slanted politically in references to "Negroes," never mentioning their positive accomplishments. John Caughey, professor of history at the University of California at Los Angeles, specifically disputed this claim by providing evidence from the text of references to "Negroes" and their significant activities.

In a detailed critique published in *The Tablet*, a Catholic newspaper of the Brooklyn, New York, diocese, Assemblyman Conrad quarreled with the lack of balance in the book. "The authors virtually ignore whole periods of our nation's history, apparently because the authors dislike the political philosophy of those times. On the other hand, whole pages are devoted to trivia." He complained against the elimination of facts about the Harding, Coolidge, and Hoover administrations and their depiction as having done little while in office; he claimed that "school children have the right to know that these men believed the federal government should act only in times of emergencies, that during periods of prosperity we should reduce taxes and attempt to pay off the national debt." Comparably, Conrad found lack of balance in the amount of representation of the Eisenhower administration and its misrepresentation in its response to communism. The treatment of communism was questioned as well; it was presented not as negatively as fascism, both in the sympathetic treatment of accused communists in the United States and the absence of identification of Russian atrocities in Hungary, its invasion of Finland, and its seizure of Poland. "This is the current liberal line that, of course, Stalin was a tyrant, but that Communism, at least Russian Communism has changed its image and can now be trusted." Conrad asserted that this treatment "doubtlessly reflects the feelings of . . . Caughey." In this context, he referred to the fact that author Caughey had refused to sign the California regents loyalty oath in the 1950s, for which he was dismissed from teaching at UCLA for two years until he signed the so-called Levering Oath. Conrad also objected to the omission of American deaths at Pearl Harbor while listing the casualties at Hiroshima and devoting more than a page to the Japanese sent to "detention camps."

Because of "public pressure," the state Curriculum Commission convened a panel of noted historians to review the book and the criticisms. The panel's list of suggested revisions was forwarded to the authors. Rafferty indicated he would ask Governor Ronald Reagan "to withhold the money for its distribution" if the recommended corrections were not made.

In December 1966, after the requested changes were made, Max Rafferty supported the approval of the book for use in California schools. The state board of education unanimously approved it. Its use was to begin in eighth-grade classes in fall 1967.

A tangential censorship incident occurred at the United Republicans of California (UROC) convention in May 1967. The UROC's board of governors ordered the excision of the last two pages of a book being sold outside the convention hall. The 60-page pamphlet, *The Story Behind the "Land of the Free"* by Ford Sammis, was critical of the book itself as well as Superintendent of Public Instruction Max Rafferty. The last two pages made unflattering allusions to Rafferty, who was supported by many delegates as a prospective 1968 candidate for the U.S. Senate. Rafferty's shift in position from hostile criticism to praise is noted; he is quoted as saying, "I almost singlehandedly succeeded in getting this book so extensively changed. The book is 500 percent better than a year ago, largely due to my efforts." (Telephone conversations with the text's two living authors, John Hope Franklin and Ernest R. May, reveal that there were "not many" and "very few" changes. Some were resisted, such as the request to identify W. E. B. DuBois as a communist.) With the two pages of Sammis's book excised, permission for the book's sale was granted despite the presence of comparable criticism of Rafferty on other pages of the text.

Sammis's criticism of the *Land of the Free* refers particularly to its statements about "civil rights and Negro affairs." The treatment of these matters was deemed slanted as were those of liberalism and patriotism.

Despite the approval of the California state board of education and the ruling of the state attorney general that the book must be used, opposition to the text continued in the fall of 1967. The Charter Oak school trustees on August 7 went on record in opposition to the book, while the school administration scheduled a meeting of the teachers using the text to discuss the book and district policy "laid out as to its use." (The Charter Oak staff described the book as "highly readable, colorfully illustrated and [able to] serve as an excellent teaching instrument if carefully used and industriously supplemented.")

Challenges to the book appeared in other California school districts. The Paso Robles school district voted to use *Land of the Free* under protest; the Downey school district refused to order the textbooks, despite being subject to losing state appropriations; the Arcadia school district considered similar action, and the Tuolumne (Sonora) County Board of Education voted to oppose the use of the text. Richard Pland of the Sonora County board objected to the book as "negative. It's designed to build a segment of the country at the expense of the rest of the country. . . . it tears down instead of building up . . . like they are trying to instill a guilt complex in us." Altogether 14 school districts declined to order this text, but by mid-December only three—Downey, Los Angeles County; Fruitvale, Kern County; and Allensworth, Tulare County—were holding out. By January only Downey had not done so; its school trustees voted unanimously on January 8, 1968, to reaffirm their rejections of the state-required textbook. One of the board's objections to this textbook was to its interpretive level: "Eighth-graders aren't ready for interpretations of history—particularly biased interpretations, be they liberal or conservative." They also objected to the content, for example, "down-grading our heroes": Nathan Hale and Davy Crockett are not mentioned, nor are the military exploits of Generals George Patton or Omar Bradley. A speech by Patrick Henry is called a "tirade," and the Boston Tea Party is described as a "mob scene . . . hijacking British ships." On December 14, 1967, the state board of education decided to insist on the book's use; in mid-January, the Downey Unified School District board voted to challenge in court the right of the state board of education to force the use of the book. It contended that the state education code did not prescribe mandatory textbooks in junior high school.

Parent groups and individuals also expressed objections. The Concerned Parents of Rialto on August 23, 1967, objected to the "numerous inaccuracies" and the failure to emphasize what they viewed to be significant events in history. In Wheatland-Chili, three residents asked for a replacement book because in their view *Land of the Free* "runs America down." The Santa Paula school district also received "several calls . . . from concerned parents." The Rialto parents were told that the school district had no choice about books to be used in the eighth grade; the Wheatland-Chili residents' request was denied by the trustees because they trusted the judgment of the book selection committee of teachers.

A citizens' group, *Land of the Free* Protesters, was formed to seek expulsion of the controversial text from Orange County classrooms. The group circulated petitions and was ready in June 1968 to submit "200 to 300" signatures to one of four school boards. The goal of the group was 10,000 signatures. Its specific charges claimed that the text

> fails to develop the great traditions of America, e.g., love of country, strong individualism, worship of God and private enterprise . . . and places undue emphasis on minor historical people, indoctrinates toward collectivism, mocks American justice, projects negative thought models and promotes propaganda alien to the American Ideal.

Individual parents expressed their objections to the textbook by preventing their children from attending the class in which it was being used. Their objections charged that it was "not a true portrayal of the history of this country" and that it presented a "slanted version of history and ridicules religious beliefs held in our home." The child of each set of parents was expelled because of the parents' refusal to allow class attendance; a criminal complaint was filed against the parents by each school district. In April 1968, one couple was found guilty of violating the state education code and was sentenced to a $10 fine or five days in jail. The verdict in effect ordered the parents to allow their son to return to school. (The outcome of the second case is not available.)

Although David Shaw asserts in his account that *Land of the Free* is "being used virtually without protest in Cleveland, Denver, Philadelphia, Kansas City, Detroit, Washington and Milwaukee," Gerald Grant identifies a specific case outside of California in Columbus, Ohio. The book was a target of the Let Freedom Ring group, which attacked it as unpatriotic and communist-inspired because one of the authors had once refused to take an academic loyalty oath. They also charged that the textbook teaches "guilt and shame" about America's past, and they found it unthinkable that there was no picture of Betsy Ross sewing the American flag.

In January 1968, the National Education Association reported, based on questionnaire responses of 1,700 educational leaders, that *Land of the Free* received the most criticism from private groups and the public. The report also listed groups that ranked high in handing out "destructive criticism," that is, criticism that caused difficulty rather than helping. The John Birch Society and teachers' unions were first and second, respectively.

Seventeen California teachers contributed to a 45-page document, *Land of the Free and Its Critics*, in which they reviewed the credentials of the major critics of *Land of the Free*—only one was a historian, but he was an Irish and European history specialist—and analyzed the questions raised about the book. The teachers quoted specific passages in the text that belied the criticisms, either in the language used, the data presented, or both. Several examples follow:

- In response to a "soft on communism" charge: "upgrades radicals and communists, treats American documents carelessly, promotes world government." Authors write: "Communism *seemed* more idealistic than Fascism or Nazism. Its apparent aim was to ensure everyone a fair share; its benefits *supposedly* would go to workers rather than an elite or master race. But Communism *attached no value to any freedom* except freedom from want. The Communist leaders believed *they alone knew* what was good for the people. *All other parties were suppressed.* So were all churches. *Speech and writing were controlled. Critics were jailed or killed.* Every effort was made to force all the people to accept Communism and *obey* the party leaders *unquestioningly.* In practice, Communist Russia was as *brutal a police state as Mussolini's Italy or Hitler's Germany.*" (Emphasis added in the document.)
- In response to criticism that patriots are omitted: "Perhaps this is why another of his [Patrick Henry] legendary sayings, 'Give me liberty or give me death!' is buried without credit in a Lyndon

Johnson speech. . . ." Authors wrote: "Discussion of the meaning of liberty came to a high point in the 1760's and 1770's." ". . . Other efforts by individuals included . . . Patrick Henry's 'GIVE ME LIBERTY OR GIVE ME DEATH!'"

- In response to the accusation that historical events are sullied, critics quote: "This mob scene, showing the hijacking of the British ships in Boston Harbor, has come down in history under the more cheerful name, The Boston Tea Party." Research is cited: ". . . a mob disguised as Mohawk Indians and Negroes rushed down to the waterfront and emptied 342 big chests of precious tea into the harbor." Samuel Eliot Morison, *Oxford History of the American People* (New York, 1965).

FURTHER READING

Allen, Shirley, et al. *Land of the Free and Its Critics*. Millbrae: California Council for the Social Studies, 1967.

Conrad, Charles. "*Land of Free* Skimpy with Facts." *The Tablet*, July 28, 1966, n.p.

Franklin, John Hope. Coauthor of text. Telephone interviews. November 1996.

Grant, Gerald. "Radical Rightists Try to Suppress Texts Sympathetic to Minorities." *Washington Post*, December 11, 1996, pp. A1, 6.

Hasegawa, Ann. "*Land of Free* Causes Delay in State Budget." *UCLA Daily Bruin*, May 18, 1966, n.p.

"History Texts Declared 'Sick.'" *Sonora Union-Democrat*, March 12, 1968, pp. 1, 6.

May, Ernest R. Coauthor of text. Telephone interview. October 1996.

Newsletter on Intellectual Freedom 16 (1967): 14, 67; and 17 (1968): 15, 20, 22, 52, 55, 63.

"Rafferty Finds Two Dirty Words." *San Francisco Chronicle*, May 13, 1966, p. 43.

Shaw, David. "History 'Interpretation' Stirs Tempest in Downey." *Long Beach Press-Telegram*, February 19, 1968, pp. B1, 4.

"Textbook Issue Causes Suspension of Morongo Student." *Riverside Enterprise*, February 13, 1968, n.p.

"Tuolumne Education Board Opposes History Text." *Stockton Record*, March 12, 1969, n.p.

LAUGHING BOY

Author: Oliver La Farge
Original date and place of publication: 1929, United States
Publisher: Houghton Mifflin Company
Literary form: Novel

SUMMARY

Set in the American Southwest in 1915, *Laughing Boy* expresses the disparate lives and natures of its two Navajo protagonists, Laughing Boy and Slim Girl, and explores their relationship. It reveals as well features of the Navajo culture and people through its representation of their attitudes and behaviors.

In a foreword written for the 1962 edition, Oliver La Farge, an anthropologist, says that he chose 1915 as the setting because it was "a less corrupted, purer era" and notes that for the Navajos it was an "age of innocence." "The general scene, the appearance and behavior of those Indians, their dress, their camps, their games, their weapons, their land, were honorably set down. . . ." He continues that he and the Navajos believed "that their general condition and mode of life, with all its hardships, simplicity, and riches, could continue indefinitely if only they were not interfered with. The collapse of that way of life began in 1933."

Laughing Boy is a traditional Navajo. Indeed, he has had next to no contact with whites. The reader meets him when he is en route to a dance, riding the 100 miles easily on his pony; he wants to race his horse. He sings, he considers the silver and turquoise bracelet he wants to make. He welcomes the talk and boasting with other young men he meets. Young, handsome, innocent, he values his life, his people, his friends, and his skills; he values "traveling in beauty," being in harmony with the world around him. For him, wealth is momentary; honor is more valued.

Slim Girl has been Americanized. Taken from her parents as a child, she is sent to a boarding school to learn American ways. Now, she lives near a white-man's town. Her history, which is not fully revealed until the climactic events of the story, is troubled. After she completes her schooling, while working for a preacher and his wife, she falls in love with a cowpuncher. He seduces her, impregnates her, and abandons her. The preacher condemns her. Only a group of prostitutes take care of her. When her baby is stillborn, she joins them but looks for a way out. She leads a lonely white man to believe she is more innocent than she is and, pretending she is to be married to an old Navajo, talks him into a liaison. By thus falsely taking his money, she is avenging herself at the same time that she is amassing wealth.

The dance offers Slim Girl an opportunity, a next step of her calculated plan: to lure a Navajo toward marriage. Her ultimate goal is to use him so she can return to the Navajo way of life—but with misgivings.

> She had no intention of herding sheep and slaving away her youth in a few years of hard labor, herding sheep, hoeing corn, packing firewood, growing square across the hips and flat in the face and heavy in the legs. No; she had seen the American women. First there was money; the Americans must serve her a little while yet . . .

She selects Laughing Boy as her instrument: "All Navajo, even to his faults, he would teach her the meaning of those oft-repeated phrases, *bik'e hojoni*, the trail of beauty; through him she would learn the content, and she would provide the means."

After a brief courtship at the dance, Laughing Boy goes with Slim Girl. He rejects his uncle's innuendo about her and defies his disapproval of their marriage. They are married according to Navajo custom at his insistence; their life is essentially smooth and happy. Yet, there are a few tense undercurrents caused by competing values and strengths. She progresses in her plan. She buys him jewelry tools and silver; keeping him out of town on a ruse, she sells his jewelry profitably. They set up a loom; he teaches her to weave. They buy horses, which he tends. She "binds" him to her with whiskey. He loves her and she, against her will, comes to love him. They prosper. She, however, continues to meet her lonely American.

Questions and unease brew trouble in Laughing Boy's consciousness. Slim Girl's absences, ostensibly to work for a preacher's wife, and her strangeness upon her return gnaw at him. Though proud of their unconventional life and of her, his love blossoming, he misses his accustomed lifestyle. A trip to a 10-day night chant, including a meeting with his family—a dangerous, ultimate test for her—and attendance at other dances both mitigate and whet his need for these contacts. He fears he will lose her; he feels he is losing himself. "What is happening to me? I am losing myself. She holds the reins and I am becoming a led horse." He begins to question Slim Girl's need for money and wonders about her unwillingness to leave the American life.

The climactic events are initiated when Laughing Boy, trailing a wandering horse, glances into an adobe house and sees his wife with her American. Automatically, he shoots the American, wounding him with an arrow in his shoulder and, with painful deliberation, his wife. The arrow lodges in her forearm. Though he determines to leave, at their house Slim Girl asks him to remove the arrow and to hear her story. They are reconciled.

En route to the north, happily planning their renewed life, Slim Girl is fatally shot by a jealous former suitor, Red Man; he had aimed for Laughing Boy. Red Man, too, had been tainted by white-man contacts. Brokenhearted but finding peace in his memory of Slim Girl and her strength, Laughing Boy returns to his home, alone but "Never alone, never lamenting, never empty. *Ahalani*, beautiful."

With this personal tragedy, La Farge represents the tensions between cultures and the eroding, destructive effects of one culture upon another. On the personal level, Laughing Boy's free, honest spirit and his traditional innocence are undermined by the luxuries, the ease, and the excitement of the unconventional offered by Slim Girl. Considerably more wrenching in impact are the Americanization of Slim Girl and her subsequent dislocation, the effect of the attitudes and behaviors of the whites toward her when she attempts to live among them. These dual processes demonstrate and predict the "collapse" referred to in La Farge's foreword.

CENSORSHIP HISTORY

Laughing Boy was one of 11 books removed from the school libraries in Levittown, New York, in March 1976. When in July the Island Trees School

District voted to continue the ban on nine of these, *Laughing Boy* was returned to the shelves. This censorship situation, which eventually was reviewed and adjudicated by the United States Supreme Court in 1982, is detailed in the censorship history discussion of BLACK BOY by Richard Wright. The case is identified as *Board of Education, Island Trees v. Pico*, 102 S.Ct. 2799, 457 U.S. 853, 73 L. Ed., 2d 435 (1982).

A protest by librarians and teachers fighting an order by the St. Tammany Parish school board in January 1984 to remove two young adult novels—*Edith Jackson* by Rosa Guy and THEN AGAIN, MAYBE I WON'T by Judy Blume—from the Covington, Louisiana, junior and senior high school libraries, boiled over to reveal a history of censorship incidents. High school librarian Bonnie Bess Wood reported that, among other titles, she had been asked to remove *Laughing Boy* in 1975–76.

In 1961, under the leadership of J. Evetts Haley, Texans for America, a right-wing group, supported by the Daughters of the American Revolution (DAR) and the John Birch Society, attacked the language and concepts of a range of history books. They succeeded in causing the State Textbook Committee to reject 12 books opposed by the Texans for America and four opposed by the DAR. In addition, substantial changes in their texts were required of publishers for specific books. These textbook battles spilled over to affect library books. *Laughing Boy* was banned from the four Amarillo high schools and at Amarillo College. The cited reason was its political ideas.

FURTHER READING

"Covington, Louisiana." *Newsletter on Intellectual Freedom* 33 (1984): 69–70.
La Farge, Oliver. "Foreword." In *Laughing Boy*. Boston: Houghton Mifflin, 1929.
Nelson, Jack, and Gene Roberts, Jr. *The Censors and the Schools*. Boston: Little, Brown, 1963.

EL LIBRO NEGRO DE LA JUSTICIA CHILENA (THE BLACK BOOK OF CHILEAN JUSTICE)

Author: Alejandra Matus
Original date and place of publication: 1999, Chile
Publisher: Planeta
Literary form: Investigative journalism

SUMMARY

El libro negro de la justicia chilena (The black book of Chilean justice) by journalist Alejandra Matus was launched on April 13, 1999, in a ceremony presided over by the chief editor of Planeta publishing house, Carlos Orellana. Fewer than 24 hours later, a ban had fallen on the book. On April 14, 1999, the Santiago Court of Appeals ordered the confiscation of the entire edition of the book and the arrest of the author and Planeta's CEO, Bartolo Ortíz, and chief editor, Orellana. It is interesting to note that this happened 10 years after Chile had been freed from military dictatorship under General Augusto Pinochet. Despite the country's state of democracy, freedom of expression was still limited in 1999.

In spite of being banned, the book was quickly published on the Internet, and soon, photocopies of it circulated freely, causing it to become the most widely read book in Chile. It was publicly commented on, criticized, and defended by all manner of people, including politicians and parliamentarians, as though no ban existed.

What terrible secrets had been revealed in this book? What hidden truth could be so powerful as to move the heavy machinery of the Chilean judicial system at such an unprecedented speed?

The book was the result of six years of investigation to explain why, historically, the judicial system has been the least respected of Chilean institutions. Negligence, abuse of power, venality, and corruption are characteristics repeatedly found among many of the Supreme Court justices mentioned in the book. As a young journalist working for the newspaper *La Época*, Matus was assigned to cover the judicial sector. Long hours in the cold hallways of the Palacio de Justicia, where there was neither a press room nor a ladies' room, allowed her to witness the daily routine of justices and court officials for five years. What she saw and heard there incited her to undertake an investigation of the Chilean judicial system, a topic never before addressed by journalistic research and almost untouched by historians.

El libro negro de la justicia chilena is a journalistic account of the hidden history of the Chilean judicial system. The book has six chapters, which can be read in any order. Chapter 3, entitled "From the Real Audiencia to the Coup d'État," describes the deficiencies of the judiciary from its inception during the 19th century until Salvador Allende's administration from 1970 to 1973, which ended with the coup d'état led by Pinochet. Although concerns were raised throughout, no administration did much to reform and modernize this important branch of the Chilean government. "Other priorities," says Matus, always deterred governments from tackling the issue.

Chapters 2, 4, and 5 give a powerful account of the state of Chilean justice during the 17 years of military rule from 1973 to 1990. The role of the Supreme Court during that period is characterized in the book as one of total subordination to the executive branch. The judicial system simply renounced its responsibility as the third power of state. Matus employs this as her thesis, stating that

> ... there has not existed, in the history of Chile, a judicial power that has been understood and has conducted itself as such; what we have had—save, I reiterate, the isolated acts of judges as brilliant and brave as they are rare—has been

a judicial "service," no more modern, ethical or independent than any other [service] of the public administration.*

The book begins in 1990, an important year in Chilean history. It was the year in which Chile celebrated the end of the Pinochet dictatorship. President Patricio Aylwin had been entrusted with the difficult task of leading the country in its transition to democracy. It was a year of protests—the victims of human rights abuses demanded justice and reparation—and a year of battles between the government and the army, which threatened to seize power again. This was also a year when the problems within the judicial system needed urgent attention. In Matus's words, "1990 was the lowest point in a long process of degradation in the judicial system." President Aylwin recognized that there was a crisis and took steps to reform the judicial system. Supreme Court justices received Aylwin's assessment and initiatives with hostility. From their point of view, there was no such crisis. Aylwin appointed the Commission for Truth and Reconciliation to investigate human rights abuses carried out during the military regime. After a long investigation, the commission released a report in which it accused the Supreme Court of not having done enough to prevent human rights violations. This accusation caught the Supreme Court justices off guard, and their hostility toward the executive power grew exponentially. It was for this reason that Aylwin's proposals for reform would not bear fruit until the next administration.

Chapter 1, entitled "Degraded Power," illustrates extensively the corruption of the Supreme Court in the 1990s. Matus gives testimony of what she witnessed during five years working as a court reporter. She tells of the moral degradation of Supreme Court justice Servando Jordán and district attorney Marcial García Pica, among others.

She recalls the first time she saw Jordán. He was walking unsteadily out of the courthouse, assisted by his chauffeur. He was clearly intoxicated. She soon realized the justice always arrived late and left early, often without completing his daily work. As president of the third chamber, Jordán was expected to sign all the day's resolutions so that they could be processed. His neglect of the task interfered with the work of others.

García Pica was an old man known for his taste for young girls. It was common to see schoolgirls between the ages of 13 and 15, in uniform, sitting outside his chambers shortly before commencement of the day's activities and again shortly after their closure. They claimed they were there to visit their "Uncle Marcial," a different niece every time. He did not bother being discreet, as Matus soon found out from secretaries and janitors.

Bribery was another common practice. Matus was told of a colleague of hers who had been asked by a lawyer to take a briefcase to one of the justices. He found out later that he had been used to deliver bribe money. It was also

---

*All translations are by Cecilia Bustamante-Marré.

well known that when a case became too complicated or inconvenient, a clerk would be paid and entire case files would disappear.

Negligence was omnipresent in the courts. Matus explains the procedure a case should follow before the sentence. The final step, after the panel of justices pronounces the verdict, is to write the proceedings. A magistrate from the panel is assigned to perform this task, which involves recording the resolution and submitting it to his colleagues for their approval and signature. If this is not done, the verdict does not legally exist and the case officially remains open. At the beginning of the 1990s there was a long list of cases that had been left unfinished for 10 years or more. Some of the justices had retired without completing the simple task of recording their rulings. A few justices had left not one but many cases in the same state. There was even a case Matus mentions in which the plaintiff died 10 years after the verdict had been pronounced, yet his case was never finalized because of the magistrate's negligence.

As the author was able to confirm, these were all well-known practices, yet no one made a move to correct them. As Matus puts it, the motto was, "if you don't accuse me, I won't accuse you." Matus was most surprised to find that major media reporters were also in the know, yet no one had ever informed on these issues. When she discussed this with her colleagues, they would advise her to "only write what is written on official paper." They further told her that it was not wise to inform on a verdict before it had been signed. "Advanced publicity—they maintained, based on their own experience— could cause the judges or ministers to change their minds." Matus did not agree with this stance:

> A certain sense of reverence prevented them from reporting the behind-the-scenes details of the judicial decisions. It was the legacy of times past which we, newcomers, were not willing to venerate.

The Supreme Court of the 1990s was the legacy of the dictatorship. It had been carefully crafted so as to continue to serve the interests of the dictator long after his time had expired. This court was the work of Hugo Rosende, Pinochet's last minister of justice who, realizing that military rule was coming to an end, managed to pass the so-called Ley Caramelo (Candy Law). Matus devotes an entire scathing chapter to this lawyer. Rosende had worked behind the scenes as a personal adviser to Pinochet for most of his administration. He entered the public scene as a minister of justice in 1984, at a critical moment for Pinochet's administration. The economic crises, the battles between the dissident wing of the judiciary and the executive, the international pressure for human rights violations, all were shaking his government's stability. Pinochet needed Rosende to neutralize opposition within the judicial branch.

Rosende foresaw the end and worked fast. He knew that the work of the military regime would be threatened by an avalanche of lawsuits for human rights violations. He even feared that the Amnesty Law, instituted by Pinochet to protect himself and his supporters, might be eliminated. He felt he had to do something.

Most Supreme Court justices were loyal to the regime, but most of them were also close to retirement. Rosende saw he needed to renew the court in order to ensure continued support. The Candy Law consisted of offering lavish compensation to those who were willing to retire before September 15, 1989. Many accepted the generous offer, which allowed Rosende to fill 12 of the 17 seats with loyalists to the regime. When Aylwin took power in 1990, 14 out of 17 justices were Pinochet's appointees. Among them were Jordán, in spite of his known proclivity for alcohol and brothels, and Hernán Cereceda, whose nepotism and venality caused Congress to indict him, putting an end to his career. Merit was clearly not the most important consideration in the selection of magistrates. What mattered most was their unconditional loyalty to the regime.

Matus argues that the Chilean judiciary has historically lacked integrity, but none more so than that of the Pinochet era. This was, by far, the darkest period in Chile's history, as *El libro negro* extensively documents. Three chapters are devoted to illustrating the magnitude of injustice and impunity under the dictator and how the judicial system allowed that to happen.

Chapter 4, "The Rites of Power," shows the evolution of the relations between the military junta and the Supreme Court from the very day of the coup d'état, September 11, 1973. As soon as the military junta took control of the country, it dissolved Congress but guaranteed that the prerogatives of the judicial system would be preserved. In turn, the chief justice of the Supreme Court, Enrique Urrutia, declared total support of the new authorities on behalf of the judicial branch. Nonetheless, by the end of the first week, the military junta had given authority to the commanders in chief of each region to establish military tribunals to deal directly with the massive number of arrests they were making as they implemented martial law. The Supreme Court justices did not seem to notice how their power was being quickly undermined. The relations between the executive and the judicial powers continued to be cordial.

In the meantime, the Santiago Court of Appeals was receiving dozens of appeals for arrests, disappearances, and executions. The appeals court ordered investigations, but if magistrates made inquiries about a detainee held in one of the new military detention camps, they found they were denied access. These magistrates protested before the Supreme Court for what they considered a clear obstruction of justice. The Supreme Court ignored them. When the situation seemed to be getting out of hand, the chief justice of the Santiago Court of Appeals, José Cánovas, decided to take the complaint directly to the Ministry of the Interior. He informed the minister, General César Bonilla, that the secret police were violating the appeals regulations. Bonilla seemed genuinely surprised and ordered the resolution of some 300 stagnant cases. "But the attitude adopted by Bonilla, who died in a mysterious airplane accident, would not be taken up by his successors."

Impeded from doing their job, appeals court justices stopped investigating. More and more suits were rejected for lack of information or access to the detainees, and their work became a "ceremonial routine," as Matus calls it.

Human rights violations continued to escalate. The chief justice of the Supreme Court received a visit from Amnesty International officials: "They expressed concern for the indifference of the judicial system regarding the complaints for human rights abuses. They were particularly alarmed by the Supreme Court's decision to renounce its supervising powers over the military courts, which had already ordered several executions." Chief Justice Urrutia consistently backed the military government, defended it from international criticism, and justified arrests and executions as perfectly legal and necessary measures.

During the first two years of the military government, with Urrutia as head of the Supreme Court, all manner of Machiavellian tactics were implemented in order to remove political opposition. The judiciary was no exception. A purge that affected all levels below the Supreme Court soon began. Pinochet communicated directly with Urrutia who ensured everything under his jurisdiction ran according to the dictator's wishes. Black lists were kept at all levels, and the Supreme Court had absolute power to dismiss, demote, or transfer personnel throughout the country.

> According to a study conducted by the National Lawyers Association in 1986, between 1973 and 1975, more than 250 magistrates and functionaries were transferred, removed, or forced to resign. Among them, some 20 prosecutors and appeals court justices, more than 50 judges and court officials, and around 180 members of the secondary echelon (functionaries, public counsels, notaries). Most of them had never had a fault in their professional record.

The same study indicates that the 1925 Constitution, in effect at that time, stipulated very specific circumstances for the removal of magistrates. This article was, therefore, clearly violated from September 11 until December 6, 1973, when Decrees 169 and 170, which modified this article, were dictated.

The new decrees gave the Supreme Court authority to evaluate magistrates and functionaries and place them on one of three lists: List One would be for meritorious performance, List Two for satisfactory performance, and List Three for unsatisfactory performance. Those included in List Three were automatically removed from the judicial system. Evaluations would take place on the second day of January each year, in closed sessions and by secret ballot. The evaluation could not be contested. Magistrates could be voted onto List Three by the simple majority of the Supreme Court members present. Therefore, the new decrees entitled the Supreme Court to remove magistrates and court officials without trial, denying them the right to know the charges against them and contest the accusations.

On March 1, 1975, Urrutia announced his retirement. On February 2, 1975, in his final address to inaugurate the judicial year, the Chilean newspaper *El Mercurio* quoted him as saying, ". . . I declare, with the veracity required by the solemnity of this ceremony, that the tribunals have continued to act with the independence that the law confers upon them, according to its real knowledge and understanding, free from any intervention of the government that currently rules the country."

Supreme Court members continued the tradition of electing the senior justice to preside over the court. The practice was an easy way to make sure that, in turn, each justice would have the chance to hold the position. Urrutia's successors followed in his footsteps in that they maintained a public show of support to the executive power. In private, however, not all were as unconditionally loyal as Urrutia had been. Some expressed their concerns, though cautiously. But they had their hands tied; any disobedience would have meant the end of their career. The government was always ready to bend the law, if necessary, to eliminate opposition. This was clear in 1981 when it was Rafael Retamal's turn to take the top position of the Supreme Court. The government did not like him because of his proclivity to accept lawsuits for human rights violations. Since the members of the Supreme Court seemed determined to continue with the tradition of electing the senior-most member, the government, in an unprecedented move, extended the Supreme Court chief justice's term by two years. Many magistrates protested the affront, but the minister of justice simply said that it would not happen again.

Two years later, it was again Retamal's turn. This time, not only could the government not stop him from becoming chief justice, but Retamal would now hold the position for two additional years. His election came about following the first massive protest against Pinochet, which Retamal legitimized.

In his first speeches as chief justice, Retamal openly repudiated the irregularities that had been taking place in the country under military rule. He dared to speak against the practice of exile, for instance, and was, as a result, sanctioned by his peers.

This was the beginning of dissent. During the 1980s many of the magistrates who had originally believed that the stories of disappearances and torture were fabrications by the "Marxists," were now realizing their error. The efforts of the Catholic Church in defense of the victims convinced many that something really wrong was going on in the country. Dissent was dangerous, but many could not remain indifferent. A group of younger judges began to meet to discuss the state of Chilean justice. They had to be very cautious; they vented their opinions only within the academic circles of Universidad Diego Portales and Centro de Promoción Universitaria. By the mid-1980s, these magistrates were creating reforms that needed to be implemented. Some publications resulted from these discussions; all those who contributed articles were placed on List Two in their evaluations. Despite this, they continued the work that would later form the basis of the reforms of the 1990s.

As Pinochet's term neared a close, more and more magistrates dared to confront the feared secret police and the government. Risking persecution and sanctions, they did their best to enforce the law. Though they did not always succeed, their integrity and courage made it clear that the entire judiciary was not corrupt. The book thus ends with a note of hope but also some concern: hope, because reform was under way; concern, for the many traps still present in Chilean law.

As Matus discusses in chapter 6, the long awaited reform of the judicial system finally arrived in 1997, during the administration of President Eduardo Frei Ruiz-Tagle and Soledad Alvear in the Ministry of Justice. This was the most ambitious effort ever made to modernize the judiciary. However, Matus warns of the dangers of habit and custom, which may obstruct change: "It remains to be seen if habit and tradition will not twist the arm of changes implemented in the law. Certainly, it will be necessary to fine-tune imperfections in the future." She emphasizes the importance of the qualities of integrity, independence, and good sense in a judge. "The success of the reforms to the judicial power will depend, in great measure, on the personality of the judge," she writes.

These minor concerns in the last pages of *El libro negro* seem to be a premonition of what was yet to come once her book was released. A magistrate, unable to see himself as he was, made her experience the full weight of the law—a law that should not exist in a modern society. In June 2002 Matus published a new book entitled *Injusticia duradera: Libro blanco de "El libro negro de la justicia chilena"* (Lasting injustice: The white book of "the black book of Chilean justice"), a compendium of her odyssey after the publication of *El libro negro*. It also includes the stories of others who, like her, suffered the consequences of laws that limit the right to free speech. She concludes that while steps have been taken in the right direction, there is still much that needs to be done. In any case, she affirms in her follow-up that *El libro negro* is now "a legal and public document, which as yet has not been refuted."

—Cecilia Bustamante-Marré
University of Wisconsin–River Falls

CENSORSHIP HISTORY

Events relating to the censorship of *El libro negro* are set against a backdrop of significant media restriction, heightened during the 15 years of Pinochet's authoritarian regime. The freedoms guaranteed by the constitution were effectively refuted by other clauses in the same document, and these refutations further supported by laws governing libel and slander. The notorious Articles 6(b) and 16 of the Law for Internal Security, a major instrument of control, criminalized insulting or defaming senior state officials (with stiff penalties); the privacy law made it illegal to publish material concerning an individual's private life that damages or could damage the individual; and the Law on Publicity Abuse empowered judges to ban press coverage of court cases.

A cause célèbre erupted when Matus announced, on April 13, 1999, the publication of *El libro negro*, a book that reveals, in her words, "a six-month investigation that recounts the observations of an inconspicuous witness . . . an immersion in the history of the Chilean judicial system." Under an order by the Santiago Court of Appeals with authority from Article 16 of the State Security Law, 1,200 books were confiscated the next day from the warehouse of Editorial Planeta under the watchful eyes of reporters and camera crews who had been notified by Planeta's chief editor, Carlos Orellana. Matus was warned by her brother, Jean Pierre Matus, a lawyer and law professor, that the authorities had accused her of violating the National Security Law. Faced with an imminent arrest warrant, Matus fled into exile before a detention order could stop her, first to Argentina, then to the United States where "political refugee" status was granted. She stayed in the United States for two and a half years.

On April 14, 1999, Rafael Huerta, a judge of the Santiago Court of Appeals, pressed charges in response to a complaint filed by Judge Servando Jordán, former chief justice of the Supreme Court. As one of the justices whose professional and personal life had been criticized in the book (Jordán had narrowly escaped impeachment on corruption charges in a scandal in which court officials allegedly protected accused drug traffickers), Jordán invoked Article 6(b) of the State Security Law, which condemned contemptuous criticism of high-ranking political, military, and judicial officials. According to Chilean law, the offense of contempt of authority was considered an "attack on public order" and was punishable by a maximum of five years in prison.

On June 16 Bartolo Ortíz, Planeta's CEO, and Orellana were arrested and charged with conspiracy to violate the State Security Law by publishing *El libro negro* and were detained. On July 29, the appeals court dismissed their case. In the United States, Matus filed a lawsuit against Chile before the Inter-American Commission on Human Rights of the Organization of American States for flagrant violation of freedom of expression and the right to be informed.

Events initially followed a predictable course in the case against Matus, but parallel actions by the president and legislature had the effect of redirecting the outcome. In the Santiago Court of Appeals case, Judge Jaime Rodríguez in December 2000 temporarily suspended review of Matus's case, allowing the arrest warrant to stand, and in February 2001 rendered his final decision, upholding the arrest warrant, in effect exiling her for 13 years. The ban on *El libro negro* was also upheld.

Shortly after *El libro negro* was confiscated, President Eduardo Frei Ruiz-Tagle sent a bill to Congress to modify the press law. (That problem had not been overlooked by the administrations that followed the Pinochet regime; in the early 1990s, a commission had been set up to create a new press law.) The intent of the bill would revise the infamous Article 6(b) and make it more difficult for authorities to ban publications entirely. The proposal was stalled in the legislature. President Ricardo Lagos, Frei's successor, sent a revised bill to Congress; the so-called Press Law—Law on Freedom of Opinion and Information and the Practice of Journalism—was enacted in May 2001 and signed by Lagos. (The success of its passage was due, in no small part, to the national and international controversy created by the Matus case.) The notorious Articles 6b and 16 of the Law for Internal Security were abolished. It also ensured greater protection for journalists.

Subsequent to the Press Law's enactment, after four months of appeals and counterappeals by Jordán, Matus's case in the courts moved forward. Her lawyer, Jean Pierre Matus, requested that Santiago Court of Appeals judge Rubén Ballesteros close the case, drop the detention order against Alejandra Matus, lift the ban on *El libro negro*, and release all impounded copies of the book. Ballesteros did dismiss all charges related to the violation of Article 6(b) of the State Security Law but upheld the detention order, pending the ruling of the appeals court. On July 10, 2001, the Fifth Chamber of the Santiago Court of Appeals unanimously accepted the appeal by Matus's defense attorney and annulled the detention order, enabling Matus to return to Chile. However, both the Santiago Court of Appeals and the Supreme Court declined in August 2001 to lift the ban on her book, declaring the writ inadmissible. Then, on October 19, 2001, Judge Ballesteros lifted the three-year ban on *El libro negro*, based on the Press Law, which had been signed in May; concurrently, he ordered the Department Investigating Economic Crimes of the Investigative Police (Chile's civil police) to return more than 1,000 confiscated books to the Planeta publishing company. Further, Ballesteros issued a temporary stay on the still-pending case for bribery and insult, also filed against Matus for violating Article 6(b). Matus returned to Chile at the end of 2001.

—Nicholas J. Karolides, with Cecilia Bustamante-Marré

FURTHER READING

"Action Alert Update: Ban on Book Lifted." IFEX: International Freedom of Expression Exchange. October 24, 2001. Available online. URL: http://www.ifex.org/en/content/view/full/14850. Accessed December 8, 2005.

Brett, Sebastian. "Chile, When Tyrants Tremble: The Pinochet Case." Human Rights Watch. October 1999. Available online. URL: http://hrw.org/reports/1999/chile/index.htm#TopOfPage. Downloaded January 15, 2005.

Matus, Alejandra. "The Chill of Chilean Justice." IPI Global Journalist Online, No. 4. 2000. Available online. URL: http://www.globaljournalist.org/archive/Magazine/chill=20004q.html. Accessed December 6, 2005.

———. *Injusticia duradera: Libro blanco de "El libro negro de la justicia chilena."* Santiago, Chile: Planeta, 2002.

———. *El libro negro de la justicia chilena.* Santiago, Chile: Planeta, 1999.

———. "Sueño con libros." *El Heraldo.* August 22, 1999. Available online. URL: http://www.elheraldo.com.co/revistas/dominical/99-08-22/noti8.htm. Downloaded January 15, 2005.

THE MAN DIED: PRISON NOTES OF WOLE SOYINKA

Author: Wole Soyinka
Original date and places of publication: 1972, United States and Canada
Publisher: Harper and Row
Literary form: Autobiography

SUMMARY

It is evident in the early chapters of *The Man Died* that Wole Soyinka is readily identified even by ordinary prisoners. He is a well-known figure—poet, playwright, learned university professor, and political activist. Within a day of his arrest, the foreign newspapers had published the news. This both astounded and alarmed his interrogator and his captors, referred to as the "Nigerian Gestapo" by Soyinka.

> My arrest . . . was prompted by the following activities: my denunciation of the war in the Nigerian papers, my visit to the East, my attempt to recruit the countries' intellectuals within and outside the country for a pressure group which would work for a total ban of the supply of arms to all parts of Nigeria; creating a third force which would utilize the ensuing military stalemate to repudiate and end both the secession of Biafra, and the genocide-consolidated dictatorship of the Army which made both secession and war inevitable.

The date is August 1967. Soyinka had ensured, as a safety measure, that he would be arrested by the police rather than army intelligence or the government Gestapo from Lagos, both of which had organized a manhunt to locate him. The plan—negotiated with "guarantees"—had been that he would be taken to Lagos for a short interview with the military head of state, Yakubu Gowon. This never happened. Instead, he was interrogated at length by the Security Branch. He was not allowed to return to his home; his legs were chained together, and he was kept in an isolated room overnight. The next day, Soyinka, after further interrogation, was incarcerated in Shaki, a maximum-security prison, before later being assigned to a medium-security prison, Kiri-Kiri. Subsequently, he was transferred to Kaduna prison, much of his time there being in solitary confinement. He was released from prison in October 1969.

The autobiography focuses on Soyinka's experiences in prison and their effects on him. Beyond the "chain-gang in South Alabama or Johannesburg," indignity, and insinuating, trap-intending questions to elicit admissions of guilt, an attempt is made to bribe him—a cabinet post if he will sign a statement implicating a member of the civilian cabinet to, in effect, force his resignation. He is humiliated—forced, disregarding his protests, to be examined by a "stool-pigeon" doctor. He is framed by an October 29, 1967, press release falsely declaring his confession, that is, his admitting to complicity with a rebel leader to an antigovernment arrangement, but had "changed his mind on this" and had also agreed to help in the overthrow of both the government of Western Nigeria and the federal military government. Subsequently, he is also warned of a plot to liquidate him, removing him from the prison to an airplane with "no destination."

The prison conditions are dehumanizing; the treatment of prisoners is cruel and brutal. The prison block is two floors with cells along the sides of an intervening corridor; bathrooms, toilets, sinks, and a lounging area are at the dead end of the corridor. Army and civilian detainees and prisoners are permitted to use the compound's encased recreation grounds—"But not the Ibo detainees [an ethnic group, victimized by the social-civil tensions]."

[The Ibo] were let into the corridor and bathrooms twice a day for an hour at a time. They occupied one entire line of cells on the lower floor. Opposite them was the other line, empty except for beddings stacked high against the walls,—reaching sometimes to the ceiling. . . . They slept on the bare floor, they had a clear view across the passage of blankets and beds, at the empty cells these beddings occupied. Some of them had no blankets and some cells were occupied by up to eight people. The cells were designed for only one man apiece, at the most, two.

Later they were locked in permanently except for 30 minutes a day, all 60 men at the same time. There was but a small window close to the ceiling for fresh air. An informer among them was always present to report any suspicious conversation.

Examples of brutality pervade the text. When the Ibos decided to reject their food for a day, the cells were raided, the prisoners marched out of their cells and manhandled.

Their effort at a concerted defiance was bound to end like others, the scapegoats would be carted off to the back cells where they would be chained to the wall and the cell flooded. They would be scientifically beaten. One thing they could not fear to lose was privilege. They literally had nothing to lose but their stench.

Flogging, apparently, was not uncommon: ". . . a back of purulent sores. There was no skin. None at all. It was a mass of sores which no longer had definition as each weal had merged with another."

Soyinka is denied adequate clothing; when transferred to Kiri-Kiri, his possessions include "comb, an off-white vest shrunken from wash and usage, a spare pair of trousers glossy from usage, a hand-towel, toothbrush and paste"; during a harmattan—a dry, parching dust-charged windstorm—the wardens wear great capes, woolen vests, ear muffs, and, at night, thick leggings, while Soyinka is in shirtsleeves and a blanket. A request for an additional blanket is ignored; he is consistently denied medical attention and supplies, for example, ointments for dry, scaled skin and cracked heels. He is, except very occasionally, denied books, paper, and pencils, and those he's had are taken away from him during searches. He asserts to a doctor in the presence of the prison superintendent:

> I have been here months. Alone. I have no books, no occupation whatever. Do you think this is good for my health?. . . . But do you think it is right? Do you think it is human? Because if you don't you ought to do something about it. I am accustomed to using and feeding my mind. Is it right I should be subjected to such a prolonged starvation?

Incarceration affected Soyinka both physically and psychologically, but he was able to withstand the pressures and travail. His sharp intelligence, political savvy, and ability to evaluate people enabled him to outmaneuver the interrogators and officials, avoiding the language traps. His ability to relate to others gained him support among the prisoners and some of the prison warders, occasionally being able to send messages to the outside world via the latter. (He notes: "I owe my life to the vigil" of two "faithfuls" who maintained contact with an army-officer friend, caroused with prison warders and soldiers, and communicated with prisoners working outside the prison walls.) However, the prison walls, the treatment of incarcerated men, and the extended solitary confinement eat away at his self-control:

> In an animal cage, in the spiritual isolation of the first few days, the prospect became real and horrifying. It began as an exercise to arm myself against the worst, it plunged into horrors of the imagination. I had begun to lose some distinction between the supposition and the reality. Even long after I had re-established contact with the outside world, had been assured that the truth was known where it mattered most, it took only a little trigger of recollection to plunge me back into that cauldron of racing pulses and nervous stress.

Soyinka experiences desolation, the abandonment of hope, an occasional sense of a "brave quest," rage—being close to violence or surrender—panic, hallucinations, and detachment. At least twice he resorts to fasting as a tactic to achieve recognition for his needs, once, a "mild partial fast of 21 days after [an] aborted release," which rapidly emaciated his body, referred to as a "token" fast. The second is cumulative: "The first week I would go one day without food, the second week two days, the next three . . . until the seventh week, and then—what?" The authorities were fearful of his demise and oversensitive to bad publicity.

Soyinka's imprisonment is politically based. Thus, there are political references and conversations, notably to the massacre that occurred in 1966 and its aftermath. An extensive flashback recalls the past events—the turmoil and chief players of the fateful months; it recounts Soyinka's attempts—at the urging of Lieutenant Colonel Adekunle Fajuyi, first military governor of the west, apparently an honest and concerned leader—to communicate with the north and avert conflict. Soyinka failed in this mission, perhaps arriving too late; Fajuyi was murdered by participants in the June 29 coup.

Interspersed among the prison revelations are comments about the atrocities committed on the national scene. Several quotes reveal the extent and nature of these:

> Man-hunts, publicized by machine-gun stutters, took place around Ikoyi where Gowon lived, and the executions and torture games that went on in his official residence, Dodan Barracks, on civilians who were simply arrested on the public road—Ikorudu checkpoint was the favourite kidnap point—were common daylight occurrences known to Yakuba Gowon.
>
> ... in ATROCITIES-free nation an ATROCITIES commission will now be set up to inquire into butchery and torture of the mid-west Ibo civilians by Federal troops and their civilian aides. In Shaki before my transfer I received eye-witness accounts from a Federal soldier, a young school-leaver who saw his ideals shattered by the wanton execution of civilians. . . . The daily executions and torture were still in progress when he left. He saw entire families wiped out in cold blood. ATROCITIES? Or simply—war?

Upon the fall of Umuahia to his military forces, Major General Gowon announced to assembled dignitaries that it was "unfortunately a few days late, as it had really been planned as a present for him on his wedding day!" Soyinka reacts:

> But the inside of the man, the deadness of mind and sense was summed up in the final unedifying revelation: that the taking of a rebel stronghold, the taking even of the smallest bow-and-arrow defended hamlet in a civil war was not to him the sum of lives on both sides, of mutilation and sacrifice, was not even the weighty dilemma and disquieting decisions of human sacrifice but—a wedding present! A glorification of a private and personal bond between himself and some unknown, irrelevant quantity. Nothing but a feudal dynastic mentality could have conceived such irreverence, nothing but power drunkenness could have bilged forth such grandiloquent vomit on the entire national sacrifice.

Excerpted from an address of welcome to His Excellency, Major General Yakubu Gowon:

> But the high-handedness of some of these soldiers has astonished us and left many gasping for breath. To cite a few instances; may we mention Mr Dennis Okparaku Edim of Okanga who in 1968, was shot in his house for no cause whatsoever, Mr Ajom Agvor who was killed at Nkum, in 1969, for refusing to allow his school daughter to be raped and Mrs Aggie Ntue, who was stabbed to death. Recently, a third year student of Ikom Secondary School, Master Agbor Nohor, who was beaten to death when the School was besieged by a group of armed soldiers. Their only reason was that the school authorities had denied them the use of the secondary school compound for cattle grazing.

Two men who had drafted the address of welcome were identified. His excellency ordered his soldiers to strip the men—H. E. Eyala, aged 42, the general secretary of the Ikom Divisional Farmer's Union, and Philip Ntui, aged 52, a private businessman—and flogged—50 strokes of the cane each—in front of his entourage, the local chiefs, and pressmen.

At a party a governor's wife complained about being insulted by the television boys. The governor, agitated, ordered them to leave immediately and to be taken to his house where they were held at gunpoint until he arrived.

> When he came he said, "Take them away and give them a thorough beating and then bring them back here to me in the morning. If any of them tries any tricks gun him down." Fortunately the officer in charge was a man of God and so instead of taking us to the barracks he took us to Iyaganku police station. We were ordered to strip and the Mobile Police boys were jumping on us with their heavy boots. At the time we were made to lie on the concrete floor. After the beating we were thrown into an overcrowded cell of hardened criminals.
> . . .

The ankle of one of the men was smashed. After making the rounds of hospitals in Nigeria, he was then sent to England where amputations took place. The wound badly infected with gangrene, he was returned home. After only six weeks, the man died.

CENSORSHIP HISTORY

First published in 1972, Soyinka's book was banned in 1984 in Nigeria. After his release from prison in 1969, Soyinka left Nigeria and did not return until a change of government took place in 1975. At that time General Yakuba Gowon, who had become head of state in 1966 after army officers from the north had overthrown the military government, killing General Johnson Aguiya-Ironsi, was himself overthrown by a military coup d'état. After a period of civilian, elected government another coup established a military government headed by Major General Muhammadu Buhari. This regime issued repressive decrees, particularly the infamous Decree 4 on January 1, 1984. The Public Officers Decree—Protection Against False Accusation—"made it a criminal offence to publish any article that brought the government or any public official into disrepute." Thus, any published statement, true or false, that could embarrass any government official was forbidden. (Subsequent directives banned public meetings, statements to the press by academics, and all forms of political debate.) It was in this context that this regime censored *The Man Died*.

This was not Soyinka's first experience with censorship, several radio plays having been banned in 1962. A discussion of Soyinka's difficulties with Nigerian government officials and laws may be found in the censorship discussion of Soyinka's THE OPEN SORE OF A CONTINENT: A PERSONAL NARRATIVE OF THE NIGERIAN CRISIS.

Soyinka has been honored with academic and literary awards. He received the Nobel Prize in literature in 1986. Also, Amnesty International has awarded him the Prisoner of Conscience Prize.

FURTHER READING

Siollun, Max. "Buhari and Idiagbon: A Missed Opportunity for Nigeria." October 2003. Available online. URL: http://www.nigerdeltacongress.com/barticles/buhari_and_idiagbon_a_missed_opp.htm. Accessed December 8, 2005.
"Special Report on Nigeria (4): Why General Buhari Failed the Coup." *Guardian* (London), September 13, 1985, n.p.

THE MANIFESTO OF THE COMMUNIST PARTY

Authors: Karl Marx and Friedrich Engels
Original dates and places of publication: 1848, Great Britain; 1872, United States (English translation)
Publishers: Communist League; Woodbull and Claflin's Weekly
Literary form: Nonfiction

SUMMARY

In the "Preface to the English Edition of 1888," Engels noted that "the history of the *Manifesto* reflects the history of the modern working-class movement" and identified it as the most international of all Socialist literature. Yet, he acknowledged significant differences between the Socialists of 1847, "adherents of the various Utopian systems," and Communists, "Whatever portion of the working class had become convinced of the insufficiency of mere political revolutions and had proclaimed the necessity of a total social change. . . ."

This definition lends itself to a central issue of section 1: class struggle. Such struggle between the oppressor, or the bourgeoisie, and the oppressed, or the proletariat, has existed throughout history and existed in the mid- and late 19th century. The bourgeoisie, equated with capital, developed in the same proportion as the proletariat developed. The latter is defined as "a class of laborers, who live only so long as they find work, and who find work only so long as their labor increases capital."

The bourgeois class developed from the feudal economic system, which was replaced by a manufacturing system to meet the demands of new markets that kept expanding, even establishing world markets. Politically oppressed by the feudal nobility in the preexisting system, the manufacturing middle class, itself revolutionized by the advance of industrialization, had achieved the position of power and control. "The executive of the modern state is but a committee for managing the common affairs of the whole bourgeoisie."

Beyond gaining political supremacy and massively altering the forms and extent of production, the bourgeoisie changed the face of society. By expanding the means of communication, all nations, even the most primitive, were drawn into civilization. The towns came to dominate the country, with significant increases in urban populations. The outcome of this was the creation of patterns of dependence: rural regions dependent on towns and cities; the primitive countries dependent on the developed ones. Also, the bourgeoisie destroyed the feudal patriarchal relations, "stripped of its halo every occupation, . . . and reduced the family relation to a mere money relation."

It has resolved personal work into exchange value, and in place of the numberless indefeasible chartered freedoms, has set up that single, unconscionable freedom—Free Trade. In one word, for exploitation, veiled by religious and political illusions, it has substituted naked, shameless, direct, brutal exploitation.

Another outcome of centralized production was the concentration of property in a few hands and the creation of "more colossal productive forces than all preceding generations together." This means of production and its control are equated with social-political power. These movements of change are identified as constant, the "revolt of modern productive forces against modern conditions of production" leading to commercial crises during which existing products and previously created forces are destroyed. "The weapons with which the bourgeoisie felled feudalism to the ground are now turned against the bourgeoisie itself." The men who will wield the weapons of destruction are the modern working class, the proletarians.

Industrialization caused the work of proletarians to lose all its individual character. As a mere appendage of a machine, the worker's value is decreased, equal essentially to the cost of production, subsistence for his maintenance and for the propagation of his race.

As privates of the industrial army they are placed under the command of a perfect hierarchy of officers and sergeants. Not only are they slaves of the bourgeois class, and of the bourgeois state; they are daily and hourly enslaved by the machine, by the over-looker, and, above all, by the individual bourgeois manufacturer himself. The more openly this despotism proclaims gain to be its end and aim, the more petty, the more hateful and the more embittering it is.

The worker is further exploited, beyond the factory, by other members of the bourgeoisie—the landlord, the shopkeeper—who take his wages from him.

In 1848, the proletariat was not yet organized in the worker's own behalf. Its struggle with the bourgeoisie was scattered and individualized or by factory, locale, or trade; it was misdirected against the instruments of production rather than the bourgeois conditions of production. However, the predicted change, given the development of industry—thus, the concentration of masses of workers and the equalization of life within the workers' rank and of wages at the same low level—was that the workers would unify.

The unifying force: communism. Defined as not forming a separate party in opposition to other working-class parties and as having no interests "separate and apart from those of the proletariat as a whole," the Communists' immediate aims are the formation of the proletariat into a class, the overthrow of bourgeois supremacy, and the conquest of political power by the proletariat. Marx and Engels saw the Communist Party as the only one that had as its purpose the advancing of the true interests of the proletariat as a class.

The "abolition of private property" was central in the theory of the Communists. This abolition focused on bourgeois property, "the final and most complete expression of the system of producing and appropriating products that is based on class antagonisms, on the exploitation of the many by the few." (The "hard-won, self-acquired, self-earned property . . . of the petty artisan and of the small peasant" was perhaps excluded from this abolition; the issue was sidestepped by the view that such property had already been destroyed by the development of industry.)

Wage-labor does not create property for the laborer; it creates capital— "the kind of property which exploits wage-labor, and which cannot increase except upon condition of begetting a new supply of wage-labor for fresh exploitation." The solution to this antagonism between capital and wage-labor, given that capital is not a personal but a social power, was to convert capital into common property. The intention, further, was to change the "miserable character" of the "personal appropriation of the products of labor" so as "to widen, to enrich, to promote the existence of the laborer."

> The proletariat will use its political supremacy to wrest, by degrees, all capital from the bourgeoisie, to centralize all instruments of production in the hands of the state, i.e., of the proletariat organized as the ruling class; and to increase the total of productive forces as rapidly as possible.

The "Communist revolution is the most radical rupture with traditional property relations . . . [and] with traditional ideas." The *Manifesto of the Communist Party* is a call to arms, to revolutionary activity.

While recognizing the variation of this undertaking in different countries, the following goals were identified as generally applicable:

1. Abolition of property in land and application of all rents of land to public purposes.
2. A heavy progressive or graduated income tax.
3. Abolition of all right of inheritance.
4. Confiscation of the property of all emigrants and rebels.
5. Centralization of credit in the hands of the state, by means of a national bank with state capital and an exclusive monopoly.

6. Centralization of the means of communication and transport in the hands of the state.
7. Extension of factories and instruments of production owned by the state; the bringing into cultivation of waste lands, and the improvement of the soil generally in accordance with a common plan.
8. Equal obligation of all to work. Establishment of industrial armies, especially for agriculture.
9. Combination of agriculture with manufacturing industries; gradual abolition of the distinction between town and country, by a more equitable distribution of the population over the country.
10. Free education for all children in public schools. Abolition of child factory labor in its present form. Combination of education with industrial production.

The concluding pages of the text define and differentiate between communism and several socialism movements. Three broad categories of socialism are discussed: reactionary socialism, including feudal socialism, petty-bourgeois socialism, and German, or "true," socialism; conservative, or bourgeois socialism; and critical-utopian socialism. Each of these socialist movements is dismissed as inadequate, focusing on the dethroned aristocrat or the petty bourgeois; the preservation of the present state of society; the "redressing of social grievances, in order to secure the continued existence of bourgeois society"; and the rejection of political and revolutionary action, seeking to improve conditions through appeals to society at large, chiefly the ruling class.

CENSORSHIP HISTORY

Censorship of Karl Marx's works began before the publication of *Manifesto of the Communist Party*. The political and social journal, *Rheinische Zeitung*, was suppressed in 1843, one year after Marx became editor. He was exiled in Paris and Brussels. He was expelled from France about 1845 for contributing to the radical magazine, *Vorwarts*. In 1849, the *Neue Rheinische Zeitung*, edited by Marx, advocated nonpayment of taxes and armed resistance against Emperor Frederick William. The journal was suspended, and Marx was tried for treason; though acquitted by a middle-class jury, he was expelled from Germany.

Action to ban the *Manifesto* in Germany occurred in 1878. It grew out of two assassination attempts—on May 11 and June 2—on the life of Emperor William I, the second of which wounded him seriously. Chancellor Otto von Bismarck exploited the fact that the first assassin had once belonged to the Social Democratic Party and caused a bill to be drafted against the "socialists and their press." It failed because of opposition from the National Liberal Party. Though there was no evidence that the second assassin was a Socialist, Bismarck again "conjured up the red peril" and dissolved the Reichstag. The next election gave him a stronger conservative party base, which easily passed his antisocialism bill, the "Exceptional Law." In addition to limiting rights to form associations and organizations in support of social democratic, Socialist or Communist activities which "are designed to subvert the existing political order in ways that threaten the public order and particularly the harmony of the social classes," the law forbade the publication of newspapers or books, including the *Communist Manifesto*.

The Catholic Church undertook its anticommunist stance in the 19th century—"since *The Communist Manifesto* first appeared in 1848." Donald Crosby points out, "[T]he popes taught that communism was essentially atheistic and irreligious," representing the very Antichrist. They regarded the Communists as "anarchistic, violent and opposed to what was best for man," and their materialism as contrary to "the heart of the church, the world of God and of the spirit." The savage persecution of Russian Catholics after the Bolshevik Revolution intensified the church's hostility. The *Communist Manifesto* during this time was listed on the Index librorum prohibitorum, or Roman Index.

In the United States in the late 1930s, Catholics identified anticommunism as demonstrating compatibility with American patriotism and the greater American society. The anticommunism of the church's leaders did not waver and was indeed solidified by the "martyring" of Archbishop Aloysius Stepinac of Yugoslavia and Joseph Cardinal Mindszenty of Hungary. Two positions of anticommunism emerged, particularly evident in the post–World War II period: a militant, conservative effort that allied with Senator Joseph McCarthy in zealous pursuit of subversives and "fellow travelers" in government and other aspects of society; and a liberal effort that, while equally opposed to communism, believed the answer was not "an extension of Red hunts and repressive legislation but an expansion of social programs designed to end hunger, disease, deficient housing and other social and economic ills that drove men into the hands of the Marxists." This group vehemently opposed Senator McCarthy and his tactics.

Given this historic position and current attitudes, the revelations of a poll of libraries in 30 cities, reported in the *New York Times* in 1953, are understandable. While public institutions did not curb books by Communists— texts by Marx, Lenin, and Stalin could be borrowed without restriction— some private religious education institutions did limit their availability. Roman Catholic universities such as Loyola University in New Orleans, Creighton University in Omaha, and Marquette University in Milwaukee placed these texts under restricted access. Students could borrow them if related to assignments or if being used for reference under direction when studying the theories of communism for thesis work. At Marquette, the instructors submitted the names of students who borrowed these books; the list was subsequently turned over to the archbishop. The Marquette University spokesperson indicated as explanation for the restricted access of the *Manifesto* that it was listed on the Index.

The 1950–53 period in the United States was one of extensive criticism of Marx's works as well as other Communist writings. The period was dramatically punctuated by the activities and accusations of Senator Joseph McCarthy and of the House Committee on Un-American Activities. It included such disparate situations as a 1950s report before the Illinois legislature's Seditious Activities Investigation Committee in 1950 that urged limiting access of many books by Marx in the public library. "They develop the subject at length and by so doing put in the young mind a yearning for that." At another level in 1953, after students in Brooksfield, Florida, who were working on papers about Russia, reported finding materials favoring that country, Paul B. Parker, a retired colonel and a library board member, set himself up as a one-person censorship committee. He removed an unspecified number of books and magazines from the nearby Brooksville public library because they were "communist propaganda." These included the *Manifesto of the Communist Party, Mission to Moscow* by Joseph E. Davies, former United States ambassador to Russia, and both the *New Republic* and *Reporter* magazines. Mayor Howard B. Smith demanded their return despite Parker's threat to label him a "fellow traveler." With the library board also insisting on the return of the material and further rejecting Parker's motion that the books and magazines be stamped "Propaganda," some were returned. One exception: *Manifesto of the Communist Party*.

The Boston Public Library came under attack on September 23, 1952, when the *Boston Post*, recently purchased by John Fox, revealed that the library subscribed to the pro-Soviet monthly *New World Review* and to Russian newspapers *Pravda* and *Izvestia;* it also disclosed it had a lobby display of the *Manifesto* and "thousands" of Communist publications. The *Post* argued: "We believe that pro-Soviet literature should be suppressed in our public libraries. . . ." This position was counterargued by the director of the library, Milton E. Lord, who was supported by the *Boston Herald*. Lord was quoted: "It is essential that information in all aspects of the political, international and other questions be available for information purposes in order that citizens of Boston be informed about the friends and enemies of their country." Supporters of the *Post* included the American Legion and the Veterans of Foreign Wars; joining the *Herald* were the *Pilot*, a Catholic diocesan paper, and the *Christian Science Monitor*. On October 3, the Boston Public Library board voted 3-2 to maintain its collection of Communist materials.

The idea of "branding" books emerged in San Antonio, Texas, in 1953. Mayor Jack White suggested to the city council that it "consider branding all Communist-written volumes in the library," that is, books whose authors had been accused of affiliation with subversive organizations. The organizer of the San Antonio Minute Women, Myrtle Hance, provided a list of 600 titles by authors whose names had been gleaned from congressional investigation testimony. After the 15-member library board protested vehemently and the public's negative reaction to the proposal emerged, the branding idea was dropped.

During 1953, international repercussions resulted from the national debate. Senator McCarthy attacked the overseas libraries of the International Information Administration (IIA), claiming that there were some "30,000 volumes subversive of American interests" by 418 authors whose loyalty to the United States was suspect. The purpose of the libraries in the postwar period was to provide a balanced view of the opinion and thinking of the United States, to provide books that were nonpolitical in nature to accurately portray the American scene—without regard to the politics of the authors. The idea was to demonstrate the free marketplace of ideas to contrast and combat, in Germany, for example, the intellectual stagnation of the Nazi period. However, in practice during this period, according to David Oshinsky, "The rule of thumb, then, was to include 'controversial' books while excluding blatantly pro-communist or anti-American propaganda." The State Department, under its secretary, John Foster Dulles, reacted to McCarthy's attack by directing, with some confusion, the removal of all books by controversial authors—"communists, fellow-travelers, leftists, et cetera"—and books critical of U.S. policies. Even books without any political content were barred, including, for instance, the mysteries of Dashiell Hammett. In Australia and Singapore, the overseas library staffs actually burned books.

In his address to the graduating class of Dartmouth College on June 14, 1953, President Dwight D. Eisenhower spoke out against censorship: "Don't join the book-burners." He defended reading Marx and others as a way of maintaining awareness of the world crisis and the purposes of the Soviets; he defended the retention of "merely controversial" books in American libraries and overseas. However, at a subsequent press conference he objected to books advocating the overthrow of the United States and agreed to the elimination of books written by Communists, while recommending books written by anticommunists about communism.

Censorship on the international scene had been prevalent. In the 19th century, from 1882 to 1900, the Russian Federation banned the *Manifesto of the Communist Party* for political reasons. In 1878 in Prussia, Bismarck persuaded the Reichstag to prohibit the literature of the Social Democrats, including the *Manifesto.* Anne Haight identifies the attempts of the Nationalist Government of China in 1929 to stop the reading of the *Manifesto* and DAS KAPITAL. Marx's works were among the 25,000 volumes publicly burned in Berlin, Germany, in 1933 in a large-scale "symbolic" bonfire demonstration. The destruction of books by the Nazis continued until World War II: In Austria, Vienna (1938) and Salzburg were notable sites; in Czechoslovakia, the education minister ordered all "unpatriotic" books, particularly by patriots, to be removed from public libraries and destroyed.

The entry "Marx, Karl" in *The Encyclopedia of Censorship* summarizes: "It is impossible to itemize every country in which Marxist works are prohibited, nor do such countries remain consistent in their bans, but it may be generally assumed that those governments pursuing right-wing totalitarianism or dictatorial policies are keen to ban the founder of communism." Germany suppressed the *Manifesto* in all occupied countries, as well as allied countries from 1940 to 1945: Denmark, Norway, France, Luxembourg, Belgium, the Netherlands, Lithuania, Latvia, Estonia, Belarus, Poland, Yugoslavia, and Greece. In this vein, a 1950 survey reported in the *New York Times* listed 16 countries as having outlawed the Communist Party, "legally or otherwise, and have taken steps in that direction." The list included Greece, Turkey, Lebanon, Syria, Korea, Burma, Indonesia, Indo-China, Malaya, Portugal, Spain, Peru, Bolivia, Chile, Brazil, and Venezuela. Other nations that then were considering such action included South Africa, Australia, Egypt, and Denmark.

In 1946, the coordinating council of the American military government in Germany ordered the destruction of Nazi memorials in order to eliminate the "spirit of German militarism and Nazism as far as possible." Darkly ironic, the "placement of books by Hitler, Goebbels, Mussolini and Karl Marx on restricted lists in libraries, or in some instances pulped," was ordered on the 11th anniversary of the Nazi book-burning demonstration.

On two occasions, October 18, 1988, and March 8, 1989, customs officials in Grenada confiscated boxes of books being shipped by Pathfinder Press, a publisher of political, historical, and academic books based in New York. The *Manifesto of the Communist Party* was one of the confiscated books. (See the censorship history of ONE PEOPLE, ONE DESTINY: THE CARIBBEAN AND CENTRAL AMERICA TODAY by Don Rojas for details of this situation.) Other notable books then banned included THE STATE AND REVOLUTION by V. I. Lenin, THE STRUGGLE IS MY LIFE by Nelson Mandela, *Maurice Bishop Speaks: The Grenada Revolution 1979–83* by Maurice Bishop, *Malcolm X Speaks* by Malcolm X, and *Nothing Can Stop the Course of History: An Interview with Fidel Castro* by Congressman Mervyn Dymally and Jeffrey M. Elliott.

FURTHER READING

"Book Burning." *New Republic* 128 (June 29, 1953): 7–17.

"Branding of Books Stirs Texas Battle." *New York Times,* June 7, 1953, p. 61.

Cook, Fred J. *The Nightmare Decade: The Life and Times of Senator Joe McCarthy.* New York: Random House, 1971.

Crankshaw, Edward. *Bismarck.* New York: Viking Press, 1981.

Crosby, Donald F. *God, Church, and the Flag: Senator Joseph R. McCarthy and the Catholic Church, 1950–1957.* Chapel Hill: University of North Carolina Press, 1978.

"Firefighting." *New Republic* 129 (September 7, 1953): 5.

Green, Jonathon, and Nicholas J. Karolides, reviser. *The Encyclopedia of Censorship, New Edition.* New York: Facts On File, 2005.

Haight, Anne Lyon, and Chandler B. Grannis. *Banned Books 387 B.C. to 1978 A.D.* 4th ed. New York: R. R. Bowker, 1978.

Importation of Publications (Prohibition) Order. Grenada. Statutory Rules and Orders No. 6 of 1989. Gazetted April 14, 1989.

Inter-American Commission on Human Rights. Report No. 2/96, Case 10, 325 Grenada. Washington, D.C.: Organization of American States, March 1, 1996.

Kipp, Lawrence J. "Report from Boston." *Library Journal* 77 (1952): 1,843–1,846, 1,887.
Oshinsky, David M. *A Conspiracy So Immense: The World of Joe McCarthy.* New York: Free Press, 1983.
Pathfinder Press Releases. New York: October 19, 1988; March 10, April 5, and April 27, 1989.
"Poll of Libraries Shows Free Choice." *New York Times,* June 16, 1953, p. 22.
"St. George's, Grenada." *Newsletter on Intellectual Freedom* 38 (1989): 141–142.
"16 Countries Outlaw Reds, Survey Shows." *New York Times,* May 16, 1950, p. 20.

MARXISM VERSUS SOCIALISM

Author: Vladimir G. Simkhovitch
Original date and place of publication: 1913, United States
Publisher: Columbia University Press
Literary form: Nonfiction

SUMMARY

Marxism, one of history's most controversial economic theories since its inception in 1848, remains important today. Writing in 1913, Simkhovitch discusses not only the merits and faults of marxism, but also why it became so important. He also differentiates it from socialism, a term many incorrectly assume is synonymous with marxism.

Simkhovitch first criticizes the critics who have attempted to devalue marxist economics by using emotion instead of reason. Unlike these critics, he has great respect for the theory and believes it is an important part of any economic student's education. He believes, however, it will never work in practice and disproves each segment of the theory, based on the information available to him at the time.

First he distinguishes marxism from previous theories of socialism. Simkhovitch is careful to point out that "all pre-Marxian socialism was distinctly ethical; every peroration against capitalism contained or implied an appeal for social justice." However, "whatever the faults and merits of Marx's theory of value may be, it was not intended as an ethical basis for socialism."

Simkhovitch next examines the individual theories of marxism. Whereas many economic theorists before Karl Marx brought up the possibility of social revolution caused by industrialization, Marx's concentration of production theory considered social revolution unavoidable. As the small producers are squeezed out of competition by new, centralized industries, the proletariat class grows until revolution is the only option. This is the center of Marx's economic theories and most necessary for the socialists who accepted his theories. In order for socialism to be possible, capitalism must centralize and the people must take it away. Simkhovitch, though, says centralization is not occurring. Trusts, combinations of firms or corporations, have developed and yet have not hindered free competition because each one is so different from the next that the only real change has been steadier maintenance of prices.

In agriculture, Marxian theory sees small farmers as the equivalent of small producers. They will be forced out by centralization and will join the displeased masses. As Simkhovitch points out, however, despite the passage of initiatives by the German Socialist government in the 1890s meant to protect the peasants' interests and win them over to socialism, they still ardently opposed Marx's theories. The reforms attempted by Germany are just the difference between socialism and Marxism to which Simkhovitch had earlier alluded: While the Socialists feel sorry for the peasants and want to help them, the marxists feel it is economically necessary for the class to fall. Simkhovitch also says that statistics from the German census of 1895 and from other countries, including the United States, showed that, when compared to 1882, there was in fact a rise in peasants, not a decrease, disproving the doctrine of concentration of agriculture and another part of Marx's theory, for "if certain conditions and tendencies make socialism inevitable, do not the absence of these conditions and the existence of contrary tendencies make socialism impossible?"

Marx believed the entire middle class would disappear, sinking into the working class or proletariat. While the workers of the past were apprenticed and had hopes of someday gaining control themselves, the factory workers of his day would never gain such control. Simkhovitch says that Marx idealized the past because few journeymen and apprentices ever did gain control, for they were continually blocked by guild masters. Marx also said small-scale capitalists would be killed off by the bigger capitalists. Using statistics from Germany, Simkhovitch proves there is not a mass of people sinking into the lower classes, but that the number of wealthy people is increasing. He attributes the problem in Marx's theory to the emergence of a new kind of company that sells stock to gain capital, thus allowing the masses to share some of the wealth. This "army of stockholders" has prevented the demise of the middle class and the decentralization of wealth.

Marx's theory of increasing misery proposes that as the masses become proletariats, their living conditions worsen until revolution is necessary for survival. Marx rejected previous theories that said that wages would increase with the cost of living. Were this true, there would be no real need for revolt. A wage that remains the same while cost of living increases, however, causes suffering and eventually rebellion. Marx said that not only did wages not rise with the cost of living, they actually decreased. Simkhovitch agrees that this did, in fact, happen at the beginning of the 19th century, due to belief in the wage-fund theory: An increase in the number of workers causes more division of money, and thus lower wages; the suffering caused by lowered wages prompts a decrease in the population and a rise in wages. The theory was held for so long because economists and governments preferred to write off the human suffering as a natural tendency of economics rather than blame themselves and believed any person calling for a reform of labor laws or for trade unions was challenging the laws of God.

Marx felt this suffering was a necessary component of revolution and also did not support any type of labor reform. However, while Marx agreed with the necessity of suffering, he thought it was produced by the concentration of industry and the production of new and better machinery, which made many workers obsolete, thus creating a surplus labor force. The eventual passage of labor laws and the creation of labor unions caused the demise of Marx's theory, which was dependent upon a laissez-faire system. Simkhovitch also shows the statistics of the day, which clearly reveal improvement in the standards of living in Germany between 1885 and 1895 and a decrease in the death and suicide rates, thus effectively disproving the theory of increasing misery. Statistics show similar growth in England and America.

Simkhovitch, while refuting the Marxian doctrine of class struggle, shows a fundamental respect for it.

> Marx's scientific forecasts are but class yearnings. His doctrine of class struggle has the same quality: it is a doctrine exaggerated and intensified by his class bias, by his hatred of the past, by his hope for the future. Here his passions come to a focus, here his raptures are too exultant to bother about conventionalities of objectivity, to care about outward consistency. Here he failed, but failed magnificently. The failures of the great often surpass the achievements of mediocrity. Marx's doctrine, with all its bias and all its faults, marks a signal advancement of our science.

Marx believed that, while past societies had several classes, society would begin to move toward only two—bourgeoisie and proletariat. The latter is incapable of raising its social status except through revolution. When this occurs, all class lines will be broken down and there will be no more class struggle. Marx's economic interpretation of history said that the seizure of power by the working class was inevitable in light of all previous class struggles. In 1850, however, he believed this seizure would occur soon, but it still had not happened by the time Simkhovitch was writing. Simkhovitch sees many problems with the doctrine. First, he says, while class struggle is an important part of history, history cannot be reduced to nothing but class struggles. Many important historical events are outside the realm of class, such as the invention of the printing press. Also, for most of history, there was in fact no struggle, but rather a lack of it, evident in an entire nation bowing to a king, unable and unwilling to struggle against him. Second, there is no proof of the move toward only two classes. Third, a large portion of the actual proletariat class cannot be relied upon to join the revolt, but rather will most assuredly fight against it, if properly paid by the bourgeoisie. Fourth, the development of a democratic form of government lessens the intensity of class struggles, as disputes are decided by ballot rather than by sword. While disenfranchised classes will fight for their right to vote, once they have it, fighting generally ceases. Democracy also promotes a feeling of patriotism, which goes directly against the class consciousness necessary for revolution. So, this class struggle does not appear to have the force necessary for a revolution, nor does it appear to be increasing in intensity.

By disproving all of Marx's theories individually and statistically, Simkhovitch demonstrates rationality over emotionalism and the invalidity of Marx's theories. Three years after publication of this book, however, Marx's theories would begin to come into play in Russia because of the increasing misery caused by World War I.

CENSORSHIP HISTORY

This book contains what was thought by many in the emerging Communist regime of Russia to be dangerous materials. Bertrand Russell in his book *The Practice and Theory of Bolshevism* says that "the materialistic conception of history, as it is called, is due to Marx and underlies the whole Communist philosophy." Since this book explained why Marxism, which is the foundation of Bolshevik thought, would never work in practice, the Bolsheviks decided it would be in their best interests to make sure no one read it. Therefore, the book, along with thousands of others, was burned during the period of the Bolshevik revolution in 1917.

The evolution of Bolshevism is long and involved, but must be touched on for an understanding of the theory. Before the revolution, Russia was ruled by the autonomous czar Nicholas II. Although there was a legislative body, the Duma, it was made up of upper-class landowners and served largely to carry out the wishes of the monarch. The outbreak of World War I in 1914 caused extreme tension in the country, due to an ever-decreasing amount of resources. The people became increasingly displeased with the monarchy, and even certain members of the Duma, known as the Progressive Bloc, wanted to institute political reforms, including releasing political prisoners and allowing democratically governed towns. Nicholas refused to allow such undermining of his authority and dismissed all those who supported the changes. The sentiments behind the desired changes, however, could not be so easily dismissed, and unrest continued to build in the country. A general shortage of food and other supplies caused by the war brought about a series of strikes starting in the summer of 1915. By February of 1917, the workers in the cities were banding together and calling for an end to the monarchy. The refusal of the Cossacks, the peace-keeping organization, to disband the insurrectionists led to the overthrow of the czar and the Duma.

Nicholas abdicated the throne, and a new provisional government was formed until the Constituent Assembly, a democratic parliament, could be established. The Mensheviks, a moderate socialist group made up of the middle class, or bourgeoisie, held the majority of the seats in the provisional government. The Bolsheviks, a more radically socialistic group working under the guidance of Lenin, represented the working and peasant classes. As Russell says, "The chief thing that the Bolsheviks have done is to create a hope, or at any rate to make strong and widespread a hope which was formerly confined to few." They brought to the lower classes a feeling that their lives could become better, and they would no longer have to be ruled by anyone except themselves.

The Mensheviks wanted a continuation of capitalism, which would eventually and naturally become socialism. The Bolsheviks, however, favored the immediate formation of a socialist state. Knowing that with the support of the working and peasant classes the Bolsheviks would gain a majority of the seats in the Constituent Assembly, the Mensheviks closed down two newspapers run by the Bolsheviks. The Bolsheviks responded with a nearly bloodless revolution and an overthrow of the provisional government. Thus, they brought an end to the incipient democracy of the provisional government and the beginning of communism.

Anne Haight notes that the Russian translation of *Marxism Versus Socialism* was burned at the "outbreak of the revolution." Although Marxist theory was warped by Lenin because he put power in the hands of a ruling elite instead of the general population (see summary of TODAY's ISMS: COMMUNISM, FASCISM, CAPITALISM, SOCIALISM for full explanation), the entire existence of communism was centered, at least in theory, on Marxist philosophy. Simkhovitch's disproval of the theory was thus unacceptable.

FURTHER READING

Carmichael, Joel. *A Short History of the Russian Revolution.* New York: Basic Books, 1964.
Haight, Anne Lyon, and Chandler B. Grannis. *Banned Books, 387 B.C. to 1978 A.D.* 4th ed. New York: R. R. Bowker, 1978.
Mel'gunov, S. P. *The Bolshevik Seizure of Power.* Santa Barbara, Calif.: ABC-CLIO, 1972.
Russell, Bertrand. *The Practice and Theory of Bolshevism.* New York: Simon and Schuster, 1964.

—Jane Graves

MEIN KAMPF

Author: Adolf Hitler
Original dates and places of publication: 1925, Germany; 1933, United States
Original publishers: Eher Verlag; Houghton Mifflin
Literary form: Biography

SUMMARY

Tormented and impoverished as a youth, optimistic yet often disappointed as an adolescent, determined and ultimately revered as a young man, Adolf

Hitler's life echoes his work's title, which translates as *My Struggle*. In spite of the victories attained while rising to power and during his reign as führer, he met many failures; his success can be attributed to sheer determination and will to see a "dream" fulfilled, even though for most it was and will always be a nightmare.

Hitler was born in 1889 on Easter Sunday in Braunau, a small Austrian border town on the Inn River that was highly concentrated with people of German heritage. Depending on whose viewpoint one believes, Hitler's childhood was either an exercise in the development of discipline or pure hell. Charles B. Flood, author of *Hitler: The Path to Power*, paints a macabre beginning for the man who would one day rule the German empire. Alois Hitler, Adolf's father, was labeled "a small-town Henry VIII" for his exploits with women. Before Adolf he produced two children by two different women. The first was a widow who bore him a daughter. They would marry and be together for seven years until she filed for separation because Alois had moved on to a 19-year-old kitchen maid in the hotel where they were living. After his estranged first wife died, he and the kitchen maid had a son, Alois Jr. They married, but she too died, which allowed Alois to marry Klara Polzl, the children's nursemaid, 23 years younger than he. She was Adolf's mother. According to Alois Jr., Hitler's half brother, Alois Sr. would at times beat Junior unmercifully, and when Junior moved out at 14, the father's abusive behavior was shifted toward seven-year-old Adolf. Young Adolf bore many beatings by his father until one day he decided not to cry. After a total of 32 strikes with a stick, his father ceased, never to beat him again. This example of childhood misery, which some say worked to forge the mind of Hitler, goes unmentioned in the opening pages of *Mein Kampf*, due to the fact that, according to Otto D. Tolischus, reviewer for the *New York Times Magazine*, one of Hitler's primary goals was that the book be a tool of propaganda, not a solely biographical depiction highlighting, among other topics, his imperfect upbringing. This would explain Hitler's view of his father, which is very different from the account given by Flood. *Mein Kampf* has Hitler revering his father as "a gentleman . . . whose most ardent desire had been to help his son forge his career, thus preserving him from his own bitter experience (which had been growing up poor and without direction)." After his mother passed away, when Adolf was 18, his father having died when he was 13, Adolf said that "I honored my father, but my mother I had loved."

Mein Kampf is a work consisting of two volumes. The first, "A Reckoning," describes the period of Hitler's life when his thoughts on politics and the German Fatherland were combined to form his tenet of National Socialism; the second, "The National Socialist Movement," expands many of the ideas presented in the first volume. Those ideas stemmed from feelings and experiences of a young ambitious Hitler trying to forge a way of life for himself other than his father's suggestion of becoming a civil servant. Hitler's first love was art, which was squelched by his nonacceptance into the academy (few thought as highly of Hitler's work as he). As a result, he turned his attention to architecture, but because of his intolerance for study at the Realschule, this also became an unfulfilled dream.

As his misfortune grew, he began making connections with other Austrian Germans, noting many shortcomings that he and they shared. He sensed a lack of pride toward the German heritage, not only from other Germans, but also from all with whom he came into contact, as though somehow Germans were second-rate. He felt misplaced along with many other Austrian Germans, as if they were removed from a righteous existence. He saw the prevalence of Social Democrats in positions of power, positions that undermined the dignity of the working class, keeping the masses in line, obedient, and helplessly stuck in positions of servitude.

Hitler learned to despise Jews because, in his viewpoint, they were the Social Democrats who made life miserable for Hitler and other Austrian Germans in the working class. Slowly, he began to notice that the most prominent members of the Social Democratic movement, the authors of the press, those who protested against restraints upon business, and those against whom he argued about the policies of marxism, the tool he directly related to Social Democracy, were all Jews. His greatest revelation in all of this was that these people were not of the Austrian nation or the German nation, but were foreigners who had come to take total control. They had no nation really. Even if a Jew had been born in Austria or Germany and was a citizen of either country, it made no difference to Hitler. His goal and the goal of all Germans would be to fight against the people whose purpose, according to Hitler, was the defilement of all humanity and destruction of all established cultures and nations. He reasoned that if the German nation was preserved and advanced by self-propagation, then that was upholding the work of nature and performing the will of God: "By defending myself against the Jew, I am fighting for the work of the Lord."

Not only did his experience in Vienna further sour his feelings toward Jews and marxism, he also saw other inadequacies that shifted him into a career in politics where his involvement with the National Socialist movement blossomed. In Austria, Hitler viewed parliament as a self-serving system that totally neglected the working masses. If a problem or need arose that could not be remedied by the governing body, there seemed to be no blame placed upon anyone from within. Hitler could not recognize good government in a bureaucracy that did nothing but advance its own idleness and satisfaction of the status quo. Hitler was further infuriated with how the parliament continued to maintain power by lulling the people into a status-quo satisfaction which, especially before times of election, seemed to ice any chance of change or revolution, which he desperately desired.

Upon his arrival in Austria in 1904, Hitler became involved in the Pan-Germanic movement. He idolized Georg von Schonerer and Dr. Karl Lueger, who both worked to save the German people from ruin and to destroy the Austrian state. However, the movement ultimately failed. According to Hitler, the movement lost all momentum because 1) the social problem had an unclear conception, 2) the tactics of trying to win support from within parliament had failed, and 3) the public lacked the will to see the revolution take place. Each of these elements brought the movement to a standstill. However, these elements would not be forgotten by Hitler, who saw each as direct opposition to what must happen in order for all German people to one day be reunited and prosper over all of Europe and ultimately the world.

Hitler returned to Munich shortly before the outbreak of World War I, which he called the happiest time in his life. He immediately requested in writing to be enlisted, and was given permission via King Ludwig III to don the tunic of the Bavarian regiment, in which he served for six years. This experience led Hitler to another key discovery in terms of his personal philosophy. Throughout the war Hitler noticed that propaganda was a tool keenly utilized by the enemy, who portrayed the Germans as fierce, bloodthirsty fighting machines—but not by his own government. He claimed this as one of the factors that led to Germany's hard loss. He saw propaganda, when properly utilized, as one of the most effective tools of war, a means by which the masses are uniformly persuaded: simple, true in essence, and proven in methodology and message. He stored what he learned from this failure for certain future use.

Because the fall of the Reich happened so quickly, the defeat was recognized and immediately put aside, which according to Hitler provided more time for the rebuilding mentality to rapidly set in and grow. Building upon the earlier aims of the failed pan-Germanic movement from his time in Austria, Hitler's focus became the full development of National Socialism, rallying a lost nation around the concept of strength through a united Germany. Within this goal was the operating premise that only those of pure German heritage were worthy of citizenry; all others were deemed expendable for the good of the nation.

Any crossing between two beings of not quite the same high standard produces a medium between the standards of the parents. That means: the young one will probably be on a higher level than the racially lower parent, but not as high as the higher one . . . if it were different, every further development towards higher levels would stop, and rather the contrary would happen . . . just as little as Nature desires a mating between weaker individuals and stronger ones, far less she desires the mixing of a higher race with a lower one, as in this case her entire work of higher breeding, which has perhaps taken hundreds of thousands of years, would tumble at one blow . . . The result of any crossing, in brief, is always the following: (a) Lowering of the standard of the higher race; (b) Physical and mental regression, and, with it, the beginning of a slowly but steadily progressive lingering illness. To bring about such a development means nothing less than sinning against the will of the Eternal Creator.

In Germany, *Mein Kampf* was responsible for the banishment of the Bible. In 1942, Dr. Alfred Rosenberg, a key supporter of the "new national church," released a 30-point doctrine of the National Reich Church, which outlined the plan for all churches to be transformed into instruments of the state and for Christianity to be systematically eliminated from all facets of religious existence. Seven of the 30 points specifically refer to the banishment of the Bible, which is to be subsequently replaced by *Mein Kampf*:

13) The National Reich Church demands the immediate cessation of the printing of the Bible, as well as its dissemination, throughout the Reich and colonies. All Sunday papers with any religious content also shall be suppressed.

14) The National Reich Church shall see that the importation of the Bible and other religious works into Reich territory is made impossible.

15) The National Reich Church decrees that the most important document of all time—therefore the guiding document of the German people—is the book of our Fuehrer [sic], *Mein Kampf*. It recognizes that this book contains the principles of the purist ethnic morals under which the German people must live.

16) The National Reich Church will see to it that this book spread its active forces among the entire population and that all Germans live by it.

17) The National Reich Church stipulates that the future editions of *Mein Kampf* shall contain its present number of pages and contents unmodified.

18) The National Reich Church will remove from the altars of all churches the Bible, the cross and religious objects.

19) In their place will be set that which must be venerated by the German people and therefore is by God, our most saintly book, *Mein Kampf*, and to the left of this a sword.

Hitler's observations in youth came to represent the foundations of Nazi Germany. To him the Aryan, Hitler's master race, was the strong, powerful, and culturally creative prototype of an ideal human being, the building block for humanity that reverberated the philosophy of the National Socialist Party. Diversity among races was a liability, not an asset; one race must rise above all others and claim absolute control. Only when Germans stood alone as the elite rulers of the world would his vision be complete. Until then, Hitler would use any tactic and force to attain that position.

The years leading up to World War II saw the most intense scrutiny of *Mein Kampf*, due to the fact that much of the world by now was certain that the text was a blueprint for Hitler's plan of world domination. Otto D. Tolischus, reporting for the *New York Times Magazine*, stated, "In content *Mein Kampf* is ten percent autobiography, ninety percent dogma, and one hundred percent propaganda. Every word in it . . . has been included . . . solely for the propagandist effect. Judged by its success, it is the propagandistic masterpiece of the age." The "masterpiece" also contains representations of Hitler's values: He recognized the futility of a government that was too large to uphold accountability and solve problems effectively; he identified one downfall of education as information taught yet never utilized while he promoted the Greek ideal of a balance between the development of mind and body as one; and he identified merit and strength in a nation bound by patriotism and the will to succeed.

CENSORSHIP HISTORY

Mein Kampf had many challenges from the time of its publication to the height of World War II and, again, in the 1990s. In *The Encyclopedia of Censorship, Mein Kampf* is identified as one of the "most often" censored books. But perhaps the most documented history comes courtesy of James and Patience Barnes's text, *Hitler's Mein Kampf in Britain and America,* which highlights not only the publication wars in the United States, but also key censorship cases that both directly and indirectly were brought on by *Mein Kampf.*

The first U.S. publication in this country was in 1933 by Houghton Mifflin in Boston; that version was published in London the same year by Hurst and Blackett. The titles were, respectively, *My Battle* and *My Struggle.* The translator for the text was Edgar T. S. Dugdale. The translation had a complicated history: In 1928 Curtis Brown Limited was given the translation rights from Eher Verlag, the German publisher. However, Cherry Kearton, a former Curtis Brown employee who shifted over to work for rival Hurst and Blackett, had left the text when he transferred companies, figuring that nothing would ever come of Hitler. When Hitler's chancellorship was announced, Kearton tried to obtain the copy of the text in hopes of beating out his former firm with the publication. However, Curtis Brown now demanded a hefty sum for just the untranslated text, a move that made the decision to purchase it more difficult. That was when Dugdale stepped in and offered his translated abridged version to Kearton and Hurst and Blackett gratis. They accepted and went ahead with publication.

The Dugdale abridgment had been approved by Eher Verlag, but further expurgation of the text was accomplished by the Nazi government before the approval was granted. (According to Barnes and Barnes, "during the 1930s it was generally assumed, officially and unofficially, that Hitler would not authorize a full translation of his autobiography.") Some of the most blatant features, thus, were censored in the expurgated text by the Nazi government in addition to omissions at the hands of the translator. These included Hitler's tirades to details of German and Austrian politics and Hitler's reactions to them, much of Hitler's discussion of Austria-Hungary in chapters 1–4, Hitler's anti-Semitic theme of race pollution (though there remained many anti-Jew sentiments, including semi-obscene allegations), the Aryan race as the bearer or perpetuator of higher culture, Hitler's detailed pseudoscientific views about population growth, the impact of syphilis on modern society, and menacing passages about France. The complete translated text was issued in 1939, one published in London and two competing versions in the United States. The latter competition was resolved in favor of Houghton Mifflin by the U.S. Circuit Court of Appeals for the Second Circuit in October 1939.

The reactions to *Mein Kampf* in Britain and the United States varied. The British populace, facing a significant potential threat, did not respond with censorial protests. In the United States, within a month of Houghton Mifflin's contracting with Hitler's German publisher, groups and individuals organized protests in an effort to suppress the book's publication. In August 1933, the *American Hebrew and Jewish Tribune* attacked the publisher: "We charge these publishers with an attempt to cash in on the misery and catastrophe of an important segment of the human family." The *New York Times* on August 18, 1933, included a quote from an *American Hebrew and Jewish Tribune* editorial: "that if Houghton Mifflin Company is bent on publishing Hitler's book 'they would do well to print the text in red, as symbolic of the blood that has dripped from Nazi bludgeons in the Third Reich. . . .' " David Brown, publisher of the Jewish periodical, stated, "we protest emphatically against the publication, sale and distribution of the English translation of Hitler's *Mein Kampf* in the United States."

Letters from Jews were written to Houghton Mifflin "by the hundreds," to President Roosevelt, urging his intervention, and to publishers such as the *Chicago Israelite*. One stated: "It is the utterance of venomous untruths about a large law-abiding peoples and I was wondering if there was not some way to stop publication of this book." A group of New York City residents petitioned the board of education to discontinue purchasing books from Houghton Mifflin: "an American firm that knowingly lends its assistance in spreading the lying propaganda of a common gangster—propaganda that strikes at the very foundations of American institutions—should have no right to participate in the distribution of taxpayers' money." In rebuttal, Edward Mandel, associate superintendent of education, asserted that the text must be placed so all "may see whether the book is worthy or is an exhibition of ignorance, stupidity, and dullness." The American Jewish Committee acted to counteract the effect of *Mein Kampf* by issuing a translation of a collection of excerpts from the original German text that had not been included in the abridged volume: "The diluted and bowdlerized version of the book as issued did not represent either the views or the temperament of its author."

In response to the public outcry, Roger L. Scaife, an officer with Houghton Mifflin, stated:

> In confidence I may add that we have had no end of trouble over the book—protest from the Jews by the hundreds, and not all of them from the common run of shad. Such prominent citizens as Louis Kirstein and Samuel Untermeyer and others have added their protest, although I am glad to say

that a number of intellectual Jews have also written complimenting us upon the stand we have taken.

The prepublication challenges did not succeed.

As domestic complaints were high in number, so, too, did the banning of *Mein Kampf* begin to happen more frequently on a global level. Three incidents occurred in the latter part of 1933. The first occurred in Prague, Czechoslovakia, on September 18, when Hitler's book was banned from sale or circulation because of its fierce militaristic doctrine, along with two other Austrian monarchist books of propaganda. The government was targeting not only Hitler, but also a number of other National Socialist publications.

The second incident happened not a week later in Munich, Germany, where it was reported that the one millionth copy of the book had been put into circulation. Part of that article stated that Hitler's response to the apparent crushing of the National Socialist movement at the time he was thrown into Landsberg prison for his involvement in the famous "putsch" of 1923 was, "Give me five years after I am out of this and I shall have the party restored."

The third event occurred on October 1, 1933, when the court at Katowice in Warsaw, Poland, banned Hitler's book for being "insulting." German booksellers had previously protested a court-ordered confiscation of the work, but the court upheld its prior decision. Hitler's response to the ban was that the Poles had not been sufficiently Germanized before the world war.

Three years later, and on the eve of World War II, the Soviets began to increase their armaments significantly, fearing that an attack from Germany was imminent. Premier Vyacheslav M. Molotov, speaking before the Congress of the Central Executive Committee, stressed that "Hitler, in *Mein Kampf*, states it is necessary for Germany to acquire new territory, and he points to Russia and the Baltic Region"; therefore, he urged that it was essential to make marked increases in the military budget. Whether the book was ever banned by the Soviets is not identified.

The sale of *Mein Kampf* was also prohibited in Austria until July 12, 1937. On that date Austria and Germany signed a "press truce," which permitted the sale of the autobiography under the condition that it could not be used for propaganda purposes.

In the post–World War II period the most recent translation of *Mein Kampf*, by Ralph Manheim, was readily available in the United States. A new edition was not available in Great Britain until 1965, although the American edition could be imported. In Germany there was a total ban of the auto-biography, which was initially suppressed by American de-Nazification efforts but then continued by the Federal Republic (West Germany) for reasons of national self-interest. Indeed, the Bavarian state government as executor of all surviving Nazi property, sought to prohibit the sale of the book throughout the world. In this regard, in the 1960s, when the Hutchinson Publishing Group, the British copyright holder, decided to reissue a British edition, its chairman encountered resistance from the West German government, the Board of Deputies of British Jews, and most Jewish organizations on the grounds that *Mein Kampf* would promote anti-Semitism and play into the hands of postwar fascist organizations. Opposition was surmounted on legal grounds; it was published in 1969.

In the decade of the 1990s, and the first years of the millennium, the European scene has evidenced considerable state-censored activity, driven in part by hate speech legislation and concerns for human rights; the rise of neo-Nazi activity appears to be an additional catalyst. Under German law, books promoting Nazi philosophy are banned from public display or sale, *Mein Kampf* having been barred for close to 60 years. The state of Bavaria, which still owns the copyright, in agreement with the federal government of Germany, does not allow any copying or printing in German. (It opposes copying or printing in other countries, as well, but with less success.) Owning and buying the book is legal, as is trading in old copies, unless such activity promotes hatred or war. Most libraries in Germany hold excerpted versions with numerous comments. Unexpurgated editions are available only to academic researchers, the original being too contentious for open sale. The book has been available for purchase on the Internet; however, German authorities have urged Internet booksellers to cease this activity. In late 1999, both Barnes&Noble.com and amazon.com had agreed to stop selling *Mein Kampf* in Germany. Pressure had also been exerted on these companies by the Simon Wiesenthal Center in Los Angeles. In 2001, a German court decided not to prosecute Yahoo! Deutschland for offering a copy of *Mein Kampf* in an online auction, recognizing it was only a supplier of Internet services and not responsible for their content.

In the Czech Republic action was taken against a publisher and an Internet distributor. The government ordered police raids on bookstores to confiscate copies of new nonexpurgated editions—without annotations or Nazi disclaimers—of *Mein Kampf*, the first in more than 50 years, part of the publisher's Books That Changed the World project. Of the more than 100,000 copies of the book that were printed, 90,000 were sold before the confiscation raids. Protests by Jewish and German groups led to the government's decision; Czech criminal code bars the dissemination of "national, racial, social or religious hatred or publicly expressing sympathy for fascism or other similar movement." Charged with disseminating Nazi propaganda—the book was alleged to promote hate groups and racism—the publisher, Michael Zitko, was found guilty of promoting a movement that suppresses human rights by three successive courts. Upon appeal, however, the Czech Supreme Court in 2002 overturned these convictions, asserting that Zitko could not be prosecuted for promoting fascism or Nazism because these movements are extinct. In 2004, Zitko was reconvicted, this time for repressing human rights. Zitko vowed to appeal this decision to the Supreme Court and perhaps the European Court of Human Rights. Subsequently, the Czech supreme court overturned the conviction, ruling he had not aimed to propagate the book's racist ideas. In a parallel case, Vitko Varak, who offered *Mein Kampf* for sale on the Internet, was fined in 2001, having been convicted of supporting and spreading a movement aimed at repressing the rights and freedoms of others. Vitko refused to pay the fine.

Several other European countries, as well as Canada, have had new editions of *Mein Kampf* translated into their native languages. The sales of the autobiography have been generally high, amid protest from Jewish groups that have led to actions by authorities. In Hungary, retail sales were suspended in December 1996, followed by a 1997 ban, on the grounds of incitement of hatred against minorities and a violation of human rights. The suspension initiated a debate over protecting free speech versus limiting viewpoints some persons considered offensive. In 1999 it was still being sold by street and subway vendors, despite complaints by the Jewish community. Sales in Portugal were blocked in 1998 after intervention by the German embassy. The copyright issue was cited, Bavaria not having granted the right to distribute the book to the Portuguese publisher; 4,000 books had already been sold, a large number in Portugal. A 1997 ban on publication in Sweden was upheld by Sweden's Supreme Court in 1998 on the grounds it would infringe copyright. A 2000 edition of *Mein Kampf* had been banned in Bulgaria; however, a 2001 edition (200,000 print run) circumvented the ban and was being sold, despite protests. The situation in Canada had a different orientation. The CEO and chair of Chapters and Indigo bookstore, Heather Rusman, withdrew the copies of *Mein Kampf* from the shelves. Considering the autobiography "hate literature," she said: "With freedom of expression, the line is drawn on hate literature. It's a corporate decision. It's what we stand for." The banning seems to have had the effect of increasing sales of the book.

The Netherlands, however, has maintained the banning of *Mein Kampf.* As recently as November 2007, Hitler's memoir was reported to be the only book not fully available since the end of World War II. As the former basis of Nazi ideology, it is regarded as "inciting hatred of, amongst others, the Jews." Thus, it remains on the blacklist. The Dutch Minister of Education, Ronald Plasterk, wants to maintain this status; yet he acknowledged that making it available in bookstores would educate readers about the "horrifying events of World War II"; however, this personal attitude is not reason enough to make *Mein Kampf* fully available.

In the context of these contradictory positions, Geert Wilders, a member of Parliament and leader of the Freedom Party, argued that the Quran is "also a hate inciting book that ought to be banned . . . as encouraging violence against disaffected Muslims and also endorsing violence by Islamic extremists." This action would parallel the blacklisting of *Mein Kampf.*

In contrast, authorities in Poland decided in 1992 to lift the ban on printing *Mein Kampf,* its publication having been determined to be legal and not in violation of Communist-era laws against fascism. Before it was re-banned in 1992 on the grounds of "eulogizing Fascism," 20,000 copies had been sold out in days, in part a response to the protests against its publication. Comparably, in 1993, Romania's chief state attorney acted against President Ion Iliescu's request to ban the book on the ground that it spreads fascism, which is forbidden by the constitution. Sales had been barred in the city of Sibiu until prosecutors released the prohibition. In 2001, *Mein Kampf* was published legally in Bulgaria for the first time.

Today only one version of *Mein Kampf* is easily attainable in the United States. Copyrighted in 1971, published by Houghton Mifflin, and translated by Ralph Manheim, it represents the work of, as the translator labels Hitler, "a half-educated writer, without clear ideas, [who] generally feels that to say a thing only once is rather slight." He also states that Hitler's style attempts to come off as highly educated and cultured but is at best redundant and without an edge.

Controversy over the republication has ensued as a result of the proposal in 2005 of the Institute for Contemporary History, based in Munich, to publish an academic edition—authoritative, annotated with comprehensive footnotes—of *Mein Kampf*. The Bavarian state government, which took over the rights of the main Nazi publisher, Eher-Verlag, after World War II as part of the Allies' de-Nazification program, has rejected this proposed project. The copyright, however, runs out in 2015; the German copyright law provides that an author's work enters the public domain 70 years after his or her death.

The basis for the rejection by the Bavarian Finance Ministry, which controls the copyright, is to prevent the distribution of Nazi ideology and the belief that publication might promote right-wing extremism. In contrast, Horst Möler, director of the Institute for Contemporary History, argues that "an academic edition could break the peculiar myth which surrounds *Mein Kampf*." Such a publication is perceived as the "best defense against those who might want to use the book to advance racist or anti-Semitic agendas." Although many German Jews still oppose the reissuing of Hitler's memoir, in 2009 the general secretary of Germany's Central Council of Jews backed the proposal as a method of informing future generations of the evils of Nazism. The Bavarian Finance Ministry hopes to prevent publication beyond 2015 under laws against incitement of hatred. An interesting paradox: Courts might rule that forbidding publication after 2015 constitutes a breach of freedom of expression.

Hitler's memoir has been under a de facto publishing ban in Germany, but it is not actually banned. While possession is not illegal, resale of old copies is tightly regulated, essentially limited to research purposes.

FURTHER READING

Baetz, Juergen. "Historians Hope to Publish *Mein Kampf* in Germany." *Washington Post*, February 5, 2010.

Barnes, James J., and Patience P. Barnes. *Hitler's Mein Kampf in Britain and America: A Publishing History 1930–1939.* Cambridge: Cambridge University Press, 1980.

Cohen, Carl, ed. *Communism, Fascism, and Democracy.* 2nd ed. New York: Random House, 1972.

"Czechs Ban Hitler's Book." *New York Times,* September 19, 1933, p. 12.

Flood, Charles Bracelen. *Hitler: The Path to Power.* Boston: Houghton Mifflin, 1989.

Green, Jonathon, and Nicholas J. Karolides, reviser. *The Encyclopedia of Censorship, New Edition.* New York: Facts On File, 2005.

Haight, Anne Lyon, and Chandler B. Grannis. *Banned Books: 387 B.C. to 1978 A.D.* 4th ed. New York: R. R. Bowker, 1978.

"Hitler Book Is Banned as 'Insulting' in Poland." *New York Times,* October 1, 1933, sec. 4, p. 2.

"Millionth Copy of Book by Hitler Off the Press." *New York Times,* September 28, 1933, p. 16.

"Nazi State Church Plan Proposes to Oust Other Faiths and Ban Bible." *New York Times,* January 3, 1942, p. 1.

Newsletter on Intellectual Freedom. "Amsterdam, Netherlands" 56 (2007): 271; "Munich, Germany" 58 (2009): 155–156.

Paterson, Tony. "German Jews Want *Mein Kampf* Reprinted." *Independent,* 10 August 2009.

"Publisher Scored for Hitler's Book." *New York Times,* August 18, 1933, p. 16.

"Reich and Austria Reach Peace Truce." *New York Times,* July 13, 1937, p. 15.

Sabine, George H., and Thomas L. Thorson. *A History of Political Theory.* 4th ed. Hinsdale, Ill.: Dryden Press, 1973.

"Soviets to Increase All Arms, Fearing Reich and Japan." *New York Times,* January 11, 1936, p. 1.

Tolischus, Otto D. "The German Book of Destiny." *New York Times Magazine,* October 28, 1936, pp. 1–2, 23.

—Eric P. Schmidt
Updated by Nicholas J. Karolides

LES MISÉRABLES

Author: Victor Hugo
Original dates and places of publication: 1862, France and Belgium; 1862, United States
Original publishers: La Croix; Carleton
Literary form: Fiction

SUMMARY

The French word *misérables,* easily understood by English readers in a literal sense, translates more appropriately as "wretchedly poor." Hugo provides an assortment of *misérables* in this novel set primarily in the first quarter of the 19th century. The protagonist is Jean Valjean.

Just released from prison after 19 years of hard labor on the galleys—five for stealing a loaf of bread to feed his widowed sister's children, 14 more for several failed attempts to escape—Valjean steals six silver plates from the bishop Monseigneur Bienvenu. The ultra-humane bishop had taken him in when both innkeepers and citizens had rejected him because of his record. When Valjean is caught and brought before him to be accused, the bishop denies the theft, says they were a gift, and speaks these not-to-be-forgotten words:

> "Forget not, never forget that you have promised me to use this silver to become an honest man. . . . Jean Valjean, my brother: you belong no longer to evil, but to good. It is your soul that I am buying for you. I withdraw it from dark thoughts and from the spirit of perdition, and I give it to God."

The bishop is a saintly man as shown by his good deeds to the needy and weak and his self-effacement. However, it is revealed at the bedside of a dying former member of the revolutionary assembly that the bishop lacks a political consciousness and seems to have without thought favored the royalists. The confrontation between these two old men teaches the bishop a greater sense of equality. At the end of the political radical's life, the bishop kneels, asking for his blessing.

Valjean's life does turn. Having rescued two children from a burning building, he is accepted by a community. Under an assumed name, Monsieur Madeleine, he becomes a successful manufacturer based on his invention; he transfers his good fortune into jobs and beneficence for the community. He has become a humane man, a man of honor, living so for eight years.

Another of life's unfortunates is Fantine. Deserted by the father of her child, destitute and unable to find work, she leaves Paris for her own province. En route, she feels forced to leave her two-year-old daughter, Cosette, with an innkeeper's wife, Madame Thenardier. She pays for Cosette's board in advance and plans to come for her as soon as she has earned money. Fantine does not realize the Thenardiers are unscrupulous and mean; they demand more and more money, which they use for themselves. They treat Cosette "a little better than a dog, and a little worse than a cat." Nor does Fantine, living in the same community as M. Madeleine, fare well. Her life is a misery; she suffers. She is unable to retrieve her daughter though several years pass.

Enter another villain, Javert, a policeman, suspicious, cold, and cruel. When Fantine attacks a dandy who has been maliciously taunting her, Javert takes her into custody and, acting as judge and jury, sentences her to six months for "insulting a citizen." M. Madeleine intercedes and takes her under his care, determined to bring Cosette to her. Unfortunately, Fantine dies before he can accomplish this.

Javert recognizes Valjean and denounces him to the prefect over the matter of the stolen silver. But, coincidentally, a man arrested for stealing some cider apples is identified as Valjean. M. Madeleine hears of this from Javert and, initially fraught with indecision, makes the difficult choice. He puts his affairs in order, including a letter to his Paris banker, then honorably denounces himself to save the innocent man.

Valjean accomplishes his mission. Imprisoned, he escapes, is retaken, then dramatically escapes again. He rescues Cosette from the Thenardiers and brings her to Paris, where they live discreetly as father and daughter in a dismal tenement. Their safety is broken by Javert. A chase at night ensues, but Valjean and Cosette elude Javert and his police; eventually they find safe haven in a walled convent where they are rescued rather melodramatically by the gardener, a man whose life M. Madeleine/Valjean had once saved. Valjean takes on a new alias, Ultimas Fauchelevent, the name of the gardener's deceased brother. For five years they live thus in seclusion, Valjean as an assistant gardener, Cosette as a student.

At this juncture, Hugo inserts a long diversion from his plot to focus on this convent of the Perpetual Adoration, its origin, atmosphere, and key principles, as well as the "convent as an abstract idea." The atmosphere of this "gloomy and stern house" is conveyed as much by the nuns' daily rules (for example, they "never bathe or light fires; chastise themselves every Friday; observe the rule of silence; only speak during recreation, which is very short") as by their strict and severe dogma ranging from complete renunciation of the world, except the students, to acts of severe abasement for all the sins, iniquities, and crimes on earth. Each of them performs in turn what they call the "reparation." "For twelve consecutive hours, from four in the evening till four the next morning, the sister . . . remains on her knees, on the stone before the Holy Sacrament, with her hands clasped and a rope round her neck." Admitting the usefulness of the monastery and convent in the past, Hugo discounts the usefulness of these antiquated institutions in the present. He labels them "abodes of error and innocence, of lost paths and good intentions, of ignorance and piety, of torture and martyrdom." He asserts, "A convent is a contradiction, the aim is salvation, the means sacrifice, supreme egotism resulting in supreme self-denial." While Hugo believes that "One can no more pray too much than love too much," he clearly sees convents and monasteries as anathema to progress.

In Paris at the end of this period, living in the same tenement vacated by Valjean is a student, Marius de Pontmercy. He had become alienated from his grandfather and maiden aunt who had raised him, because he had dramatically come to love his deceased father, a former soldier/officer under Bonaparte. His grandfather had taught him to hate his father, primarily for political and class reasons. Marius's life is constrained, inside the edge of poverty; he sells his clothes for food. Good-hearted but innocent and a dreamer, he is connected with a group of idealistic students who preach revolution, but he initially prefers isolated walks. During these he chances upon Cosette and Valjean, again living in obscurity in Paris. Observing them day by day, Marius falls in love with Cosette and takes to following them. This alarms Fauchelevent/Valjean into secretly relocating. Marius becomes distraught.

At this juncture Marius becomes acquainted with his neighbors, none other than the Thenardiers (under an alias), who have lost their previous livelihood to bankruptcy and are now living on beggarly schemes. The parents and two young daughters live in slovenly misery; their even younger son, Govcoche, unwanted and unloved, is on the streets. Marius, peeping through a crack in the wall, witnesses the family's duplicity with a philanthropist, Fauchelevent/Valjean, and Cosette, and then Thenardier's attempt to defraud Valjean with the help of a den of cutthroat thieves. Javert, whom Marius had warned, arrives to terminate the attempted crime, but Valjean escapes during the melee without being seen. Marius, benumbed by these events, loses this opportunity to connect with his beloved.

The lovers are united, however. They pledge their love, meeting secretly evening after evening in the secluded garden. At first unsuspecting, Valjean becomes outraged after intercepting a note from Marius and determines to thwart the romance.

The explosion of a street insurrection against King Charles X, led by middle-class intellectuals and students and supported by "the people" who are suffering from hard times, interrupts Valjean's plan to leave Paris for London with Cosette. He goes to the barricades, knowing Marius is there, and witnesses the heroic, courageous, and selfless defiance of the revolutionaries, including the valiant, life-risking behavior of Marius. The revolutionaries are, however, overwhelmed.

Valjean, ever watchful, rescues Javert first, and then the unconscious Marius and escapes, carrying Marius across his shoulders, into the sewers of Paris. The journey through this dark, slimy labyrinth is arduous, torturous, and exhausting. At an exit he is accosted by Thenardier who, without recognizing him, requires a bribe to unlock the gate. Outside the exit he is stopped by Javert, who is tracking Thenardier, and taken into custody. However, Javert agrees to take Marius to his grandfather's home and to allow Valjean to go to his home. There, he uncharacteristically leaves him. Javert has at last been affected by Valjean's good deed but, in an emotional trauma, resulting from his dilemma between the pledge to duty and the payment of debt, he commits suicide. Valjean's escape is now permanent.

There is a happy-ever-after conclusion, though it is marred by near tragedy, reflecting the conscience of both Valjean and Marius, but relieved by Thenardier's further duplicity. Marius recovers from his wounds and is reconciled with his grandfather, who admits his errors. Valjean recognizes his paternal selfishness in at first attempting to separate the lovers and reunites Cosette with Marius; they marry and receive Valjean's (M. Madeleine's) fortune. Valjean privately admits his past to Marius, intending to permanently absent himself so as not to endanger Cosette's future. Marius, not aware that Valjean had been his savior and suspecting him of greater misdeeds—indeed robbery of M. Madeleine's fortune—coldly agrees. Cosette is deeply saddened by her father's strange removal at this time of her life's greatest bliss. Valjean himself suffers emotionally to the point of death.

Enter Thenardier: Intent on another scheme to defraud Marius of M. Madeleine's fortune, he reveals some data, some valid, some erroneous, which connect with and correct what Marius knows about Valjean. The whole truth is revealed. Cosette and Marius rush to Valjean's home, indeed to his deathbed, and make peace with him and themselves.

CENSORSHIP HISTORY

Censorship was not foreign to Victor Hugo. Authorities in France were antagonized by his depiction of royalty, specifically Louis XIII, in his drama *Marion de Lorme;* he is shown to be a "weak, superstitious and cruel prince." Performance was prohibited in 1829. In 1832, the performance of *Le Roi s'amuse* was prohibited after its first performance because of derogatory allusions to Louis-Philippe. Copies of *Napoléon le petit,* a satire written in 1852, a year after Hugo went into exile upon the coup d'état of Louis Napoléon, were seized by French police in 1853.

Les Misérables escaped seizure. In his biography of Hugo, Matthew Josephson writes: "Dealing as it did with events of thirty years before, the book was tolerated by the Imperial censorship. But some have said that the wide circulation of *Les Misérables* helped to pierce the political gloom of France."

All of his works were banned in Russia in 1850 by Nicholas I, who saw them as potentially subversive.

Hugo also had works listed in the Index librorum prohibitorum, or Roman Index, which was published, initially in 1559, by the Congregation of the Inquisition (or Holy Office) of the Roman Catholic Church. *Notre Dame de Paris* was listed in 1834; *Les Misérables* was listed in 1864 and remained there until 1959. Books were condemned for doctrinal reasons or for being anticlerical, that is for criticizing or seeming to criticize the papacy and the church, or for moral reasons.

In her chapter "The Librarian as a Censor, 1900–1908," Evelyn Geller discusses the ambivalence and tensions in values of librarians in the context of the Progressive movement, which was marked "by a curious blend of political liberalism and moral conservatism." In the context of the library, this became a tension found between freedom and censorship, the former representing a tolerance for the "rich and varied literature on social problems" and a standard of freedom, the latter expressing protectiveness of moral sensibilities. Distinctions were drawn between "immorality, which confused vice with virtue, from indecency." Literary merit complicated the issue. In this charged atmosphere of moral versus immoral decision making, *Les Misérables* was rejected in 1904 from a library by a Philadelphia school committee (with the single dissent of one woman) because it mentioned a *grisette* (a word associated with prostitution at the turn of the century). Corinne Bacon, a faculty member of the Albany Library School and future editor of the *H. W. Fiction Catalog,* scorned this ban as a mistaken overprotection of the young and of women, in particular. She distinguished immorality from coarseness. The latter, perhaps superficial and unpleasant, was acceptable; the former, which "confused our moral sense," was not.

When the right-wing forces of Carlos Castillo Armas (the Liberator) seized control of the government of Guatemala in 1954, Castillo Armas's subordinates undertook the burning of "subversive" books. These included *Les Misérables* along with the novels of Miguel Angel Asturias, including EL SEÑOR PRESIDENTE, STRONG WIND, and THE GREEN POPE.

FURTHER READING

Geller, Evelyn. *Forbidden Books in American Public Libraries, 1876–1939: A Study in Cultural Change.* Westport, Conn.: Greenwood Press, 1984.

Green, Jonathon, and Nicholas J. Karolides, reviser. *The Encyclopedia of Censorship, New Edition.* New York: Facts On File, 2005.

Haight, Anne Lyon, and Chandler B. Grannis. *Banned Books: 387 B.C. to 1978 A.D.* 4th ed. New York: R. R. Bowker, 1978.

Josephson, Matthew. *Victor Hugo: A Realistic Biography of the Great Romantic.* Garden City, N.Y.: Doubleday, Doran, 1942.

Schlesinger, Stephen, and Stephen Kinzer. *Bitter Fruit: The Untold Story of the American Coup in Guatemala.* Garden City, N.Y.: Doubleday, 1982.

A MONTH AND A DAY: A DETENTION DIARY

Author: Ken Saro-Wiwa
Original dates and places of publication: 1995, United Kingdom; 1995, United States
Publisher: Penguin Books
Literary form: Memoir

SUMMARY

Ken Saro-Wiwa's memoir is both a representation of his illegal "arrest" on June 21, 1993, near Port Harcourt, by armed security men and his detention without charges and also a manifesto about the corruption of the Nigerian government of the military dictator Ibrahim Babangida. Chapters 1 through 3 and 9 through 11 detail the detention events; in between, chapters 4 through 8 reveal the politics of Nigeria, focusing on the calamitous situation of the Ogoni people, an ethnic minority in the Nigerian nation.

> Suddenly, my car screeched to a halt. I raised my head in surprise. Before me was an armed security man flagging the car down, his rifle pointing at my chauffeur's head. Then, just as suddenly, more security men in mufti headed for the rear door of the car, swung it open, and ordered me to get down. I refused to do so. They spoke more gruffly and I remained just as adamant.

So Saro-Wiwa's troubles begin. He is taken first to the State Security Service (SSS) offices and then to the Central Police Station. After filling out a form, having his request to see his lawyer rejected, and being interrogated, and waiting a long time, he is taken by bus on a long drive of "roughly twelve hours" to Lagos.

Arriving in the morning, after not having eaten for 18 hours (prisoners are expected to provide their own food), he is transferred to the Federal Investigation and Intelligence Bureau (FIIB). The procedure is repeated— filling out a form, being interrogated, waiting. Saro-Wiwa is joined by an inmate from the infamous guardroom, a journalist who has been held in custody for a month without being informed of the crime he had committed. A plea from a human rights lawyer saves Saro-Wiwa from the guardroom—crowded, cramped, the inmates violent toward new inmates— and gains him "special consideration,"—that is, spending the night in the "reception desk," an open area without doors, windows, or a toilet. He is brought food by a lawyer friend and his briefcase and shoulder bag by his brother. Nevertheless, he cannot sleep.

The next day, a decision is made to return him to Port Harcourt, where Saro-Wiwa is transferred to the IMO State Police Command, arriving there at about 10 o'clock on June 23. Two other detainees have been picked up along the way.

> We were led into a room next to the guardroom. There was no light in it, the only available light coming from a beam which fell from the fluorescent tube in the corridor. There was no door, the only door having fallen off its hinges. . . . There were a few tables and chairs. . . . Opposite the room was a bathroom from which came the stinking odour of human waste.

While this "favour" saved them from the "indignities" of the guardroom, Saro-Wiwa has had enough of police brutality and dehumanizing conditions. He complains:

> I launch into a diatribe of the black man's inhumanity to his own kind, the trait responsible for the retardation of all blacks. It is inconceivable, I assert, that a man of my achievement and age can be subjected to the terrible indignities that have been meted out to me merely on suspicion and which I feel sure cannot be sustained in a court of law.

They are moved to the senior police officers' waiting room which has a fan, two dirty settees on which they could stretch, and the senior police officers' toilet.

The detention began to seem indefinite. Saro-Wiwa's legal team decided to go to court to demand his release. The immediate captors had not received further orders from superior officials. The assistant commissioner did, however, grab all of Saro-Wiwa's papers and go through them, including his diary of his first week of detention. "He warned that I did not have the right to write, and that if I was not on good behaviour [sic], he would have no option but to treat me according to the book."

His health having been affected, Saro-Wiwa is transferred to the police clinic, and, after delays and obstructions, transferred to Port Harcourt Prison. There, after examples of bureaucratic incompetence, on his doctor's orders he is taken to the University of Port Harcourt Teaching Hospital. He was saved from a further conspiracy to remove him. Then on July 22, he was informed that he would be granted bail.

The weighty segment of this memoir may be divided into four major features: the political-economic conditions of ethnic minorities in Nigeria, particularly the Ogoni people; the economic and ecological devastation that the Ogoni have experienced; assessing and asserting the flaws and negligence of oil companies; and the development of strategies to alleviate the situation, including a bill of rights. An international exposure is a further step. Saro-Wiwa's ultimate "efforts being bent to the improvement of the life of the Ogoni people and, by implication, the ethnic minorities and indigenous people of Nigeria, of Africa."

A primary source of the problem of ethnic minorities in Africa was the 1884 conference in Berlin when the European powers divided Africa according to geographic features and meridians without any concern for the ethnic groups. Nigeria, comprised of 200 or so ethnic groups, is dominated by three or four of them—with larger populations and areas of control, who thus control the politics of a confederated government with a strong central government. Adopting a unitary approach, "the resources of the Ogoni and other ethnic minorities in the Niger River Delta could be more easily purloined while paying lip-service to Nigerian federalism and unity." The military, who seized power, did not allocate profits of oil appropriately to the areas where it was produced.

The Ogoni live in poverty: no pipe-borne water, no electricity, and no job opportunities. Their once self-sustaining agriculture in a lush river delta has been destroyed, the land devastated by oil companies prospecting for and mining oil.

Oil exploration has turned Ogoni into a waste land: lands, streams, and creeks are totally and continually polluted; the atmosphere has been poisoned, charged as it is with hydrocarbon vapours, methane, carbon monoxide, carbon dioxide and soot emitted by gas which has been flared twenty-four hours a day for thirty-three years in very close proximity to human habitation. Acid rain, oil spillages and oil blowouts have devastated Ogoni territory. High-pressure oil pipelines crisscross the surface of Ogoni farmlands and villages dangerously.

Strategies designed and promoted by Saro-Wiwa were both conventional and creative as well as controversial. He organized groups like the Movement for the Survival of the Ogoni People (MOSOP), generating interest among the young, emphasizing a nonviolent approach; Ethnic Minority Rights of Nigeria (EMIRON); and Ethnic Autonomy, Resource and

Environmental Control (ERECTISM). He brought together an elite group to write an Ogoni bill of rights, summarized as follows:

> The Bill called for (a) political control of Ogoni affairs by Ogoni people (b) the right to control and use a fair proportion of Ogoni economic resources for Ogoni development (c) adequate and direct representation as of right in all Nigerian national institutions (d) the use and development of Ogoni languages in Ogoni territory and (e) the right to protect the Ogoni environment and ecology from further degradation.

A dynamo, he sought advice and assistance from other nations' experts and United Nations agencies, gaining significant international exposure for his Ogoni people and other ethnic minorities in Nigeria.

Saro-Wiwa's text concludes with a judicial ruling in his favor that the state had held him illegally; the judge ruled that the state owed Saro-Wiwa compensation and that he should be set free. A positive note, indeed, but clouded by the ominous truth about the author's death.

CENSORSHIP HISTORY

The introduction of the memoir, written by William Boyd and first published in the *New Yorker* on November 27, 1995, recounts that in May 1994, Ken Saro-Wiwa was on his way to address a rally but was turned back by a military roadblock. During the riot that occurred after the rally, four Ogoni elders, believed to be sympathetic to the military, were killed.

Saro-Wiwa and 15 others were arrested and accused of incitement to murder. Imprisoned for more than a year, he was tried before a special tribunal, which permitted no appeal. He and eight codefendants were found guilty and sentenced on November 2; he was executed by hanging on November 10, 1995.

Boyd writes: "The 'judicial process' has been internationally condemned as a sham. It was a show trial in a kangaroo court designed to procure the verdict required by the government."

Wole Soyinka, Nigeria's Nobel Prize in literature winner (1986), in his *The Open Sore of a Continent: A Personal Narrative of the Nigerian Crisis*, writes that Saro-Wiwa was held in detention, under inhuman conditions "in chains in a hidden prison, incommunicado." Further, he and the others were held "without a charge and without any indication of the slightest intention of bringing them to trial."

The special tribunal, handpicked by General Sani Abacha, who had overthrown the previous regime, was convened on January 16, 1995; however, various delays stalled the trial until early March. "One such delay, lasting several weeks, was caused by the admission of two principal prosecution witnesses that they had been bribed by the authorities to give false evidence against the accused." Having been "routinely harassed and assaulted by security agents" and prevented from seeing their clients, the defense lawyers eventually removed themselves from the case, "declaring that their continued participation would only give a semblance of legality to a patent circus spectacle."

Soyinka claims that the "death by hanging" was "predictable." Ken Saro-Wiwa's "fate had long been sealed. The decision to execute him and his eight companions was reached before the special tribunal was asked to reconvene and pronounce a verdict that had been decided outside the charade of judicial proceedings." The Abacha regime was known for its attacks on freedom of the press; journalists were arrested and beaten for writing about the regime's impounding of Ken Saro-Wiwa's books. His execution was the ultimate form of state censorship.

FURTHER READING

Boyd, William. "Introduction." *A Month and a Day: A Detention Diary*. By Ken Saro-Wiwa. New York: Penguin, 1995.

Hunt, J. Timothy. *The Politics of Bones*. Toronto: McClelland & Stewart, 2005.

Soyinka, Wole. *The Open Sore of a Continent: A Personal Narrative of the Nigerian Crisis*. New York: Oxford, 1996.

Wiwa, Ken. "The Trials of Ken Saro-Wiwa." *In the Shadow of a Saint: A Son's Journey to Understand His Father's Legacy*. New York: Alfred A. Knopf, 2000.

MY BROTHER SAM IS DEAD

Authors: James Lincoln Collier and Christopher Collier
Original date and place of publication: 1974, United States
Publisher: Four Winds Press
Literary form: Novel

SUMMARY

The action of *My Brother Sam Is Dead* centers on the Meekers, a Connecticut village family during and after the American Revolution. The Meeker family's loyalties are divided—as are those of the community, the father being a Tory but promoting a neutral stance, anxious to protect his family and his livelihood. The elder son, Sam, drops out from college to join the rebel forces, leaving young Tim, the narrator, uncertain about whom and what to support. The emotional tensions and battlefield violence cause Tim to reconsider his values and political position over the span of the novel, from 1775 to 1778.

Disputes in the family—politics and relationships—upset its dynamics. Sam desires acknowledgment of his decision to fight with the Patriots; his father rejects this and demands that Sam remove his uniform and return to college or not come home. Sam requests the use of the family's Brown Bess during the war, the family's only gun, and is denied. He steals it. When Tim questions his father's decision in another instance, Mr. Meeker insists on Tim's obedience.

Disputes between the Tories, the colonists loyal to the king, and the Patriots, those loyal to the Continental Congress and the war effort, increase enmity between them. The war comes to the family and the community. A rebel group enters their tavern home and demands their weapon; when they are told the family no longer has it, an officer whips the flat side of his sword across Mr. Meeker's face. In 1776, en route to a Hudson River community to sell cattle, Tim and his father are surrounded and threatened by hostile men with rebel sympathies who are probably cowboys—cattle thieves; they are rescued by a Loyalist Committee of Safety. Attacked again on the way home during a blizzard, Mr. Meeker is captured, although Tim, using a ruse, escapes. (Later, the family learns that Mr. Meeker died of cholera on, unaccountably, a British prisoner ship.) Tim takes on the management of the household and business affairs with his mother, seeing himself suddenly to have achieved adult status. The British enter the community in 1777, taking several prisoners, including a nine-year-old boy, shooting down a messenger, and laying siege to a building. They attack, killing those inside and beheading a slave; these actions, witnessed by Tim, affect him physically as well as intellectually.

Later that year, the Continentals return and establish an encampment. The culminating event, the arrest and trial of Sam Meeker, occurs. The thieves, who Sam and Tim had chased, accuse Sam of stealing his family's cows. The court-martial goes against him; he is condemned to death by firing squad. General Putnam is steadfast in his decision to use Sam's case as an example for his troops to prevent such pillaging and theft. Putnam denies Mrs. Meeker's and Tim's requests for clemency. Sam's innocence may not be clear to the court or the general—evidence was lacking—but it is clear to the reader.

Against this backdrop of rite of passage, this novel focuses on questions of freedom—the sons' freedom from the authority of their father and the colonists' political freedom from the British Crown. Loyalties, competing at personal and political levels, are fraught with tension and hostility. While the novel opens with an eager-to-fight Sam, imbued with patriotic zeal, admired by an envious Tim, an antiwar stance evolves. This may be deduced by Tim's doubts and eventual rejection and from such comments as these from Mrs. Meeker, a sympathetic character: "War turns men into beasts. It's cheaper to shoot a boy than to feed him" and "Bah, patriotism. Your patriotism has got my husband in prison and one of my children out there in the rain and muck shooting at people and likely to be dead at any minute, and my business half ruined. Go sell your patriotism elsewhere. I've had enough of it." The violent events solidify this impression.

CENSORSHIP HISTORY

James Lincoln Collier and Christopher Collier, a professor of history at the University of Connecticut and the Connecticut state historian, collaborated in the writing of eight historical novels, most of them set during the Revolutionary War. *My Brother Sam Is Dead* is the most often challenged; it ranks 12th on the American Library Association's (ALA) "The 100 Most Frequently Challenged Books of 1990–2000." It also placed seventh in the ALA's annual rankings of the top 10 challenged books of 1996 and on the comparable lists of People For the American Way, which ranked it 11th in 1995–96 and 10th in 1994–95. Acclaimed for its literary quality and historical accuracy, it was named a Newbery Honor Book, a Jane Adams Honor Book, and a finalist for a National Book Award, all in 1975.

The two most frequent arguments presented by challengers and occasionally successful censors, often in relation to age appropriateness for elementary school readers, were foul and vulgar or profane and inappropriate language and too much violence. Specific words objected to include *dammit, Jesus, damn you, bastard, hell, Goddamn,* and *son of a bitch.* The diversity of these challenges in terms of time and place is widespread, reported from 1983 through 2004 in a range of states, among them California, Georgia, Pennsylvania, Ohio, Kansas, and Colorado. Some typical assertions are the "persistent usage of profanity" as well as references to "rape, drinking, and battlefield violence"; "In our house we do not allow God's name to be used in vain. Since God has been removed from our schools, how can we now speak about God in a derogatory way?" This complaint drew this response: "The literary, political, social, and historical significance outweighed the thirty occurrences of offensive language." Another explained: "We are obviously concerned about the decay in the way we speak to one another and the way we express ourselves. What we're trying to say is that it's not OK." A review committee in Maine countered the language complaint by explaining that the book had "a very strong moral theme, of benefit to students that outweighs the infrequent negative language. . . . It matters that the uses of bad language occur in emotional and difficult times and are not part of the normal speech." The graphic violence complaints refer to but do not often identify the decapitation and the execution scenes. A few complaints object to references to drinking, rape, and antireligious sentiments. A minister's request to ban the book asserted, in addition to obscene language, that it presented "a negative approach to God. . . . This is not about censorship, and it's not about First Amendment rights"; he indicated it was a matter of taste and whether the schools should "endorse the use of profanity." A member of a Florida school board, an air force veteran who was shot down in Vietnam, defended the language as realistic—"portrayal of war included profanity."

In 2009, this novel was challenged—because of a parent's concern about profanity—in Muscoggee County, Georgia; it was retained in all elementary school libraries.

Direct confrontation with the unorthodox presentation of this war is mostly avoided by challengers. Two examples reflect this concern: In Connecticut, a challenger accused the book of "inflammatory propaganda" and as being "an inaccurate depiction of the Revolutionary War." Another challenger objected to the portrayal of "Americans as barbaric, unfeeling and almost inhumane."

FURTHER READING

Attacks on Freedom to Learn, 1992, 1993, 1995. Washington, D.C.: People For the American Way, 1991–92, 1992–93, 1994–95.

Collier, Christopher, ed. *Brother Sam and All That: Historical Context and Literary Analysis of the Novels of James and Christopher Collier.* Orange, Conn.: Clearwater Press, 1999.

Doyle, Robert P. *Banned Books: 2001 Resource Guide.* Chicago: American Library Association, 2001.

"Muscogee County, Georgia." *Newsletter on Intellectual Freedom* 58, no. 3 (May 2009): p. 93.

MY NAME IS ASHER LEV

Author: Chaim Potok
Original date and place of publication: 1972, New York
Original publisher: Alfred A. Knopf
Literary form: Novel

SUMMARY

Asher Lev has a gift. It is a gift that at once fulfills him and torments him, for it scrapes harshly against the grain of the doctrines of the Ladover Hasidim community in which he was born and raised. His parents, Rivkeh and Aryeh, are deeply committed to their faith; their daily lives are oriented around its prayers and practices. Aryeh Lev, a respected official of the sect centered in Brooklyn, New York, serves as emissary of the rebbe (rabbi, international leader of the sect) to governments and Ladover Hasidim communities.

Asher's gift is art. His artistic impulses find early expression in childhood when "his dearest companions were Eberhard and Crayola." As he matures, his skill and passion advance, as does the tension with his father, who refers to Asher's childhood occupation as "foolishness." Asher's drawing, however, carries him through his mother's emotional collapse when her brother, on a mission for the rebbe, is killed in an automobile accident. But his father becomes increasingly distressed when, after watching his young son concentrating on a drawing of his mother, realizes Asher's activity is not child's play.

Asher enters the Ladover Yeshiva and Rivkeh enters Brooklyn College, after being permitted by the rebbe to undertake her brother's studies, which were his mission. During this period, Asher has stopped drawing. Afraid of the world around him, frightened by his mother's blaming the rebbe for her brother's death, he feels the making of "lines and shapes on pieces of paper was a futile indulgence in the face of such immutable darkness, a foolishness I would certainly leave behind when I entered the world beyond the window of our living room." He is not, however, a good student, seemingly distracted and incomplete; he cannot seem to give his attention to academic subjects.

During this period, too, Asher is awakened to the plight of Russian Jews and his father's work in trying to help individuals escape from Russia. He learns of the Jewish writers who have been shot: "Those who didn't die in prison were taken out and shot. . . . The Russians kill people the way people kill mosquitoes. What kind of human being kills another human being that way?" This is followed by the announcement of the so-called doctor's plot: They had confessed to trying to kill top Soviet leaders by misdiagnosis and harmful medical treatment. At Yeshiva, the students' religious mentor makes this speech:

> Dear children. Today the enemies of the Jewish people have again shown us how much they hate us and our Torah. The Russian bear has cast six of our people into the pit. Our tears and our prayers go out to our brothers the children of Israel in this moment of darkness. For hundreds of years, Jews have suffered from the murderous hatred of the Russians, first under the czars and now under the Bolsheviks. The Russian government is different, but the Russian hatred of the Jew is the same. . . .

Stalin's death is celebrated in the synagogue with deeply intense prayers of thankfulness.

The photograph of Stalin in his casket rekindles Asher's need to express himself through drawing. He unconsciously recreates Stalin's image in his notebook from memory; this leads to more drawings. During this period, the tension between Asher and his father is intensified. Asher refuses to go to Vienna, where his father is being sent on a special mission. He is afraid of losing his gift—unwilling "to lose it again." Asher's neglect of his studies, interpreted as a denial of the father, in contrast to his fixed concentration on his art, feeds the conflict. However, a deeper issue, less easily resolved, dominates: the teachings and mission of the Ladover Hasidim in conflict with elements of secular and non-Hasidim society that would intrude on these teachings and mission. In the context of this mission, "to bring the

Master of the Universe into the world" through the teachings of the Torah and helping Jews to escape tyranny and establish communities to practice their faith, Aryeh fears his son's passion for art and foresees trouble in the future:

In the week that 13-year-old Asher will become a bar mitzvah, the rebbe, in a private conversation with Asher, says,

> A life should be lived for the sake of heaven. One man is not better than another because he is a doctor while the other is a shoemaker. One man is not better than another because he is a lawyer while the other is a painter. A life is measured by how it is lived for the sake of heaven. Do you understand me, Asher Lev?

He arranges for Asher to study art for five years with a master sculptor-painter, Jacob Kahn, a nonobservant Jew whose father had been a member of the sect. Aryeh is not reconciled to this decision: "He is my son. I want to raise my son in my own way. . . . How can I reconcile myself to this, Rivkeh? . . . There will be trouble from this. When a son goes so far away from a father, there can only be trouble."

The relationship between Kahn and Asher proves bountiful, in both artistic and human terms. He also learns to confront himself as an artist and his responsibility as an artist. Kahn initiates this confrontation:

> "As an artist you are responsible to Jews?" Listen to me, Asher Lev. As an artist you are responsible to no one and to nothing, except yourself and to the truth as you see it. Do you understand? An artist is responsible to his art. Anything else is propaganda. Anything else is what the Communists in Russia call art. I will teach you responsibility to art. Let your Ladover Hasidim teach you responsibility to Jews. . . .

Asher takes a major step in this regard when he draws with trembling hesitation his first nude from a model. The task becomes easier with time; separating his religious self from his artistic self also becomes easier. Summers are spent gloriously at Provincetown with Kahn and his wife, Tanya, after Rivkeh joins Aryeh in Vienna. Asher seems to be released into brightness and color. A few years later, in his first year at Brooklyn College, Asher becomes the "youngest artist ever to have a one-man show in a Madison Avenue gallery."

Asher's parents return from Europe. There is now a "permanent high wall of uncertainty and hostility" between Asher and his father. Aryeh believes the tradition of respecting one's father should supersede the tradition of art. Asher's response is to depart for Europe to visit museums and to paint.

In Italy, he sketches people, the *Pietà*, the *David*. In Paris, where he decides to stay for one or two years, he paints from his sketches, from his memories, and from the stories of his ancestors that he had heard. He thinks of his mother and her

> years of anguish. Standing between two different ways of giving meaning to the world, and at the same time possessed by her own fears and memories, she had moved now toward me, now toward my father, keeping both worlds of meaning alive, nourishing with her tiny being, and despite her torments, both me and my father.

He recalls her vigils at their living room window, watching the street, waiting for one or the other. Asher twice paints his mother at the window. The first painting seems incomplete; he puts his father and himself in the second one, on either side of her. With her arms outstretched, the painting takes the form of a crucifixion.

Asher returns to New York for the exhibition of his European work. The crucifixion paintings are considered masterpieces and have been purchased by a New York museum, but because they reveal so much, he dreads showing them and having his parents see them. But they do, and then are horrified, speechless. The wall between his father and him becomes a chasm; Aryeh will not listen to explanations, nor is he able to communicate. His mother listens but does not understand. Community members, feeling angered and betrayed, shun him. Even the rebbe, who had long supported him, counsels him to return to Paris.

> You are too close to people you love. You are hurting them and making them angry. They are good people. They do not understand you. It is not good for you to remain here. . . . Go to the yeshiva in Paris. You did not grow up there. People will not be so angry in Paris. There are no memories in Paris of Asher Lev.

He departs the next day. As he steps into a cab, looking up, he sees both parents watching him through the living room window.

CENSORSHIP HISTORY

My Name is Asher Lev was one of 49 books barred from the Moscow International Book Fair in 1983; they had been part of the U.S. Association of Jewish Book Publishers exhibit. They also included, notably KEEPING FAITH: MEMOIRS OF A PRESIDENT by Jimmy Carter and MY PEOPLE: THE STORY OF THE JEWS by Abba Eban. This event is detailed in the discussion of *Keeping Faith*.

FURTHER READING

"Exiled Writers Differ with U.S. Publishers." *Publishers Weekly*, September 22, 1983, 14–15.
Hartzell, Richard. "Eye on Publishing." *Wilson Library Bulletin* 58 (1983): 200.

Macrae, John, III. Letter: "The Moscow Book Fair." *New York Times Book Review,* September 4, 1983, p. 30.

"Moscow, USSR." *Newsletter on Intellectual Freedom* 32 (1983): 201.

Reuter, Madalynne. "Fourth Moscow Book Fair: Controversy as Usual." *Publishers Weekly,* September 23, 1983, 14.

Schmemann, Serge. "Moscow Bars 49 Books of U.S. Jewish Group." *New York Times,* September 12, 1983, p. A9.

MY PEOPLE: THE STORY OF THE JEWS

Author: Abba Eban
Original date and place of publication: 1968, United States
Original publisher: Behrman House
Literary form: Nonfiction

SUMMARY

Abba Eban's extensive work traces the Jews from the origins of the Hebrew tribes of Mesopotamia to the mid-20th century and their struggles with the Palestinians. Eban, an Israeli statesman, illustrates the relationship between the Russians and the Jews; the first dictate terms of living, economics, and social status to the second, just one example of the many difficult struggles that have tested the strength of the Jews. However, this has not made them buckle in defeat but instead rise to meet the challenges and prosper.

As early as the first century of the common era, Jewish communities settled on the Russian shores of the Black and Azov Seas, where they remained unchanged through the sixth century. They remained in what was known as the Khazar Empire until its collapse in the 10th century, which led to mass migration and assimilation. Those who left settled in Kiev, where they prospered for the next half millennium.

As the 16th-century czardom was setting out to unify Russia into a single empire, Ivan the Terrible declared Jews to be "importers of poisonous medicine and misleaders of the Christian Faith," which led to further discriminatory legislation against them, such as a double tax on merchants and burghers. In 1827, under Nicholas I, the situation worsened, as Jewish youth were subjected to what Eban refers to as "military martyrdom," whereby they were conscripted, then served an additional 25 years of military service. The effect struck terror into the Jewish community, physically to the youths, spiritually to all. Meanwhile, the government was introducing secular studies into Jewish schools. According to Eban, this only increased the desire of the Jews to hold onto their traditional values.

The 19th century saw a resurgence in anti-Semitism, in particular with the concept of "blood libel," the blaming of Jews for the ritual murder of Christians so their blood could be used in preparation of Passover matzo. When a high-ranking priest disappeared in 1840, the Jews were held responsible. Further, they were given restrictions in residence, marriage, and economic opportunities. Jews were blamed for the spread of liberal ideas, even though few attended colleges where these ideas actually originated. With the notion shortly after the turn of the 20th century that Jews were destroying the foundations of Christianity, many were ruthlessly exterminated, whether the fault was not assimilating well enough or having blended in too well.

The Russian-Jewish community was torn asunder near the turn of the 20th century when many individuals who at one time had been indifferent to Gentiles (non-Jewish people) now began to abandon Jewish traditions in order to gain acceptance in that society. Nevertheless, when Czar Alexander II was killed by a terrorist's bomb in May 1881, the blame was placed on the entire Jewish community. The result was a mass exodus to America and other countries. Russian policy toward the Jews took a turn for the worse under Nicholas II, whose adviser, Constantin Pobiedonostsev, predicted for Russian Jews that "One-third would die out, one-third would leave the country, and one-third would be completely dissolved in the surrounding population."

The period between the 1880s and World War I saw 2.3 million Jews emigrate from Eastern Europe and Russia, yet some 8 to 10 million remained despite powerful persecution. For those who remained, a slight break in hardships occurred with the onset of the Bolshevik Revolution in 1917. The new government promised to eliminate restrictions on Russian citizens due to nationality and religion, and the Russian Jews worked toward developing national-cultural autonomy. This change was thwarted within two years, however, when the Soviet government cut off all contact between Russian Jews and all Jewish peoples worldwide. Five million Russian Jews were now left to start anew within the Soviet realm that had been decimated by war and shut off from the rest of the world.

Eban paints the period between the world wars as a time when persecution continued for the Jews in Russia despite noted gains. Additionally, he reports, "In the two decades between the wars the Jewish people had neither squandered its opportunities nor fully used them. . . . there was soon to break around the head of the Jewish people the most violent and destructive torrent of hate that ever afflicted any family of the human race." That torrent was the Holocaust of Nazi Germany.

The end of World War II saw the recognition of the Israeli nation, but not without conflict: Jews wanted not to be in a subservient role in their own homeland, Palestinians were not eager to allow the Jews in on equal terms. The Soviet Union's stance was one of "understanding for Jewish national aspirations." On November 29, 1947, the Palestinian partition gained majority vote in the United Nations General Assembly session. This event was unique in that the cause garnered United States and Soviet agreement. However, the gain of the Jews was accompanied by an emerging threat, unified Arab opposition to the partition.

My People: The Story of the Jews was published in 1968; world political climate has changed tremendously since then. However, at that time, the Soviet government's policy of containment was still in effect, which kept more than 3 million Jews in isolation from their worldwide kin. Also, the anti-West posture of the Soviet Union was a principal factor in its support of the Arab nations during the Six-Day War against Israel. Eban comments that the Soviets had much more to gain on the plane of "Great Power Competition" by supporting 14 Arab states versus a lone Israel.

CENSORSHIP HISTORY

Soviet authorities confiscated six out of 150,000 books at the third Moscow International Book Fair in September 1981. In 1979, at the previous fair, more than 40 titles had been confiscated from Americans alone. (The American Association of Publishers [APP] declined the invitation to the 1981 book fair.) Among the books confiscated in 1981 from the Association of Jewish Book Publishers was the children's version of Eban's *My People: A History of the Jews;* the original version was not removed. The children's version of *My People,* along with *The American-Jewish Yearbook: 1981,* were censored because they included passages incorrectly depicting Soviet attitudes toward the Jews, these being declared offensive. Another title, *History of the Jewish People* by Shmuel Ettinger, was also removed because of references to Joseph Stalin's designs against what he saw as a "doctor's plot."

Then, in 1983, the original version of *My People* was one of 49 books barred from the Moscow International Book Fair, all part of the U.S. Association of Jewish Book Publishers exhibit. They also included, notably, KEEPING FAITH: MEMOIRS OF A PRESIDENT by Jimmy Carter and MY NAME IS ASHER LEV by Chaim Potok. This event is detailed in the discussion of *Keeping Faith.*

FURTHER READING

Butz, Arthur R. *The Hoax of the Twentieth Century.* Brighton, U.K.: Historical Review Press, 1975.

"Exiled Writers Differ with U.S. Publishers." *Publishers Weekly,* September 22, 1983, 14–15.

Hartzell, Richard. "Eye on Publishing." *Wilson Library Bulletin* 58 (1983): 200.

Lind, Carol. "Soviets Steal More Than a Glance at U.S. Books on Display in Moscow." *Christian Science Monitor,* September 2, 1981, 1.

Macrae, John, III. Letter: "The Moscow Book Fair." *New York Times Book Review,* September 4, 1983, p. 30.

"Moscow, USSR." *Newsletter on Intellectual Freedom* 32 (1983): 201.

Reuter, Madalynne. "Fourth Moscow Book Fair: Controversy as Usual." *Publishers Weekly*, September 23, 1983, 14.

Schmemann, Serge. "Moscow Bars 49 Books of U.S. Jewish Group." *New York Times*, September 12, 1983, p. A9.

—Eric R. Schmidt
Updated by Nicholas J. Karolides

NELSON AND WINNIE MANDELA

Authors: Dorothy Hoobler and Thomas Hoobler
Original date and place of publication: 1987, United States
Original publisher: Franklin Watts
Literary form: Biography

SUMMARY

This juvenile biography of Nelson and Winnie Mandela also provides an overview history of the struggle against apartheid in South Africa. The struggle is told chiefly from the perspective of black Africans.

Nelson Mandela, born in 1918 in Cape Province, South Africa, is introduced in childhood, growing up in a back-country environment relatively protected from racism. From the tribal elders he heard stories of the past before South Africa was occupied by Europeans, when blacks enjoyed democratic self-government, freedom of movement, and African ownership of the land and its wealth. Also described was the defense by his ancestors against the invaders. He attended Fort Hare College, a Methodist college, intent on studying law, but was suspended for joining a protest. Working first in the Johannesburg gold mines, he experienced for the first time the "horrendous conditions" of his fellow black Africans. Subsequently in Alexandra, he was helped to complete his college degree through correspondence courses, then his law studies with the sponsorship of a firm of white lawyers. These events occurred prior to the initiation of the apartheid system in 1948.

Born in 1936, Winnie Mandikizela was early impressed with the need for an education; she also became conscious of whites feeling superior to blacks and their victimization of blacks. Intelligent, keeping a low profile, she graduated with high honors from high school and the Jan Hofmeyr School of Social Work in Johannesburg, having witnessed as part of her studies the dismal conditions of blacks living in rural areas. She accepted upon graduation a position as medical social worker, the first black to hold such a position in South Africa.

The conditions under which blacks lived were fostered by restrictive legislation resulting from the whites' felt sense of superiority. Males (later, women were included) were required to carry government-issued passes that controlled their movements; this ensured that the majority of blacks were forced to stay in rural areas. Regions of the country were designated for each of the several races and mixed races to live, own property, and conduct business, the best being reserved for whites; the black "homelands" occupied 13 percent of the total area though blacks constituted 70 percent of the population. Schools were not only segregated but also, after apartheid, limited for blacks in type and amount of education, thus ensuring their low status. The government also issued banning orders against blacks who opposed their policies; these orders restricted their mobility to a prescribed area and severely limited their ability to meet with other banned persons. Blacks were arrested and imprisoned—for long periods, even indefinitely, without benefit of trial—for infractions such as accepting rides from banned persons, or on mere suspicion.

In addition to such regulations, townships outside of cities where blacks lived were slums; ramshackle houses without electricity or sewage facilities crowded next to each other. In the rural areas the "scope of miserable conditions" was broad. "Many of the houses were merely shacks made of iron sheets and cardboard. Scraps of rags and newspapers plugged up the cracks." Poverty was extreme; mothers were unable to afford food for their children and themselves. Government policy separated families. Conditions in the jails, apart from detention without trial, often in solitary confinement, were comparable: filthy, often bedless cells; enforced silence; nonsubsistence diet (water in which rice had been boiled); no exercise.

Nelson joined the African National Congress (ANC) in 1944, determined to change the status and humiliating conditions imposed on blacks. Rising to leadership positions, he initially maintained a "moderate" stance, recognizing that the different racial groups would stay in South Africa but "insist[ing] that a condition of interracial peace and progress is the abandonment of white domination, and . . . exploitation and human misery will disappear." Charged in December 1956 with violation of the Suppression of Communism Act, Nelson was arrested and tried for treason, a trial that lasted six years. (Nelson and Winnie were married during this period, in 1958.) He defended himself and the others, winning their acquittal. Subsequently, he went underground to avoid arrest and to be able to move "freely" about the country.

Because the ANC's nonviolent protests were answered with government violence against the participants, such as the shooting of peaceful demonstrators at the Sharpeville Massacre in 1960, some ANC members undertook violent protests against government buildings and installations; Nelson was placed in charge. These attacks caused the government to intensify its search for him. With the help of an informer, he was picked up upon his return from an illegal speaking tour, primarily in Africa, found guilty, and sent to prison. When a government raid in 1963 discovered the headquarters of the outlawed ANC, he was removed from prison and tried again with other leaders. Charged with "recruiting members for sabotage and violent overthrow of the government," he again led the defense. This time, however, he and all but one of the others were found guilty. The judge, however, exercised "the only leniency I can show" and sentenced the defendants to life imprisonment.

In his behavior and statements, Nelson expressed his dedication to obtain freedom for his people.

No, [my freedom] is not a direct threat to the Europeans. We are not anti-white; we are against white supremacy and in struggling against white supremacy we have the support of some sections of the European population. . . . We said that the campaign we were about to launch was not directed against any racial group. It was . . . directed against laws which we considered unjust.

During my lifetime I have dedicated myself to this struggle of the African people. I have fought against white domination, and I have fought against black domination. I have cherished the ideal of a democratic and free society in which all persons live together in harmony and with equal opportunities. It is an ideal which I hope to live for and to achieve. But if needs be, it is an ideal for which I am prepared to die.

During the first trial in 1956, the government accused the ANC of being Communist because it had accepted aid from the Communist Party. In fact, the South African Communist Party was the only white party willing to work with Africans. The ANC joined forces with it and the Indian National Congress in calling for a national demonstration. Nelson, who had refused to join the Communist Party, had misgivings about this union. In court, he argued against the accusation of like aims of the two groups:

The ANC, unlike the Communist Party, admitted Africans only as members. Its chief goal was, and is, for the African people to win unity and full political rights. The Communist Party's main aim, on the other hand, was to remove the capitalists and to replace them with a working-class government. The Communist Party sought to emphasize class distinctions whilst the ANC seeks to harmonize them. This is a vital distinction.

In his finding of not guilty, the judge specified that the prosecution had not proven the ANC to be Communist or that the ANC's Freedom Charter advocated a Communist state.

While Nelson was imprisoned after the second trial, Winnie's life was one of deliberate government harassment and deprivation: In 1965, she received a five-year banning order; her employers were pressured to fire her, job after job; their children were expelled from one school after another; her home was broken into and searched; she was jailed, and in 1977 she was banished to an outlying community. Throughout this period, Winnie continued the struggle, first attempting to follow Nelson's footsteps, then infusing her efforts with her own social work experiences. She developed an independent view of the reality of the black experience.

The book concludes with several pages bringing the text toward the mid-1980s. In January 1985, South Africa's president Pieter W. Botha offered to release Nelson Mandela if he renounced violence unconditionally. Mandela responded that he was not a violent man.

> It was only then when all other forms of resistance were no longer open to us that we turned to armed struggle. Let Botha show that he is different. . . . Let *him* renounce violence. Let him say that he will dismantle apartheid. Let him unban the people's organization, the African National Congress. Let him free all who have been imprisoned, banished or exiled for their opposition to apartheid. Let him guarantee free political activity so that the people may decide who will govern them.

In April 1986, Winnie was released from banishment; Nelson was still in prison.

CENSORSHIP HISTORY

The first annual report of the Oregon Intellectual Freedom Clearinghouse, released by the Oregon State Library, identified *Nelson and Winnie Mandela* as one of 17 library books that had been formally challenged between May 1987 and June 30, 1988. (The other books were challenged variously for sexual content, profanity, or being scary and violent.) The challenge occurred at the Hillsboro Public Library. The challenger was a patron who charged that the "Mandelas and the African National Congress of which they are members are Communist backed." John Thommes, the patron, specified on the library's Request for Reconsideration of Library Materials form that the theme of the book was "to glorify revolutionary heros [sic] of Marxist ideology. It has no literary value per se unless you condone violence and racism against blacks." Reading the work, he asserted, would result in "a misleading impression favoring ANC, a violent (to their own people) Communist organization." He recommended the purchase of *Other End of the Lifeboat* by Otto Scott.

After being reviewed, the book was retained in the library's collection. The final decision was made by the library director and the children's librarian. The latter also suggested that an additional book to "balance" coverage of the subject be ordered. The Scott text, however, was unavailable since it had gone out of print. Thommes donated his copy. Debra Brodie, the library director, reported in November 1996 that it was still in the Hillsboro Library collection, but inexplicably, *Nelson and Winnie Mandela* was not. It is available at three other county libraries, offering easy interlibrary loan access.

FURTHER READING

Brodie, Debra. Library Director. Hillsboro [Oregon] Public Library. Correspondence. November 1, 1996.

"Library Censorship in Oregon." *Newsletter on Intellectual Freedom* 38 (1989): 3.
"Request for Reconsideration of Library Materials." Hillsboro [Oregon] Public
Library. Calif. April 1988.

1984

Author: George Orwell
Original date and places of publication: 1949, London and United States
Publishers: Secker and Warburg; Harcourt Brace Jovanovich
Literary form: Novel

SUMMARY

The time after World War II was one of great turmoil. Although the immediate danger was over, many feared that the Communist ideologies that had
taken over the USSR and parts of eastern Europe would spread throughout
the world, meaning an end to the democracy and capitalism under which the
United States and many other countries flourished. The novel *1984* took these
fears to their furthest point, projecting a future world that is entirely totalitarian and describing in-depth the problems of humanity in such a world.

Winston Smith lives in London on the landmass known as Airstrip One in
the country Oceania. The 39-year-old man is sickly and balding with a bleeding, open sore on his ankle that never heals. Every day he must climb the
seven floors to his apartment, for the elevator never works. His main subsistence is the stale bread and pasty stew with unidentifiable meat that he can get
for lunch at work. In order to keep sane, he drinks a lot of Victory Gin, which
makes his eyes water as it painfully slides down his throat, and smokes many
Victory Cigarettes, which he must always remember to hold carefully so the
tobacco does not fall out. He is constantly surrounded by the lies his government tells, forced to listen to them at all hours from the telescreens blaring
away in every room. He is one of the few aware that what is heard are lies, for
he works as a fact-changer at the Ministry of Truth, which is responsible for
all publications, propaganda, and entertainment for Oceania.

> What happened in the unseen labyrinth to which the pneumatic tubes led,
> he did not know in detail, but he did know in general terms. As soon as all
> the corrections which happened to be necessary in any particular number of the
> *Times* had been assembled and collated, that number would be reprinted, the
> original copy destroyed, and the corrected copy placed on the files in its stead.
> This process of continuous alteration was applied not only to newspapers,
> but to books, periodicals, pamphlets, posters, leaflets, films, sound tracks,
> cartoons, photographs—to every kind of literature of documentation which
> might conceivably hold any political or ideological significance. Day by day
> and almost minute by minute the past was brought up to date. . . . In no case
> would it have been possible, once the deed was done, to prove that any falsifi-
> cation had taken place.

At the same time as history is being revised, statistics are being faked so they are in accordance with the image the Party wishes to project:

> But actually, he thought as he readjusted the Ministry of Plenty's figures, it was not even forgery. It was merely the substitution of one piece of nonsense for another. . . . For example, the Ministry of Plenty's forecast had estimated the output of boots for the quarter at a hundred and forty-five million pairs. The actual output was given as sixty-two millions. Winston, however, in rewriting the forecast, marked the figure down to fifty-seven millions, so as to allow for the usual claim that the quota had been overfilled. In any case, sixty-two millions was no nearer the truth than fifty-seven millions, or than a hundred and forty-five millions. Very likely no boots had been produced at all. Likelier still, nobody knew how many had been produced, much less cared. All one knew was that every quarter astronomical numbers of boots were produced on paper, while perhaps half the population of Oceania went barefoot.

In addition to the faking of statistics, historical facts are changed. Besides Oceania, the only other countries in the world are Eastasia and Eurasia. If Oceania is at war with one of these, it has always been at war with it. So, when the country changes allies and begins warring with a different nation, all of the past newspaper articles detailing the war must be changed to fit into this new world order. Then every individual must change the past in his or her mind, known as doublethink, and forget that anything other than this new truth was ever known.

It is this kind of deception that has Winston questioning his entire upbringing. He has always been told that Big Brother, the leader of the Party, saved the country from the terrible oppression of the capitalists. But he looks around him at the lack of many necessities and substandard quality of others and wonders if it has always been this way. If the Party lies about war, could it not also lie about saving society?

He has decided to begin consciously fighting the Party and attempting to discover the truth by keeping a diary of his thoughts, most of which are against Big Brother. He is careful to point out, though, that his first act of defiance began long ago. When one thinks about defying Big Brother, he or she has already committed a crime against him, known as thoughtcrime, which in and of itself is punishable by death. For this reason, Winston thinks he may as well go as far as possible in his defiance because he is essentially already dead.

Some day the Thought Police will catch him and he will die. Every room has a telescreen that simultaneously broadcasts Party news and monitors whatever is happening in the room for the Thought Police. People he knows could turn him in to save themselves. He has already reconciled himself to the fact that he will be caught someday and has given up any hope for his future. But he wants to find out the truth before he is discovered.

Winston's journey to discover this truth while rebelling against the Party encompasses many levels. The first is his fascination with the past. Winston frequents an antique shop where many relics of the age of capitalism are present—things that have no real purpose other than beauty, such as a blown glass paperweight filled with coral. He purchases the paperweight and takes the opportunity to talk with the proprietor about the time before Big Brother took over. The man does not know much, but he gives some credence to Winston's idea that the world was better before the reign of Big Brother.

A second level of rebellion is sexual. The Party does not like people to bond in that way, fearing that they may love one another more than they love the Party, and has set up many antisex leagues to promote its view. Winston is approached one day by a beautiful young woman named Julia, who also works at the Ministry of Truth. After many difficult encounters where they attempt to hide from the telescreens, they agree to meet in a clearing in the woods. Here they are able to be free with one another and have sex for the first time. They do it because they have been told not to, and the more rebellious they are, the better they like it. After a few more such meetings Winston gets the proprietor of the antique store to rent them the furnished room above his shop. There they have many encounters, which are more than just sex, but a sharing of feelings and desires.

The third level is a more active form of rebellion against Big Brother. Julia and Winston decide to attempt to join the underground organization called the Brotherhood. Winston has always felt a special comradeship with a member of the Inner Party who works in his building, O'Brien. In the hall one day, O'Brien tells him how much he admires his work and to stop by his house for a new edition of the dictionary of Newspeak, the official language of Oceania. Winston and Julia take the chance that this is a secret message and arrive at O'Brien's house together in order to proclaim their hatred of Big Brother and their alliance with the Brotherhood. O'Brien, after questioning them, agrees to let them join and gets a copy of the book that details the truth about Big Brother and the formation of Oceania.

The book, entitled *The Theory and Practice of Oligarchical Collectivism*, was written by the man on whom most of the anger and hatred of the Party members is focused, Emmanuel Goldstein. It appears that years before he was a highly influential charter member of the Party, but as its views changed, he was eliminated and has now become the scapegoat for all of the problems of Oceania. During the Two Minutes Hate, a daily ceremony in which all members are required to participate, his face is constantly shown so it can be insulted. The book discusses the truth behind the three Party slogans—"Ignorance is Strength," "War is Peace," and "Freedom is Slavery." For instance, war is peace because the constant preparation for war allows the economy to remain steady by using up surplus goods. Although battles rarely take place, war is a socially acceptable excuse for constant rationing. It also keeps the citizens in the state of fear, which makes them believe they need the protection of the government.

After receiving the book and reading it, Julia and Winston are caught in their room above the antique shop. A picture falls down to reveal the telescreen, which has been monitoring them the whole time. Then the proprietor, who has removed his disguise, is seen in his true form, a member of the Thought Police. They are brought to the Ministry of Love and put in separate jail cells. After much physical torture and starvation, which is standard procedure for all criminals, Winston begins his special sessions with O'Brien, who, along with the Thought Police, had been monitoring Winston for seven years. During these sessions O'Brien uses a type of shock therapy to get Winston to realize the power of the Party and the futility of opposing it. Winston holds firm to his belief that the Party cannot take the truth from him, believing there are certain truths that cannot be controlled. For instance, he thinks that $2 + 2 = 4$, and there is no other way to think. O'Brien, though, gets him to believe that $2 + 2 = 5$, which proves the end of his resistance and final acceptance of everything the Party tells him.

After he is released from the Ministry of Love, Winston is a pitiful shell of what he once was. He does not really work anymore, but spends his time drinking at a café and playing chess with himself. He sees Julia once, but their desire to be together has been taken from them, and both accept the Party's truth. He knows one day, when he is not paying attention, he will be shot in the back of the head. But he believes that he has discovered the ultimate truth of Big Brother and has been saved, so he is ready. The final lines of the novel show his ultimate acceptance of that which he vehemently denied his entire life.

> He gazed up at the enormous face. Forty years it had taken him to learn what kind of smile was hidden beneath the dark mustache. O cruel, needless misunderstanding! O stubborn, self-willed exile from the loving breast! Two ginger-scented tears trickled down the sides of his nose. But it was all right, everything was all right, the struggle was finished. He had won the victory over himself. He loved Big Brother.

CENSORSHIP HISTORY

Many attempts have been made to rid school libraries of *1984* in the nearly 50 years since its publication. In his introduction to *Celebrating Censored Books*, Lee Burress identified the 30 most frequently challenged books from a compilation of data from six national surveys of censorship pressures on American schools (1965–82); *1984* ranked fifth. This was especially true in the 1960s and 1970s when the nation was gripped by fear over the possibility of nuclear war with the Soviet Union, whose mere existence as a successful communist country threatened the United States and its democratic ideals. As such, the novel was frequently called into question.

More often than not, though, these claims surround the immorality and profanity of the novel. The sexual explicitness was often called inappropriate for adolescents or for any age group. Some did object to the study of the book because of its communistic ties. In the Lee Burress study of censorship in Wisconsin schools conducted in 1963, the John Birch Society is cited as objecting to the book for its "study of communism." A 1966 national survey completed by Burress, which does not cite specific names or places, identifies a principal who thought the novel "shows communism in a favorable light." A parent on the same survey complained that the "socialistic state shows utopia which is wrong." While in the latter case the request was denied, the principal's objection prevented the book from being purchased.

In a case cited in Jack Nelson and Gene Roberts's *The Censors and the Schools*, a teacher in Wrenshall, Minnesota, refused to remove *1984* from his reading list, leading to his dismissal. He was reinstated, though, after arguments "that the book 'illustrates what happens in a totalitarian society.'"

Nelson and Roberts also discuss the censoring of *1984* as a consequence of the "textbook battles" of the 1960s in Texas. Ten novels were removed from the libraries of the four Amarillo high schools and Amarillo College, including MacKinlay Kantor's ANDERSONVILLE, Aldous Huxley's BRAVE NEW WORLD, John Steinbeck's THE GRAPES OF WRATH, and Oliver La Farge's LAUGHING BOY. According to Nelson and Roberts, most objections were raised because of obscenities in the novels, but some charges were due to the books' "political ideas or because the authors had once belonged to groups cited by the House Un-American Activities Committee."

As late as 1981, similar complaints were still being lodged. A Baptist minister in Sneads, Florida, Rev. Len Coley, attempted to have the book banned from school use on numerous occasions, often claiming the support of other church groups that later denied involvement. He said it was procommunist and contained explicit sexual material. As cited in the *Newsletter on Intellectual Freedom*, though, on January 13, 1981, the Jackson County school board voted unanimously to retain the novel as a "parallel reading text in a course on 'anti-communism' offered at Sneads High School."

However, many objections to the novel end with its removal from the classroom or the library or with it not being purchased. The continual objections to the novel are well evidenced by the fact that in a national survey completed by Burress in 1966, although the book was already considered a classic by many critics, it was present in only 43 percent of school libraries.

FURTHER READING

Burress, Lee. *Battle of the Books: Literary Censorship in the Public Schools, 1950–1985.* Metuchen, N.J.: Scarecrow Press, 1989.

——. *Censorship Report.* Unpublished: 1966.

——. "The Pressure of Censorship on Wisconsin Public Schools." *Wisconsin English Journal* 6 (October 1963): 6–28.

Karolides, Nicholas J., and Lee Burress, eds. *Celebrating Censored Books.* Racine: Wisconsin Council of Teachers of English, 1985.

Nelson, Jack, and Gene Roberts, Jr. *The Censors and the Schools.* Boston: Little, Brown, 1963.

Newsletter on Intellectual Freedom 30 (1981): 73.

—Jane Graves

NOVEL WITHOUT A NAME

Author: Duong Thu Huong
Original date and place of publication: 1995, United States
Publisher: William Morrow and Company
Literary form: Novel

SUMMARY

Quan, a captain in the Vietcong who is fighting to evict the Americans from Vietnam and to defeat South Vietnamese forces, is the narrator-protagonist of *Novel Without a Name*. He was mobilized at age 18 from a northern village amid exuberant patriotic festivities. Now in 1975, 10 years later, Quan, despairing and increasingly cynical, recounts events and feelings of his present life against a backdrop of poignant recollections of his past and responses to the undesecrated environment amid the bombed ruins.

The war seems endless. One battle drags into another, some of them ending in victories, others in retreats. The battles themselves are not particularly represented; the after-effects tell the story.

> Every night, through a twilight swirling with ash, smoke, and dust, we dragged the corpses of our comrades away from the battlefield, from an earth soaked in blood, strewn with human flesh—that of the day's combat, the putrid shreds of the previous day, the rotting debris of a whole week shrouded in fog. No words will ever be able to describe the stench. . . . Cries dripping with blood and flesh. Caked in dried blood and sweat, we dragged our rifles and our dead on our backs. Some bodies were intact, some truncated, missing a head or a leg, others had their stomachs ripped open, their intestines dangling. The blood of our comrades mingled with our sweat and soaked into our clothes. We marched, stunned by exhaustion and despair. We threw our last remaining energy into each retreat, not in the hope of saving our lives, but with the feverish desire to participate in the next day's butchery. We wanted to live so that in twenty-four or forty-eight or seventy-two hours we could spit fire on the enemy, watch the bodies tumble, the blood spurt forth, the brains shatter . . . to redress the balance.

At the end of the novel, the Vietcong momentum carries through to swift victory. Quan's company, however, has been decimated: Only 12 veterans are alive to participate in the celebration, 142 of the original group having been killed.

The effects of the war are visited upon individuals and groups, soldiers and the general populace. Aside from the deaths and wounds, there is rampant illness. Quan fights bouts of malaria. Once, when his company is ordered into battle, a third of them are stricken with malaria, but their order to march is maintained; that night "the company advanced single-file, a fierce, icy wind at our backs. Two able-bodied combatants carried each of the sick men and the weapons." While en route across the country, on a mission to rescue a childhood companion who is reported to have gone mad,

Quan meets a soldier who has been suffering from dysentery for four years and seven months. Hunger and destruction are ubiquitous on his journey:

> At the front we had often been tortured by a hunger that blanched men's stares, that melted their bones. Sometimes the supply division would suddenly shower us with food. But here, behind the lines, people lived with a kind of hunger that raged without cease-fire, that went on and on: the hunger for protein.

Half-starved villagers eat manioc (cassava, source of tapioca) so the troops can have rice. Quan, on his mission, is insistently offered food despite meager rations and the hungry bellies of children. He is given refuge in makeshift bunkers during bombardments.

Behind the lines he begins to acknowledge another kind of brutality among the Vietcong forces and officials toward their own people. Quan finds his friend, Bien, not mad but pretending successfully to be so by throwing himself onto and rolling on barbed wire and banging his head against nails in a wall. Bien, a powerful yet gentle man, can no longer endure the carnage of war. He is kept locked up in a small shack with only a small peephole in his own excrement; he had not been allowed to bathe for two months. Bien is emotionally scarred by the war and its patriotic requisites as well; offered the opportunity by Quan to be discharged to return to the village's normal life, he cannot face the humiliation of returning without honor: "He dreamed of returning to the village, of decorating his obscure, colorless life with trophies of victory."

Another kind of brutality becomes evident. Quan, after his rescue mission, returns to his village on leave for the first time since he was mobilized. He discovers that his sweetheart, Hoa, to whom he had pledged himself, had been doubly violated: "Last year, the village Party committee drafted her. Poor girl. By the end of the year, she was pregnant. No one wanted to claim the child. She refused to denounce the father. Shamed, her parents threw her out." When Quan goes to her, their loneliness and anguish over lost years and lost love overwhelm them. However, Quan's bitterness and alienation seem to take over as he admits that the "beautiful dream that once bound us to each other had died."

These personal and global brutalities are experienced through the veil of patriotism and the rhetoric of marxism. Ten years later, Quan is haunted by his day of mobilization—the red flags in the courtyard, the beautiful girls singing, the slogans on the wall—"LONG LIVE THE NEW COMBATANTS FOR OUR COUNTRY!"—"THE YOUNG PEOPLE OF DONG TIEN VILLAGE UPHOLD ANCESTRAL TRADITION!"—"LONG LIVE INVINCIBLE MARXISM-LENINISM!"—and his own sense of "marching toward a glorious future." The war is perceived not merely as "against foreign aggression" but also as a "chance for a resurrection. . . . [O]ur country would become humanity's paradise. Our people would hold a rank apart. At last we would be respected, honored, revered." Armed with the "dialectical materialism of Marxist thought," the Vietcong victory would be more than success of a tiny country against the imperialists. It would be a victory for marxism—to build communism on earth, to realize the dream of a paradise for humankind.

These memories are tainted with irony, recalled as they are in moments of despair, jarred as they are by the reality of mud and carnage: "The blood and filth had filed words down, gnawed through them just as they had rotted through the soles of our soldier's shoes. I had my dose of glory and adulation."

Quan's doubts may have been initiated by coincidence when he had read an old issue of the Communist Party daily; it was celebrating the glorious victories during the Tet Offensive:

> We had been there. I had buried with my own hands countless numbers of my companions, had dragged away from the line of fire little Hoang's corpse, one of the many angels lost in the war. All he had left was one arm, one leg, and a diary filled with gilded dreams.

Quan frequently mentions the deaths of gentle and intellectual youths, including his younger brother, and the agony of mothers over their lost sons.

The questioning deepens as the Communist Party officials are implicated. Bien's father is derisive about the local village secretary:

> Before, out of every ten of them you could find at least seven who were honest, civilized. Even during the worst intrigues, at least they feared public disgrace. Now the ones who hold the reins are all ignoramuses who never even learned the most basic morals. They study their Marxism-Leninism, and then come and pillage our vegetable gardens and rice fields with Marx's blessing. In the name of class struggle, they seduce other men's women.

He continues his diatribe in the safety of an isolated field.

> And no one dares say it. Even I don't, and I'm the most rebellious person in the village. I brought you out here to speak freely. For so long, it's just been misery, suffering, and more suffering. How many have died since the great De Tham, Phan, and Nguyen Thai Hoc—how many lives were sacrificed to gain independence? The colonialists had only just left Vietnamese soil and these little yellow despots already had a foothold!

An overheard conversation in a train compartment further unsettles Quan. A pair of elitist, middle-aged Party functionaries, having usurped seats from sleeping soldiers, reveal hypocritical cynicism and corruption about the ideals and doctrines of the revolution. One of them is arrogant about the use of power to subdue the people to Party purposes.

> All you need to do is mount a podium perched above a sea of rippling banners. Bayonets sparkling around you. Cannons booming. Now that's the ultimate pleasure: the gratification of power. Money. Love. Why, next to it, they're nothing. So we need a religion. . . . We demolished the temples and emptied the pagodas so we could hang up portraits of Marx, enthrone a new divinity

for the masses. Remember the army's ideological rectification campaigns? With the cadres from 1952 to 1953? Were those really any different from confessions in church? We invented sins. We tortured ourselves. We repented in exchange for a pure soul, hoping it would bring us one step closer to the Supreme Being. Today, it's the same story.

Karl Marx is slandered:

Obviously, a great man can't be judged on the basis of his private life. But just for a laugh, do you know what kind of a man Karl Marx was in real life? Well, he was a debauched little dwarf. As a student, he hung out in brothels. He particularly liked gypsy girls. As for his mature years, everybody knows that he got his own maid pregnant. It was only when he died that his wife Jenny forgave him and adopted the bastard kid. Ha ha ha ha!

The final "truth" is revealed to Quan by one of his soldiers who points out after he is reprimanded for destroying medicine containers and television sets—the people's property—in a South Vietnam warehouse that "the people, that's my mother, my father, your parents, the soldiers . . . will [never] get a crumb." He illustrates from a personal experience that money collected for charity was confiscated by officials for personal use.

Weary in body and spirit as the war draws to a close, old before his time, Quan realizes he has lost everything. He feels "barren, emptied, beaten." His dreams are shadowed by Hoa's youthful image, the memory of his brother's birth and his bright talent and a warrior ancestor. This ancestor, a wraith, speaks to Quan of "triumphal arches"; Quan curses him in response. The dream closes with Quan remarking, "My poor ancestors. Wretched architects of glory."

In discussing the future with his deputy, who is worried about what they will do, he tells him, "You think too much! Try to concentrate on your nerves and muscles instead so you can get out of this war alive. After that, we'll see about the rest." At the victory celebration, having noted that "glory only lasts so long," he responds to the question "What happens afterward" by saying, "How do I know? We're all in the same herd of sheep." He hears nothing more of their conversation, only the sounds of: a mournful chant, "rising from the fields, from the solitude of the countryside."

CENSORSHIP HISTORY

For 10 years, starting at age 21, Duong Thu Huong led a Communist Youth Brigade unit at the front during the Vietnam War, living in tunnels and underground shelters alongside regular North Vietnamese troops. She was part of a theatrical troupe, responsible for arranging performances to entertain soldiers and people in bombed-out areas. Their purpose: to enhance morale. She was one of three survivors of a unit of 40 men and women.

After decades of activism with the Vietnamese Communist Party, Duong became disillusioned; in the 1980s she wrote and spoke about the political and spiritual chaos of Vietnam, for the most part at official Party and Writers' Union Congress functions or in interviews with official Party literary magazines. The first censorship and banning of Duong's books occurred in the early 1980s. In 1982 she publicly protested, at the Third Congress of the Writers' Union, the censorship of a screenplay. Between 1982 and 1985, a party banning order ensured that none of her work was published. A documentary she had independently produced during 1985–87, *A Sanctuary for the Despairing*, about the inhumane conditions in a camp for 600–700 "mentally ill" war veterans, was destroyed by security police under orders of party secretary Nguyen Van Linh. In 1988, PARADISE OF THE BLIND, Duong's third novel, was denounced by Nguyen, who issued a second banning order. In 1990 *Novel Without a Name* was sent to France and the United States since publication was forbidden in Vietnam; the third banning order identified this novel. None of her recent novels or screenplays, including *Memories of a Pure Spring* (1996) and *No Man's Land* (1999), has been published in Vietnam.

An advocate of democratic reform, specifically supporting multiparty politics, Duong in July 1989 was expelled from the Communist Party (party officials say she resigned), accused of espousing heresies about democracy and human rights. On April 13, 1991, she was arrested and imprisoned without trial. She was charged with having contacts with "reactionary" foreign organizations and with having smuggled "secret documents" out of the country. Duong responded to these charges by asserting that she was expelled from the Party because of her dissident views; the "secret documents" were her writings, including the manuscript of *Novel Without a Name*. She was held in prison for seven months, first in a compound outside Hanoi and then in a prison. She described her cell as having "no windows—only a door with a hole for me to look out of." She was not done any physical harm, but she lost nearly 35 pounds because of inedible prison food. She commented: "They wanted to know if I had communications with anybody who was dangerous—foreigners or overseas Vietnamese. It was all a pretext to harass me, to frighten me." She was released in November 1991.

In 2002, having published one of her controversial articles in a Vietnamese newspaper in Australia and another, "The Flap of Raven Flock" (*"Tung Vo Canh Cua Bay Qua Den"*) in the *Saigon Times*, she was identified as a "national traitor," a "woman ungrateful for what Vietnamese martyrs have done for the country's liberty." In the cited articles, she expresses Vietnam's past as "the ill-fated history of a humble nation in which any brave soldier can become a dim-witted and cowardly citizen . . . and authority in Vietnam lies in the barrel of a gun held by right-wing extremists and village bullies."

An alternative interpretation of the banning of Duong's works indicates that they are not formally banned except in effect: "Government-controlled publishing houses will not reprint the popular old works, nor will they publish her new works." Her books, among the most beloved works in modern Vietnamese literature, are difficult to obtain. A bookseller in Hanoi said, "We all love her novels, but we cannot have them on our shelves."

During a 2005 visit to France—only the second time that she has been allowed to travel to Europe—Duong asserted that her priority is to denounce the Hanoi government as irremediably corrupt and abusive. "It is my mission to do so on behalf of those who have died under this shameful regime. . . . I have to empty what is inside me to keep my conscience clear. The people have lost the power to react, to reflect, to think. Perhaps I will give people courage." Duong has been living in exile in France since 2006, but she has not chosen—nor sought—political asylum.

Duong Thu Huong was nominated for the 1991 Prix Femina Étranger. On December 13, 1994, she was awarded the French chevalier order of arts and letters. The Vietnamese government in Hanoi expressed unhappiness over this "deplorable action"; the incident caused a rift—*un coup de froid*—between the two countries. France was accused of "a new form of colonialism" for giving an award to a dissident Vietnamese writer.

FURTHER READING

Klepp, Lawrence. "In Dubious Battle." *Far East* (April 4, 1994): 37.
McPherson, Nina. "A Note about the Author." In *Paradise of the Blind*, by Duong Thu Huong. New York: William Morrow, 1993, pp. 268–70.
Proffitt, Nicholas. "The Mission of Comrade Quan." *New York Times Book Review*, February 12, 1995, pp. 13–14.
Riding, Alan. "Vietnamese Writer Won't Be Silenced!" *New York Times*, Jully 11, 2005.
Shenon, Philip. "In This Author's Book, Villains Are Vietnamese." *New York Times International*, April 12, 1994, p. A43.

OIL!

Author: Upton Sinclair
Original date and place of publication: 1927, United States
Publishers: Albert and Charles Boni
Literary form: Novel

SUMMARY

J. Arnold Ross, Jr., "Bunny," is a wide-, wide-, wide-eyed innocent/idealist who just happens to be the son of a wealthy oil distributor, who, in turn, happens to be a decent and fair man, but who has class interests that he cannot escape. At the heart of the novel is this father-son relationship. J. Arnold Ross, Sr., "Jim," has to act in certain ways in order to preserve his business, which he has taught his son from Bunny's pre-high school days, while Bunny does not feel bound by those interests when they conflict with social justice. The only conflict in the relationship comes when the father's worldly ways conflict with Bunny's impeccable, abstract morality. So Jim's justifications twist through the book, playing out Sinclair's consistent theme, the lack of moral will in decent people to attempt to make a difference individually.

Jim is portrayed through the eyes of his son as such a kind father and caring employer that readers can easily sympathize with this industrialist, even when he takes as his business partner the jovial, unscrupulous "Verne" Roscoe. As long as Verne's past sins (illegally depriving landowners of their oil rights) and present illegitimate power plays (buying the 1920 presidential election) contribute to the Ross family wealth and are committed against undeveloped characters, the reader even accepts Jim's outlook, despite the undeniably ethical warnings of his son. But, in an important plot turn, Bunny's insistence on the necessity of justice in all of society is brought home to the reader as Verne turns his power against the protagonist of the novel, about whom the reader does care.

Verne's brutal dishonesty toward Bunny may be even more effective in emphasizing the need for social justice than the more obvious attempt to inculcate the lesson through Verne's dishonest brutality toward his oil workers. The character central to representing their interests is Paul Watkins, who starts as an uneducated worker, becomes a union organizer, takes on socialist views, and ends as an earnest Communist who travels to Moscow to receive directions on organizing workers in the United States. Bunny and Paul meet when they are still children and become close friends—much closer from Bunny's side—since he idolizes his friend's fierce honesty.

Oil! also features Paul's brother, a religious leader of a wealthy Angel City (Los Angeles) church. He is seen by Jim and Bunny at an out-of-the way hotel with a woman. At one point he seems to have disappeared by the seashore. During his absence, coincidentally a time when a blonde-haired woman from his church has also disappeared, a man who looks like him is seen as a passenger in a convertible driven by a woman with blonde hair. After several men lose their lives searching for him in the sea, he reappears with a story: While swimming, he was taken by the devil until an angel of god rescued him. He even produces a feather from the angel.

As Bunny grows throughout the novel from a boy of about 10 to a young man of about 30, we witness his initiations into the world, including his sexual introductions. His first lover, Eunice Hoyt, initiates the sexual advances and assures Bunny that even at her high school age she has taken birth control measures. She controls her parents by her knowledge of their illegitimate sexual liaisons, to the point of having Bunny sleep with her at her parents' house. She controls Bunny through sex, which she desires more often and desperately than Bunny. Bunny learns more about life through his sister, Bertie, who intentionally gets herself pregnant to trap her preferred man and then gets an abortion when her scheme fails. Verne's lifestyle is also new to Bunny. Verne lives on a Xanadu of a private ranch, with stables, a private zoo, and a house that is described as a secular cathedral with an "altar," a projection surface on which guests watch an idol of the silver screen. Verne has, in addition to a wife, a mistress, who has been made into a film star by his millions. Verne pimps for Bunny an even more attractive movie star, Vee Tracy, with whom Bunny wakes up in well-described bedroom scenes. At the conclusion of Bunny's education, he speaks of his decision to marry Rachel

Menzies as merely a concession to bourgeois tastes that might otherwise hinder their lives' work.

Bunny grows up under the political influence of his father's opinions of socialism:

> Dad explained the difference between public and private business; in your own business, you were boss, and you drove ahead and pushed things through; but when you ran into public authorities, you saw graft and waste and inefficiency till it made you sick. And yet there was [sic] fools always rooting for public ownership; people who called themselves Socialists, and wanted to turn everything over to the government to run, and when they had their way, you'd have to fill out a dozen application blanks and await the action of a board of officials before you could buy a loaf of bread.

Bunny, who volunteers for World War I, sees the Russian Revolution as his father does:

> Dad would read paragraphs out of the papers, details of the horrors that were happening in Russia—literally millions of people slaughtered, all the educated and enlightened ones; the most hideous tortures inflicted, such obscenities as you could not put into print. Before long they began applying their Communist theories to the women of the country, who were "nationalized" and made into public property by official decree; the "commissars" were raping them wholesale. Lenin was killing Trotsky, and Trotsky was throwing Lenin into jail. It was a boiling up from the bottom of the social pit, such savagery as we had hardly dreamed existing in human nature.

But Paul continually provides the open-minded Bunny with a different perspective; so does Rachel, as when she and Paul debate the merits of socialism versus communism in front of Bunny.

> "That is my criticism of the Socialist movement, it fails to realize the intellectual and moral forces locked up in the working class, that can be called out by the right appeal."
>
> "Ah," said Rachel, "but that is the question—what is the right appeal? I want to appeal to peace rather than to violence. That seems to me more moral."
>
> Paul answered, that to make peace appeals to a tiger might seem moral to some, but to him it seemed futile. The determining fact in the world was what the capitalist class had done during the past nine years [spanning World War I and its aftermath]. They had destroyed thirty million human lives, and three hundred billions of wealth, everything a whole generation of labor had created. So Paul did not enter into discussions of morality with them; they were a set of murderous maniacs, and the job was to sweep them out of power.

By novel's end, five characters cover the political spectrum: At the center is Bunny, who always sees the other person's point of view; on his immediate right is his father, who helps the workers and socialists he knows with his oil money; and to the right of him is Verne, at war with anyone who threatens his interests, however indirectly; on Bunny's left is his wife, Rachel, whose moderate socialism contrasts to Paul's espousal of violence as the path to social revolution.

CENSORSHIP HISTORY

According to Robert Doyle and also Anne Lyon Haight and Chandler B. Grannis, *Oil!* was forbidden in Boston in 1927 because of its comments on the Harding administration, but legally it was Sinclair's sexual explicitness and discussion of contraception that caused the ban. Boston's municipal judge John Duff fined book clerk John Gritz $100 for selling material "manifestly tending to corrupt the morals of youth." Sinclair seized upon the censorship as an opportunity for publicity. He made a trip to Boston and declared to reporters that the real reason for the suppression of *Oil!* was, as Leon Harris, Sinclair's biographer, relates, "its description of how the oil interests bought the Republican Convention that nominated Harding."

The reference is to Harding's Teapot Dome scandal. Although the scandal takes its name from the location in Wyoming of a government oil reserve, Teapot Dome encompassed other reserves, including the Elk Hills Naval Oil Reserve in California, the novel's setting. Edward L. Doheny (Peter O'Reilly, Sr., in Sinclair's novel) was charged with bribing Secretary of the Interior Albert B. Fall ("Secretary Crisby") with $100,000. Comparing the strange history as recounted by Burl Noggle to what Sinclair wrote reveals the similarity of detail.

According to Noggle,

> During his testimony, Doheny also produced a mutilated note, which he claimed as the one signed by Albert Fall when he received the $100,000 [as merely a friendly loan, not a bribe]; but Fall's signature was torn off. Doheny said that he had torn it from the note himself, since, if he should die before Fall could repay the loan, Fall might be pressed for repayment to the Doheny estate at an inconvenient time. He gave the signature to his wife, so that the two together still held Fall's entire note. Edward Doheny, Jr., knew of this arrangement.

According to Sinclair, in *Oil!*,

> [T]he committee grabbed "Young Pete" O'Reilly, and "grilled" him, and made him admit that he had carried the trifling sum of a hundred thousand dollars to Secretary Crisby in a little black bag—more stuff right out of a movie! And then they grabbed "Old Pete," and he claimed it was just a loan—he had got a note, but he couldn't recollect where the note was. He finally produced a signature which he said had been cut off the note, but he couldn't tell what had become of the rest of it; he was very careless about notes, and thought he had given it to his wife, who had misplaced all but the signature.

Verne's character was based in part on that of Harry F. Sinclair, whose first trial for bribery was dismissed because of jury intimidation. Sinclair benefited from Fall's release of the Teapot Dome reserve and was charged with paying a $68,000 bribe to Fall's ranch foreman. In testimony before the Senate, Sinclair's private secretary in "utter seriousness . . . claimed to have referred to 'six or eight cows' " and was misunderstood to have said "$68,000 in some manner, 'hearing thous' instead of 'cows.' " Upton Sinclair includes this detail as well: "Now the senators put the badly rattled foreman on the witness stand, and he had to explain that it was all a misunderstanding—what he had said was not 'sixty-eight thousand dollars,' but 'six or eight cows.' You can see how easy it was for such a mistake to happen!" Sinclair's inclusion of such details, including the exact amounts of money involved in each case, easily made the novel a roman à clef to some degree.

Other scandals of Harding's administration are referred to at the beginning of part six of the chapter entitled "The Exposure."

> Barney Brockway [Attorney General Harry M. Daugherty, whom Coolidge forced to resign] had given one of his henchmen a desk in the secret service department; this was the "fixer," and if you wanted anything, he would tell you the price; . . . if you wanted to recover a ten million dollar property [seized during World War I], you turned over half a million in liberty bonds to the "fixer." Bootlegging privileges were sold for millions. . . . Dan heard from insiders that more than three hundred millions had already been stolen from the funds appropriated for relief of war veterans.

To dramatize the fact that many of his sexual descriptions were taken from the Bible's Song of Songs, Upton Sinclair sold a copy of a Bible wrapped in *Oil!*'s cover jacket to a policeman. Charges were dropped when the identity of the real book was revealed. Leon Harris further describes Sinclair on this trip to Boston: "A picture of Sinclair with sandwich boards in the shape of two fig leaves hawking this edition was reproduced in papers all over the world and helped the book become an international best seller."

The book was banned from public libraries in 1929 in Yugoslavia, burned by the Nazi bonfires because of Sinclair's socialist views in 1933 in Germany, and banned in 1956 in East Germany, where Sinclair was called an "irate foe of communism." Sinclair was considered a socialist who exposed the complicity of big business and government and a writer who addressed sex realistically in his novels, so the Nazi condemnation is understandable. That the German Communists also banned the book may have had to do with some of the comments against the Russian Revolution or against socialism (quoted above). If the revolution was not a "boiling up from the bottom of the social pit," Stalin's reign of terror might by 1956 be perceived as one. Jim's comment about needing to wait for a board of officials before buying a bread loaf also might have struck home to Communists who lacked consumer goods and waited years for apartments or cars. The novel also makes reference to some unflattering historical acts by Germany. When Bunny's respected history teacher, Mr. Irving, relates "the hope of the German ruling class to win back to responsibility [after their World War I defeat] by serving the allies against the Russian revolution," East Germany's role against its then-current (1956) ally was emphasized. Germany's role in attempting to suppress communism is also mentioned as one Communist son rages to his socialist father (both, father and son, friends of Bunny): " 'What are your beloved Social-Democrats doing now [mid-1920s] in Germany? They have got charge of the police, and they are shooting down Communist workers for the benefit of the capitalist class.' "

Wide Is the Gate, Sinclair's 1943 novel, has also been censored with the collection en masse of Sinclair's other works.

Dedicated to "my millions of friends in the Soviet Union, who, while this book was being written, have been defending our common cause," *Wide Is the Gate* is one in a series of stories that basically follow the front page news of the *New York Times* by means of a central character, Lanny Budd. Budd uses his profession as an art adviser to the wealthy to gain information to pass to his socialist friends. For the censorship history, see THE JUNGLE by the same author.

FURTHER READING

Bullard, F. Lauriston. "Book-Banning Issue Burning in Boston." *New York Times,* July 3, 1927, sec. 2, p. 2.

"Boston Stops Sale of Nine Modern Books." *New York Times,* March 12, 1927, pp. 1, 3.

Doyle, Robert P. *Banned Books: 1994 Resource Guide.* Chicago: American Library Association, 1994.

Haight, Anne Lyon, and Chandler B. Grannis. *Banned Books, 387 B.C. to 1987 A.D.* 4th ed. New York: R. R. Bowker, 1978.

Harris, Leon. *Upton Sinclair: American Rebel.* New York: Crowell, 1975.

Noggle, Burl. *Teapot Dome: Oil and Politics in the 1920's.* Baton Rouge: Louisiana State University Press, 1962.

"Upton Sinclair Works Banned." *New York Times,* May 18, 1956, p. 23.

—Marshall B. Toman
University of Wisconsin–River Falls

ONE DAY IN THE LIFE OF IVAN DENISOVICH

Author: Aleksandr Solzhenitsyn
Original dates and places of publication: 1962, Soviet Union; 1963, United States
Publishers: Novy Mir; Penguin Books
Literary form: Novel

SUMMARY

Reveille sounds at 5:00 A.M. as one of the guards hits a hammer on a length of rail. Ivan Denisovich Shukhov awakes. He is 40 years old with two years left to serve of his 10-year imprisonment. Ivan, a Russian soldier, was captured by the Germans in February of 1942. Along with several other prisoners, he escaped and returned to his own lines. The Russians accused him of spying for German intelligence and sentenced him to a prison camp in Siberia.

On this particular morning, the outside temperature is 17 degrees below zero. Ivan is concerned that his squad, the 104th, will be sent to work on the "Socialist Way of Life Settlement." This is a new construction site, and there is no place for the prisoners to warm themselves while they work or to build fires. Ivan hopes that Tiurin, the squad leader, will be able to buy off the senior official and send another squad to the site.

It is time for morning roll call. The prisoners must go outside to be counted. "There is nothing as bitter as this moment when you go out to the morning roll call—in the dark, in the cold, with a hungry belly, to face a whole day of work. You lose your tongue. You lose all desire to speak to anyone." Today the prisoners are forced to strip to make sure they aren't wearing anything under the regulation shirt and undershirt. Finally, roll call is completed and the squads line up to march to the power station to work. Luckily, the 104th is not going to the "Socialist Way of Life Settlement." The prisoners are counted again, and then they are escorted by guards across the Siberian landscape. Once they reach their destination, the prisoners are counted again. Following this, the squad leaders must get their assignments. This allows a brief interlude in the activities and time for the prisoners to relax. Fortunately, today this takes 20 minutes.

The work assignment for the day is to continue building a second-story cement block wall. The prisoners work hard because it is the only way to warm themselves, and the entire squad will suffer if one person doesn't do his share of the work.

The prisoners receive lunch consisting of oatmeal and bread in the early afternoon. Shukov recalls feeding oats to the horses when he was young. "Never had it occurred to him that there'd come a time when his whole soul would yearn for a handful of them." Through a daring and lucky trick, Ivan is able to obtain two extra bowls of oatmeal. One goes to Pavlo, the deputy squad leader, and Ivan is given the second bowl.

The squad goes back to work on the wall after lunch. Ivan is able to temporarily forget his situation by concentrating on his work.

Thanks to the urgent work, the first wave of heat had come over them—when you feel wet under your coat, under your jacket, under your shirt and your vest. And after about an hour they had their second flush of heat, the one that dries up the sweat. Their feet didn't feel cold, that was the main thing. Nothing else mattered. Even the breeze, light but piercing, couldn't distract them from the work.

Their progress continues until quitting time at 6:00 P.M. The prisoners must be counted before they return to camp. Once they reach camp, they are counted again and searched. Dinner tonight consists of black cabbage stew and bread. Ivan is lucky to get some fish in his stew. At 9:00 P.M. the prisoners are counted again before lights go out.

The 104th squad is made up of men from various backgrounds. Senka was captured by the Germans two times and deafened by a severe blow to the skull. On his second capture he was put in Buchenwald and escaped. The Russians imprisoned him for associating with the enemy. Gopchik is a young prisoner who was sentenced to 25 years when he was 14 years old. His crime was that he brought a pail of milk to outlaws.

Tsezar was a young filmmaker before he was imprisoned. He is rather wealthy, and he is able to pay off the officials. His money has gotten him an office job as the assistant to the rate inspector. Tsezar receives many packages from home. Fetiukov, a former big shot in an office, was disclaimed by his wife and children when he was sentenced. He never receives anything in the mail, and Ivan describes him as a "jackal." The Moldavian is truly a spy for the Germans. He misses the end of the day count because he has fallen asleep in a warm corner. His absence leads to several recounts in which the prisoners and the guards must endure the outside temperature. Once he is found and brought to the counting area, the prisoners and the guards beat him.

Alyosha is serving a 25-year sentence for being a Baptist. He continues to pray frequently, and at times he even seems happy. He has a Bible hidden in a niche in the wall by his bunk and reads it whenever possible. At the end of the day, Alyosha, and Ivan discuss the merits of prayer and religion. Alyosha says, "Ivan Denisovich, you shouldn't pray to get parcels or for extra stew, not for that. Things that man puts a high price on are vile in the eyes of our Lord. We must pray about things of the spirit—that the Lord Jesus should remove the scum of anger from our hearts. . . ." He also tells Ivan not to pray for freedom. When Ivan complains that praying doesn't shorten an individual's time in prison, Alyosha is upset and says there is a positive side to being in prison: "Here you have time to think about your soul."

A former navy commander, Captain Buinovsky was a liaison officer on a British ship. The British admiral sent the captain a gift after the war so the Russians put the captain in prison for 25 years. The captain is a high-ranking prisoner who still believes in communism and has only been in camp for three months. During the morning strip search, the captain cites article nine of the criminal code and says that the guards have no right to strip search the prisoners. He tells the guards, "You are not behaving like Soviet people, you're not behaving like Communists." The captain receives 10 days in the guardhouse for his comments. The guardhouse is described as follows:

Brick walls, cement floor, no windows, a stove they lit only to melt the ice on the walls and make pools on the floor. You slept on bare boards, and if you'd any teeth left to eat with after all the chattering they'd be doing, they gave you nine ounces of bread day after day and hot stew only on the third, sixth, and ninth. Ten days. Ten days "hard" in the cells—if you sat them out to the end, your health would be ruined for the rest of your life. T.B. and nothing but hospital for you till you kicked the bucket.

The prisoners are not allowed to see a clock or a watch. They must address the guards as "Citizen," not the Communist greeting "Comrade." They must enter the mess hall in double file. They are not to walk through the camp on their own. An entire squad is to go together whenever possible. The prisoners are to have Sundays off, but if there happen to be five Sundays in a month, the guards give the prisoners three and take two as workdays.

At the end of this day, Ivan Denisovich goes to bed feeling that he has had a good day. This has been "a day without a dark cloud. Almost a happy day." By the end of his prison term, Ivan will have served 3,653 days remarkably similar to this one.

CENSORSHIP HISTORY

Nikita Khrushchev was the leader of the Soviet Union when *One Day in the Life of Ivan Denisovich* was published in 1962. Wanting to expose some of the truths regarding Stalin's regime, Khrushchev granted permission for Solzhenitsyn's prison camp book to be published. J. M. Coetzee quotes Dina Spechler's study of the phenomenon of "permitted dissent" in which she refers to Khrushchev as an "ambitious reformer." Against the nagging resistance from the party and bureaucracy, he used *Novy Mir* as a vehicle to "expose and dramatize problems and reveal facts that demonstrated . . . the necessity of the changes he proposed." In his struggle, Khrushchev wanted to win the support of both the moral humanist" and the "historical revisionist" (anti-Stalinist) intellectuals. Solzhenitsyn's works were banned from publication in the Soviet Union in 1964 after Khrushchev lost power. Solzhenitsyn himself in THE GULAG ARCHIPELAGO footnotes the objection of the "retired bluecaps"—the interrogators—to the publication of *One Day in the Life of Ivan Denisovich;* their complaint was that "the book might reopen the wounds of *those who had been imprisoned* in camp." Solzhenitsyn continues, "Allegedly they were the ones to be protected." The situation worsened for the author, and in 1974 he was deported and stripped of his Soviet citizenship.

This book has been censored many times in the United States. In schools, the primary reason for the censorship has been "vulgar language." In most cases, the requests for censorship have been denied. However, in Utah and Michigan, students were allowed to substitute another book for their assignments.

The Lincoln County, Wyoming, school board removed the novel from its high school curriculum in 1995. The novel was objected to for its "considerable obscenities." The superintendent of the district said that the book would remain on the library shelves.

In 1981, a Buckland, Massachusetts, parent asked the superintendent of the Mohawk Trail Regional High School to remove the book from a 12th-grade required reading list. His son had shown him a passage from the novel, and the parent was upset by the profanity. The objector felt that there was "plenty of good literature in the United States, without taking something out of Russia that doesn't even use the English language properly." The district superintendent, saying that Solzhenitsyn was a "very important author," was reluctant to remove his work. He also stated that he had read the novel before the complaint and felt it was a "good book with a good message."

The novel was one of four books that parents in Omak, Washington, asked to have reviewed because of "profane language" in 1979. *One Day in the Life of Ivan Denisovich* was a recommended, but not required, book for several English classes. An ad hoc review committee was appointed by the district superintendent to determine whether the book should be removed from the school library.

A New Lisbon, Maine, school board objected to the classroom use of the book, stating it did not comply with the *New York Times* language guidelines. In this instance, the book was removed from classroom use but remained in the school library. In 1976, the book was actually removed from the Milton, New Hampshire, high school library because of objectionable language.

Mahwah High School's trustee, William Buhr, challenged the inclusion of *One Day in the Life of Ivan Denisovich* in the school library. Buhr objected to the use of obscenities in the book; he even threatened to use profanity at all board of education meetings until the book was removed from the library. Buhr, a Nazi labor camp survivor, also argued that the book was not a true depiction of life in a Siberian labor camp. Board president Howard Geiger objected, too: "If I was the author of this book, I'd walk around with a bag on my head! If we permit this filth to be read, what next?" The board of education voted against the challenge in September 1976. A 1999 challenge at the Storm Lake (Iowa) High School objecting to the novel's profanity also failed.

The entire book contains fewer than a dozen objectionable words. The instances where these words occur are realistic in light of the situations and the setting. The book's focus on Ivan's desire to maintain human decency and self-respect while surrounded by evil was not recognized by these objectors.

FURTHER READING

Burress, Lee. *Battle of the Books: Literary Censorship in the Public Schools 1950–1985.* Metuchen, N.J.: Scarecrow Press, 1989.

Coetzee, J. M. "Censorship and Polemic: The Solzhenitsyn Affair." *Pretexts* 2 (Summer 1990): 3–36.

Dixon, Ron. "A Book Debate Splits Mahwah." *Paterson News,* September 14, 1976, p. 17.

Doyle, Robert P. *Banned Books 1994 Resource Guide.* Chicago: American Library Association, 1994.

Haight, Anne Lyon, and Chandler B. Grannis. *Banned Books 387 B.C. to 1978 A.D.* 4th ed. New York: R. R. Bowker, 1978.

Miller, Robert Keith. "Defending Solzhenitsyn: One Day in the Life of Ivan Denisovich." In *Celebrating Censored Books!* edited by Nicholas J. Karolides and Lee Burress, 89–92. Racine: Wisconsin Council of Teachers of English, 1985.

Newsletter on Intellectual Freedom 28 (1979): 75–76; 31 (1982): 10–11; 44 (1995): 100.

Pohl, Frederik. "One Day in the Life of Ivan Denisovich by Aleksandr Solzhenitsyn." In *Censored Books: Critical Viewpoints*, edited by Nicholas J. Karolides, Lee Burress, and John M. Kean, 395–398. Metuchen, N.J.: Scarecrow Press, 1993.

Solzhenitsyn, Aleksandr. *The Gulag Archipelago.* Vol. 1. New York: Harper and Row Publishers, 1973.

Spechler, Dina. *Permitted Dissent in the U.S.S.R.* New York: Praeger, 1982.

—Laurie Pap

ONE PEOPLE, ONE DESTINY: THE CARIBBEAN AND CENTRAL AMERICA TODAY

Author: Don Rojas
Original date and place of publication: 1988, United States
Original publisher: Pathfinder
Literary form: Nonfiction

SUMMARY

Sponsored by the Anti-Imperialist Organizations of the Caribbean and Central America, this text is comprised primarily of speeches by leaders of this organization presented at its plenary meetings or other assemblies. There are also three declarations, one of which opens and another of which closes the text. All were presented from 1984—when the organization was founded—to 1988.

In 1988, the Anti-Imperialist Organizations was composed of 38 political parties and movements from 23 countries in the English-, Spanish-, French-, Dutch-, and Creole-speaking Caribbean and Central America. These parties represented divergent political views, identifying themselves as social democratic, revolutionary democratic, Communist, and workers' parties.

> Despite these diverse origins and philosophies, however, all have united around a common anti-imperialist and anti-colonialist platform and a shared opposition to the aggressive, interventionist policies of Washington. We have united as well to seek ways and means of combating the grave social and economic crisis pressing down hard on the backs of our peoples.

In many respects the speeches and documents are repetitive, each expressing and illustrating the concerns and issues noted above. The discussion of these problems is balanced by salutes to individual and national efforts to accomplish real liberation, by statements of goals for the organizations and the people of these nations and with the recognition of their inherent unity.

Colonialism and imperialism are not synonymous, but they are perceived to have similar goals and effects. In a significant way imperialistic practices, occasionally referred to as neocolonialism, are expressed as an extension of the domination of outsiders upon the peoples of these lands. Colonialism is a force of genocide, bringing about the extermination of the indigenous inhabitants, slavery and indentured servitude, and the imposition of one-crop economies. A further obtrusion is the different languages, religions, and cultures of the colonizers, which artificially divide the peoples of the Caribbean and Central America. Grenada's revolutionary prime minister Maurice Bishop is quoted as condemning "the curse of colonialism": "We see it as one of our historic duties and responsibilities to pull down these artificial barriers of colonialism and to develop that oneness and that unity that we nearly lost. We are one people from one Caribbean with one struggle and one destiny."

Colonialism still exists in the region: "France still denies independence to Guadalupe, Martinique, and French Guiana. The Dutch still rule Curacao and several other islands. Britain too still has several colonies in the Caribbean." The United States practices "direct colonial rule" by its presence in Puerto Rico. The enforced integration of the island is a deficit to its people, particularly in economic aspects, which has social consequences. The people are deprived, which affects their standard of living.

The United States, synonymous with imperialism in this text, replaced the European colonial powers. "It exercises total economic, political, and military domination over the countries of the area, except for those still under European influence, and more recently, Cuba and Nicaragua, which have freed themselves of their bonds." Military and political intervention is a paramount issue. The "criminal U.S. invasion of Grenada in 1983" after a counterrevolutionary coup that overthrew the Bishop government is an oft-repeated example, as is "its murderous mercenary war against Nicaragua, its support to repressive, rightist regimes from El Salvador to Haiti to Jamaica." The "low intensity" conflicts in Central America are promoted by the United States to stop "the people's struggle" against conditions of poverty and oppression of the existing regime. As an example, "It is estimated that U.S. aid for the war in El Salvador runs about $3 million per day." In supporting the leaders of Haiti, inheritors of the mantle of bloody, repressive dictatorships, the United States was acting against the Haitian peoples' efforts to eradicate these conditions. The U.S. government also used political and economic measures to destabilize the government of Panama, which it perceived to be hostile to its interests.

Military-political manipulation by the United States is evident in both Panama and Puerto Rico, where the United States maintains military bases. According to the 1977 canal treaties, negotiated by President Jimmy Carter and General Omar Torrijos, the U.S. Armed Forces were to have a limited role, in contrast to the past, "exclusively to provide protection and defense of the canal"; however, these forces assert their presence more broadly. "The Southern Command . . . is an enormous complex dedicated to military control, espionage, and intervention against all the countries of Latin America and the Caribbean." Similarly, Puerto Rico—site of more than 60 military installations and bases—is used as a staging ground for invading troops as well as for training of troops.

The tactics of the United States are censured.

> On March 2, 1917, the U.S. Congress approved a law called the Jones Act, imposing U.S. citizenship on Puerto Ricans. Leaving aside the dramatic implications that such an imposition has on a people struggling to defend its nationality and independence, the Jones Act paved the way for the use of Puerto Rico and Puerto Ricans for military purposes.

Such imposition denied the voice of the local populace to mediate against the militarization of the island.

A frequently named culprit in this current military-political-economic imperialism is President Ronald Reagan and his government. Identified respectively as arrogant and warmongering, they are held accountable for the Grenada invasion, launched on "trivial pretexts," which was accompanied by CIA payoffs to Caribbean governments that supported the invasion, and other "dialogue[s] of war." The Reagan doctrine "is based on the most enormous nuclear arms race and on support for military counterrevolution in the Third World that has two sides to it: counterinsurgency and insurgency." The attempts to "trampl[e] underfoot" the Panama Treaties and undermine Panama's government by economic reprisals, developing a united front of right-wing political parties and initiating a process of "social subversion," are also assigned to the Reagan administration. The latter is analogous to a "Trojan horse to guarantee U.S. penetration and rule of the Caribbean."

A ribbon of sentences intoning calls for collective action and for unity ripple through these speeches:

> This unity is necessary so that the Caribbean will no longer be a sea of war, plowed by imperialist fleets that stifle popular rebellions, drown national revolutions in blood, overthrow patriotic governments, threaten and menace with giant military maneuvers, and impose puppet governments.
>
> What good will unity serve if it does not hold out the promise for more social and economic justice, if it does not guarantee more human rights, more democracy, more cultural and intellectual sovereignty, high standards of living, and better quality of life?

These calls express the ultimate goals of the Anti-Imperialist Organizations of the Caribbean and Central America.

CENSORSHIP HISTORY

On two occasions, October 18, 1988, and March 8, 1989, customs officials in Grenada confiscated boxes of books being shipped by Pathfinder Press, a publisher of political, historical, and academic books based in New York. *One People, One Destiny: The Caribbean and Central America Today* was one of the confiscated books.

The first shipment of several boxes accompanied a Pathfinder representative who had been invited to participate in activities commemorating the fifth anniversary of the murder of Prime Minister Maurice Bishop. According to a Pathfinder release from March 1989, the representative was informed that the books could not be admitted because they were "against our system" and the titles were being checked against "a list of banned books." The second shipment of four boxes had been shipped to Terence Marryshow, leader of the Maurice Bishop Patriotic Movement (MBPM), via Federal Express. Another box of books belonging to Grenadian journalist and political activist Einstein Louison, being delivered by Pathfinder director Steve Clark, was also confiscated. Clark was told that the books were restricted in Grenada, but the official would not cite the laws or explain how the list of restricted books was determined.

In the months succeeding these seizures, protests, in addition to those of Pathfinder Press, were issued by PEN American Center and the Committee to Protect Journalists. Condemnatory statements were also made by novelist Graham Greene, British member of Parliament Tony Benn, U.S. representatives George Crockett and Ronald Dellums, and Canadian New Democratic Party leader Roland Marin. A petition protesting the book banning was signed by 34 representatives of publishers, bookstores, and distributors attending the Eighth International Book Fair of Radical, Black and Third World Books in London.

In a related action, officials of the Grenadian government barred the conference participation of four persons from the United States—Steve Clark, Meryl Lynn Farber, Argiris Malapanis, and University of Minnesota professor August Nimtz—by granting only three-day visas and refusing to extend them.

On March 20, 1989, a suit was filed by MBPM leader Terry Marryshow in Grenada's High Court of Justice to challenge the constitutionality of the 1951 law, enacted during the British colonial rule, under which the books had been banned. The suit charged that the book-banning law violated 13 sections of Grenada's 1973 constitution: The law "is in conflict with the rights guaranteed me by the said Constitution and . . . cannot reasonably be justified in a democratic society." The lawsuit further seeks "an injunction restraining [the government of Prime Minister Herbert Blaize] from sending [Marryshow's] publications out of Grenada or otherwise parting with same until the trial of the Motion or further order of the Court."

According to Kendrick Radix, attorney for the plaintiff, the British colonial law had been repealed by the People's Revolutionary Government led by Maurice Bishop after it gained power in the March 13, 1979, revolution. Radix, who had served as attorney general in the revolutionary government, also argued that if a claim was made that the 1951 law was in effect and constitutional, the seized books could not be among the titles banned in that legislation. He pointed out that the government could not keep a secret, unpublished list of barred books.

The trial, scheduled for April 7, 1989, was postponed at the request of government lawyers on April 7 and again on April 21. In the interim, on April 11, the Importation of Publication (Prohibition) Order was issued by British Commonwealth governor general Paul Schoon and the Cabinet of Prime Minister Herbert Blaize. On the grounds that it "would be contrary to the public interest," the order prohibited "importation into the State of any past, present, or future issue of any of the publications mentioned. . . ." Eighty-six titles were identified, including *One People, One Destiny*.

Although legal documents have been presented, the High Court had not as of March of 1997 ruled on the case despite several written requests to the judges and a written request to the chief justice. The decree remains in effect.

On March 1, 1996, the Inter-American Commission on Human Rights, an agency of the Organization of American States, issued a 12-page report that concluded with three findings:

> The "right to freedom of thought and expression" of the petitioners has been violated by the Government of Grenada. This right to "freedom of thought and expression" is one which is contained in Article 13 of the American Convention on Human Rights.
>
> The Government of Grenada must lift the ban on the books which remain under the banning order.
>
> The Government of Grenada must adopt the necessary measures to ensure that its Legislation is brought into conformity with Article 13 of the American Convention on Human Rights.

These findings resulted from an investigation of allegations that Grenadian officials had attacked freedom of speech, press, and information. Requests of information on May 2 and September 21, 1989, and again, subsequent to the Marryshow suit challenging the constitutionality of the 1951 British Colonial Law, on October 2, 1992, were followed by five others from April 28, 1993, to June 21, 1995.

Because Grenada is a party to the American Convention on Human Rights, having ratified it on July 18, 1978, the Commission analyzed the evidence in accordance with its procedures (Article 46) and rules (Article 13). The latter is concerned with "the right to freedom of thought and expression . . . includ[ing] freedom to seek, receive and impart information and ideas of all kinds." The Commission found that the Grenada government's "act of seizing and banning the books has the effect of imposing 'prior censorship' on the freedom of expression and therefore has violated the two-fold aspects of the right to receive and impart information to 'everyone' both within and outside the community."

Other notable materials barred include THE STRUGGLE IS MY LIFE by Nelson Mandela; *Maurice Bishop Speaks: The Grenada Revolution 1979–83* by Maurice Bishop; *Malcolm X Speaks* by Malcolm X; *Nothing Can Stop the Course of History: An Interview with Fidel Castro* by Congressman Mervyn Dymally and Jeffrey M. Elliott; and many works reflecting socialist and communist doctrine, including THE MANIFESTO OF THE COMMUNIST PARTY, by Karl Marx and Friedrich Engels, and THE STATE AND REVOLUTION, by V. I. Lenin.

FURTHER READING

Baumann, Michael, and Michael Taber. Pathfinder Books. Telephone conversations. November 1996 and March 1997.
Importation of Publications (Prohibition) Order. Grenada. Statutory Rules and Orders No. 6 of 1989. Gazetted April 14, 1989.
Inter-American Commission on Human Rights. Report No 2/96, Case 10.325. Grenada. Washington, D.C.: Organization of American States, March 1, 1996.
Pathfinder Press releases. New York. October 19, 1988; March 10, April 5, April 27, 1989; and April 9, 1996.
"St. George's Grenada." *Newsletter on Intellectual Freedom* 38 (1989): 49–50, 141–142.

THE OPEN SORE OF A CONTINENT: A PERSONAL NARRATIVE OF THE NIGERIAN CRISIS

Author: Wole Soyinka
Original date and place of publication: 1996, United States
Original publisher: Oxford University Press
Literary form: Nonfiction

SUMMARY

Novelist, playwright, poet, and 1986 Nobel Prize winner, Wole Soyinka is also an educator, political analyst, and human rights activist. In *The Open Sore of a Continent: A Personal Narrative of the Nigerian Crisis*, Soyinka takes a political stance, diagnosing and revealing the issues his country faced and the corruption of its government officials. The book is divided into four segments, the commentary in these segments being interlocking.

In the first segment, "A Flawed Origin—but No Worse Than Others," Soyinka asks the critical question, What is a nation? Several possible answers are offered in the context of considering Nigeria's future as a nation or nations. (Alternative questions are also asked: When is a nation? At what price is a nation?) Some of the answers are subjective; a nation could be a condition of the collective mind or an expression of the will to nationhood. Ireland serves as an example of the latter. It could also be formed through the ruthless repression of nationalist claims, as was the case with the Soviet Union. Or it could be a political entity, such as France, Sweden, Japan, or Ghana. Yet, evidence of separatist movements—the Basques in Spain, the Kurds in Turkey—disrupts the conditioned response to these nations. Even geographical coherence does not necessarily offer nation-state certitude—witness the separation of Pakistan from India, and then Bangladesh from Pakistan.

The problem of nationality, exhibiting an international concern with ethnicity and statehood, is exemplified by Nigeria. It has experienced a bitter and horrific civil war, a "so-called war of unity and ended up intact—geographically at least," and had a section of eastern Nigeria that split off, deciding to join Cameroon. The non-negotiability of national boundaries declared by every military junta is questioned. "The inviolability principle of national boundaries is therefore a fictitious concept, born out of nothing more substantial than faith, and therefore every bit as questionable for those of the rational world." Soyinka asserts that the occupants of the nation as a whole must decide whether it serves the collective self-interest to continue as one nation.

The election of June 12, 1993, was a potential turning point for Nigeria. "No need for illegal or contestable improvisation was encountered anywhere; the structures of voting and counting were unimpaired. Order was the order of the day." Soyinka asserts with this national triumph that the Nigerian people proclaimed their readiness to evolve into a single entity. Chief Moshood Abiola was the clear winner. Then, the dictator, Major General Ibrahim Babangida, who in 1985 had ousted the previous military dictator, Major General Muhamadu Buhari, annulled the election. Soyinka declares, "It is 100 percent certain that there never again will be an acceptable election exercise in this country." Babangida gets full measure of negation, both for the mismanagement and corruption of his regime—he served no one so well as himself—and this electoral "crime against the Nigerian humanity."

As the second segment's subtitle indicates, "The Spoils of Power: The Buhari-Shagari Casebook" focuses on two government leaders: Shehu Shagari, elected to the presidency in 1979, and Buhari, who gained that office through the 1983 coup d'état. The "spoils of power" are defined as far more lethal than the spoils of office: "The spoils that accompany power are not as particularized as those of office, but they nevertheless constitute a brutal exaction from the populace, savaging their psyche and intimating to them a kind of essential worthlessness." Bequeathed by the former British colonial masters, this phenomenon is tenacious: Selected "scions are groomed in the tradition," power being "routinely handed down from villain to villain and extended retroactively to shield past villains," thereby perpetuating protection and immunity from retribution. Features of such power are revenge and violence. Revenge is the response to exposure of inadequacies of the governments and its rulers toward those who are critically perceptive of the ruled and "reject the actuality of social retardation that continues to be their portion." And a significant outcome is corruption on a massive scale.

Shagari, perceived by Western powers to be a "quiet, unassuming, committed democrat," initiated the breakdown of Nigeria's economy, according to Soyinka, through an "import license" policy, a party-member patronage scheme whereby party loyalists were able to pad private accounts. This policy represented a loss of billions of dollars to the state and caused the national debt to spiral out of control, Nigeria becoming a "beggar nation." Shagari is also accused of turning Nigeria into a police state as the 1983 election campaign approached by investing authority in an "uncouth, power-crazed police chief, one Sunday Adewusi, who promptly inaugurated a scorched-earth policy in order to ensure his master's second tenure as Nigeria's head of state." A "Kill-and-Go" approach was applied: For example, six members of a rival party traveling in a minibus were ambushed by "thugs of the National Party of Nigeria" and fired upon, the bus was set on fire, and the occupants were clubbed back as they tried to escape while more than 100 armed police sat in four open-sided vans and watched. In another incident, a medical doctor was arrested for picking up some injured survivors of one of Adewusi's assaults on unarmed citizens, locked up, accused of being a doctor of rebels, and tortured.

The "villainous despot," General Buhari, ousted Shagari, placed him under house arrest, and instead of taking action against Adewusi—he was allowed to retire with full benefits and entitlements—acted against opposition leaders to "discredit the entire caste of politicians . . . a selective discrediting agenda . . . largely the intellectuals and politicians both of the north and south. They wrote themselves into Nigerian, African and possibly global history by staging a *coup d'état*, not against an incumbent government but against the opposition to that government." The Buhari regime replaced the "import license racket" with "counter trade," a version of trade by barter, which was "massively corruptible"; "there is no question that [Buhari's] colleagues within the military and the usual business partners did" so, to the detriment of the state. Buhari introduced record-breaking prison sentences of 200 and 300 years and nation muzzling decrees, including Decree No. 2, which "declared a journalist guilty, with a penalty of prison without option of a fine, not for publishing lies against the government or its officials but for publishing the truth, if such truths brought the government or any of its officials into public ridicule and contempt."

In "The National Question: Internal Imperatives," segment three, Soyinka is largely concerned with the postelection 1993 present and the future. The dictatorial regime of General Sani Abacha established by a coup in 1993 continued the repression and violence against the Nigerian people. Under Abacha's direct command, more than 200 peaceful demonstrators, intent on expressing resistance, were gunned down on the streets of Lagos, for example. Abacha arrested Chief Moshood Abiolo, charged him with high treason, and imprisoned him. Abacha's dictatorship put a stranglehold on the once vibrant press—now "officially dead." Abacha sent to Ogoniland, having declared it a military zone, a murderous "pacification team" that has subjected its people to "ethnic cleansing" including "arbitrary displacement, expropriation of their property, violence on their persons, and the rape of their womanhood," as well as massacre activities. It was after one of these events, the murder of four traditional chiefs, that the leader of the Movement for the Salvation of the Ogoni People (MOSUP), Ken Saro-Wiwa, was charged with complicity in the murders. He was not present, having been prevented by the police at a roadblock on security grounds. A special Civil Disturbances Tribunal tried the case and convicted Saro-Wiwa, who was subsequently hanged. (See A MONTH AND A DAY: A DETENTION DIARY.)

Having indicated and condemned the infringements on political and civil liberties by several military governments, having documented human rights violations, having further identified significant lapses in public services—health services, potable water, public transportation, education, and sufficient food—Soyinka asserts, "Under dictatorship, a nation ceases to exist." A dictatorship annuls the process of choice and participation.

> When we espouse the cause of democracy, therefore, our minds encompass more than the ritual of the polling booth and the change of baton at the end of an agreed-upon number of years. Side by side with the eradication of the uniformed mutants who erupt from time to time on our national landscapes, we consider also a dispensation that enables all humanity to breathe freely, to associate freely, to think freely, and to believe or not believe without a threat to their existence and without discrimination in their social rights. Implicit in that freedom of association is, difficult as it may be to accept, the right of collective dissociation.

In his conclusion, Soyinka recognizes that the history of many nations is flawed but that the human mind can encompass this recognition and develop "new directions that redress the history of societies and humanize the destiny of their peoples." (Author's note: Both military dictator, Sani Abacha, and the duly elected claimant to the presidential office, Chief Moshood Abiolo, died in 1998.)

CENSORSHIP HISTORY

Soyinka has not been averse to voicing his opinions. In 1994 in a public statement, he identified the then Nigerian head of state General Sani Abacha as a psychopath who suffered from an inferiority complex. By early November of 1994, plans to eliminate Soyinka finalized, and he was put under surveillance. Asked to report to the State Security Service in Lagos but forewarned that he was to be detained—his international passport having been seized, his United Nations documents confiscated—he escaped through the borders. He lived in exile until 1998, when he returned to Nigeria.

During his exile he became an outspoken critic of the Abacha regime. He was charged with treason in 1997. *The Open Sore of a Continent* was published in the United States and the United Kingdom but not in Africa. It was available in Cape Town, South Africa, in 1998, but, as Kole Omotoso notes, "thanks to the tumbling rand, it is well beyond the pockets of those who would best benefit from what it contributes to the debate about the state of Africa."

Yet these difficulties with Nigerian authorities and its censors were not Soyinka's first. Soyinka's works have been censored in Nigeria: first, several radio plays in 1962, then his 1972 autobiography, THE MAN DIED: PRISON NOTES OF WOLE SOYINKA, in 1984. He was in and out of prison two times: in 1965 for three months, having been falsely accused of broadcasting false election results on the radio, and in 1967 for 27 months, arrested but never charged, falsely accused of supporting the rebels during the Nigerian civil war.

Soyinka's first exile was self-imposed. It occurred after his imprisonment and after the civil war had ended. It was during this period that he wrote *The Man Died*. A second exile was involuntary in 1983 during President Shagari's civilian government and Inspector-General Adewusi's regime. He had denounced the election as fraudulent and had been active in attempting to get the results rejected. Again, he had been warned of the intention and the details of the plan by members of the police force, who actually at the impending time took him to the airport to effect his escape. During this exile he was constantly on the move, his life threatened repeatedly.

FURTHER READING

Omotoso, Kole. "The Necessity of the State." *Black Renaissance* 1, no. 3 (1993): 90–93.
Ononuga, Bayo. "Soyinka Tells His Exile Story." In *Conversations with Wole Soyinka.* Ed. Biodun Jeyifo. Jackson: University of Mississippi Press, 2001.

OUR LAND, OUR TIME: A HISTORY OF THE UNITED STATES

Author: Joseph Robert Conlin
Original date and place of publication: 1985, United States
Publisher: Coronado Publishers
Literary form: Textbook

SUMMARY

Our Land, Our Time, a chronological history of the United States, begins with the arrival of the first people in the Americas in 25,000 B.C. and concludes in the 1980s with the Reagan administration. It is a standard text with respect to covering the major events, people, and movements of American history in its 10 units (34 chapters). It also includes numerous vignettes of lesser-known but significant events and citizens. Most challenges to this

11th-grade textbook have focused on its alleged "one-sided presentation" and its coverage of the 20th century.

After a 10-page summary of the migration of Indians across the Bering Strait corridor and the general variations among their cultures according to the large geographic regions of the continent, the text turns to explorations, quarrels among nations, and colonial settlements. The familiar deeds of discovery and less familiar (to young readers) misdeeds are recounted. For instance, brave but ruthless Hernando Cortez (Hernán Cortés), the Spanish conquistador, and his army killed more than 17,000 Aztec in battle and through diseases. "Hundreds of thousands more died when forced to work at a pace to which they were not accustomed" and under poor conditions in the mines and on the plantations. Among the other colonies there were contrasts: The Dutch of New Amsterdam and the English Quakers in Pennsylvania treated the Indians honestly, buying land from them, as did Roger Williams who established a settlement in Rhode Island; the other English colonists took the land they wanted. The Dutch and the Quakers did not suffer reprisals.

President Andrew Jackson was "quite ruthless" in his treatment of southeastern tribes. Despite the treaty of 1791, despite their having made peace with the whites and having adopted many of their customs, despite a Supreme Court ruling supporting them, the so-called Civilized Tribes were forced to give up their lands.

> Georgia ignored the court and Jackson refused to enforce the decision. By 1835 the Cherokees too were worn down and agreed to move to Oklahoma. Their tragic 800-mile (1,300-kilometer) trek in 1838 became known as the "Trail of Tears." Neglected and abused by the soldiers that accompanied them, the Cherokees and other southeastern tribes lost thousands of people to disease and starvation.

Contrasts in religious attitudes are also evident in the text. A group of Protestants, the Separatists (given the name "Pilgrims" in the 1800s), and the Puritans, who suffered from religious intolerance in England, were themselves militantly intolerant of other religions. In Rhode Island and Pennsylvania religious tolerance was practiced; religious persecution was rare outside of Massachusetts.

Suggested initially in connection with the introduction of slavery among the colonies, the issue of equal rights is found throughout the text. The significance and the idealism of the Bill of Rights and the Declaration of Independence for both the beginning and later United States are expressed, in part, by adverse examples. Wealthy eastern South Carolina colonists refused to allow back-country settlers to organize county governments of their own for fear they would grow and gain control of the colonial assembly. Although it is unclear what Jefferson meant by "men" when he wrote "all men are created equal" in the Declaration of Independence, in practice a married woman was "required to turn over the management of her property to her husband in every colony ... [and] could not engage in business without [his] permission"; nor could women vote. Slaves were denied the right to pursue happiness (the opportunity to own property, the right to pursue economic security and riches) as well as liberty.

Even these supposedly inalienable rights were qualified. Only in Massachusetts were black people thought to be covered by a bill of rights. The Massachusetts Supreme Court ruled that slavery was abolished because the state constitution said that "all men are born free and equal," and the state bill of rights guaranteed personal liberty. Nowhere else was this action taken soon, and some southern states explicitly stated that their bills of rights did not apply to slaves or even to free blacks.

After the United States was established, the right to vote was expanded generally to grant suffrage to every male who paid taxes; previously only white male heads of households could vote; there also was a property ownership requirement. The voting privilege gradually was extended by the end of the 1820s to all adult white males. Women did not achieve that right until 1920, although the struggle to achieve it started formally in 1848. Blacks were given the vote after the Civil War, but black southerners lost this right and other civil liberties after white Democrats regained control of these states. Although steps had been initiated in the 1940s, not until the civil rights movement in the 1960s were these denied liberties more fully achieved.

The transformation of the United States from an agricultural to an industrial economy began as early as the first decade of the 19th century. Fueled by American ingenuity—inventions designed upon inventions in both machinery and manufacturing processes, supported by a growing banking system and available labor—the nation was catapulted toward the future. Agriculture itself was altered by advanced farm equipment. These marvelous feats and advances in lifestyle—from transportation to processed foods—and standard of living were marred by greed and corruption, and by inhumane working conditions and long hours, particularly for women and children. In addition to slavery, there was a bias against immigrants, other nonwhites, and Catholics.

The disparity between the earning power of industrial magnates and merchants and that of working people and farmers became sharply evident in the late 19th century. Reform movements to improve working and financial conditions punctuated the 19th and 20th centuries. Reformer presidents like Republican Theodore Roosevelt and Democrat Franklin D. Roosevelt, both of whom were inconsistent and politically conscious, effected changes as did the success of labor unions. Reform crusades led by citizens and politicians took action against corruption in government and a great variety of social ills ranging from slavery and civil rights to unsanitary food processing, education, health, and hygiene.

The representation of the political administrations over the 20th century is necessarily constrained by space. Some administrations are highlighted, given the events and issues during their terms in office; both Roosevelts, for example, are afforded more space than Harding, Carter, or Reagan (whose administration is in its third year when the text concludes). Of the presidents themselves, efforts to acknowledge their perceived character strengths and deficiencies are evident; their accomplishments and failures are recounted. Republican "Teddy" Roosevelt, described as "exuberant, assertive," took "bold action" against some trusts, was the "worker's friend," supporting conservative labor unions, but was "hostile and aggressive" toward those who advocated socialism. He is also credited as a major conservationist. FDR is perceived as helping the working class through instituting jobs programs. A "man of action," "decisive," and "a compassionate man who was truly concerned about others," Roosevelt's "first great strength" was a practical attitude of flexibility: "It is common sense to take a method and try it. If it fails, admit it frankly and try another." Both men were criticized by members of their own party and the opposition party.

Woodrow Wilson is acknowledged for "honesty, integrity, and a refusal to deal with corrupt party bosses" and for being an idealist about a "new world order." His stubbornness against any changes in the League of Nations Treaty is cited as the reason for its defeat. Warren G. Harding, "a likeable, humane man" who persuaded the leaders of the steel industry to reduce the workday in their mills to eight hours, was not an active president; he was also a victim of several of his unscrupulous cabinet appointees. Herbert Hoover, described as a "cool, brilliant administrator" and "humane," became, undeservedly, "the villain of the Great Depression"; Calvin Coolidge's policies were identified as instrumental in depressing the economy. Hoover's philosophy of rugged individualism caused him to delay action but measures taken in 1931 and 1932 did create jobs and shore up the economy. Idealistic Jimmy Carter failed to get congressional support for his attempts to solve economic and energy problems but did negotiate a Panama Canal Treaty and the Camp David Accords, a treaty between Israel and Egypt. Carter "dedicated his administration to the cause of human rights everywhere in the world." Ronald Reagan's "administrative ability . . . made a better impression than did that of Jimmy Carter"; he acted quickly on "the most innovative legislative program since [President Lyndon B.] Johnson's Great Society." Reagan argued against huge government expenses and reduced spending on social programs, but increased military spending in order "to restore America's prestige in the world."

> In 1981, because of the President's spending, the accumulated national debt reached $998 billion. In 1982, for the first time, the national debt rose to over $1 trillion. The critic of big government spending had borrowed and spent more money than any president before.

CENSORSHIP HISTORY

Education Research Analysts (ERA) is best known for its textbook reviews and its lists of disapproved books, which are circulated to other groups around the country. Its directors, Mel and Norma Gabler, testify every year at the Texas state textbook adoption proceedings, and they have been successful in persuading publishers to modify books to meet their demands, according to the 1986–87 report, *Attacks on Freedom to Learn*, by People For the American Way (PFAW). They have also been successful in promoting textbook and classroom library book challenges across the country.

On November 9, 1985, however, the Texas State Board of Education declined to reject the U.S. history textbook *Our Land, Our Time*; it also refused to require publishers to identify the political affiliation of every person quoted in their history books. Michael Hudson, PFAW's Texas director, applauded the decision. "Today the State Board of Education showed the nation that Texas was not backing down on its commitment to improve textbook content. Sound history won out over sectarian bias."

The Gablers had charged that the history textbook was "negative" and biased against Republicans, conservatives, and Reagan: "They give children a one-sided presentation that is totally biased, using glowing terms every time they refer to a Democrat and derogatory terms every time they refer to a Republican." *Attacks on Freedom to Learn* quotes Mel Gabler, who offered the Gablers' view of history on a 1982 PBS broadcast:

> One thing that we have to consider in the American history [books] is that so much emphasis is put upon so many of the minorities. The great majority of Americans are being short shrifted throughout American history. . . . And then Mrs. Rosa Parks, now I believe this was put in to get the woman mentioned. I think to resurrect people that were hardly known and give them predominant space is not fair to the great men who did accomplish something in this country.

Since *Our Land, Our Time* does include a sidebar featuring Rosa Parks, the quotation is pertinent to this 1985 challenge. (The text offers a series of such spotlights on individuals under the heading "Movers and Shakers"; individuals so honored include such diverse figures as Benjamin Franklin, Sojourner Truth, Clara Barton, Montgomery Ward, Jane Addams, and John Muir. Spotlight profiles of every president are also included.)

A contrasting evaluation was expressed by Raymond J. Lockett, chair of the history department at Southern University and a member of the local school system's Multicultural Committee. In this capacity he reviewed books used in public school classrooms. While he found aspects of the 1987 edition of *Our Land, Our Time* to be positive—for example, the book "explain[s] a lot about slavery and the subservient role"—he also stated that "Blacks were dissatisfied with the institution of slavery, but you would never learn that from reading the text." Also, the text "gives no information about black soldiers' contributions to the American Revolution, the Civil War and World War I." Lockett also asserts, among other concerns, that there is little discussion about the different civil rights movements through the 1950s and 1960s although "this was the movement that changed the face of America."

Two school challenges of *Our Land, Our Time* occurred in 1986, both of them in Texas, despite the state board ruling. In Richardson and Pasadena, the text was maintained on close votes of 3-2 (March 4) and 4-3 (March 31), respectively. The Richardson challenge was initiated by community members, while the Pasadena objections were raised by school board trustees. In Pasadena, the trustees had previously voted to request that its 47-member district textbook committee review its original recommendation. Four committee representatives, one from each high school, attended the school board meeting, and again recommended the text, indicating that it "meets all of the criteria" and included the essential elements. Jack Ray, supervisor of social studies for the district, commended the committee members' commitment and expertise, based on 60 years of classroom teaching. He also noted that the claims that the book opposed the free enterprise system were "evidently taken out of context"; he added that the same claim had been made at the state textbook committee hearing.

A third challenge, more indirect, occurred in Boise, Idaho, in the context of a proposal by a state legislator to require that the membership of the 13-member State Textbook and Improvement of Instruction Committee be changed to include two members who would not be professional educators. The legislation would also require local school boards to create district textbook committees, one-fourth of whose memberships would be noneducators. Representative Jerry Callen's purpose in this legislation was to curb the adoption of textbooks found to be objectionable. He cited examples of such books that were brought to his attention by Concerned Women of America, founded by Beverly LaHaye, wife of televangelist Tim LaHaye, and by the fundamentalist Christian Coalition Association. The charge levied against *Our Land, Our Time* was that it gave the Soviet Union and the United States equal weight, instead of emphasizing America's position. (Of the text's 832 pages, as evident in the index, a total of about three pages in nine entries offer discussion of the Soviet Union; there are also six additional instances when the Soviet Union is mentioned.) Two examples of the text's representation of the Soviet Union are revealing: "The President [FDR] did not like Soviet communism or Joseph Stalin's dictatorship. . . . [but] to continue nonrecognition was unrealistic"; "Americans thought of Soviet Communists as ruthless, brutal atheists who were bent on destroying democracy and capitalism." The Boise school board approved the text.

FURTHER READING

Attacks on Freedom to Learn: 1985–1986 Report and *1986–87 Report*. Washington, D.C.: People For the American Way, 1986 and 1987.
Newsletter on Intellectual Freedom 35 (1986): 21–22, 82, 137.
Warren, Chante Dionne. "Black History Month: History Text Called Incomplete." [Baton Rouge, La.] *Advocate*, February 1, 1996, p. 2B.

PARADISE OF THE BLIND

Author: Duong Thu Huong
Original dates and places of publication: 1988, Vietnam; 1993, United States
Publishers: Women's Publishing House; William Morrow and Company
Literary form: Novel

SUMMARY

Paradise of the Blind is set in the Soviet Union and Vietnam in the 1980s. Its narrator heroine, Hang, a Vietnamese woman in her early 20s, is forced by her economic need (and the economic plight of Vietnam) to be an "export worker" in a Russian factory. She supports her mother, Que, whose leg has been amputated after having been struck by an automobile. A gifted student, Hang has cut short her university education to undertake this responsibility.

A telegram—"Very ill. Come immediately."—comes from her despised Uncle Chinh, her mother's younger brother, who has used his connections in a Communist Party cadre to secure a position in Moscow. Hang does not know it, but the illness is a fraud. Though rebellious about her duty, ill and short of funds, she takes the train to Moscow to fulfill her family obligation, a tradition of honoring a male family member maintained initially by her mother. En route she recounts family history and relives her childhood experiences.

Orphaned in their late teens, Que and Chinh followed different paths. Que stayed in their northern village and married "handsome Ton"; Chinh joined the Liberation Army and became a Communist Party functionary. Upon his return to the village, in charge of the campaign for land reform and needing to protect his own image and status, he insists on the break-up of his sister's marriage. Ton's family has been designated as belonging to the "exploiting class"—they owned a few acres of rice paddy, and during the harvest season they hired migrant workers. Working in the fields herself, Aunt Tam, Ton's older sister, is considered a "pillar of the countryside," yet the family is to be "denounced and punished." Ton, unable to face the humiliation, feels forced to flee, assisted by his sister. Hang reveals:

> My mother never understood the tragedy that had befallen her. Like so many others at this time, she began to live in constant terror. Uncle Chinh struck hard and fast. My grandmother and my aunt were forced to prostrate themselves, heads bowed, arms crossed behind their backs, in the communal village courtyard. Facing them, behind a blaze of torches, sat the people of our village. They obeyed orders: "Listen to our denunciation of their crimes. Then, shout a slogan: 'Down with the landowning classes!' Raise your fist like this and scream: 'Down, down!'"

Land reform devastates fields and rice paddies and also foments misery and anger. Some years later, when the Rectification of Errors program is initiated to return rice paddies to their rightful owners, Chinh goes into hiding, so the villagers turn on Que as the target of their vengeance. Rescued by Aunt Tam, Que escapes to Hanoi, where she earns her livelihood as a food vendor. During this interval, Ton, who has made another life for himself, locates Que; the love rekindled, Hang is conceived, but Ton dies before being able to settle the affairs of his second life in order to return to Que.

Hang's memories weave two tapestries: Que and Hang's relationship with Aunt Tam, who, with constant hard work, persistence, and cleverness, reestablished herself and became wealthy; and Que and Hang's relationship with Uncle Chinh and his wife, who have achieved some party hierarchy. These memories encompass Hang's childhood through her 20th year.

Hang meets Aunt Tam during her childhood. The event is fraught with emotion. Aunt Tam, recognizing her brother in Hang's face—"She's a drop of his blood. My niece"—is ecstatic. In keeping with family tradition and the legacy of male authority, she undertakes to provide for Hang with feasts of food, gifts of jewelry, money, clothes, and university living expenses. The bond between the two grows beyond duty to include respect and affection, although Hang is troubled by the excess of gifts.

Que maintains the same obeisance to tradition in her response to her brother. Despite Chinh's criticism of her working as a vendor in the manner of a capitalist entrepreneur and refusing to take a job in a factory—that is, refusing to join the working class at a lower salary—Que fawns on him and his family. She expends her energy and her funds to provide food for them to supplement his meager party salary. She deprives herself and Hang, becoming in her fervor significantly self-destructive, emotionally and physically. Hang, recognizing her uncle as a fraud—corrupt, conniving, self-aggrandizing, arrogant, and cruel—distances herself.

The sisterly relationship between Que and Tam is undermined and ultimately destroyed by Chinh. When Tam sees how Hang's well-being is affected, holding Chinh in contempt as the de facto murderer of Ton and destroyer of their lives, she accuses Que of misplaced loyalty. She determines to support only Hang. This creates a schism between mother and daughter that Hang is unable to bridge. Indeed, before her mother's accident, Hang had left home, expelled by her mother's anger, to live in the university dormitory. Later, when Hang goes to her uncle to seek aid for her disabled mother, she receives excuses and avoidance. This leads to her employment in the Soviet Union and her abhorrence of Uncle Chinh.

Superimposed on this tapestry of family relationships are the manifestations of the Communist Party and the corrupt manipulation of the government officials who betray the revolution. Uncle Chinh is the party's champion and its embodiment, although not the only one. He berates an erring subordinate:

The party has led the people to victory, a huge victory. It has made us humanity's conscience, the flame of the liberation of oppressed people everywhere.
Of the three great international revolutionary trends, we are the touchstone,
the standard. You must commit yourself to this truth.

Ironically, on another occasion he lectures, "Comrades, you must behave in
an exemplary manner while you are in this brother country. Each one of you
must show you are capable of perfect organization and discipline." Yet he
engages in illicit trading of goods, using his position to access Vietnamese
goods to exchange for Russian consumer products to be resold in Vietnam
for his profit. He leeches on Hang to serve this purpose, the real reason for
the "Very ill" telegram.

Other examples of corruption: Aunt Chinh, a senior party member, is
the dean of an entire philosophy department; she supervises truly educated
persons, though she has completed but two short remedial courses designed
"for workers and peasants." The vice president of the village, misusing his
power, evicts a widow from her land, upon which she is dependent for her
livelihood, and he brags about his accomplishment because he wants it for
his daughter, who is to be married. There are other examples of repression
and misery, fear and humiliation. Hang comes to grips with the overpowering effect of these evils when she watches a small group of young Japanese
traveling in the Soviet Union.

What did these people have that we didn't have? Hundreds of faces rose in
my memory: those of my friends, people of my generation, faces gnawed with
worry, shattered faces, twisted, ravaged, sooty, frantic faces. . . . Our faces
were always taut, lean with fear. The fear that we might not be able to pay for
food, or not send it in time, the fear of learning that an aging father or mother
had passed away while waiting for our miserable subsidies.

Hang leaves Moscow to return to her factory dormitory, even more disillusioned with Uncle Chinh, even more conscious of his corruption. His life
is a lie, she has discovered, for in Moscow he works as a cook/servant for a
group of young men.

Learning of Aunt Tam's imminent death, Hang hurries back to Hanoi.
There, she is partly reconciled with her mother; Uncle Chinh's legacy stands
between them. Upon Aunt Tam's death, she participates in the funeral and
orchestrates the several necessary ceremonies. As Aunt Tam's beneficiary,
she becomes wealthy. However, as she contemplates the village around her,
she comes to a resolution:

And I saw the pond again, the stagnant water, stinking, bloodied by the
sunset. . . . I saw my village, this cesspool of ambition, all the laughter and
tears that had drowned in these bamboo groves. . . .
    Comets extinguish themselves, but memory refuses to die, and "hell's
money" has no value in the market of life. Forgive me, my aunt: I'm going to

sell this house and leave all this behind. We can honor the wishes of the dead with a few flowers on a grave somewhere. I can't squander my life tending these faded flowers, these shadows, the legacy of past crimes.

CENSORSHIP HISTORY

For 10 years, starting at age 21, Duong Thu Huong led a Communist Youth Brigade unit at the front during the Vietnam War, living in tunnels and underground shelters alongside regular North Vietnamese troops. She was part of a theatrical troupe, responsible for arranging performances to entertain soldiers and people in bombed-out areas. Their purpose was to enhance morale. She was one of three survivors of a unit of 40 men and women.

After decades of activism with the Vietnamese Communist Party, Duong became disillusioned; in the 1980s she wrote and spoke about the political and spiritual chaos of Vietnam, for the most part at official Party and Writers' Union Congress functions or in interviews with official Party literary magazines. The first censorship and banning of Duong's books occurred in the early 1980s. In 1982 she publicly protested, at the Third Congress of the Writers' Union, the censorship of a screenplay. Between 1982 and 1985, a party banning order ensured that none of her work was published. A documentary she had independently produced, *A Sanctuary for the Despairing*, about the inhuman conditions in a camp for 600–700 "mentally ill" war veterans, was destroyed by security police under orders of Party Secretary Nguyen Van Linh.

Published in 1988, *Paradise of the Blind*, Duong's third novel, was denounced by Nguyen Van Linh, who issued a second banning order. It outraged Vietnamese leaders, particularly the sections describing the 1953–56 land reform campaign—its excesses and its mismanagement, its destructive effects. Nguyen publicly excoriated Duong as "a whore"; he issued a second banning order. However, all 60,000 copies were already sold out; no copies were available for confiscation and destruction.

Duong, in an interview in 1995, acknowledged that most of the reprehensible characters are based on party functionaries: "In general, my writing is based on what I see in life. . . . [Chinh is] based on a man who is a leading cadre of the Vietnamese trade unions. He lives in Hanoi, and unfortunately his type is very common in Vietnam."

The land reform program, the spine of the novel, is based on the reality of the 1953–56 campaign which, as translator Nina McPherson declares,

> triggered a wave of violence: terrified villagers were forced to denounce their "landlord" neighbors to guerrilla "security committees"; and by 1956, tens of thousands of villagers—some of them with only a few acres of land—had been arrested. Nearly 100,000 "landlord" farmers were sentenced to forced labor camps by courts that were often composed of no more than a handful of illiterate peasants. In the chaos, many of the Communist cadres administering

the land reform engaged in factional struggle, and some took advantage of their power to spare their own relatives or seize the property of the accused for themselves.

Duong's depiction of these situations and their repercussions established her leadership of the dissident movement, leading to her arrest and the banning of her works. Please see the censorship history of NOVEL WITHOUT A NAME for an expanded discussion.

FURTHER READING

McPherson, Nina. Translator's note to In *Paradise of the Blind*, by Duong Thu Huong. New York: William Morrow, 1993.
Shenon, Philip. "In This Author's Book, Villains Are Vietnamese." *New York Times International*, April 12, 1994, p. A4.

THE PATRIOT (*HA PATRIOT*)

Author: Hanoch Levin
Original date and place of publication: 1987, Israel
Publisher: Hakibbutz Hamevchad
Literary form: Drama

THE QUEEN OF THE BATHTUB (*MALKAT AMBATYA*)

Author: Hanoch Levin
Original date and place of publication: 1987, Israel
Publisher: Hakibbutz Hamevchad
Literary form: Drama

SUMMARY

At least three of Hanoch Levin's plays were written in response to an Israeli war. *You and Me and the Next War* was staged in 1968, one year after the Israeli victory in the Six-Day War. *The Queen and the Bathtub* was produced in 1970 during the war of attrition with Egypt and Syria. *The Patriot* was staged in 1982, during the war in Lebanon. All three were satirical reviews.

In contrast to Israeli euphoria and self-congratulation after defeating three Arab armies in the Six-Day War, Levin, in *You, Me and the Next War*, criticized the capture of East Jerusalem, the West Bank (from Jordan), the Golan Heights (from Syria), the Gaza Strip, and the Sinai Peninsula (from Egypt), through which Israel became the military ruler of thousands of Palestinians. He charged the nation with hypocrisy, scorning those, particularly the hard-liners, who hoped to retain the West Bank and the Gaza Strip despite these being lands of another people. The Israeli mainstream was also criticized for insisting that Israel had no choice but to launch the war. He evidently opposed Israeli expansionist politics. He also called attention to the heavy human loss—the dead and wounded young soldiers. He was one of the earliest critics of the war and its aftermath, the play predicting dire consequences.

The Queen of the Bathtub lampooned Prime Minister Golda Meir, the Queen, who is surrounded by absurd characters, such as the Prince of the Rump and the Lord Keeper of the Enema. It also made fun of the war being waged against Egypt and Syria. The play included a parody of the Genesis story of Abraham's sacrifice of his son, Isaac. In this version, Abraham tells Isaac that he is going to kill him in obedience to God's request, asking for Isaac's forgiveness. Isaac assents to this request, indicating his understanding. However, Abraham, whose hearing is impaired, does not hear the voice of the angel calling out to him to save his son. Isaac, who does hear the angel, convinces his father of God's message. The scene ends with Isaac wondering what will happen if other fathers who are about to sacrifice their sons are not able to hear the voice of the angel.

A song was inserted in the play immediately after the revised version of the sacrifice of Isaac (see Censorship History below). A son lying dead in his grave sings it to his father, who is burying him. The son tells his father not to be proud or lift his head, but to weep; he also asserts that "Something greater than honor / Now lies at your feet, father dear." The concluding stanzas express the poignant plea of the victim, the dead son:

And don't say you've made a sacrifice,
For the one who sacrificed was me here,
And don't say other high flown words
For I am very low now, father dear.

Father dear, when you stand over my grave
Old and tired and forlorn here,
And you see how they bury my body in the earth—
Then you beg my pardon, father dear.

Intensely satiric, *The Patriot* is written in the form of a fable, which follows an idealistic and patriotic Israeli through a series of skitlike encounters with official hypocrisy, military boasting of preparedness for war, and ethnic hatred. The play further focuses on such issues as the occupation of the West Bank and Israeli-Arab relations. The Israeli army in one sequence is likened to Nazi storm troopers. The average Israeli is portrayed as a brutal imperialist and a mixture of blind nationalism and crass materialism. In one scene, the central character, the "patriot," as a condition for buying land in the occupied West Bank of the Jordan River—to prove his patriotism—is forced to kick an Arab shoeshine boy in the face. Although depicted as chauvinistic, the patriot is desperate to immigrate to America, so much so that he debases himself in front of an American consular official: He is obliged to spit in his mother's face to prove to the U.S. consul that he is not taking his family along. In a concluding skit, the patriot is killed while on military service in Israeli-occupied Albania, Levin's far flung location of Israeli military conquests. Upon reaching heaven, he insults and dethrones God.

CENSORSHIP HISTORY

Levin gained fame and notoriety with the production of *You and Me and the Next War;* it aroused a storm of criticism. Initially staged in an acting style inspired by American fringe theaters protesting the Vietnam War, it was tried out on a left-wing kibbutz audience: People angrily threw chairs at the actors, interrupting the performance in the middle. Older members of the kibbutz left in protest. Younger members stayed until the end; they had experienced the war directly. Subsequently, a softer, more personal style of presentation proved to be effective: The play's scenes and language were apparently extreme and outspoken enough in themselves.

The *Queen of the Bathtub* caused riots and a storm of protest unprecedented in Israeli theater history. The criticism of national beliefs accepted as truths and the political establishment fueled a scandal even before the play's premiere when one of the national newspapers, *Ma'ariv,* published several passages. Initially, the government censorship board, to which the play had been submitted for prior approval in accordance with the law, censored two sections from the show, one of them being the parody of the Genesis story of Abraham's sacrifice of his son. Levin's subversion of the Genesis text was considered by the Censorship Boards to be offensive to the fathers of the soldiers serving in the army. The theater appealed to the High Court, which issued an injunction to compel the board to give reasons for its demands; the play was approved, the dialogue included, though the original text was revised. Although the play was approved by the censors, the public uproar and the publicity and criticism—particularly from some of the religious members of the Tel Aviv municipality, who threatened not to support the theater—led to demands that the mayor ban the play; he refused. The deputy prime minister, who served also as the minister of education and culture, Yigal Allon, supporting artistic freedom, denounced the banning request, as did many others. However, riots, nightly protest demonstrations, and many letters to the cast—including some death threats—forced the board of the theater to close the show after 19 performances. "The actors, who felt threatened by the sometimes violent and aggressive reactions of some of the spectators, agreed to this decision," according to Freddie Rokem.

The Israeli Film and Theater Censorship Board banned *The Patriot* initially without a reason, later saying it was totally unpatriotic. It indicated that the play depicts Israelis as "corrupt and degenerate, ruthlessly killing Arab children and degrading the Arabs" and as "gravely offensive to the

447

fundamental values of the state, the Jewish tradition and wide segments of the population, both Jewish and Arab," as noted in Levin's obituary.

The initial suppression of the entire play itself drew criticism, the debate about the principle of freedom of speech intensifying. Critics of the Censorship Board claimed it was the first time a play had been banned for political contents only. Attorney General Yitzhak Zamir noted that the board's first duty was to honor free speech, be tolerant toward political satire, and censor works containing criminally offensive material. In contrast, Deputy Education Minister Miriam Tasa-Glazer, supporting the ban, said, as quoted in an AP article by Marcus Eliason, that it was not political censorship: "This play questions our entire existence, experience, the right of the people of Israel to exist. It is filled with hatred and destructiveness." About the chain of events Glenda Abramson wrote:

> . . . protests, meetings, marches, and demonstrations took place, organized by the Israeli Union of Performing Artists, supported by the Hebrew Writers' Association, with satirical material specially written by leading playwrights. These protested against the threat to artistic freedom of speech and called for the repeal of censorship, which, they claimed, contradicted democratic principles. Meanwhile, amid such publicity, the theater staged *The Patriot* without obtaining the Board's permission to do so. Two illegal performances of the play took place, each instigating arguments with the police. In Israel, as in most countries, police and censorship worked closely together. The police attended the first performance in order to inform the management that criminal charges were being brought against it and insisting that the performance be canceled, at the same time confirming that they would not stop it.

The theater management's appeal to the High Court led to the board agreeing to pass the play, with three cuts, which was condemned by pro–freedom of speech groups. The play, however, was staged, the banned sections read aloud by a stagehand—not an actor—with the auditorium house lights up, this reading being preceded by a satirical reiteration of the terms of the ban. In a 1984 court case—the criminal offense being disobedience of the Censorship Board—Judge Yoram Galin "concluded that the banned sections had not been *acted* but read, that the reading of these portions constituted the transmission of information to the public rather than a 'show,' " noted Abramson. He acquitted the accused, asserting it was a freedom of speech issue.

Government and opposition members of the Knesset demanded abolition of the Censorship Board. The Knesset, taking the first step, on October 27, 1982, voted 44-33 to end Israel's system of film and theater censorship, thus sending it to committee. (After committee action a final vote would take place in the Knesset. This appears not to have happened.)

Levin won top honors in the Israeli Theater Prize awards in 1997 for *Murder* and the Edinburgh Festival award in 1983 for *Sohare ha-gumi* (Rubber merchants). After Levin's death, Prime Minister Ehud Barak called him "one of the greatest playwrights that Israel had ever had," and Education

Minister Yossi Sarid said, "[he] showed us what we really looked like when we were still saying 'Surely, that can't be us'. . . . Levin saved us because without him we wouldn't have known that the social and political ulcer was about to explode."

FURTHER READING

Abramson, Glenda. "Theater Censorship in Israel." *Israel Studio* 2, no. 1 (1997): 111–135.
Bronner, Ethan. "Hanoch Levin, 56, Leading Israeli Playwright." *New York Times,* August 20, 1999, p. C17.
Eliason, Marcus. "Bitter Dispute over Censorship of Play." Associated Press, October 26, 1982.
"Hanoch Levin: Obituary." *Scotsman Publications,* August 20, 1999.
Rokem, Freddie. "Introduction." *The Labor of Life: Selected Plays,* by Hanoch Levin. Trans. Barbara Harshav. Stanford, Calif.: Stanford University Press, 2003.

THE POLITICS OF DISPOSSESSION

Author: Edward W. Said
Original date and place of publication: 1995, United States
Publisher: Vintage Books
Literary form: Nonfiction

SUMMARY

Subtitled *The Struggle for Palestinian Self-Determination, 1969–1994, The Politics of Dispossession* is a collection of 38 political essays by Edward Said. These are divided into three sections, "Palestine and Palestinians," "The Arab World," and "Politics and Intellectuals"; the essays in each section are organized chronologically, dated between 1969 and 1993. Written for different media, often in relation to particular circumstances or events, they are repetitious, tending toward generalizations, and sometimes inconsistent with data. Over this range of years, Said's purpose is to make sure that the past and the present that derives from it are not forgotten; the range of the work raises cognizance of the continuing plight of Palestinians and the forces operating against them.

In the first section, Said relates the history, situation, and goals of the Palestinians, describing their dispossession and the emergence of their political presence. In this context, he displays the policies and actions of the Israeli government, the attitudes of the American public, and the actions of the U.S. government. Several prominent strands of thought develop through the collection.

The Palestine problem began during World War I. The British had promised the Palestinian Arabs independence if they joined the war against the Ottoman Empire. Yet, in 1917, the British promised Palestine to the

Zionists, even though the region's population at that time was about 90 percent Arab. In 1948, just before all but 120,000 Palestinians were driven out in a "terrifying mass exodus," the population was about 70 percent Arab and 30 percent Jewish.

> Zionist settlers still owned only 6 percent of the land surface of Palestine, the Arabs owning the rest. Yes, the Arabs contested the Partition project of 1947 [to create Israel] for perfectly sound reasons then: that it would allot 55 percent of Palestine (and the best part of the country, at that) to a Jewish state comprising less than a third of the total Arab and Jewish populations.

In June 1967, Israel's military occupied the West Bank and Gaza, representing 22 percent of Palestine's land. In 1991, this land held approximately 2 million Palestinians.

The confiscation of land was the primary act of dispossession, a policy that continued. About 400 of the original 500 Palestinian villages have been destroyed, according to Said, "Israel not only eradicat[ing] a society but dispossess[ing] its people and occupy[ing] the remainder of its territory." And "the settlements continued, their number increasing to more than two hundred; more land was confiscated, especially around Jerusalem." Said cites David Ben-Gurion, first prime minister of the state of Israel, as having made it clear that "partition was a step toward acquiring *all* of the territory."

Palestinians have also been denied their humanity, their very personhood; as "non-Jews" (their official designation) living within Israel, they are deprived of their legitimacy as Palestinians, that is, they are not a people, but rather only individuals who are Arab. The Arab citizens of Israel have a "radically subordinate and consequently disadvantaged position." Dispossession has a more universal application. Said expresses Israel's rigid separation between Jew and non-Jew. Through an ideology of difference it relegates the rights of non-Jews to an inferior or lesser status: "Zionism divided reality into a superior 'us' and an inferior, degenerate 'them'. Today [1977] if you are an Arab in Israel, you are a third class person; you cannot ever be equal, so far as land owning and immigration rights, free movement, and state institutions are concerned." Said asserts that the Israelis have "dispossessed, alienated, and brutalized" the Palestinians in such disparate acts as bombing, strafing, and punishing the civilian refugee population and "exacting a dreadful price from students who have no schools or universities, men and women who have little food, no jobs, no political rights, no certainty at all of life, residence, or even subsistence nourishment a week hence." Cruel and inhumane policies and practices of the Israeli government and military are underscored through repetition. In 1980, after the Camp David agreement, Said, wrote:

> Israeli spokesmen in the meantime have been unyielding on important points: no Palestinian self-determination, no Israeli withdrawal, no change

in an increasingly aggressive settlement policy, no Palestinian control over anything as important as water resources or security, or foreign policy, or immigration, or East Jerusalem.

As for the Palestinians, Said chronicles their attitudes toward and resistance against the Israeli occupation and mistreatment, often galvanized in reaction to critical events. After the catastrophe of 1967—the Israeli military had defeated the Arab nations in six days—the Palestinian national movement of resistance emerged, reinvigorating the Palestinians, men and women, to take up arms on their own behalf for the first time.

> Thus, [the battle of Karameh—a village built by refugees—in March 1968] divided the Palestinian experience into a *before* that had refused an encounter, which meant accepting the Palestinian Arab past, and an *after* that finds the Palestinian standing in, becoming, fighting to dramatize the disjunction of his and her history in Palestine before 1948 with his history at the peripheries since 1948.

Palestinianism emerged: "Previously a classless 'refugee,' since 1967 he has become a politicized consciousness with nothing to lose but his refugeedom; that isn't much of a possession, and it is his only political possession at present."

In one essay Said refers to 3,500 acts of resistance to the occupation in 1987. That same year, in December, the so-called intifada, an uprising of unarmed civilians, began, lasting at least through 1991 (the last essay in this section is 1992). Aside from thwarting the Israelis, it brought together the three major sections of the Palestinian people: those living in Israel—Israeli citizens, the inhabitants of occupied Gaza and the West Bank, and the exile population dispersed throughout the Arab world and in Europe, Africa, and North America. Achieving widespread television coverage, the intifada re-created the Palestinian image:

> For those of us who live in the West, the change in public opinion has been very slow in coming, but by the late 1980s it did come, although after the 1982 Israeli invasion, the PLO [Palestine Liberation Organization] had become a far-diminished, not to say enfeebled, organization located quite improbably in Tunisia. The *intifadah*, which broke out in Gaza in December 1987, suddenly thrust a population of almost two million unarmed Palestinians before huge television audiences in the West and, with them, an inevitable number of Israeli soldiers who were seen beating and shooting them. No longer confined to the image of a gang of skulking terrorists, the Palestinians began to acquire in 1988 the irrevocable status of a people dispossessed and under a brutal military occupation in international consciousness, a status consolidated by the Palestine National Council meeting held in Algiers later that year.

These events were a catalyst for encouraging the goal of self-determination of the Palestinian people based on nationalist aspirations. Several options emerged, among them complete liberation; a negotiated settlement; equality in a shared territory, an approach formulated by PLO leader, Yasir Arafat; and statehood based on United Nations Resolution 181, signaling Palestinian sovereignty on whatever Palestinian territories were vacated by the occupation, based on principles of equality, mutuality, and social justice. "The *priority* in this mode of trying to settle the conflict would have to be getting Israel for the first time in its history to recognize Palestinian national rights unequivocally," as well as achieving equal representation between PLO and other participants during negotiations, an expectation rejected heretofore by both Israel and the United States.

In this context, Said occasionally refers to the "heavy emotional pressure of the Holocaust." While recognizing its impact on the European community,

> It cannot be emphasized enough, I think, that no Arab feels any sort of guilt or shame that every Westerner (apparently) feels, or is impelled to show he is feeling, for that horrible chapter in history. For a Palestinian Arab, therefore, it is not taboo: to speak of "Jews" in connection with Israel and its supporters, to make comparisons between the Israeli and the German occupations, to excoriate journalism that reports Jewish suffering but ignores, or discounts, Israel's razing of Arab homes and villages, Israeli napalm bombing, Israeli torture of Palestinian resistance fighters and civilians, Israel's deliberate attempt to obliterate the Palestinian Arab, Israel's use of its understanding of "Arab psychology" to offend the Arab's human status, Israel's callous use of Jewish suffering to blackmail Christians and Muslims by toying with (and then implementing) "plans" for Jerusalem—and so on.

In this context Said asserts that as a consequence of Western guilt for the Holocaust, Israel is exempted from normal criteria by which nations are measured and judged:

> The question to be asked is how long can the history of anti-Semitism and the Holocaust in particular be used as a fence to exempt Israel from arguments and sanctions against it for its behavior toward Palestinians, arguments and sanctions that were used against other repressive governments such as that of South Africa. How long are we going to deny that the cries of the people of Gaza—a recent visitor told me that she could not open her window for three days, so great was the stench—are directly connected to the policies of the Israeli government and not to the cries of the victims of Nazism?

Said's righteous indignation transfers also to the uncritical Western—particularly American—media that, empathizing with the Jews, actively adopt a pro-Israel stance, taking on Israel's cause while denigrating the Palestinians as terrorists and ignoring Israel's punishing acts against them. Said argues that essentially, American media failed to give the American public any understanding of the suffering endured by the Palestinians until the onset of the intifada.

The portrayal of Arafat, credited as the major leader of the PLO, shifts during the course of these essays. In 1983, Said describes him as "the decisive and psychological fact of [the Palestinians'] national identity," having shaped them into a national community. Two "surprisingly important" accomplishments are identified: He made the PLO a genuinely representative body, and he "formulated the notion that Palestinian Arabs and Israeli Jews would—indeed must—seek a future together on equal footing in a shared territory." Modest in manner, personally incorruptible, and having an unlimited commitment to his people and cause, he is nevertheless tolerant of corrupt and incompetent subordinates. Said notes, however, that Arafat has been criticized for his vacillations, his questionable involvements with extremist groups and nations, and his frequent inability to seize political opportunities. Said is critical of the Israeli-Palestinian agreement, the Oslo Declaration of Principles, which he terms an "instrument of Palestinian surrender to which Arafat 'acquiesced' . . . without establishing any plan for proceeding and without getting much in return but a grudging recognition of the PLO as the representative of the Palestinian people." In 1994, writing in the Epilogue, Said calls for the PLO hierarchy to "step aside"; Arafat's leadership is questioned by everyone, his manner autocratic, arbitrary, and unresponsive to appeals for reform and opening up the decision-making process. "No leadership can expect forever to be in sole control of money and political authority and to dole these out according to its whims," asserts Said.

A significant thought, highlighted in "The Arab World" section, is Said's castigation of Arab nations: "the Right Wing thinking which dominates Arab capitals and governments and institutions, is . . . fundamentally schizophrenic. It is quite able to carry out brutality at home and alleged sweetness and light abroad, with no necessarily felt sense of hypocrisy or contradiction." The Arab states take progressive international positions and at home regressive political and economic positions. He cites "economic adventures" that include building luxury hotels and numerous airports, importing quantities of consumer goods, real estate speculation, and purchasing new stocks of military goods, as well as investing in castles in England, Cadillacs, and Lockheed jets, but no "investments in universities and libraries, in hospitals, in projects that will improve the moral, physical, and intellectual lot of our teeming underprivileged masses" or investments in Western universities to promote the study of Arab and Islamic civilization. In contrast, he notes the neglect of the "rapidly increasing masses whose accelerating poverty probably outstrips the increase in the birthrate." In this context, Said asserts:

I could go on and on—but my point is clear. We are living through a period in the Arab world of unparalleled economic prosperity on the one hand, and of unparalleled political and social and intellectual poverty on the other hand. In what Arab capital is it possible to write and publish what one wishes, to say the truth, to stem the tide of repressive central state authority, intolerant of everything except its own fantasies and appetites? Most of our best writers and intellects have either been co-opted or jailed into silence. It is not only in Israel—I must remind you—that human rights are trampled. . . . Everywhere the individual is brutalized by the secret police, by huge unthinking bureaucracies, by a heedless Central State authority. Everywhere the democratic opposition is not tolerated, its leaders silenced, its voices muffled.

U.S. Middle East policy and its consequences are expressed through Said's interpretive lens. Several chronological statements reveal his understanding and attitudes.

1973—"Thus, whether it is the Senate Foreign Relations Committee, or a U.S. Army handbook, the accepted view has come to find disorder and instability in need of pacification and stability. But since the United States has interests 'that command concern,' a policy must steer a course between maintaining 'traditional Friendships' and a net dollar inflow of some $1.7 billion per year from the Middle East."

1973—"While there is no gainsaying the supply of Soviet arms to some Arab countries, I think it can be confidently said that the U.S.-supplied arms are delivered with two principal objectives in mind, both of them more flexibly adaptable to U.S. interests than the monolithic (and only modestly successful) Soviet policy of arming a very few Arab states for defense against Israeli attacks. The two U.S. objectives in arms supply are: (1) preserving an internal balance within the Middle East and assuring oil supplies; and (2) outflanking the Soviets to the east and south."

1984—"U.S. aid levels to Israel received roughly half of the entire American foreign aid budget, most of it in outright gifts and in subsidies to Israeli industries directly competitive with American counterparts."

1989—"Secretary of State [James] Baker's May 22 speech to AIPAC [American Israel Public Affairs Committee] appeared to be, and was greeted by some of his audience and some Arabs, as a new departure for U.S. Middle East policy. He was explicit about ending the occupation of the West Bank and Gaza; he told the Israelis and Palestinians to give up ideas about Greater Israel and the whole of Palestine respectively; he reiterated the principles of exchanging territory for peace, of confidence-building measures, of an emerging new political reality for Palestinians."

1991—"Who has given us the right to project our power all over the world, at the same time proclaiming our higher purpose and superior wisdom? The United States is in fact repeating the practices employed by the British and French in the nineteenth century. The big differences are, first, that today we are capable of much greater destruction than they were, and, second, that we are unable to state openly and candidly our engagement in the business of empire, and damn the results."

1991—"Since 1973 the United States has wanted a physical presence in the Gulf: to control oil supply, to project power, and above all, recently, to refurbish, refinance, reinvigorate its military, still supposedly suffering the Vietnam syndrome. With his crude brutality no match for the U.S. and Israeli propaganda, Saddam [Hussein] became the perfect target, and the best excuse to move in. The United States will not soon leave the Middle East."

As a counterpoint, Said urges concern for the dispossessed, the Palestinians, answering to their needs, responding to their desires—economic, political, and cultural—and recognizing their humanity. He challenges the United States—government and citizens:

> For two generations the United States has sided in the Middle East mostly with tyranny and injustice. I defy anyone to tell me of one struggle for democracy, or women's rights, or secularism, and the rights of minorities that the United States has supported. Instead we have propped up compliant and unpopular clients, and turned our backs on the efforts of small peoples to liberate themselves from military occupation, while subsidizing their enemies.

CENSORSHIP HISTORY

In late July 1996, copies of *The Politics of Dispossession* and another collection by Said were removed from West Bank and Gaza bookstores by Arafat's security men, the confiscation reportedly having been ordered by the Ministry of Information. The first raid occurred on a small bookstore in central Ramallah. Sales of the books were banned, although, in an interview, Said indicated they could be purchased surreptitiously. (The books, he noted, are available in Israel.)

Reports noted the sharp criticism of the landmark Israeli-Palestinian agreement signed in September 1993 in the books' essays. Said called the signing of the Oslo accords by Arafat a "capitulation" and the agreement an "instrument of surrender." Arafat, according to Said, was greatly angered by Said's persistent critique.

FURTHER READING

Barsamian, David. "Edward W. Said." *The Progressive* 65, no. 11 (November 1998): 41–45.
"He Won't Gag Me." *Guardian* (London), August 23, 1996, p. 13.
Schmemann, Serge. "Palestinian Security Agents Ban Books by a Critic of Arafat." *New York Times*, August 25, 1996, sec. 1, p. 12.

THE PRINCE

Author: Niccolò Machiavelli
Original dates and places of publication: 1532, Italy; 1640, England
Publishers: Antonio Blado; R. Bishop
Literary form: Nonfiction

SUMMARY

Dedicated to Lorenzo de' Medici (though initially to Giuliano de' Medici, his uncle, who died in 1516), *The Prince*, or *Il Principe*, was written in 1513–14, against a backdrop of 16th-century Italian intrigue, strife, and political upheaval. Machiavelli had been a casualty of this upheaval when the republican government of Florence in which he had been a civil servant, chiefly in the diplomatic corps, fell and the Medici family returned to power. (Three generations of Medicis had ruled prior to the formation of the republican government in 1494.)

Machiavelli's purpose in this treatise on politics, at least on the surface, is to offer advice on successful governance, including gaining and maintaining control of territories. Ultimately, he wanted a "strong state, capable of imposing its authority on a hopelessly divided Italy" and the expulsion of foreign powers. Underlying his analysis is a basic tenet: "the real truth of things rather than an imaginary view of them," favoring political realism and rejecting idealist views of human behavior, including rulers and the ruled, with regard to political practice and response. In this context of politics, Machiavelli subordinated morals to political expediency.

Having minimized the problems of princes of hereditary states in maintaining control of their territory—"it is simply a matter of not upsetting ancient customs, and of adjusting them instead to meet new circumstances," for the people have grown accustomed to their prince's family—Machiavelli turns his attention to the greater difficulties of "mixed principalities," that is, a new territory grafted onto the old states, and of new states. These difficulties increase when the language, customs, and laws of the new possession differ from those of the conquering prince.

One of the chief difficulties is the conquered, some of whom may have welcomed the opportunity to change masters but are fickle in their friendship when they discover that their expectations of bettering their lives have not been borne out. Additionally, those who have been harmed in the power seizure become enemies. Machiavelli recommends extinguishing the family line of the previous prince but maintaining the old way of life and customs, laws and taxes, thus earning the good will of the people, so as to incorporate the new territory into the old in the shortest possible time.

For new possessions, Machiavelli recommends that the new prince go to the new territory to live; troubles may be spotted and dealt with before they expand. Another tactic is to establish colonies rather than maintain any army because fewer are hurt and they are poor and scattered.

All the others remain untouched, which is a persuasion to keep quiet; yet they also become fearful of making a mistake and suffering like those who have already been despoiled. . . . And in this connection it should be remarked that men ought either to be caressed or destroyed, since they will seek revenge for minor hurts but will not be able to revenge major ones. Any harm you do to a man should be done in such a way that you need not fear his revenge.

Further, the conqueror should become the protector of his weak neighbors, should act to weaken his strong neighbors, and should fight an invading force of a powerful foreigner. In this vein, Machiavelli asserts, using the Romans as his example, that war should not be avoided: ". . . wars don't just go away, they are only postponed to another's advantage." A critical error in this regard is to allow or assist another state to become powerful. "From this we can draw a general rule, which never fails or only rarely: the man who makes another powerful ruins himself."

Machiavelli distinguishes between those princes who acquire territories through chance or good fortune and those who acquire territories through their own arms and energy. While the latter may endure more problems in gaining and securing power, they will more easily hold power because of the strength of character they exhibited. "Such men meet with great difficulties in their rise to power; all their dangers are on the way up, and must be overcome by their talents (*virtù*) but once they are on top, once they are held in veneration, and have destroyed all their envious rivals, they remain powerful, secure, honored, and happy." In contrast, men who achieve new states with other people's arms and by good luck are at a loss because they are dependent on the goodwill and good fortune of those who elevated them. They cannot command because they lack capability and do not have their own loyal troops unless they corrupt them.

Cesare Borgia exemplifies one who became established through the power of his natural father, Pope Alexander VI, and his troops. However, Cesare, a man of shrewdness and ambition, solidified his position by attacking neighboring cities. Having taken control of the Romagna and realizing the people had been plundered by their former masters and had become lawless, he created peace and obedience by establishing good government based on absolute authority and cruelty. When his ends were achieved, he caused his agent, the man held responsible for the excessive harshness, to be publicly and savagely murdered, thus removing the onus of blame from himself. Machiavelli does not condemn Cesare but offers him as a model for those who rise to power through the fortune and arms of others.

While he credits their courage and their ability to overcome adversity, Machiavelli does not acknowledge as excellent those who come to power by crime. It is a factor neither of fortune nor of virtue to "murder his fellow citizens, betray his friends, to be devoid of truth, pity, or religion."

In discussing empowerment to rule in a civil princedom, Machiavelli identifies two forces: the nobles, who desire to command and oppress the people, and the people, who desire not to be dominated and oppressed. Becoming a prince with the help of the nobles is more difficult than with the help of the people. The nobles claim equality, so he cannot command or manage them; also, the nobles are apt to be self-interested and independent and, thus, not dependable in times of adversity. If the people have selected him, the prince needs only take them under his protection and provide benefits for them; he should do this even if they did not select him in order to gain their support and obligation. This is all the more important when it is recognized that a prince cannot make himself safe against a hostile people; there are too many of them. He can, however, safeguard against hostile nobles who are few. "And because men, when they receive benefits from a prince whom they expected to harm them, are especially obligated to him, such a prince's subjects may feel more warmly toward him than if he had risen to power with their help."

Several chapters focus on character and behavior attributes of princes that lead to praise or blame. In introducing these, Machiavelli identifies basic generalizations: "I know everyone will agree that among these many qualities a prince certainly ought to have all those that are considered good. But since it is impossible to have and exercise them all, because the conditions of human life simply do not allow it, a prince must be shrewd enough to avoid the public disgrace of those vices that would lose him his state." These also reveal a practical imperative: success of the enterprise.

Machiavelli compares several key virtues and vices. Among these are generosity and stinginess; he opts for the latter because by being stingy a prince can save his resources to support the defense of his state and to engage in wars and ventures without taxing his people. Generosity is not recognized unless it is so ostentatious as to deplete his funds, causing him to raise money through taxes. Princes can afford to be generous with what belongs to strangers.

While being thought merciful is preferable, princes will find cruelty advantageous. Cesare Borgia used cruelty to unify, to restore order and obedience. Cruelty can also compel loyalty and respect, particularly among soldiers. However, such behavior should be tempered with humanity to avoid being hated. For a prince to be feared is more advantageous than to be loved. Men—"ungrateful, fickle, liars and deceivers, fearful of danger and greedy for gain"—don't worry about offending a man who makes himself loved when it is to their advantage; fear, however, involves dread of punishment from which there is no escape. To avoid being hated, though feared, a prince should refrain from taking the property of his subjects and citizens and from taking their women. "Cruelty is badly used when it is infrequent at first, but increases with time instead of diminishing."

Comparably, Machiavelli argues that a crafty, cunning, manipulative prince is more successful than one who keeps his word. A prince needs to be flexible in this regard to suit his interests. He cites Pope Alexander VI as a master at such deception; while appearing virtuous, convincing in his assertions and solemn in his oaths and using these characteristics, when possible, he was ready for the contrary when the situation warranted. Men judge by appearances. The prince's task is to "win victories and uphold his state."

By avoiding contempt and hatred, by demonstrating in his actions that he isn't fickle or frivolous, that he is courageous, sober and strong, the prince will be highly esteemed. This respect and the goodwill of his people whom he keeps satisfied will avert internal subversion against which the prince must be on guard. Conspirators will not act against him if they know the people will be outraged and will not support them. The prince must also be on guard against foreign powers. This defense is secured by good weapons and good friends; "if he has good weapons, he will never lack for good friends."

The Prince concludes with an impassioned "exhortation to restore Italy to liberty and free her from barbarians," a plea seemingly connected to his dedication. The times are propitious; the country is ready to be released from "cruel insolence of the barbarians." He calls particularly on the House of the Medici to raise a citizen army to disperse and defeat the invaders.

Machiavelli's name has become synonymous with unscrupulous political behavior. He has been identified as an agent of Satan and charged with "deliberately advocating evil." Segments quoted out of context, as exemplified by the Gentillet publication (see Censorship History), effectively illustrate Machiavelli's iniquity. Such interpretations still obtain, as exemplified by the opinion of Leo Strauss: "If it is true that only an evil man will stoop to teach maxims of public and private gangsterism, we are forced to say that Machiavelli was an evil man."

A more modern interpretation focuses on Machiavelli's intent to express the reality of political action based on analysis of history in contrast to the ideal behavior. J. R. Hale infers that Machiavelli "was concerned only with *il vero*, the true picture of what actually happened, and that he only talked about politics in terms directly deduced from the way in which men had behaved and did behave." An extension of this position, as identified by numerous critics, is Machiavelli's low esteem of men, evident in *The Prince* in his derisive language and attitude describing the populace, the nobles, and the rulers themselves.

Robert M. Adams relates a 180-degree variation in the 20th century, which is, "tradition [which] has emphasized the idealistic, enthusiastic, patriotic, and democratically minded Machiavelli." In this context he acclaims Machiavelli as "a great moral conscience"; "he resurrects . . . the undying worm of man's bad conscience at pretending to rule his fellow men."

CENSORSHIP HISTORY

Despite Antonio Blado having received permission from Pope Clement VII (Giulio de' Medici) to publish Machiavelli's writing, in 1559 all of

Machiavelli's works were placed on the Index librorum prohibitorum, the Roman Index of Paul IV, in the "banned absolutely" category. Compiled by the Holy Inquisition in Rome at the urging of Pope Paul IV (described as "implacably anti-heretical"), the Index forbade Catholics to read the works, including *The Prince*, or even own copies. The prohibition resulted from the Council of Trent, meeting from 1545 to 1563 in order to strengthen the discipline of the Roman Catholic Church against Protestantism. Pope Paul IV, a lifelong inquisitor and mortal enemy of heresy, widened the scope of the Index to include, beyond heresy, morality and manners in general. This was the first appearance of Machiavelli on an Index list.

This censorship system was finally abandoned in 1966; the last Index, that of Leo XIII, had been published in 1881 with supplements in 1884, 1896, and 1900. Books previously banned but published prior to 1600 were removed from the Index, "although," as noted in the *Encyclopedia of Censorship*, "they are to be considered as much condemned today as they ever were."

The 1572 massacre of some 50,000 French Huguenots by Catholic leaders, beginning on Saint Bartholomew's night and extending for several weeks, was blamed on Machiavelli by the Protestants. This was because Catherine de' Medici, the queen mother and power behind the throne of her 22-year-old son, was a reader of Machiavelli; she was hated as an Italian and a Medici and as a secret and treacherous person. The irony of the accusation against Machiavelli is that the Catholics were at this time forbidden to read him.

In 1576, a French Huguenot, Innocent Gentillet, published (in French) *A discourse on the meanes of evel governing and maintaining in good peace, a kingdome, or other principalitie: Divided into three parts, namely, the counsele, the religion, and the policie, which a prince ought to hold and follow. Against Nicholas Machiavelli, the Florentine.* It was translated and published in English in 1602. Gentillet, who held Machiavelli directly responsible for the Saint Bartholomew massacre, used selected maxims to attack *The Prince*. His text was considerably influential since translation of *The Prince* itself into the languages of Protestant countries was delayed for many years. The English translation was published in 1640 when the episcopal censorship broke down. See the Censorship History discussion of AREOPAGITICA by John Milton. The Elizabethans' understanding of and hostility to *The Prince* derived from Gentillet's book.

Most recently, in 1935, Benito Mussolini, Fascist dictator of Italy, encouraged the distribution of *Il Principe*, thereby demonstrating Italy's need for an all-powerful dictator supported by a national army. And shortly after Fidel Castro overthrew the Batista government in Cuba in 1959, a newspaper reported that *The Prince* was on his revolutionary reading list.

FURTHER READING

Adams, Robert M. "The Interior Prince, or Machiavelli Mythologized" and "The Rise, Proliferation, and Degradation of Machiavellism: An Outline." In *The Prince*, edited by Robert M. Adams, 238–250. New York. W. W. Norton, 1977.

Bull, George. "Introduction." In *The Prince*. Trans. George Bull. Baltimore: Penguin Books, 1961, pp. 9–26.

Green, Jonathan, and Nicholas J. Karolides, reviser. *The Encyclopedia of Censorship, New Edition*. Facts On File, 2005.

Haight, Anne Lyon, and Chandler B. Grannis. *Banned Books 387 B.C. to 1978 A.D.* 4th ed. New York: R. R. Bowker, 1978.

Hale, J. R. "The Setting of *The Prince*." In *The Prince*, edited by Robert M. Adams, 141–152. New York: W. W. Norton, 1977.

Magill, Frank N., ed. *Masterplots*. Rev. ed. Englewood Cliffs, N.J.: Salem Press, 1976.

Strauss, Leo. "Machiavelli the Immoralist." In *The Prince*, edited by Robert M. Adams, 180–185. New York: W. W. Norton, 1977.

PRINCIPLES OF NATURE

Author: Elihu Palmer
Original dates and places of publication: 1801, United States; 1819, England
Publisher: [s.n.]; Richard Carlisle
Literary form: Nonfiction

SUMMARY

In the two decades from 1790 to 1810, the idea of a rational religion, which had steadily developed in 18th-century America, became a significant force, giving rise to debate and controversy. Elihu Palmer's *Principles of Nature; or, a Development of the Moral Causes of Happiness and Misery among the Human Species* is credited as being the catalyst of this religious controversy. It also demanded attention to social issues such as the relationship between church and state, the immorality of slavery, and the rights of women. In addition, it identified the hazards of a strongly centralized government and proposed secular ethical models versus theologically based ones.

Identifying himself as a Deist, Palmer promoted a rational religion of nature in opposition to Christianity's supernaturalism and aspects of other religions. He primarily argued for naturalistic ethics based on the ideas of "reciprocal justice" and "universal benevolence." The world view of revealed religion was perceived as incompatible with the principles of natural philosophy and the lessons of ordinary experience; its teachings were seen to not jibe with rational analysis, and to be antithetical to the enhancement of human happiness and virtue.

Palmer asserted that the happiness of society depended on the "exercise of equal and reciprocal justice." Within his naturalistic ethics he acknowledged that each human was equally endowed with both sensation and liberty.

> . . . whatever be the active power, the moving cause that directs the universe
> . . . it has also given [men] the same rights to use of its benefits, and that in

the order of nature, all men are equal. . . . that all men are constituted independent of each other, that they are created free, that no man can be subject, and no man sovereign, but that all men are the unlimited proprietors of their own persons. Equality, therefore, and liberty, are two essential attributes of man, two laws of the divinity. . . . it follows that the balance of receipts and payments in political society, ought to be rigorously in equilibrium with each other; so that from the idea of equality, immediately flows that other idea, equity and justice.

He argued, therefore, that all individuals—men, women, blacks, whites, "aborigines"—be treated equitably. This equitable treatment was deemed to be self-serving because individuals are linked; thus, avoiding injury of another reciprocates to the self. This necessary feature of individual morality affects society as well.

The slavery issue is joined in Palmer's discussion of the origins of earth and the laws of nature.

Among the human species, there is evidently a great diversity of external appearance; the white and the black man are as different in some other respects, as they are in the color of their skin; the long straight hair of the one, and the curled wool of the other, is a verification of this remark. Both races are intelligent, and it is presumed that the intellectual powers are not in any essential degree dissimilar. Improvement has made more difference than nature, and the immoral opinion, that the whites have a right to enslave the blacks, is a complete abandonment of the principle of reciprocal justice, and a violation of the fundamental laws of Nature.

While Palmer does not overtly address the women's rights issues in *Principles of Nature*, it is evident in his ethical system; in a published oration, delivered on July 4, 1797, Palmer expressed the political and social equality of women:

Among those causes of human improvement . . . that are of most importance to the general welfare, must be included, the total annihilation of the prejudices which have established between the sexes an inequality of rights, fatal even to the party which it favours. In vain might we search for motives by which to justify this principle, in difference of physical organization, of intellect, or of moral sensibility. It had at first no other origin but abuse of strength, and all the attempts which have since been made to support it are idle sophisms.

The concept of universal benevolence extends from that of reciprocal justice. "It is the duty of every man to be just and benevolent; an opposite conduct would become the signal of universal discord. . . ." Palmer expressed this tenet in both individual and national terms. The narrow prejudice that creates enmity between men and between nations is subversive to the best interests of human society. He held political governments accountable for nurturing these prejudices.

Two keystones to Palmer's philosophy are the permanence of the laws of nature and the immutability of God. Nature, he wrote, is "constant, stable and uniform," and "God is just, immutable and eternal; that he regards with parental benevolence, the creation which he has made, and that he will not wantonly destroy it to gratify the imaginary whims of a blind and bigoted fanaticism." Linking nature's laws with rational belief and the evidence of human experience, "the testimony of our own senses," Palmer contended the falsity of such doctrines as miracles, prophecy, and scriptural authority. Given the basis that "God is infinite in all his perfections; the laws of nature are an effect of the divine attributes, and must have been modified in the best possible manner, and to answer the best and wisest purposes," he argued for the study of nature:

> Philosophy teaches us to seek in nature, and the knowledge of her laws, for the cause of every event, and when this knowledge shall become universal, man will relinquish with elevated satisfaction his attachment to those supernatural schemes of a vindictive theology, which have served only to destroy the harmony of nature and demoralize the intelligent world. O, man! Return in thy inquiries to the basis of physical existence, develop its principles, cultivate science, love truth, practice justice, and thy life shall be rendered happy.

In this context, Palmer reasoned that supernatural dogma violated both the immutability of nature and rational experience. He rejected miracles such as the Virgin Birth and the Resurrection as being outside the uniformity and continuity of nature, a contradiction of reason. Further, he argued that if God is perfect, miracles are "an insult to the dignity" of God, for they suggest he is imperfect and willing to violate the system of natural laws he had created. In like vein, Palmer disputed the fulfillment of prophesies; he noted that in man there is "a pride and vanity which induces him to pretend to a knowledge of futurity, and that his knowledge is the result of a secret and mysterious intercourse with celestial powers."

Palmer invalidated, in large measure, the morality of the Bible, deeming it "distorted, deficient, or wicked." While he admitted to "some good moral maxims"—those that encourage love, charity, and compassion—he denied that Christianity "contains anything like a pure *system* of genuine morality." He cited contradictions: A passage in Luke, "If any man come to me, and hate not his father, and mother, and wife and children . . . he cannot be my disciple," versus another in Matthew, which commands the love of enemies, and another in the Epistles of John, "If any man say that he is in the light and hate his brother, he is in darkness, even until now." Palmer identified features of the "grossest violation of theoretic moral excellence and practical purity"; these are made worse because they are attributed to God: "bloody commands of vengeance and slaughter . . . abominable crimes of unrelenting murder and universal pillage"; orders to prophets to lie and deceive and to the Jews "to borrow from the Egyptians, jewels of silver and jewels of gold without any intention of ever returning them." The Son of God comes "with a sword" and sends "his disciples secretly to take and carry away a colt which did not belong either to him or his disciples." Moses and Mahomet are described as "active villains . . . eminent murderers, and their debaucheries have been signalized by acts of barbarous brutality. . . ." The Jews "took the liberty of exercising a principle of indiscriminate extirpation toward all heathen nations"; Mahometans pursued, similarly, destructive wars; the Christians, too, "not a whit behind either of these two grand divisions in the exercise of a censorious and military spirit. The crusader and the domestic quarrels of the Christian church will furnish an abundant verification. . . ." Palmer denounced the "double despotism" of church and state.

> It is the peculiar office of reason to look at the utter demolition of the ancient regimen of Church and State. These twin sisters of iniquity are the moral giants, which have stalked with huge devastation over the face of the whole globe. Political despotism and supernatural religion have done more to render the human race vicious and depraved, than all other causes conjointly combined. If the passions of man and the impulses of his nature have frequently produced a moral eccentricity in his conduct, it is certain that a corrupt government and a corrupt religion have rendered him habitually wicked; have perverted all the conceptions of the mind upon moral and political subjects, and brutalized his intellectual existence.

CENSORSHIP HISTORY

The *Encyclopedia of Censorship* identifies *Principles of Nature* as one of the "most often" censored books. It appeared, along with Thomas Paine's *THE AGE OF REASON*, more often in the courts of England for blasphemous libel than any other book.

Palmer was not a stranger to censorship in the United States. His attacks on Christian doctrines in the North, particularly in puritan New England, were found shocking. Before he located an audience in New York City for his increasingly radical deism, he was relieved of pulpits in Massachusetts and New York State, and denied the opportunity to speak in Philadelphia, particularly. There, the Episcopal bishop, William White, so threatened with reprisals the owner of the Church Alley meeting house, which had been rented for Palmer's oration, that the contract was broken. According to T. J. Moore, "The bishop had placed blinders on the whole city to prevent Palmer's points from being seen." Palmer's response, a notice in a daily newspaper, alluded to the Bill of Rights, in effect for three months, having been inhibited by "laws of opinion."

Palmer's deistic movement had political ramifications. He was identified by Kerry Walters, as "Unquestionably the chief of American deists." Palmer "metamorphosed Enlightenment deism into a popular movement that rocked the Early Republic's religious and moral sensibilities in the opening years of the nineteenth century." He joined his deism to social activism. At the time when a "Theistic Church" (theism was an alternate name for deism) was being founded, a deistic liberal, Jefferson, was elected to the presidency. Throughout the campaign of 1800, however, political and religious conservatives vilified Jefferson, charging that he and his party desired to overthrow Christianity. He was accused of daring to disbelieve the deluge, "reducing the Flood—and therefore the Bible—to mythology," defining "the Old Testament as the written tradition of a tribal people," equating it with flood traditions of other ancient peoples. A New England newspaper identified Jefferson and his associates as "philosophical infidels" who were planning to establish the "heretic 'Age of Reason.' " Walters in his essay on Jefferson's writings asserts that among the American deists who were regularly defamed as "godless apostates," Jefferson "suffered the most from the calumny his deism prompted." Church and state were not separated; Jefferson's religious beliefs were easy prey for those who disapproved his politics.

These accusations resurfaced in 1815 when Jefferson offered to sell his personal library, "the largest and finest in the country," to the Congress to replace the Library of Congress—3,000 volumes—which had been burned by the British during the War of 1812. Jefferson's library—6,487 volumes—would expand the scope of the Library of Congress beyond the original legislative orientation of primarily legal, economic, and historic works to include philosophy, the arts, architecture, and science. Opposition to the purchase was raised in the House of Representatives, chiefly from Massachusetts Federalists, who claimed that the library's "philosophical and infidel productions" were of no use to congressmen and insulting to the nation.

On the other side of the Atlantic, the deistic controversy was "the chief product of eighteenth-century theology in England," according to Leslie Stephen. At the end of the century, *The Age of Reason* by Paine, who was acknowledged by Palmer as an associate thinker, "shocked all of respectable England." Edmund Burke in 1790 had exclaimed that no one had read the deists for 40 years; in 1793–95 with Paine's irreverent appeal to the masses, in Stephen's words, "Deism appeared again ferocious and menacing." Paine offended many because of his radicalism in both religion and politics (see THE RIGHTS OF MAN).

The 1819 publication of *Principles of Nature* in England aroused a like controversy. Richard Carlisle, the publisher of *Principles* and also of Paine's *The Age of Reason*, who was already in jail serving a sentence for another publication, was further sentenced—a 500-pound fine and a year imprisonment for *Principles of Nature* and 1,000 pounds and two years imprisonment for *The Age of Reason*. His wife, Jane, who had done the work in printing *Principles*, proceeded to print a full account of her husband's trial, including passages he had quoted from the two works; she was tried for blasphemous libel in 1820 and found guilty but escaped sentence on a technicality. Subsequently, in 1821 she was tried and found guilty (a two-year sentence), as was Mary Anne

Carlisle, Richard's sister (a one-year sentence), and, from 1821 until 1824, a procession of other publishers.

FURTHER READING

Cole, John Y. *A Brief History of the Library of Congress.* Washington, D.C.: Library of Congress, 1993.

Green, Jonathon, and Nicholas J. Karolides, reviser. *Encyclopedia of Censorship, New Edition.* New York: Facts On File, 2005.

Haight, Anne Lynn, and Chandler B. Grannis. *Banned Books: 387 B.C. to 1978 A.D.* 4th ed. New York: R. R. Bowker, 1978.

Kerber, Linda K. *Federalists in Dissent: Imagery and Ideology in Jeffersonian America.* Ithaca, N.Y.: Cornell University Press, 1980.

Moore, Terry Jonathan. *Neither True nor Divine: Elihu Palmer's Opposition to Christianity.* Ph.D. diss. New Orleans Baptist Theological Seminary, 1994.

Morais, Herbert M. *Deism in Eighteenth Century America.* New York: Russell and Russell, 1960.

Palmer, Elihu. *An Inquiry Relative to the Moral and Political Improvement of the Human Species.* New York: John Crookes, 1797.

Peterson, Merrill D. *Thomas Jefferson and the New Nation: A Biography.* New York: Oxford University Press, 1970.

Stephen, Leslie. *History of English Thought in the Eighteenth Century.* Vol. 1. New York: Peter Smith, 1949.

Thomas, Donald. *A Long Time Burning: The History of Literary Censorship in England.* New York: Praeger, 1969.

Walters, Kerry S. *The American Deists: Voices of Reason and Dissent in the Early Republic.* Lawrence: University Press of Kansas, 1992.

Walters, Kerry S. "Elihu Palmer & the Religion of Nature: An Introductory Essay." In *Principle of Nature,* by Elihu Palmer. Wolfeboro, N.H.: Longwood Academic, 1990.

PROMISE OF AMERICA

Author: Larry Cuban and Philip Roden
Original date and place of publication: 1971, United States
Original publisher: Scott Foresman Spectra Program
Literary form: Textbook

SUMMARY

Promise of America is a junior high school history text in five volumes. Book One, "The Starting Line," covers the early history of America. Book Two, "Struggling for the Dream," discusses slavery and the move west. Book Three, "Breaking and Building," deals with post–Civil War society. Book Four, "Sidewalks, Gunboats, and Ballyhoo," takes readers into the early part of the 20th century. Book Five, "An Unfinished Story," brings students up to the year of publication.

Cuban and Roden had taught high school history, trained teachers at the Cardozo Project and Northwestern University (respectively), and had prior experience in writing and developing curricula.

In *Promise of America*, the authors use a variety of perspectives. These include excerpts from writers of fact and fiction, including Booker T. Washington, Nat Turner, and Benjamin Franklin; and from such newspapers as the *Wall Street Journal* and the *Washington Post*, along with slave songs and the Resolution Adopted by the Seneca Falls Convention. Young African Americans were interviewed for the book to give their views on racism; pictures and drawings from past and present abound to give readers a feel for what life was like for different peoples in different times.

A second area of importance is the authors' use of discussion questions. In this text, no student will be asked a question like, "What would you have done if you were in George Washington's place when his father caught him chopping down the cherry tree?" Instead, typical discussion questions ask students to compare and contrast slavery in Latin America and in the United States to see where conditions were worse. Students are asked to make connections between segregated schools and poverty among African Americans; they read letters from a slave owner to a runaway slave and the slave's answer to the "wretched woman" who still claims that he owes her money for his freedom; the level and types of questions asked consistently challenge students to use their critical faculties and to think for themselves.

A third aspect of the series is that the authors deemphasize dates of events and the "Great Man" concept of history and emphasize instead how common people lived and how the past relates to the present. For example, while many history textbooks give little attention to the role of religion in American life, *Promise of America* discusses such issues as the religious persecution that drove the Mormons to travel beyond the frontier. The series also examines such often ignored topics as the role of women in Native American societies and how one cannot really speak of a single culture for the indigenous peoples, the struggles of the labor movement and poor people in general, and the disappearance of the "mountain man" as civilization crept westward. In addition to using famous writers, Cuban and Roden also excerpt letters and diaries from common people of the time.

CENSORSHIP HISTORY

A textbook generally does not have a long lifespan. Thus, most of the challenges to *Promise of America* occurred in the early 1970s.

In 1972, in St. Charles, Missouri, a group of parents banded together under the name of Concerned Citizens for St. Charles and protested to the local school board about *Promise of America*. They disliked open-ended questions, feeling that the questions might actually lead to "socialism and anti-Americanism." Even more alarming, they felt, was that Cuban and Roden had apparently approved of some forms of civil disobedience and included what the parents called "gutter language." Nevertheless, Assistant Superintendent W. D. Grigsby defended the book before the board, explaining that these books promoted democracy by opening up the marketplace of ideas and encouraging the students to think. While the Concerned Citizens for St. Charles promised more action, it is not known if they were ever successful in removing the text from the eighth-grade curriculum.

The set of volumes met with a harsher fate in 1976 in Eugene, Oregon. It was removed from the required reading list and put into the supplementary category at the school at Fern Ridge. The school board decided to take the action after a six-member panel could not come to an agreement; the three teachers voted to retain the books as basic texts, while the three community members who were not teachers voted to remove them. The issue was first initiated by Ellie Placek, who described herself as "an American citizen and a concerned Christian parent." Placek objected to the books on many grounds. For example, Book Two includes a photograph of a Native American man standing by his car, which has a bumper sticker reading "Custer Died for Your Sins." Placek found this to be blasphemous. She also objected to the series' inclusion of Martin Luther King, Jr.'s "I Have a Dream" speech. King, asserted Placek, was "a pro-communist race agitator." Although she succeeded in getting the books removed from the required list, Placek vowed to continue the fight and hoped that the books would be removed from the school and destroyed.

However, in Warren, Michigan, the most troubling events occurred. In 1975, Warren Consolidated Schools superintendent Olin L. Adams, Jr., ordered that the school bow to parental opposition and remove the books entirely from the school. This happened in part because of a school board that was unwilling to compromise at all; although Adams suggested that the books be at least retained on the supplementary lists, only one board member agreed with him, noting that "history is not a matter of all good or all bad." The board agreed with parents that the texts were aimed at inner city children (and that this was bad) and that the historical excerpts often contained racially derogatory terms.

But the fight did not end there. The Warren Educational Association brought a grievance before the National Labor Relations Board, claiming that removing the books violated the academic freedom clause of their contract with the school board. However, the National Labor Relations Board determined that the school board was not overstepping its bounds or violating the contract, and that the board had the right "generally to manage the school system and specifically to choose appropriate texts."

FURTHER READING

Newsletter on Intellectual Freedom 21 (1972): 128; 24 (1975): 111–112; 25 (1976): 37.

—Mitchell Fay
University of Wisconsin–River Falls

REPORT OF THE SIBERIAN DELEGATION

Author: Leon Trotsky
Original dates and places of publication: 1903, Geneva, Switzerland;
1980, Great Britain
Publisher: [s.n.]; New Park Publications
Literary form: Nonfiction

SUMMARY

The Second Congress of Russian Socialist Democracy was decisive for the future of the Russian Revolution, decisive in a direction that had not been anticipated. Leon Trotsky in his *Report of the Siberian Delegation* reveals the nature of the split between the Bolsheviks and the Mensheviks, how that split emerged and was defined. Lenin's tactics are exemplified, throwing light on the character of this man.

Prior to the congress, the editorial board members of the London-based paper *Iskra* had assumed a leadership role, urging change in Russian social democracy. The internal discussions and disputes of these editors developed into a rift at the congress between the minority (the soft "Iskraists") and the majority (the hard "Iskraists")—the Mensheviks and the Bolsheviks respectively—led by Julius Martov and Vladimir I. Lenin. Trotsky, who had been neutral, apparently joined the moderate minority group at the meeting.

The rift surfaced in the phrasing of paragraph one of the rules, which established who might be considered a member of the newly formed party.

> Lenin's formula: "A member of the Party is one who recognizes its programme, supports it materially and participates in the activity of one of the organizations of the Party." Martov's formula: "A member of the Party is one who recognizes its programme, supports it by material means and renders it regular personal collaboration under the direction of one of its organizations."

Lenin advocated strict centralism and severe discipline, which meant control over the members of the party. "This control can only be assured if it is possible to reach each member. Now, this can be done if *all the members of the Party* are formally fixed, that is *registered* in the appropriate manner with one of the Party organizations." Martov, in contrast, envisioned a less centralized organization, including such sympathetic bodies as workers organizations, which would be excluded by Lenin unless they dissolved themselves and joined the legitimate organizations of the party.

The schism was codified by the divisive arguments, manipulation, and outcomes in developing the structure of the party center. In addition to a "single indivisible Central Committee, a prospect seductive because of its very simplicity, for ideological leadership," a need was seen for a group to be concerned with practical, organizational work, the Organizing Committee.

The ideal of a third group, "a conciliatory, unifying organism," materialized as the Council and developed into the supreme body of the party, composed of five members. Trotsky points out that the last development in effect, by bestowing supremacy on the Council, subverted the original intention of denying the idea of a "single centre" and terminated the idea of two independent centers.

Gaining control of the Council expressed the underlying power struggle between the Mensheviks and the Bolsheviks. Maneuvers and manipulation ensued:

> The question of the elections acquired for both parties a meaning of the first order, because in this question was summed up and so to speak personified the struggle of principle between the tactics of normal constitutional order and the tactics of the "state of siege" backed up by dictatorship.

Lenin achieved his purpose:

> The "state of siege" on which Lenin insisted with such energy, requires "full powers." The practice of organized distrust demands an iron hand. The system of Terror is crowned by a Robespierre. Comrade Lenin reviewed the members of the Party in his mind, and reached the conclusion that this iron hand could only be himself. And he was right. The hegemony of social democracy in the struggle for emancipation meant, according to the "state of siege," the hegemony of Lenin over social democracy.

In the subsequent elections, with all 20 of the 20 minority members abstaining from voting, Lenin's followers were seated.

In closing pages of his document, Trotsky uses prophetic words to define the personality of Lenin and the outcome of the congress. Having identified Lenin as energetic and talented, he added "disorganizer" and *victory not of centralism but of ego-centralism.*" Lenin's demand for unanimity in the appointment of new members on the Central committee was perceived as permitting him to veto "anyone possessed of the vice of *personal initiative and independence.*"

Lenin's success is identified as potentially disastrous to the party. Trotsky likens Comrade Lenin's need "to take on the role of the Incorruptible" and his transformed Council to a caricature of Robespierre and his all-powerful Committee of Public Safety. With "creatures of the Incorruptible . . . placed in all important State posts," Trotsky foresaw the threat of grave danger.

> Such a regime cannot last forever. The system of Terror ends up in reaction. The Parisian proletariat had raised up Robespierre, hoping he would drag them out of their poverty. But the dictator gave out too many executions and not enough bread. Robespierre fell, dragging with him the Montagne, and with them, the cause of democracy in general.

CENSORSHIP HISTORY

The first inkling, perhaps, of imminent censorship is suggested by Trotsky himself in "A few words by way of conclusion" appended to the report (for the published pamphlet but not part of the report itself). He refers to a "Letter to the Editorial Board of *Iskra*" written by Comrade Lenin in which he complained of "clandestine" literature, including the *Report of the Siberian Delegation*, being circulated. Lenin reacted to "the most amusing accusations" against himself of "autocracy" and of having created a "Robespierre-style regime of executions." Trotsky queries whether Lenin is "quite simply not prepared to recognize this right [of publishing documents] to the 'minority.' "

The *Report* was banned by the imperial government in 1903 and by the government of the Soviet Union in 1927. In both cases the reason was the same, opposition to the existing philosophies of government, although they represented ideologically polar positions. The latter censorship was part of the complex struggle to maintain the Revolution and to gain power. Upon Lenin's illness, Gregory Zinoviev, Leo Borisovich Kamenev, and Joseph Stalin joined forces, forming in 1923 the notorious "Triumvirate"; their common bond was to oust Trotsky, the most popular Communist Party member, and to assume the succession. Within two years Trotsky, who was advocating the democratization of the party, had been politically isolated, and in 1925 he was removed from his chairmanship of the War Council and other duties. Within two more years, Stalin exerted control and stripped Zinoviev and Kamenev of their powers; they then joined Trotsky to form the Joint Opposition. Their defeat resulted in Trotsky's condemnation by the Fifteenth Party Congress in December 1927. In January 1928, Trotsky was arrested: "The GPU agents produced a warrant for Leon Davidovich's [Trotsky] arrest, as well as a copy of the sentence pronounced on him in secret and in his absence by Political Security Council." He was exiled to Central Asia; in 1929 he was deported to Turkey. Stalin had consolidated his power.

In the 1930s, Trotsky's works were banned in quite disparate venues: the United States (in Boston), 1930; Germany, 1933; Soviet Union, 1933; and Italy, 1934. The situation in Germany is memorable. On May 10, the first large-scale book-burning demonstration occurred. Students gathered 25,000 volumes by Jewish authors and burned them in the square in front of the University of Berlin. Joseph Goebbels, the minister of public enlightenment, delivered a speech at the occasion about "the symbolic significance of the gesture." Similar book-burning demonstrations were held at other German universities. Marxist literature was consigned to such public fires in Munich, where 5,000 schoolchildren were admonished, "As you watch the fire burn these un-German books, let it also burn into your hearts love of the Fatherland." Students took books they considered appropriate for the bonfire from bookstores, but they were prevented from confiscating books from the university library.

FURTHER READING

Haight, Anne Lyon, and Chandler B. Grannis. *Banned Books: 387 B.C. to 1978 A.D.* 4th ed. New York: R. R. Bowker, 1978.

Howe, Irving. *Leon Trotsky.* New York: Viking Press, 1978.

Serge, Victor, and Natalia Sedova Trotsky. *The Life and Death of Leon Trotsky.* New York: Basic Books, 1975.

Trotsky, Leon. *My Life: An Attempt at an Autobiography.* New York: Pathfinder Press, 1970.

THE RIGHTS OF MAN

Author: Thomas Paine

Original dates and places of publication: 1791 (Part 1), 1792 (Part 2), England; 1791 (Part 1), 1792 (Part 2), United States. The first part was also serialized in New York City in summer 1791

Publishers: Jeremiah Samuel Jordan; Graham (serialized by the *Daily Advertiser*)

Literary form: Nonfiction

SUMMARY

In the latter part of the 1700s, as England saw its prized colony slip away from control and witnessed revolution in France, it attempted to suppress the flow of ideas from America, whose independence served as an inspiration to others who would fight for liberty and was seen as a danger to the British Crown. Much of the efforts centered on the works of Thomas Paine. *The Rights of Man* was among the most prosecuted books in the 1790s in England. Most often it was prosecuted on the charge of seditious libel.

Paine began writing *The Rights of Man* within two days of the publication of Edmund Burke's 1790 book, *Reflections on the Revolution in France.* Burke, who bitterly denounced the French Revolution, had heretofore been much admired by Paine, but Paine turned on what he saw as flaws in Burke's writings as well as the inherent evil of the British government.

Paine's writing style is recursive. In addition, many of his ideas focus on the history of his time, but the historical data were not what got Paine into trouble with the censors.

Paine begins by refuting Burke's assertion that the ascension of William and Mary in 1689 bound the nation of England in fealty forever to the monarchy. Paine claimed that it was absurd to believe that today's generation could be bound by the promises of earlier generations. The living must have precedence over the dead, and the Parliament that gave the oath of loyalty had no power to do so; hence, the actions of that earlier generation are not binding on those people living in the present.

Paine also argues against the notion of hereditary superiority. "Man" is the highest title that one can receive or need. As there is no inherent quality in a title, such titles are merely meaningless nicknames, but a "unity of man" stems from the natural rights of all human beings. As all people are equally children of God, so all are equal in rights to each other.

Among the natural rights that humans have simply because of existence are intellectual rights, which include liberty to read and hear, to speak, and to think. The rights of the mind also include spiritual rights. Paine forcefully argues that freedom of religion is not simply tolerance. Humans have no right or power to simply "tolerate" another religion; to speak of tolerance would be tantamount to a deliberative body passing a law allowing God to receive the worship of the Jew or to prevent God from doing this. Clearly, no earthly power exists that could pass such a measure. To God, all beliefs are equal and one. Besides intellectual rights, humans have the right to act in the interests of their own happiness, so long as the pursuit of happiness is not injurious to the rights of others.

Out of these natural rights are derived civil rights. To exist in society requires a certain sacrifice of some portion of natural rights. But this sacrifice must be a part of a social compact; no government can summarily take these rights from its people. People enter into society in order to ensure enjoyment of civil rights, which individuals acting on their own might not be able to guarantee.

Paine then builds on these ideas of rights by examining the ways in which a government may rule. Governments can exist through superstition and be led by priests; they can exist through the force of power and be led by conquerors; or they can be based on rights and rule through reason and the will of the people. The last is the only government that deserves to exist. By contrast, an aristocracy is equal to tyranny for several reasons: As there is no heredity of ability, there is no justice in passing power within a particular family from one generation to another; aristocratic classes are not accountable to the people and thus are inherently unjust; the aristocracy is based on power instead of rights; the aristocratic class (in part due to rules of primogeniture) necessarily degenerates over the course of time.

In contrast to England, Paine presents France. Much of the first part of *The Rights of Man* is devoted to countering claims of tyranny and excess in the French Revolution. Unfortunately for Paine, only a few years would pass before such tyranny would occur, and he himself would become one of the victims of it, a prisoner in France after the revolution. But France, says Paine, is superior to England because it has a real constitution and because its legislature is responsive to the people. Where the government can claim to "reform itself," there is no real chance for reform, because there is no accountability. Paine asserts that everything about the government of England is the opposite of what it should be.

The second part of *The Rights of Man* was published in 1792. Again, it was well received by the reading public. Paine explains why representative government is best. Using America as a model and harbinger of change, Paine demonstrates that monarchies are, by their nature, militaristic. In addition, their quest for further conquest represents a drain on the nation's finances through taxation and debt. To end this despotism, Paine calls for the liquidation of the monarchy and for the monies of England to be distributed among the poor and to promote employment of those who are currently unemployed. In addition, these monies would promote new marriages and the raising of children.

After showing the problems of monarchism, Paine distinguishes between the possible types of government and tells us that the "more perfect civilization is, the less occasion has it for government." Furthermore, government should be "nothing more than a national association acting on the principles of society." But a monarchy acts in the best interests of the monarch; an aristocracy acts in the best interests of the aristocratic class. It is only a republic, such as found in America, that acts in the best interests of the welfare of the people.

To develop this argument in greater detail, Paine takes his readers through the development of the Constitution of Pennsylvania, the Articles of Confederations, and the Constitution of the United States of America. He ends with the optimistic thought that revolution, and the desire for the freedom that a representative democracy can bring, might spread throughout Europe and could mean an end to war and tyranny.

CENSORSHIP HISTORY

While most of Paine's *The Rights of Man* seems, to modern Americans, a basic and accepted part of political beliefs, it presented a clear challenge to Great Britian. Although essentially free of the censor's ire in our time, Paine himself was persecuted in his lifetime; in fact, this book has also been included on *The Encyclopedia of Censorship*'s list of works "most often" censored.

In 1791, Charles James Fox introduced a bill to the House of Commons that would allow juries to decide what was and was not libelous. Although it was thrown out by the House of Lords, in 1792 Fox's Libel Act survived attacks by Lord Kenyon and his cronies to become law. Although judges were still allowed to give their opinions to the juries, juries were now empowered to disregard judges' advice. At the same time, an increasing number of books and newspaper articles had attacked the monarchy; some suggested that Prime Minister William Pitt was using the king's madness as an excuse to take over the government.

In this situation, Paine's publication was like holding a match to tinder. The first printing of *The Rights of Man* was discontinued in February 1791. The printer, known today variously as Johnson and Chapman, decided that the book exhibited a "dangerous tendency" and ceased his work. The next month in England, Jeremiah Samuel Jordan released the book to the public with a much larger printing. The initial printing of 10,000 copies sold out overnight in London. However, in the summer of 1792, Jordan was arrested and pled guilty to a charge of seditious libel for printing the second part of *The Rights of Man*. By some estimates, the first part of *The Rights of Man* may have sold as many as 2 million copies within its first year and was available at low cost.

William Pitt agreed that Paine was probably correct in many of his attacks, but asserted that his writing could cause "a bloody revolution" if not checked. Although he did not take the drastic step of burning all copies of *The Rights of Man*, Pitt is reported to have paid demonstrators five shillings a man to take to the streets and denounce Paine. On a single night in February of 1792, Paine was burned in effigy in four separate places in London. He was hanged in effigy in London, Worcester, Canterbury, and elsewhere. When the British discovered that the American version of Paine's book restored a section that had been left out of the British one, the charge that government in Britain was in every way the opposite of what it should be, Pitt took more extreme action.

An initial summons on the charge of seditious libel was made against Paine on May 21, 1792; on June 8, he appeared in trial, but the actual court date was postponed until December. Paine did not relent in his attacks, but as time went on, his friends began to fear for his life. Legend has it that the poet William Blake urged him to flee the country. One step ahead of a warrant for his arrest and imprisonment without bail, Paine fled England for France on September 18. Unfortunately, he was later imprisoned while in France because of his hostility to the Jacobins and his efforts to prevent the execution of Louis XVI.

Thomas Erskine, the attorney general to the Prince of Wales and an advocate for freedom of the press, served as Paine's spokesman at the trial over *The Rights of Man*. Erskine argued against using passages out of context as grounds for finding a book to be seditious. He was often successful in winning acquittals for those charged with libel and frequently published on the subject of press freedom. He would even invite juries to set aside the laws as written. Although Thomas Erskine agreed to take on Paine's case, not everyone was happy with his decision, including Lord Loughborough, who was to become the lord chancellor.

The trial, held on December 18, 1792, was presided over by the same Lord Kenyon who had led the fight against the Fox Libel Act. While Erskine objected to the prosecution's reading of a letter from Paine as evidence (Erskine contended that the charges were brought against Paine for *The Rights of Man* and not for any other private correspondence), Kenyon overruled. Facing a hostile jury, Erskine argued for three hours and 40 minutes that the book should be viewed as a whole, without items taken out of context. He stated that Paine was not guilty because he had not attempted to incite his readers to break the law. Writers, he argued, have a right and a duty to point out error by the government. However, the jury was so keen to convict that they had lost the patience to hear Erskine's summing up. Under British law, seditious libel meant that if the words could topple the established order, their truth or falsity had no bearing on the case. On December 20, Paine was found guilty, not only of libel, but of high treason. He was forbidden, on pain of death, to set foot in England ever again.

After Paine's trial, a spate of prosecutions for seditious libel resulted, including against the works of Paine. However, in June 1793, a jury found Daniel Isaac Eaton guilty only of publishing *The Rights of Man;* they denied that Eaton was guilty of criminal intent. This was the verdict in a like suit against him in July 1793 for publishing *Letter Addressed to the Addressers on the Late Proclamation,* although in early 1793, the publisher Henry Delaney Symonds was sentenced to a year in prison and fined 100 pounds for selling the same pamphlet. And in 1819, Richard Carlile was found guilty of publishing THE AGE OF REASON, incurring a fine of 1,000 pounds and two years' imprisonment. Still, despite *The Rights of Man* and *The Age of Reason* being condemned by the courts, comments Donald Thomas, "throughout the first quarter of the nineteenth century there was no shortage of willing martyrs prepared to go . . . to Newgate [prison] for six months or a year, in order that the philosophy of Thomas Paine should not go unread or unheard." Erskine himself was allowed to print an account of the trial of Paine. Samuel Taylor Coleridge and Jeremy Bentham would later join the cause for the free press. Coleridge asked, "How many of Thomas Paine's hundreds of thousands of readers have been incited to acts of political violence by reading him?" He averred that few, if any, had been so moved. In the 19th century, Britain largely came to agree with Erskine's argument that sedition existed only when an author actually attempted to incite readers to violence against the government.

But because Paine never hesitated to speak his mind, by the end of his life he had become an outcast in America, Britian, and France. Although he spent his final years in America, he was ostracized and shunned as an atheist and as a traitor to the cause of freedom. He survived a murder attempt, was stripped of his right to vote, and was labeled a blasphemer. The man who may have done more than any other to promote the causes of the American Revolution and liberty died on June 8, 1809, in relative obscurity. Even long after his death, Teddy Roosevelt called Paine "a filthy little atheist." Robert B. Downs notes, "He was none of these . . . few figures in American history are as controversial as Thomas Paine and few made contributions as notable as his toward the beginning of the United States as a nation."

FURTHER READING

Downs, Robert B. *Books That Changed America.* London: Macmillan, 1970.
Edward, Samuel. *Rebel! A Biography of Tom Paine.* New York: Praeger, 1974.

Green, Jonathan, and Nicholas J Karolides, reviser. *Encyclopedia of Censorship, New Edition*. New York: Facts On File, 2005.

Thomas, Donald. *A Long Time Burning: The History of Literary Censorship in England*. New York: Praeger, 1969.

—Mitchell Fay
University of Wisconsin–River Falls

RUSSIA

Author: Vernon Ives
Original date and place of publication: 1943, United States
Original publisher: Holiday House
Literary form: Nonfiction

SUMMARY

"Russia is the New World of the Twentieth Century. Just as the United States was the growing giant among nations in the last half of the last century, so was Russia in the first half of the present." With this opening, Vernon Ives sets the tone for his short, adolescent-level illustrated book, in which comparison to the United States is to be a dominant format for describing both the history and the current political system in Russia. Russia's eastward expansion into Siberia is compared to the U.S. push westward; the enslavement and eventual emancipation of the Russian serfs is compared to slavery and emancipation in the United States; the Russian Revolution is compared to the American Revolution; Soviet Russia's achievements in developing and industrializing a vast new country are compared to similar U.S. achievements; even the two current systems of government are compared in certain aspects.

The first half of the book is devoted to prerevolution Russian history, beginning 1,000 years ago when the Vikings came to the Dnieper Valley, established Kiev as their capital, and began a trading route to Constantinople, from where they brought Greek Orthodoxy back to Russia. In the mid-13th century, the Mongol warriors of Chinggis (Genghis) Khan swept westward across Asia and conquered Kiev, ruling for 200 years over the Russians, with only the "backwoods town of Moscow" keeping Russian sovereignty alive. By 1500, the Mongols, "fighters, not colonizers," had grown careless; the Viking descendants managed to regain power and made Moscow their new capital, thus beginning the period of the czars. When the last Viking czar died at the end of the 16th century, after ousting a Polish ruler who took over briefly, the Russians chose their own ruler and initiated the 300-year reign of the House of Romanov.

Throughout its history, Russia was pulled both east and west. After 200 years of Asian influence during the Mongol period, the czars turned the country's cultural, linguistic, and religious focus toward its Slavic brethren in central Europe, with Peter the Great going so far as to establish a new capital in St. Petersburg. This, however, didn't stop Russian pioneers from pushing east into Siberia, "a land for the taking." Three factors aided Russia's expansion eastward. First, Russian geography consists of east-west belts of similar terrain (southernmost are the deserts, then the grassy steppes, the forests and, northernmost, the tundra), which enables people living at a particular latitude to feel "at home" due east. Second, the extensive network of rivers forms almost a continuous link from the Ural Mountains to the Pacific. Third, the high price paid for fur in poorly heated 16th- and 17th-century Europe lured many a fortune-seeker eastward. In addition, the fiercely independent Cossacks made natural leaders. They were a band of "outlaws" who, during Mongol rule, had evaded both Mongol subjugation and Moscovite taxation and conscription, by holding out in an area between the two territories. They became the czar's finest imperial soldiers and defeated the Mongol khan of Siberia.

Peter the Great is credited for achieving his main goal of making Russia a great European power. By forcing the serfs to fight in his great army and navy or to work where assigned, he introduced science and industry to the country but set up a pattern of war and peasant labor that lasted 150 years after his death. The serfs were freed in 1861 (two years before the U.S. slaves were freed), but even then the land was given to groups of peasants who were responsible for payment. "Thus the freed serf still owned no land of his own and the inevitable revolution had only been delayed."

Ives describes four factors leading up to the revolution: the suppression of all liberal thinking for the 300-year Romanov rule; the failure to make the peasants truly free; poor leadership by the czar in World War I, which caused discouragement among soldiers who were dying for lack of supplies; and the complete collapse of the autocratic political structure in 1917. In an atmosphere of chaos, with peasants looting and killing across the countryside and political factions vying for power, the Bolsheviks finally took control, led by Vladimir Lenin, "one of the greatest leaders of modern times." The 1917 Bolshevik revolution was complicated by the continuing war with Germany and Austria; by rivalry among factions, some supported by other countries that feared the communist "experiment" because it aimed to propagate itself throughout the world; and by the confused masses, who were already used to czarist repression and were not convinced that communism would be better.

Although the Communists came out on top of the struggle, "the change in society was too sudden" to be smooth. Private ownership of farms and factories was abolished, as was money. Obligatory work was done in exchange for state provision of basic necessities. There was no regard for the individual; only the common good of Russia mattered.

But as new plans were being made to correct mistakes and progress the state, Lenin died, and the execution of the plans was left to "the strong leadership of Joseph Stalin." With three Five Year Plans, Stalin aimed to transform the ignorant, unskilled, agricultural Russia into a literate, trained, industrial USSR as fast as possible. This was "a bigger job than Americans were ever called upon to do. No nation in history ever did so much so fast." In order to achieve what had been Lenin's first goal—nationwide electrification—massive dams were constructed. Further, the state established huge collective farms, which hired workers as a factory would, used modern machines and fertilizers and attempted to teach the peasants the new methods. This plan almost failed: Peasants were slow to learn; "wealthier" peasants who resisted giving up their own land were sent to remote prison camps or construction jobs; and crop failures killed millions. "But whatever the cost, however harsh the means and different from our way of life, the fact remains that the collective farms worked." Ives writes that by 1937 less than half the Russian population was producing twice the food of czarist Russia, releasing millions of farmers to work in industry. "The old Russian village was gone forever." Huge mines and factories were built to capitalize on Russia's vast resources, which included one-fifth of the world's known supply of coal and iron, one-third of the world's forests and half its oil.

Ives describes Russia's undaunted push to navigate the Arctic, "sparing no pains to bring every known means of science to the Arctic problem." He states that Russians have "shown the way" to the day when routine flights will cross the North Pole, making the United States and Russia close polar neighbors. He adds, "Close neighbors should be good friends. . . . That people of different stock, education, language and religion can live together in one united nation has been proven by the Soviet Union no less than the United States, which in many ways are remarkably alike." Though three-quarters of Russia's population are Slavs, Ives claims that ever since Stalin's days as first commissar for minor nationalities, the Soviets have seen to it that their minority populations (including Muslims, Buriats, Jews, Aryans, Caucasians, and Yakut nomads) have lost no rights. Their languages and cultures are honored, and as citizens they have equal shares in the government.

Ives shows the USSR made up of 16 member republics—similar to our states. The Soviet of Nationalities corresponds to the U.S. Senate, with each republic holding equal representation; the Soviet of the Union corresponds to the U.S. House of Representatives with members elected according to district population. Government administration is conducted by the Council of People's Commissars, headed by Premier Stalin. With its citizens forbidden to join any other party, the Communist Party in effect *is* the government, and party membership is an honor eagerly sought. Ives concludes that this system is "not the American way." Americans do not like one-party politics, no private ownership, government control of information, or the idea of being told what to do. But, he says, Americans do admire people who get things done and people who have developed a vast new country and overthrown an oppressive rule.

"A way of life not one's own is not necessarily the wrong way." but "this has been very hard for both Russia and other countries to keep in mind." In a later edition of the book, Ives describes a distrustfulness growing out of the end of World War II (1945) that "put the entire world into a state of anxiety about another global war, in which civilization itself might be destroyed. . . . Civilization has at last come to a point where it can keep on growing only in the climate of peace."

CENSORSHIP HISTORY

Russia was removed from library shelves at Proctor and New Hartford high schools in September 1955 on the advice of a textbook commission of the Education Department of the state of New York. According to the commission, the book, while not seditious or disloyal, contained passages "that are either untrue or almost certain to evoke untrue inferences." Some teachers and parents had complained that the book is favorable to the Soviet Union, perceived at times as a country with which the United States might potentially be at war.

In 1966, after Ives's book had been in the Marksville Elementary School library for 13 years, the Avoyelles Parish school board in Marksville, Louisiana, followed the advice of board member S. R. (Pete) Abramson and passed a motion to ban the book from school libraries. Abramson charged that the book was pro-Russian in comparing Russia to the United States. He objected especially to the passage, "That people of different stock, education, language and religion can live together in one united nation has been proven by the Soviet Union no less than the United States, which in many ways are remarkably alike." Additional criticisms of the book included the passage "Many small government positions are held by non-party Russians but almost all important posts are filled by Communists," and the paragraph that notes that this is not the American way but acknowledges that "we do admire people who get things done as we do."

The point was raised by J. B. Lepke of Bunkie, Louisiana, that in 1943 the United States and Russia were allies in the war, which initiated a discussion of political philosophy. Though this discussion might have recognized that the book reflected the more favorable American attitude toward the Soviet Union that was current in 1943 when the book was written, in the end the motion to ban the book was passed unanimously.

The superintendent, Lynden Couvillion, further suggested that, in addition to banning this book, a committee of teachers in each school be set up to continue to screen library books.

FURTHER READING

"Banned after 13 Years." *Newsletter on Intellectual Freedom* 15 (1966): 21.
"School Board Bans Russian Book, Fails to Change Reading." *Bunkie Record,* February 3, 1966, pp. 1, 8.

—Alexis Karolides

SECRECY AND DEMOCRACY: THE CIA IN TRANSITION

Author: Stansfield Turner
Original date and place of publication: 1985, United States
Publisher: Houghton Mifflin
Literary form: Nonfiction

SUMMARY

This book, written by the former director of central intelligence (DCI) of the Central Intelligence Agency (CIA), details his time at the agency in order to show both its strengths and its weaknesses and to give support for the changes he felt were necessary to keep the agency effective in this changing world. Secrecy is an important part of staying ahead in the world; each nation struggles to find out the secrets of other nations, called intelligence, while attempting to keep those nations from discovering theirs, called counterintelligence. Both the CIA and the Federal Bureau of Investigation (FBI) aid the United States in this endeavor. The FBI conducts intelligence and counterintelligence activities inside the United States, while the CIA does the same outside the country.

The CIA, essentially, is a balancing act. There is a fine line between national security and individual rights. Because the United States is a democracy, it is not allowed to use the same invasive tactics on its citizens as did its Soviet counterpart, the KGB. When it was discovered in the seventies that this code was not being honored, the American public became outraged. They felt that the CIA had no right to invade their privacy, which was done, as Turner says, in many ways: "Countless 'dangerous' citizens were placed under surveillance, with bugs on their telephones, microphones in their bedrooms, or warrantless break-ins of their homes." Because the United States honors the privacy of its citizens, Turner says, it will never be as good as the Soviet Union at counterintelligence.

In addition to balancing between the security of the nation and the rights of the individual, the CIA, in conjunction with the Congress, must decide on the proper balance of oversight and secrecy. In the past, the CIA operated with relatively little supervision by Congress or the general public because, as Turner says: "Honesty, openness, and respect for the rights of the individual are important elements of our international reputation, and the public doesn't like to think of compromising them. Generally the public has preferred to let the CIA do what it needed to do, but only if it didn't have to know about it." Once the veil of secrecy was dropped in the 1970s and the public became aware of CIA atrocities, it became apparent that with little supervision by the government, or even their superiors in the CIA, many individual agents can abuse that trust and misuse their power. For example, when a former KGB officer, Yuri Nosenko, defected to the United States in 1964, he told CIA agents that he could not remember any KGB involvement with Lee Harvey Oswald, the eventual assassin of President Kennedy. The CIA agent in charge, James Jesus Angleton, refused to believe Nosenko and concluded that he was a double agent who must be forced to confess, so Nosenko was placed in solitary confinement for more than three and a half years, where he was underfed and forbidden to have any connection with the outside world. Once this type of behavior was exposed, the need for more oversight became clear. Congress, according to Turner, must be made aware of and approve of the actions of the CIA, in a way that does not compromise the information.

The CIA is a large and multifaceted organization. Its intelligence and counterintelligence activities include the collection of data, both through human and technological means, and the analysis of that information. When Turner was DCI from 1977 to 1981, the importance of technological collection of data was just becoming acknowledged. While technology will never replace human espionage, he writes, it is still a valuable resource. It can collect many minute details that are out of reach to humans, such as photographs from space satellites, with no risk to human life. On the other hand, human-to-human contact is necessary to determine the state of affairs in a country, particularly the feelings and morale of its inhabitants. Turner said he discovered during his term as DCI that, while the espionage branch was too large, both it and the technological branch were extremely effective. What was lacking was correct analysis of the information gathered by them. He also said that any changes he attempted in the size and methods of the espionage branch met resistance, and that the problems still existed at the time he wrote the book. In order to better the department, he would like to see communication between CIA analysts and social and physical scientists throughout the country. Unfortunately, this communication is seen by many in the CIA to be dangerous to the state of secrecy. Also many universities forbid contact between their professors and the CIA because it could become a conflict of interests for the professor and could, if exposed, blacken the image of the university as a whole.

Covert action, which is "[America's] efforts to influence the course of events in a foreign country without [its] role being known," is important to national security as well. It is used as a response to "despotic acts" and against countries whose political backgrounds are perceived as threatening to the United States, such as Communist countries, however poor and unmilitarized they are. Covert action ranges from the proliferation of propaganda to convincing inhabitants to revolt to actually aiding in that revolt by sending money or supplies or by giving paramilitary support.

CIA and Congress disagree on what is an appropriate amount of oversight. Congress desires to have control of covert action, especially to be informed prior to all covert operations. While Turner agrees that a higher level of supervision is necessary, he objects to the idea that all operations would have to be disclosed prior to their initiation because then the degree of secrecy required for successful completion would be endangered. Turner expresses concern, however, that covert action taken under President Ronald Reagan and his DCI, William Casey, was improper; they did not make Congress fully aware of their actions, and thus brought the country into the position where a declaration of war was a possibility without permission. In reference to the Reagan administration's involvement in Nicaragua in the early 1980s, Turner says, "Covert Action should be brought back from the Reagan administration's excesses to the limits prescribed by law." In Nicaragua, covert action consisted of aiding a guerrilla force, known as "contras," to attempt to wear down and undermine the Nicaraguan government through continual warfare. The CIA later helped place bombs in the Nicaraguan harbors and plotted to assassinate several civil officials, such as judges and police officers. These types of activities are against the American ideals of democracy and reflect the actions of a more totalitarian government. All this was done with little involvement of Congress, for the CIA failed to inform Congress of its actions and ignored congressional restrictions. As such, Congress continually attempted to bring Casey under control, to no avail.

> The [Reagan] administration's willingness repeatedly to flout the Congress reflected a view that oversight was an impediment rather than a necessity for good intelligence in a society like ours. . . . In thirty years we had shown that the secrecy of intelligence presents temptations and that oversight is needed to keep people from overstepping the bounds tacitly stipulated by the public.

The major problem that Turner sees with the intelligence community is that it is not a true community. Although the Defense Intelligence Agency, which is made up of the intelligence branches of each military organization, and the National Security Agency are supposed to report their information to the DCI, and all agencies are supposed to share information among one another, little sharing goes on. Rather, each agency strives to discover the big secret and be rewarded.

CENSORSHIP HISTORY

As secrecy is of utmost importance to the CIA, all writings of former CIA agents must be screened to make sure that none of the information contained within them is classified. All agents have to sign a document upon entering and another upon leaving the agency that says they will submit all of their writings regarding the CIA to a review board. While Admiral Turner was DCI, he urged the attorney general to prosecute Frank Snepp, whose book, DECENT INTERVAL, was written and published without being submitted to the review board.

Although Turner agrees that the review board is necessary, he says in the appendix to his book that it has problems with "timeliness and arbitrariness."

As he says, each chapter would take anywhere from six weeks to five months to review, which would cause added expense to the publisher. Also, he had several unresolvable objections to decisions of the board to remove portions from his book. He cites two reasons for his objections. First, he feels that much of what was censored was not really confidential; some material, in fact, was already in the public domain, thus "making a mockery of the secret label." For example, Mitgang, writing for the *New York Times*, cites him as saying:

> "While I was director of the CIA, I gave a number of unclassified speeches to audiences with no security clearances. In one of those I gave a hypothetical example of how we integrate various types of intelligence collection. When I attempted to quote my own unclassified speech in my book, I was denied permission. Yet, I obtained quite freely a copy of my speech from the CIA and assume, since it is not classified, that you or any citizen could so so today."

Second, while he realizes that CIA agents give up their First Amendment rights because national security is more important, Turner feels that many of the items removed from his memoir had more to do with a petty desire of the Reagan administration to remain uncriticized than with national security.

In another example cited in the appendix, Turner tells how he had made an objection to the board, and it had replied that he could publish the information if he deemed it " 'appropriate,' " but that the administration would respond with " 'whatever action it deemed appropriate.' " Eight months after deciding to give in because he did not want to appear to be giving away secrets that "could encourage less responsible individuals to be cavalier about releasing secret information," that information was declassified, and he asked again for permission to use it. His objection was still under consideration when his book went to press. He was disappointed because, as he says, "I was, in effect, denied permission to say the same things the CIA was having said in public. The citizens of our country deserve better assurance that their interests are truly being served by the CIA's review process." He believes this arbitrariness stems from the irritation the administration felt with "the book's highly critical view of the Reagan administration's mishandling of our intelligence activities, especially its indifference to any oversight of the CIA. . . . Clearly the Reagan administration does not understand that oversight of intelligence in our society includes constructive criticism from outsiders like me."

FURTHER READING

Green, Jonathon, and Nicholas J. Karolides, reviser. "CIA." In *Encyclopedia of Censorship, New Edition.* New York: Facts On File, 2005.
Mitgang, Herbert. "Book Notes." *New York Times*, August 31, 1988, p. C22.
Newsletter on Intellectual Freedom 37 (1988): 216.
Turner, Stansfield. "Appendix: A Word on Censorship." In his *Secrecy and Democracy: The CIA in Transition.* New York: Harper and Row, 1985.

—Jane Graves

EL SEÑOR PRESIDENTE (THE PRESIDENT)

Author: Miguel Angel Asturias
Original dates and places of publication: 1946, Mexico; 1963, United
States
Publishers: Costa-Amic; Murray Printing Company
Literary form: Novel

SUMMARY

The events of *El señor presidente*, or *The President*, are immediately precipitated
by the "murder" of Colonel José Parrales Soriente, a favorite officer of the
president of an unnamed country that is believed to be Guatemala. However,
the machinations behind the events reveal that the president and his regime
are the chief catalyst for the terrors and tyranny that emanate from the death
of the colonel.

There are other victims, including the "murderer," a "halfwit beggar"
called "the Zany," who is traumatized by the word *mother*. Having been terrorized by hearing the word jeered at him, he reacts violently when Parrales
Soriente creeps up to him while he is asleep and shouts it in his ear. The witnesses, other beggars, are captured, imprisoned, interrogated, and tortured—
all at the orders of the judge advocate general—until at last they change their
story of the Zany's guilt to betray two men, General Eusebio Canales and
Abel Carvajal, the lawyer, whose names are provided by the judge advocate.
Thus, Canales and Carvajal, though innocent, become political victims, as do
a host of others.

The president, who is portrayed as a self-centered, suspicious, and vindictive man, orders his favorite confidential adviser, Miguel Angel Face (Don
Miguel Cara de Angel), to secretly warn Canales of his anticipated arrest so
that he will "take to flight at once" because "it doesn't suit the government
for him to go to prison." Angel Face orchestrates the escape with help from
Lucio Vasquez, a member of the secret police whom he chances to meet in a
bar, under the guise of kidnapping Camila Canales, the general's daughter,
so they might elope. Angel Face succeeds in capturing Camila while accompanied by a collection of rough men who are to loot the house so as to create
a diversion. The police join in the looting.

General Canales does escape. The failed attempt to kill him during his
escape brings down the wrath of the judge advocate. Arrests are made, the
first being that of Fedina Rodas, who has innocently come to warn Camila,
after hearing the plan from her husband, who was told about it by Vasquez.
She is incarcerated in a tomblike cell and interrogated. She tells her story,
but the judge advocate prefers to disbelieve her. She is mistreated and beaten;
her captors bring her infant son, crying for nourishment, to the next room
to force her to reveal the "truth" of the general's whereabouts. Since she cannot, the child is allowed to die within earshot; she goes mad. Subsequently,

the judge advocate sells her for 10,000 pesos to a madam of a brothel to be enslaved in prostitution.

The judge advocate causes the arrests of Carvajal and Vasquez. Astounded (and innocent), Carvajal is charged with sedition, rebellion, and treason. After days in the dungeon, he is brought to trial before the Council of War. Actually, there is no trial, only ritual; he is sentenced to death by the tribunal, whose members are drunk. No indulgences are granted to political prisoners.

> A few steps further on they entombed him in an underground dungeon three yards long by two and a half wide, in which twelve prisoners condemned to death were already standing packed together like sardines, motionless for lack of space, satisfying their physical needs where they stood and trampling on their own excrement. Carvajal was Number 13. When the soldiers left them, the painful breathing of the mass of doomed men filled the silence of the cell, already disturbed by the distant cries of a walled-up prisoner.

Vasquez is also sentenced to death for shooting the Zany, though he claims that he was an agent of the secret police and had orders to do so.

Meanwhile, Angel Face has had a change of mind and of heart, both before and after the abduction of Camila.

> And the more he thought about his project the blacker it seemed; the idea of kidnapping the daughter of a man doomed to die seemed to him as horrible and repugnant as it would have been congenial and pleasant to help him to escape. It was not good nature which made such a naturally unfeeling man dislike the thought of ambushing a trusting and defenceless citizen. . . . No. Very different were the sentiments which made Angel Face bite his lips with silent disapproval of this desperate and diabolical plan. He had believed in all good faith that as the general's protector he possessed certain rights over his daughter, but he now saw them sacrificed to his accustomed role of unreasoning tool, myrmidon and executioner.

Afterward, upon looking into her pale face and anguished eyes, he abandons the prospect of forcing his attentions on her, becoming first fatherly, then protective. He attempts to place her in the homes of her uncles and aunts; one after the other, they reject her. Out of fear for their own lives, reputations, and fortunes, they repudiate their brother and, thus, his daughter.

During this interlude, Camila becomes seriously ill with pneumonia. At the point of death, having received final absolution, she is married to Angel Face. This step is predicted to bring about the miracle of saving her life: "[T]he only thing that can fight death is love." He has come to love her and, after she recovers, she also loves him. Briefly, they share a life of dangerous bliss. The danger, of course, is that the president's confidential adviser has married the daughter of the president's presumed enemy—without his permission. Beneath the surface, the terror cauldron bubbles. The judge advocate submits a letter denouncing Angel Face, whom he feels has insulted him. The president acts as if he still trusts Angel Face and sends him to Washington as his special envoy to mend international relations. It turns out to be a trap. (Though it is not stated, the president is implicitly the activator.) At the border, Angel Face is arrested, given no opportunity to defend himself and beaten. Another man who resembles him takes on his identity and his papers. Angel Face is cast into solitary confinement in the most foul and dire conditions. He wastes away and dies.

General Canales becomes a changed man. His journey across his country opens his eyes to the deceptions and injustices perpetrated on his countrymen by the government he had been defending. He hears stories of his benefactors—a farmer who rescues him in the mountains and three elderly sisters who take him in to hide him and arrange for him to be smuggled across the border. They have been defrauded by local government officials in league with greedy, dishonest lawyers. They lose their lands, property and, in the farmer's case, the lives of his wife and sons.

> A storm of feelings was raging in old Canales' breast, such feelings as are always aroused in the heart of a good man when confronted with injustice. He suffered on behalf of his country. . . . It is a more despicable and therefore a sadder thing to be a soldier simply in order to keep a gang of ruffians, exploiters and self-important betrayers of their country in power, than it is to die of hunger in exile.

Canales leads a revolutionary army to reassert justice but dies just when he is about to lead his troops of defrauded men into action. Empowering these activities is the president. He hates his countrymen, as he reveals:

> "Ungrateful beasts!. . . . I loved and shall always love Parrales Soriente; I was going to have made him a general, because he trampled on my countrymen and humiliated them, and if it hadn't been for my mother he would have finished them off altogether and avenged me for all the grudges I bear against them, things I alone know about. Ungrateful beasts!"

Indeed, the best way to get on his right side is "to commit a public outrage on defenceless people," "to demonstrate the superiority of force to public opinion," or "to get rich at the expense of the nation."

The text is steeped in treachery and riddled with ironies. The police called to rescue Camila loot her home, allowing her to be abducted. Vasquez bludgeons Camila's nurse with a massive iron bar and groans when her inhuman cries pierce the air. The bordello madam's private apartment is crowded with engravings, sculptures, and religious images and relics. The major whom Angel Face warns against informers and advises to get on the good side of the president is the very officer who is in charge of his entrapment and who mercilessly has him brutalized. The overpowering irony is the honoring of the president—"Long live the President! Long live the Constitutional President of the Republic!"—a celebration at its height during those events.

The focus of another work by Asturias, his so-called Banana Plantation trilogy—with its implicit political orientation—also invited censorial attention. Composed of *Viento fuerte* (STRONG WIND), 1950, *El papa verde* (THE GREEN POPE), 1954, and *Los ojos de los enterralos* (*The Eyes of the Interred*), 1960 (respectively issued in the United States in 1967, 1971, and 1973), the novels describe the exploitation of plantation workers and the influence exercised by U.S. companies in Guatemala until the second half of the 20th century.

CENSORSHIP HISTORY

The political life of Miguel Angel Asturias is significantly interwoven with his literary career. His participation as a student in opposing the dictatorship of Manuel Estrada Cabrera in Guatemala and subsequent activity as a political journalist led to 10 years of voluntary exile, beginning in 1923. The Cabrera regime had been overthrown in 1920, but Cabrerista forces soon regained power. *El señor presidente* was written in 1932. Its situations and events are identified as being based on the author's experiences with the totalitarian Cabrera regime.

Asturias returned to Guatemala in 1933. Elected to the National Assembly in 1942, he again actively participated in an overthrow, this time in 1944 of the dictatorial regime of General Jorge Ubico. Diplomatic assignments for Asturias followed during the brief period of democracy in the succeeding years until the 1954 counterrevolution.

Once empowered, the right-wing forces of Carlos Castillo Armas ("the Liberator") banished Asturias in 1954, stripping him of his Guatemalan citizenship. (He never returned, but his passport was returned in 1959 at the insistence of the University of Guatemala.) Among the actions taken by Armas subordinates was the burning of "subversive" books. These included Asturias's novels *El señor presidente*, *Strong Wind*, and *The Green Pope*. (Also burned were Victor Hugo's LES MISÉRABLES, Dostoyevsky's novels, and the writings of Juan José Arvalo Bermejo and other revolutionaries.) The first two books of the trilogy were banned because of their evidently strong criticism of a U.S. corporation (the United Fruit Company). It is reported that United Fruit actively promoted the intervention of the United States to overthrow the government of Jacobo Arbenz. The action was supported by the Central Intelligence Agency (CIA).

Journalists Stephen Schlesinger and Stephen Kinzer make a detailed case, based on U.S. State Department documents released to them through the Freedom of Information Act, of U.S. complicity in the overthrow of the democratic government of Arbenz in 1954. CIA director Allen Dulles is identified as the "godfather of Operation Success, the plot to overthrow Arbenz," while Secretary of State John Foster Dulles is represented as planning the

Guatemalan coup; he is depicted as building justification for his planned coup at the 10th Inter-American Conference at Caracas, Venezuela, where he lobbied for two weeks for passage of a resolution condemning communism in the Americas and, subsequent to the coup, insisting that Arbenz's followers in asylum in foreign embassies be seized and prosecuted as communists.

When Miguel Angel Asturias was awarded the Nobel Prize in literature in 1967, *El señor presidente* was one of the works specifically identified in the award statement.

FURTHER READING

Callan, Richard J. *Miguel Angel Asturias.* New York: Twayne, 1970.

Flynn, Gerard, Kenneth Grieb, and Richard J. Callen. *Essays on Miguel Angel Asturias.* Milwaukee: University of Wisconsin Press, 1973.

Grieb, Kenneth. "Miguel Angel Asturias as a Political Propagandist." In *Essays on Miguel Angel Asturias,* edited by Gerard Flynn et al., 10–22. Milwaukee: University of Wisconsin Press, 1973.

Schlesinger, Stephen, and Stephen Kinzer. *Bitter Fruit: The Untold Story of the American Coup in Guatemala.* Garden City, N.Y.: Doubleday, 1982.

Wiskari, Werner. "Guatemalan Author of Anti-U.S. Works Wins Nobel Prize." *New York Times,* October 20, 1967, pp. 1, 44.

SLAUGHTERHOUSE-FIVE, OR THE CHILDREN'S CRUSADE

Author: Kurt Vonnegut, Jr.
Original date and place of publication: 1969, United States
Publisher: Delacorte Press
Literary form: Fiction

SUMMARY

Many years after World War II, Kurt Vonnegut visited Bernard V. O'Hare, a friend from the war, to discuss the destruction of Dresden. The Allied forces annihilated Dresden with so much firepower that it resembled the ruins one might imagine seeing after an atomic bomb had been dropped. Vonnegut and other American prisoners of war (POWs) survived the ordeal in "Schlachthof-fünf," Slaughterhouse-Five, a cement fortress originally used as a stockyard killing shed. The two men later returned to Dresden, which, along with personal experience, provided Vonnegut with material to write his "famous book about Dresden."

Billy Pilgrim, the protagonist, was born in Ilium, New York, in 1922. He served in the army as a chaplain's assistant. After his father is accidentally killed in a hunting accident, Billy returns from furlough and is assigned as an aide to a regimental chaplain whose assistant has been killed. However, the chaplain is killed in the Battle of the Bulge, leaving Billy and three other Americans lost and wandering deep in German territory. One of the other Americans, Roland Weary, is an antitank gunner who has been plagued throughout his life by being the unpopular person everyone likes to ditch. More than once Weary pushes Billy out of the line of enemy gunfire, but Billy is so exhausted and in such poor condition that he does not realize his life has been spared. This attitude infuriates Weary, who "had been saving Billy's life for days, cursing him, kicking him, slapping him, making him move." Weary and the other two in the quartet, both scouts, have become "The Three Musketeers" in Weary's mind. However, as Weary's obsession to keep the hallucinating Billy alive grows, the scouts' contempt of Billy and Weary also grows, and they ditch Billy and Weary. Weary is set on destroying Billy, but just as he is about to send his heel crashing through Billy's exposed spine, the two are discovered by a band of German soldiers and taken as prisoners of war.

Billy and Weary are searched, deprived of their weapons and valuables, and paraded away to a cottage that has been transformed into a holding place for POWs. The men are placed with about 20 other Americans. For a propagandist technique, Billy is singled out and photographed as an example of how the American army prepares its men for the war. The Germans and the POWs travel on and meet with more POWs until they form a human river. They arrive at a railyard and are separated by rank, privates with privates, colonels with colonels, and so on. Billy and Weary are separated, but Weary's continuous testimony of how Billy was responsible for the breakup of "The Three Musketeers" eventually spreads to the car where Billy is being held, causing a general feeling of hatred from the occupants of the car toward Billy. On the ninth day of their journey, Weary dies of gangrene. On the 10th day the train finally stops and the occupants are released into a prison camp. Billy is the next to last to leave his car. A corpse stays behind.

The men are stripped, they shower, and their clothes are sanitized. Among them is Edgar Derby, a middle-aged man whose son is fighting in the Pacific theater, and Paul Lazzaro, a tiny shriveled-up man who is covered with boils. Both men were with Weary when he died; Derby cradled his head, and Lazzaro promised to enact revenge upon Billy. The men are given their clothes and dogtags, which they must wear at all times. They are led to a shed that houses a number of middle-aged Englishmen who have been POWs since the beginning of the war. Unlike their American counterparts, however, the Englishmen have made the most of their imprisonment by keeping themselves in shape and properly groomed. They have also cleverly hoarded enough rations that they can afford to trade with the Germans for supplies like lumber and other building materials that they use to maintain their shed.

In poor condition and in a hallucinatory state, Billy is billeted in the hospital portion of the British compound, which is in reality six beds in another room of the shed. Here he is injected with morphine and watched by Derby, who reads *The Red Badge of Courage* to pass the time. Billy awakens from his morphine-induced sleep, not knowing where he is or what year it is. Derby and Lazzaro are sleeping in adjacent beds. Apparently Lazzaro's arm has been broken for stealing cigarettes from an Englishman, and he is now lecturing Billy and Derby on how he will someday enact revenge for that and for Weary's death, for which he holds Billy responsible.

The Americans are informed by the head Englishman that they will be "leaving this afternoon for Dresden—a beautiful city. . . . [they] needn't worry about bombs. . . . Dresden is an open city. It is undefended, and contains no war industries or troop concentrations of any importance." The Americans arrive to find that what they have been told is true. They are led to a cement fortress that had been a slaughterhouse of livestock and is now their dwelling place—"Schlachthof-fünf." The Americans are assigned to work in a factory that produces malt syrup enriched with vitamins and minerals, to be used by pregnant German women.

Four days later, Dresden is destroyed. Billy, some Americans, and four German guards are safe in the underground slaughterhouse while the entire city is firebombed. As they emerge the next afternoon, "the sky was black with smoke. The sun was an angry little pinhead. Dresden was like the moon now, nothing but minerals. The stones were hot. Everybody else in the neighborhood was dead." The soldiers order the Americans to line up in fours, and they all march away until they come to a country inn that is far enough removed from Dresden to not have been affected.

Two days after the war ends, Billy and five other Americans ride back to Dresden, looting through abandoned homes and taking as many souvenirs as they please. The Russians come along soon afterward and arrest the Americans, who are sent home on the *Lucretia A. Mott* two days later.

Throughout his war experience, Billy Pilgrim is a time traveler. His trips stem from a few incidents, namely, when he is near death or when he is on drugs. As he is being pushed along by Weary, he travels in time forward and backward. For example, he goes back to when he was a boy, when he and his father were at the YMCA. His father wanted to teach Billy how to swim by using the "sink-or-swim" technique. Having been pushed into the deep end, Billy ended up "on the bottom of the pool, and there was beautiful music everywhere. He lost consciousness, but the music went on. He dimly sensed that somebody was rescuing him. [He] resented that." From the pool he goes forward in time to 1965 to visit his mother in Pine Knoll, a rest home; then he returns to 1958 to his son's little league banquet; from there he goes ahead to a New Year's Eve party in 1961, where he is caught cheating with another woman; finally he is back in the German outland, being shaken against a tree by Weary.

While under the morphine-induced sleep in the British-run prison camp, Billy travels through time to 1948, to the veterans' hospital near Lake Placid. He is being introduced by Eliot Rosewater, a former infantry captain, to the works of Kilgore Trout, a little-known science fiction writer who will become Billy's favorite author and whom Billy will meet some years later. Billy also goes ahead to a time when he is 44 years old and a captive in the zoo on Tralfamadore. The Tralfamadorians, telepathic beings who live in four dimensions and have a firm understanding of the concept of death, have captured Billy and put him into a "human exhibit," where he is naked in a setting consisting of furniture and appliances from the Sears & Roebuck warehouse in Iowa City, Iowa. Not long after Billy is captured, the Tralfamadorians capture a female earthling, Montana Wildhack, a 20-year-old motion picture star whom they hope will mate with Billy. In time she gains Billy's trust and they mate, much to the awe and delight of the Tralfamadorians.

Not long after their sexual experience, however, Billy wakes up. It is 1968, and he is sweating profusely because his electric blanket is on the highest setting. His daughter had laid him in bed upon his return from the hospital, where he had been placed after being the lone survivor in a plane crash in Vermont, en route to an optometrists' convention in Canada. His wife, the former Valencia Merble, is the daughter of a well-to-do optometrist, who had placed Billy in charge of his business in Ilium, thus making Billy a wealthy man. She died while rushing to visit Billy in the hospital after the plane crash, apparently from carbon monoxide poisoning.

Billy Pilgrim drives to New York City the next day, hoping to be on a television show so he can tell the world about the Tralfamadorians. Instead, he ends up on a radio talk show where the topic is "Is the novel dead or not?" Billy speaks of his travels, Montana, the Tralfamadorians, multiple dimensions and so on, until "He was gently expelled from the studio during a commercial. He went back to his hotel room, put a quarter into the Magic Fingers machine connected to his bed, and he went to sleep. He traveled back in time to Tralfamadore." Billy Pilgrim dies on February 13, 1976.

CENSORSHIP HISTORY

As one of the most censored books in recent years—ranked 15th, according to Lee Burress on his national surveys–based list of the 30 most challenged books from 1965 to 1985 and ranked 69 on the American Library Association's list of "The 100 Most Frequently Challenged Books of 1900–2000"—*Slaughterhouse-Five, or the Children's Crusade: A Duty-Dance with Death* can boast dozens of cases when students, parents, teachers, administrators, librarians, and members of the clergy have called for the removal or destruction of the Vonnegut novel for one or many of the following reasons: obscenity, vulgar language, violence, inappropriateness, "bathroom language," "R-rated" language, ungodliness, immoral subject matter, cruelty, language that is "too modern," and an "unpatriotic" portrayal of war.

In an early suit in Michigan—*Todd v. Rochester Community Schools* (1971)— circuit judge Arthur E. Moore told an area high school to ban the book for violating the Constitution's separation of church and state; the novel "contains and makes references to religious matters," was a "degradation of the person of Christ," and was full of "repetitious obscenity and immorality." Thus, it fell within the ban of the establishment clause. The Michigan Appellate court reversed the circuit court's decision; the court had overstepped its bounds in venturing into the area of censorship. According to the appellate court, judgments about books resided with "students, the teacher, and the duly constituted school authority. Such action [by the circuit court] is resolutely forbidden by the Constitution."

June Edwards focuses on the charge of parents and the religious right: "The book is an indictment of war, criticizes government actions, is anti-American, and is unpatriotic." This charge defies the reason why Vonnegut wrote the novel, which was to show that "there is nothing intelligent to say about a massacre." Edwards supports this position by also countering the final two arguments: "Young people may refuse to serve in future combats after reading about the horrors of war in novels like *Slaughterhouse Five* . . ., but this does not make them un-American. They do not want their country to engage in violence, to exterminate whole populations, but to find other ways to resolve conflicts."

Nat Hentoff reports that Bruce Severy, the only English teacher in North Dakota's Drake High School in 1973, used *Slaughterhouse-Five* in his classroom as an example of a "lively contemporary book." Severy submitted the text to the superintendent for review and, after receiving no response, went ahead and taught it. A student's objection citing "unnecessary language" led to a school board meeting where the text was denounced and labeled "a tool of the devil" by a local minister. The school board decided that the novel would be burned, even though no board member had read the entire book. Severy, after discovering his contract would not be renewed, stated, "A few four-letter words in a book is no big deal. Those students have all heard these words before; none learned any new words. I've always thought the purpose of school was to prepare these people for living in the 'big, bad world,' but it evidently isn't so." Severy, with help from the American Civil Liberties Union, sued the school district; the following verdict was reached in an out-of-court settlement: 1) *Slaughterhouse-Five* could be used by teachers in Drake High School in connection with the teaching of English in grades 11 and 12; 2) Severy's performance could not be in written or oral terms deemed unsatisfactory; and 3) Severy was awarded $5,000.

The Librarians Guide to Handling Censorship Conflicts gives a detailed account of the suits and countersuit of the *Pico v. Board of Education*, Island Trees Union Free School District cases of 1979, 1980, and 1982. It is noted for being the first case of school library censorship to have reached the Supreme Court. The case stemmed from the actions of school board members attending a meeting in 1975 of Parents of New York United (PONY-U), where one of the issues concerned "the control of textbooks and library books in the schools." Using a list that contained books considered objectionable in other high school libraries, Richard Ahrens, then president of the school board, along with board member Frank Martin, descended upon the school library one evening to see which listed books were shelved there. They discovered nine, including *Slaughterhouse-Five*. At a subsequent meeting in February 1976 with two high school principals, the board decided to remove the nine books, along with two others from the junior high school. Two of the books were removed from classrooms as well. That decision prompted a memo from Superintendent Richard Morrow, who stated, "I don't believe we should accept and act on someone else's list. . . . we already have a policy . . . designed expressly to handle such problems." At the March 30 meeting, President Ahrens disregarded the memo and ordered the books removed from the district's libraries. After the media got word of the brewing controversy, the board wrote a rebuttal that stated:

> This Board of Education wants to make it clear that we in no way are BOOK BANNERS or BOOK BURNERS. While most of us agree that these books have a place on the shelves of the public library, we all agree that these books simply DO NOT belong in school libraries where they are so easily accessible to children whose minds are still in the formulative [sic] stage, and where their presence actually entices children to read and savor them. . . .

Superintendent Morrow responded that it was "wrong for the Board—or any other single group—to act to remove books without prolonged prior consideration of the views of both the parents whose children read these books, and the teachers who use these books to instruct . . . and to by-pass the established procedure for reviewing the challenged books." On April 6 the board and Morrow voted to appoint a review committee of four parents and four teachers to review the books and make recommendations concerning their future status. In the meantime, Morrow requested that the books be returned to the shelves until the review process was completed. They were not. In subsequent meetings, the review committee determined that six of the 11 books, including *Slaughterhouse-Five*, should be returned to the school shelves. Three were not recommended, and two others could not be decided upon. However, on July 28, the board in an open meeting voted to return only one book, LAUGHING BOY, to the shelves without restrictions and one, BLACK BOY, with restrictions despite the committee's stance. Ahrens stated that the other nine books could not be assigned as required, optional, or suggested reading, but could be discussed in class.

A lawsuit was filed on January 4, 1977, by Stephen Pico and other junior and senior high school students, who were represented by the New York Civil Liberties Union. Pico claimed that First Amendment rights had been violated via the board's removal of the books.

As entered in the court record, the school board condemned the books as "anti-American, anti-Christian, anti-Semitic, and just plain filthy"; it cited passages referring to male genitalia, to sexuality, to lewd and profane language, and to sacrilegious interpretations of the Gospels and of Jesus Christ. According to Leon Hurwitz, "A federal district court gave summary judgment for the board, but an appellate court remanded the case for a trial on the students' allegations." The Supreme Court to which the school board appealed this decision, in a 5-4 decision, upheld the appellate court, rejected the idea that "there are no potential constitutional constraints on school board actions in this area." The case came full circle on August 12, 1982, when the school board voted 6-1 to return the books to the school library shelves, with the stipulation that the librarian send a notice to the parents of any student who might check out a book containing objectionable material. (For further discussion of this case, refer to the censorship history of *Black Boy*.)

Many other incidents have occurred throughout the seventies, eighties, and nineties concerning *Slaughterhouse-Five*. According to *Banned Books: 387 B.C. to 1987 A.D.*, an unidentified Iowa town's school board in 1973, the same year as the Drake burning, ordered 32 copies burned because of objectionable language. The teacher who assigned the text had his job threatened. In McBee, South Carolina, a teacher using the text was arrested and charged with using obscene materials.

Newsletter on Intellectual Freedom reports that a review committee in Lakeland, Florida, in 1982 voted 3-2 to ban *Slaughterhouse-Five* from the Lake Gibson High School library, citing explicit sexual scenes, violence, and obscene language. The complaint originated from a board member and was backed by then Polk County deputy school superintendent Cliff Mains, who stated that the book review policy maintained the decision's legal validity.

On May 27, 1984, in Racine, Wisconsin, William Grindeland, the district administrative assistant for instructional services, barred the purchase of *Slaughterhouse-Five*, stating, "I don't believe it belongs in a school library." Unified school board member Eugene Dunk countered, "Denial of quality reading materials for our youngsters is criminal." This stirred up a heated controversy, which was compounded by the board's banning of five textbooks, three in social studies and two in home economics, on June 12. Board member Barbara Scott proposed that a "reserved list" be developed that contained books for which written parental permission would be required for students to check them out. Meanwhile, the Racine Education Association (REA) threatened to take legal action and file a lawsuit in federal court against the United school board if the book was banned. REA executive director Jim Ennis said the suit's goal would be to "prevent the school board from excluding 'contemporary and relevant literature' from Unified libraries and courses." On June 14, a committee of administrators did recommend that the school district purchase a new copy of *Slaughterhouse-Five* and also recommended a new library book selection policy, which called for the formation of a committee consisting of parents, librarians, and directors of instruction, who together would be responsible for the selection of new library materials. This news prompted the REA to hold off on any legal action against the school district.

On May 15, 1986, Jane Robbins-Carter, president of the Wisconsin Library Association, wrote to inform the Racine Unified School District that a resolution of censure had been developed "due to the conflict between the policies and practices of the District as they relate to library materials selection and purchase and the principles of intellectual freedom as supported by the Library Bill of Rights of the American Library Association." The charges stemmed from the actions undertaken by William Grindeland, which allowed him "the authority to delete orders for library materials 'not in keeping with the standards of the selection policy,'" to use "vague and subjective criteria" in choosing what materials could be used, and to refer "requests for materials of a highly controversial nature . . . to the public library, local bookstores or newsstands." Robbins-Carter added that "the censure will remain in effect until such time as the Board of Education adopts a revised Library Materials Selection and Purchase Policy." The Racine Unified School District adopted a policy in June 1985; on December 9, the Racine Unified School District's Library Materials Review Committee voted 6-2 to place *Slaughterhouse-Five* under limited access to students with parental permission. Grindeland, a member of the committee that reviewed the book, said, "I objected to the book being in a school library, and I still do. But restricting it is a good compromise."

In October 1985, in Owensboro, Kentucky, parent Carol Roberts filed a complaint stating that *Slaughterhouse-Five* was "just plain despicable," referring to the passages about bestiality, Magic Fingers, and the sentence, "The gun made a ripping sound like the opening of the zipper on the fly of God Almighty." She had also prepared a petition with the signatures of over 100 parents. In November, a meeting consisting of administrators, teachers, and parents voted unanimously that the text remain on the school library shelves. Judith Edwards, director of the city schools' department of instruction, commented that the committee "felt the book was meritorious." In April 1987, in LaRue, Kentucky, the LaRue County Board of Education refused to remove *Slaughterhouse-Five* from the school library shelves despite numerous complaints citing foul language and deviant sexual behavior. Principal Phil Eason defended the book, stating that it "show[s] the obscenity of war," and "We don't make them [the people opposing the text] read them [books in the library]."

In August 1987, in Fitzgerald, Georgia, school officials decided that a policy used to ban *Slaughterhouse-Five* from all city schools would also offer the same protection against other "objectional" materials. The book was permanently banned by a 6-5 vote after Farise and Maxine Taylor, whose daughter had brought the book home, filed a formal complaint in June, citing that "[I]f we don't do anything about it, they're putting that garbage in the classroom and we're putting our stamp of approval on it."

In February 1988, in Baton Rouge, Louisiana, school board member Gordon Hutchinson stated that he wanted to ban *Slaughterhouse-Five* and all books like it, which he described as being "a book of dirty language." The complaint was brought to his attention by parent Brenda Forrest, whose daughter had selected the book from a suggested reading list at Central High School. Baton Rouge District PTA president Beverly Trahan commented, "You can get into some very serious problems with book bans." Dick Eiche, executive director of the East Baton Rouge Association of Educators, echoed Trahan's view supporting the book. School board president Robert Crawford, a Vietnam veteran, agreed with Eiche and Trahan's views when he stated, "I think it's dangerous to start banning books. We could clean out the libraries if we wanted to." In March, Superintendent of Schools Bernard Weiss said a committee would be formed to evaluate the book. The 12-member committee voted 11-0 with one abstention to retain the book. Community member Bill Huey stated, "I can hardly believe this community . . . is even discussing removing a book from library shelves. I don't want to live in a community that sanctions bingo and bans books."

Slaughterhouse-Five was challenged, but retained, in Monroe, Michigan, in 1989, as required reading in a modern novels course for juniors and seniors because of its language and the portrayal of women: "Many similes or metaphors are used to describe things or events, but they are generally stated in sexual terms. . . . Or the language is just plain offensive. Any claim to be using this language for emphasizing is invalidated by its frequent use. I feel this book is degrading to life, sex, women and men, and above all, God." Another attack occurred in 1991, in Phemmer, Idaho, where parents objected to the book's use in an 11th-grade English class, citing profanity. Because the school had no policy in effect to deal with the challenge, an official ordered that the book be removed from the school and that the teacher using the book throw away all copies. In Round Rock, Texas, in 1996, 12 novels used in honors or advanced placement classes were charged with portraying excessive violence and sexual situations. The challenger, a school board member, claimed the request for removal was not censorship: "It's deciding what is consistent with society's standards and appropriate for everyone to use in the classroom." A student remarked, "The whole thing is motivated by fear. They're afraid we're actually going to have to think for ourselves." The novel was retained.

Complaints in Prince William County, Virginia, in 1998 centered on profanity and explicit sex scenes. A school board member, responding to excerpts from three challenged novels, indicated he was "completely appalled. I feel that this is a degradation to the human race." In Coventry, Rhode Island, in 2000, the novel was removed as required reading in the summer reading program although retained as an option; the challenger complained of vulgar language, violent imagery, and sexual content. After the novel was challenged in 2001 as being too graphic for high school students in Moreno

Valley, California, the school board voted unanimously against a request to withdraw it from the Advanced Placement English curriculum.

A controversy over books deemed inappropriate for students ensued in May 2006 in a suburban Chicago school district, Arlington Heights–based Township High School District 214. The district includes six high schools of about 13,000 students. School board member Leslie Pinney identified nine books, including *Slaughterhouse-Five*, as containing explicit sexual images, graphic violence, and vulgar language; their educational value was questioned. The school board voted 6-1 to retain the nine books after a school board meeting attended by some 500 persons. Other books on the list included *Beloved*, by Toni Morrison; THE THINGS THEY CARRIED, by Tim O'Brien; *The Awakening*, by Kate Chopin; *Freakonomics*, by Steven D. Levitt and Stephen J. Dubner; *The Botany of Desire: A Plant's-Eye View of the World*, by Michael Pollan; *The Perks of Being a Wallflower*, by Stephen Chbosky; *FALLEN ANGELS*, by Walter Dean Myers; and *How the García Girls Lost Their Accents*, by Julia Alvarez.

In February 2007, a citizens' group, the Livingston Organization for Values in Education (LOVE), complained to the Howell school board about the sexual content of four books in the Howell (Michigan) High School curriculum: *Slaughterhouse-Five*, by Kurt Vonnegut; *Black Boy*, by Richard Wright; THE BLUEST EYE, by Toni Morrison; and *The Freedom Writers Diary*, by Erin Gruwell. Their challenge demanded that the books be removed from the curriculum; a LOVE spokesperson compared the books to *Penthouse* and *Playboy* magazines, asserting that they "contain similarly graphic materials in written form [and] are equally inappropriate." *The Bluest Eye* was described as a "graphic child rape book." Letters were also sent to the offices of the U.S attorney, state attorney general, and Livingston County prosecutor, requesting opinions about whether the books violate laws on obscenity and distribution of materials that are harmful to minors. The federal and state offices forwarded the request to the FBI, a routine procedure with such complaints.

On February 12, the school board voted 5-2 to reject LOVE's complaint. The books will continue to be used in AP classes. The district superintendent explained, "We should also be very careful about dismissing literary works because they test our own belief system or challenge our values." David Morse, the county prosecutor, concluded that the books are legal on two grounds: 1) Since the school board has approved use of these books, the teachers and administrators have complied with school codes and are exempted from criminal prosecution; 2) To qualify as obscene, a book must be found to appeal only to readers' prurient interest in sex and have no literary or educational merit. ". . . it is clear that the explicit passages [in the books] illustrated a larger literary, artistic or political message and were not included solely to appeal to the prurient interest of minors." Michigan attorney general Mike Cox and U.S. Attorney Stephen Murphy concurred with Morse and indicated in mid-March that they would not prosecute.

FURTHER READING

"Board Reverses Censorship Stand." *Racine Journal Times,* June 22, 1984, n.p.

"Book Banning." *Racine Journal Times,* June 13, 1984, n.p.

Burress, Lee. "Introduction." In *Celebrating Censored Books!,* edited by Nicholas J. Karolides and Lee Burress. Racine: Wisconsin Council of Teachers of English, 1985.

Edwards, June. *Opposing Censorship in the Public Schools: Religion, Morality, and Literature.* Mahwah, N.J.: Lawrence Erlbaum Associates, 1998.

"FBI, State Deem Books Legal after Obscenity Complaints." Available online. URL: www.familiesaretalking.org/index.cfm?useaction=feature.show feature & feature ID= 1069. Accessed June 14, 2010

Foerstel, Herbert N. *Banned in the U.S.A.: A Reference Guide to Book Censorship in Schools and Public Libraries.* Westport, Conn.: Greenwood Press, 1994.

Francisco, Jamie. "School Board Averts Ban." *Chicago Tribune* (May 26, 2006). Available online. URL: http://www.alliancelibrarysystem.com/pdf/2006Schoolboard avertsbookban.pdf. Accessed February 18, 2011.

Haight, Anne Lyon, and Chandler B. Grannis, *Banned Books: 387 B.C. to 1978 A.D.* 4th ed. New York: R. R. Bowker, 1978.

Hentoff, Nat. *The First Freedom: The Tumultuous History of Free Speech in America.* New York: Delacorte Press, 1980.

Hurwitz, Leon. *Historical Dictionary of Censorship in the United States.* Westport, Conn.: Greenwood Press, 1985.

Jenkinson, Edward B. *Censors in the Classroom: The Mind Benders.* Carbondale: Southern Illinois University Press, 1979.

Jones, Frances M. *Defusing Censorship: The Librarian's Guide to Handling Censorship Conflicts.* Phoenix, Ariz.: Oryx Press, 1983.

Newsletter on Intellectual Freedom 23 (1974): 4; 29 (1980): 51; 31 (1982): 155, 197; 33 (1984): 158; 35 (1986): 9–10, 57, 114; 36 (1987): 51, 224; 37 (1988): 86–87, 139–40.

"OK for *Slaughterhouse Five.*" *Racine Journal Times,* June 14, 1984, n.p.

"Unified Bans 5 Books." *Racine Journal Times,* June 12, 1984, n.p.

"Unified Lifts Book Ban." *Racine Journal Times,* June 19, 1984, n.p.

"Unstocking the Shelves." *Racine Journal Times,* May 27, 1984, n.p.

—Eric P. Schmidt
Revised by Nicholas J. Karolides

SNOW

Author: Orhan Pamuk
Original dates and places of publication: 2002, Turkey; 2004, England and United States
Publishers: İletişm; Faber & Faber; Alfred A. Knopf
Literary form: Novel

SUMMARY

An exile living in Germany for 12 years for having been part of a Marxist-Leninist movement as a student, Ka (an appellation he prefers to Kerin Alakuşeğlu) returns to Istanbul to attend his mother's funeral, then travels by bus to Kars (Kar is the Turkish word for snow), an isolated community on the Turkey-Armenia border. When asked why he's there, he claims to be a journalist, covering the upcoming municipal elections and the spate of suicides by young women. In fact, Ka is a poet; he is traveling to Kars to connect again with a university classmate, İpek, who is extraordinarily beautiful. He imagines himself to be in love with her.

As the bus exits from Erzurum, it begins to snow, heavy and thick, continuing throughout the trip and the four days he stays in Kars. The blizzard blankets the city, at once masking the streets, covering the grime and the evidence of poverty, creating an aura of silence and wonder. It spoke to Ka of purity, a sense of innocence that is soon lost. The roads leading into Kars are blocked to all traffic, Kars becoming in effect totally isolated.

Kars's turbulent history—"endless wars, rebellions, massacres, and atrocities . . . , occupied alternately by Armenian and Russian armies" in the past, the Turkish army arriving in 1920—predicts the ethnic diversity and divisiveness of the present. There are animosities among political, religious, and ethnic factions: democratic republicans, secularists, Muslims, atheists, separatist Kurds, revolutionaries, old-style socialists, and the military. There is also hostility toward the Westerner attitude of the central government and distrust of those, like Ka, who reflect Western behaviors—or, on the contrary, envy of these individuals. Tension seems a constant, propelled by corruption: poverty and joblessness, a sense of constant surveillance, police (brutal) invasion of homes, bugged rooms, double agents, informers, an oppressive military presence, and the MIT—National Intelligence Agency.

The suicide phenomenon (Ka was given details of six incidents) was fraught with rumors and religious-political accusations. With one exception, the young women's stories revealed that marital abuse, paternal repression, poverty, and a besmirched reputation were critical causal factors. Yet, the exception, the "head scarf girl," became the cause célèbre. Many women and girls refused to obey the edict of national authorities that outlawed the wearing of head scarves in educational institutions. This led to these girls being barred from the classroom—in effect, from an education. The head scarf was perceived as a symbol of political Islam: "When a girl has accepted the head scarf as the Word of God and the symbol of faith, it's very difficult for her to take it off." Despite the Islamic condemnation of suicide as a major sin and the urging of her parents to remove her head scarf, this girl "began to tell her father that life had no meaning and that she no longer wanted to live," and she committed suicide.

Ka becomes embroiled in the Kars political and religious maelstrom on his first day. He and İpek witnessed the murder of the director of the Education Institute, who had ordered the head scarf removal; then he is taken to meet Blue, identified in Turkish papers as a terrorist, a militant political Islamist, rumored to be a murderer, who is hiding out in Kars for reasons unknown. Later, Ka is confronted by three boys, who assert Ka is an atheist and question his motives for being in Kars.

There are two strands to the plot: Ka's relationship with İpek, which becomes intense, and her family, including her sister, Kadife; Ka's becoming involved in a plan to bring a proclamation to a German reporter (actually a person of Ka's invention), professing a statement of values, signaling a kind of unanimity among oppositional forces in Kars. Ka agrees to Blue's insistence that he convince İpek's father to attend a secret meeting to write and sign the "announcement."

Readers witness or are informed of inhumane practices and degrading conditions. We visit the district of shanties; some residents who "opened their doors fearfully, assuming, after so many years of police intimidation, that this was yet another search." We are told of Muhtar's (İpek's former husband who is a mayoral candidate) "look of miserable resignation . . . he knew he would get a beating,"—and he did, apparently simply by being with Ka. We are part of the audience with Ka at the National Theatre when a "revolution" occurs on stage; seemingly part of the play's plot, a violent secular/antipolitical group mounts a coup, taking over the city government; soldiers on the stage fire at the audience, five volleys, killing 17. At a second performance at the National Theatre, a character, played by Kadife (a head scarf wearer), is required to remove her head scarf and shoot the hero; she does, but the gun is unexpectedly loaded. Taken to the police headquarters to identify the suspects in the murder of the Education Institute's director, we look with Ka's eyes into one cell "about the size of a double bed . . . five people inside, one of them a youth with a bloody face." Ka did not as a matter of principle identify anyone in any of the cells, though he recognized two of them from the theatre episode.

Almost two-thirds through the novel, leaving Ka and İpek in a passionate embrace, the text shifts to Frankfurt four years later; the narrator (the author) enters the novel. He has come to Germany to reclaim Ka's possessions—especially his green notebook in which he had written his Kars poems—and to uncover the details of his death. Ka had been shot at about midnight outside a shop, three bullets in his body. The green notebook was not found. But he did find a packet of love letters, written to İpek but never sent.

Conversations and debates among the characters reveal significant concerns. Faith is a primary one, as evident in the head scarf controversy: the "'covered girls' who have put everything at risk for the sake of their faith. But it is the secular press that calls them 'covered girls.' For us, they are simply Muslim girls, and what they do to defend their faith is what all Muslim girls must do." When an actress on stage attempted to burn a head scarf, a boy from the religious high school in the audience shouted, "Down with the enemies of religion! Down with the atheists! Down with the infidels." The head scarf agitation pits the secular government's suppression against Islamic militants. The women speak of pride in honoring the "Word of God and the symbol of faith."

The "disease" of atheism is a parallel concern. It is not uncommon for Ka to be asked if he is an atheist as is the case with his exchange with three students from the religious school. They lecture him about believing in God, and they assume as an atheist he has an urge to commit suicide.

State-sponsored oppression is frequently represented in the novel. Blue's proposed proclamation to the West is a critical feature of the novel: "Will the West, which takes its great invention, democracy, more seriously than the Word of God, come out against this coup that has brought an end to democracy in Kars?" The "Announcement" that is created at the secret meeting, beyond calling attention to the interruption of the democratic election process, includes also "A brief reference . . . to the Kurds who'd been shot or taken from their homes and killed, and to the torture and intimidation suffered by the boys from the religious high school. . . . An assault on the people, the spirit and religion." It called for the "whole world to unite in protest against the Turkish Republic."

The overarching theme of *Snow* is the conflicting nature of life in Turkey, the challenge to the secular government and attitudes by the Islamic militants. This is expressed in the rejection of the Westernization attitudes of the state, the rejection of Ka's European attitudes and character. This friction is evident also in the Turks' defensive inferiority complex, at once resentful and self-protective about their situation. Conscious of the people's poverty and the stereotypical reaction of contempt by Westerners, a passionate Kurd asserts, "We're not stupid, we're just poor!"

The plot, intrigue-filled and convoluted, draws Ka into the center of the action as a conspirator and mediator. Yet, his personal goal—to gain happiness with İpek—which he seems to have achieved when she agrees to join him in Germany, is affected by his actions on behalf of the political-social life of the city. At the conclusion of the "present" of the novel, Blue has been located in his hiding place and killed, and Ka sends a note to İpek stating that he is under military "protection" and "they are forcing me to leave on the first train." He asks İpek to join him at the train station, as they have planned, with their luggage. She did not.

CENSORSHIP HISTORY

Orhan Pamuk's statement, quoted in the Swiss newspaper *Tages Anzeiger* in February 2005 that "a million Armenian and 30,000 Kurds were killed in these lands, and nobody but me dares to talk about it" was the catalyst for the onslaught leveled against him and his books. He was charged under Turkey's Article 301 in the then new penal code, which states: "A person who being a Turk, explicitly insults the Republic Turkish Grand National Assembly, shall be punishable by imprisonment of between six months to three years." Pamuk was retroactively charged in June; the newspaper interview occurred four months earlier. Such accusations of genocide are rejected by Turkey in both the deaths of ethnic Armenians in the early 20th century and, more recently, the deaths of Kurdish separatists.

The trial began on December 16, but it was suspended; another law requires that ex post facto charges be approved by the Ministry of Justice. On January 22, 2006, the Justice Ministry asserted it had no authority to open a case against Pamuk under the new penal code, thus refusing to issue an approval of the prosecution. Nevertheless, there was an outcry in the international press against this "repressiveness," and members of the European Parliament reacted against the case as "unfortunate" and "unacceptable."

The reactions in Turkey by conservative nationalist groups were much less benign. A hate campaign forced Pamuk to flee the country; during the trial nationalists shouted traitor and threw eggs at his car. Censoring attacks also occurred. A local government authority in Isparta ordered the "seizure and destruction" of Pamuk's books in libraries within his jurisdiction in protest of the author's remarks. The Turkish press reported that in Bilecik, a community about 93 miles (150 km) south of Istanbul, Pamuk's books were burned at a "Respect the Flag" rally. These were "calls from fellow journalists for Pamuk to be forever 'silenced.'"

In a BBC News interview, Pamuk asserted that his purpose was to defend freedom of speech in Turkey: "What happened to the Ottoman Armenians in 1915 was a major thing that was hidden from the Turkish nation; it was a taboo. But we have to be able to talk about the past."

This was not the first instance of Pamuk's legal trials. A supporter of Kurdish political rights, in 1995 he was among a group of authors tried for essays that criticized Turkey's treatment of the Kurds, a minority group within its borders.

The so-called Ergenekon scandal was the outcome of the arrest in January 2008 of 13 ultranationalists, including retired military officers and Kemal Kerinçsiz (who had led the attempt to bring Pamuk to trial in 2005). These participants in a Turkish nationalist underground organization named Ergenekon were suspected of conspiring to assassinate political figures, such as the Turkish-Armenian newspaper editor and intellectual Hrant Dink, who was murdered in 2007; Orhan Pamuk was among the figures targeted by the group. The author himself acknowledged that the police informed him of the assassination plan.

Orhan Pamuk was awarded the 2006 Nobel Prize in literature.

FURTHER READING

"The Curious Case of Orhan Pamuk." *Harvard Political Review* (April 1, 2009).

Hacaoglu, Selcan. "Turkish Court Drops Charges against Novelist." *Independent*, January 23, 2006.

Hitchens, Christopher. "Mind the Gap." *Atlantic Monthly* (October 2004): 188–93.

"International PEN Calls for Government Condemnation of Attacks on Author Orhan Pamuk." *International Freedom of Expression Exchange* (IFEX) (April 6, 2005).

Lea, Richard. "Plot to Kill Nobel Laureate." *Guardian* (London), January 28, 2008.

Tonkin, Boyd. "From Public Enemy to National Hero." *Independent*, October 16, 2008.

Updike, John. "Anatolian Arabesques." *New Yorker*, August 30, 2004, 98–99.

SPYCATCHER

Author: Peter Wright
Original dates and places of publication: 1987, Australia; 1987, United States
Publishers: William Heinemann; Viking Penguin
Literary form: Autobiography

SUMMARY

Subtitled *The Candid Autobiography of a Senior Intelligence Officer*, *Spycatcher* reveals the activities of MI5, the "Security Service" of Great Britain, while focusing on the role of Peter Wright. MI5's central function is domestic counterintelligence in contrast to the foreign intelligence mission of MI6, alias the "Secret Service." The MI stands for "Military Intelligence," but MI5 is operated entirely by civilians.

Wright entered the service initially prior to 1955 as a research scientist and worked as an agent for MI5 from 1955 to 1976. Wright's first appraisal was that the services were woefully out of date technologically, needing new techniques of eavesdropping that did not require entry to premises. His first project, a sensitive microphone, established the underpinnings of his reputation. This success was followed by the development of other devices. He describes the early 1950s as "years of fun," detailing a series of spysearching and eavesdropping incidents that illustrate technological inventiveness.

The saga continues through the 1960s, but the tone begins to change with the appointment of Roger Hollis as director-general of MI5 in 1956. Clearly, Wright doubts Hollis's ability to lead the Security Service and questions his negation of or hesitation to pursue active measures. Nevertheless, targets were pursued, among them the Egyptian government. Wright was able to develop a method of determining the settings of the cipher machines in the Egyptian embassies, thus enabling the British to decode the cipher. This ability was significantly helpful during the Suez Crisis.

In the context of the Suez conflict, Wright also mentions that MI6 developed a plan to assassinate Gamel Abdel Nasser, the president of Egypt. Two alternative plans, he claims, had been approved by Prime Minister Anthony Eden. Another revelation is that MI5 had gone beyond attempting to bug the avowed cold war enemy, Russia, but had also bugged the embassies of Britain's ally, France. This intelligence eavesdropping occurred during the 1960–63 interval when Great Britain was attempting to enter the Common Market.

A persistent, sometimes overriding concern relates to the infiltration of the British intelligence operations at the hands of an elaborate "Ring of Five" spy group. A Russian defector had so identified a conspiracy group. Double agents Guy Burgess, former executive officer of the British Foreign Service, and Donald Maclean, British diplomat, had defected to Russia in 1951.

Harold "Kim" Philby, a high-level British diplomat and senior intelligence officer, was cleared after interrogation by MI6; however, Philby's reinterrogation by MI5 in 1962 led to his confession that he, too, was a double agent. He defected to Russia in 1963. In 1964, Sir Anthony Blunt, about whom there had been suspicions for years, also confessed to being a Russian spy. Wright, at the heart of these investigations, provides extended details of them along with his efforts to track down the fifth man. He reveals evidence that MI5's plans and procedures had often been leaked; he is sure that the culprit is in a high-level position. He and a colleague narrow down the choices to the director himself, Roger Hollis. Wright time and again asserts his belief in this finding even after Hollis is cleared after he has retired in 1965.

With regard to these revelations Wright reports considerable dismay and embarrassment within the intelligence community and the government. The revelations cast doubt on the effectiveness of the services, in particular their ability to maintain secrecy.

Another major operation, which may have grown out of fervor to track down subversives in government, is directed against Prime Minister Harold Wilson. Wilson came under suspicion, a suspicion, according to Wright, fed by James Angleton, chief of counterintelligence of the CIA, who would not reveal his source. Wilson's office was bugged while he was prime minister. Wright claims that MI5 had enough information to cause "a political scandal of incalculable consequences" that would have led to Wilson's resignation. He further states that he was approached by a group of MI5 officers to participate in a plot to leak information to "contacts in the press and among union officials . . . that Wilson was considered a security risk." The purpose was to bring down the government.

The book closes with Wright's retirement. He reiterates in the last chapter his conviction that Hollis was the "fifth man" and that "fear of scandal" became the most important consideration affecting everyone for the "turmoil of the 1960s." Throughout the book he asserts his own devotion to the cause represented by MI5 and acknowledges his many efforts on behalf of that cause.

CENSORSHIP HISTORY

The censorship challenge of *Spycatcher* emerged on two fronts: the publication of the book and the publication of excerpts and reports of its contents in newspapers. The government of Prime Minister Margaret Thatcher argued that publication would cause loss of confidence in MI5's ability to protect classified information, would damage national security, and would violate secrecy oaths taken by intelligence officers.

The Book

In September 1985, having learned of the planned publication of *Spycatcher* in Australia, thus avoiding litigation in Britain (the publisher had sent an advance copy to the attorney general, suggesting he could remove offensive passages, but a review of the text had determined that the book should be totally suppressed), the British government began legal action to suppress release of the book. It sought and was granted a temporary injunction by an Australian court, blocking publication until a trial had settled the legal issues.

The civil suit was tried in the New South Wales Supreme Court, Sydney, in November 1986, having been preceded by pretrial hearings. Essentially two major arguments emerged, those of national security and those of Wright's violation of his lifetime agreement to maintain secrecy about his MI5 activities. The defense argued that a previous publication, *Their Trade Is Treachery* by Chapman Pincher, published in 1981, had already revealed the information in *Spycatcher* (Wright had been an unnamed consultant to Pincher) and that the government had not taken action to prevent its publication. Thus Wright was not violating the secrecy code. The government claimed that Pincher the journalist was different from Wright the public official. The five-week trial ended on December 20, 1986, with Justice Philip Powell questioning the veracity of British cabinet secretary Sir Robert Armstrong, the chief witness for the Thatcher government.

Justice Powell announced his ruling on March 13, 1987. In a 286-page document, he rejected the claim of the government that *Spycatcher* would be harmful to British security and denied the request for a permanent injunction. He reasoned that the material in Wright's book was either harmless or already disclosed. He agreed that the government had the right to expect intelligence agents to keep secrets. However, two general reasons were offered why the British government could not claim that right in this instance: Earlier books and other publications had not been banned; disclosure to the public should be permitted when intelligence officers conducting secret operations break the law.

Within days, the British attorney general announced that the ruling would be appealed. The appeal hearing began on July 27, 1987, and the verdict on that appeal was announced on September 24, 1987. The New South Wales Court of Appeals rejected the government's request on a 2-1 vote. The court allowed the injunction against publication for three days. The government then appealed this decision that would have allowed publication to the High Court, Australia's highest judicial body. It was denied on September 27, 1987, allowing publication of the book in Australia. (About 240,000 copies of *Spycatcher* were sold in Australia after the lower court had ruled in favor of publication.)

The appeal to the High Court went forward, scheduled for March 8, 1988. The High Court's seven judges announced their unanimous decision on June 2, 1988, rejecting the government's attempt to ban further publication. These judges also accepted Britain's reasoning that Wright was bound by his lifetime oath to remain silent. They indicated, however, that the Australian court had no jurisdiction to enforce a British security regulation.

The Newspapers

In June 1986, the British government obtained legal rulings barring two newspapers, the *Guardian* and the *Observer*, from publishing leaks of Wright's allegations. The two newspapers had already each published an article in relation to the Australia trial. The newspapers appealed on the grounds that the information was already in the public domain and in the public interest since serious wrongdoing of the secret service was alleged. The appeal was denied: If the original publication was unauthorized, then republication would also be unauthorized.

Three different newspapers published articles on April 17, 1987. The *Independent* first included a full front-page summary of Wright's allegations with verbatim quotes from his book; the *Evening Standard* and the *Daily News* followed suit. The attorney general charged them with criminal contempt of court, citing the existing ban on the first two newspapers. The initial verdict supported the newspapers on the grounds that one newspaper was not bound by an injunction on another. However, on July 15, the appellate court overturned this verdict, in effect setting wide-ranging restrictions on any newspaper that published any material that another had been prevented from publishing.

Meanwhile, the *Sunday Times* on July 12, 1987, had begun a serialization of *Spycatcher*. This series, however, was stalled by a temporary injunction by the government on July 16.

In the succeeding week, the *Sunday Times*, the *Guardian*, and the *Observer* appealed the injunction. Days later, a High Court judge sided with the newspapers by dismissing the injunction. However, the government's appeal to the court of appeals resulted in a decision favorable to the government, but modified: Extracts were disallowed, but publication of Wright's allegations was legitimate news. Both parties appealed to the law committee of the House of Lords, the "Law Lords," Britain's highest appellate body. Its decision, a 3-2 ruling, on July 30, 1987, not only favored the government, but also extended the original ruling to include any evidence or arguments from the Australian court hearings. The Law Lords stated in their written opinions, issued in mid-August, that their ruling was temporary, pending a full trial. Further publication would destroy the government's case in advance of a trial. The minority opinion, calling attention to the release of *Spycatcher* in the United States and its availability in Britain, indicated that the claim of confidentiality was an empty one since it had already been lost; another point noted that the attempts to insulate the British public were "a significant step down the very dangerous road of censorship."

In the interim between ruling and opinions, the newspapers had violated the ban: The *Guardian* had reported the Australian court's hearings; the *News on Sunday* printed excerpts from *Spycatcher*. The attorney general announced it would prosecute the *News on Sunday* for contempt of court. Prime Minister Margaret Thatcher indicated the fight was a matter of principle because of the violation of a lifelong vow. Editor Brian Whitaker's reaction: "It is unacceptable that in a democracy like ours the British press should not be allowed to print stories concerning this country which are appearing in other newspapers throughout the world."

The trial to determine whether the injunctions should be permanent began in late November 1987; it concluded on December 21, 1987, when the High Court judge found in favor of the newspapers, rejecting a permanent injunction. Justice Richard R. F. Scott was critical of the government: The duty of the press to inform the public had "overwhelming weight" against potential government embarrassment because of scandal. "The ability of the press freely to report allegations of scandal in government is one of the bulwarks of our democratic society. . . . If the price that has to be paid is the exposure of the Government of the day to pressure or embarrassment when mischievous or false allegations are made, then . . . that price must be paid."

The court of appeals, to which the government had immediately appealed, ruled unanimously in favor of the newspapers in February 1988. The ban on press publication remained in effect while the government appealed to the House of Lords. In October, that body unanimously upheld the court of appeals, lifting the temporary injunctions barring the newspapers from printing news about and excerpts from Wright's book and the trial. The government lost a two-and-a-half-year struggle.

The language of the ruling did not express a legal right to publish. Rather, the finding in favor of the newspapers was based on the reality of the information no longer being secret. In the majority opinion, Lord Keith declared, "[G]eneral publication in this country would not bring about any significant damage to the public interest beyond what has already been done."

The *Guardian*, the *Observer*, and the *Sunday Times* filed a suit against the British government with the European Court of Human Rights, which issued its final judgment on November 16, 1991. The first ruling, unanimous, determined that the British government had violated the European Convention on Human Rights in its attempt to prevent the three newspapers from disclosing the evidence of serious wrongdoing by MI5 contained in *Spycatcher*. Specifically, Article 10, which guarantees "the right of freedom of expression" to everyone, was violated. The second ruling, however, on a 14-10 vote, upheld the principle of prior restraint, supporting the government's injunctions on the *Guardian* and the *Observer* after they published the first articles about Wright's allegations. In confirming the legality in banning the publication of potentially sensitive material, the majority of the European Court acknowledged an "interests of national security exception." The dissenting judges were critical of a government being able to suppress disclosures before they are published. Once published—as was the case in the United States in July 1987—the contents could no longer be described as secret. In this context, the government's continuing the gag after July 1987 prevented newspapers from exercising their right and duty to provide information on a matter of legitimate concern.

U.S. Publication

With regard to the publication of *Spycatcher* in the United States, letters dated between March 6 and July 5, 1987, and published in London's *Independent* revealed that Assistant Treasury Solicitor David Hogg suggested to Viscount Blankenham, chair of Pearson—owner of Pearson, Inc., in the United States whose subsidiary, Viking Penguin, was considering publishing *Spycatcher*—that Blankenham could "remove the directors of the American subsidiaries" if they persisted in their plans. Blankenham, while admitting his sympathy for the government's position, nevertheless stated:

> "[P]redisposition to sympathy [cannot] lead—in an international publishing group—to any insistence by Pearson . . . that overseas publishing houses in the group acknowledge and act on that sympathy." It is not open to an English court, he said, to control the exercise of power arising in the internal management of a foreign company.

Spycatcher was published in the United States in July 1987.

FURTHER READING

"British Official Suggests Ousting Viking Board to Stop *Spycatcher.*" *Publishers Weekly,* August 7, 1987, 311.
Clines, Francis X. "*Spycatcher* Judge Rules Against Thatcher." *New York Times,* December 22, 1987, p. 16.
Fysh, Michael, ed. *The Spycatcher Cases.* London: European Law Centre, 1989.
Kirtley, Jane E. "The Law Lords Take a Detour: Chapter Two of the *Spycatcher* Saga." *Government Information Quarterly* 7 (1990): 53–58.
———. "A Walk Down a Dangerous Road: British Press Censorship and the *Spycatcher* Debacle." *Government Information Quarterly* 5 (1988): 117–135.
Newsletter on Intellectual Freedom 36 (1987): 229.
Pincher, Chapman. *The Spycatcher Affair.* New York: St. Martin's Press, 1988.
———. *Their Trade Is Treachery.* London: Sidgwick and Jackson, 1981.
Turnbull, Malcolm. *The Spycatcher Trial.* Topsfield, Mass.: Salem House Publishers, 1989.

THE STATE AND REVOLUTION

Author: Vladimir I. Lenin
Original date and place of publication: 1917, United States
Publisher: Marxian Education Society (with the permission of the Communist Party of Great Britain)
Literary form: Nonfiction

SUMMARY

Shortly before the October Revolution of 1917 catapulted him and his party to power, Vladimir Lenin began writing a pamphlet on the nature of governments and the need for violence in overthrowing them. As he was rather busy trying to lead both the Bolsheviks and the nation of Russia, Lenin never completed the work to its original design. However, within weeks of his triumph, the first part of Lenin's book was released as *The State and Revolution*.

Lenin begins by discussing the nature of class and state. Throughout the work, he extensively quotes Karl Marx and Friedrich Engels. It is Engels's contention that the state arose when humans began to congregate in larger units than simple extended families or small villages. As larger groups of humans gathered together, class differences arose. The state exists solely for the purpose of allowing the oppressors to maintain their advantages over the oppressed. Even when changes in power occur, they invariably retain the structure of the previous state, and so no real changes ever take place.

To maintain power, the state employs "special bodies of armed men placed above society and alienating themselves from it," the police and a standing army. The use of prisons is a further extension of the state's power in protecting itself from the masses. Although until recent times, Lenin maintains, countries such as England and America had resisted the move to greater enforcement of state power, the actions of World War I demonstrated that such power generally grows stronger. Inevitably, such power is used to maintain the inequities of the class structure. Lenin explains that those who do not understand this also tend to misinterpret the idea of the "withering away of the state." This process is not a gentle, nonviolent disappearance of government. Rather, the proletariat seizes the means of production and transforms itself into an armed body of workers. Lenin contends that almost no one (his numbers are about one in 1,000 of those who have read Marx and Engels) understands that Marx and Engels did not mean anything short of violent revolution. The "withering away of the state" is not possible so long as the former oppressor class has any ability or desire to regain power. Thus, the bourgeois state will be abolished by force; only the proletarian state, which will exist after the socialist revolution, will peacefully wither away.

In much of the writing, Lenin attempts not only to shore up support for his own movement but also to demonstrate how others who would claim to follow Marx and Engels are subverting their writings in order to prevent the needed changes and revolution. Lenin points to revolutionary activity in France and Germany to show that revolutions that did not smash the apparatus of state power only succeeded in perfecting its oppressive force. Only when such special bodies as the police and army are recognized as parasites upon the people will the real revolution come.

Yet as long as the state exists, there will be a dictatorship by a single class. Lenin argues that Marx was the first to recognize this as scientific truth (although Lenin notes that Marx did not "invent" the theory any more than any scientist invents a truth). But the experience of the Communards in France demonstrated again to Marx that the workers could not simply use existing state mechanisms if a revolution were to be successful. What is required as the first step is a dictatorship of the proletariat. The preconditions for any society to begin the move to communism are universal literacy and "the training and disciplining of millions of workers by the huge, complex, socialized apparatus of the postal service, railways, big factories, large-scale commerce," and so on.

Only an armed dictatorship of the proletariat can "smash the bureaucratic-military machine"; bourgeois revolutions like those in Portugal and Turkey could not really succeed. The army of workers is not a "special force" because it is composed of the people and will automatically enforce the will of the people. Yes, they will have to "suppress the bourgeois and crush their resistance," and while government lasts, it will be necessary to reduce the salaries and prestige of those who work for the government. These government workers must also be subject to recall by the people at any time and must be elected by the people. The revolution cannot work if there is a special class of professional politicians and parliamentarians, nor can elections held every few years with little accountability pave the way for a workers' paradise.

As this move is made, all workers will initially receive equal wages for equal work. All citizens are essentially the hired workers of the state. Of course, it may be required to simply get rid of members of the former oppressor classes who refuse to cooperate, but this does not trouble Lenin much. This is the first phase of Communist Society. But as a new generation is raised, they will be brought up in the philosophy of communism. In time, they will come to embrace the idea that each should contribute according to his ability and each should take according to his need. There will be no greed or parasitism, because all will see that such beliefs and actions are wrong.

Only at this point, when communism is safe within itself, will the state begin to wither away. This is the ultimate goal of Lenin's revolution, but he clearly points out that Russia is far from this point. In other words, his critics should not expect the withering away to happen soon; rather, they should expect the armed masses to continue the dictatorship of the proletariat.

Although Lenin had hoped to write on the experience of the Russian Revolutions of 1905 and 1917, *The State and Revolution* itself was written in August and September of 1917. Lenin was interrupted from further work by the October Revolution. As he explained, "[s]uch an 'interruption' can only be welcomed . . . [i]t is more pleasant and useful to go through the 'experience of the revolution' than to write about it."

CENSORSHIP HISTORY

As with the writings of Karl Marx, the works of Lenin have been censored so often and by so many that it is difficult to catalog all the challenges. (See DAS KAPITAL and MANIFESTO OF THE COMMUNIST PARTY for more information.) *The State and Revolution* also made *The Encyclopedia of Censorship*'s list of works "most often censored."

Lenin's *The State and Revolution* was seized in Boston in 1927 as obscene and was suppressed in Hungary during that same year, charged with being "subversive."

A massive book burning was held in Nazi Germany in the city of Munich on May 10, 1933. The purging was designed to rid the fatherland of communist and socialist influences that sought to destroy the nation. All works of Lenin, including *The State and Revolution*, were burned at that time.

In 1954, in Providence, Rhode Island, the local post office tried to prevent the shipment of 75 copies of the book to Brown University; again, the books were labeled "subversive."

In 1989, the nation of Grenada showed just how successful Ronald Reagan's six-day war had been in preserving freedom and democracy in that nation. On March 8, five boxes of books were seized from Pathfinder Press director Steve Clark; four of these boxes were the property of the publishing house, while the remaining box was in Clark's personal possession. This followed an October seizure of other Pathfinder Press shipments. Included among the books confiscated on March 8 by the Grenada government was Lenin's *The State and Revolution*. On April 11, Grenada officially banned 86 titles, including Lenin's, from ever entering the country again. The response of the United States government? It was "obviously lawful and clearly within the purview of the Grenadian Constitution. There is freedom of the press, but the government has the wherewithal to allow books into the country as it sees fit." (See ONE PEOPLE, ONE DESTINY for details.)

Aside from these individual cases, two periods of American history illustrate censorship using the full force of Lenin's "special bodies of armed men" to enforce the oppression of thought and action.

After World War I, America's fears turned away from Kaiser Wilhelm and toward Communists at home and abroad. Fearing the influence of the now-powerful Lenin, U.S. attorney general A. Mitchell Palmer led an attack against the "Red Menace," bolstered by the Espionage Act of 1917 and the Sedition Act of 1918 (an amendment to the 1917 law). These laws allowed the government to crack down on those who failed to show proper support for the United States. For example, a salesman in Waterbury, Connecticut, was sent to jail for six months in 1920 for telling a customer that Lenin was "the brainiest" or "one of the brainiest" political leaders in the world. In all, more than 100 different publications were banned from being shipped through the mail, and at least 2,000 people were convicted under either the Sedition Act or the Espionage Act.

During World War II, the hysteria didn't wait for American participation. Perhaps the most important examples of censorship in relation to *The State and Revolution* revolve around the Supreme Court case of *Dennis v. United States* and the Smith Act of 1940 that was challenged by the case. The Smith Act of 1940 (also known as the Alien Registration Act) regulated political dissent to ensure national loyalty. This was the first peacetime sedition act passed into law since the infamous Alien and Sedition Act of 1798. In 15 separate trials, over 100 defendants were charged with violations of the law.

In 1949, Eugene Dennis, then the secretary of the American Communist Party, was convicted for violating the Smith Act. He and his codefendants had been arrested mainly because of their possession of four books: *The Foundations of Leninism* by Joseph Stalin, *The State and Revolution* and *The History of the Communist Party* by Lenin, and the MANIFESTO OF THE COMMUNIST PARTY by Karl Marx and Friedrich Engels. The case reached the Supreme Court in 1951. In a 6-2 decision, the Court upheld Dennis's conviction, abiding by former justice Oliver Wendell Holmes's standard of "clear and present danger." While the court determined that advocacy of ideas or doctrine was protected under the law, it denied that advocacy of action was protected if it involved or encouraged a violent or forceful overthrow of the government of the United States of America. Dennis responded that force was needed only because the present system would not allow for peaceful change. But the Court, under the leadership of Chief Justice Fred Vinson, was willing only to go as far as distinguishing between the theoretical and practical advocacies. At the time this seemed to be a blow against freedom.

However, while the decision went against Dennis, this case did mark a change in precedent in favor of greater freedom. Vinson's separation of advocacy proved to work in favor of the freedom to possess unpopular (even revolutionary) writing. In the 1957 case, *Yates v. United States*, the Court held that a lower court judge had failed to instruct the jury as to the difference between advocacy of doctrine and advocacy of action. The Supreme Court reversed the conviction of Yates, and from that time on, the Smith Act was essentially dead. It was finally repealed in 1978.

FURTHER READING

Connor, James E., ed. *Lenin on Politics and Revolution.* New York: Pegasus, 1968.

Green, Jonathon, and Nicholas J. Karolides, reviser. *The Encyclopedia of Censorship, New Edition.* New York: Facts On File, 2005.

Haney, Robert W. *Comstockery in America.* Boston: Beacon Press, 1960.

Harer, John B. *Intellectual Freedom: A Reference Handbook.* Santa Barbara, Calif.: ABC-CLIO, 1992.

Importation of Publications (Prohibition) Order. Grenada. Statutory Rules and Orders No. 6 of 1989. Gazetted April 14, 1989.

Inter-American Commission on Human Rights. Report No 2/96, Case 10.325. Grenada. Washington, D.C.: Organization of American States, March 1, 1996.

Lamont, Corliss. *Freedom Is as Freedom Does.* New York: Continuum, 1956.

Pathfinder Press releases. New York: October 19, 1988; March 10, April 5, April 27, 1989; and April 9, 1996.

"St. George's Grenade." *Newsletter on Intellectual Freedom* 38 (1989): 49–50, 141–142.

—Mitchell Fay
University of Wisconsin–River Falls

STRONG WIND (*VIENTO FUERTE*)

Author: Miguel Angel Asturias
Original dates and places of publication: 1950, Guatemala; 1967, United States
Publishers: Editorial del Ministerio de Educación Pública; Owen (*The Cyclone*)
Literary form: Novel

THE GREEN POPE (*EL PAPA VERDE*)

Author: Miguel Angel Asturias
Original dates and places of publication: 1954, Argentina; 1971, United States
Publishers: Editorial Losada; Delacorte
Literary form: Novel

STRONG WIND: SUMMARY

The novel opens with Adelaido Lucero and his friend Cucho performing the back-breaking work of gathering rocks to be crushed for the raw material with which Guatemala is being industrialized. But Asturias's first book of his trilogy soon focuses on an odd "Gringo" vendor, Cosi, who meets his future wife, Leland Pyle, at Lucero's home. Having been a laborer all his life, Lucero's dream is to buy farming land for his sons, Lino and Juan. He anticipates that all will be well for his sons and his friend Cucho's godson, Bastián, whom he has talked into buying land as well. The Luceros, Bastián Cojubal, and Bastián's in-laws, the Ayuc Gaitáns, begin farming their land, which is adjacent to that of Leland and Cosi, now also banana planters. The four families of planters make progress until Tropical Banana refuses to pay the accustomed price for bananas, preferring instead to achieve a vertical monopoly and run the entire operation rather than to buy from independent farmers. As "Tropbanana" begins to put the independent growers under economic pressure, Cosi, whose last name is Mead, organizes the Mead-Lucero-Cojubal-Ayuc Gaitán growers organization and fights the corporation.

He travels to Chicago to get an audience with Tropbanana's CEO, referred to in the narrative as "the green pope," and urges him to support the labor and dignity of the independent growers through fair prices. Eventually shown the door by a previously hidden, machine gun-bearing bodyguard, Cosi then buys a truck and begins to sell the cooperative's fruit in the larger nearby towns. Mysteriously, but perhaps with Tropbanana's encouragement, a family of wealthy, degraded landowners begins to undercut the cooperative's prices in those towns. The cooperative is forced to travel farther to the capital. Then Bastián and Juan Lucero are arrested. Knowing that Tropbanana is

STRONG WIND/THE GREEN POPE

behind the arrests, Cosi visits the corporation's on-site lawyer, who disclaims responsibility and blames the press for inciting the authorities.

Aware that the press is misinformed by Tropbanana, Cosi goes to the capital's newspapers to give a different report. With "Franciscan softness," an editor explains, on " 'the commercial side it would be going against the best interests of one of our best advertisers, Tropical Banana, Inc.,' " to publish a different version of the facts than the one presented to the paper by Tropical Banana, Inc. When Cosi states that " 'the frank thing would be to call [the newspapers] what they are: organs for the interests of Tropical Banana, Inc.,' " the editor responds, "'Bravo, bravo! Except that in that case we'd lose our customers, because if it were exposed to the public eye, we'd lose our usefulness.' " Thus, only through a large, quiet bribe to the military is Cosi able to free Bastián and Juan. Later, when the cooperative again goes to the capital to sell its fruit, there is no one at the market to buy. "Excess" fruit has been distributed freely by Tropbanana. And so the fight continues.

The book's title has three meanings. Meteorologically, the term refers to hurricane-force gales. One of the most compelling reasons for Tropbanana's choosing this area of Guatemala to plant was its supposed topographical immunity to the strong wind. Second, Cosi speaks of the strong indigenous wind in a political metaphor when he prophesizes that small, dignified, indigenous, independent growers will sweep away Tropbanana's large, monopolistic, foreign, authoritarian conglomerate like a strong wind. By novel's end, the term asserts its literal meaning but assumes a new metaphorical resonance.

Toward the book's conclusion, Cosi takes a trip to New York with Leland. Now, several unexplained events surrounding Cosi are cleared up: his having lawyers, his access to the green pope, his expensive purchases. He himself is a major stockholder in Tropbanana, but one who is trying to lead a revolt of stockholders to reverse the company's short-term, disreputable, and exploitative policy for one of long-term, honorable cooperation with the people who actually do the work. As he says in his address to the minority holders:

"Things can't go on like this in the American tropics, unless we want to lose our prestige and our investments forever. Practice shows that if we go there with hands clean of bribery and if we cooperate in the welfare of those people, without the sacrifice of a single cent of our current profits and perhaps even increasing them, they will look on us as friends and not as enemies. We are not honest and we have no respect for the laws of the countries where we operate. They're not against us because we're Americans, but because we're bad Americans. It's sinister to crush every day the hopes of men who have planted their fields and want to live in peace. Those men make war on us because we went to them on a war footing. . . . the hatred of those people will follow us, multiplied by the number of bunches of bananas that our inspectors reject each day."

Cosi and Leland go back to run their model cooperative, both for itself and to convince Tropbanana stockholders of the appropriate way of interacting with the people in the tropics. Unfortunately, the people have already suffered too much from Tropbanana. An independent farmer named Hermenegilo Puac has his hope for an economically secure future crushed when Tropbanana puts economic pressure on him to sell his land by rejecting his bananas. Hermenegilo Puac's hatred will follow Tropbanana, even after his death. With the potent magic of Hermenegilo Puac's severed head, Shaman Rito Perraj calls forth the strong wind, in which the plantations are severely damaged and Cosi and Leland perish; the third meaning of "strong wind" thus becomes the natural revenge that blindly wreaks.

THE GREEN POPE: SUMMARY

This second novel of Asturias's trilogy traces George Maker Thompson's (GMT) rise to the presidency of Tropical Banana. GMT begins as a small-time boat owner engaged in hard business practices in the Caribbean, but soon he amasses enough capital with the sale of his boat to become both a stockholder and the on-site manager of Tropical Banana's Central American holdings. The end of the novel's first part finds GMT poised to oust the current president of Tropical Banana. Having created an economic empire, GMT now aggressively advocates the political annexation of territory as well. In so doing, he gains the backing of the wealthy stockholders, as one of them, Mr. Gray, explains at a party in New Orleans.

> "But as I said, Thompson, times are changing. The most noble traditions, the ones that Kind throws into our faces, have fortunately been replaced by the trusts, and since we're part of one of the hundred trusts that manipulate politics in the United States, why hesitate about annexing those countries to assure our wealth and to do away with the governments that we maintain there. . . ."
>
> Thompson . . . heard footsteps. Other people were arriving. Bankers and powerful stockholders whom Gray introduced, from Socony-Vacuum Oil Company, one billion four hundred million dollars; the Gulf Oil Corporation, one billion two hundred million dollars; the Bethlehem Steel Corporation, a billion dollars; General Electric, a billion dollars; the Texas Company, a billion dollars; General Motors, two billion eight hundred million dollars; the U.S. Steel Corporation, two billion five hundred million dollars; the Standard Oil Company, three billion eight hundred million dollars.
>
> "I didn't bother to invite the small fry," Gray said, smiling before going out to greet his guests. . . . "All big stockholders, and all on your side."

A buoyant GMT does receive one disappointing piece of news in New Orleans, however. His daughter, Aurelia, tells him she is pregnant with the child of a Portuguese-American archaeologist who had been studying the Maya ruins on Tropical Banana's land. GMT resolves to put his money to work to find the archaeologist, Ray Salcedo, in order to address the issue, then confidently heads to Chicago to become "the green pope," the president of the company.

When he arrives in the current president's office, however, he learns that a stockholder named Richard Wotton, concerned with the company's immoral ways, has been investigating Tropical Banana's illegal appropriation of land and corruption of government officials. Wotton has turned his findings over to the State Department, which will now block any annexation plans. GMT is doubly shocked since he had arranged to have Wotton murdered long ago. Unfortunately, the man GMT had thought was Wotton in disguise turned out to be Charles Peifer, another concerned stockholder who had come to Central America promising the natives to help them regain their land. Wotton had indeed investigated Tropical Banana's operation in disguise: as Ray Salcedo. GMT is forced to relinquish his aspirations to head Tropical Banana.

But the novel's second part demonstrates that unscrupulous titans like GMT with big problems simply employ big solutions. The second part shows GMT as director of Tropical Banana's Central American operations troubleshooting for the company. A minor problem arises in the form of the heirs to Lester Mead's millions in Tropical Banana stock. In the trilogy's first book, Mead tried to work cooperatively with the natives. When his native partners suddenly become rich upon Mead's death, their previously egalitarian politics threaten Tropical Banana. However, each one, except Adelaido Lucero (and his family), is easily neutralized by being exposed to the lifestyle of the fabulously wealthy. (One of their primary concerns becomes the type of hat they wear.)

A big problem is solved by winning an international dispute in a virtual Central American war that was manufactured by Honeyfruit, a competing American fruit company. Tropical Banana owns land in one country, and Honeyfruit owns land in another. Honeyfruit revives a boundary dispute, hoping for a war that it knows its puppet country can win. The last part of the book shows peasants of one country ready to kill peasants of the neighbor, and soldiers preparing to die for the patriotic honor of "their land," all so that one or the other of the American companies can exploit more people and land. GMT's solution is simple. He bribes the mediating commission; the settlement thus preserves Tropical Banana's dominance. In the uncertain hours before the settlement, when war and thus the diminishment of Tropical Banana's holdings seem imminent, GMT uses his inside information to buy Tropical Banana's slipping stock. He becomes the main stockholder and president, the green pope at last.

CENSORSHIP HISTORY

Because of their thinly disguised and strong criticism of a U.S. corporation (the United Fruit Company), *Strong Wind* (1950) and *The Green Pope* (1954), the first two books of Asturias's "Banana Trilogy," were banned when Carlos Castillo Armas, supported by the CIA, overthrew the Guatemalan government in 1954. Their censorship history is thus similar to that of EL SEÑOR

PRESIDENTE (1946), banned for its exposure of the effects of American imperialism. (The trilogy's third novel is *Los ojos de los enterrados* [1960], translated as *The Eyes of the Interred* [1973].)

FURTHER READING

Callan, Richard J. *Miguel Angel Asturias*. New York: Twayne Publishers, 1970.
Flynn, Gerard, Kenneth Grieb, and Richard J. Callan. *Essays on Miguel Angel Asturias*. Milwaukee: University of Wisconsin, Milwaukee, 1973.
Grieb, Kenneth. "Miguel Angel Asturias as a Political Propagandist." In *Essays on Miguel Angel Asturias*, edited by Gerard Flynn et al., 10–22. Milwaukee: University of Wisconsin, Milwaukee, 1973.
Schlesinger, Stephen, and Stephen Kinzer. *Bitter Fruit: The Untold Story of the American Coup in Guatemala*. Garden City, N.Y.: Doubleday, 1982.
Wiskari, Werner. "Guatemalan Author of Anti-U.S. Works Wins Nobel Prize." *New York Times*, October 20, 1976, pp. 1, 44.

—Marshall B. Toman
University of Wisconsin–River Falls

THE STRUGGLE IS MY LIFE

Author: Nelson Mandela
Original date and place of publication: 1978, United Kingdom
Publisher: International Defense and Aid Fund for Southern Africa
Literary form: Nonfiction

SUMMARY

Highlights from Nelson Mandela's political life introduce the third edition of *The Struggle Is My Life* (1990), which is composed primarily of his speeches and writings as well as some other documents relating to the South African struggle for liberation. Threaded into the highlights are short quotations from these, including the source of the book's title, an open letter from the underground to explain that situation:

> I have had to separate myself from my dear wife and children, from my mother and sisters, to live as an outlaw in my own land. I have had to abandon my profession and live in poverty and misery, as many of my people are doing. . . . Only through hardship, sacrifice and militant action can freedom be won. The struggle is my life. I will continue fighting for freedom until the end of my days.

The speeches, writings, and documents are arranged chronologically, from the first in 1944 to the last in 1990. This arrangement provides a historical framework that reveals the development of the struggle for liberation—

the policies of the government and responses of the Africans to them. Also revealed are the roles that Mandela played and the progression of his thinking.

The initial documents—the "Manifesto" of the African National Congress (ANC) Youth League (1944), its "Basic Policy Statement" (1948), and its "Programme of Action" (1949)—delineate the goals and demands of the ANC and its program and policies. The basic goals were the unification and consolidation of African youth, cutting across tribal associations, so they could more successfully resist white domination, promoting liberation, and self-determination. Equality and democracy were ultimately the foundation premises. As Mandela himself defined the program of action during the treason trial, 1956–60, the ANC had determined upon a shift in action policy from "merely pleading [its] cause to the authorities to the exerting of pressure through political and economic action." A related shift was the change from a centralist organization to a grassroots orientation with the establishment of regional and local liberation groups.

The National Day of Protest in 1950, the Defiance Campaign in 1952, and the Congress of the People in 1955 illustrate the nonviolent tactics, as does the later Stay-at-Home general strike in 1961. The protest, a national nonwork day, was organized to express opposition to the Unlawful Organizations Bill, which was enacted as the Suppression of Communism Act, but perceived by the ANC as a government vehicle to suppress African organizations. The Defiance Campaign targeted unjust laws, including pass laws, curfews, and the railroad apartheid regulations; it "released strong social forces which affected thousands of our countrymen" and "inspired and aroused our people from a conquered and servile community of yes men to a militant and uncompromising band of comrades-in-arms."

The "Call to the Congress" was addressed to all South Africans, Europeans and non-Europeans. On June 25, 1955, more than 2,000 Africans and 200 to 300 each of Indians, Coloured people, and whites attended the Congress of the People and adopted a Freedom Charter. The charter established essential human and political rights: suffrage rights for all; equal status and rights in the courts and schools; restoration of the national wealth to the people; redivision of the land; guarantees of basic freedoms; the right to work and achieve equal benefits; and the right to medical care and decent housing without racial barriers. A significant preamble statement underscored this equality: "That South Africa belongs to all who live in it, black and white, and that no government can justly claim authority unless it is based on the will of the people. . . ."

Articles written by Mandela for *Liberation* during the 1955–59 period spotlight critical problems: the effects of apartheid on the lives of individuals and communities; the ulterior motive of the rehabilitation scheme to undermine communities and to sever laborers from their land; the relegating of "Africans to a position of perpetual servitude" as a result of the Bantu Education Bill, which established a separate education system for Africans and denied them access to the universities; and the self-government plan for the tribal reserves, which is unmasked as an undemocratic, state-dominated mechanism. In a discussion of the waning European imperialism in Africa after World War II, the United States is identified as a new menace in Africa: "The American brand of imperialism is imperialism all the same in spite of the modern clothing in which it is dressed and in spite of the sweet language spoken by its advocates and agents."

After the Sharpeville shootings of unarmed persons in March 1960 and the subsequent banning of the ANC, in December 1960, Mandela and 156 other political leaders were acquitted in a trial that lasted four years. In December, Mandela also participated in an All-African Conference of 40 leaders. These leaders viewed the proposal by the apartheid government to establish a republic as a threat that would further institutionalize racialist policies; they resolved not to accept the results of the vote of the white minority (one-fifth of the population), and instead to demand the calling of a National Convention of elected representatives "on an equal basis irrespective of race, colour, creed or other limitation." If that tactic failed, they resolved to stage a countrywide general strike. Elected secretary of the National Action Council, Mandela (the only identified member so as to protect the others) went underground to organize the three-day "stay-at-home" strike in May 1961.

Two events occurred during this period that significantly affected Mandela's life: the organization of the Umkhonto we Sizwe (Spear of the Nation), a group formed to fight repression and violence at the hands of the government with a violent response (i.e., sabotage), and Mandela's breaking the law by illegally leaving the country to attend and address (the text is included) the conference of the Pan-African Freedom Movement of East and Central Africa held in Ethiopia in January 1962. Arrested on his return in August 1962, Mandela was charged and convicted three months later for inciting persons to strike illegally and for leaving the country without a passport. Conducting his own defense, Mandela challenged, before responding to the charges, the right of the court to hear his case and requested that the judge withdraw on the grounds of prejudice. His challenge was based on the fear that he would not be given a fair and proper trial and that he considered himself "neither legally nor morally bound to obey laws made by a parliament in which [he had] no representation." He argued extensively that Africans were not equal before the law, that they had no right to participate in making the laws, that laws and courts are used to punish Africans, thus he could not be fairly tried.

In October 1963, Mandela was charged and brought to trial again, along with nine other men, principally on charges of sabotage. In his court statement, Mandela clarified the separation of the Umkhonto group from the ANC and the reasons behind its formation, given the long ANC tradition of nonviolence and negotiation. "Fifty years of non-violence had brought the African people nothing but more and more repressive legislation, and fewer and fewer rights." The government's policy of responding to nonviolence with violent acts had the effect of intensifying feelings of bitterness and hostility, which would inevitably lead to "outbreaks of terrorism." To channel these emotions and energies, Umkhonto was formed to focus on "properly controlled violence"—managed sabotage, avoiding bloodshed, avoiding civil war. In June 1964, Mandela and seven other defendants were found guilty and sentenced to life imprisonment.

After Mandela spent more than 20 years in prison, the state president of South Africa, P. W. Botha, offered Mandela his freedom in January 1985 on the condition that he would "unconditionally reject violence as a political weapon." (This was the sixth offer of release reported.) Mandela rejected it; his statement read, in part:

> . . . I cherish my own freedom dearly, but I care even more for your freedom.
> . . . Not only I have suffered during these long, lonely, wasted years. I am not less life-loving than you are. But I cannot sell my birthright, nor am I prepared to sell the birthright of the people to be free. I am in prison as the representative of the people and of your organization, the African National Congress, which was banned.
> What freedom am I offered while the organization of the people remains banned? What freedom am I offered when I may be arrested on a pass offence? What freedom am I offered to live my life as a family with my dear wife who remains in banishment in Grandfort? What freedom am I offered when I must ask for permission to live in an urban area? What freedom am I offered when I need a stamp in my pass to seek work? What freedom am I offered when my very South African citizenship is not respected?
> Only free men can negotiate. Prisoners cannot enter into contracts. . . .

In July 1989, Mandela met with Botha and subsequently with F. W. de Klerk, who had succeeded Botha as state president. (He had previously met with other officials.) The documents prepared for these meetings reveal his intent to promote negotiations between the ANC and the government. He focuses on the need of the government to renounce violence and to accept the sharing of political power with blacks. In February 1990, Mandela was released from prison, nine months after the release of the others convicted with him. The Mandela section of the book concludes with four speeches, each delivered at a rally after his release.

Two supporting texts, prison memoirs of inmates each convicted of sabotage, close the book. They describe the conditions and practices of the prison. They also report on the treatment of Mandela, impressions of him, his morale, and his political development while in prison.

CENSORSHIP HISTORY

The Struggle Is My Life was banned in South Africa. The ban was lifted on March 30, 1990, after Mandela was released from prison, February 11, 1990.

The government stated that Mandela's autobiography was now "part of the accepted political rhetoric" in South Africa.

On two occasions, October 18, 1988, and March 8, 1989, customs officials in Grenada confiscated boxes of books being shipped by Pathfinder Press, a publisher of political, historical, and academic books based in New York. *The Struggle Is My Life* was one of the confiscated books. Other notable works included ONE PEOPLE, ONE DESTINY: THE CARIBBEAN AND CENTRAL AMERICA TODAY, by Don Rojas; *Maurice Bishop Speaks: The Grenada Revolution 1979–83*, by Maurice Bishop; *Malcolm X Speaks*, by Malcolm X; *Nothing Can Stop the Course of History: An Interview with Fidel Castro*, by Congressman Mervyn Dymally and Jeffrey M. Elliott, and many works reflecting socialist and communist doctrine, including MANIFESTO OF THE COMMUNIST PARTY by Karl Marx and Friedrich Engels and THE STATE AND REVOLUTION by V. I. Lenin. Please refer to the censorship history of *One People, One Destiny* for the details of this situation and its outcome.

FURTHER READING

Frankel, W. H. Legal consultant to International Defense and Aid Fund for South Africa. Personal letter. October 7, 1994.
Importation of Publications (Prohibition) Order. Grenada. Statutory Rules and Orders No. 6 of 1989. Gazetted April 14, 1989.
Inter-American Commission on Human Rights. Report No 2/96, Case 10, 325 Grenada. Washington, D.C.: Organization of American States, March 1, 1996.
Pathfinder Press Releases. New York: October 19, 1988; March 10, April 5, and April 27, 1989.
"St. George's, Grenada." *Newsletter on Intellectual Freedom* 38 (1989): 141–142.

A SUMMARY VIEW OF THE RIGHTS OF BRITISH AMERICA

Author: Thomas Jefferson
Original date and place of publication: 1774, Pennsylvania Colony
Publisher: John Dunlap
Literary form: Nonfiction

SUMMARY

The immediate audience for *A Summary View of the Rights of British America* was the Virginia delegation to the proposed Congress of the Colonies. Recognizing Virginia's prominence among the colonies and particularly in the establishment of the Congress, Thomas Jefferson proposed these strong arguments to serve as instructions to the Virginia delegates. The convention of delegates did not adopt Jefferson's proposal, as he acknowledged, "the leap I proposed being too long, as yet for the mass of our citizens." The document was written as a resolution directed to the king, who is referred to as "his Majesty" but identified as the "Chief Magistrate of the British Empire."

The first position Jefferson takes is to assert the rights of the colonies—which God and the laws have given equally and independently to all—to their own laws and regulations within their new societies. This assertion is made "humbly" but in "the language of truth, and divested of those expressions of servility which would persuade his Majesty that we were asking favors, and not rights. . . ." This position is based on the argument that the immigrants to the colonies had been inhabitants of Britain and possessed the "right which nature had given to all men" to emigrate, comparable to their Saxon ancestors who had come to the island of Britain from northern Europe. "Nor was ever any claim of superiority or dependence asserted over them by that mother country from which they had migrated." The colonists, having shed their own blood and expended their own fortunes in acquiring lands for settlement and in making those settlements effectual, "themselves alone . . . have right to hold." They themselves adopted the system of laws of the mother country and themselves thought it "proper . . . to continue their union with her by submitting themselves to the same common Sovereign."

The oppression of the colonies by the king and the legislature spans the years and life of the colonists. These include the presumption of dividing and distributing the lands among the king's favorites and followers, lands that had been acquired by the lives, labors, and fortunes of individuals. Repudiating the prohibition of free trade and the curtailment of free manufacture, Jefferson attacks the British Parliament for assuming the power of imposing taxes on American exports, prohibiting sales of excess products to and the purchase of products from other countries. Avaricious British merchants, confident of exclusive trading rights, had doubled and trebled charges for commodities sold to the colonies and reduced payment for purchases. He declares the prohibition of manufacturing of articles of American raw materials for use in America an act of despotism whose purpose is to support industry in Britain.

Jefferson cites the increasing frequency of instances of legislation passed by Parliament that "intermeddled with the regulation of the internal affairs of the colonies." These range from an act establishing a post office in America to accommodate the king's ministers and favorites to several acts that grant duties on stamps, paper, tea, and other items, and an act suspending the legislature of New York. In this last instance, Jefferson asks, "Can any one reason be assigned why 160,000 electors in the island of Great Britain should give law to four million in the states of America, every individual of whom is equal to every individual of them, in virtue, in understanding and in bodily strength?"

Two acts are particularized because of the great injustice they express. The first act discontinued shipping from the harbor in Boston as punishment for the violent action of throwing a cargo of tea into the ocean because of opposition to the tea tax. Many innocent persons in Boston were made to suffer because of the act of "not the hundredth part of the inhabitants." The second act determined, in order to suppress riots and tumults in Boston, that a murder committed in Boston would be tried in Great Britain if the governor so decided.

> And the wretched criminal, if he happen to have offended on the American side, stripped of his privilege of trial by peers of his vicinage, removed from the place where alone full evidence could be obtained, without money, without council, without friends, without exculpatory proof, is tried before judges predetermined to condemn. The cowards who would suffer a countryman to be torn from the bowels of their society, in order to be thus offered a sacrifice to parliamentary tyranny, would merit that everlasting infamy now fixed on the authors of the act!

Within the context of these acts and others, the document urges the king to "resume the exercise of his negative power, and to prevent the passage of laws by any one legislature of the empire, which might bear injuriously on the rights and interest of another."

Several other issues are drawn. The "wanton exercise of this power which we have seen his Majesty practice on the American legislature" describes actions taken by the king to defeat attempts by the colonies to exclude all further importation of slaves from Africa and to abolish domestic slavery; the king thus prefers the "immediate advantages of a few African corsairs to the lasting interests of the American states, and to the rights of human nature deeply wounded by this infamous practice." Jefferson identifies this as "so shameful an abuse of power."

This attitude is also applied to England's inattention to the laws passed by the colonial legislatures; requiring the king's assent is deemed a grievous oppression. A like consequence is the practice of attempting to restrict the representative membership of legislatures and of dissolving a house of representatives and then refusing to call another.

> While those bodies are in existence to whom the people have delegated the powers of legislation, they alone possess and may exercise those powers; but when they are dissolved by the lopping off one or more of their branches, the power reverts to the people, who may exercise it to unlimited extent, either assembling together in person, sending deputies, or in any other way they may think proper. We forbear to trace consequences further; the dangers are conspicuous with which this practice is replete.

Jefferson further denies the king the right to bring large bodies of armed forces to American shores. He argues that such troops are subject to "our laws made for the suppression and punishment of riots, and unlawful assemblies"; otherwise they are considered "hostile bodies, invading us in defiance of the law." The introduction of troops is aggravated by making the civil powers subordinate to the military rather than the reverse as prescribed by "our laws."

In his concluding paragraph, Jefferson alludes to "that freedom of language and sentiment which becomes a free people claiming their rights, as derived from the laws of nature and not as the gift of their chief magistrate." In this context he acknowledges that "kings are the servants, not the proprietors of the people" and urges him to deal with all parts of the empire with "equal and impartial right." Jefferson asserts that upon the king's action depends "the preservation of that harmony which alone can continue both in Great Britain and America the reciprocal advantages of their connection. It is neither our wish nor our interest to separate from her." After enumerating the grievances to be redressed, he conveys a closing suggestive sentiment: "The God who gave us life gave us liberty at the same time; the hand of force may destroy, but cannot disjoin them."

CENSORSHIP HISTORY

Although the Virginia convention of delegates thought Jefferson's proposed resolution too bold to approve, they adopted "tamer sentiments." Initially identified as "Draft of Instructions to the Virginia Delegates in the Continental Congress," it had been considered by assembled delegates, after being placed on the table so it might be read by Peyton Randolph, the chair of the assembly. (He had received if from Jefferson, who had become ill en route and was unable to attend.) It was applauded by some and approved by many, but their awareness of "its unsuitability to the existing state of things" was such that at least one historian, Parton, wrote, "Probably not one member would have given it the stamp of his official approbation." Another historian, Bowers, says, "Not a few [of the delegates in Williamsburg] shied away from a statement so robust. Not a few of the more conservative unquestionably felt . . . [it] delved too deep and required too much."

However, it was admired sufficiently to be printed in Philadelphia and circulated among the delegates to the First Continental Congress, most of whom admired it. When copies reached England, it was read there and applauded by some. Members of the opposition of the group in power had it printed after Edmund Burke "changed it here and there, added sentences" (in Jefferson's words, "shaped it to opposition views"). This "weapon of offense against the ministry" went through several editions.

The result was Jefferson's emergence as an important leader on the American scene, but also the identification of his infamy. In Jefferson's words, it earned him "the honor of having my name inserted in a long list of proscriptions, enrolled in a bill of attainder commenced in one of the Houses of Parliament." Claude Bowers suggests that beyond forbidding his name and the loss of civil rights, implied by a bill of attainder, Jefferson "had been found an eligible candidate for the Tower of London." However, Jefferson wrote, the bill "was suppressed in embryo by the hasty step of events which warned them to be a little cautious."

Fawn Brodie, specifying further, defines the penalty for treason, assigned by British judges in sentencing Irish rebels in 1775:

> You are to be drawn on hurdles to the place of execution, where you are to be hanged by the neck, but your bodies are to be taken down, your bowels torn out and burned before your faces, your heads then cut off, and your bodies divided each into four quarters, and your heads and quarters to be then at the King's disposal; and may the Almighty God have mercy on your souls.

Jefferson's authorship of *A Summary View of the Rights of British America* led to his selection as the author of the Declaration of Independence.

In Russia under Czar Nicholas I (1833), *Melanges Politiques et Philosophiques: Extracts des Memoires et de la Correspondence de T. Jefferson* was banned for political reasons.

FURTHER READING

Bowers, Claude G. *The Young Jefferson: 1743–1789.* Boston: Houghton Mifflin, 1945.

Brodie, Fawn M. *Thomas Jefferson. An Intimate History.* New York, W. W. Norton, 1974.

Ford, Paul Leicester. "Introduction." In *A Summary View of the Rights of British America,* by Thomas Jefferson. Brooklyn, N.Y.: Historical Printing Club, 1892. Reprint, New York: Lenox Hill Publishing and Distribution, 1971.

Haight, Anne Lyon, and Chandler B. Grannis. *Banned Books: 387 B.C. to 1978 A.D.* 4th ed. New York: R. R. Bowker, 1978.

Huddleston, Eugene L. *Thomas Jefferson: A Reference Guide.* Boston: G. K. Hall, 1982.

Jefferson, Thomas. *Autobiography of Thomas Jefferson.* New York: Capricorn Books, n.d.

Parton, James. *Life of Thomas Jefferson.* Boston: James R. Osgood and Company, 1874.

SYLVESTER AND THE MAGIC PEBBLE

Author/Illustrator: William Steig
Original date and place of publication: 1969, United States
Publisher: Windmill Books
Literary form: Fantasy fiction

SUMMARY

Sylvester, a young donkey, collects pebbles of unusual shape and color. One day he is astonished to find a "flaming red, shiny, and perfectly round" one with magic properties. Hurrying home in excitement to tell his parents of this marvel, he is startled by a mean, hungry lion and, panicking, turns himself into a rock. The pebble rolls to the ground. The "confused, perplexed, puzzled, and bewildered" lion slouches away, muttering.

Night falls. Sylvester's parents, frantic with worry through the night, begin their search for Sylvester at dawn. They inquire of neighbors (one, a sympathetic homemaker, is a pig) and all the children (puppies, kittens, colts, and piglets). They seek help from the police. (The police, wearing blue uniforms and expressions of concern, are pigs). A search party (all dogs) sniff throughout the neighborhood. Sylvester is not to be found. His parents fear the worst.

The seasons pass, summer to fall and then to winter. With the coming of spring, Sylvester's parents decide to picnic in an attempt to ease their pain. They find a rock (Sylvester) and arrange their picnic foods about it. His mother sits on him and awakens Sylvester from a deep winter sleep. He tries to shout aloud, but he is stone-dumb. His father finds the magic pebble and puts it on the rock, saying, "What a fantastic pebble! Sylvester would have loved it for his collection."

A mysterious excitement stirs Sylvester's mother, who senses that her beloved son is nearby. She reveals her thoughts to her husband. As they look at each other sadly, Sylvester responds by thinking to himself, "I wish I were my real self again!" In less than an instant, he is.

> You can imagine the scene that followed—the embraces, the kisses, the questions, the answers, the loving looks, and the fond exclamations!

As for the pebble, it is put in an iron safe. Some day it might be needed, but for the present the family members have all that they want.

CENSORSHIP HISTORY

Sylvester and the Magic Pebble received the Randolph J. Caldecott Medal for the best illustrated children's book of 1969. In March 1971, the Intellectual Freedom Committee of the American Library Association noted a "nationwide campaign to remove [the book] from school and public libraries."

The *Newsletter on Intellectual Freedom* identified a May 1970 incident in Lincoln, Nebraska, as the first instance of *Sylvester and the Magic Pebble*'s being "exposed," followed that summer by numerous others; over the protest of 18 librarians, the book was removed from public school libraries. In June, a Queens Borough public librarian, Rudolph Bold, complained in a letter published in *American Libraries:*

> The 1969 winner . . . should have been disqualified . . . because of the extremely poor taste of one of the illustrations. . . . One could attempt a defense of the author and claim coincidence or a lack of malicious intent on his part. But the author/illustrator would have to be a hermit not to realize the insulting significance of "pig" as applied to a law officer. Inserted in a book for the preschool child, it assumes the stature of subtle propaganda that would make a Goebbels smile.

Of like mind, the elementary school library staff of the Palo Alto, California, United School District voted to remove the book from its shelves. They claimed that the drawing of the police officers as pigs "reinforces prejudices and misconceptions learned outside the school environment, and destroys the conscientious efforts of socially concerned teachers and librarians to guide children toward becoming objective and just citizens."

Momentum against the book gathered force during the fall of 1970. Between September and December, challenges to *Sylvester and the Magic Pebble* were made in many parts of the country. The American Library Association's Office for Intellectual Freedom and the Children's Services Division received requests for information and assistance from libraries in Maryland, Ohio, Pennsylvania, Kansas, South Carolina, Wyoming, and Illinois. Besides Lincoln and Palo Alto, it was reported that the book was removed "for re-evaluation" in Toledo, Ohio, and East Alton and Woodriver, Illinois. Libraries in Prince George's County and Wicomico County, Maryland, however, retained *Sylvester and the Magic Pebble*.

The Toledo, Ohio, event resulted from a complaint from Patrolman James Caygill, president of the Toledo Police Patrolman's Association, who threatened to take court action if the book was not removed. School officials did remove *Sylvester and the Magic Pebble*, pending a review of a committee of public and school library representatives. It was revealed that teachers had been warned about the illustration when the staff had originally recommended the book.

In Prince George's County, Maryland, Deputy Sheriff Donald Belcher, irate when his young daughter brought the book home, filed a complaint with school officials, the American Federation of Police, the National Sheriff's Association, the Maryland Sheriff's Association, and the International Conference of Police Associations (ICOPA). ICOPA, which claims to represent 150,000 law enforcement officers, issued a letter on November 12, 1970, which included the following statement: "no wonder that the children and some adults have no respect for the law enforcement officer. [W]e demand that the book be removed." Prompted by these and protests from parents and other law enforcement associations, a special 10-member school board panel was formed to investigate the complaints. The panel, ruling that *Sylvester and the Magic Pebble* did not contribute to the "development of negative attitudes toward police officers," recommended that the book remain available in all elementary school libraries. It cited Steig's reaction, when interviewed, that the drawings had "no political or derogatory connotations whatsoever"; a questionnaire to students and teachers with mostly favorable responses; critical acclaim of the book; and the fact that other characters as well as the police are depicted as pigs. The report was sent to the school board for review.

The board of directors of the International Conference of Police Associations at its December meeting in St. Louis considered *Sylvester and the Magic Pebble*. After concluding that it contained "a dangerous slur against policemen," the board members decided to call attention to the book. On December 20, Victor J. Witt, secretary-treasurer of the Illinois Police Association, sent letters to all Illinois law enforcement officers. Citing the offending illustration and his concern that the depiction would "mold the minds" of children, causing them "to think of policemen as pigs rather than their good friends," he wrote:

> Please check your grade school libraries and public library to see if this book is there. If it is, ask them to remove it, and if they do not, please go to your local press. I am sure they are in favor of proper recognition of the police officer. Liberty and Democracy without controls are chaos. You represent this Liberty, this Democracy and supply the controls.

Subsequently, in a telephone interview with Seth S. King, Witt, while acknowledging that the statement had been in his letter, indicated that it had not been the intention of his organization to remove the book from libraries.

In response to this letter and a deluge of requests for help by Illinois librarians, the Office of Intellectual Freedom of the American Library Association prepared a packet of information for these librarians. "Almost all librarians who received the materials advised the office that, when law enforcement officers were shown the book, they agreed the entire furor was unnecessary. Consequently, the book remained in most of the Illinois libraries where it had been challenged."

Another response to Witt's letter came from Gerald S. Arenberg, chief of staff for the American Federation of Police, who accused Witt of an "abuse of police power." Arenberg wrote:

> While we do not like or approve of police officers being called "pigs" or depicted as such I believe your letter may cause the law enforcement profession much more criticism . . . that of acting as a censor. . . . It would only tend to prove to the critics of today's police that we are on the path to book-burning and thought control. I think such publicity is more degrading to our profession than the "pig" image you are trying to erase by abuse of police power.

Witt denied that IPA was attempting to censor or act as a book burner.

The head librarian of the Freeport (Illinois) library in January 1971 ordered the removal of the controversial page showing police officers as pigs; a "library patron" had complained that the "picture depicting policemen as pigs was offensive." William Wilman insisted that he had acted on his own, prior to the Illinois Police Association's urging the local police department to remove the book. The removal of one page necessitated the removal of three others because of their locations; however, Wilman claimed that their elimination did not "ruin the continuity of the story."

In a *New York Times* article on May 4, 1969, prior to the first challenge of *Sylvester and the Magic Pebble* and to the announcement of the Caldecott award, Steig had written of his "affection for pigs." After the challenges emerged, in a letter dated February 23, 1971, and published March 3, 1971, Steig noted that all the characters in *Sylvester and the Magic Pebble* are domesticated animals (except for the villain lion) and very likable. "It should be obvious that no insult to anyone could possibly have been intended. The story was written in 1968 when, as far as I know, the word 'pig' had not yet been used as a designation for a policeman." Denying that he would write political propaganda for children, he asserted, "the police who complained are yelling 'fire' where there is no fire and calling attention to something that doesn't exist."

Though the controversy seems to have quieted after 1971, *Sylvester and the Magic Pebble* did appear on a list of more than 250 books considered "unsuitable for elementary school libraries" issued by the Hamilton County (Tennessee) school system.

FURTHER READING

Bold, Rudolph. "Rocky!" *American Libraries* 1 (June 1970): 525.
King, Seth S. "Book's 2 Pigs Stir Censorship Row." *New York Times*, February 20, 1971, p. 29.
Newsletter on Intellectual Freedom 20 (1971): 5, 27, 44–45, 60–61, 77–78; 24 (1975): 139.
"School Censors Hit New York, Ohio, Maryland and California." *Library Journal* 96 (1971): 228–230.
Steig, William. Letter. "Steig's Likable Pigs." *New York Times*, March 3, 1971, p. 42.

TEN DAYS THAT SHOOK THE WORLD

Author: John Reed
Original date and place of publication: 1919, United States
Publisher: Boni and Liveright
Literary form: Reportage

SUMMARY

During the October Revolution of 1917 that saw the Bolsheviks rise to power in Russia, few outsiders were given a chance to witness the historic events. One outsider who was there was an American named John Reed. Reed's 1919 account of the events is told in *Ten Days That Shook the World*, a "slice of intensified history," which was later "unreservedly" recommended by Lenin himself and hailed as a "National Classic" and taught in Russian public schools. Indeed, upon Reed's death, he was buried in the Kremlin, the only American ever to be so honored by the Soviet Union.

Since this book was written while all of the major players were still widely known, it is not a "history" in the normal sense of that term. Although Reed does give some background information, modern readers may need to become familiar with the general events before they can make sense of Reed's eyewitness to the events.

The book is extremely sympathetic account. There can be no mistaking Reed's feelings as to the rightness of the actions when he describes the

Bolshevik leader as "great Lenin" and describes him as "unimpressive [in appearance], to be the idol of a mob, loved and revered as perhaps few leaders in history have been. A strange popular leader—a leader purely by virtue of intellect . . ." Reed's praise of Lenin and Trotsky will get him into trouble with the censors in two very different societies.

Ten Days That Shook the World opens with notes and explanations of the different factions and the general process of Russian political life. Reed recognizes that the many different factions and Russian terms can confuse readers, so his brief description serves as an introduction and as a reference point.

Chapter 1 explains the background of the conditions that could lead to Revolution, although it presupposes some knowledge. This is more of a work of journalism than it is introductory history. Chapter 2 describes General Kornilov's attempt to "make himself military dictator of Russia." Kerensky forms yet another new government but excludes the Bolsheviks; this will have a profound effect on Russia, as the Bolsheviks (or "Bolsheviki," as Reed calls them) feel they should have their rightful place in guiding Russia. Meanwhile, Kerensky must also wrestle with what to do with the Cossacks and the military Cadets. Failure to keep these groups aligned with the government could only help General Kornilov.

Chapter 3 argues that Kerensky was losing his grip. "In the relations of a weak Government and a rebellious people there comes a time when every act of the authorities exasperates the masses, and every refusal to act excites their contempt. . . ." At the same time, issues do not bode well for Lenin and his followers; they are being lambasted by the press. One paper reported that "the Bolsheviki are the most dangerous enemies of the Revolution." The Bolsheviki sought to organize a new government made up of the representatives of the Soviets. In Trotsky's words, the provisional government was "absolutely powerless," and it was time for new and vital leadership—namely, the Bolsheviki.

Chapter 4 describes how the provisional government was no longer able to hold power, in part because other groups, socialist and otherwise, were beginning to sympathize with the Bolsheviki being denied any voice in Kerensky's government. Prisoners were taken by virtually every group that could muster the required force to do so, and the Duma, or city government, "declares war" against the Bolsheviki. Trotsky declared the provisional government fallen, and the Second Congress of Soviets of Workers and Soldiers' Deputies gave a majority to the Bolsheviki. The immediate result was that the Winter Palace was taken under control by the Bolsheviki.

Reed writes: "So. Lenin and the Petrograd workers had decided on insurrection; the Petrograd Soviet had overthrown the Provisional Government and thrust the coup d'etat upon the Congress of Soviets. Now there was all great Russia to win—and then the world! Would Russians follow and rise? And the world—what of it? Would the peoples answer and rise, a red world tide?"

Chapter 5 indicates that it was not time to celebrate just yet. Kerensky had fled, and capital punishment in the army had been abolished. In a triumphant display, the Bolsheviki announced that temporary commissars (all party members) were appointed. But there was a possible threat from the Cossacks. The bourgeoisie believed that Lenin's group would fall, and offered no cooperation. The Railway Union refused to recognize the Bolsheviki and closed down means of transportation, supply, and communication. "It was war—war deliberately planned, Russian Fashion: war by strike and sabotage." Chapter 5 also contains one of only two references to Josef Stalin. Stalin was named as a temporary commissar (the last person listed); Reed reports that the crowd that had gathered to hear the announcement of these temporary commissars applauded each name as it was called out, "Lenin's and Trotsky's especially."

Chapters 6 through 9 describe growing dangers. The air was thick with rumor. Kerensky was said to be marching on Petrograd; the army might support Lenin. No, the soldiers supported Lenin, but the officers supported Kerensky. Enraged by opposition, Trotsky stood up at a meeting and proclaimed that "we wanted to settle matters without bloodshed. But now that blood has been spilled there is only one way—pitiless struggle. . . . We've won the power, now we must keep it!" And keep it they do, for Kerensky managed to insult and anger the Cossacks, costing him any chance he had of their support. He fled in disguise, losing "whatever popularity he had retained among the Russian masses."

In chapter 10 the Bolsheviki at long last gained control of the city of Petrograd. Soon after, Moscow joined Petrograd in recognizing the authority of the Bolsheviki. A ceremony of rejoicing is described, and Reed's partisan character is again revealed. "I suddenly realized that the devout Russian people no longer needed priests to pray them into heaven. On earth they were building a kingdom more bright than any heaven had to offer, and for which it was a glory to die."

The final two chapters tell something of the aftermath. Republics are declared autonomous by Stalin (in his only other appearance in the book), government employees strike, banks try to derail the revolution through noncooperation, other socialist groups try to grab a share of power. Threats to their power are met by the Bolsheviki. Freedom of the press is not allowed for those who criticize them; Lenin urges that the people should move the Revolution forward by force; a new Duma is elected in Petrograd; and counterrevolutionists are arrested everywhere. The book actually ends much later than "ten days" after it began, as the peasants are seen to be won over at a meeting the next summer. In some ways, these last two chapters detract from the force and pace of earlier parts of the book, although they are needed to complete the story. By the close of *Ten Days That Shook the World*, Lenin, Trotsky, and the Bolsheviki are firmly in control of Russia.

CENSORSHIP HISTORY

There are really two separate censorship histories of *Ten Days That Shook the World*, one in America, and the other in the Soviet Union. Both nations disagreed with the politics expressed in the writing, although for different reasons.

The Federal Espionage Act of 1917, passed during the height of war hysteria, made it much easier for the government to crack down on "radical" or "anarchist" groups; the Industrial Workers of the World (IWW, or the Wobblies) was a frequent target of government raids. A cable, written by Reed in Petrograd on November 15, 1917, was delayed by U.S. censors for a week because they feared it might incite revolution here.

On his return to America, Reed was advised by his friend, the writer Lincoln Steffens, that conditions were not ripe for an enthusiastic account of the revolution. Reed was told that if he felt he must write of the events in Russia, he should at any rate not try to publish them. The only article that Reed was able to publish initially was "hedged with a disclaimer of his 'Socialist' views," and Reed himself was arrested under the Federal Espionage Act of 1917. More troubles followed; Reed was heckled in Boston, denied a permit to speak and subsequently arrested in Philadelphia for inciting a crowd to riot; his papers were confiscated in Cleveland, and he was arrested for using "disloyal, scurrilous and abusive language about the Military and Naval Forces of the United States." Although he was not indicted, sentiment against the Communists and Reed ran high. One newspaper editorial described Reed as "One Man Who Needs the Rope." He testified before the Senate on Russia, but mostly because he had already been identified as "the chief Bolshevik propagandist in the country."

Against these odds, Reed showed great courage in getting *Ten Days That Shook the World* published. Biographer Robert Rosentone notes that it is surprising how well the book was received, garnering both critical and popular acclaim. *Ten Days That Shook the World* was not only received favorably in the radical journals, but it was also praised in such conservative papers as William Randolph Hearst's *New York American* and the *Los Angeles Times*. The book sold more than 9,000 copies in its first three months of release.

However, not everyone was an admirer. In 1919, Paul Paine, the president of the New York Library Association, argued against exposing women to Reed's *Ten Days That Shook the World* because he feared it was too much for their delicate sensibilities. Worse still, official reaction against Reed was negative. After returning to Russia, he found that he was being charged, in absentia, for criminal anarchy. Reed attempted to travel to America via Finland, but he was arrested on trumped-up charges. Eventually, he leaked a story of his own execution to try to get the State Department to get involved, but his passport was denied. He was returned to Russia, where he died soon after.

America certainly did not take a more sentimental view of John Reed in death. A cold war version of *Ten Days That Shook the World*, edited by Bertram D. Wolfe, attempted to discredit the author for his political views. Indeed, if it were not for the efforts of Warren Beatty in his movie *Reds,* which appeared in 1981, the memory and legacy of John Reed might have been fully suppressed for most Americans.

Curiously, complete suppression of Reed did happen for a time in the Soviet Union. Reed had made an enemy in Stalin, who felt slighted by his minor role in Reed's account of the October Revolution. Further, Trotsky, who was later virtually "erased" by Stalin from the history of the revolution, appears in Reed's book as a personage second in importance only to Lenin. Reed himself had remarked early on that Stalin, while not an intellectual, "knows what he wants. He's got will power, and he's going to be on top of the pile some day." This prophecy certainly came true. With Stalin's rise to power, a book that had been hailed as a "National Classic" in Russia was first thoroughly "edited" and then suppressed altogether. Yet Stalin was to use the book later as support for his own practice of purges and executions. Eventually, Stalin encouraged the "John Reed Societies" in America as a means of recruiting those who might be sympathetic to Soviet Russia.

Yet, to have survived the hostility against him in getting this book published Reed demonstrated that political pressures cannot always stop the spread of ideas and that the political censors cannot always prevent writers, readers, and publishers from exercising their rights.

FURTHER READING

de Jonge, Alex. *Stalin and the Shaping of the Soviet Union.* New York: William Morrow, 1986.

Geller, Evelyn. *Forbidden Books in American Public Libraries, 1976–1939.* Westport, Conn.: Greenwood Press, 1984.

Gunther, John. *Inside Russia Today.* New York: Harper and Brothers, 1958.

O'Connor, Richard, and Dale L. Walker. *The Lost Revolutionary: The Biography of John Reed.* New York: Harcourt, Brace and World, 1967.

Rosenstone, Robert A. *Romantic Revolutionary.* New York: Alfred A. Knopf, 1975.

—Mitchell Fay
University of Wisconsin–River Falls

THE THINGS THEY CARRIED

Author: Tim O'Brien
Original date and place of publication: 1990, United States
Publisher: Houghton Mifflin/Seymour Lawrence
Literary form: Fiction

SUMMARY

A true war story, according to Tim O'Brien, is never moral, never able to separate fact from fiction, never ending, never diminutive, never uninquisitive, and never about war. Instead, a true war story is about the things that war is not: "sunlight . . . the way dawn spreads out on a river . . . love and memory." A true war story serves as a healing tool to anesthetize the sting of war. In *The Things They Carried*, O'Brien has a true war story for every path that he, Lieutenant Jimmy Cross, and Alpha Company travel. The purpose of O'Brien's story, which is made up of many smaller stories, is to make the reader think about not just the Vietnam War, but also the aspects and experiences that take place before and after the war within the hearts of those directly and indirectly involved. For those who were in the war, the book raises many questions and provides some answers. For those who were not involved with combat, the book sheds light on aspects least thought of when Vietnam is mentioned, including the feelings, thoughts, and challenges raised by the experience.

At first Tim O'Brien is strongly against U.S. involvement in Vietnam, perhaps more so than a typical 21-year-old, but he, like the rest of a nation divided, is mostly confused and unsure as to how the whole experience will develop. "Certain blood was being shed for uncertain reasons," and he wants no part of the turmoil. In fact, he did work for various antiwar factions toward the end of his college days, nothing to be jailed for, but his activism still served to solidify his liberal views. When his draft notice arrives, it is as though his entire life has been shrouded with a cape of hopelessness and desperation. Feeling already defeated, as though this can only be the passage to an early death, O'Brien one day sets out for a haven from his future.

Fear drives O'Brien to a derelict old resort in northern Minnesota run by one Elroy Berdahl, an old man who has seen nothing too surprising lately and can pretty easily surmise O'Brien's peril. For six days O'Brien fantasizes about the many ways he can escape his predicament. However, the reality of what others will think of him clamps down his motivations, keeping them well in check. During the last day of his stay, the two take to the river for a fishing excursion. Wise in his years, Berdahl pilots his old watercraft to a quiet inlet, which O'Brien immediately recognizes as his opportunity to escape. Twenty yards astern and up a rocky and jagged shoreline lays the thick brush of the undisturbed Canadian border. His body, tense yet eager, will not budge, not because he does not want to jump, but because he fears what others will say. He cannot face his family or friends as one labeled an abandoner. He can only sob and resign himself to the war, and the many stories in which he will partake.

O'Brien's time on Rainy River with Elroy Berdahl shows another side to the peril of Vietnam: the battle within. The actual battle in the field is well enough documented; what of the battles that occur away from that venue? What becomes of the young man with a prosperous future when faced with the gripping apprehension of a bleak situation: Kill or be killed? What happens to the weary yet ever thankful patriot who finds less than a sliver of a hero's welcome upon returning home after a hellish ordeal? The most intense battles may be those that take place internally, like his time on Rainy River, not in a wet, sticky, smoldering trench.

One particular mind battle occurs when O'Brien is injured and nearly dies of shock, due largely to the inexperience of the new medic, Bobby Jorgenson, who replaces Rat Kiley as the medic of Alpha Company well into the war. O'Brien is more than bitter about Jorgenson and wants to take revenge. He strikes one night while Jorgenson has night watch: Carefully rigging trip lines, sheets and devices designed to emit strange sounds, O'Brien carefully plays hell with Jorgenson's nerves, leading the medic to believe that he not only is being watched, but also stalked and possibly a sitting-duck target. O'Brien is near giddiness as he pulls on a line that makes a sharp rustling sound, and Jorgenson pivots toward it, furiously clutching his rifle and peering into the blackness. However, as this goes on, O'Brien wonders if it has been too much. He thinks about how it must have been for Jorgenson to be thrust into a difficult situation, and if he could have performed any better, considering the circumstances. O'Brien decides to end the game but cannot because the friend he enlisted to help him is now more wrapped up in the prank than O'Brien ever was and refuses to back down. O'Brien is now a powerless spectator as the prank continues throughout the night, tormenting Jorgenson while inflicting guilt on O'Brien as well. The next day, O'Brien confesses to Jorgenson and offers an apology, which is accepted. Both become friends, but O'Brien still feels as though his retaliation went too far.

The Things They Carried is told by an older, more critical, yet more inquisitive O'Brien. Storytelling is combined with fierce antiwar sentiment and the belief that, right or wrong, the soldiers were justified because they had to do their patriotic duty. O'Brien fictionalizes events that actually occurred on the line along with those that happened just before the war, directly after the war, when he was a boy growing up, and in the present. O'Brien invents names and places to make the action seem more real to those who actually were there and to those who can only read about it. The author Tim O'Brien was in Vietnam for about one year and saw the enemy in human form only once. The character Tim O'Brien is a 21-year-old kid going off to war. The only link between the two is the feelings such as fear, doubt, excitement, and anger they both experienced.

CENSORSHIP HISTORY

Attacks on the Freedom to Learn: 1992–1993 Report cites an attempt to ban *The Things They Carried*. The incident occurred in Waukesha, Wisconsin. The school board was presented with a teacher's request to order 120 copies of the text for classroom use in a modern literature class. Objections raised at the school board meeting on September 9, 1992, cited the text "for profanity and for discussion of the Vietnam War." The motion to vote on the adoption of the text was brought up by L. Brecka and seconded by J. Cuevas. The discussion that ensued was highlighted with concerns including "anti-American attitudes, offensive language, political bias, and disturbing fiction. . . ." A vote of 8-1 against adoption was the end result, with the request that the book remain suitable for library reference but not for required classroom reading. Also noteworthy is the fact that the teacher who originally requested the book for classroom use was not mentioned in the meeting minutes, perhaps disabling the defense of the book even further. Since that decision was made, none of the members serving on the 1990 Waukesha school board remain and were thus unavailable for comment.

Two challenges, one in Pennridge, Pennsylvania (2001), the second in George County, Mississippi (2003), both for the book's language, had opposite results. The novel was retained in Pennridge, despite the protest of its "strong language"; the novel was removed in George County for profanity and violence, along with *FALLEN ANGELS*, by Walter Dean Myers, and *OF MICE AND MEN*, by John Steinbeck. The negative vote resulted despite the explanation by Principal Paul Wallace of the school's policy of parental approval of readings, based on information about the works' contents and the provision of alternate reading materials.

A controversy over books deemed inappropriate for students ensued in May 2006 in a suburban Chicago school district, Arlington Heights–based Township High School District 214. The district includes six high schools of about 13,000 students. School board member Leslie Pinney identified nine books, including *The Things They Carried*, as containing explicit sexual images, graphic violence, and vulgar language; their educational value was questioned. The school board voted 6-1 to retain the nine books after a school board meeting attended by some 500 persons. Other books on the list included *Beloved*, by Toni Morrison; SLAUGHTERHOUSE-FIVE by Kurt Vonnegut, *The Awakening*, by Kate Chopin, *Freakonomics*, by Steven D. Levitt and Stephen J. Dubner; *The Botany of Desire: A Plant's-Eye View of the World*, by Michael Pollan; *The Perks of Being a Wallflower*, by Stephen Chbosky; *Fallen Angels*, by Walter Dean Myers; and *How the García Girls Lost Their Accents*, by Julia Alvarez.

FURTHER READING

Attacks on the Freedom to Learn 1992–1993 Report. Washington, D.C.: People For the American Way, 1993, p. 189.
Francisco, Jamie. "School Board Averts Book Ban." Available online. URL: alliancelibrarysystem.com/PDF/2006. Accessed October 25, 2010.
Harris, Robert R. "Too Embarrassed Not to Kill." *New York Times Book Review*, March 11, 1990, p. 8.
Prescott, Peter S. "The Things They Carried." *Newsweek*, April 2, 1990, p. 57.

—Eric P. Schmidt
Updated by Nicholas J. Karolides

THIS EARTH OF MANKIND

Author: Pramoedya Ananta Toer
Original dates and places of publication: 1980, Indonesia; 1991, United States
Publishers: Hasta Mitra Publishing House; William Morrow and Company
Literary form: Novel

CHILD OF ALL NATIONS

Author: Pramoedya Ananta Toer
Original dates and places of publication: 1980, Indonesia; 1993, United States
Publishers: Hasta Mitra Publishing House; William Morrow and Company
Literary form: Novel

THIS EARTH OF MANKIND: SUMMARY

It is 1898. Java, the setting of *This Earth of Mankind*, is under colonial rule of the Netherlands. "Colonial rule" signals a recognition of two factions, at least: the rulers and the ruled. The culture of these two groups, their interactions and the tensions between them are revealed through the situations and difficulties that beset the two central characters, Minke and Nyai Ontosoroh (also identified as Sanikem, her birth name).

Minke, a Native Javanese (differentiated from an Indo who is of mixed race—Native and Dutch), is an 18-year-old student in the prestigious Dutch-language high school, the H.B.S. Surabaya. He is the only Native in the school, though there are a few Indos. He is a top student, having become fluent in Dutch and having acknowledged European training, science, and learning. Minke does not reveal his family name or origins, preferring, it seems, to be judged for himself. We learn that his family is upper-class Javanese; during the time period of the book, his father is appointed by the Dutch to the role of *bupati*, that is, the chief administrator of a region, a most important credential for a Native Javanese.

The word *nyai* identifies a Native concubine of a European man in the Indies; it is used as a title of address. When she was 14, Sanikem's father, in order to fulfill his ambitions to become a paymaster, sold her to Herman Mellema, with whom she was forced to live. She bore him two children, Robert and Annelies, but he would not marry her, though he acknowledged the children as his. He did proceed to educate her and train her to operate his dairy business. Eventually, Nyai takes over its operation; through her careful stewardship the business and their land holdings have expanded. She maintains her control when there is a break in their relationship caused by the appearance of Mellema's Dutch son of his first marriage. (Nyai wisely does not formalize the break, for she wants to protect her children.) Led to believe that this marriage is still in force and confronted by financial and social demands, Mellema apparently loses a large measure of control of his sanity.

Through a school acquaintance, a surface "friend," Minke is introduced to the Mellema family, initially excepting the father, in their luxurious home. Warmly accepted by Nyai and Annelies, who is quite lonely, shortly after that first visit, Minke is invited to establish residence in their home; Annelies has become dependent on his presence. He accepts, though he senses that there are strained relationships emanating from Robert. He refuses to acknowledge his mother. He also has rejected his nativeness and is associating with whites or Indos. Minke learns that Robert had attempted to engage Nyai's bodyguard to assassinate him. Robert is jealous of Minke's relationship with Nyai. Minke also learns, after he becomes intimate with Annelies, that Robert has raped his sister.

The lives of these people explode when Herbert Mellema's body is found in a nearby upscale brothel. Robert is also discovered to be living there, but he escapes through a window and disappears. (Nyai has been receiving the two men's bills from the proprietor for months and has been paying them.) Nyai and Minke are both under suspicion. Their innocence is eventually established, but not before Minke's relationship with Annelies and Nyai's apparent knowledge and approval of it are made public. They are thus made to seem contemptible.

Three events occur to bring the novel to its close, two of them celebratory occasions. The first is the graduation exercises. The awards ceremony is telling: The top-ranking student in the state exams is from H.B.S. Batavia; the second-ranking student is Minke (therefore the top-ranking student in his own school). When the school's second-rank placement is announced, "Everyone cheered loyally"; when Minke's name is announced as the winner, he is tendered only "weak clapping." The second occasion is the marriage of Annelies and Minke, a gala affair, which everyone attends.

The third event, six months later, breaks this euphoric spell. Herman Mellema's legitimate son had sued before the Amsterdam district court to inherit his father's wealth and property. Having discredited the rights of Nyai on every count of property and motherhood, the court awards him four-sixths of the property and Annelies and Robert one-sixth each; guardianship of Annelies and management of Robert's property are also awarded to him. Annelies's marriage to Minke is ignored as not legal. All attempts (protestations of the Dutch assistant resident, outcries from Islamic scholars against the discrediting of their laws, legal efforts with assistance from a formidable attorney, and riots in the streets) to reverse this ruling and avert the catastrophic loss fail. Annelies, the fragility of her spirit again affecting her health so that she is in severely weakened condition, is forcibly removed from her home and taken to a ship to sail for the Netherlands. She packs a few of her belongings in the same suitcase used by her mother when she forcibly left her parents' home.

The situations and character relationships of this novel are replete with such examples of racial bias and tension. Clear distinctions in intelligence and capacity as well as in political and social position are drawn among the Pures (i.e., the Europeans), the Indos, and the Natives. This hierarchy is enforced in the court case when Nyai, a Native, is denied maternity rights since she is not Mrs. Mellema. "Annelies Mellema is under European law; Nyai is not. Nyai is a Native. Had Miss Annelies Mellema not been legally acknowledged by Mr. Mellema she too would be a Native and this court would have had nothing to do with her." The dehumanizing system and its assumptions are challenged by Nyai when on the witness stand she reviles the Europeans who demean the offspring of Europeans and their nyais but do not rebuke or challenge the behavior of the men who enslave these women and count them as without worth simply because they are Natives.

Class consciousness among nonwhites concomitantly feeds on these biases. It is an overlay on the existing class structure. Minke's invitation from the Dutch assistant resident, for example, immediately gains for him a respectful notoriety. Such associations generate power; such cooperation with the Dutch colonialists (Minke's father is appointed and empowered by the Dutch to be the *bupati* of the region, the administrator whom other Natives must honor with obeisance) suggests adherence and fosters deeper division and distinction among the Native groups. Minke himself exemplifies a central tension. Although he is a Native, through his education and contacts he has become infused with European values to the neglect of the Javanese language, culture, and his own family.

The portrayal of Nyai reflects this tension. She breaks through political, social, and gender boundaries and does not accept "her place." She asserts her presence on social occasions and in business situations, establishing her strength as an individual. Nyai dramatically succeeds in representing the repositioning of Native women in Javanese society, who are ignored, as well as contesting the Dutch mentality.

These several themes coalesce to express the novel's political statement: opposition to oppression, to the dehumanization and disempowerment of the Natives by the Dutch. Nyai and Magda Peters, Minke's Dutch teacher, state the underlying psychology:

> "They can't stand seeing Natives not being trodden under their feet. Natives must always be in the wrong. Europeans must be innocent, so therefore Natives must be wrong to start with. To be born a Native is to be in the wrong."
>
> "Yes, this is how it is in all colonies: Asia, Africa, America, Australia. Everything that is not European, and especially if it is not colonial, is trodden upon, laughed at, humiliated, for no other reason than to prove the supremacy of Europe and of colonial might in every matter—not excluding ignorance. Don't forget, Minke, those who first came to the Indies were mere

adventurers, people Europe itself had exiled. Here they try to be even more European. Trash."

Oppression by Natives is more muted, largely expressed through the willingness of Natives in positions of authority to work with the Dutch, perhaps to maintain their status. Minke has great potential because he has risen above the "slavish attitude" of his people in having adopted a European attitude; he is perceived as being "totally European." Magda Peters recognizes, however, that Nyai belies this Association Theory: "If there were just a thousand Natives like that in the Indies . . . these Netherlands Indies could just shut up shop." Peters is considered a "fanatical radical" who supports the "Indies for the Indies" movement, that is, equality for the Indies with the Netherlands. It is evident that Minke, in his enthusiasm for his teacher and the positions he takes in his articles, is moving in this direction.

CHILD OF ALL NATIONS: SUMMARY

After reports of Annelies's decline and death in the Netherlands, effected in part by the neglect of her Dutch half relatives, despite her evident ill health, and in part by her emotional alienation, the lives of Minke and Nyai spin into despair and deterioration. Minke seems unable to concentrate on his tasks. His feelings of impotence are further confused by criticism from Nyai and two good friends, a French artist, Jean Marais, and a journalist, Kommer, about his writing in Dutch rather than Malay, which would reach an audience of his own people. His disorientation is heightened by contact with an illegal immigrant from China, one of the "Chinese Younger Generation" whom he is asked to interview for an article. These situations set the thematic issues of *Child of All Nations*. They also reinspire Minke's activity.

The threat of the "yellow peril from the north" first surfaces in the colonial newspaper for which Minke writes. He is still innocent of its political agenda to support the Dutch colonial regime without regard for the Native people of Java. He begins to recognize its bias when his sympathetic article about the Chinese youth is drastically altered in its statements and tone. He is intrigued by the Chinese youth's intensity and ideals, which focus on freedom from oppression, condemnation of corrupt European domination, and the insistent need to shake off the shackles of the older generation, which, corrupt and ignorant, is obedient to the oppressors in order to maintain its elite position.

Minke's realignment to the Javanese condition and culture begins in earnest during a journey to Nyai's birthplace, which is in the center of extensive sugar cane fields and dominated by a sugar mill. He meets "Old Truno," that is Trunodongso, an unusual Javanese peasant farmer who is "suspicious of his superiors"—including Minke—and "who refused to fit himself to the mold." Truno has been battling the economic and political forces around him. He refuses to sell his five *baku* of land inherited from his parents—about which he is intimidated and insulted—and overtly demands honest payment for its rental, of which he is deceived. He defends his land and family with a machete. From him Minke learns the plight of peasant farmers, their virtual enslavement by the Dutch-controlled sugar company, and their meager, impoverished existence. They are kept under the heel by woefully low wages, additional enforced labor without recompense over long hours, illiteracy, and a deliberate aura of fear and suspicion. Implicated in this treachery are village officials, civil officials, and factory officials—all Natives.

Minke adopts Trunodongso's cause as his own and pledges himself to it; feeling the man's passion and recognizing his people's cause, he writes his best article—"a protest against the injustices suffered by who knows how many thousands of Trunodongsos. I would reveal to the world the conspiracy of blood-sucking vampires who were cheating those illiterate farmers of their rents"—and submits it to his editor. It is rejected to the accompaniment of a severe lecture denouncing the accusations as lacking proof and being libelous. "There are no peasant farmers who have become poor as a result of renting their land to the sugar mills. They receive a fair rent. They are happy to work as plantation laborers on their own land that they have rented out." He further insinuates that Minke would be in deep trouble if the contents of the manuscript were to become known. The incident leaves Minke with a lost political innocence, a full recognition of the degree to which his thought has been controlled, and an initial sense of danger. Later, Kommer confirms that the editor is in the pockets of the sugar interests and is paid to protect the sugar lobby.

Later in the book, the newspaper reports a peasant rebellion that necessitated calling in the army. After three days it is quashed, and its suspected leaders are punished. The sugar factory manager orders that the chief suspect receive 80 lashes before standing trial; he dies on the 70th. Minke is devastated, deeply concerned that his article in the hands of his former editor in effect betrayed Trunodongso. But he, wounded in body and spirit, and his family escape; they arrive at Nyai's estate, where they are given refuge and promises of work.

Minke attempts an "escape" as well by boat to Betawi to enter medical school. His political-economic education continues aboard ship through the auspices of a shipmate, a liberal Dutch journalist, who paints a detailed picture of the sugar interests' control of newspapers in order to maintain order and prices, and the Dutch government's role—capital and security—in underwriting the sugar companies. International intrigue is also identified, Java being inevitably the pillaged victim. The destructive influence and power of trade and production on humanity are made clear, contradicting Minke's schoollearned belief system of science and laws.

The journey to Betawi is not completed. Minke is intercepted and returned home for the reconvened trial to ascertain Herman Mellema's murderer or, as Nyai and Minke believe, to discredit them in anticipation of Maurits Mellema's arrival to lay claim to their land and business. The prosecution is thwarted when key evidence, a letter from now remorseful Robert Mellema, Nyai's son, is published by Kommer. The letter implicates the owner of the brothel, who confesses.

The novel concludes with a confrontation between Nyai, accompanied by Minke, Kommer, and Jean Marais, and Maurits Mellema. Maurits, who had arrived with arrogant and superior mien, leaves "stooped . . . look[ing] small, insignificant." This battle of truth is won by Nyai.

CENSORSHIP HISTORY

Pramoedya Ananta Toer was imprisoned for political reasons for 14 years and under house or city (Jakarta) arrest for an additional 20 years—from 1979 to 1999. He was first imprisoned by the Dutch from 1947 to 1950 for his role in Indonesia's anticolonial revolutions; he had been a member of the revolutionary underground and had printed and distributed revolutionary pamphlets.

In the years after his release, Pramoedya was politically active in the sense of participating in the struggle of ideas. While he never joined the Communist Party of Indonesia, he had been a member of LEKRA, a cultural organization associated with the Indonesian Communist Party, and had published a sympathetic history of the Chinese in Indonesia that was banned by the country's founding president, Sukarno. He was again jailed, for 10 months. In 1965, after a failed coup on September 30 that was blamed on the Communists, Pramoedya was picked up by the army on October 13, along with thousands of others suspected of having Communist sympathies. (As many as 1 million others were killed in what has been termed one of modern history's bloodiest massacres in a move by General Suharto to wipe out the party in Indonesia.) At this time, Pramoedya's manuscripts and personal library were burned, and all his books were banned. Without benefit of trial, he was imprisoned and subsequently interned at a remote penal island, Buru. Although he could not write there, he began to tell the *This Earth of Mankind* tetralogy (sometimes referred to as the Buru Quartet) orally to the other prisoners, in part to lift their morale and, through the character of Nyai, to give them a new sense of their own self-worth.

In late 1973, under an edict from the president's office that allowed prisoners to "retool their skills," Pramoedya was allowed to write. Wisely, because his own copies were later confiscated, he prepared carbon copies of his writings that he traded to other prisoners. Upon his release from prison in 1979, he obtained the carbons from other prisoners who had managed to safeguard their copies. In 1980, *This Earth of Mankind* was published; *A Child of All Nations* appeared two months later. Both books were banned on May 29, 1981, by the government of Indonesia. Pramoedya's publisher was ordered to cease publication of all his books; magazine editors were told not to print any of his stories, nor to mention him.

The official reason for the ban is that the books were "subversive"; they constituted a surreptitious attempt to disseminate Marxist-Leninist thought. Paul Tickell, in his analysis "Righting History," published in *Inside Indonesia*, identifies other reasons: The suggestion that the elite of Java was "little more than tools of Dutch colonialism" was offensive to those in power, as was the depiction of a society divided by class and race; the parallel suggestion that the elite were indifferent to the needs of ordinary people was also an affront. Another reason for banning Pramoedya's books was that they "contain misleading writings, which could create the wrong opinion about the government of Indonesia." They are accused, also, of containing "agitation and propaganda" and "profound Communist theories."

The third and fourth books in the tetralogy, *Footsteps* and *House of Glass*, were also censored in May 1986 and June 1988, respectively. They are all still banned in Indonesia. The attorney general of Indonesia, on April 19, 1995, banned Pramoedya's *Silent Song of a Mute* just two months after it went on sale. The decree read, "Allowing the circulation of the book will cause commotion or restlessness, which can disturb public order." Accordingly, all copies of the book throughout Indonesia were ordered to be withdrawn from circulation; persons with copies were to turn them in to the nearest prosecutor's office. Individuals caught with these books in their possession have been sentenced to prison on charges of subversion.

According to *Asia Watch*, a student, Bambang Subono, was arrested in 1988 for trying to sell *House of Glass*. A search of his home uncovered a copy of a novel, *Mother*, by Maxim Gorky, which had been translated by Pramoedya into Indonesian, as well as other novels by Pramoedya. Bambang's friend Isti Nugroho, who had borrowed the Gorky novel from the library, was also arrested. Both men were sentenced to prison on charges of subversion for seven and eight years, respectively. Both men had been held in military detention for two months; Itsi was tortured. In addition to reading Pramoedya's books, the two were charged with having discussed what the prosecutor considered Marxist-Leninist themes, such as the gap between the rich and the poor, the growing power of the state, and the elitist, undemocratic nature of Indonesian education.

The bans on Pramoedya's works—30 novels and books—have not been officially removed, although the books have been available since the overthrow of Suharto in May 1998. Earlier, his writings circulated clandestinely. It was estimated that 500,000 photocopies of *House of Glass*, the final part of his *This Earth of Mankind* tetralogy, were being circulated from individual to individual. However, at a rally in Jakarta in 2001, two groups, identified as the Islamic Youth Movement and the Anti-Communist Alliance, staged a series of book burnings. Dozens of books, including those of Pramoedya, were bonfired. Bookstores have been raided; as a result of threats to seize communist books, police in Yogyakarta impounded 49 books from 11 bookstores, including those of Pramoedya, while other bookstores have withdrawn his books and others.

In 1950, after Indonesia won its independence, THE FUGITIVE (1949) won the H. B. Yassin Award for the best first novel of the year and the Balai Putaska literary prize. Pramoedya was awarded the 1988 PEN Freedom-to-Write Award, the 1995 Ramon Magsaysay Prize for his contribution to Asian culture, and a UNESCO award in 1996. He was the recipient of the Grand Prize at the 11th Fukuoka Asian Culture Prizes in 2000. In the same year, he was nominated for the Nobel Prize in literature. In 1999 he was awarded an honorary doctorate by the University of Michigan. He died April 30, 2006.

FURTHER READING

Bald, Margaret. "For Indonesia's Rulers, the Fiction Hurts." *Toward Freedom* (August–September, 1992): 17–18.
Charle, Suzanne. "Prisoner without a Cell." *Nation*, February 3, 1992, 134–135.
Crosette, Barbara. "Banned in Jakarta." *New York Times Book Review*, January 19, 1992, p. 24.
Jones, Sidney. *Injustice, Persecution, Eviction: A Human Rights Update on Indonesia and East Timor:* New York: Asia Watch, 1990.
McDonald, Hamish. *Suharto's Indonesia.* Blackburn, Australia: Dominion Press/Fontana Books, 1980.
Scott, Margaret. "Waging War with Words." *Far Eastern Economic Review* (August 9, 1962): 26–30.
Tickell, Paul. "Righting History." *Inside Indonesia* (May 1986): 29–30.

365 DAYS

Author: Ronald J. Glasser
Original date and place of publication: 1971, United States
Publisher: George Braziller
Literary form: Nonfiction narrative

SUMMARY

The title, *365 Days*, refers to the standard maximum tour of duty in Vietnam. The title is apt, for there is throughout the text a consciousness of time already served and time remaining in the tour of duty. "You've been in Nam how long?" "How much longer do you have in country?" The months, the weeks, the days are counted.

Glasser, a physician serving during the Vietnam War in an army hospital in Japan that received medical "evacs" from the casualty staging area, establishes his purpose in the foreword. He writes not "in desperation" or "to prove a point," but to offset the sinking feeling "that nothing would be remembered except the confusion and the politics." His focus is on the men and their experiences. He tells their true stories, in their language. He was part of the stories set in Japan, the hospital stories; the stories set in Vietnam are "from the boys I met."

This collection of 17 sketches reflects a wide range of situations and men, giving the reader a sense of broad contact with the war from multiple perspectives. The several hospital sketches are set in different units: surgical, psychiatric, burn. The combat scenes vary: an infantry company on a "sweep," an ambush team, a mechanized "track" battalion, a search-and-destroy mission, a cooking unit, and a helicopter "chopper" rescue mission. The personnel range, too, from the neophyte to the massively trained and experienced, enlisted men and officers; from medics to nurses and doctors.

"Go Home, Kurt," the first sketch, sets the action and the tension, both the physical-emotional and the ethical-political. Kurt is brought in by chopper, bleeding profusely, close to death. In an exhausting two-hour operation, Peterson, the surgeon, cleans out the infection, ties a perforated artery, and closes the wound. The operation takes ten units of blood, but the leg stays on. Kurt survives. The ethical-political tension takes shape during the recovery period: Kurt's sense of duty to the men in his unit begins to falter as he talks with other evacs, friends from the unit. He questions, doubts, fears; yet he's nagged by the thought of a "lot of guys still there." Tension is expressed among the surgeons: A couple send the patients back as soon as they are well, no matter how many days are left of their tours; others, like Peterson, seeing the young soldiers as victims, arrange medical extensions to use up the last days.

"Mayfield" and "Track Unit" portray company and battalion operations respectively, establishing the nature of the fighting and the quality of the men. Sweaty-hot, muddy, dusty, explosively hazardous, the fighting is dominated by a kill-or-be-killed mind set. The men crawl through mud, wade through muck and paddies, scratch through tangled underbrush. The land is laced with mines, some spewing thousands of steel balls, others propelling explosive charges capable of blowing off legs, shattering arms and heads.

The men are described as sloppy, fatalistic, but professional: They fight well when they fight; they follow orders and do what is expected of them, including killing, but without illusions or convictions. They fight for each other. They are weary.

> The time thing of 365 days just nailed it down: no matter what these kids did or how they acted, they knew they had only 365 days of it and not a second more. To the kids lying around him, Nam simply didn't count for anything in itself. It was something they did between this and that, and they did what they had to do to get through it—no more.

The suddenness and frequency of casualty and death are striking. These and other sketches offer statistics. The Tet offensive resulted in 4,114 killed, 19,285 wounded, and 604 missing in action; taking hills 837 and 838 led to 80 percent casualties in two companies. Mayfield muses, "A first sergeant, and he couldn't keep up with the replacements. Five times in the last week, he'd had to bend over the wounded and ask their names. . . . He couldn't keep a second lieutenant; they ran through his fingers like the mud they worked in. He'd lost three that month alone, one right after another."

Several young lieutenants are featured, each exquisitely trained, superbly capable of survival in Vietnam War-style battle. An account of airborne and ranger training is detailed in "The Shaping-Up of McCabe"; the evolution of the man to a sharpened, hardened killer is evident. Responsive to fighting, the lieutenants are nevertheless dedicated to their men and to saving their lives, as illustrated by Dennen in "Track Unit."

An older officer, Bosum, is presented, perhaps as contrast. He is described as sincere and dedicated, but "locked into the early 1940's" mentality—". . . they desperately want to win, or at least not to lose, and are always, even within the shifting quagmire of Nam, pausing a bit, trying for a better way." As brigade commander, Bosum's better way in effect sacrifices men. There are no reserves; there is less rest. Intent on driving out the Vietcong, Bosum orders a push and no pull back. Whole platoons are wiped out. After the battle, an expensive victory, a grenade is rolled into Bosum's tent.

Individual heroism and loyalty are represented throughout, but particularly in "Medics" and "Choppers." The medics' skill and calm efficiency are matched by their selflessness, their apparent disregard of danger to themselves.

> Growing up in a hypocritical adult world and placed in the middle of a war that even the dullest of them find difficult to believe in, much less die for, very young and vulnerable, they are suddenly tapped not for their selfishness or greed but for their grace and wisdom, not for their brutality but for their love and concern.

Likewise, the chopper pilots are shown to be risk takers, daring landings under fire out of an awareness of the need of their service to bring in supplies, to bring out the wounded and deceased.

Awareness emerges from the text of the ages of the combatants: 17, 18, 19; again and again Glasser identifies them as "boys" or "kids." He alludes often to healthy adolescent bodies shattered.

A sense of futility and loss permeates the text. The last sketch, "I Don't Want to Go Home Alone," heightens this feeling as Edwards, a burns specialist who has just returned from taking his brother's body home, tries to save the life of David, suffering from 80 percent second- and third-degree burns. We participate in David's fear, his confusion and anxiety, his anger and defiance—and his dying.

CENSORSHIP HISTORY

365 Days was removed from the shelves of the Baileyville, Maine, high school library in 1981 by the school committee, which subsequently rejected an appeal by two students to return the book on a "restricted" basis. The committee chair indicated that the reason for the removal was the excessive use of four-letter words rather than the book's theme of death and dying in Vietnam or its antiwar tone. In January 1982, U.S. District Court judge Conrad Cyr temporarily enjoined the Baileyville School Committee from banning the book.

In ordering "interim injunctive relief," Judge Cyr ruled that the plaintiffs had demonstrated "(1) that [they] will suffer irreparable injury if the injunction is not granted; (2) that such injury outweighs any harm which granting injunctive relief would inflict on the defendant(s); (3) that plaintiff(s) [have] exhibited a likelihood of success on the merits; and (4) that the public interest will not be adversely affected by the granting of the injunction." He ordered the book returned to the library shelves. In his memorandum, he wrote:

> . . . the right to receive information and ideas has been recognized by the United States Supreme Court. . . . Courts recognizing a constitutional right to receive information emphasize the societal importance of fostering the free dissemination of knowledge and ideas in a democratic society. . . .
>
> The robust traditions of public education in our constitutional jurisprudence contradict assertions that the Bill of Rights constrains the abridgement of free expression for the exclusive benefit of the speaker. . . .
>
> Public schools are major marketing places of ideas, and First Amendment rights must be accorded to all "persons" in the market for ideas, including secondary school students, seeking redress of state action banning a book from the "warehouse of ideas." The way would be open to pare the protections of the First Amendment to constitutional insignificance in our public schools were courts to accede to suggestions . . . that the banning of a library book, the least obtrusive conventional communication resource available, does not at least presumptively implicate the reciprocal First Amendment right of secondary school students to receive the information and ideas there written. . . .
>
> How anomalous and dangerous to presume that state action banning an entire book, when the social value of its content is roundly praised and stands unchallenged by the state, does not directly and sharply implicate First Amendment rights because the ban was not intended to suppress ideas.
>
> The social value of the conceptual and emotive content of censored expression is not to be sacrificed to arbitrary official standards of vocabular [sic] taste. . . . As long as words convey ideas, federal courts must remain on First Amendment alert in book banning cases, even those ostensibly based strictly on vocabular [sic] considerations.

In August 1982, a consent decree forbidding the book's removal was signed after the committee agreed to settle the case out of court.

FURTHER READING

"*365 Days* Returned to Maine School Library." *Newsletter on Intellectual Freedom* 31 (1982): 33, 67–69.

TODAY'S ISMS: COMMUNISM, FASCISM, CAPITALISM, SOCIALISM

Author: William Ebenstein
Original date and place of publication: 1954, United States
Original publisher: Prentice-Hall
Literary form: Nonfiction

SUMMARY

In the preface to *Today's Isms: Communism, Fascism, Capitalism, Socialism*, William Ebenstein establishes his central purpose: analysis of the four main isms of the contemporary world to reveal their basic principles and policies. He indicates that particular attention will be given to their psychological roots—the personality traits and psychological motivations to which they each appeal—and the "distinct conceptions of the nature of man" which underlie them. The historical context is also analyzed.

Communism

The opening strategy is to identify and discuss several significant principles of Karl Marx's theory, their origins and import, and then to establish their flaws or failed promise in relation to the reality of change of the economic and social world. A major marxist doctrine that Ebenstein questions is that basic social change can be brought about only by violent revolution. Marx argued that social change is necessitated when "technological knowhow ('forces of production') begins to outstrip the existing social, legal, and political institutions ('relations of production')." The owners of the means of production, the ruling class, resist social change because they identify their own values with universally valid ones. This Marxian class struggle inevitably meant the "forcible overthrow of all existing conditions." In contradiction to this thesis, two major revolutions—the passage of the Reform Act in England in 1832 and the Jacksonian revolution in the United States—were nonviolent; other nonviolent changes have led to greater political and social democracy in these countries and others.

Still another failed prediction is Marx's view of the inevitable proletarianization of society in a capitalist economy, a significant feature of its revolutionary overthrow that would lead to the establishment of communism. A factor in this failure was the upgrading of the labor force; affected individuals took on middleclass values and lifestyles, further reducing the impulse toward proletarianization. In a related discussion, Ebenstein explains that contrary to the marxist expectation and official Soviet claims, a classless society has not been achieved.

Having delineated other forces in the physical, social, and human environments—conservation of natural resources, bureaucracy, specialization, and nationalism—which affected the operation of Marx's theory,

Ebenstein expresses Lenin's active interpretation of the theory. In short, while Marx believed in the primacy of economics over politics, Lenin gave primacy to politics over economics.

> Whereas Marx expected that a communist revolution would lead to the *dictatorship of the proletariat*, an essentially economic entity, *over the bourgeoisie*, also a basically economic category . . . Lenin's concept of dictatorship meant, in more political terms, *dictatorship of the communist party over the proletariat* since he had little faith that the working class had the political understanding or spontaneous ability to secure the existence and expansion of a communist state.

Strengths of the communist system are represented in rapid industrialization, economic growth, education, and science. Weaknesses of the communist system are largely expressed in human terms: a stress on conformity, political and intellectual orthodoxy, and coerced adherence to policies dictated from the top of the ruling hierarchy, such as Stalin-mandated collectivism, which transformed the independent peasant into a dependent agricultural proletarian. Political and intellectual orthodoxy also has been marked by repressive controls of literature and publications.

Fascism

"Stripped to essentials, fascism is the totalitarian organization of government and society by a single-party dictatorship, intensely nationalistic, racist, militaristic, and imperialist." In contrast, "Whereas communism is very largely the product of predemocratic and preindustrial societies, fascism is *postdemocratic* and *postindustrial:* fascism is unlikely to seize power in countries with no democratic experience at all." These may, however, be subject to dictatorships.

Fascism has appealed to two groups: small groups of industrialists and landowners who are able to exert power through money in countries where democracy has been weak, and the lower-middle-class salaried group (not the proletariat class), which seeks "salvation of status and prestige." Persons in this group, caught between big business and labor, feel jealous of the former and fearful of descending into the latter. Fascism encourages a sense of usefulness and belonging and mitigates the sense of disorientation and destruction of traditional values that are frequently undermined by industrialization and urbanization.

The psychological roots of totalitarianism—applicable to communism as well as fascism—are grounded in an authoritarian tradition. Identifiable characteristics of a fascist-authoritarian personality include

> First, a tendency to conform compulsively to orthodox ideals and practices; emotional rigidity and limited imagination; excessive concern with problems of status and strength; strong loyalty to one's own group coupled with vehement dislike of outsiders; and stress on discipline and obedience rather than

freedom and spontaneity in human relations (education, sex, family, religion, industry, government). The "herd-minded" (or ethnocentric element in the fascist personality) is perhaps the single most important one, although no one element in itself conclusively defines a personality as authoritarian.

Dependence and submission in a totalitarian society provide a sense of security and the "comforts of irresponsibility." The superiors direct their subordinates to express their hostility and aggressiveness against real or imaginary enemies, thus promising mastery over others.

Seven principal elements of fascism are detailed: 1) distrust of reason— fanatical and dogmatic rather than reflective and open-minded; 2) denial of basic human equality; 3) code of behavior based on lies and violence; 4) government of the elite, denying the capabilities of the people as a whole; 5) totalitarianism in all human relations, employing authority in social as well as political relations; 6) racism and imperialism, reflecting hierarchy and superiority; and 7) opposition to international law and order.

In concluding this section, the author expresses several fascist aspects in United States society that threaten democratic principles: an anti-intellectual tendency that undermines faith in rational processes, and acts of extremism—terrorism and other violence and racism. However, "possibly the most dangerous softening up of democratic resistance to fascism is the destruction of democratic habits and institutions, not by outside attacks. . . . It derives its parasitic strength from the inertia and apathy of the citizens of a democracy. . . ."

Capitalism

Based on the premise that there is "a close link between capitalism and democracy, Ebenstein devotes about half of this section to an expression of democracy, revealing thus a critical facet of capitalism. Democracy is defined as including free elections; a free press; freedom of political association; freedom of religion, thought, and speech; equality before the law; the right to oppose the government; the right to form unions; and the right to move freely within one's country and abroad. "Above all, *freedom from fear* is basic in the Western concept of democracy. No society can be called free unless its citizens feel safe from unwarranted intrusion into their affairs by governmental authorities, particularly the secret police."

The standards and criteria of a democratic society are not always attained. Among those discussed are rational empiricism, the "confidence in reason and in the applicability of reason not only to physical nature but also to human relations"; emphasis on the individual, social, and political institutions existing to serve the individual; the concept of the law behind the law, which recognizes the state's authority being derived from the consent of the governed; that discussion and consent are the means of settling divergent viewpoints and interests; and basic equality of all human beings.

The psychological roots of democracy, in contrast to totalitarianism's authoritianism, are the nurturing and maturation of security within the self and the recognition that freedom implies choice between alternatives. Democracy is also rooted in a sense of equality between genders and among races, joined with tolerance and cooperation, which may result in the democratic process of consultation, discussion, and free exchange.

Capitalism, which developed historically as part of the movement of individualism, is more than a particular type of economy, but rather a whole social system, a capitalist civilization. In classical capitalism, "ownership of the means of production (land, factories, machinery, natural resources) is held by individuals, not by the state." This does not exclude the possibility of government ownership of natural monopolies, or basic public services or land. The diffusion of such ownership among many property owners is perceived to be preferable because ownership of productive property signifies power over people.

The second principle, market economy, is based on the specialization of labor; its fundamental aspect is the "comparatively unregulated operation of supply and demand" (in contrast to the command economy of fascism and communism in which the state controls the workings of the economy). A significant feature of market economy is consumer sovereignty: Consumers have the freedom to choose what goods they will buy, thus ultimately determining how much will be produced. Other essential characteristics include competition, research, and profit.

Modern capitalism has moved away from classical capitalism first in the separation of ownership from management and collectivization, and the concentration of manufacturing in giant corporations. Second, the traditional hierarchical pattern of control has been modified by organized labor, legislation, public opinion, and the growth of a sense of responsibility toward the community. Third is the modification of the orthodox philosophy of laissez-faire by government interference in the business-economic realm, conjoined with social principles. This interference has led several capitalist countries to evolve into welfare states. "The main principles of the welfare state are . . . first the recognition that every member of the community is entitled, solely because he is a human being, to a *minimum standard of living*; second, the welfare state is committed to putting *full employment* at the top of social goals to be supported by public policy." The United States adapted its economy in this direction through legislation that provided for parity support for farmers, Social Security, education loans and aid; regulated labor-management relations; and redistributed income through taxation to bring about greater equality.

Socialism

Socialism is defined as being akin to capitalism, having originated as a result of modern industrial capitalism and sharing its liberal and democratic concepts. It is opposed to the authoritarianism of communism and fascism, which operate by command and coercion. Socialism features a protest against social inequality and against money as the chief tie among human beings. Socialism puts faith in collective productive property and effort, while capitalism puts faith in individual property and effort. However, in "both systems—classical liberal, capitalism and democratic socialism—there is the underlying assumption that *the right to property ultimately rests on work, effort, and industry, rather than on formal law, custom, or birth."*

Socialists reject several premises and behaviors of communists. The marxist doctrine of revolutionary upheaval and civil war is renounced in favor of constitutional procedures and peaceful persuasion; socialist perception adheres to the "installment plan," the gradual adjustment of industrial and social conditions. The idea of the proletariat, people as a mass, is also rejected in acknowledgment of the individual. With regard to public ownership, socialists deny the necessity of total state ownership and insist on due process and compensation when a citizen is faced with potential loss of property. The elite concept of government by a minority party's minority cadre of professional revolutionaries is also rejected.

The success of socialist principles is evident in several European countries, as well as the welfare principles affecting social programs in the United States. A principal variation among the applications is in the degree of nationalization of industry and other social services. These very successes undermine the future of the socialist movement.

In the concluding pages, Ebenstein differentiates between European socialism and that of developing countries seeking better living standards, health, and education for their people. For these regions, socialism, while not identically practiced, projects three central positions: the ideal of social justice, a commitment to raise the living standards of the masses and narrow the gap between the classes across the spectrum of life; the ideal of human brotherhood and world peace through law; and a commitment to planning.

CENSORSHIP HISTORY

Today's Isms: Communism, Fascism, Capitalism, Socialism was one of four books challenged in Roselle, New Jersey, in 1972. The others were THE AFFLUENT SOCIETY, by John Galbraith; THE AGE OF KEYNES, by Robert Lekachman; and *The Struggle for Peace* by Leonard Beaton. Please refer to the censorship discussion of *The Affluent Society.*

FURTHER READING

Cohen, Robert. "Educational Groups Deplore Roselle Book Ban." *Newark Star-Ledger,* June 23, 1972, p. 17.
———. "Roselle Board President Defends Book Bannings." *Newark Star-Ledger,* June 15, 1972, p. 11.

————. "State Education Official Assails Book Bannings," *Newark Star-Ledger,* June 27, 1972, p. 15.

Moffatt, George. "Book 'Ban' Challenged in Roselle." *Newark Star-Ledger,* June 28, 1972, p. 18.

————. "Roselle Will Buy 'Banned' Books and 4 'Balancers.' " *Newark Star-Ledger,* July 6, 1972, p. 20.

"A School Board Head in Jersey Orders 'Liberal' Books Deleted." *New York Times,* June 18, 1972, p. 50.

"Success Stories." *Newsletter on Intellectual Freedom* 21 (1972): 147.

THE UGLY AMERICAN

Authors: William J. Lederer and Eugene Burdick
Original date and place of publication: 1958, United States
Publisher: W. W. Norton and Company
Literary form: Fiction

SUMMARY

The Ugly American begins with a note from the authors stating the story is fiction but based on fact. They write, "The names, the places, the events, are our inventions; our aim is not to embarrass individuals, but to stimulate thought—and, we hope, action."

Louis Sears is the American ambassador to Sarkhan, a fictional country in Southeast Asia near Burma and Thailand. For 18 years, Sears was a U.S. senator. While awaiting an appointment as a federal judge, he is offered the ambassadorship to Sarkhan. Sears does not know anything about the country; in fact, he is not even sure where it is located. Accepting the appointment in the early 1950s, he goes to Sarkhan, but he never learns anything about its culture or language. He considers the native people "damned little monkeys" and manages to alienate and offend most of them with his rudeness and his assuming ways.

Russian ambassador Louis Krupitzyn arrives in Sarkhan one week after Sears. He and his wife have rigorously studied the culture for the past two years. Krupitzyn knows how to read and write the language. He has molded himself into the ideal man by Sarkhanese standards: He lost 40 pounds, he took ballet lessons, he read Sarkhanese literature and drama, he became a skillful player of the nose flute, and he regularly attended lectures on Buddhist religion and practices. The day after his arrival in Sarkhan, Krupitzyn goes to the great monastery to pay his respects to the chief abbot, the leader of all Buddhists in the area, to whom he speaks with reverence in classical Sarkhanese.

Sears and Krupitzyn are in competition to win the favor of the Sarkhanese government and people, although Sears does not understand the full implications. The Russians, primarily due to Krupitzyn's knowledge and skill, are moving toward their goal of turning Sarkhan to communism within 30 months. Krupitzyn and his staff are victorious in portraying the Russian government as more helpful and supportive than the American government.

Reading of the threat of communism in Sarkhan in 1952, John Colvin, former Office of Strategic Services (OSS) agent in Sarkhan during the war, writes many letters to his congressman, explaining Sarkhanese culture and offering suggestions for helping the people. He decides to aid the situation himself when he receives inadequate replies from the government. His plan is to introduce powdered milk into the culture and eventually bring in Texas cattle that could feed on the useless grasses found throughout the country. He will support the initial investment of the venture, but he plans to turn the operations and revenues over to the native peoples who help him run the business.

Colvin, in Sarkhan for two weeks selling powdered milk, is beaten by his former friend and military associate Deong, now a Communist, who accuses him of trying to poison the people. A group of women beat, kick, and scratch him; they drop him naked on the embassy sidewalk with a note pinned to his bare chest saying he raped a native woman. Ambassador Sears does not believe Colvin's version of the events.

In 1952, Father Finian is assigned to Burma as overseer of Catholic missions. In his quest to help the Burmese people fight communism, Father Finian lives among the native people, learns their language, and suffers through weeks of severe dysentery in order to eat their food and drink their water. He gathers eight native men and facilitates a plan to help them rid the countryside of communism. They publish a newspaper called *The Communist Farmer*, which exposes communist doctrine and illustrates the truth about the Communist Party to the people. Through the efforts of the "nine friends," the Communists are run out of the Burmese countryside. Father Finian plans to move to Sarkhan next and begin a similar operation.

In a letter to a State Department official in Washington, Louis Sears writes,

> We got another crackpot here, too—Father Finian. This priest has to be handled with kid gloves. I don't want to get into a beef with the Roman Catholics. But this Finian has just come from Burma where he started a small revolution; now he's organizing here in Sarkhan way up north, and the local papers are beginning to raise hell. If Cardinal Spellman is for him, I can tolerate him, I suppose. But if the Catholic bigshots are down on him, I'll get him shipped back to the States.

After several major political blunders, Sears is awarded his judgeship earlier than expected and immediately leaves Sarkhan. Before leaving the country, he takes three courses of action: He refuses to extend protection to Father Finian; he advises the Sarkhanese government to refuse a visa to John Colvin; and he writes a letter to the State Department, noting his accomplishments in Sarkhan.

Gilbert MacWhite, a recognized expert on Soviet theory and practice, is the new ambassador. Excited about his new appointment, MacWhite learns the Sarkhanese language and reads about Sarkhan's history and political life. MacWhite is determined to destroy the communist stronghold in Sarkhan. His complex plan, however, is revealed to the communists by two trusted Sarkhanese servants. MacWhite decides to go to the Philippines and Vietnam to learn how they deal with the communists and to gain a better understanding of Asian peoples. During his travels, he invites several Americans to Sarkhan to help improve the situation.

Homer Atkins, an engineer, and his wife, Emma, move to a small village in Sarkhan. Homer employs the help of the villagers in the designing, building, and selling of pumps that will move water from the rivers up the hillsides to the rice paddies. Emma, who notices that all of the old people have stooped backs caused by sweeping with short-handled brooms, locates a tall natural reed and uses it to construct a longer broom handle, thus helping the villagers. James Wolchek, an army paratrooper who has learned to adapt communist tactics in battle, comes to Sarkhan to instruct recruits in guerrilla tactics. U Maung Swe, a well-known and respected Burmese journalist, tells MacWhite that John Colvin was framed by the Communists; he recommends that Colvin be brought back to continue his work.

When U Maung Swe is asked about American prestige in Southeast Asia, he responds, "Poor America. It took the British a hundred years to lose their prestige in Asia. America has managed to lose hers in ten years. And there was no need for it. In fact, she could get it all back in two years, if she wanted to." He explains that Americans in foreign countries isolate themselves socially, live pretentiously, and they are loud and ostentatious.

The chair of the Senate Foreign Affairs Committee, Senator Brown, decides to tour Asia and the Far East. His plan is to visit as many countries as possible, talk to the natives and low-ranking employees, and find out what is really happening in these countries. The ambassador to Vietnam, Arthur Alexander Gray, forewarned of the senator's arrival, plans to keep him away from the truth about the situation in Vietnam. He hires an interpreter to "make sense" out of what the natives say to the senator. He instructs his staff to stay at the embassy, working until at least eight o'clock at night, to ride bicycles instead of driving their cars, to stay out of the French restaurants and cafés, and to generally prove their "sense of drive and dedication." The plan to keep Brown from learning too much is successful, and Senator Brown returns to the United States pleased with his positive interactions abroad.

Ambassador Gilbert MacWhite is an honest man. His reports to the U.S. government directly conflict with the reports of Senator Brown, a discrepancy that results in a reprimand from the secretary of state. In response, MacWhite writes that he was not prepared for "the silent desperation with which the battle between the communist world and our world is being fought here." He states that the Russians have not suffered a major defeat since the end of World War II and advises the U.S. government and its representatives to engage in moral acts in the real interest of the people. "To the extent that our foreign policy is humane and reasonable, it will be successful. To the extent that it is imperialistic and grandiose, it will fail."

In the final section of MacWhite's letter, he requests that every American sent to Sarkhan be able to speak and read Sarkhanese; that no dependents be allowed to come to Sarkhan unless the American employee is willing to serve there for at least two years; that the American commissary and PX be withdrawn with no supplies for Americans except toilet articles, baby food, canned milk, coffee, and tobacco; that Americans not be allowed to bring their own automobiles to Sarkhan; and that Americans coming to Sarkhan be well read in books by communist leaders. MacWhite indicates that if these requests are not met he will resign his position. Three weeks later, all requests are denied for being "highly impractical," and MacWhite is requested to return to the United States.

In the final chapter of the book, "A Factual Epilogue," the authors again state that the book is based on fact. They substantiate the characters and stories in the book with real-life individuals and instances from their time in Southeast Asia. Finally, they offer their own statement about U.S. foreign policy in that part of the world:

> We have been offering the Asian nations the wrong kind of help. We have so lost sight of our own past that we are trying to sell guns and money alone, instead of remembering that it was the quest for the dignity of freedom that was responsible for our own way of life.

CENSORSHIP HISTORY

In 1953, Senator Joe McCarthy led an investigation of the Overseas Library Program. The libraries, overseen by the International Information Agency (IIA), existed with the objective of providing a balanced view of U.S. beliefs to people in foreign countries. Books were chosen "based on content without regard to authorship." Controversial books were included, while blatantly anti-American or procommunist books were excluded from the library shelves. McCarthy and his team planned to "investigate the way in which controversial books were allowed to reach" the libraries. Carl McArdle, assistant secretary for public affairs, in response to the investigation, stated, "no material by any controversial persons, Communists, fellow travelers, etc., will be used by the IIA."

The repercussions of this new policy were far-reaching. After testimony before the House Un-American Activities Committee, a list, published in 1953, named those who had been mentioned unfavorably throughout the hearings. Many respected individuals had their works removed from libraries. (Please refer to the censorship discussion of MANIFESTO OF THE COMMUNIST PARTY for more details.)

Immediately after publication, *The Ugly American* was temporarily censored by George V. Allen, director of the U.S. Information Agency, previously the IIA. The agency had an information media guaranty program in which booksellers abroad were given dollars for local currencies derived from the sale of American books. Allen, undoubtedly influenced by McCarthy's investigation five years earlier, felt that permitting the book to be sent abroad under this program "would not be in the interests of the United States." In December 1958, Allen changed his mind. An agency spokesperson said, "One facet in Mr. Allen's decision to approve the book for the program was his desire not to create any impression of 'another Pasternak' case by 'censorship at home.'" He was referring to the Soviet Union's ban on DOCTOR ZHIVAGO by Boris Pasternak.

Senator J. W. Fulbright, Arkansas Democrat and chair of the Senate Foreign Relations Committee, criticized the novel from the Senate floor in 1959. He was upset by the portrayal of Americans overseas as "boobs or worse," while Russian diplomats were portrayed as "talented, dedicated servants of communism." He said the book had "misled a number of gullible Americans, including a few Senators," into thinking it was an accurate portrayal of American personnel abroad.

The Ugly American is listed in Lee Burress's 1963 survey of censored books completed by Wisconsin English Department chairpersons and school administrators. The teachers who reported felt that some objectors had hidden motives; the objectors professed to object to the language in the books they attacked, but they were actually objecting to the ideas found within the pages. It was believed that those who objected to ideas found more support for their objections by attacking the morality and/or language of those books. *The Ugly American* falls into this category, according to the survey.

According to the same survey, a Wisconsin teacher and a group of parents objected to *The Ugly American* because of its critical pictures of Americans abroad. This same group also objected to what they deemed immorality and obscenity. The unpublished 1966 National Survey of Objections to Books by Lee Burress cites three further challenges to the book based on its "filthy language and references to sex" and its profane and vile language. These requests for censorship were denied.

FURTHER READING

Burress, Lee. *Battle of the Books: Literary Censorship in Public Schools.* Metuchen, N.J.: Scarecrow Press, 1989.

———. "The Pressure of Censorship on Wisconsin Public Schools." *Wisconsin English Journal* 6 (October 1963): 6–28.

"Fulbright Attacks 'The Ugly American.'" *New York Times*, May 20, 1959, n.p.

Oshinsky, David M. *A Conspiracy So Immense: The World of Joe McCarthy.* New York: Free Press, 1983.

"A Special New Republic Report on Book Burning: Who Are the Book Burners? What Happened in San Antonio, St. Cloud and Boston? Senate Transcript— McCarthy vs. Conant." *New Republic,* June 29, 1953, 7–9.
"U.S.I.A. in Reversal on 'Ugly American.'" *New York Times,* December 6, 1958, n.p.

—Laurie Pap

UNCLE TOM'S CABIN

Author: Harriet Beecher Stowe
Original date and place of publication: 1852, United States
Publisher: John P. Jewett
Literary form: Novel

SUMMARY

When Harriet Beecher Stowe wrote *Uncle Tom's Cabin,* her main goal was to paint a picture of slavery so heartrending as to cause white people to rise up against it. Her goal was not one of political change, however, for she believed that change that did not include a change of heart would not last. She thought the only way to effect a proper change was through conversion of the entire nation to Christianity. If everyone believed not only in but also practiced an equality ordained by God, the slaves would necessarily be set free and everyone would be able to go to Heaven. As such, every plot line focuses on a character who is a model of acceptance of Christianity, or a character whose faith is tested. Whether characters are good or evil depends upon their religious nature more than their deeds.

One plot line tells of the slave Eliza, her husband, George, who lives on another plantation, and their son, Harry. When Eliza discovers that her owner, Mr. Shelby, has sold her son to pay off a debt, she decides her only option is to run away. Her husband has already done so, as he is afraid his master will not allow his marriage to Eliza to continue, but will instead force him to live with another woman on his plantation. George feels his only hope is to run away to Canada and earn enough money to buy his wife and child. Once Eliza decides to escape, she realizes that her only hope, too, lies in Canada. She runs with her child toward the river that separates her home state of Kentucky from the free state of Ohio. With the slave trader Haley about to capture her, she has few choices; she crosses the ice-covered Ohio River, baby in her arms and no shoes on her feet, and arrives on the free side, tired and full of gashes. Unfortunately, due to the Fugitive Slave Law of 1850, being in a free state means relatively little. The new law forbids the people of the free states from helping runaway slaves and requires the slaves to be captured and returned to their proper owners. Quakers, notorious for their hatred of slavery, reject this law, becoming her main assistants, offering her food and shelter and reuniting her with her husband. The family is still in danger, however, as the slave trader has hired two men to find and capture Eliza and Harry, and they have set up a posse toward that end. The family attempts its escape to Canada, then is cornered by the posse, but George is unwilling to give up easily and begins shooting, wounding one of the group and scaring the others away.

Eliza and George are virtuous Christians, while Haley and the men he has hired are not. Eliza has faith that God will do what is best, as shown by her belief that He will help her across the river. George's faith, however, is tested. He feels that he and all blacks have been deserted by God. According to the beliefs of the narrator, George must accept Christianity as a necessary part of becoming a good man. This acceptance comes when, at the home of a Quaker with his wife and son, George is treated as an equal for the first time. The narrator says that "a belief in God, and trust in His providence, began to encircle his heart, as, with a golden cloud of protection and confidence, dark, misanthropic, pining, atheistic doubts, and fierce despair, melted away before the light of a living Gospel. . . ." George has converted in his soul, and thus is saved; Haley and the two slave trackers, however, are seen as evil, not because they sin daily by treating humans as property, but because they are not Christians. The narrative makes clear that their lack of Christian virtue will most certainly be dealt with harshly on Judgment Day.

The second major plot line follows the journeys of a virtuous man, Uncle Tom. He was also sold to Haley, but unlike Eliza, he is not willing to run away. He believes that he must do what his master says in this life and in the next. The plantation owner has put his trust in Tom, and Tom feels he cannot disobey. More important, Tom believes that whatever is to happen is ordained by God, and he will not risk becoming wicked by breaking His laws. While Tom has a wife and several children, he passively allows himself to be taken away and is soon found on a ship going down the Mississippi River. Also aboard is a young girl, little Eva. Tom is drawn to befriend her because she is angelic and pure. When he saves her life after she falls into the river, her father, Augustine St. Clare, agrees to purchase him.

Tom is brought to his new home in New Orleans, where the reader is introduced to a variety of characters. Eva's mother, Marie, is an extremely selfish hypochondriac who cares more for her own fabricated illnesses than the real illness of her child. St. Clare, on the other hand, cares deeply for his child and for his slaves. He believes slavery is wrong but does not see any way he can stop it. He believes it is his own fault if his slaves misbehave because being slaves has made them immoral. St. Clare also does not care much for religion because, as he says, religious slave owners are hypocritical, and he does not want to attend a church where the ministers tell the owners what they want to hear instead of the truth. Miss Ophelia is St. Clare's cousin from Vermont, whom he has engaged to run his household while his wife is "sick." She is hypocritical in a different way because she is religious and believes slavery is wrong, but she cannot stand to think of black people as her moral or intellectual equals.

St. Clare, while himself against slavery, details why his brother, Alfred, is in favor of it. Alfred, an "aristocrat," gives several arguments in defense of slavery by comparing it to other political systems.

". . . . 'the American planter is only doing, in another form, what the English aristocracy and capitalists are doing by the lower classes;' that is I take it, *appropriating* them, body and bone, soul and spirit, to their use and convenience. . . . there can be no high civilization without enslavement of the masses, either nominal or real. There must, [Alfred] says, be a lower class, given up to physical toil and confined to an animal nature; and a higher one thereby acquires leisure and wealth for a more expanded intelligence and improvement, and becomes the directing soul of the lower."

Eva is the ideal type of person Stowe wanted everyone to become—purely Christian and not hypocritical. Even in death, Eva remains pure, for she welcomes the opportunity to see her savior and converts others to the path of righteousness. Unlike her mother, she does not use the Bible to prove that God made slavery for a reason. Unlike Ophelia, she practices love and kindness. Unlike her father, she believes ending slavery is possible and that it is her mission to change the feelings of those around her so they feel compelled to free their slaves. She accomplishes this goal through her death. Her father is so moved that he becomes more religious and begins the paperwork necessary to free Tom, while Topsy, a mischievous and self-proclaimed "wicked" young slave girl, becomes good, and Ophelia begins to think of Topsy as a human, capable of loving and being loved.

Unfortunately, the papers that would give Tom his freedom have not been completed by the time St. Clare is stabbed trying to break up a fight—the ultimate act of Christian selflessness—so Tom is sold by Marie. He is bought at an auction by Simon Legree, a man who uses constant beatings to keep his slaves in line and drives them until they die, then buys new ones. More than his lack of respect for human life, his desire to make Tom give up his religion makes him a villain; when he finds Tom's hymnbook while rooting through his belongings, he says, "'Well, I'll soon have *that* out of you. I have none o' yer bawling, praying, singing niggers on my place; so remember. Now, mind yourself . . . *I'm* your church now! You understand,—you've got to be as I say.'" When Tom refuses Legree's order that he beat another slave, Legree becomes incensed. He tells Tom that he owns him, body and soul, but Tom responds:

"Mas'r Legree, as ye bought me, I'll be a true and faithful servant to ye. I'll give ye all the work of my hand, all my time, all my strength; but my soul I won't give up to mortal man. I will hold on to the Lord, and put his commands before all,—die or live; you may be sure on't. Mas'r Legree, I an't a grain afeard to die. I'd as soon die as not. Ye may whip me, starve me, burn me,—it'll only send me sooner where I want to go."

This attitude forces Legree into a state of fear because he knows himself to be wicked and that, in the end, he will go to Hell. This fear manifests itself in a hatred of Tom so strong that he eventually beats him to death. Tom is another exemplary Christian who would rather accept his own death than inflict pain on another. His death causes the conversion of Cassy, an older slave woman who has turned away from God because she believes He has turned away from her. He also converts Sambo and Quimbo, Legree's slaves, who run the plantation and willingly beat their fellow slaves; when he dies, they realize the wrongs they have done to him and others and repent. Finally, Tom's death causes a different kind of conversion, when George Shelby, son of Tom's old owner, frees all of his slaves.

CENSORSHIP HISTORY

Uncle Tom's Cabin, from the moment it was published, was extremely controversial. The topic of slavery lay at the ideological heart of America and caused a great split, for how could a nation founded on principles of equality support a system in which 5 million of its populace were degraded and forced into submission? For this reason, the novel spurred many debates. Many in the North wanted to know if the stories were true; not living in slavery and seeing it firsthand, they could not believe that it was so cruel. That is why at the end Stowe included a chapter entitled "Concluding Remarks," in which she vouches for the truth of each incident she details, including the flight of Eliza across the icy Ohio River and the sad tales of familial separation on the auction block. Despite the controversy surrounding the novel and the fact that, as Joseph Conlin says in his book *Our Land, Our Time*, it "was banned in the South," the novel quickly became a best seller, with 3 million copies in print before the Civil War. In addition to responding to censorship, a dialogue was created between the proslavery and antislavery activists of both the North and the South. Those who disagreed with Stowe's conclusions countered them with criticism of her novel and with what John Tebbel calls "'anti–Uncle Tom' books," such as *Aunt Phillis's Cabin; or, Southern Life as It Is*.

Uncle Tom's Cabin was not only potentially dangerous to the American system of slavery, however. The idea of equality offended many others. Anne Haight notes that in 1852 it was "banned under the 'censorship terror' of Nicholas I." Censorship was a large part of Russian history, not just of books, but also of periodicals, plays, music, and other forms of expression. This trend was started long before Nicholas became czar, but his reign reinforced and extended the prohibitions. According to the statute on censorship of 1828:

> Works of literature, science, and art are to be banned by the censorship: (a) if they contain anything that tends to undermine the teachings of the Orthodox Greco-Russian church, its traditions and rituals, or in general the truths and dogmas of the Christian faith; (b) if they contain anything infringing upon the inviolability of the supreme autocratic power or upon the respect for the imperial house, or anything contradicting basic government legislation.

Uncle Tom's Cabin was seen as a threat to both of these conditions and was, therefore, censored. The system of aristocracy that Stowe criticizes as inhumane existed in Russia as well. The czar and other nobles prospered, while the lower classes worked very hard for relatively little. The free circulation of such ideas was understood as dangerous to the czar, so the novel was censored. Similar censorship took place for many other authors.

Also based on the statute of 1828, the novel was censored for undermining religious ideals. While the novel is extremely pro-Christian, it often takes sides against the church and the clergy. Both St. Clare and Stowe herself discuss the hypocrisy of the Christian church, which twists scripture to the advantage of slaveholders. When Marie tells how a sermon discussed scripture that showed how slavery was properly ordained by God, St. Clare scoffs at the idea: "'This religious talk on such matters,—why don't they carry it a little further, and show the beauty, in its season, of a fellow's taking a glass too much, and sitting a little too late over his cards, and various providential arrangements of that sort, which are pretty frequent among us young men; we'd like to hear that those are right and godly, too.'" Stowe, in her final paragraph, says, "Both North and South have been guilty before God; and the *Christian Church* has a heavy account to answer. . . ." She believed that it was the church's responsibility to teach the Christian virtues of kindness and equality, not to help support the unkind and unequal system of slavery.

The belief that the church allows so unjust a system to continue was also the reason behind papal censorship of this novel. Haight notes that in the Italian states and in the papal state in 1855 "the sale of the volume was prohibited, though not listed on the index." The Index librorum prohibitorum, or Roman Index, listed the works Catholics were forbidden to read, due to their blasphemous nature.

In addition to censorship in other countries, the novel was often protested and censored in the United States in later years by people who felt it was racist. Haight writes that in Bridgeport, Connecticut, in 1955, "a dramatized version . . . was protested by blacks as a caricature of reality." Stowe's novel, in fact, presents a stereotypical view of blacks and whites. For example, while Aunt Chloe is delightedly describing a dinner she made, she compares herself to her mistress, and several implicitly racist statements are made:

> "I and Missis, we come pretty near quarreling about dat are crust. . . . and, finally, I got kinder sarcy, and, says I, 'Now Missis, do look at dem beautiful white hands o' yourn, with long fingers . . . and look at my great black stumpin' hands. Now, don't ye think dat de Lord must have meant *me* to make de pie-crust, and you to stay in de parlor?'"

Remarks like these, found throughout the narrative, upset readers. Elsewhere in the story, Stowe paints a picture of blacks who are so happy as slaves that when George Shelby gives them their freedom, they refuse it. She also ends the plot of George and Eliza by sending them to Liberia, a colony in Africa set aside for freed slaves, making it obvious that educated, free blacks are not welcome in America. Also, many felt the character of Tom to be overly passive and unwilling to fight for his own life and freedom or that of his family. As Haight points out, during the 1950s, "'Uncle Tom' was becoming a derogatory phrase implying submissiveness."

In 1984, in Waukegan, Illinois, the book was protested by Alderman Robert B. Evans, Sr., along with Mark Twain's *ADVENTURES OF HUCKLEBERRY FINN*, Harper Lee's *TO KILL A MOCKINGBIRD*, and Margaret Mitchell's *Gone with the Wind*. As Lee Burress points out, students and parents joined the protest in objection of "'racism' and 'language.'" Specifically, as the *Newsletter on Intellectual Freedom* says, Evans objected to the books' use of the word *nigger* and requested that they be removed from the curriculum: "There are no books in the district that talk about 'honkies,' 'dagos,' 'spics,' 'polacks,' or 'Hymies.' Just like people of those nationalities are offended by use of those words, black folks are offended by use of the word 'nigger.'" Since only *Huckleberry Finn* was required reading, the result was removal of this novel from the required reading list.

FURTHER READING

Burress, Lee. *Battle of the Books: Literary Censorship in Public Schools, 1950–1985.* Metuchen, N.J.: Scarecrow Press, 1989.

Conlin, Joseph R. *Our Land, Our Time: A History of the United States.* San Diego, Calif.: Coronado Publishers, 1985.

Haight, Anne Lyon, and Chandler B. Grannis. *Banned Books: 387 B.C. to 1978 A.D.* 4th ed. New York: R. R. Bowker, 1978.

Monas, Sidney. *The Third Section: Police and Society in Russia under Nicholas I.* Cambridge, Mass.: Harvard University Press, 1961.

Newsletter on Intellectual Freedom 33 (July 1984): 105.

Tebbell, John. *A History of Book Publishing in the United States.* Vol. 3: *The Creation of an Industry: 1630–1865.* New York: R. R. Bowker, 1972.

Vernadsky, George, ed. *A Source Book for Russian History from Early Times to 1971.* Vol. 2. New Haven, Conn.: Yale University Press, 1972.

—Jane Graves

UNITED STATES–VIETNAM RELATIONS, 1945–1967 (*THE PENTAGON PAPERS*)

Commissioned by: U.S. Department of Defense
Original date and place of publication: 1971, United States
Publisher: U.S. Government Printing Office
Literary form: Nonfiction

SUMMARY

The publishing history of *The Pentagon Papers* deserves detailing. Initially, it was an extensive Defense Department study commissioned by Secretary of Defense Robert S. McNamara on June 17, 1967, and completed on January

15, 1969, a narrative of about 3,000 pages and about 4,000 pages of documents, totaling 47 volumes. On June 13, 1971, the *New York Times*, having secretly received a copy, began printing a series of nine sets of articles and supporting documents; interrupted by an extended court restraining order, the series was completed on July 5, 1971. Other newspapers, principally the *Washington Post*, but also the *Boston Globe*, the *Chicago Sun-Times*, the *St. Louis Post-Dispatch*, and the *Christian Science Monitor*, also published articles during this time.

On June 29, U.S. senator Mike Gravel of Alaska attempted to read portions of the Pentagon study into the *Congressional Record* from the Senate floor. When this tactic was unsuccessful because of a parliamentary maneuver, he achieved his goal through the Senate Subcommittee on Public Buildings and Grounds, of which he was chair.

The New York Times *Series*
While the government's challenge involved the entire set of narratives and documents in its attempt to retrieve the materials and retain their "top secret" designation, the immediate catalyst was the publication of summaries of portions of the study and related documents by the *New York Times*.

June 13, 1971: Two front-page pieces introduce the series. One describes the "Vietnam Archive," summarizes the broad conclusions of the study, from the initial involvement of the Truman administration to the build-up of American political, military, and psychological stakes leading to open warfare in 1965. The second details the origins and development of the report itself.

The substantive articles related to the Tonkin Gulf destroyer incident of August 1964. "The Covert War" reveals that for six months prior to the August incident, the U.S. government had operated an elaborate program of covert military operations, sabotage, commando raids, and destroyer patrols in the gulf against the state of North Vietnam. The intent was to force the Hanoi government to order the withdrawal of guerrillas through substantial destruction and psychological harassment. Prior to its onset, both the intelligence community and the Joint Chiefs of Staff gave this program little chance of success.

The progressive buildup of a take-charge and war mentality is expressed. These were fed by the perceived failure and inability of the South Vietnam government to control the Vietcong rebellion, which persisted in gaining strength. Administration leaders reacted strongly against a negotiated compromise political settlement or "neutralization" because either would signify a communist victory and signal the destruction of the American position in South Vietnam. President Lyndon Johnson is revealed as "pushing his Administration to plan energetically for escalation while . . . continually hesitating to translate these plans into military action." At the same time, he is perceived as "calculating international and domestic political conditions before making any of his moves in public." The underpinnings of these policy decisions were the "domino" theory, which predicted the fall of all Southeast Asia to communism one country at a time unless it was stopped; the threat of China; and the fear of loss of prestige and U.S. world dominance.

The planning of the bombing strategy and the government's political and psychological maneuvering blended in with the chain of events leading to the Tonkin Gulf incident. Public statements at the time by Secretary of State Rusk and Secretary of Defense McNamara obscured U.S. involvement in pre-incident attacks against North Vietnam. A significant outcome of the Tonkin event and the congressional and public discussions that ensued was the preparation of the American public for escalation, a major recommendation of a strategy conference the previous June.

June 14, 1971: The consensus to bomb North Vietnam was reached at a White House strategy meeting in September 1964 in concert with the emerging view that the war needed to be escalated if the situation was to be saved. Publicly Johnson (at the height of the presidential election contest) took a position of restraint, against enlarging the war. However, there is evident relentless progress toward a war mentality, expressed by the concept of "provocative strategy," provoking a response that would allow a retaliatory air attack. Evident also is a hardening of options: the elimination of "extreme withdrawal" and "fall back" positions; the rejection of tactics like a selective bombing campaign, which would lead to negotiations.

In late November a bombing strategy of "progressively more serious air strikes" was designed, yet the president was reassuring the press at a news conference that "speculating and taking positions" about expansion of the war were premature. Both the Joint Chiefs of Staff and the intelligence agencies dissented from this decision, the former advocating a willingness to apply unlimited force, the latter pessimistically not giving the plan "very strong chances for breaking the will of Hanoi." Reluctant to even hint at the existence of the plans as late as January 3, 1965, Secretary Rusk ruled out "either a U.S. withdrawal or a major expansion of the war." Two reprisal air strikes occurred on February 8 and 11. The order to begin sustained bombing was given on February 13.

June 15, 1971: The third set of articles expresses the decision of April 1, 1965, to launch a ground war using U.S. troops. This decision was tied to the recognition that the bombing strategy was not going to work. President Johnson ordered that this decision be kept secret, that subsequent increases in military support forces, initially 18,000–20,000 men, not receive premature publicity and that the "appearance of sudden changes in policy" be minimized. On July 17, "swiftly and in an atmosphere of crisis," President Johnson approved the deployment of 200,000 troops, as requested by General William C. Westmoreland.

These decisions were not without warnings of failure and recommendations against committing ground forces. Undersecretary of State George W. Ball "proposed that the United States 'cut its losses' and withdraw from South Vietnam." Director of Central Intelligence John A. McCone also warned against committing ground troops and becoming mired in jungle combat. On the other side were the many voices advocating a tough stand. President Johnson was responding to these and to the advice of General Westmoreland. The president publicly took a posture of compromise, but the offered conditions for peace were "more akin to a 'cease and desist' order," perceived by the North Vietnam government as a demand for surrender.

July 1, 1971: The focus of this day's articles dips back to the Kennedy administration, 1961–63. The study indicates that Kennedy shifted the direction and involvement of the Vietnam strategy from the "limited-risk gamble" of the Eisenhower administration to one of "broad commitment." The underlying objective was to prevent communist domination of South Vietnam. While Kennedy resisted pressures to commit ground-combat units, the number of troops was increased, initially by 500 on May 11, 1961, but up to 16,000 by the end of his 34 months in office; he also approved of covert operations involving U.S. military advisers. These commitments were not disclosed to the public. In taking these steps, Kennedy ignored the advice of the intelligence community, which was "conspicuously more pessimistic (and more realistic)" than other senior advisers. The Joint Chiefs of Staff, advocating a range of combat operations, estimated "a good chance of . . . arresting things and giving Diem a chance to do better and clean up. . . ."

According to the Pentagon's study, the Kennedy administration, despite its disavowal, "knew and approved of plans for the military coup d'etat that overthrew" the government of President Ngo Dinh Nhu on November 1–2, 1963. The study indicates that "Our complicity in his overthrow heightened our responsibilities and our commitment." There was internal friction in the administration—at least two officials recommended disengagement; however, the decision was made largely in recognition of the failures of Diem to control the country, manage the war effort, and achieve popular support through political, economic, and military reforms. Further, Washington was upset that Diem's promise of conciliatory actions toward Buddhists who protested religious persecution was repudiated by repeated brutalities. The study acknowledges that this was a "watershed" period for the United States when the Vietnam policy could have been reconsidered, even to the point of disengagement. Apparently, the direction chosen was a greater commitment to maintaining a noncommunist South Vietnam.

July 2, 1971: The mid-1965 to late 1966 period represented a rapid expansion of American forces, jumping incrementally from 175,000 men in June 1965 to 542,000 in June 1966. Neither the requests for troops nor the approvals of all but the last by President Johnson were made public. The build-up was based on a "colossal misjudgment" about the effect of the bombings on both the North Vietnam military capabilities and morale; it did not consider the "escalation reactions" of North Vietnam. The American military commanders were confident of victory, General Westmoreland pinning his expectations on "search-and-destroy strategy," taking "the war to the enemy, denying him freedom of movement anywhere in the country. . . ." A program of expanding the bombing, targeting oil tanks, was urged by the Joint Chiefs and, against a negative recommendation of the CIA, approved by President Johnson on June 22, 1966. However, civilian leaders, including Secretary of Defense Robert McNamara, began to reveal doubts as early as fall 1966 about both the effectiveness of the bombings and the ground war. By summer's end it was clear that, though the major oil storage capacity of North Vietnam had been destroyed, the enterprise had failed in its ultimate purposes: The bombing had not persuaded Hanoi to negotiate, nor had it limited Hanoi's ability to infiltrate men and supplies to the south.

July 3, 1971: The schism in the Johnson administration with regard to the conduct of the war deepened in the October 1966 to May 1967 period. The study identified three groups: the "disillusioned doves," the McNamara group, which tried to set limits on the war and then reduce it; the military group, urging the widening of the war; and, in the middle position, President Johnson along with senior civilian White House officials. Early in this period, McNamara, having recognized the failure of U.S. policy to produce both the necessary reforms and morale in South Vietnam and the military-psychological reversals to North Vietnam, recommended cutting back the bombing and seeking a political settlement; in May 1967, he advocated that the United States stop trying to guarantee a noncommunist South Vietnam and be willing to accept a coalition government that included the Vietcong. He wrote: "(1) Our commitment is only to see that the people of South Vietnam are permitted to determine their own future. (2) This commitment ceases if the country ceases to help itself." When General Westmoreland requested an additional 200,000 troops, President Johnson resisted, authorizing a 55,000-man increase, drawing the line at mobilization of reserve forces and reflecting on the concomitant increase in North Vietnam's forces. Johnson did side with the military in escalating the bombing. A proposal to reduce bombing did not reemerge until March 1968, several days after Secretary McNamara left office, opening the way toward the May negotiations in Paris.

July 4, 1971: The Tet Offensive occurred in February 1968. The turmoil at the front—for this North Vietnam offensive took the White House and Joint Chiefs by surprise (though this was denied)—was matched by the turmoil of the debate in February and March among advisers and among the public. According to the study, the president himself was severely shocked and disappointed because he had discounted negative analyses and attended to optimistic reports. The military's renewed requests for more troops to meet the offensive were heavily resisted by civilian advisers—only a 10,500-man contingent was authorized. A review of U.S. policy, led by Clark M. Clifford, secretary of defense-designate, concluded that sizable troop increases would not alter the course of the war; the group's recommendation, however, was a compromise. In conjunction, the CIA indicated that a bombing halt could result in Hanoi's offer to negotiate.

In his speech to the American people on March 31, 1968, President Johnson gave evidence that he had reversed the decisions to send 30,000 additional troops and to continue the bombing. He also announced he would not be a candidate for his party's nomination for president. The president's new strategy signaled a turn in policy on the road to peace; two considerations had fueled the decision: 1) additional troops "would not make a military victory any more likely; and 2) a deeply felt conviction of the need to restore unity to the American nation."

July 5, 1971: This final article returns to the 1945–60 period to reveal early policy decisions that set the stage and the commitments of the United States to Vietnam. The Truman administration initially rejected assistance to both the French and the Vietminh in their conflict but, on December 30, 1949, decided, after the takeover of mainland China by the Communists, to provide military aid to the French against the Communist-led Vietminh. Subsequently, the Eisenhower administration pledged to abide by the Geneva Accords of 1954 (though it had termed them a "disaster"); however, it approved actions, including the introduction of American troops, that had "a direct role in the ultimate breakdown of the Geneva settlement." Secret operations were already being conducted during the Geneva conference. Further, despite the recognition of the instability of Premier Diem's regime, his lack of support and his ineffectual measures to help the peasants, a decision was made to back him. The U.S. role in blocking the elections scheduled in the Geneva Accords or in being responsible for Diem's refusal to hold them is also questioned. The fear was that elections would lead to unification of the two Vietnams under Ho Chi Minh. But U.S. aid (almost entirely for security with minimal funds for community development, social welfare, health, and education) did not curb the North Vietnam insurgency.

CENSORSHIP HISTORY

The first articles and documents of the Pentagon study—what came to be known as the "Pentagon Papers"—were published by the *New York Times* on Sunday, June 13, 1971. There was no immediate reaction, but on the next day, U.S. attorney general John Mitchell requested that the *Times* voluntarily stop publishing and return the materials. The *Times* declined to accede to the request.

On Tuesday, July 15, the *Times*, upon the request of the government, was ordered by Federal District Court judge Murray I. Gurfein to halt publication for four days. (The third set of articles had appeared on this day.) The hearing on the government's civil suit to permanently enjoin the *Times* from further publication was set for Friday, June 18. On the succeeding day, Judge Gurfein refused to order the *Times* to return the report immediately; he indicated that temporary harm to the *Times* "far outweighed" the "irreparable harm that could be done to the interests of the United States." The *Times* had argued that the release of the documents would cause their source to be identifiable, because the copying machine could be traced, as could some handwriting. Instead, on July 17, a list of descriptive headings was submitted to the Justice Department.

At this stage, the gist of the government's argument was that the *Times* had violated a statute that made it a crime for persons who had unauthorized possession of government documents to disclose their contents when such disclosure "could be used to the injury to the United States or to the advantage of any foreign nation." The *Times* claimed that this antiespionage law was not intended by Congress to be used against newspapers; and that this was a classic case of censorship of the press, forbidden by the First Amendment.

On Friday, June 18, the Justice Department requested a restraining order against the *Washington Post*, which had initiated its series of articles on sections of the "Pentagon Papers" on the previous day. However, Judge Gerhard Gesell of the Federal District Court of the District of Columbia refused to grant even a temporary restraining order, claiming there was no evidence of a threat to national security. However, this decision was reversed on June 19 by a 2-1 circuit court of appeals vote that ordered Judge Gesell to hold a hearing on the government's request. The two judges supporting the government indicated that they had acted on the belief that "freedom of the press, important as it is, is not boundless." The third judge objected to the decision as a "suppression of one of our most important freedoms."

In the *New York Times* case, on June 18, Judge Gurfein extended the restraining order another day so he could come to a decision. At the hearing, the government argued that the *Times* had violated the law and presidential orders; by publishing secret documents the *Times* had declassified them and thus had "compromised our current military and defense plans and intelligence operations and [had] jeopardized our international relations." The *Times*'s position was that the government overclassified documents to hide embarrassing information and that the First Amendment forbids the executive and judicial branches of the government to use "national security" as a reason for censoring articles, except as they might reveal troop movements.

On June 19, Judge Gurfein announced his decision: He refused to enjoin the *Times* from publishing further articles based on the Pentagon study. His finding was that the government had failed to show harm to the national security to justify prior restraint. He noted, "The security of the nation is not on the ramparts alone. Security also lies in the value of our free institutions." However, Judge Irving Kaufman of the Court of Appeals of the Second Circuit extended the injunction against further publication, pending the government's appeal of the decision.

The *Washington Post* case also moved to the Court of Appeals of the District of Columbia after Judge Gesell's ruling on Monday, June 21, that the *Post* could resume publication. As had Judge Gurfein, he also found that the government had failed to show "an immediate grave threat to national security, which in close and narrowly defined circumstances would justify prior restraint on publication." He added, "it should be obvious that the interests of the Government are inseparable from the interests of the public, and the public interest makes an insistent plea for publication."

On June 22, the Justice Department requested and received a restraining order from Federal District judge Anthony Julian against the *Boston Globe*, which had published materials from the Pentagon study on this date.

Wednesday, June 23 was a day of conflicting decisions. Having first, on June 21, decided in New York that the cases were too significant to be heard by the usual three judge team, the full complement of court of appeals judges—eight in New York, nine in Washington—held hearings. However, while the District of Columbia Court of Appeals ruled on a 7-2 vote that the *Washington Post* had the "Constitutional right to publish," the Second Circuit Court of Appeals on a 5-3 decision permitted the *Times* to publish, but only those materials cleared by the government as not being dangerous to national security. The three dissenting judges voted to approve the decision of the district court. In this case, Judge Gurfein was instructed to hold hearings to determine which documents would "pose such grave and immediate danger to the security of the United States as to warrant their publication being enjoined."

The *Chicago Sun-Times* started publishing articles on June 23 based on the Pentagon study. However, the Justice Department did not take action to enjoin this newspaper, claiming the materials used had been declassified.

President Richard M. Nixon announced on June 23 that 47 volumes of the Pentagon study would be made available to Congress, but that the secret classification must be maintained, pending review of the documents by the executive branch. When delivered, the documents were placed in a vault.

After the *New York Times* and the Justice Department appealed their respective negative decisions on June 24, the Supreme Court agreed on June 25 to hear arguments. Four justices—Hugo L. Black, William O. Douglas, William J. Brennan, Jr., and Thurgood Marshall—dissented from this decision, voting instead to allow publication without a hearing.

The *New York Times* indicated it would not resume publishing under the authorized circumstances because its case was pending. To print articles defined as acceptable by the government would in effect be submitting to censorship. The *Washington Post* also indicated it would not resume publishing until the case was adjudicated. Chief Justice Warren E. Burger placed both papers on equal publication restraint, using the Second Circuit Court of Appeals ruling as the basis.

Though eight of 11 newspapers in the Knight Newspapers group (a newspaper chain mainly in the eastern third of the country) along with the *Los Angeles Times* began publishing features of the Pentagon study on June 24, the Justice Department did not attempt to enjoin them. The *St. Louis Post-Dispatch* was restrained by court order on June 26 after it initiated an article series. However, the *Christian Science Monitor* series, initiated on June 29, was not enjoined.

On Wednesday, June 30, the Supreme Court issued its 6-3 decision, upholding the right of the two newspapers to publish materials from the Pentagon study. The restraining orders against the *Boston Globe* and the *St. Louis Post-Dispatch* were immediately dissolved.

Within the broad assertion that any attempt to ban news articles prior to publication bears "a heavy presumption against its constitutionality. . . . the Government has not met that burden," the justices' opinions fell into three groups:

1. The absolutists (Hugo L. Black, William O. Douglas, and Thurgood Marshall)—The First Amendment forbids any judicial restraint: Justice Black indicated that a paramount responsibility of the free press "is the duty to prevent any part of the Government from deceiving the people and sending them off to distant lands to die of foreign fevers and foreign shot and shell. . . . far from condemnation [the newspapers] should be commended for serving the purpose that the Founding Fathers saw so clearly." Beyond this, Marshall argued that Congress had twice (1917 and 1957) considered and rejected such power for the courts; the Supreme Court would be "enacting law" if it had imposed restraint.

2. The middle position (William J. Brennan, Jr., Potter Stewart, and Byron White)—The press could not be blocked except to prevent direct, immediate, and irreparable harm; this material did not pose such a threat. White added, however, that he "would not have any difficulty in sustaining convictions" under the law even if the security threats did not justify prior restraint.

3. The dissenters (Warren E. Burger, John M. Harlan, and Harry E. Blackmun)—The courts should not refuse to enforce the executive branch's decision that the materials were confidential, affecting foreign policy; they also agreed with Justice White's position regarding convictions.

This case was significant beyond the immediate decision related to these documents and these two (or four) newspapers. It was the first time in the nation's history that a newspaper had been restrained by a court from publishing an article; it was, further, the first time the Supreme Court had ruled on a case of prior restraint of a newspaper by the government.

FURTHER READING

Butterfield, Fox. "Pentagon Papers: Eisenhower Decisions Undercut the Geneva Accords." *New York Times*, July 5, 1971, pp. 1, 13.

Graham, Fred P. "Court Denies U.S. an Injunction to Block *Times* Vietnam Series." *New York Times*, June 20, 1971, pp. 1, 26.

———. "Court Restrains the *Times* Again; A Hearing Today." *New York Times*, June 22, 1971, pp. 1, 18.

———. "Judge, at Request of U.S., Halts *Times* Vietnam Series Four Days Pending Hearing on Injunction." *New York Times*, June 16, 1971, p. 1.

———. "*Times* Asks Supreme Court to End Restraint on Its Vietnam Series." *New York Times*, June 25, 1971, pp. 1, 12.

———. "*Times* Case Heard, Restraint Extended; U.S. Action Halts a *Boston Globe* Series." *New York Times*, June 23, 1971, pp. 1, 22.

———. "*Times* Series Is Delayed Again; Paper to Appeal to High Court." *New York Times*, June 24, 1971, pp. 1, 16.

———. "*Times* Series Still Held Up Pending Court Ruling Today." *New York Times*, June 19, 1971, pp. 1, 11.

———. "Supreme Court Agrees to Rule on Printing of Vietnam Series, Arguments to Be Heard Today." *New York Times*, June 26, 1971, pp. 1, 10.

———. "Supreme Court, 6-3 Upholds Newspapers on Publication of the Pentagon Papers." *New York Times*, July 1, 1971, pp. 1, 15-19.

———. "U.S. Asking Court for Order to See *Times* Documents." *New York Times*, June 17, 1971, pp. 1, 18.

———. "U.S. Fails to Get Immediate Court Order to Force *Times* to Turn Over Documents." *New York Times*, June 18, 1971, pp. 1, 14.

Halloran, Richard. "Ruling for *Post*." *New York Times*, June 22, 1971, pp. 1, 27.

Naughton, James N. "Panel Backs *Washington Post*." *New York Times*, June 24, 1971, pp. 1, 16.

———. "*Post* Case Opinion." *New York Times*, June 20, 1971, pp. 1, 27.

———. "U.S. Loses in Move to Curb *Post*." *New York Times*, June 25, 1971, pp. 1, 13.

———. "*Washington Post* Restrained: Appeals Court Reversed Decision Favoring Paper." *New York Times*, June 19, 1971, pp. 1, 11.

Salter, Kenneth W. *The Pentagon Papers Trial.* Berkeley, Calif.: Justa Publications, 1975.

Shapiro, Martin. *The Pentagon Papers and the Courts.* San Francisco, Calif.: Chandler Publishing, 1972.

Sheehan, Neil, Hedrick Smith, E. W. Kenworthy, and Fox Butterfield. *The Pentagon Papers.* New York: Bantam Books, 1971.

Turner, Robert F. *Myths of the Vietnam War: The Pentagon Papers Reconsidered* (Southeast Asian Perspectives, #7). New York: American Friends of Vietnam, 1972.

Ungar, Sanford J. *The Papers and the Papers.* New York: E. P. Dutton, 1972.

THE VANĚK PLAYS

Author: Václav Havel
Original date and place of publication: 1978, Germany
Publisher: Rowohlt
Literary form: Drama

SUMMARY

Václav Havel's trio of plays, *Audience, The Unveiling (Vernisáž)*, and *Protest*, each focus on the same partly autobiographical character, Ferdinand Vaněk. (The original Czech version of the Vaněk character in *The Unveiling*, however, was Bedřich Frederich, but for the sake of uniformity and meaning, he is renamed.) The setting shifts—respectively, a brewery office, an apartment, an author's study—and the scenarios are individualized. There are, however, a few references to *Audience* in the other two plays. The plays are written in the Theatre of the Absurd dramatic form.

In *Audience*, Ferdinand Vaněk, dressed in a heavy workcoat and boots, enters the brewmaster's office and is invited to sit down and imbibe beer. Timid, he declines but is given a glass anyway. In response to Brewmaster's opening "Well? So how is it goin'?" Vaněk responds, "Fine, thank you —." Thereafter, the brewmaster converses; Vaněk responds briefly, mostly monosyllabically, for example: "Right," "Yes—," "I'm not down—."

Brewmaster raises the issue of trust several times, in essentially the same language, cautioning Vaněk: "If you don't mind me givin' you a little tip, I wouldn't wanna get too close to any of these people here—Me, I don't trust anybody! People are real assholes! Real assholes! You'd better believe it. So you just do your job—don't get into no deep discussions—that really ain't worth it—especially in your case—." Mid-play he admits that he has been deceived by another employee.

> You know what they did to me? They accused me of splitting five hundred barrels of lager—this surplus we had here—with this one restaurant manager. Ain't that something? The whole thing didn't happen that way at all of course, but this son of a bitch—this Mlynařik from fermenting upstairs—you know who I'm talkin' about?

He acknowledges his respect for Vaněk, given his significantly changed circumstances—"now outta the blue" from a stay-at-home writer to a barrel roller in a physically uncomfortable workplace. Yet, Vaněk does not shirk his tasks.

> It'll all be okay, Vaněk! Don't you worry, I won't let you down! You're a quiet, hardworking guy. You check in regular every day, don't talk crap like all the others, you don't beef about the pay—and condsiderin' the shortage of manpower, eh?

Brewmaster asserts that Vaněk can count on his standing by him. Vaněk's having been hired by Brewmaster is a matter of principle—Vaněk is "not some old sock." He offers Vaněk the possibility of a desk job, for which Vaněk expresses gratefulness, yet essentially asks for two favors: that Vaněk invite Bohdalová, a popular stage and television actress, to the brewery for some drinks; and against a backdrop warning, "They come here to ask about you—" and that he's "runnin' outta ideas about what to keep on tellin' em every damn week," so he asks Vaněk to record something about himself:

You're what they call an intellectual, right? You keep up with politics, don't you? You're writing stuff, ain't you? Who the hell should know whatever the fuck it is they wanna know if not you?

Brewmaster pleads in the context of their relationship: "Damn it, didn't we just finish sayin' that we're all in this together? That we gotta give each other a hand? That we're gonna be a team here? Didn't we just toast to that now? You tell me—did we or did we not just toast to that?" When Vaněk declines on principle—"I can't be snitchin' on myself," Brewmaster is shattered, accusing Vaněk of intellectual self-orientation. Seeming hysterical and isolated, without a future, his head on Vaněk's breast, he sobs. After a while, he falls asleep. Vaněk exits.

Soon, a knock on the door causes Brewmastser to wake up, sobered. Vaněk comes in, is invited to sit down, and to have a drink. This time, he accepts and in response to the question, "Well? So how is it goin'?" Vaněk responds, "Everything's all fucked up."

Three characters are featured in *Unveiling*. In addition to Ferdinand Vaněk, there is a married couple, Vera and Michael, who have completely redesigned their home's interior with a collection of eclectic eccentricities. Their best friend, Vaněk, is invited to the "unveiling" of their masterpiece setting which they've worked so hard to create. He arrives, a bouquet of flowers in hand.

The couple is determined to change the lives of Ferdinand and his wife Eva, to enhance their living conditions and behaviors, to cause them to become more like them. After each self-congratulatory episode, one or the other asserts to Ferdinand, who has little to say: "You don't like to talk about it, I know. But you know, Michael and I have been talking about the two of you lately; we've been thinking about you a lot—and we really care about how you live!"

Their advice ranges from furnishing decor—"When you have what we call a place with character, your whole life suddenly—like it or not—acquires a certain face, too—as sort of new dimension—a different rhythm, a different context, a different order"; cuisine—"an interesting dinner, some small gourmet surprise, . . . these represent a kind of cement that holds a family together"; raising a child—"You know a child really changes you a lot—suddenly you begin to understand everything differently, more deeply—life—nature—people—and all of a sudden your own life—like it or not—acquires sort of a new dimension—a different rhythm, a different content, a different order—."

Another feature of the couple's concern is the relationship of Ferdinand and Eva; they focus on sexual relationships, extolling their own, and assuming inadequacy of Ferdinand, they offer to demonstrate a sexual encounter so he can learn their techniques. Indeed, they initiate a demonstration, Michael having opened Vera's blouse, revealing her breasts.

Further, they are critical about Ferdinand's activities—his job at the brewery, which is beneath his abilities, given his proven talent as a writer and his basic intelligence. Ferdinand's statement, "I'm sorry, but it was the only thing I could do in my situation—" is essentially disregarded, that "if only you really wanted to and tried a little harder," he could get a job in an editorial office, Michael proclaims:

> Life is rough and the world is divided. The world doesn't give a damn about us and nobody's coming to our rescue—we're in a nasty predicament, and it will get worse and worse—and you are not going to change any of it! So why beat your head against the wall and charge the bayonets?

In the middle of this scolding dialogue, Vaněk prepares to leave, quietly edging toward the door. When they notice this, Vera and Michael become increasingly upset, first declaiming their noble intentions of trying to help their best friend, then Vera hysterically accuses him: "You're selfish! A disgusting, unfeeling, inhuman egotist! An ungrateful, ignorant traitor." She throws his bouquet at Vaněk as he's leaving. He doesn't leave; he picks up the flowers, hesitantly puts them back in the vase, and sits down.

Vera and Michael instantly take on their hospitable smiling personas—and the play begins again with the opening action. The curtain fall as music booms.

Whereas implications of political fallout in Vaněk's life are unstated, only subtly alluded to in the first two plays, *Protest* focuses on the political misuse of power. Two characters, Vaněk and Staněk, meet in the latter's well-appointed study. Acquaintances in the past, they've not been in contact; this meeting is instigated by Staněk, whose purpose is not immediately revealed.

Preliminary conversation does reveal several salient ideas. First, Staněk wonders if Vaněk was followed en route to his home; then, he asks Vaněk about prison life—was he beaten, drugged, given dubious injections? Vaněk, replying negatively, is rather noncommittal. Second, Staněk's character is exposed. It is clear from the relative opulence of his office and his work as a writer for television that he has opted out of political life. As he himself admits, he is "still tolerated by the official apparatus." He declares:

> It's disgusting, Ferdinand, disgusting! The nation is governed by scum! And the people? Can this really be the same nation which not very long ago behaved so magnificently? All that horrible cringing, bowing and scraping?

The selfishness, corruption and fear wherever you turn! What have they made of us, old pal? Can this really be us?

He applauds the activities of Vaněk and other writers—"all the protests, petitions—the whole fight for human rights!" He continues:

> It's extremely important there should be at least a few people here who aren't afraid to speak the truth aloud, to defend others, to call a spade a spade! What I'm going to say might sound a bit solemn perhaps, but frankly, the way I see it, you and your friends have taken on an almost superhuman task: to preserve and to carry the remains, the remnant of moral conscience through the present quagmire! The thread you're spinning may be thin, but—who knows—perhaps the hope of a moral rebirth of the nation hangs on it.

Yet, despite his applause and solemn concern, he prefers not to be so exposed. Which leads to the raison d'être of the invitation to Vaněk: the arrest of Javirek, a pop singer, presumably for telling an unacceptable story during one of his performances. Staněk has been trying through "private intervention" to get him released. Perhaps not coincidentally, his daughter has been impregnated by him. Since his tactic has not worked, he wonders if a protest or a petition might; he seeks Vaněk's experienced help. Vaněk produces a protest document from his briefcase with some fifty signatures; after some hesitation, he asks Staněk to add his signature.

Staněk declines. His reasoning is intricate. On the positive side, if he adds his signature, he will regain his self-esteem, his lost freedom, his honor, and he will gain the regard of members of his family. On the negative side, he will lose his job and standard of living, and his son will not be able to continue his education. Further, his signature will call attention to him and away from Javirek, perhaps to the pop singer's disadvantage.

The denouement brings two surprises. During a brief contretemps between the two men about moral superiority, Staněk reveals, "Well! As far as I know, in prison you talked more than you should have." Vaněk, shocked and embarrassed, "jumps up, wildly staring at Staněk, who smiles triumphantly." The phone rings. Vaněk listens to the telephone conversation. Javirek has been released. Private intervention did work. A protest letter might have caused an opposite response.

There are meaningful parallels among these three plays, notably the character of Vaněk, whose hesitant demeanor and minimalist linguistic responses suggest, at least, discomfort and defensiveness but might in a larger sense suggest symbolic language repression. He is essentially passive. Yet, each of the plays offers a glimpse of resistance to overpowering circumstances: in *Audience*, Vaněk's rejection of "snitchin' on myself" and his closing line; in *The Unveiling*, his mild attempt to defend his life with Eva, totally rejected or ignored by his friends; and in *Protest*, the protest document and the request for a signature. The straitjacket quality of these situations suggests constraints on Vaněk's life.

The repetitive structure and language, features of the theatre of the absurd, further limit—if any—control by the characters, a dependence on the same words and phrases, especially evident in Brewmaster and Vera and Michael; they deserve Vaněk's noncommittal responses. The endings of these plays simply announce a return to the opening. Both plays, thus, reveal the emptiness of these characters' lives, despite the self-congratulatory protestations of Vera and Michael. They, in this context, reveal a focus on materialistic values, given the selection and collection of eclectic artifacts.

Staněk, in *Protest*, signifies this choice for comfort, monetary success, and safety over the taking an ethical stance both in the life he leads and his political decision not so sign the protest document. He is safe in his affluent home, as are his children, despite—or so he claims—his "bitter awareness that I've again—who knows, perhaps for the last time—missed a chance to shake off the bonds of shameless compromises in which I've been choking for years."

CENSORSHIP HISTORY

Although his pre–Prague Spring (1968) plays had been critical of society—*The Garden Party* (1963), a satire of modern bureaucratic routines, and *The Increased Difficulty of Concentration*, an attack on fashionable sociological terminology—Václav Havel did not draw overt attention from censors until the Soviet Union and its Warsaw Pact allies, reacting to the freedom orientation of the Prague Spring, invaded and occupied Czechoslovakia in 1968.

In 1968, the playwright was criticized by the Soviet trades union newspaper, *Trud*, for advocating the depolitization of the Czechoslovak Union of Writers. *Trud* interpreted this as calling for "full freedom for any views, including anti-socialist ones, and no obligation on writers to defend proletarian ideology."

During the Warsaw Pact invasion, Havel commented on the events on Radio Free Czechoslovakia. As part of the suppression of Prague Spring, his plays were banned from performance and publication. His passport was confiscated. His plays were produced elsewhere, in New York, for example, but he was barred from traveling to see them. He continued to write; in the 1970s he wrote a series of one-act plays, among them the Vaněk plays. Without access to a stage, his plays were circulated in samizdat form (that is, disseminated outside officially sanctioned channels) across Czechoslovakia, thus solidifying his reputation as a leading revolutionary. They were also circulated in Western Europe.

Havel was cofounder and spokesman of Charter 77, a human rights manifesto, the catalyst of which was the arrest and imprisonment of members of the Czech psychedelic band, the Plastic People, for political reasons. The manifesto urged the Czech government to abide by the basic human rights established by the Final Act of the 1975 Helsinki Agreement. It was signed by 243 prominent Czech intellectuals. Havel also cofounded the Committee for the Defense of the Unjustly Persecuted in 1979.

These activities led to constant surveillance and harassment by the government. Sometimes his visitors were harassed. He was arrested and imprisoned in 1997, the first time, and multiple times subsequently. His longest incarceration for subversion of the republic was four-and-a-half years, from June 1979 to January 1984 (though he was released in 1983 because of illness). One four-month stretch was served in a cell 12 feet by seven feet, which he shared with a burglar. His last internment, four months of a scheduled eight, was in 1989 for participating in a flower-laying ceremony in memory of a student who had set himself afire to protest the 1968 invasion.

FURTHER READING

Dawisha, Karen. *The Kremlin and the Prague Spring*. Berkeley: University of California Press, 1984.
Esslin, Martin. "The Theatre of the Absurd." In *Essays in the Modern Drama*, edited by Morris Freedman. Boston: D.C. Heath and Company, 1964.
Goetz-Stankiewicz, Marketa. *The Silenced Theatre: Czech Playwrights Without a Stage*. Toronto: University of Toronto Press, 1979.
Goetz-Stankiewicz, Marketa, ed. *The Vaněk Plays: Four Authors, One Character*. Vancouver: University of British Columbia Press, 1987.
Henry, William A., III, and William Maden. "Vaclav Havel: Dissident to President." *Time*, January 8, 1990.
Zeman, Z. A. B. *Prague Spring*. New York: Hill and Wang, 1969.

WAITING

Author: Ha Jin
Original date and place of publication: 1999, United States
Publisher: Pantheon Books
Literary form: Novel

SUMMARY

Set in China, *Waiting* spans about 21 years, from 1964 to 1985, in the life of Lin Kong, a medical officer. The novel is not plot driven; it follows his life shortly after his arranged marriage in 1963 and the birth of his daughter, through a divorce, and then a remarriage.

A model officer and a respected doctor, Lin is acknowledged for his kindness and thoughtfulness, his willingness to treat even common blisters. He is proud, sensitive about his image, and conscious of his status and of meeting Communist Party standards. When he first met his fiancée after the arranged marriage had been accomplished, he was dismayed by her appearance— old-looking with wrinkled and leathery skin—and her bound feet: "This was the New China; who would look up to a young woman with bound feet?" His shame is such that for two decades he had never let her visit him at the army hospital and after the birth of their daughter had slept in a separate room when at home.

In 1966, when he is about 30 years old, a major change begins in Lin's simple and peaceful life. Mannu Wu, a nurse in her mid-20s, instigates a relationship, which shifts, principally through her overtures, from friendship to a platonic romance and commitment. His yearly efforts to gain a divorce fail, the court ruling against him until the mandated 18-years-of-separation waiting period was over. The intervening years are fraught with emotional turmoil: He is intermittently indecisive and anxious, and his doubts about his love increase over time; Mannu, lonely, impatient, frustrated, becomes conscious of aging. At last married, Mannu is soon pregnant and in the eighth month has a difficult delivery of twin boys. She is diagnosed with a heart condition and is unable to care for the children, a situation that causes stress, extreme weariness, and a near collapse of the couple's relationship. The novel concludes on a bittersweet note.

Their lives are beset by regulations and prohibitions. Prominent in this novel are the rules affecting personal relationships. "According to the army hospital's rule, established by Commissar Wang in the winter of 1958, it was only after eighteen years' separation that an officer could end his marriage without his wife's consent." In his quest for a divorce, Lin Kong is berated by judges as "immoral and dishonorable" as a revolutionary officer and a poor model for civilians. Hospital regulations also prohibited a man and a woman on the staff from walking together outside the compound unless they were married or engaged to prevent "abnormal," that is, sexual, activity; they could eat together in the mess hall. To have dinner in a restaurant in town required permission from the vice director of the hospital's Political Department, but a third person had to be present. In this vein, student nurses could not have boyfriends. Only officers, not enlisted men, could have girlfriends. If an illicit love affair was discovered, or even suspected, punishment was likely: discharge from the military and, perhaps, banishment to work in the interior of China.

Place of residence is also proscribed, as is work assignment. In order for Lin's ex-wife and his daughter, Hua, to move to the city, permission had to be granted. A young officer, assigned by the Political Department, dealt with the district police in charge of the residential registry. He also conducted arrangements for Hua's employment in the city, the leaders having agreed to this transfer. There are other examples in the text of needing to gain permission to work in a city, apparently a preferred location.

The army hospital's Political Department acts also as a censorship agency, ordering the staff to hand in all books containing "bourgeois ideology and sentiments, particularly those by foreign authors." The hospital's small library collection is limited to political and medical science books: "the two dozen novels and plays it had once owned had been surrendered to the bonfires built by the Red Guards before the city hall." In a parallel act, the Red

Guards are also identified as "smashing temples and abbeys throughout the country, and monks and nuns had been either sent back home or banished far away, so they might make an honest living like the masses."

Other features of the novel may be perceived as potentially detrimental to the "New China" image. In 1988, given a top general's order, to "carry on the spirit of the Long March and restore the tradition of horses and mules," the army trains to be able to operate without modern vehicles; for a month a third of the hospital staff would march 400 miles through the countryside. Along the way they would practice treating the wounded and rescuing the dying from the battlefield. The army is also depicted as a marriage broker, locating available women as potential wives for generals and commissars. It is reported that an officer, a regimental commander, detained a young woman journalist in his barracks because he wanted to spend a week with her. And a battalion commander, befriended by Lin in the hospital, brutally rapes Mannu during Lin's absence, proving his manliness and how to handle women, in contrast to Lin, who had not ever slept with her.

The medical situation is also lacking. In the mid-1960s the hospital had only four medical school graduates on its staff, the rest of the 70 doctors having been trained by the army itself through short-term courses and experiences on battlefields. Further, technology in use in Europe that would mitigate Mannu's heart condition and lengthen her life is not available in China. A folk remedy is successful in curing the twins' acute dysentery when medically prescribed treatments had failed.

Toward the end of the novel, a TV report, "To Get Rich Is Glorious," featured individuals who had become affluent after adopting capitalist practices, having responded to the Communist Party's call. Making money was no longer illegal. One of the individuals interviewed is the former battalion commander who had raped Mannu. On the air he admitted to earning 20,000 yuan the previous year, 20 times the amount he paid his workers.

CENSORSHIP HISTORY

In 2000, the publication of *Waiting* in China by the government-owned Beijing Publishing Group was in the preparation stage, a translation half completed, when a harsh attack in a Beijing literary review, *Chinese Reading News*, June 14, 2000, denounced the work. The essay, written by a Beijing University literature professor with a Ph.D. from the University of Chicago, charged Ha Jin with attempting to portray China's backwardness and the "stupidity of the Chinese People." Jin had "cursed his own compatriots and become a tool used by the American media to vilify China." Specific features criticized were the depiction of the "extremely rustic peasant with bound feet," the resistance of fellow villagers to Lin's request for divorce, which the reviewer interpreted as showing that "Chinese do not appreciate love," and the single braid of hair featured on the cover of the U.S. edition, interpreted as a male pigtail, a symbol of the feudal era. The American press and critics who praised the book were also attacked. Subsequent to this critical essay, other newspapers followed suit with negative reviews. The Chinese publication was canceled.

Jin responded to these attacks by claiming his novel is a work of literature and not a "disguised polemic." He asserted, "It's about the human heart, about human flaws and the sinister nature of time." The bound feet of Lin's wife, based on a real-life story he had heard years before, inspired the novel.

While the chief editor of Beijing Publishing Group claimed that the decision not to publish *Waiting* was a coincidence rather than a response to an official request, news reports noted both the "near-universal shunning" of the novel by the Chinese media and the Chinese government's campaign, apparently initiated in early 2000, against works of fiction as well as books on politics and history that do not portray China in the way Beijing would like, both to its own people and to foreign readers. President Jiang Zemin, in June 2000, asserted, "Some party members and cadres are openly expressing opposition in newspapers, books and speeches to the party line. Such opposition must be stopped." The media "shunning" noted above is interpreted as the Communist Party's propaganda department, which controls all publications, having ordered the silence. Jin indicated that some Chinese reporters told him that they had been ordered not to write about the book.

Jin, a one-time soldier in the Chinese army, moved to the United States in 1985 and received a Ph.D. in literature from Brandeis University. He chose not to return to China in 1989 after the violent crackdown on democracy campaigners and was denounced for his support of prodemocracy demonstrations.

Waiting was honored by the U.S. National Book Award in 1999 and the PEN/Faulkner Award in 2000.

FURTHER READING

Eckholm, Erik. "After an Attack, Chinese Won't Print Expatriate's Novel." *New York Times*, June 24, 2000, p. B9.

O'Donnell, Lynn. "China's Doctor Zhivago Out in Cold." *Australian*, July 3, 2000, p. 13.

WHY ARE WE IN VIETNAM?

Author: Norman Mailer
Original date and place of publication: 1967, United States
Publisher: G. P. Putnam's Sons
Literary form: Novel

SUMMARY

Allegory has never been the most popular approach for a novelist to take. Bunyan's *Pilgrim's Progress* is probably the best-known example, along with medieval plays like *Everyman*. But in his 1967 novel, *Why Are We in Vietnam?* Norman Mailer uses allegory to argue that the American way of thinking is largely responsible for the prosecution of that war.

Ostensibly a story mostly dealing with a hunting trip in Alaska, Mailer uses what he calls a "stream of conch" approach to tell his tale. His main character and narrator is an 18-year-old Texan named D. J. Jethroe, who claims that he may be a white boy from Texas or an old black man from Harlem, tape recording his brain in an effort to fool God. D. J. "has ideas like nobody else" and "sees right through shit," although he continues to assert that he may be dealing us nothing but a fantasy. We are also told, ad infinitum, that D. J. is a genius.

Mailer's use of language relies on rhyme. slang, and a lot of swearing. He discusses racism, the sex life of his main character's parents, his best friend's father's fondness for masturbation, and D. J. and his friends' indulgences in anal and group sex; he almost continuously directly insults the intelligence of the reader in comparison to the narrator's own genius.

Mailer creates a sense of competition throughout the book. D. J.'s best friend is "Tex" Hyde; the two young men compete with each other while also sharing an unexpressed homoerotic attraction for each other. Of even more importance is D. J.'s competition with his father, Rusty. Years before, while playing football in the backyard, D. J. mistakenly had taken his father's challenge and humiliated the older man by running around him again and again. Finally, his father was able to tackle D. J., and he bit him on his backside. Now moving slowly because of the bite, D. J. is tackled, repeatedly and with great violence, by his father. At the conclusion of their "game," D. J. takes a pickax and hits his father on the head before running away from home for a week.

The background of all this is delivered in a rambling monologue that alternates between "Chaps" (chapters) and "Intro Beeps." We discover that Rusty is an executive for Central Consolidated Combined Chemical and Plastic, a company that added the "Combined" when it realized that, without the extra "C," their abbreviation would match that used in Russia for the Soviet Union. Rusty is a member of the Republican Party, the FBI, the RELM Cons ("the Rotary, Elks, Lambs, Masons Consolidated for corporation studs who jes ain't got the time to spread out so they put it all in one dead fuck building") and "the John Birch, natch." Rusty asserts his power over his flunkies, Medium Asshole Bill and Medium Asshole Pete. These men have the obligation, as far as the hunting trip goes, to back up Rusty in his desire to get bragging rights from the trip.

So Rusty, D. J., Tex, and the two Medium Assholes fly up to Alaska. There they are met by their hunting guide, Big Luke Fellinka. Luke tries to persuade Rusty that conditions simply aren't right for hunting a bear, but Rusty will not be dissuaded. Luke quickly learns that these men are in the hunt for all of the wrong reasons: They want to kill without a real risk of being killed; they want to be able to boast to their buddies (who are also their competitors in machismo); they want to kill to feel more in control of their own lives. Mailer thus initiates use of the hunt as allegory, showing that these men are the kinds of men who want to be in Vietnam so that they can boast and kill and show their "manliness" to the rest of the world.

Although the hunt begins well, with Tex cleanly shooting a wolf, events rapidly deteriorate. Chap Five gives an insight into the minds of the hunting party—it is all about their guns and what the guns can do. Significantly, Rusty has at least five guns. This description is filled with talk of what explosive power the guns have; again, the analogy compares "guns" with the military's slang use of that word as a synonym for the penis.

Medium Asshole Pete wounds a caribou but does not do a good enough job for the animal to die quickly, so they must track it and resort to using helicopters ("Cop Turds," in D. J.'s terms). Since Vietnam was well known as a war in which the innocent were often shot from helicopters, the analogy begins to take a sharper focus. When the animal is finally brought down, Big Luke cooks it for lunch. The meal is not pleasant, "it tasted loud and clear of nothing but fresh venison steeped in bile, shit, and the half-digested contents of the caribou's stomach—it was so bad you were living on the other side of existence, down in poverty and stink wallow with your nose beneath the fever—that was Luke's message to us."

But the message is lost on Rusty. As he ruminates on his desire to kill a bear, Rusty thinks, "Communism is going to defeat capitalism, unless properly destroyed. . . . the great white athlete is being superseded by the great black athlete. . . . the Jews run the Eastern wing of the Democratic party. . . . he, Rusty, is fucked unless he gets that bear, for if he don't, white men are fucked more and they can take no more."

Unfortunately for him, Pete kills a bear before Rusty does. Now Rusty's bloodlust is stirred even higher. He and D. J. break off from the rest of the group. They share a rare moment of intimacy and real talk. Rusty even apologizes to D. J. for not being around more often and for not being a better father. In both a literal and metaphoric sense, "D. J. can get familiar with Rusty's breath which is all right." They are hunting as father and son and as man and man. They finally spot a bear and bring it down. But while it is D. J. who makes the killing shot, when they return to camp, he refuses to take the credit, and Rusty abstains from setting the record straight. "Whew. Final end of love of one son for one father."

Without real fathers to love, D. J. and Tex head off into the woods alone. Again, the analogy suggests that the young men who volunteer to fight in Vietnam may have something to prove. D. J. and Tex strip themselves of their weapons and their civilization. Lying next to each other, both realizing that they want to have sex with the other, they divert their energies to cutting open their skin and letting their blood mingle. They become "blood brothers . . . killing brothers." They deny a chance at life and choose to follow a way of death instead. "God was a beast, not a man, and God said, 'Go out and kill—fulfill my will, go and kill.' " They follow this commandment. On the very last page of the novel D. J. and Tex are "off to see the wizard in Vietnam . . . Vietnam, hot damn."

CENSORSHIP HISTORY

The censorship history of this book raises interesting issues. *Why Are We in Vietnam?* has been kept out of libraries more by acts of omission than by commission. *Newsletter on Intellectual Freedom* reported that the book was not stocked on library shelves in Wilmington, North Carolina, even though board members had not read it; they reacted mainly on the basis of reviews. Christopher B. Deran, the director of the library, explained, "it wasn't just the words. The whole book has no valid purpose. It is a bad novel." *Why Are We in Vietnam?* was also refused by public libraries in New York, Baltimore, and the Washington, D.C., area. In Prince Georges County (near Washington), the Book Evaluation Committee stated that "a) The few sections that have good writing do not add to or have a place in the story. b) The story line gets submerged in a cess-pool [sic] of irrelevant vulgarity. c) Mailer's reputation as 'one of America's major writers' is hardly enhanced by this nonsense."

Newsletter on Intellectual Freedom also reported that the libraries in Fairfax, Virginia, and Montgomery, Alabama, refused to stock *Why Are We in Vietnam?* In Montgomery, the library claimed that "the decision was not related to Mailer's political activities," and noted that the book was not needed as the library already had a balance between pro– and anti–Vietnam War sentiments. Procensorship advocates such as Phyllis Schlafly have long argued that libraries need to avoid "unbalancing" the marketplace of ideas, as well as contending that selection itself is not censorship. These libraries seem to have agreed with her in the case of Mailer's novel.

However, the history of censorship for *Why Are We in Vietnam?* is not entirely a case of refusing to select the book. In Huntsville, Alabama, assistant city attorney E. Cantley Cooper requested that the book be removed from the public library's shelves. The library's director, Richard Covey, initially assumed that the request had been an official one and so complied. It turned out that Cooper had been acting as a private citizen, although the mayor and the city attorney also subsequently supported the removal. None of these three men had ever read the book. Fortunately, as *Library Journal* records, Covey was able to return *Why Are We in Vietnam?* to the shelves, thanks in large part to local support. The library board members rallied behind him, agreeing that the city did not have the right (especially in an unofficial action) to censor them. Letters to the editor and editorials in the *Huntsville Times* also gave backing to Covey to stand up to the city.

It is true, as many of these librarians claimed, that reviews of *Why Are We in Vietnam?* were not uniformly positive. Biographers of Mailer point out that even while some saw the novel as a brilliant allegory, the general critical reaction was unfavorable, while Peter Manso notes that *Why Are We in Vietnam?* may have been "the most obscene book ever written in American fiction." It also seems as though Mailer himself did not regard the efforts at censorship as particularly serious; he may have written the novel only to discharge his publishing contract with Putnam, and he had already begun working on other projects.

At the least, it is interesting that so many libraries acted on the advice of reviews or personal opinions of board members. As one dissenting voice noted, *any* writing at that time by Mailer was "an important literary event."

FURTHER READING

"Huntsville (Alabama) Public Library Rocked by Mailer Book." *Library Journal* (January 15, 1968): 138.
Manso, Peter. *Mailer: His Life and Times.* New York: Simon and Schuster, 1985.
Mills, Hilary. *Mailer: A Biography.* New York: Empire Books, 1982.
Newsletter on Intellectual Freedom 17 (1968): 1–3, 19.

—Mitchell Fay
University of Wisconsin–River Falls

A WOMAN IN BERLIN: EIGHT WEEKS IN THE CONQUERED CITY

Author: Anonymous
Original dates and places of publication: 1954, United States; 1959 (German edition), Switzerland
Publishers: Harcourt Brace; Kossodo
Literary form: Diary

SUMMARY

Friday, April 20, 1945, 4:00 P.M. The anonymous diarist (hereafter "She") begins her memoir with sounds of war in the background, yesterday's "distant rumble," today "a constant roar." The Russian invasion is thus forewarned, an outcome never anticipated when the war started. There is little news. She has been bombed out of her apartment and is living in a borrowed one out of her suitcase. Food is scarce; hunger is a constant. Electricity and running water are erratic—soon to disappear altogether. At night, the building's residents huddle in the basement shelter, protection from air raids, and later, briefly, from the Russians.

The atmosphere is fraught with despair and fear. "My sole concern as I write these lines is my stomach. All thinking and feeling, all wishes and hopes begin with food." Three early contrasting scenes illuminate the situation, the first of soldiers: "I stood in the doorway and watched some soldiers pass by our building, listlessly dragging their feet. Some were limping. Mute, each man to himself, they trudged along, out of step, toward the city. Stubbly chins and sunken cheeks, their backs weighted down with gear. . . . They all seem so miserable, so little like men anymore. The only thing they inspire is pity, no hope or expectation." Another scene: the discovery of food in the former police barracks, recently used by the Luftwaffe; a frantic mass in the pitch-black basement shoving, shouting, grabbing what they could find. Plunder—and anger. The author's apartment destroyed by a bomb, She moves in with the widow.

April 27 is the "day of catastrophe." The Russians have arrived, have taken over the street—troops, horses, vehicles—initially seeming friendly. Soon, since She knows a rudimentary Russian, having traveled to Russia, She is called upon to intercede in behalf of two women being molested. Though She manages to save them, She becomes a victim. Caught in a dark corridor, She is raped by two soldiers, twice each. Then, shortly thereafter back in her apartment, hemmed in by four soldiers, She is raped by one of them, who, asserting ownership, briefly becomes her protector against the others. But the next day another rapes her, an older man who spits in her mouth. She determines to find a protector, an officer who would, by rank, shield her from others. In effect, She gives herself to him, becoming his property. Anatole, a lieutenant, the chosen one, dispels other "suitors" and brings food and drinks. So begins a way of life. When his unit is repositioned, he is replaced by the major.

Few women escape these assaults—even grandmothers. Young girls, virgins, were concealed in false ceilings. Others used the same tactic as the author. One detailed event reveals the abuse of Elvira, a redhead who was hiding in a liquor distillery. She and the widow climb up to the fifth floor apartment to which Elvira had escaped

"They lined up," [the distiller's] wife whispers to us, while the redhead stays silent. "Each took his turn. She says there were at least twenty, but she doesn't know exactly. . . ." I stare at Elvira. Her swollen mouth is sticking out of her pale face like a plum. "Show them," says the distiller's wife. Without a word the redhead opens her blouse and shows us her breasts, all bruised and bitten. I can barely write this; just thinking about it makes me gag all over again.

Berlin is covered with a blanket of fear among the women and an accompanying deep sense of despondency.

In contrast, the Russian soldiers, speak of German atrocities on the eastern front. On April 27, when the German women ask an officer to protect them, he cites a Stalin decree, but one of the men being reprimanded "voices his objection, his face twisted in anger: 'What do you mean? What did the Germans do to our women?' He was screaming. 'They took my sister and . . .' and so on." Another brutality is revealed in a May 5 conversation between two German women protected it seems by the presence of two young children, an infant and a four-year old, and two young soldiers, clearly enchanted by the children. One of them, a 17-year old "looks at [the author], brow deeply furrowed, and asks me to translate that in his village German soldiers stabbed some children to death and took others by the feet and bashed their heads against a wall. Before I translate, I ask, 'Did you hear that? Or see it yourself?" He gazes off and says in a stern voice, 'I saw it twice myself.' I translate."

Distinctions among the Russians are identified. As contrasts to the brutal, lewd men who force themselves on the women and even Lieutenant Anatole, a peasant and somewhat refined, we are introduced to an intellectual sergeant, a schoolteacher by profession and an orthodox marxist; his conversations are political and economic. Another, Anatole's orderly, solicitous and linguistically sophisticated, discusses Pushkin. Having been rejected by the author, his advances were made during Anatole's absence. Another lieutenant is "distant and formal and flawlessly polite."

Aiming to replace Anatole in the author's bed, the major is discreet, politely cautious. "He speaks a sophisticated Russian: as always I can tell by the fact that whole sentences go by without my understanding a word. He seems to be well read and quite musical, and he's clearly taking pains to behave like a gentleman even now." During their first intercourse, when She complains of being miserable and sore, he is gentle and silently tender. He wants her to join him in Russia.

Early in the diary, an April 26 entry, She notes how her attitudes—and those of other women—and interpretation of men are changing.

> These days I keep noticing how my feelings toward men—and the feeling of all the other women—are changing. We feel sorry for them; they seem so miserable and powerless. The weaker sex. Deep down we women are experiencing a kind of collective disappointment. The Nazi world—ruled by men, glorifying the strong man—is beginning to crumble, and with it the myth of "Man." In earlier wars men could claim the privilege of killing and being killed for the fatherland was theirs and theirs alone. Today we women, too, have a share. That has transformed us, emboldened us. Among the many defeats at the end of this war is the defeat of the male sex.

She notes her prewar instinct with German men to "play down my intelligence for them" because a German man wants to be smarter.

The reactions of German men to the abuse of their wives was "reasonable—they react with their heads, they're worried about saving their own skins, and their wives support them in this. No man loses face for relinquishing a woman to the victors. . . . On the contrary, they would be censured if they provoked the Russians by resisting. The husband of the author's friend so acted but "torment[ed] himself with reproach" for not interceding when "the Ivans took their pleasure with his wife." He was "within hearing range."

Two exceptions to this reasonable code are represented. When a Russian attacked the bookseller's wife, her husband yelled at him, running toward him with "red-eyed wrath," thus causing the Russian to back off. Another husband, whose wife had drunk and slept with the same Russian several times, shot her in the back and then shot himself in the mouth.

While not a constant commentary, the flaws of the Nazi regime are frequently enough expressed to assert a position. Early in the diary, on April 23, She reflects on the government's abandonment of the civilians:

> There were rolls at the baker's, the last ones. My last ration cards for bread, too. No new cards in sight. No decrees and no news, either. Nothing. Not a soul cares about us anymore. We're suddenly mere individuals, no longer members of the tribe, the German Nation. Old ties are broken; friendships don't extend farther than three buildings away. There's only the group of us, huddled in the cave, a clan, just like in prehistoric times. The horizon has shrunk to three hundred paces.

On May 8, Herr Pauli, the widow's tenant, curses the government about the *Volksturm* [People's militia] "senselessly" sending old, tired men "to die at the last moment . . . just left to bleed to death, helpless with not even a rag to dress their wounds." A reference to Göering, reported as crying like a child upon his arrest, identifies him as "a colossus with feet of clay." In reacting on May 17 to a former Nazi party boss having been denounced and picked up, She reflects, "We have mixed feelings, talking about this. A bit of *schadenfreude* [taking joy in other's suffering] cannot be denied. The Nazis were too pompous and subjected the *volk* to too many harassments, especially in the last few years, so it's right that they should atone for the general defeat."

The shortage of food—hunger—is introduced on April 20 and persists throughout the eight weeks, excepting the two weeks when her Russian protectors are also providers and when She, as a drafted laborer along with other women, is fed a hearty barley soup. There are days when She and the widow lived solely on bread or nettles or a thin flour soup. Throughout the post-Army period, women are described as gaunt and hollow-eyed; on June 11, She notes, "I was very low on energy; my diet has no fat. There's always this wavy mist in front of my eyes, and I feel a floating sensation, as if I were getting lighter and lighter."

Throughout her diary, She contemplates her situation and herself: "I'm constantly repulsed by my own skin. I don't want to touch myself, can barely look at my body . . . and all for the filth I am now" (April 29). After the departure of the lieutenant and the appearance of the major, she writes, "I cannot force myself into this role, to feel at ease so quickly. I have this repulsive sense of being passed from hand to hand; I feel humiliated and insulted, degraded into a sexual thing" (May 2). When both the lieutenant and the major are on the scene, She is apprehensive: "What am I supposed to do? I'm nothing but booty-prey that has to stand back and let the hunters decide what to do with their game and how to parcel out" (May 4). "Sleeping for food is another new concept. . . ." (May 16). She also recognizes her growing resilience and strength: "On the other hand, things are looking pretty good for me. I'm healthy and refreshed. Nothing has harmed me physically. I feel extremely well armed for life. . . . I'm well equipped for the world" (May 13).

On June 16, Gerd, the author's fiancé, returns from the front in civilian dress and suntanned and bearing food; he had simply left the army. She was "feverish with joy." The relationship sours: He does not understand her unwillingness to share food with his guests. He responds negatively to her stories of her experiences, becoming angry. "You've all turned into a bunch of shameless bitches, everyone of you in the building. Don't you realize?" He grimaced in disgust. "It's horrible being around you. You've lost all sense of measure." He read her diary; when she translated her shorthand "*schdg*" as *schändung*" (rape), he "looked at me as if I were out of my mind but said nothing more." The next day he left to visit a buddy's parents and would return with food. The diary ends a page later.

By the conclusion of the diary in mid-June, some semblance of order and normality had been achieved. Running water and electricity had been restored to the apartment on May 19 and May 27 respectively. Germany had surrendered; peace had been declared. Germany had been divided into sectors, and on June 10, 1945, it was announced that Berlin, too, would be divided among the three allies. On June 15, the radio broadcasts another concentration camp report. Some rations were being distributed. Walking through the streets seemed safe. Yet, "everywhere you turn you can sense the fear. People are worrying about their bread, their work, their pay, about the coming day. Bitter, bitter defeat."

CENSORSHIP HISTORY

The republication in 2003 after 50 years of A *Woman in Berlin: Eight Weeks in the Conquered City* was received with critical acclaim, becoming a best seller in Germany for at least 19 weeks. It was praised for its unsentimental honesty, its "determination to see beyond the acts themselves" and the author's "fierce, uncompromising voice." Its style is acclaimed for its precise detail and keen observation. In contrast, the first publication in Germany in 1959 was controversial and the author felt humiliated. Thus, she had refused to allow it to be reprinted until after her death. She died in 2001.

The first publication—an incomplete translation—was in the United States in 1954 in the cold war years, presumably when western audiences might have been more receptive. In addition to English, it was translated into seven other languages. The 1959 German-language edition, published in Switzerland, perhaps because it was banned in Germany, faced a hostile or silent response. Germans, during a period of great forgetting, were not ready for "uncomfortable truths"; sexual collaboration for survival was a taboo subject. Germans were outraged, accusing the author of "besmirching the honor of German women." Further, German men were affronted by their images in the diary: standing aside or acquiescing to their women being violated. The author, in fact, does refer to the myth of the strong man as being eradicated. Thus, the diary was "virtually banned," quickly going out of print; "the book sank without trace in a country that had *decided* to deal with the horrors of its immediate past through collective silence."

Hans Magus Enzensberger, the literary executor of the author, in keeping with his perception of her wishes, maintained the "anonymous" authorship for the 2003 edition. However, Jens Bisky, a German journalist with *Süddeutsche Zeitung* revealed his discovery that the author was Marta Hillers, a not altogether confirmed fact. In response to this revelation, Enzensberger accused Bisky of "shamelessness."

FURTHER READING

Bourke, Joanna. "Living with a Brutal Bear." *Independent*, June 17, 2005.
Connolly, Cressida. "She Screamed for Help but Her Neighbors Barricaded the Door." *Daily Telegraph*, April 17, 2005.
Enzensberger, Hans. "Enzensberger and Anonyma." *Der Spiegel*, September 29, 2003.
Esch, Christian. "An Unimportant Person?" *Süddeutsche Zeitung*, September 25, 2003.
Gottesmann, Christoph. "A Woman in Berlin." *New York Times Book Review*, September 11, 2005, 6.
Grant, Linda. "The Rubble Woman." *Observer*, July 2, 2005.
Harding, Luke. "Row Over Naming of Rape Author." *Observer*, October 5, 2003.
Kanon, Joseph. "*A Woman in Berlin*: My City of Ruins," *New York Times*, August 14, 2005.

WORDS OF CONSCIENCE: RELIGIOUS STATEMENTS ON CONSCIENTIOUS OBJECTION

Editors: A. Stauffer Curry (first edition); Shawn Perry (ninth edition)
Original date and place of publication: 1951, United States
Publisher: National Interreligious Service Board for Conscientious Objectors (NISCO)
Literary form: Nonfiction

SUMMARY

Eighty-nine of the 97 pages of *Words of Conscience* are made up of "official statements of religious bodies," expressing their view of conscientious objection. Of the remaining text pages, three discuss war and three respond to the question, "Am I a conscientious objector?" to help readers establish their positions. Four kinds of objections are expressed:

1. Conscientious Objection—"a deep conviction, motivated by conscience, that prevents someone from taking part in armed combat." The Supreme Court has so defined the term as to exempt all persons "whose consciences, spurred by deeply held moral, ethical or religious beliefs, would give them no rest or peace, if they allowed themselves to become a part of an instrument of war." Federal law recognizes two groups—conscientious objectors (those who cannot participate in the military in any way) and noncombatants (those who would serve in the military but only in noncombatant duties).
2. Selective Objection—based on the "just-war theory." On this basis, nonparticipation is related to wars that are considered unjust. Federal law does not recognize the selective objector. However, most major religious bodies of the Western World have traditionally based their positions on the just-war theory.
3. Nuclear Pacifism—objection to participation in a military situation potentially leading to nuclear war.
4. Noncooperation—a belief that "cooperation with the draft, even as a conscientious objector, helps to support a war effort." These objectors may immigrate to foreign countries or refuse to register for the draft; they may attempt to thwart the draft through legal or procedural maneuvers. "Non registration is currently illegal."

Altogether 70 statements across the spectrum of religious bodies in the United States are included in the book. These statements may be grouped into several categories from overall antiwar and nonparticipation sentiment to several modified stances. Excerpts of representative samples are given below, with the recognition that variations between and among these are no doubt significant to the groups that composed them.

The first example expresses the fully antiwar conscience.

RELIGIOUS SOCIETY OF FRIENDS (QUAKERS)

We utterly deny all outward wars and strife, and fighting with outward weapons, for any end, or under any pretense whatever; this is our testimony to the whole world. The Spirit of Christ by which we are guided, is not changeable, so as once to command us from a thing as evil, and again to move us into it; and we certainly know, and testify to the world, that the Spirit of Christ, which leads us unto all truth, will never move us to fight and war against any man with outward weapons, neither for the Kingdom of Christ, or for the kingdoms of this world. . . . Therefore we cannot learn war any more.

(From a statement by George Fox, founder of the Society of Friends, and others, in a declaration made in 1660.)

A less absolute antiwar participation statement urges noncombatant or alternative service:

EPISCOPAL CHURCH

WHEREAS, the Bishops of the Anglican Communion affirmed at Lambeth in 1958, echoing similar words in 1930 and 1940, that "war as a method of settling international disputes is incompatible with the teaching and example of our Lord Jesus Christ"; and

WHEREAS, the House of Bishops of this Church, while recognizing a Christian's basic obligation to the State and for obedience to law, has affirmed on several occasions that in any conflict of loyalties he must still be guided by his conscience in obedience to God as revealed in Jesus Christ; and. . . .

RESOLVED, the House of Deputies concurring that this Convention hereby recognizes the propriety both of non-combatant service with the military and of civilian alternative service as legitimate methods for discharging one's obligation of service to his country as a conscientious objector against war; . . .

The "just war theory" leading to selective objection is also expressed:

FREE METHODIST CHURCH

1. We recognize the sovereign authority of government and the duty of every Christian to reverence the power, to obey the law, and to participate righteously in the administration of lawful order in the nation under whose protection he resides (Matthew 22:21; Romans 13:1–7). Members of our church should bear the responsibilities of good citizenship, and they have the right to act in the enforcement of law and the defense of the peace in accord with the conscience of each person.
2. We believe, however, that military aggression is indefensible as an instrument of national policy and strategy (Isaiah 2:3–4). The destruction of life and property and the deceit and violence necessary to warfare are contrary to the spirit and mind of Jesus Christ (Isaiah 9:6–7; Matthew 5:44–45). It is therefore the duty of every Christian to promote peace and goodwill, to foster the spirit of understanding and mutual trust among all people, and to work with patience for the renunciation of war as a means to the settlement of international disputes (Romans 12:18; 14–19).
3. It is our firm conviction that none of our people should be required to enter military training or to bear arms except in time of national peril and that the consciences of our individual members should be respected (Acts 4:19–20; 5:29). Therefore, we claim exemption from all military service for those who register officially with the church as conscientious objectors to war.

A large group of religious bodies identify support for both conscientious objectors and nonconscientious objectors. Often these state an understanding of loyalty and service to the United States, that is, to the responsibility of citizens, but recognize a precedence of conscience for individuals within their communities:

BUDDHIST

WHEREAS, The Buddha-Dharma (Teachings of Buddha) teaches that each person possesses the potentiality to develop his unique personality to Perfect Enlightenment, each according to his innate capacity; and . . .
RESOLVED, that the Buddhist Churches of America will give moral and spiritual support and counsel to any young Buddhist who chooses to serve his country; and be it
RESOLVED FURTHER, that the Buddhist Churches of America will give the same support and guidance to those who, according to their conscience and personal religious conviction, choose not to participate in war in any form.

After these official statements, "unofficial" statements of several American Indian groups—the Iroquois, Cheyenne, and Dakota (dated 1907) and the Hopi (dated 1949)—are inserted, followed by those of Black Muslim (from a brief for Petitioner dated 1970), Buddhist (dated 1971), and Islamic groups.

The text concludes with three statements of religious leaders reacting to nuclear pacifism. Pope John Paul II, Billy Graham, and Rabbi Isidor B. Hoffman seem to support nuclear pacifism by rejecting the arms race and nuclear war.

CENSORSHIP HISTORY

A unanimous vote of 5-0 by the school board of the Coleman, Wisconsin, Area School District in March 1982 in effect censored *Words of Conscience: Religious Statements on Conscientious Objection.* The book was placed on restricted access in the Coleman High School library because of its alleged political overtones. School board president David Rakowski clarified the restriction: "If a student needs the books for reference or resource material, he is free to check them out." (The other book restricted at the same time was HANDBOOK FOR CONSCIENTIOUS OBJECTORS, edited by Robert A. Seeley.) Apparently in support of the restriction, the school librarian, Arlene Valenti, stated, "though the freedom to read is everyone's right, a young mind is very impressionable, and so it becomes important for educators to guard against misleading ideas and writing."

A concerned mother of two teenaged sons, Donna Meyer, had initiated the request for the books. She had reacted to the fact that the school permitted military recruiters to speak with the students but did not present the other side of the issue. She argued that informed decisions by students about future choices should be based upon available balanced information.

A telephone interview with an assistant to the current librarian of Coleman High School revealed, after she checked the restricted shelves, that the two books were not in the library; they had been withdrawn "a few years ago" because they were "out of date."

FURTHER READING

"Coleman, Wisconsin." *Newsletter on Intellectual Freedom* 31 (1982): 126.

YANGTZE! YANGTZE!

Author: Dai Qing (editor)
Original dates and places of publication: 1989, China; 1994, United Kingdom and Canada
Publishers: Guizhou People's Publishing House; Earthscan Publications Ltd.
Literary form: Nonfiction

SUMMARY

The third-longest river in the world, the Yangtze (Yangzi) stretches across much of China. The Yangtze and its tributaries have been critical to the life of China and multitudes of Chinese people. The PBS web page for *Great Wall Across the Yangtze* states,

> Throughout history, people have been drawn to the Yangtze River for trade, transport, and spiritual pilgrimage [. . .] The Yangtze is revered for its role in providing sustenance to those who inhabit its banks. For thousands of years, these people have tilled its fertile plains, fished its deep pools and navigated its channels.

The idea for a dam at the Three Gorges region of the Yangtze originated in 1919 with Sun Yat-sen, but it had only been under serious discussion since the 1950s when Chairman Mao Zedong proposed building the dam. The dam was proposed to generate hydroelectric energy, control floods, and improve navigation. The large dam was preferred by party officials in part because of its very grandiosity: Instead of harnessing the natural resources of the river with smaller projects, they wanted a massive dam to make a statement about national strength. *Yangzte! Yangzte!* features letters, interviews, and essays by those who advise postponing the beginning of the Three Gorges project or abandoning the project altogether. Dam opponents featured in *Yangtze! Yangtze!* include scientists, engineers, journalists, environmental experts, and many officials with experience in economic issues. Lawrence Sullivan notes in the preface to the 1994 edition that

The contributors to this volume are generally *not* liberal, Westernized dissidents. Many are long-time loyal communists; others are veteran members of China's normally compliant satellite parties. These are [. . .] largely elderly officials with scientific and technical backgrounds who have opposed the dam out of a genuine concern for China's economic health and political stability.

It was compiled quickly in 1989 to be distributed to delegates of the National People's Congress (NPC), which would be voting on the project.

Most critics of the dam shared similar objections. The main objections and concerns were the following:

1. *The tributaries should be harnessed first with smaller projects.* The benefits of electricity and income from the Three Gorges project would not be seen for a very long time; Li Rui, a secretary of industrial affairs under Mao Zedong, vice-minister in the Ministry of Water Resources and Electric Power, and longtime dam opponent, says "it will take 12 years for the dam to generate power, and a total of 20 years to complete construction and resettle the people who are displaced. How then can the immediate problem of acute energy shortage be solved?" Smaller projects spread out among the Yangtze's tributaries would, according to Sun Yueqi, a government official specializing in economic issues, "produce quicker economic results and which can improve flood control, electricity generation, and navigation within this century." Such smaller projects would be cheaper, more efficient, and more effective in producing energy. Scientist and former president of Beida University Zhou Peiyuan says that "smaller hydro-electric projects on the upper reaches of the Yangtze have the advantage of quicker completion, smaller investment, and immediate profits." There are also smaller ways to develop flood control capabilities: according to Lu Qinkan, a specialist on flood control who first started assessing the Three Gorges project in 1944, "the best way to control floods is to improve dikes, securing the facilities for flood diversion areas; build more reservoirs on tributaries, and continue work on soil conservation at the upper reaches."

2. *Budgetary.* The estimated cost of the project is far too low and will likely cost much more: Wu Jiaxinag, an economist and former researcher under the Communist Party, says "the Three Gorges project will become a 'bottomless pit' demanding endless investment." The national economy is not strong enough to sustain such a project. Furthermore, the project would hinder rather than help the goal of quadrupling the GNP by the year 2000. Critics also point out that the dam will take longer to build than proponents claim.

3. *Population relocation.* The dam project would require the relocation of at least 1.1 million people, quite possibly more. The area

requiring relocation includes 13 cities and hundreds of factories. Many critics complain of the economic costs of relocating so many people, but Dai Qing says that "population relocation is far more than a political and economic problem. It is directly related to environmental and social issues," and that "the Three Gorges resettlement program would stir up social unrest and create many unforeseen environmental effects." Jin Jun, a former researcher at the Institute of Sociology, Beida University, complains that relocation was assessed largely from an economic perspective, and that sociologists and anthropologists should be included in the assessment.

4. *Sedimentation.* Former vice minister of the Ministry of Communication Peng De says that "[s]ome Chinese experts regard sedimentation as the cancer of the project, which would become incurable if discovered too late." According to Peng, the Yangtze's "sediment load at present is the fourth highest in the world. Due to deforestation along the river banks, [. . .] the Yangtze will soon rank as the third most silted river in the world." The dam would cause the sediment to aggregate, causing serious problems to navigation. The sediment could render the Chongqing port unusable, and eventually it would take up significant reservoir space, diminishing the dam's productivity: "after the construction of the Three Gorges project, sediment would continue to increase during each flood season; little would be washed away and the reservoir would gradually lose its capacity to generate power."

5. *Navigation.* In addition to the danger of sedimentation halting navigation, the dam itself would make ship navigation slow, with any malfunction halting navigation significantly. According to Zhou Peiyuan, the dam "will have five sluice gates, which means that a much longer time will be needed for boats to pass through. If any of the five sluice gates breaks down, this important channel will be totally blocked."

6. *Environmental Damage.* Critics point out it is difficult to predict the potential environmental hazards of the project, but with a project this immense, the risks are substantial. Possible consequences include pollution, induced earthquakes, landslides, soil erosion, loss of farmland, and reduced fish populations. Botanist Hou Xueyu, an adviser to the Experts' Group on Ecology and Environment, also notes that "the natural beauty and cultural heritage of the area would be permanently damaged as well."

7. *National defense threat.* The dam would be a military and terrorist target; according to deputy director of the Department of Domestic Political Affairs at *China Youth News,* Yang Lang, experts claim the project "would threaten our national defense," and that it "has not

been adequately assessed in terms of national defense and the threat of war." According to Yang, the mere threat of a military attack on the dam would have severe economic consequences and an actual attack would be catastrophic.

8. *Unscientific assessment process.* Those charged with assessing the viability of the Three Gorges project were already inclined to support the project, making the findings biased. A letter written by 10 members of the Chinese People's Political Consultative Conference claims "the assessment has been carried out by the department responsible for the project, and by no means is it an objective and comprehensive one." In particular, former leaders in the Ministry of Water Resources and Electric Power dominated the process, hindering an objective overview. Some also accuse dam proponents of deliberate distortion and deceit in order to advance the project. More broadly, it was pro-dam arguments that dominated the media, as anti-dam views were suppressed.

CENSORSHIP HISTORY

The 1994 English-language edition of *Yangtze! Yangtze!* (available in its entirety online at http://www.threegorgesprobe.org/pi/documents/three_gorges/Yangtze/) includes additional material, including information on the publication and censorship of *Yangtze! Yangtze!* and the eventual approval of the Three Gorges project.

Yangtze! Yangtze! was written partly in response to a campaign that promoted pro-dam arguments and suppressed anti-dam arguments; it is not surprising, then, that Dai Qing and the book became targets of that same suppression. *Yangtze! Yangtze!* was considered controversial for specific reasons—it opposed a specific policy desired by authorities—and broader reasons—it questioned the wisdom of officials and suggested need for more open debate on the issue. Getting the book published was itself a struggle: most media outlets were under state control, and they primarily published pro-dam arguments. Dai Qing had a great deal of trouble getting the material for *Yangtze! Yangtze!* published, but she did finally find a publisher (Guizhou People's Publishing House) willing to publish arguments opposing the dam.

Though *Yangtze! Yangtze!* was compiled and published months before the 1989 pro-democracy protests, and the book focuses mostly on technical issues involving the dam, the protests provided the opportunity for dam proponents in power to suppress *Yangtze! Yangtze!* According to the English-language edition, after the Tiananmen Square massacre, "Dai Qing was publicly denounced by the official media, and in July she was arrested." She was in jail for 10 months, as the book was accused of "abetting the turmoil." The Yangtze Valley Planning Office communicated to the Party Committee of Guizhou, "claiming that the publishing of the book was driven by the 'ulterior motives' of the disturbance activists," and the YVPO also asked the Media and Publication Administration to censor the book. The book and its authors were also accused "of advocating 'bourgeois liberalization.'" Eventually,

> the Media and Publication Administration and the Publishing Bureau of Guizou province denounced and banned *Yangtze! Yangtze!* The Party Commission of Guizhou issued a resolution [which] accused the book of launching a political attack under the guise of scholarly debate. The Party argued that the book's authors had disguised their true intentions, and were guilty of "engaging in preparing opinions for the chaos (i.e., the period of the prodemocracy movement prior to the [Tiananmen Square] military crackdown on June 4) and riot (i.e., the days of the crackdown itself)." The resolution ordered the publishing company to recall the remaining 30,000 copies of the book and destroy them immediately.

The resolution also required "self-criticisms" from the publishers. The 25,000 copies that were sold before the ban still circulated.

Engineer Wang Weiluo later noted he believes that it was the head of state himself, Premier of China Li Peng, who worked "behind the scenes" to have Dai Qing arrested and *Yangtze! Yangtze!* banned.

Yangtze! Yangtze! may have contributed to the Three Gorges project being postponed in 1989, but the victory was temporary. In 1992, the NPC approved the Three Gorges project and, while construction of the dam has been completed, work to solve problems and make it fully operational continues. Numerous recent reports on problems associated with the dam seem to suggest the criticisms of the dam project in *Yangtze! Yangtze!* have been validated, especially regarding the cost, the consequences of population relocation, and the environmental devastation of the dam.

FURTHER READING

Bosshard, Peter. "Nature Strikes Back at Three Gorges Dam" (January 25, 2010). International Rivers. Available online. URL:http://www.internationalrivers.org/blog/peter-bosshard/nature-strikes-back-three-gorgesdam. Accessed September 23, 2010.

"China's Three Gorges Dam: A Model of the Past" (October 20, 2009). International Rivers. Available online. URL: www.internationalrivers.org/files/3Gorges-FINAL. pdf. Accessed January 24, 2011.

Great Wall Across the Yangtze. PBS. Available online. URL: www.pbs.org/itrs/greatwall.

Hvistendahl, Mara. "China's Three Gorges Dam: An Environmental Catastrophe?" (March 25, 2008). *Scientific American*. Available online. URL: www.scientificamerican.com/article.cfm?id=chinas-three-gorges-dam-dissater. Accessed January 24, 2011.

Kuhn, Anthony. "Concerns Rise with Water of Three Gorges Dam" (January 2, 2008). National Public Radio. Available online. URL: www.npr.org/templates/story/story. php?story ID-17723829. Accessed January 24, 2011.

Watts, Jonathan. "Three Gorges Dam May Force Relocation of a Further 300,000 People." *Guardian* (London) (January 22, 2010). Available online. URL: www. guardian.co.uk/enviorment/2010/jan/22/wave-tidal-hydropower-water. Accessed January 24, 2011.

Weiluo, Wang. "June 4 Incident, Dai Qing and the Three Gorges Dam Project (June 30, 2009)." Probe International. Available online. URL: www.probeinternational. org/three-gorges-probe/june-4-incident-dai-ging-and-three-gorges-dam-project. Accessed January 24, 2011.

Wong, How Man. *Exploring the Yangtze: China's Longest River*. San Francisco: China Books & Periodicals, 1989.

Yang, Lin. "China's Three Gorges Dam Under Fire." *Time* (October 12, 2007). Available online. URL: www.time.com/time/world/article/0,8599,1671000,00.html. Accessed January 24, 2011.

—Joseph K.M. Fischer
University of Wisconsin-River Falls

BIOGRAPHICAL PROFILES

PHILIP AGEE (1935–2008)

Agee spent 12 years as an operative of the Central Intelligence Agency (CIA). After his resignation from the CIA he worked on several exposés, editing *Dirty Work I: The CIA in Western Europe* (1978) and writing *Inside the Company: CIA Diary* (1975) and *Dirty Work II: The CIA in Africa* (1979). He also wrote the autobiographical *On the Run* (1987), in large measure about his experiences as an object of CIA attention. In 1979, his United States passport was revoked by the United States secretary of state on national security grounds in relation to the Iran hostages confrontation.

GABRIEL ABRAHAM ALMOND (1911–2002)

Almond was a professor of political science at Stanford University for many years after teaching at several other institutions, including Yale and Princeton. A prolific writer and editor, in addition to *Comparative Politics Today: A World View* (1974), his publications include *Freedom and Development* and *Comparative Politics: System, Process and Policy;* those coedited include *Progress and Its Discontents* (1982) and *The Civic Culture Revisited* (1989). The American Political Science Association honored him with its James Madison Award.

RAJAA ALSANEA (1982–   )

Alsanea was born in Saudi Arabia, receiving international acclaim for her 2005 novel *Girls of Riyadh*. She has a dentistry degree from King Saud University and is a dental graduate student in Chicago. She plans to return to Saudi Arabia to practice as a dentist. She was nominated for the 2009 Dublin Literary Award.

ANONYMOUS (1911–2001)

Identified (though not absolutely) as Marta Hillers, the author of *A Woman in Berlin: Eight Weeks in the Conquered City*, was a German journalist who studied at the Sorbonne and traveled extensively in Europe, including Russia. She wrote for German newspapers and magazines, as well as doing some work for the Nazis. *A Woman in Berlin* was her only major work.

MIGUEL ANGEL ASTURIAS (1899–1974)

Born in Guatemala, Asturias received his doctor of laws there in 1923. He left Guatemala for political reasons for the first time in 1923, studied South

American cultures at the Sorbonne until 1928 and also wrote for Central American newspapers. He returned in 1932 and was elected to the national congress in 1942. From 1945 to 1954, he served in the Guatemalan diplomatic corps but was exiled from Guatemala from 1954 to 1966; then he became Guatemala's ambassador to France. A writer in all genres, his major forms were folk studies, poetry, and the novel. He won the Prix du Meilleur Roman Étranger in 1952 for *El señor presidente* (1946), the International Lenin Peace Prize in 1966, and the Nobel Prize in literature in 1967.

THOMAS ANDREW BAILEY (1902–1983)

Bailey combined two distinguished careers—professor of history at Stanford University and writer of history. *The American Pageant* (1956) is acknowledged his best-known work. His awards include the Commonwealth Club of California Silver Medal in 1941 for *A Diplomatic History of the American People* (which went through 10 editions) and Gold Medals in 1945 for *Woodrow Wilson and the Lost Peace* and in 1951 for *America Faces Russia: Russian American Relations from Early Times to Our Day*.

ANDRE BRINK (1935–)

Born to a Dutch family and educated in South Africa, Brink returned to his homeland in 1968 from studies in France to record the turmoil and injustice there and "to accept full responsibility for what I write." His numerous publications include *Looking on Darkness* (1974), the first Afrikaans book to be banned by South African censors; *Rumours of Rain* (1978); and *An Act of Terror* (1991). Among his eight awards are the Martin Luther King Memorial Prize and the Prix Medicis Étranger, both in 1980, for *A Dry White Season* (1979). He also was honored three times with South Africa's prestigious CNA Award for literature and by France with the Commander of the Order of Arts and Lettes from the Legion of Honor. Recent works include *The Blue Door* (2007), *Other Lives* (2008), and *A Fork in the Road: A Memoir* (2009). He is a professor of Afrikaans and Dutch literature at Rhodes University.

DEE ALEXANDER BROWN (1908–2002)

Historian and novelist, Brown has also served as librarian and professor of library science at the University of Illinois at Urbana-Champaign. In addition to nonfiction, he has authored adult and juvenile novels, throughout his career examining the history of the settling of the West, its hardships and triumphs, and the injustices suffered by American Indians. He has been honored by the American Library Association in 1971 with the Clarence Day Award for *The Year of the Century* (1966), by New York Westerners in 1971 with the Buffalo Award for *Bury My Heart at Wounded Knee* (1970), and by the Western Writers of America in 1981 with the Best

Western for Young People Award for *Hear That Lonesome Whistle Blow* (1977).

EUGENE L. BURDICK (1918–1965)

A Rhodes Scholar at Oxford University, Burdick joined the faculty of the University of California, Berkeley, in 1950 and served as a professor of political theory until his death. Burdick coauthored *The Ugly American* (1958) and *Sarkhan* (1965, republished as *The Deceptive American*) with William J. Lederer. *Fail-Safe*, which he wrote with Harvey Wheeler, was published in 1962. These books each involved themes that created intense debates and controversy, that is, the ineptitude of Americans abroad and the overdependence on machines and armaments to control war.

ARTHUR R. BUTZ (1933–)

A professor of electrical engineering on the faculty of Northwestern University in the Department of Electrical Engineering and Computer Sciences, Butz is the author of numerous technical papers along with *The Hoax of the Twentieth Century* (1975).

JIMMY (JAMES EARL) CARTER (1924–)

The 39th president of the United States, Carter has extended his public career with diplomatic and public service. He has been honored with the International Institute for Human Rights' Gold Medal in 1979, the International League of Human Rights' Human Rights Award in 1983, and the Albert Schweitzer Prize for humanitarianism in 1987 and has been the recipient of many honorary doctorates. His books (two with his wife, Rosalynn) encompass autobiography (*Keeping Faith: Memoirs of a President*, 1982, 1995), political insight (such as *Negotiation: The Alternative to Hostility*, 1984, 2003, and *The Blood of Abraham: Insights into the Middle East*, 1985, 1993), and fiction (*The Hornet's Nest: A Novel of the Revolutionary War*, 2003). Recent works include *An Hour Before Daylight: Memories of a Rural Boyhood* (2001), *Christmas in the Plains: Memories* (2001), *Sharing Good Times* (2004), *Palestine: Peace, Not Apartheid* (2006), and *Beyond the White House: Waging Peace, Fighting Disease, Building Hope* (2008). Carter received the Nobel Peace Price in 2002. Carter is the first U.S. president to publish a work of fiction.

JOHN WALTON CAUGHEY (1902–1995)

Caughey gained prominence as a civil libertarian and as the author and editor of many history books. He authored *In Clear and Present Danger: The Crucial State of Our Freedom* (1958) and *The American West: Frontier and Region* (1969), coauthored *Land of the Free* (1965), and edited *Los Angeles: Biography of a City* (1976). His teaching career at the University of California, Los Angeles, spanned 40 years.

CHRISTOPHER COLLIER (1930–)

After teaching in public schools from 1955 to 1961, Collier taught history at the University of Bridgeport from 1961 to 1981. He has been a professor of history at the University of Connecticut since 1981. His *The Pride of Bridgeport: Men and Machines in the Nineteenth Century* (1979) is one of his history texts of Connecticut. Collier has collaborated with his brother, James Collier, on a number of history textbooks, including *The United States in the Cold War, World War Two*, and *The Middle Road: American Politics, 1945 to 2000* (all in 2001), as well as having cowritten the novel *My Brother Sam Is Dead* (1974) and other historical fiction.

JAMES LINCOLN COLLIER (1928–)

A freelance writer, Collier has published many books about musical instruments, musical theory, and musicians; he earned the London Observer Book of the Year Award for *The Making of Jazz: A Comprehensive History* (1978). Collier has also written many adolescent novels, some with his bother, Christopher Collier. These books include *The Bloody Country* (1976); *The Winter Hero* (1978); *War Comes to Willy Freeman* (1983); *Jump Ship to Freedom* (1981); and *My Brother Sam Is Dead* (1974), which was honored with the Newbery Honor Book Award, American Library Association notable book citation, and the Jane Addams Peace Prize.

JOSEPH ROBERT CONLIN (1940–)

Conlin is a professor of history at the University of California, Davis. In addition to *Our Land, Our Time: A History of the United States* (1985), his writings include *Bacon, Beans and Galantines: Food and Foodways on the Western Mining Frontier* (1986), *American Anti-War Movements* (1968), and *The Troubles: A Jaundiced Glance at the Movement of the Sixties* (1982).

ROBERT EDMUND CORMIER (1925–2000)

Radio and newspaper writer and author of fiction, Cormier received honors for his news writing and his novels for adolescents. In 1959 and 1973, the Associated Press of New England honored him for the best human interest story of the year. Among other awards, the American Library Association honored four of his novels as Best Book for Young Adults: *The Chocolate War* (1974); *I Am the Cheese* (1977); *After the First Death* (1979); and *The Bumblebees Fly Away* (1983). The novels explore themes of the abuse of power, the struggle of individuals with institutions, and the relationship between good and evil.

LARRY CUBAN (1934–)

Cuban has had a distinguished career as an educator, teaching in public schools in Pennsylvania, Ohio, and Washington, D.C. He has also been employed as superintendent of schools in Virginia and as director of the U.S. Commission on Human Rights. He is a professor of education, emeritus of Stanford University. In addition to *Promise of America* (1971), which he wrote in collaboration with Philip Roden, his writings include *The Black Man in America* (1971); *To Make a Difference: Teaching in the Inner City* (1970); and *How Teachers Taught: Constancy and Change in American Classrooms, 1890–1980* (1984).

A. STAUFFER CURRY (1931–1994)

Clergyman and psychologist, A. Stauffer Curry was executive secretary of the National Service Board of Religious Objectors from 1949 to 1955. Subsequently, he served in several capacities, including moderator of the Church of Brethren; program analyst in drug abuse education in the department of psychiatry, Beth Israel Medical Center; and staff member of the Westchester County (New York) Community Health Board.

DAI QING (1941–)

A Chinese journalist, Dai Qing was a columnist for *Enlightenment Daily* from 1982–1989. She has received numerous recognitions and awards, including Harvard's Nieman Fellowship for journalists in 1991 and the Goldman Environmental Award in 1993. In addition to publishing *Yangtze! Yangtze!*, she has written numerous other books, most recently *Tiananmen Follies: Prison Memoirs and Other Writings* (2003). She currently lives in Beijing.

RICHARD MERCER DORSON (1916–1981)

Acknowledged as influential in "presenting the study of folklore as something approaching an exact science" and as a well-defined branch of our cultural history, Dorson's teaching career was primarily divided between Michigan State University and Harvard University. He was the author of such books as *America in Legend: Folklore from the Colonial Period to the Present* (1973); *Buying the Wind: Regional Folktales of the United States* (1974); and *Folklore and Fakelore: Essays Toward a Discipline of Folk Studies* (1976). He was also editor of several folktale anthologies. He was awarded the Chicago Folklore Prize three times.

DUONG THU HUONG (1947–)

Identified as among the most popular writers of contemporary Vietnam, Duong served as a cultural activities guide in Vietnam prior to 1975 and as a member of a performing arts group for Vietnamese troops on the front during the war. She also has worked as a screenwriter; she was a producer-director for the film *The Sleepwalker.* The unflattering portrayals of Vietnam Communist Party functionaries exemplified in *Novel Without a Name* (1995) led to official harassment, arrest, and incarceration. She was honored with the Chevalier des Arts and des Lettres in 1994, the Prince Claus Foundation Award in 1999, and the Ginzane Cavour literary award in 2005. *Paradise of the Blind* (1988) was short-listed for the 1992 Prix Femina Etranger, and *Novel Without a Name* was short-listed for the 1997 International IMPAC Dublin Literary Award. Recent novels include *Memories of a Pure Spring* (2000), *Beyond Illusions* (2002), *No Man's Land* (2005), and *Au zénith*, a translation of *Dinh Cao Choi Loi* (2009).

ABBA EBAN (1915–2002)

Born in South Africa, Eban is noted for becoming the first permanent United Nations representative for Israel, a post he held from 1949 to 1959. Elected to the Knesset (legislature), he later became deputy prime minister in 1963. He served as foreign minister from 1966 to 1974. He received honorary degrees from more than a dozen universities. In addition to *My People: The Story of the Jews* (1969), his works include *Voice of Israel* (1957), *Israel in the World* (1996), *Promised Land* (1978), *Heritage: Civilization and the Jews* (1984), and *Israel: The First Forty Years* (1987).

WILLIAM E. EBENSTEIN (1916–1976)

Austrian born, educated in both Austria and the United States, Ebenstein culminated his academic career as professor of political science at the University of California, Santa Barbara. His texts tend to focus on political systems; among them are *Fascist Italy* (1939); *The German Record: A Political Portrait* (1945); *Totalitarianism: New Perspectives* (1962); *American Democracy in World Perspective* (1967); and *Today's Isms: Communism, Fascism, Capitalism, Socialism* (1954).

FRIEDRICH ENGELS (1820–1895)

A German Socialist philosopher, Engels was the closest collaborator of Karl Marx. He co-authored the *Manifesto of the Communist Party* (1848) and edited, after Marx's death, the second and third volumes of *Das Kapital*. Engels led a double life, operating effectively in the business and social worlds, while pursuing revolutionary thought. The latter involved writing articles on communism and developing associations with radical leaders and workers.

HOWARD MELVIN FAST (1914–2003)

Essentially a freelance writer, Fast was also a war and foreign correspondent. His first novel was published at age 18 in 1933, followed by close to 100 other works, including those written under pseudonyms, principally E. V. Cunningham. *Citizen Tom Paine* (1943) was written in his first decade as a novelist, when he explored America's heritage of freedom. After World War II he joined the Communist Party, which he renounced around 1960. After his contempt of Congress conviction in 1950 for withholding records concerning an organization listed as subversive, he was blacklisted for years.

His honors include literature, news writing, screen writing, and television awards as well as the Schomburg Award for Race Relations in 1944 for *Freedom Road* (1944) and the International Peace Price from the Soviet Union in 1954. *Freedom Road* and *Spartacus* (1951) were best sellers.

JOHN HOPE FRANKLIN (1915–2009)

Franklin has been identified as a pioneer in the study of African-American history and life. His prolific writings include *Slavery to Freedom, A History of Negro Americans* (1947), *A Southern Odyssey: Travelers in the Antebellum North* (1976), *Racial Equality in America* (1976), and *George Washington Williams: A Biography* (1985), which won the Clarence L. Holte Literary Award in 1986, and *Land of the Free* (1965, co-authored with John Caughey and Ernest May); he has also edited and contributed to many volumes. His academic career as a historian was primarily at the University of Chicago. He has been presented with more than 100 honorary degrees.

JOHN KENNETH GALBRAITH (1908–2006)

The greater part of Galbraith's teaching career was at Harvard University, but he spent the 1941–43 period as administrator of the U.S. Office of Price Administration. He also served as U.S. ambassador to India. He was awarded the Medal of Freedom, the President's Certificate of Merit, and 15 honorary doctor of laws degrees. Galbraith attacked the errors of conventional economic principles and policy in such texts as *American Capitalism: The Concept of Countervailing Power* (1952), *The Affluent Society* (1967), *The New Industrial State* (1967), and *Economics and the Public Purpose* (1973). The middle two were best sellers.

GAO XINGJIAN (1940–)

Born in China, Gao made his reputation as a playwright and director in the 1980s with *Signal Alarm* (1982), *Bus Stop* (1983), *Wild Man* (1985), and *The Other Shore* (1986). Since *The Other Shore* was banned in China, none of Gao's plays has been performed in China. Gao left China in 1987, settling in Paris as a political refugee and becoming a French citizen in 1998. Gao has also written a novel (*Soul Mountain*, 1999) and several works of literary criticism and theory. He received the Nobel Prize in literature in 2000.

JEAN CRAIGHEAD GEORGE (1919–)

Noted for her meticulous expression of the environment and the evocation of animals, George's many works of juvenile fiction and nonfiction include *My Side of the Mountain* (1959, selected a Newbery Medal Honor book in 1960 and recipient of four other awards), *Julie of the Wolves* (1972 a Newbery Medal in 1973 and finalist citations from the American Library Association and National Book Award), and *The Talking Earth* (1983). Her nonfiction works include *Spring Comes to the Ocean* (1965), *Everglades Wildguide* (1972), and *How to Talk to Your Animals* (1985). Recent works include *Charlie Raven* (2004), *Snowboard Twist* (2004), and *Frightful's Daughter Meets the Baron Weasel* (2007).

RONALD J. GLASSER (ca. 1940–)

Since his discharge from the Army Medical Corps, Glasser has practiced pediatric medicine in Minnesota. He has authored a war novel, *Another War, Another Peace* (1985), in addition to his nonfiction *365 Days* (1971), and several medically related texts, *The Body Is the Hero* (1976), *Ward 402* (1973), *The Greatest Battle* (1978), *The Light in the Skull: An Odyssey of Medical Discovery* (1997), and *Wounded: Vietnam to Iraq* (2006).

JUNE GOODWIN (UNKNOWN–)

A freelance writer, Goodwin has been a foreign correspondent for the *Christian Science Monitor*, which included assignments in African countries. *Cry Amandla!* (1984) resulted from these contacts and experiences. A recent work is *Heart of Whiteness: Afrikaners Face Black Rule in the New South Africa* (1995).

NADINE GORDIMER (1923–)

Identified as the "literary conscience" of her South African homeland, Gordimer focuses many of her works on the effects of apartheid. Along with novels, such as *July's People* (1981) and *A Sport of Nature* (1987), she has authored short story collections, television plays, and documentaries and essays. The winner of the 1991 Nobel Prize for literature, she has also received South Africa's prestigious CNA Award for literature for *Burgher's Daughter* (1979) in 1980, James Tart Black Memorial Award in 1973 for *Guest of Honour* (1970), and Commonwealth Award for Distinguished Service in Literature in 1981. She has been honored with 15 honorary doctorates. In South Africa she has been an outspoken antagonist of censorship.

JOHN GUNTHER (1901–1970)

A reporter with Chicago's *Daily News* who became famous for travel books, beginning with *Inside Europe* (1936), Gunther also wrote well-received books on Asia, Latin America, the United States, Africa, Russia, South America, and Australia, in addition to the memoir *Death Be Not Proud* (1949), about the death of his 17-year-old son.

WILLIAM HARRISON HARTLEY (1906–1997)

Co-author of *American Civics* (1967), Hartley also prepared a range of materials for teachers of social studies. These included textbooks, such as *Conservation and Citizenship* (1940); manuals; pedagogical texts, such as *Your Heritage of Freedom: Suggestions for Teachers* (1948) and *Selected Films for American History and Problems* (1940); and audiovisuals, such as *Paul Revere and the Minute*

Men (1955). Hartley was on the faculty of Towson State College, Baltimore (now Towson University).

RICHARD E. HARWOOD (1948–)

Harwood is the pseudonym used by Richard Verrall for the publication of *Did Six Million Really Die?* (1972). Verrall was a member of the British National Front and editor of *Spearhead* magazine from 1976 to 1980.

VÁCLAV HAVEL (1936–)

Born to an upper-middle-class family, Havel faced barriers from the Communist regime. His bourgeois background limited his formal education to the required grade level. Subsequent to his achieving secondary education through night and technical college classes, he was not accepted into a post-secondary school with a humanities program. Nevertheless, he became a celebrated and a renowned playwright (more than 20 plays), essayist, and dissident—writing and speaking significantly against the repression of human rights and urging democratic reforms. After the Velvet Revolution, he was elected the 10th and last president of Czechoslovakia (1989–92) and subsequently was elected to be the first president of the Czech Republic (1993–2003). His awards include the Philadelphia Liberty Medal (1994), International Gandhi Peace Prize (2002), Amnesty International's Ambassador of Conscience Award (2003, the inaugural recipient), and Presidential Medal of Freedom (2003), as well as multiple honorary doctorates.

JOHN HELY-HUTCHINSON (1724–1794)

A lawyer, Hely-Hutchinson served in the Irish parliament and subsequently as provost of Trinity College, the latter under considerable fire, both for his lack of qualifications for the position and for his evident efforts to aggrandize his family. The publication of the *Commercial Restraints of Ireland* (1779) helped to remove from the public mind his reputation of being subservient to the government.

NAT (NATHAN IRVING) HENTOFF (1925–)

Hentoff's career started in radio as a writer, producer, and announcer. It evolved into reviewing, reporting, and editing for newspapers, chiefly the *New York Herald Tribune* and the *Village Voice*. In 2009, he joined the Cato Institute as a senior fellow. The passions evident in his writing have been jazz, as seen in *Jazz Country* (1965), which received the Children's Spring Festival Award, *New York Herald Tribune* in 1965, and social reform, as seen in adult novels, such as *Blues for Charlie Darwin* (1982); adolescent novels, such as *The Day They Came to Arrest the Book* (1982), which received the Acton Public Library Award in 1983; and nonfiction, such as *The First Freedom: The Tumultuous History of Free Speech in America* (1980), which received the Hugh M. Hefner First Amendment Award, in 1981, among many others.

ADOLF HITLER (1889–1945)

Born in Austria, Hitler was the leader of the German Nazi Party. Under coercion, President Hindenberg in 1933 appointed Hitler to the chancellorship; Hitler then succeeded Hindenberg in 1934, adopting the title Führer. He was named *Time*'s Man of the Year in 1938. His works, in addition to *Mein Kampf* (1925), include *Hitler's Zweites Buch* (written in 1928 and discovered in 1958), *The Speeches of Adolf Hitler, 1922–August 1939* (1942), and *Hitler's Table Talk, 1941–1944* (1953).

DOROTHY HOOBLER (1941–)

A freelance writer, Hoobler has also worked as an editor and genealogist. She and her husband, Thomas Hoobler, have written collaboratively. Among their many titles are *Nelson and Winnie Mandela* (1987), *Vietnam: Why We Fought* (1990), *Drugs and Crime* (1988), *Cleopatra* (1987), *Your Right to Privacy* (1986), and *Stalin* (1985). They have also written textbooks and several nonfiction series, such as *American Family Album*. Recent publications include *A Samurai Never Fears Death* (2007), *Seven Paths to Death* (2008), and *The Crimes of Paris* (2009).

THOMAS HOOBLER (1944?–)

In addition to freelance writing, Hoobler has taught English and photography in a private school. Aside from Nelson and Winnie Mandela (1987), some of his collaborative writings with his wife, Dorothy, are identified above.

CLAIRE HOY (1940–)

Hoy has been a political columnist for several Toronto, Canada, newspapers. In addition to coauthoring *By Way of Deception* (1990) with Victor Ostrovsky, he has written *Bill Davis: A Biography* (1985), *Friends in High Places: Politics and Patronage in the Mulroney Government* (1987), *Margin of Error: Pollsters and the Manipulation of Canadian Politics* (1989), *Nice Work: The Continuing Scandal of Canada's Senate* (1999), and *Stockwell Day: His Life and Politics* (2000).

VICTOR HUGO (1802–1885)

Poet, dramatist, novelist, Hugo is identified as the most important of the French Romantic writers. In later life he was a politician and a political writer. Although his most famous works are *Notre-Dame de Paris* (1831) and *Les Misérables* (1862), both of which express condemnation of aspects of society, his early renown came from his plays. One of these, *Marion de Lorme*, gained him attention because its stage performance was prohibited in 1829. In 1841, Hugo was elected to the Académie Française, and in 1845, he was nominated to the Chamber of Peers. Hugo escaped France into exile from 1851 to 1870 after he attempted resistance to a coup d'etat that established the Second Empire under Napoleon III.

VERNON ARTHUR IVES (1908–)

In addition to *Russia* (1943), Ives has written *The Rich Papers: Letters from Bermuda, 1615–1646* (1984), *Turkey* (1945), and *Jaufry the Knight and the Fair Brunessende* (1935).

THOMAS JEFFERSON (1743–1826)

The principal author of the Declaration of Independence, Jefferson was the first U.S. secretary of state and the third president of the United States. He was previously active in the politics of Virginia, serving as governor (1779–81); *A Summary View of the Rights of British America* (1774) emerged from this period. Subsequently, he served in the Continental Congress and as a diplomat. Jefferson's only book was *Notes on Virginia* (1785). He is also acknowledged for his interests and abilities in the arts and sciences.

HA JIN (1956–)

Jin was born in China and moved to the United States in 1985. He earned a Ph.D. in literature at Brandeis University in 1993. He is currently a professor of English at Boston University. Jin has won several awards for his fiction, including the PEN Hemingway Award for *Ocean of Words* (1996) and the Flannery O'Connor Award for short fiction for *Under the Red Flag* (1997). His first full-length novel, *Waiting* (1999), won the 1999 National Book Award for fiction and the 2000 PEN/Faulkner Award for fiction. *The Bridegroom* (stories 2000) won the Asian American Literary Award. His recent novels are *The Crazed* (2002), *War Trash* (2004), and *A Good Fall: Stories* (2009).

MACKINLAY KANTOR (1904–1977)

The author of 43 books, Kantor's career also included other writing situations: newspaper reporter and columnist, war correspondent, and scenario writer for Hollywood film studios. He was awarded the Pulitzer Prize for *Andersonville* (1955) and the O. Henry Award for "Silent Grow the Guns" in 1935. Other well-known works are *Long Remember* (1934); *Glory for Me* (1945), which became the Oscar-winning film *The Best Years of Our Lives* (1946); and *The Voice of Bugle Ann* (1936). He was the recipient of five honorary doctor of literature degrees.

ROSS Y. KOEN (1918–2008)

A specialist on East Asian affairs, Koen was a professor of government and politics at Humboldt State College, California, and later served as an executive secretary of the Association of California State College Professors and associate editor of its monthly newsletter. He has also worked as a private consultant. He published *The China Lobby in American Politics* in 1960.

RON KOVIC (1946–)

After serving in Vietnam, where he was awarded the Purple Heart and the Bronze Star, Kovic became a political activist and writer. He was nominated for Academy Awards for the best adapted screenplay and best film and the Golden Globe for best screenplay in 1990, all for *Born on the Fourth of July*, based on his 1976 autobiography. He has also written a novel, *Around the World in Eight Days* (1984).

MILAN KUNDERA (1929–)

Initially interested in music—he was a jazz pianist—Milan Kundera published his first volume of poetry in 1953. His plays were highly regarded in Czechoslovakia, particularly *The Keeper of the Keys* (1962). *Žert (The Joke)* (1967) was his first published novel. With the publication in France of *The Unbearable Lightness of Being* (1984), he made his international breakthrough. He has been politically active, joining the Czech Communist Party in 1947 in protest of Nazism. He was expelled from the Party in 1950, automatically reinstated in 1956, and was expelled again in 1970. *Žert (The Joke)* won the Czechoslovak Union Prize in 1968. Kundera has also been awarded the Prix Médicis Étranger (1973), the Austrian State Prize for European literature (1987), the Nelly Sachs Prize (Germany 1987), and the Jerusalem Prize for the Freedom of the Individual in Society (1985). He received an honorary doctorate from the University of Michigan in 1983 and the Czech medal of merits for his contribution to the renewal of democracy (1995).

OLIVER LA FARGE (1901–1963)

Although he taught ethnology and writing, La Farge's principal career was as a writer of novels, short stories, and nonfiction. He won the Pulitzer Prize in fiction for *Laughing Boy* (1929), his first novel, and the O. Henry Memorial Prize for "Haunted Ground" in 1931. Among his other works are novels—*The Copper Pot* (1942) and *The Enemy Gods* (1937)—short story collections—*A Pause in the Desert* (1957) and *All the Young Men* (1935)—and nonfiction—*As Long as the Grass Shall Grow* (1940).

JANE LANGTON (1922–)

The author of children's books and suspense novels, Langton's titles include *The Memorial Hall Murder* (1978), *The Transcendental Murder* (1964), and *The Fragile Flag* (1984). *The Fledgling* (1980) was named a Newbery Honor Book by the American Library Association. Her recent novels include *The Deserter: Murder at Gettysburg* (2003), *The Mysterious Circus* (2005), and *The Dragon Tree* (2008).

WILLIAM J. LEDERER (1912–2010)

A graduate of the Naval Academy, Lederer served in the U.S. Navy from 1930 to 1958; after wartime duty in Asia and with the Atlantic Fleet, he was special assistant to the commander in chief of the Pacific from 1950 to 1958. He later became a freelance writer and a lecturer on the college circuit. Lederer's writings include *The Ugly American* (1958) and *Sarkhan* (1965), both co-authored with Eugene Burdick; *Ensign O'Toole and Me* (1957); and *A Nation of Sheep* (1962).

ROBERT LEKACHMAN (1920–1989)

Economist, educator, and author, Lekachman was distinguished professor of economics at Herbert H. Lehman College of the City University of New York from 1973 to 1989. He was also selected by *Change* magazine in 1986 as having made a significant contribution to American education. His writings reflect his belief that economic growth should coincide with social justice. Among his titles are *A History of Economic Ideas* (1959), *The Age of Keynes* (1966), *Greed Is Not Enough: Reaganomics* (1982), and *Visions and Nightmares: America After Reagan* (1987).

VLADIMIR I. (ULYANOV) LENIN (1870–1924)

A devout marxist, Lenin was the founder of the Bolshevik Party in Russia and the first head of the Soviet Union. After a three-year exile in Siberia from 1897 to 1900 for revolutionary activities, followed by 17 years of living in western Europe, he returned to Russia during World War I to help lead the October Revolution of 1917. Among his writings are *The State and Revolution* (1917) and *Imperialism: The Highest Stage of Capitalism* (1917).

HANOCH LEVIN (1943–1999)

Born in Tel Aviv, Levin studied philosophy and Hebrew literature at Tel Aviv University. He wrote 56 plays, 34 of which were produced during his lifetime. In 1972, Levin began his career with the play *Ya 'akobi and Leidental* and went on to direct another 22 of his own plays. In 1998, he received the prize of the Israeli Theatre Academy for *Requiem* (1998). His works include *You, Me and the Next War* (1968), *The Queen of the Bathtub* (1970), *The Patriot* (1982), *Everyone Wants to Live* (1985), and *The Dreaming Child* (1993).

(HARRY) SINCLAIR LEWIS (1885–1951)

Employed first as a journalist and editor, Lewis's major career was as a writer of novels, short stories, plays, and screenplays. His 1920s novels *Main Street* (1920); *Babbitt* (1922); *Arrowsmith* (1925), which won the Pulitzer Prize (which he declined); and *Elmer Gantry* (1927) analyzed the sociology of American middle-class life and commercial culture. *It Can't Happen Here* (1935) used elements of American society to re-create the United States as a fascist dictatorship. Lewis was awarded the Nobel Prize in literature in 1930; he also received the *Ebony* magazine award for promoting racial understanding in *Kingsblood Royal* (1947).

LIAO YIWU (1958–   )

A prominent author—poet, screenwriter, and novelist—Liao Yiwu has lived life at the bottom rung of society. Throughout the 1980s, he was a popular new poet in China. His poem "Massacre," an intense reaction to the Tiananmen Square event of June 4, 1989, altered his career and changed his life. Intense interrogations, detentions, imprisonment, abusive punishment, torture—and censorship. He has compiled *The Fall of the Holy Temple*, an anthology of underground poems (1998), and *The Corpse Walker: Real-Life Stories, China from the Bottom Up* (2008). (A shortened version in Chinese, *Interviews with People from the Bottom Rung of Society*, was published in 2002.) He has received a Freedom to Write Award from the Independent Chinese PEN Center (2007) and a Human Rights Watch Hellman-Hammett Grant (2003).

NICCOLÒ MACHIAVELLI (1469–1527)

Machiavelli was an Italian statesman and writer. He served the Florentine republic for 14 years as second chancellor and secretary, in diplomatic missions and in the organization of the militia. With the fall of the republic, Machiavelli was deprived of his positions. He turned to writing. Among his books are *Il Principe* (*The Prince*) (written in 1513 and published in 1532 after his death), *Discorsi* (1531), *Dell'arte della Guerra* (1520), and *Vita di Castruccio* (1520).

NORMAN MAILER (1923–2007)

Mailer is chiefly known for his novels, although he also claims to be working in a field akin to journalism. Some of his best-known works are *The Naked and the Dead* (1948), *Why Are We in Vietnam?* (1967), and *Tough Guys Don't Dance* (1984). He has also been a film producer, director, and actor. He has been awarded two Pulitzer Prizes, in 1969 for *Armies of the Night* (1968) (general nonfiction) and in 1979 for *The Executioner's Song* (1979) (letters); the latter also received a National Book Critics Circle nomination and Notable Book citation and an American Book Award nomination.

NELSON R. MANDELA (1918–   )

A practicing lawyer, Mandela's response to the mistreatment of black Africans in his native South Africa was to become a political activist and a leader of the African National Congress. He was sentenced first to five years for inciting Africans to strike and then to life imprisonment for sabotage and treason. In 1991, he was freed unconditionally and in 1994, was elected president. His writings are political and include collections of his speeches and letters, including *No Easy Walk to Freedom* (1965); *Nelson Mandela, Symbol of Resistance and Hope for a Free South Africa* (1990); and *Nelson Mandela, Speeches 1990: Intensify the Struggle to Abolish Apartheid* (1990). He has been honored with two doctor of laws degrees and three awards for international understanding and human rights from India, Austria, and UNESCO. Mandela received the Nobel Peace Prize (with F. W. de Klerk) in 1993.

VICTOR MARCHETTI

Most of Marchetti's work while he was employed with the CIA was devoted to analysis of data; he was a specialist on the military affairs of the Soviet Union. His last three years of service were in the capacity of staff officer in the office of the director. He resigned in 1969 after 14 years of service, "disenchanted and disagreeing with the agency's policies and practices." His novel, *The Rope-Dancer* (1971), and his co-authored nonfiction exposé, *The CIA and the Cult of Intelligence* (1974), were both challenged by the CIA for their revelations of the agency's activities.

JOHN D. MARKS (1943–)

Co-author of *The CIA and the Cult of Intelligence* (1974), Marks had been a foreign service officer with the U.S. State Department, stationed in Washington and Vietnam. Part of his assignment in Washington was as staff assistant to the department's intelligence and research director. He resigned in 1970, working subsequently as executive assistant to Senator Clifford Case and in various research and staff positions for agencies such as the Union of Concerned Scientists. *The Search for the "Manchurian Candidate"* was named Best Book of 1979 by Investigative Reporters and Editors. He is a fellow of Harvard Institute of Politics and director of the Nuclear Network in Washington.

KARL HEINRICH MARX (1818–1883)

Together, Marx and Friedrich Engels were largely responsible for the development of communism, triggered by their famous *Manifesto of the Communist Party* (1848). Earlier articles by Marx went beyond socialist doctrine to stress political struggle and revolution. In 1864, he became the head of the newly founded International Working Men's Association. His writings include *Das Kapital* (the first volume, 1867)—the second and third volumes edited by Engels; *The Economic and Philosophic Manuscripts* (1844); and, co-authored with Engels, *The German Ideology* (1845).

PETER MATTHIESSEN (1927–)

Cofounder in 1951 of *The Paris Review*, Matthiessen's writing includes award-winning fiction and nonfiction. *Far Tortuga* (1975) was cited "Editor's Choice" by the *New York Times Book Review*; *The Snow Leopard* (1978) received the Brandeis, National Book and American Book Awards; *Sand Rivers* (1981) received the John Burroughs Medal and the African Wildlife Leadership Foundation Award; and *Wildlife in America* (1959) earned permanent installation in the White House library. Matthiessen is widely considered one of the most important wilderness writers of the 20th century; however, human victims form the core of his most recent writings, as in *In the Spirit of Crazy Horse* (1983).

ALEJANDRA MATUS (1966–)

Matus is a journalist from Chile. After she wrote *El libro negro de la justicia chilena* in 1999, she fled her country for the United States. Upon returning to Chile in 2001, she wrote for the state-run newspaper *La Nación* before she and the entire Sunday edition editorial staff resigned in 2003 after a conflict over the censorship of a story she had written. She is currently the editor of *Plan B*, an independent biweekly magazine she founded with the rest of her former *La Nación* coworkers in 2003. She received the 2000 Vasyl Stus Freedom to Write Award and was one of the recipients of the 2000 Hellman/ Hammett Grant.

ERNEST RICHARD MAY (1928–2009)

May's academic career as professor of history has been primarily at Harvard University. He advocates "more and better use of history by those charged with making decisions." May co-authored *Land of the Free* (1965) with John W. Caughey and John Hope Franklin and co-edited *The Kennedy Tapes: Inside the White House During the Cuban Missile Crisis* (1997) with Philip Zelikow. Among his later texts are *Knowing One's Enemies: Intelligence Assessment Before the Two World Wars* (1984) and *A Proud Nation* (1983). He received the American Historical Association George Louis Beer Prize in 1959 for *The World War and American Isolation, 1914–1917.*

JOHN MILTON (1608–1674)

One of the great English poets, Milton is best known for his epic *Paradise Lost* (1667). He was also an active writer of political tracts, including *The Doctrine and Discipline of Divorce* (1642) and *Areopagitica* (1644).

HERTA MÜLLER (1953–)

Born in a German-speaking town in Romania, Herta Müller emigrated to Germany in 1987. An uncensored copy of a short story collection, *Niederungen* (*Nadirs*), was smuggled into Germany and published in 1982. Her first published novel, *Drückender Tango* (Oppressive Tango) (1984), was followed by 17 others. Those translated into English include: *The Passport* (1989), *The Land of Green Plums* (1996), *Traveling on One Leg* (1988), and *The Appointment* (2001). For *The Land of Green Plums*, she won the German Kleist and the Irish IMPAC awards; in 2009 she was awarded the Nobel Prize in literature.

ABDUL RAHMAN MUNIF (1933–2004)

Born in Jordan of a Saudi father and an Iraqi mother, Munif studied law at Baghdad and Cairo Universities. He earned a Ph.D. in petroleum economics at the University of Belgrade. He served as an oil economist in Baghdad and director of planning of the Syrian Oil Company and later as director of crude oil marketing. From 1981, Munif devoted himself entirely to writing. His first novel (1972) was *Trees and the Assassination of Marzoug (Al-ashjar wa-ghtyal Marzuq)*. His quintet (1984–89), of which *Cities of Salt* is the first volume, was his most important work. Another of his celebrated works is *East of the Mediterranean* (1975). Munif won two distinguished Arab awards for his novels, which have been translated into 10 languages.

TIM O'BRIEN (1946–)

O'Brien served in Vietnam from 1968 to 1970, receiving the Purple Heart. He was a national affairs reporter for the *Washington Post* from 1973 to 1974. He has taught at Texas State University–San Marcos. His works include *Northern Lights* (1975); National Book Award winner *Going After Cacciato* (1978); *Nuclear Age* (1985); and *The Lake of The Woods* (1994), which won the *New York Times Book Review* Best Book Award in 1994 and the Cooper Prize in 1995 for best novel on a historical theme. His recent novels include *Tomcat in Love* (1998) and *July, July* (2002).

VICTORIA ORTIZ (1942–)

Ortiz has been a high school and college teacher of French, Spanish, and Latin American literature, a coordinator of a Spanish humanities program, and a caseworker for various social agencies. She is the assistant dean of student services and director of admissions, University of California–Irvine. She translated Che Guevara's *Reminiscences of the Cuban Revolutionary War* (1968) and has written two juveniles—*The Land and People of Cuba* (1973) and *Sojourner Truth* (1974).

GEORGE ORWELL (1903–1950)

As a child in India and later as a member of the imperial police, Orwell saw many examples of British abuse of power. Calling himself an anarchist or socialist, he became an opponent of imperialism and other political organizations, which he believed ruled people unfairly. His antitotalitarian beliefs led him to write many novels and essays, including "Shooting an Elephant" (1936), *Burmese Days* (1934), *Animal Farm* (1945), and *1984* (1949). He also worked as the head of Indian service for the British Broadcasting Corporation and as the literary editor of the *Tribune*, a socialist paper.

VICTOR OSTROVSKY (1949–)

Born in Canada but raised alternately in Israel, Ostrovsky holds dual Canadian and Israeli citizenship. He was a case officer for the Institute for Intelligence and Special Operations (MOSSAD) of Israel (the equivalent of the CIA) from 1984 to 1986 before he resigned. The Israeli government took extensive and immediate steps to suppress *By Way of Deception: The Making and Unmaking of a Mossad Officer* (1980). Ostrovsky has also written a novel, *Lion of Judah* (1993), and *The Other Side of Deception: A Rogue Agent Exposes The Mossad's Secret Agenda* (1994), a follow-up to *By Way of Deception.*

THOMAS PAINE (1737–1809)

Although born in England, Paine was a leader in the American Revolution. A political pamphleteer, his *Common Sense* (1776) and "Crisis" papers were important influences in maintaining support for Washington and his troops. He has been called "the American Voltaire" for the quality of his writings, including *The Rights of Man* (1791–92), a defense of the French Revolution and republican principles; and *The Age of Reason* (1794–96), an exposition of the place of religion in society. Paine died in poverty and disrepute.

ELIHU PALMER (1764–1806)

Raised, educated, and ordained in the Calvinist tradition, Palmer soon gave evidence of doubting Christian Church doctrines. His liberal sermons caused him to be dismissed from church assignments. He turned to the study of law; however, after being totally blinded from yellow fever, he became a freelance preacher of deism. He gained a hearing in the 1796–1801 years, achieving acclaim in New York City. In addition to *Principles of Nature* (1801), Palmer published two newspapers and many of his orations and articles.

ORHAN PAMUK (1952–)

Born in Istanbul, Pamuk first studied architecture for three years before completing a journalism degree at Istanbul University. He started writing in 1974, his first novel *Mr. Cevdet and His Sons* being awarded the first prize in the 1979 Novel Contest of the Milliyet Press. Other awards include the 1984 Madarali Novel Prize and the 1991 Prix de la Découverte Européenne for *The Silent House*, his second novel, and the 1990 Independent Award for Foreign Fiction for the historical novel *The White Castle*. *My Name Is Red* has won three awards: Prix du Meilleur Livre Étranger (France 2002), Premio Grinzane Cavour (Italy 2002), and International IMPAC Dublin Literary Award (Ireland 2003). *Snow* was awarded the French Prix Médicis Étranger in 2005. In 2006 he was awarded the Nobel Prize in literature. Having been a visiting scholar at Columbia University from 1985 to 1988, he returned there in 2006 as the Robert Yik-Fong Tam Professor in the Humanities.

BORIS PASTERNAK (1890–1960)

Born a member of the upper class in Moscow, Pasternak's *Doctor Zhivago* (1957), which he referred to as "my chief and most important work," is his only novel, but he was also one of the best Russian poets of the 20th century. In addition, he wrote several memoirs, and during the repressive Stalin period, when he had stilled his own literary voice, translated many works into Russian, including several Shakespearean plays and Goethe's *Faust*. He earned the Nobel Prize in literature in 1958 but refused it six days later—not soon enough for the Soviet government, which labeled him a traitor for bowing to the anti-Soviet forces of the West.

SHAWN PERRY (1952–)

Perry worked as an archivist for and wrote the history of the National Shrine (now Basilica) of the Immaculate Conception before joining the staff of the National Interreligious Service Board for Conscientious Objectors (NISBCO) as editor of its newsletter. He also edited *Words of Conscience: Religious Statements on Conscientious Objection* (9th edition, 1980). He is now associated with the Amalgamated Transit Union, editing the magazine *In Transit* and its Internet home page, speechwriting, and handling public relations.

CHAIM POTOK (1929–2002)

Potok is known principally for his fiction expressing universal issues and themes while focusing on Jewish characters. *The Chosen* (1967), and *The Promise* (1969), both best sellers, won awards; the Edward Lewis Wallant and the National Book Awards for *The Chosen* and the Athenaeum Award for *The Promise*. Other recent novels include *Davita's Harp* (1985) and *The Gift of Asher Lev* (1972), the sequel to *My Name Is Asher Lev* (1972). Among his non-fiction works are *The Jew Confronts Himself in American Literature* (1975) and *Ethical Living for a Modern World* (1985).

PRAMOEDYA ANANTA TOER (1925–2006)

Pramoedya was imprisoned by each of his native Indonesia's three 20th-century governments for alleged subversive political activities and writings. His freedom of travel was constrained until 1999. He wrote his prize-winning novel *The Fugitive* (1950) during the first imprisonment and his "Buro Quartet"—*This Earth of Mankind* (1980), *Child of All Nations* (1980), *Footsteps* (1985), and *House of Glass* (1988)—during the last. He incorporated nationalistic principles and themes of revolutionary clashes throughout his works. *The Fugitive* was awarded the Balai Pustaka literary prize. Pramoedya was honored with the Ramon Magsaysay Award, identified as the Nobel Prize of Asia, for his contribution to Asian culture. In 1999 he was awarded an honorary doctorate degree by the University of Michigan.

MANUEL PUIG (1932–1990)

An Argentine author, Puig write, most notably, *Betrayed by Rita Hayworth* (*La traición de Rita Hayworth*), *Heartbreak Tango* (*Boquitas pintadas*), and *Kiss of the Spider Woman*. He also wrote plays and screenplays, including respectively, *Under a Mantle of Stars* (*Bajo un manto de estrellas*) and *Kiss of the Spider Woman* (*El beso de la mujer araña*), which was filmed in 1985 and a Broadway musical in 1993. The screen adaptation of *Heartbreak Tango* won the best-script prize at the San Sebastián Film Festival in 1974 as did Puig's film adaptation of Jose Donosi's *El lugar sin límites* in 1976.

ALEKSANDR NIKOLAEVICH RADISHCHEV (1749–1802)

Born into the landed gentry class, Radishchev worked in various civil service functions throughout his life. In his first book, in 1773, he established his view of autocracy as the form of government "most repugnant to human nature." In 1792, Catherine the Great sentenced him to 10 years' internment in Siberia for publishing *A Journey from St. Petersburg to Moscow* (1790). Catherine's son and successor, Paul, in 1797 permitted Radishchev to return "under observation" to his estate. Paul's successor freed Radishchev in 1801 and appointed him to the Commission on Revision of the Laws. In 1802, when the commission chair reproached him for presenting some of his old ideas, Radishchev went home distressed and killed himself with poison.

JONATHAN RANDAL (1933–   )

A former correspondent for the *Washington Post*, Randall has covered the Middle East and Europe. In addition to *After Such Knowledge, What Forgiveness?* (1999), Randal has written *Going All the Way: Christian Warlords, Israeli Adventurers and the War in Lebanon* (1983) and *Osama: The Making of a Terrorist* (2004).

JOHN REED (1887–1920)

Reed was a poet and journalist. Born in Oregon, the widely traveled Reed mixed his ability with language and his revolutionary zeal to become a leader of the American left and the first head of the U.S. Communist Labor Party. Books such as *Insurgent Mexico* (1914), *The War in Eastern Europe* (1916), and *Ten Days That Shook the World* (1919) were incisive accounts of events that few other Americans saw. He remains the only American to be given state burial at the Kremlin.

ERICH MARIA REMARQUE (1898–1970)

Born in Germany, Remarque came to the United States in 1939 and was later naturalized. He served in the German army on the western front in World War I, earning a German Grand Cross of Merit. His experiences in the war led him to write his most famous work, *All Quiet on the Western Front* (1928). Political resentment against the novel's realism forced Remarque in 1932 to escape Nazi harassment by crossing the border to Switzerland. He was an author of both novels—including *The Road Back* (1931) and *A Time to Live and a Time to Die* (1954)—and plays.

PHILIP RODEN (1940–)

In addition to coauthoring *Promise of America* (1971) with Larry Cuban, Roden collaborated on *Life and Liberty: An American History* (1984). He was a teacher of history in Evanston (Illinois) Township High School until his retirement in 1994.

DON ROJAS (1949–)

Active in political affairs, Rojas has been secretary for propaganda and information of the Anti-Imperialist Organizations of the Caribbean and Central America. During the 1970s, he served as the assistant director of communications at the National Urban League, in the 1980s as minister of information in the government of Grenada and in the 1990s as editor of the *New York Amsterdam News* and, then, press secretary of the National Association for the Advancement of Colored People. Rojas has managed the Burned Churches Project of the National Council of Churches. He has edited several books, including *One People One Destiny: The Caribbean and Central America Today* (1988). In 1996, he founded an online news site called The Black World Today (http://www.tbwt.com) and an associated radio network, Black World Radio. In 2002, he was appointed general manager of WBAI/Pacifica Radio in New York City and in 2006 press officer of Oxfam America.

THOMAS B. ROSS (1929–2002)

Ross was a reporter for the International News Service and United Press International before joining the Washington bureau of the *Chicago Sun-Times* in 1958. In 1970, he became bureau chief. He and David Wise coauthored three books: *The U-2 Affair* (1962), *The Invisible Government* (1964), and *The Espionage Establishment* (1967).

MIKE ROYKO (1932–1997)

From the moment he landed a job on the base newspaper during his stint in the air force, Royko was a journalist. As a reporter and columnist he worked for the *Chicago Sun-Times* and the *Chicago Tribune*, as well as being nationally syndicated. His work earned him the Pulitzer Prize for commentary in 1972 and the National Press Club's Lifetime Achievement Award in 1990. In addition to several collections of columns, he wrote the political biography *Boss: Richard J. Daley of Chicago* (1971).

HAROLD O. RUGG (1886–1960)

Rugg, a member of the faculty at the Columbia University Teacher's College, had a long career as a professor, trainer of educators, and author. His series, *Problems of American Culture*, was one of the most widely used texts in the 1930s and 1940s.

EDWARD SAID (1935–2003)

Said was a professor of English and comparative literature at Columbia University in New York City and also taught at Harvard, Johns Hopkins, and Yale. Said was well known as an advocate and activist for the Palestinian cause in Israel. He published *The Politics of Dispossession* in 1995. His best-known works of literary and cultural criticism are *Orientalism* (1978) and *Culture and Imperialism* (1993).

KEN SARO-WIWA (1941–1995)

One of the first graduates of Nigeria's University of Ibadan in 1965, Saro-Wiwa initially served in government administrative roles, but he was removed from office when he publically criticized corrupt practices. Subsequently, he was recognized as a writer/producer of television drama and authored many novels and collections of poetry. He was a founding member in 1990 of the nonviolent Movement for the Survival of the Ogoni People (MOSOP), the author of the Ogoni Bill of Rights, and a political and environmental activist. In *Nigeria, the Brink of Disaster* and *Genocide in Nigeria* (1992) he criticized corruption and two petroleum companies. *Sozaboy: A Novel in Rotten English* (1985) and his civil war memoir, *On a Darkling Plain* (2006), exemplify the diversity of his writing. After a trial, condemned as unfair by international observers, Saro-Wiwa was found guilty and executed. He received the Right Livelihood Award for his courage and the Goldman Environmental Prize.

ROBERT A. SEELEY (1943–)

After performing two years of alternative community service with the American Friends Service Committee, Seeley worked on the staff of the Central Committee for Conscientious Objectors from 1984 to 1994. He was a draft counselor and was responsible for the writing, designing, and producing of all publications and newsletters. Among his works are *Handbook for Conscientious Objectors* (13th edition, 1981), *The Handbook of Non-Violence* (1986), *Choosing Peace: A Handbook on War, Peace, and Your Conscience* (1994), and numerous articles. Currently he operates a desktop publishing consultation and Web design enterprise (http://www.givewings.com).

ELIF SHAFAK (1971–)

Born in France, the child of a Turkish diplomat, Elif Shafak now divides her time between Istanbul, Turkey, and Tucson, Arizona. She has published nine novels, most written in Turkish; those written in English include *The Saint of Incipient Insanities* (2004), *The Bastard of Istanbul* (2006), and *The Forty Rules of Love* (2010). She received the Rumi Award for *Pinhan (The Sufi)* in 1998. *Mahrem (The Gaze)* earned the Union of Turkish Writers Prize in 2000. She works as a political scientist, an assistant professor of Near Eastern Studies at the University of Arizona.

VLADIMIR SIMKHOVITCH (1874–1959)

Simkhovitch was born in Russia and immigrated to the United States in 1898. He became a professor of economic history at Columbia University in 1904. In addition to his contribution to the field of economic history, *Marxism versus Socialism* (1913), he was the author of *Toward the Understanding of Jesus and Other Historical Studies* (1920). He was also a trustee of Greenwich House, a cultural center in New York City directed and co-founded by his wife, Mary Kingsbury Simkhovitch.

UPTON SINCLAIR (1878–1968)

Sinclair's literary career spanned 70 years and included over 100 books, beginning with dime novels at age 15 to pay for college and ending with his *Autobiography* in 1962. One of his literary friends castigated him for insufficient character development, which detracted from books that held twice the intellectual content of most "literary" writers. This criticism is least just with respect to his three great novels: *The Jungle* (1906), *Oil!* (1927), and *Boston* (1928). Small in stature, he is best known for his fearlessness in his struggle for justice, both in his life and in his novels. He won the Pulitzer Prize in 1943 for *Dragon's Teeth* (1942) and received, in 1962, both the New York Newspaper Guild Page One Award and the United Auto Workers Social Justice Award.

AGNES SMEDLEY (1892–1950)

Smedley's career as a journalist and champion of the downtrodden in China, India, and the United States brought her repute and led to infamy. She struggled against sex discrimination, became a foreign correspondent, and later worked in the Indian freedom movement. "I have had but one loyalty, one faith," she said, "and that was to the liberation of the poor and oppressed." She wrote widely about the struggles of the Chinese people and their revolutions in newspapers and magazines such as the *New Republic*, the *American Mercury*, and *New Masses*. Her books include *China's Red Army Marches* (1934), *Battle Hymn of China* (1943), and the autobiographical *Daughter of Earth* (1929).

FRANK SNEPP (1943–)

After a brief stint as a researcher for CBS News, Snepp was recruited by the CIA. His eight-year service, from 1968 to 1976, included two tours at the U.S. embassy in Saigon. He was the chief strategic analyst of North Vietnamese political affairs and was awarded the Medal of Merit in 1975. However, he resigned a year after the collapse of South Vietnam in disagreement with the agency's cover-up of its failures and those of the State Department. In addition to numerous contributions to magazines and newspapers, he published the nonfiction works *Decent Interval* (1977) and *Irreparable Harm* (1999) and a novel, *Convergence of Interest* (1982). Snepp has numerous broadcast credits and six awards, notably the Edward R. Morrow Regional Award (2006 and 2007) and the Emmy Award (2008).

ALEKSANDR ISAYEVICH SOLZHENITSYN (1918–2008)

Solzhenitsyn was arrested in 1945, while commander of an artillery battery of the Soviet Army, and sentenced to eight years in labor camps for anti-Soviet agitation; he was exiled from 1953 to 1956. After the publication in 1962 of *One Day in the Life of Ivan Denisovich* he was forbidden to live in Moscow and banned from teaching secondary school mathematics and physics. In 1973, the KGB found his manuscript of *The Gulag Archipelago*, which led in 1974 to his being arrested for treason, stripped of Soviet citizenship, and exiled from the Soviet Union. Solzhenitsyn was nominated for the 1964 Lenin Prize and was awarded the Prix du Meilleur Livre Étranger in 1969 for *The First Circle* (1968) and *Cancer Ward* (1968) and the 1970 Nobel Prize in literature. Solzhenitsyn accepted the latter award but was unable to travel to Sweden to claim it for fear he would be denied reentry to the Soviet Union.

WOLE SOYINKA (1934–)

Born in Nigeria, Soyinka is a prolific writer of plays, novels, poetry, nonfiction, and literary essays. Soyinka has taught at the University in Ibadan, Lagos, and has been a visiting professor at Cambridge, Sheffield, and Yale. His writings include plays such as *The Swamp Dwellers* (1958), *Brother Jero* (1960), and *Strong Breed* (1963); novels such as *The Interpreters* (1965) and *Season of Anomy* (1973); poetry such as *Idanre, and Other Poems* (1967) and *Ogun Abibiman* (1976); the autobiographies *The Man Died: Prison Notes* (1972) and *Ake* (1981); and nonfiction such as *The Open Sore of the Continent* (1996). Soyinka received the Nobel Prize in literature in 1986.

WILLIAM STEIG (1907–2003)

Steig was a cartoonist, popular for his sketches in the *New Yorker* and *Vanity Fair*, a sculptor, and an author. In addition to his many collections of drawings, he published numerous children's books, including *Roland, the Minstrel Pig* (1968), Caldecott medal winner *Sylvester and the Magic Pebble* (1969), Newbery Honor recipient *Abel's Island* (1976), Caldecott Honor recipient *The Amazing Bone* (1976), American Book Award winner *Doctor de Soto* (1982), and *Shrek!* (1993), the basis for the 2001 film.

JOHN STEINBECK (1902–1968)

Throughout his many works, Steinbeck examined the theme of human dignity while pointing out the paradox between the American Dream and the harsh reality of poverty. In addition to his many novels, including *Of Mice and Men* (1937), *The Red Pony* (1937), *East of Eden* (1952), and the Pulitzer Prize–winning *The Grapes of Wrath* (1939), he wrote several stage and screen adaptations of his works, nonfiction, and poems under the pseudonym Amnesia Glasscock. He also received two Academy Award nominations for best original story; three General Literature Gold Medals, Commonwealth of California; and the 1962 Nobel Prize in literature.

HARRIET BEECHER STOWE (1811–1896)

For 18 years Stowe lived in Ohio on the border of the slave states, coming in contact with fugitive slaves and learning about life in the South. After the death of one of her children she said she understood the pain of a slave mother being separated from her child. Her vow to do service to the slaves resulted in *Uncle Tom's Cabin* (1852), which was published serially in *National Era*, an antislavery magazine edited by Frederick Douglass. In addition to antislavery novels, she also wrote studies of social life and New England Puritanism in both fiction, essays, and religious poems.

JONATHAN SWIFT (1667–1745)

One of the greatest satirists in world literature, Swift's works of prose and poetry and his pamphlets have received worldwide attention through criticism and praise. He attacked any form of oppression or injustice, in the church and in politics, as in *The Drapier's Letters* (1724). His finest satires, almost all published anonymously, include *A Tale of a Tub* (1704), *The Battle of the Books* (1704), *The Mechanical Operation of the Spirit* (1704), *A Modest Proposal* (1729), and *Gulliver's Travels* (1726), Swift was ordained in 1694 in the Church of England and served as dean of St. Patrick's in Dublin from 1713 to the end of his life.

WALLACE TERRY (1938–2003)

An African-American journalist who covered the Vietnam War for *Time* magazine, Terry later published *Bloods: An Oral History of the Vietnam War* (1984), which was nominated for a Pulitzer Prize. Several videocassettes, made up of lecture and/or discussion about the war, have been produced: "Wallace Terry on Bloods, the American Experience in Vietnam," "The Bloods of Nam," and "After Our War, How Will Love Speak?" An audiocassette, "Bloods," has also been recorded.

LEON DAVIDOVICH TROTSKY (LEV DAVIDOVICH BRONSTEIN) (1879–1940)

Trotsky became involved in revolutionary activities at age 18 and joined the Social Democratic Party movement in 1903. He became one of its foremost leaders, renowned for his writing and speeches. He wrote his *Report of the Siberian Delegation* in 1903. Since he was perceived by Stalin to be a threat because of his popularity, he was exiled to Central Asia in 1928 and deported from the Soviet Union in 1929. In exile he continued writing. Trotsky was assassinated in his home in Coyoacán, Mexico, by a Spanish Communist agent, who had won the confidence of the Trotsky household.

DALTON TRUMBO (1905–1976)

Johnny Got His Gun (1939), recipient of the National Book Award and the American Booksellers Award, was Trumbo's only well-reviewed novel; however, as a screenwriter he is identified as having the "most successful set of credits," including scripts for *Kitty Foyle* (1940), an Academy Award nominee; *Exodus* (1960); *Spartacus* (1960); and *The Brave One* (1956), an Academy Award winner. In 1971 and 1972, his film adaptation of *Johnny Got His Gun*, which he also directed, won seven film awards, including the Cannes Film Festival Special Jury Grand Prize. His refusal, as one of the Hollywood Ten, to cooperate with the House Un-American Activities Committee resulted in a prison sentence and an extended period of blacklisting by Hollywood producers, during which he wrote scripts under pseudonyms, including *The Brave One*.

STANSFIELD TURNER (1923–)

A graduate of the U.S. Naval Academy, Turner also attended Oxford University as a Rhodes scholar. Admiral Turner held many key positions in the U.S. Navy and for the government, including aide to the secretary of the navy, president of the Naval War College, commander of the U.S. Second Fleet, commander in chief of the Allied Forces in southern Europe for NATO, and director of the CIA. He is an author, a teacher, and a lecturer and wrote *Secrecy and Democracy* (1985), *Terrorism and Democracy* (1991), *Caging the Nuclear Genie* (1997), and *Spy Stories* (2003).

WILLIAM S. VINCENT (1907–1983)

Vincent worked as a professor, researcher, educational filmmaker, and author. He was the general secretary of Associated Public School Systems and the director of the Central School Boards Commission of Educational Research. His written works include *Introduction to American Education* (1954), *Roles of the Citizen* (1959), and *American Civics* (1967) (coauthored with William Harrison Hartley).

KURT VONNEGUT, JR. (1922–2007)

A freelance writer and occasional teacher Vonnegut has been acclaimed for his novels, but he has also written plays, short fiction, and essays. His works include *Player Piano* (1952), *Welcome to the Monkey House* (1968), *Breakfast of*

Champions (1973), *Cat's Cradle* (1963), and *God Bless You, Mr. Rosewater* (1965). The last two and *Slaughterhouse-Five* (1969), regarded as his finest work, have been censored. Vonnegut has been honored with two doctor of literature degrees as well as the Literary Lion Award from the New York Public Library and the Eugene V. Debs Award for public service.

JAMES H. WEBB, JR. (1946–)

An Annapolis graduate, Webb served in Vietnam and was one of the most highly decorated Marines, receiving the Navy Cross, Silver Star, two Bronze Stars, and two Purple Hearts. He also was named Outstanding Veteran by the Vietnam Veterans Civic Council in 1976. He served as secretary of the navy from April 1987 to February 1988; in 2006 he was elected to the Senate from Virginia. He has written novels such as *Fields of Fire* (1978), *A Sense of Honor* (1981), *A Country Such as This* (1983), *Something to Die For* (1991), *The Emperor's General* (1999), and *Lost Soldiers* (2001), as well as the nonfiction works *Micronesia and the United States Pacific Strategy* (1974) and *Born Fighting* (2004).

(JOHN) HARVEY WHEELER, JR. (1918–2004)

Interested in political science since childhood, Wheeler said he studied it "to try to understand why everything went wrong and what might be done to make things better." He worked as a professor and author. He wrote both academic works and political science-related fiction, including *Fail-Safe* (1962), *Democracy in a Revolutionary Era* (1968), and *Politics of Revolution* (1971). He was also the cofounder and joint chief editor of the *Journal of Social and Biological Structures.*

DAVID WISE (1930–)

Wise joined the staff of the *New York Herald Tribune* as a reporter and became the White House correspondent and bureau chief of the Washington office. In addition to *The Invisible Government* (1964), *The Espionage Establishment* (1967), and *The U-2 Affair* (1962), all co-authored with Thomas B. Ross, his recent works include *Molehunt: The Secret Search for Traitors That Shattered the CIA* (1992), *The American Police State: The Government Against the People* (1978), *Cassidy's Run: The Secret Spy War Over Nerve Gas* (2000), *Spy: The Inside Story of How the FBI's Robert Hassen Betrayed America* (2002), and *Democracy Under Pressure* (2004).

PETER WRIGHT (1916–1995)

Wright worked his way through the rural economy program at Oxford as a farmhand, and later became involved in technical projects during World War II. As a member of British intelligence organizations, he helped to convince the British government of Soviet technological superiority and to improve British technology designed for counterintelligence. After retiring, he wrote the memoir of his days in counterespionage, *Spycatcher: The Candid Autobiography of a Senior Intelligence Office* (1987).

RICHARD WRIGHT (1908–1960)

Born on a Mississippi plantation, Wright struggled for both an education and his political ideals. He was a member of the Federal Writer's Project in Chicago and New York and the recipient of a Guggenheim fellowship. These grants allowed him the time to write many works, including *Native Son* (1940) and *Black Boy* (1945). Although he became a Communist in 1932 after being refused jobs promised him by both Republicans and Democrats and was the Harlem editor of the *Daily Worker*, he later left the party in 1944 and expatriated to Europe at the end of World War II.

GERARD COLBY ZILG (1945–)

Before becoming a full-time writer, Zilg was a press secretary for a congressman and taught secondary school English and social studies. He has written *Du Pont: Behind the Nylon Curtain* (1974), *Du Pont Dynasty* (1984), and *Thy Will Be Done* (cowritten with Charlotte Donnett; 1995). The last two books are listed as authored by "Gerard Colby."

BIBLIOGRAPHY

BOOKS

Adams, Robert M. "The Interior Prince, or Machiavelli Mythologized" and "The Rise, Proliferation, and Degradation of Machiavellism: An Outline." In *The Prince*, edited by Robert M. Adams, 238–250. New York: W. W. Norton, 1977.

Agee, Philip. *On the Run*. Secaucus, N.J.: Lyle Stuart, 1987.

Allen, Roger. *The Arabic Novel: An Historical and Critical Introduction*. Syracuse, N.Y.: Syracuse University Press, 1982.

Allen, Shirley, et al. *Land of the Free and Its Critics*. Millbrae: California Council for the Social Studies, 1967.

Alsanea, Rajaa. *Girls of Riyadh*. New York: Penguin, 2007.

Anonymous. *A Woman in Berlin: Eight Weeks in the Conquered City*. New York: Henry Holt, 2005.

Attacks on Freedom to Learn: 1980–1983 Report. New York: People For the American Way, New York Regional Office, November 1983.

Attacks on Freedom to Learn: 1985–1986 Report. Washington, D.C.: People For the American Way, 1986.

Attacks on Freedom to Learn: 1986–1987 Report. Washington, D.C.: People For the American Way, 1987.

Attacks on Freedom to Learn: 1992–1993 Report. Washington, D.C.: People For the American Way, 1993.

Balderston, Daniel, and Francine Masiello, eds. *Eight Approaches to Teaching Puig's* Kiss of the Spider Woman. New York: Modern Language Association of America, 2007.

Balmuth, Daniel. *Censorship in Russia, 1865–1905*. Washington, D.C.: University Press of America, 1979.

Barnes, James J., and Patience P. Barnes. *Hitler's Mein Kampf in Britain and America: A Publishing History 1930–1939*. Cambridge: Cambridge University Press, 1980.

Bowers, Claude G. *The Young Jefferson: 1743–1789*. Boston: Houghton Mifflin, 1945.

Brady, Frank, ed. *Twentieth Century Interpretations of Gulliver's Travels*. Englewood Cliffs, N.J.: Prentice-Hall, 1968.

Brodie, Fawn M. *Thomas Jefferson: An Intimate History*. New York: W. W. Norton, 1974.

Bull, George. "Introduction." In *The Prince*. Trans. George Bull. Baltimore: Penguin Books, 1961, 9–26.

Burg, David, and George Feifer. *Solzhenitsyn*. New York: Stein and Day, 1972.

Burress, Lee. *The Battle of the Books: Literary Censorship in the Public Schools, 1950–1985*. Metuchen, N.J.: Scarecrow Press, 1989.

———. "*The Grapes of Wrath*: Preserving Its Place in the Curriculum." In *Censored Books: Critical Viewpoints*, edited by Nicholas J. Karolides, Lee Burress, and John M. Kean, 278–287. Metuchen, N.J.: Scarecrow Press, 1993.

Butz, Arthur R. *The Hoax of the Twentieth Century*. Richmond, U.K.: Historical Review Press, 1975.

Callan, Richard J. *Miguel Angel Asturias*. New York: Twayne Publishers, 1970.

Carmichael, Joel. *A Short History of the Russian Revolution.* New York: Basic Books, 1964.

Carroll, W. G. Introduction to *The Commercial Restraints of Ireland Considered*, by John Hely Hutchinson. Dublin, Ireland: M. H. Gill and Son, 1888.

Catherine the Great. "The Empress Catherine II's Notes on the Journey." In *A Journey from St. Petersburg to Moscow*, edited by Roderick Page Thaler, 239–249. Cambridge, Mass.: Harvard University Press, 1958.

Chalidze, Vallery. *To Defend These Rights: Human Rights and the Soviet Union.* New York: Random House, 1974.

Cohen, Carl, ed. *Communism, Fascism, and Democracy.* 2nd ed. New York: Random House, 1972.

Cole, John Y. *A Brief History of the Library of Congress.* Washington, D.C.: Library of Congress, 1993.

Collier, Christopher, ed. *Brother Sam and All That: Historical Context and Literary Analysis of the Novels of James and Christopher Collier.* Orange, Conn.: Clearwater Press, 1999.

Conlin, Joseph R. *Our Land, Our Time: A History of the United States.* San Diego, Calif.: Coronado Publishers, 1985.

Connor, James E., ed. *Lenin on Politics and Revolution.* New York: Pegasus, 1968.

Conquest, Robert. *The Pasternak Affair: Courage of Genius.* Philadelphia: J. B. Lippincott, 1962.

Cook, Bruce. *Dalton Trumbo.* New York: Charles Scribner's Sons, 1977.

Cook, Fred J. *The Nightmare Decade: The Life and Times of Senator Joe McCarthy.* New York: Random House, 1971.

Crankshaw, Edward. *Bismarck.* New York: Viking Press, 1981.

Crosby, Donald F. *God, Church, and the Flag: Senator Joseph R. McCarthy and the Catholic Church, 1950–1957.* Chapel Hill: University of North Carolina Press, 1978.

Cuthbertson, Ken. *Inside: The Biography of John Gunther.* Chicago: Bonus Books, 1992.

Dai Qing. *Yangtze! Yangtze!* Toronto: Earthscan Publications, 1994.

Davis, Herbert. "Introduction." In *The Drapier's Letters to the People of Ireland Against Receiving Wood's Halfpence*, by Jonathan Swift. Oxford: Clarendon Press, 1935.

de Jonge, Alex. *Stalin and the Shaping of the Soviet Union.* New York: William Morrow, 1986.

DelFattore, Joan. *What Johnny Shouldn't Read: Textbook Censorship in America.* New Haven, Conn.: Yale University Press, 1992.

DeMuth, James. "*Johnny Got His Gun:* A Depression Era Classic." In *Censored Books: Critical Viewpoints*, edited by Nicholas J. Karolides, Lee Burress, and John M. Kean, 331–337. Metuchen, N.J.: Scarecrow Press, 1993.

Downs, Robert B. *Books That Changed America.* London: MacMillan, 1970.

Doyle, Robert P. *Banned Books: 1994 Resource Guide.* Chicago: American Library Association, 1994.

Edward, Samuel. *Rebel! A Biography of Tom Paine.* New York: Praeger Publishers, 1974.

Edwards, June. *Opposing Censorship in Public Schools: Religion, Morality, and Literature.* Mahwah, N.J.: Lawrence Erlbaum Associates, Publishers, 1998.

Flood, Charles Bracelen. *Hitler: The Path to Power.* Boston: Houghton Mifflin, 1989.

Flynn, Gerard, Kenneth Grieb, and Richard J. Callan. *Essays on Miguel Angel Asturias.* Milwaukee: University of Wisconsin–Milwaukee, 1973.

Foerstal, Herbert N. *Banned in the U.S.A.: A Reference Guide to Book Censorship in Schools and Public Libraries.* Westport, Conn.: Greenwood Press, 1994.

Ford, Paul Leicester. "Introduction." In *A Summary View of the Rights of British America*, by Thomas Jefferson. Brooklyn, N.Y.: Historical Printing Club, 1892. Reprint, New York: Lenox Hill Publishing and Distribution Co., 1971.

Fysh, Michael, ed. *The Spycatcher Cases*. London: European Law Centre, 1989.

Gallo, Donald R. "Reality and Responsibility: The Continuing Controversy over Robert Cormier's Books for Young Adults." In *The VOYA Reader*, edited by Dorothy M. Broderick, 153–160. Metuchen, N.J.: Scarecrow Press, 1990.

Garbus, Martin. Afterward to *In the Spirit of Crazy Horse*, by Peter Matthiessen. New York: Viking Press, 1983, 589–96.

Gayle, Addison. *Richard Wright: Ordeal of a Native Son*. Garden City, N.Y.: Anchor Press/Doubleday, 1980.

Geller, Evelyn. *Forbidden Books in American Public Libraries, 1876–1939. A Study in Cultural Change*. Westport, Conn.: Greenwood Press, 1984.

Goetz-Stankiewicz, Marketa. *The Silenced Theatre: Czech Playwrights Without a Stage*. Toronto: University of Toronto Press, 1979.

———, ed. *The Vaněk Plays: Four Authors, One Character*. Vancouver: University of British Columbia Press, 1987.

Gordimer, Nadine. *The Essential Gesture: Writing, Politics and Places*. New York: Alfred A. Knopf, 1988.

Graham, Maryemma, and Jerry W. Ward, Jr. "*Black Boy* (American Hunger): Freedom to Remember." In *Censored Books: Critical Viewpoints*, edited by Nicholas J. Karolides, Lee Burress, and Jack Kean, 109–116. Metuchen, N.J.: Scarecrow Press, 1993.

Green, Jonathon, and Nicholas J. Karolides, reviser. *The Encyclopedia of Censorship, New Edition*. New York: Facts On File, 2005.

Grieb, Kenneth. "Miguel Angel Asturias as a Political Propagandist." In *Essays on Miguel Angel Asturias*, edited by Gerard Flynn et al., 10–22. Milwaukee: University of Wisconsin–Milwaukee, 1973.

Gunther, John. *Inside Russia Today*. New York: Harper and Brothers, 1958.

Haight, Anne Lyon, and Chandler B. Grannis. *Banned Books, 387 B.C. to 1978 A.D.* 4th ed. New York: R. R. Bowker, 1978.

Hale, J. R. "The Setting of *The Prince*. In *The Prince*, edited by Robert M. Adams, 141–152. New York: W. W. Norton, 1977.

Haney, Robert W. *Comstockery in America*. Boston: Beacon Press, 1960.

Hansen, Harry. "The Book That Shocked a Nation." In *All Quiet on the Western Front*, by Erich Maria Remarque. New York: Heritage Press, 1969.

Harer, John B. *Intellectual Freedom: A Reference Handbook*. Santa Barbara, Calif.: ABC-CLIO, 1992.

Harris, Leon. *Upton Sinclair: American Rebel*. New York: Crowell, 1975.

Havel, Václav. *The Vaněk Plays*. Germany: Rowohtt, 1978.

Hentoff, Nat. *The First Freedom: The Tumultuous History of Free Speech in America*. New York: Delacorte Press, 1980.

Hoffman, Nancy. "A Journey into Knowing: Agnes Smedley's *Daughter of Earth*," In *Tradition and Talents of Women*, edited by Florence Howe, 171–182. Urbana: University of Illinois Press, 1991.

Hosking, Geoffrey. *The First Socialist Society: A History of the Soviet Union from Within*. Cambridge, Mass.: Harvard University Press, 1985.

Howe, Irving. *Leon Trotsky*. New York: Viking Press, 1978.

Huddleston, Eugene L. *Thomas Jefferson: A Reference Guide*. Boston: G. K. Hall, 1982.

Hunt, J. Timothy. *The Politics of Bones*. Toronto: McClelland and Stewart, 2005.

Hunter, William B., ed. *A Milton Encyclopedia*. Lewisburg, Pa.: Bucknell University Press, 1978.

Hurwitz, Leon. *Historical Dictionary of Censorship in the United States*. Westport, Conn.: Greenwood Press, 1985.

Jamieson, John. *Books for the Army: The Army Library Service in the Second World War*. New York: Columbia University Press, 1950.

Jefferson, Thomas. *Autobiography of Thomas Jefferson*. New York: Capricorn Books, n.d.

Jenkinson, Edward B. *Censors in the Classroom: The Mind Benders*. Carbondale: Southern Illinois University Press, 1979.

Johnson, Chalmers. *An Instance of Treason. Ozaki Hotsumi and the Sorge Spy Ring*. Stanford, Calif.: Stanford University Press, 1964.

Jones, Frances M. *Defusing Censorship: The Librarian's Guide to Handling Censorship Conflicts*. Phoenix, Ariz.: Oryx Press, 1983.

Jones, Sidney. *Injustice, Persecution, Eviction: A Human Rights Update on Indonesia and East Timor*. New York: Asia Watch, 1990.

Josephson, Matthew. *Victor Hugo: A Realistic Biography of the Great Romantic*. Garden City, N.Y.: Doubleday, Doran, 1942.

Kagan, Richard C. "Introduction." In *The China Lobby in American Politics*, by Ross Y. Koen. New York: Harper and Row, 1974.

Karolides, Nicholas J., and Lee Burress, eds. *Celebrating Censored Books*. Racine: Wisconsin Council of Teachers of English, 1985.

Karolides, Nicholas J., Lee Burress, and John M. Kean, eds. *Censored Books: Critical Viewpoints*. Metuchen, N.J.: Scarecrow Press, 1993.

Kerber, Linda K. *Federalists in Dissent: Imagery and Ideology in Jeffersonian America*. Ithaca, N.Y.: Cornell University Press, 1980.

Knapp, Shelley Lyn. *Quoting Revolution: A Study of Agnes Smedley's Attempt to Express a Revolutionary China to the West*. M.A. thesis. University of Washington, 1987.

Kundera, Milan. *The Joke (Zert)*, fifth edition. New York: HarperCollins, 1992.

La Farge, Oliver. "Foreword." In *Laughing Boy*. Boston: Houghton Mifflin, 1929.

Lamont, Corliss. *Freedom Is as Freedom Does*. New York: Continuum, 1956.

Lauter, Paul. "Afterword." In *Daughter of Earth*, by Agnes Smedley. New York: Feminist Press, 1973.

Levine, Suzanne Jill. *Manual Puig and the Spider Woman: His Life and Emotions*. New York: Farrar, Straus and Giroux, 2000.

Liao Yiwu. *The Corpse Walker: Real-Life Stories, China from the Bottom Up*. New York: Pantheon Books, 2008.

MacKinnon, Janice, and Stephen MacKinnon. *Agnes Smedley: The Life and Times of an American Radical*. Berkeley: University of California Press, 1988.

Magill, Frank N., ed. *Masterplots*. Rev. ed. Englewood Cliffs, N.J.: Salem Press, 1976.

Manso, Peter. *Mailer: His Life and Times*. New York: Simon and Schuster, 1985.

Marchetti, Victor, and John D. Marks. *The CIA and the Cult of Intelligence*. New York: Alfred A. Knopf, 1974.

McDonald, Hamish. *Suharto's Indonesia*. Blackburn, Victoria, Australia: Dominion Press/Fontana Books, 1980.

McPherson, Nina. Translator's note to *Paradise of the Blind*, by Duong Thu Huong. New York: William Morrow, 1993.

Mel'gunov, S. P. *The Bolshevik Seizure of Power*. Santa Barbara, Calif.: ABC-CLIO, 1972.

Miller, Robert Keith. "Defending Solzhenitsyn: One Day in the Life of Ivan Denisovich." In *Celebrating Censored Books!* edited by Nicholas J. Karolides and Lee Burress, 89–92. Racine: Wisconsin Council of Teachers of English, 1985.

Mills, Hilary. *Mailer: A Biography.* New York: Empire Books, 1982.

Misurella, Fred. *Milan Kundera: Public Events, Private Affairs.* Columbia: University of South Carolina Press, 1993.

Monas, Sidney. *The Third Section: Police and Society in Russia under Nicholas I.* Cambridge, Mass.: Harvard University Press, 1961.

Moore, Terry Jonathan. *Neither True Nor Divine: Elihu Palmer's Opposition to Christianity.* Ph.D. diss. New Orleans Baptist Theological Seminary, 1994.

Morais, Herbert M. *Deism in Eighteenth Century America.* New York: Russell and Russell, 1960.

Myers, Thomas. *Walking Point: American Narratives of Vietnam.* New York: Oxford University Press, 1988.

Müller, Herta. *The Appointment.* New York: Metropolitan Books/Henry Holt, 2001.

Munif, Abdul Rahman. *Cities of Salt.* New York: Random House, 1987.

Nelson, Jack, and Gene Roberts, Jr. *The Censors and the Schools.* Boston: Little, Brown, 1963.

Noggle, Burl. *Teapot Dome: Oil and Politics in the 1920's.* Baton Rouge: Louisiana State University Press, 1962.

"A Note about the Author." In *Paradise of the Blind,* by Duong Thu Huong. New York: William Morrow, 1993, 268–270.

O'Connor, Richard, and Dale L. Walker. *The Lost Revolutionary: The Biography of John Reed.* New York: Harcourt, Brace and World, 1967.

O'Neil, Robert. *Classrooms in the Crossfire: The Rights and Interests of Students, Parents, Teachers, Administrators, Librarians and the Community.* Bloomington: Indiana University Press, 1981.

Ononuga, Bayo. "Soyinga Tells His Exile Story." In *Conversations with Wole Soyinka,* edited by Biodun Jeyifo. Jackson: University of Mississippi Press, 2001.

Orwell, George. *Animal Farm.* New York: New American Library, 1946.

Oshinsky, David M. *A Conspiracy So Immense: The World of Joe McCarthy.* New York: Free Press, 1983.

Palmer, Elihu. *An Inquiry Relative to the Moral and Political Improvement of the Human Species.* New York: John Crookes, 1797.

Pamuk, Orhan. *Snow.* New York: Alfred A. Knopf, 2004.

Parton, James. *Life of Thomas Jefferson.* Boston: James R. Osgood, 1874.

Payne, Robert. *The Three Worlds of Boris Pasternak.* Bloomington: Indiana University Press, 1961.

Peterson, Merrill D. *Thomas Jefferson and the New Nation: A Biography.* New York: Oxford University Press, 1970.

Pincher, Chapman. *The Spycatcher Affair.* New York: St. Martin's Press, 1988.

———. *Their Trade Is Treachery.* London: Sidgwick and Jackson, 1981.

Pohl, Frederik. "One Day in the Life of Ivan Denisovich by Aleksandr Solzhenitsyn." In *Censored Books: Critical Viewpoints,* edited by Nicholas J. Karolides, Lee Burress, and John M. Kean, 89–92. Metuchen, N.J.: Scarecrow Press, 1993, pp. 89–9.

Porter, Robert. *Milan Kundera: A Voice from Central Europe.* Aarhus, Denmark: Arkona, 1981.

Puig, Manuel. *Kiss of the Spider Woman.* New York: Alfred A. Knopf, 1979.

Quintana, Ricardo. *The Mind and Art of Jonathan Swift*. London: Oxford University Press, 1936.

Rosenstone, Robert A. *Romantic Revolutionary*. New York: Alfred A. Knopf, 1975.

Rowland, Mary F., and Paul Rowland. *Pasternak's Doctor Zhivago*. Carbondale: Southern Illinois University Press, 1967.

Russell, Bertrand. *The Practice and Theory of Bolshevism*. New York: Simon and Schuster, 1964.

Sabine, George H., and Thomas L. Thorson. *A History of Political Theory*. 4th ed. Hinsdale, Ill.: Dryden Press, 1973.

Saillers, Emile. *John Milton: Man, Poet, Polemist*. Oxford: Basil Blackwell, 1964.

Saro-Wiwa, Ken. *A Month and a Day: A Detention Diary*. New York: Penguin Books, 1995.

Saunders, George. *Samizdat: Voices of the Soviet Opposition*. New York: Monad Press, 1974.

Schlesinger, Stephen, and Stephen Kinzer. *Bitter Fruit: The Untold Story of the American Coup in Guatemala*. Garden City, N.Y.: Doubleday, 1982.

Serafin, Steven R., ed. *Encyclopedia of World Literature in the 20th Century*. Vol. 5. Farmington Hills, Mich.: St. James Press, 1999.

Serge, Victor, and Natalia Sedova Trotsky. *The Life and Death of Leon Trotsky*. New York: Basic Books, 1975.

Shafak, Elif. *The Bastard of Istanbul*. New York: Penguin, 2007.

Shapiro, Martin. *The Pentagon Papers and the Courts*. San Francisco: Chandler Publishing, 1972.

Sheehan, Neil, Hedrick Smith, E. W. Kenworthy, and Fox Butterfield. *The Pentagon Papers*. New York: Bantam Books, 1971.

Siebert, Fredrick Seaton. *Freedom of the Press in England, 1476–1776*. Urbana: University of Illinois Press, 1965.

Sirluck, Ernest. "Preface and Notes." In *Complete Prose Works of John Milton*. Vol. 2. New Haven, Conn.: Yale University Press, 1959.

Slater, Kenneth W. *The Pentagon Papers Trial*. Berkeley, Calif.: Justa Publications, 1975.

Smedley, Agnes. *Battle Hymn of China*. New York: Alfred A. Knopf, 1943.

Snepp, Frank. "Postscript." In *Decent Interval*. New York: Random House, 1977.

Solzhenitsyn, Aleksandr. *The Gulag Archipelago*. Vol. 1. New York: Harper and Row, 1973.

———. *The Oak and the Calf*. New York: Harper and Row, 1980.

Soyinka, Wole. *The Open Sore of a Continent: A Personal Narrative of the Nigerian Crisis*. New York: Oxford, 1996.

Spechler, Dina. *Permitted Dissent in the U.S.S.R.* New York: Praeger, 1982.

Stephen, Leslie. *History of English Thought in the Eighteenth Century*. Vol. 1. New York: Peter Smith, 1949.

Strauss, Leo. "Machiavelli the Immoralist." In *The Prince*, edited by Robert M. Adams, 180–185. New York: W. W. Norton, 1977.

Tebbel, John. *A History of Book Publishing in the United States*. Vols. 1–4. New York: R. R. Bowker, 1972–81.

Thaler, Roderick Page. Introduction to *A Journey from St. Petersburg to Moscow*, by Aleksandr Radishchev. Cambridge, Mass.: Harvard University Press, 1958.

Thomas, Donald. *A Long Time Burning: The History of Literary Censorship in England*. New York: Frederick A. Praeger, 1969.

Tittler, Jonathan. *Manuel Puig.* New York: Twayne, 1993.
Trotsky, Leon. *My Life: An Attempt at an Autobiography.* New York: Pathfinder Press, 1970.
Trumbo, Dalton. "Introduction." In *Johnny Got His Gun.* New York: Bantam Books, 1983.
Turnbull, Malcolm. *The Spycatcher Trial.* Topsfield, Mass.: Salem House Publishers, 1989.
Turner, Robert F. *Myths of the Vietnam War: The Pentagon Papers Reconsidered* (Southeast Asian Perspectives, #7). New York: American Friends of Vietnam, 1972.
Turner, Stansfield. "Appendix: A Word on Censorship." In *Secrecy and Democracy: The CIA in Transition.* New York: Harper and Row, 1985.
Ungar, Sanford J. *The Papers and the Papers.* New York: E. P. Dutton, 1972.
Vernadsky, George, ed. *A Source Book for Russian History from Early Times to 1917.* Vol. 2. New Haven, Conn.: Yale University Press, 1972.
Walters, Kerry S. *The American Deists: Voices of Reason and Dissent in the Early Republic.* Lawrence: University Press of Kansas, 1992.
Walters, Kerry S. "Elihu Palmer & the Religion of Nature: An Introductory Essay." In *Principle of Nature*, by Elihu Palmer. Wolfeboro, N.H.: Longwood Academic, 1990.
Warmbold, Carolyn Nizza. *Women of the Mosquito Press: Louise Bryant, Agnes Smedley, and Margaret Randall as Narrative Guerrillas.* Ph.D. diss. University of Texas at Austin, 1990.
Weathersby, Dorothy T. *Censorship of Literature Textbooks in Tennessee: A Study of the Commission, Publishers, Teachers, and Textbooks.* Ed.D. diss., University of Tennessee, 1975.
Webb, Constance. *Richard Wright: A Biography.* New York: Putnam, 1968.
Wong How Man. *Exploring the Yangtze: China's Longest River.* San Francisco: China Books and Periodicals, 1989.
Zeman, Z. A. B. *Prague Spring.* New York: Hill and Wang, 1967.

COURT CASES

Agee v. Muskie, 203 U.S. App. D.C. 46, 48, 629F. 2d 80, 82 (1980).
Agee v. Vance, 483 F. Supp. 729 (1980).
Board of Education, Island Trees Union Free School District #26 et al. v. Pico, 102 S.Ct. 2799, 457 U.S. 853, 73 L.Ed. 2d 435 (1982).
Haig, Secretary of State v. Agee. 453 U.S. 280: Supreme Court 1981.
Minarcini v. Strongsville City District, 541 F. 2d 577 (6th Circuit 1976).
New York Times Co. v. United States, 403 U.S. 713: Supreme Court 1971.
San Diego Committee v. Governing Board of Grossmont Union High School District, 790 F. 2d 1471 (9th Circuit 1986).
Scearcey v. Crim, 815 F. 2d 1389 (11th Circuit 1987).
Snepp v. United States, 444 U.S. 507: Supreme Court 1980.
Todd v. Rochester Community Schools, 41 Mich. App. 320 (1972).
United States v. Washington Post Co., 403 U.S. 713: Supreme Court 1971.

JOURNALS AND NEWSPAPERS

Adams, James. Review of *Sex and the City. Globe and Mail*, May 29, 2010.
"Agee Passport Ordered Restored." *New York Times*, January 29, 1980, p. 14.

Ahmed, Fatema. "Velvet Lives: Fatema Ahmed Goes Searching for Romance in Saudi Arabia." Guardian Review. *Guadian* (London), July 14, 2007.

"Anniston Coalition Targets 'Obscenity.' " *Tuscaloosa News*, October 9, 1982, n.p.

"Arbitrator's Decision: Restore *Bloods* to Shelf." *School Library Journal*, October 1987, 14.

"ASTA Release." *Anaheim Secondary Teachers Association*, September 27, 1978 and November 15, 1979.

"Author Loses Court Ruling." *New York Times*, April 22, 1982, p. 30.

Averback, Ronna. "Authors Defend Books in Ban Suit." *Strongsville News Sun*, June 27, 1974, p. 1.

Bagdikian, Ben H. "Working in Secret." *New York Times Book Review*, June 28, 1964, pp. 3, 20.

Bailey, Charles W. "Publisher Says CIA Tried to Censor Book." *Minneapolis Morning Tribune*, June 9, 1964, p. 35.

Bald, Margaret. "For Indonesia's Rulers, the Fiction Hurts." *Toward Freedom* (August–September, 1992): 17–18.

———. "Why Don't We Know about This Great Novelist?" *Toward Freedom* (June–July 1990): 13–14.

Baskin, Jason M. "The Appointment." *Chicago Review*, December 22, 2007.

"Berlin and Rome Hail Ban on Lewis Film." *New York Times*, February 17, 1936, p. 21.

Berry, John F. "Du Pont Book Contract Breach Ruled by Judge." *Washington Post*, July 24, 1982, p. D9.

Bixler, Paul. "Book Banned by Greene County Libraries, Is Offered to Public by Antioch College." *Steinbeck Newsletter* (Winter 1993): 10–11.

Blake Patricia. "A Diseased Body Politic." *New York Times Book Review*, October 27, 1968, p. 7.

———. *"The Gulag Archipelago."* *New York Times Book Review*, October 26, 1975, pp. 1, 18–21.

———. "Who Is the Rev. Wendell Runion and Why Does He Want Those Books Banned?" *Asheville Citizen*, January 31, 1981, n.p.

"Board Reverses Censorship Stand." *Racine Journal Times*, June 22, 1984, n.p.

Bold, Rudolph. "Rocky!" *American Libraries* 1 (June 1970): 525.

"Book Banning." *Racine Journal Times*, June 13, 1984, n.p.

"Book Burning." *New Republic* 128 (June 29, 1953): 7–17.

"Book Overcomes Challenge in Palmyra." (Lebanon, Pa.) *Daily News*, October 22, 1994, p. 3.

Bosshard, Peter. "Nature Strikes Back at Three Gorges Dam." International Rivers. Available online. URL: www.internationalrivers.org/blog/peter-bosshard,nature-strikes-back-three-gorges-dam. Accessed September 23, 2010.

"Boston Stops Sale of Nine Modern Books." *New York Times*, March 12, 1927, pp. 1, 3.

Bourke, Joanna. "Living with a Brutal Bear." *The Independent* (June 17, 2005).

Bowden, Kevin. "Community Split on Steinbeck Novel." *Union City Daily Messenger*, December 13, 1993, pp. 1, 2.

———. "Request for Alternate Book Denied." *Union City Daily Messenger*, January 11, 1994, pp. 1, 2.

Boyd, William. Introduction to *A Month and A Day: A Detention Diary* by Ken Saro-Wiwa. New York: Penguin, 1995.

Boyle, Maureen. "Board Nixes Book Ban, Sets Warnings Instead." [Manchester, N.H.] *Union Leader*, June 23, 1982, p. 6.

Bradley, Julia Turnquist. "Censoring the School Library. Do Students Have the Right to Read?" *Connecticut Law Review* 10 (Spring 1978): 747–74.

"Branding of Books Stirs Texas Battle." *New York Times*, June 7, 1953, p. 61.

"British Official Suggests Ousting Viking Board to Stop *Spycatcher.*" *Publishers Weekly*, August 7, 1987, 311.

Bryan, C. B. D. "Growing up the Hard Way." *New York Times Book Review*, August 15, 1976, p. 1.

Buie, Lisa. "Attempt to Have Book Banned Makes National Group's Report." [Rock Hill] *Herald*, September 1, 1988, p. 2A.

———. "Fort Mill School Won't Ban Book." [Rock Hill] *Herald*, May 6, 1988, pp. 1, 14.

———. "Parents Want Book Removed from School." [Rock Hill] *Herald*, April 27, 1988, pp. 1, 19.

Bullard, F. Lauriston. "Book-Banning Issue Burning in Boston." *New York Times*, July 3, 1927, sec. 2, p. 2.

Burress, Lee A., Jr. "The Pressure of Censorship on Wisconsin Public Schools." *Wisconsin English Journal* 6 (October 1963): 6–28.

Butterfield, Fox. "Pentagon Papers: Eisenhower Decisions Undercut the Geneva Accords." *New York Times*, July 5, 1971, pp. 1, 13.

Campbell, Duncan. "G2: The Spy Who Stayed Out in the Cold": *Guardian* (London), January 10, 2007, p. 4.

Campbell, John, Jr. "Concern Expressed over Books in Schools." *Asheville Citizen*, January 23, 1981, n.p.

———. "Large Crowd Gathers for Sessions on Books." *Asheville Citizen*, February 20, 1981, p. 17.

"Canada Blocks Book by Former Israeli Agent." *New York Times*, September 10, 1990, p. A16.

Carlson, Peter. "A Chilling Case of Censorship." *Washington Post Magazine*, January 4, 1987, pp. 10–17, 40–41.

Carmody, Dierdre. "Ex-Aide Challenges CIA's Secrecy Suit." *New York Times*, March 9, 1978, p. 19.

Chapman, Ralph. "Agnes Smedley Denies Charge of Acting as Spy for Soviets." *New York Herald Tribune*, February 11, 1949, n.p.

Charle, Suzanne. "Prisoner Without a Cell." *Nation*, February 3, 1992, 134–135.

"CIA Concerned over Book." *Newsletter on Intellectual Freedom* 13 (1964): 48.

"CIA Whistleblower Returns to UK." *Guardian* (London), November 3, 1995, p. 18.

"CIA Will Give Data to Enjoin Ex-Agent." *New York Times*, April 27, 1972, p. 7.

"CLA Cancels 'Holocaust Hoax' Publisher." *Newsletter on Intellectual Freedom* 34 (1985): 1, 30–31.

Clines, Francis X. "*Spycatcher* Judge Rules Against Thatcher." *New York Times*, December 22, 1987, p. 16.

"Club Withdraws Book on Du Ponts." *New York Times*, January 21, 1975, p. 30.

Coetzee, J. M. "Censorship and Polemic: The Solzhenitsyn Affair." *Pretexts* 2 (Summer 1990): 3–22.

———. "Educational Groups Deplore Roselle Book Ban." *Newark Star-Ledger*, June 23, 1972, p. 17.

———. "Roselle Board President Defends Book Bannings." *Newark Star-Ledger*, June 27, 1972, p. 15.

————. "State Education Official Assails Book Bannings." *Newark Star-Ledger,* June 27, 1972, p. 15.

Cohen, Roger. "Ban on Mossad Book Is Overturned." *New York Times,* September 14, 1990, p. C29.

————. "Judge Halts Publication of Book by Ex-Israeli Intelligence Officer." *New York Times,* September 13, 1990, p. A1.

"Connecticut School Bans Book on Mayor Daley." *New York Times,* April 12, 1972, p. 36.

Connolly, Cressida. "She Screamed for Help but Her Neighbors Barricaded the Door." *Daily Telegraph,* April 17, 2005.

Connolly, Kate. "Holocaust Denial Writer Jailed for Five Years." *Guardian* (International), February 16, 2007, p. 21.

Connor, Collins. "Panel Finds Book on Vietnam Too Graphic for Middle School." *St. Petersburg Times,* October 2, 1987, pp. 1, 10.

————. "Teachers' Union Official Seeks Review of Banned Reading." *St. Petersburg Times,* September 23, 1987, n.p.

Conquest, Robert. "Evaluation of an Exile." *Saturday Review,* April 20, 1974, 22–24, 30.

Conrad, Charles. "Land of Free Skimpy with Facts." *Tablet,* July 28, 1966, n.p.

"Controversy at Glenwood over Censorship of Books." *Newsletter on Intellectual Freedom* 19 (1970): 30.

"Court Backs Philip Agee in Dispute over Passport." *New York Times,* June 28, 1980, p. 6.

"Court Dismisses Janklow Suit against Viking and Matthiessen." *Publishers Weekly,* June 16, 1989, 14.

"Covers for CIA Are Big Problem." *New York Times,* January 16, 1976, p. 5.

Cowperthwait, Richard, and Alan Abbey. "Richford Parents Fermenting over *Grapes of Wrath.*" *Burlington Free Press,* November 11, 1981, pp. 1–2B.

Crawford, Tom. "Ferret out Books, Cobb Board Told." *Atlanta Journal,* May 27, 1977, p. 8A.

"Crazy Horse Suit Ends; Viking to Publish New Edition in 1991." *Publishers Weekly,* November 9, 1990, 12.

Crewdson, John M. "CIA Will Seek to Excise Parts of Book by Ex-Aide." *New York Times,* September 21, 1973, p. 18.

Crosette, Barbara. "Banned in Jakarta." *New York Times Book Review,* January 19, 1992, p. 24.

"The Curious Case of Orhan Pamuk." *Harvard Political Review* (April 1, 2009).

"Czechs Ban Hitler's Book." *New York Times,* September 19, 1933, p. 12.

Daniel, Elizabeth. "Publication Fight Takes New Turn." *Tampa Tribune,* September 25, 1987, pp. 1, 3.

"Daley Denies Wife Induced Stores to Ban *Boss.*" *New York Times,* September 2, 1971, p. 23.

De Guetteville, Harry. "Sex and the Saudi Kingdom a Hot Seller: Banned Novel Lifts the Veil on Conservative Society." *National Post,* February 8, 2006.

Dixon, Ron. "A Book Debate Splits Mahwah." *Patterson News,* September 14, 1976, p. 17.

"Do Not Ban This Book" (Editorial). *Fort Mill Times,* May 4, 1980, p. 2.

Don't Take Any Guff from a Self-Appointed Censor." *Newsletter on Intellectual Freedom* 13 (1964): 81.

Dowe, Kelly. "Conservatives' Sword Mightier Than Textbooks." *Birmingham Post-Herald*, April 19, 1981, p. C1.

Eckholm, Erik. "After an Attack, Chinese Won't Print Expatriate's Novel." *New York Times*, June 24, 2000, p. B9.

Eder, Richard. "Allegory of Oppression in Ceaucescu's [sic] Romania." *New York Times* (September 12, 2001).

———. "The Disillusion of a CIA Man: 12 Years from Agent to Radical." *New York Times*, July 12, 1974, p. 4.

———. "Why Decision in Snepp Case Disturbs Publishers." *New York Times*, March 11, 1980, sec. 3, p. 5.

Enzensberger, Hans. "Enzensberger and Anonyma." Interview. *Der Spiegel* (September 9, 2003).

Esch, Christian. "An Unimportant Person?" *Süddeutsche Zeitung* (September 25, 2003).

Esslin, Martin. "The Theatre of the Absurd." In *Essays in Modern Drama*, edited by Morris Freedman. Boston: D. C. Heath and Company, 1964.

"Ex-Agent Is Permitted to Profit from Books Not Cleared by CIA." *New York Times*, October 3, 1980, p. 16.

"Ex-CIA Agent and U.S. Settle Suit Over Profits from Book." *New York Times*, June 28, 1980, p. 14.

"Ex-CIA Man Denies He Gave Information." *New York Times*, July 11, 1974, p. 9.

"Exiled Writers Differ with U.S. Publishers." *Publishers Weekly*, September 22, 1983, 14–15.

Feldman, Gayle. "Morrow Gives Voice to Banned Indonesian Writer." *Publishers Weekly* 237 (February 9, 1990): 27.

Feldman, James. "The Right to Present Alternatives." Unpublished article.

Feigenbaum, Lynn. "S. Dade School Bans Book on Cuba." *Miami News*, March 28, 1974, p. 5A.

Fein, Esther B. "Book Notes." *New York Times*, September 23, 1992, p. C20.

Fields, Howard. "High Court Rejects Libel Appeal against Viking." *Publishers Weekly* 237 (January 26, 1990): 310, 312.

"Fifty Years of Wrath." *Newsletter on Intellectual Freedom* 38 (1989): 121–23

Filkins, Peter. "Betrayal as a Way of Life." *New York Times Book Review* (October 21, 2001).

Finn, Elaine. "Communist Passages Spark Debate over Textbook." (Charlottesville, Va.) *Daily Progress*, January 12, 1922, pp. A1, 12.

"Firefighting." *New Republic* 129 (September 7, 1953): 5.

Fowler, Susanne. "Turkey, a Touchy Critic, Plans to Put a Novel on Trial." *New York Times* (September 16, 2006).

"France Expels Agee as an Undesirable." *New York Times*, August 19, 1977, p. 10.

Francisco, Jamie. "School Board Averts Ban." *Chicago Tribune* (May 26, 2006). Available online. URL: http://www.alliancelibrarysystem.com/pdf/2006Schoolboard avertsbookban.pdf. Accessed February 18, 2011.

Fransecky, Robert B. "Censorship and the Teaching of English." *Newsletter on Intellectual Freedom* 17 (1968): 39–40.

Freely, Maureen. "Writers on Trial." *New York Times*, August 13, 2006.

"Fulbright Attacks *The Ugly American*." *New York Times*, May 20, 1959, n.p.

Gehrke, Donna. "Kanawha Bans Classic Book from Classes." *Des Moines Register*, February 12, 1980, p. 1A.

LITERATURE SUPPRESSED ON POLITICAL GROUNDS

————. "School Board May Ban *Grapes of Wrath.*" *Des Moines Register,* February 10, 1980, p. 1B.

Gent, George. "Knopf Sues Over CIA Censoring of Book" *New York Times,* October 31, 1973, p. 36.

Gillespie, Scott. "Racine Board Bans 5 Books from Curriculum." *Milwaukee Sentinel,* June 12, 1984, pp. 1, 11.

Gottesmann, Christopher. "A Woman in Berlin." *New York Times Book Review,* September 11, 2005, 6.

"Government Bans Pramoedya's Book." *Jakarta Post,* May 13, 1995, n.p.

Graf, Thomas. "Jeffco Teacher Withdraws Challenge." *Denver Post,* November 1, 1986, p. 6B.

————. "Teacher, Citizen Challenge 2 Jeffco Children's Books." *Denver Post,* October 30, 1986, p. B1.

Graham, Fred P. "Court Denies U.S. an Injunction to Block *Times* Vietnam Series." *New York Times,* June 20, 1971, pp. 1, 26.

————. "Court Restrains the *Times* Again; a Hearing Today." *New York Times,* June 22, 1971, pp. 1, 18.

————. "Judge, at Request of U.S. Halts *Times* Vietnam Series Four Days Pending Hearing on Injunction." *New York Times,* June 16, 1971, p. 1.

————. "Supreme Court Agrees to Rules on Printing of Vietnam Series, Arguments to Be Heard Today." *New York Times,* June 26, 1971, pp. 1, 10.

————. "Supreme Court, 6-3 Upholds Newspapers on Publication of the Pentagon Papers." *New York Times,* July 1, 1971, pp. 1, 15–19.

————. "*Times* Asks Supreme Court to End Restraint on Its Vietnam Series." *New York Times,* June 25, 1971, pp. 1, 12.

————. "*Times* Case Heard, Restraint Extended; U.S. Action Halts a *Boston Globe* Series." *New York Times,* June 23, 1971, pp. 1, 22.

————. "*Times* Series Is Delayed Again; Paper to Appeal to High Court." *New York Times,* June 24, 1971, pp. 1, 16.

————. "*Times* Series Still Held Up Pending Court Ruling Today." *New York Times,* June 19, 1971, pp. 1, 11.

————. "U.S. Asking Court for Order to See *Times* Documents." *New York Times,* June 17, 1971, pp. 1, 18.

————. "U.S. Fails to Get Immediate Court Order to Force *Times* to Turn Over Documents." *New York Times,* June 18, 1971, pp. 1, 14.

Grant, Gerald. "Radical Rightists Try to Suppress Texts Sympathetic to Minorities." *Washington Post,* December 11, 1996, pp. A1, 6.

Grant, Linda. "The Rubble Woman." *Observer,* October 5, 2005.

Greenhouse, Linda. "Ex-CIA Agent Loses Appeal on Passport." *New York Times,* June 30, 1981, pp. 1, B8, B9.

————. "Reviving Affirmative Action Issue, Court Will Decide." *New York Times,* January 9, 1990, pp. A1, 18.

Grisso, James L. "Amherst High Keeps *Andersonville.*" *Cleveland Plain Dealer,* August 25, 1967, n.p.

"*Gulag* in the UN" *Newsletter on Intellectual Freedom* 23 (1974): 162.

Hacaoglu, Selcan. "Turkish Court Drops Charges against Novelist." *Independent,* January 23, 2006.

Halloran, Richard. "Ruling for *Post.*" *New York Times,* June 22, 1971, pp. 1, 27.

"Hanoi reproche à Paris d'avoir décoré une dissidente." ["Hanoi reproaches Paris for having decorated a dissident".] *Le Monde*, December 27, 1994, n.p.

Harding, Luke. "Row over Naming of Rape Author." *Observer* (October 5, 2003).

Harris, Kate. "Parents Group Trains Guns on Number of Textbooks." *Birmingham News*, February 12, 1981, p. 2A.

Harris, Robert R. "Too Embarrassed Not to Kill." *New York Times Book Review*, March 11, 1990, p. 8.

Hartzell, Richard. "Eye on Publishing." *Wilson Library Bulletin* 58 (1983): 200.

Hasegawa, Ann. "Land of Free Causes Delay in State Budget." *UCLA Daily Bruin*, May 18, 1966, n.p.

Henry III, William A., and William Maden. "Vaclav Havel: Dissident to President." *Time*, January 8, 1990.

Hentoff, Nat. "Officer Arrest That Book." *Washington Post*, October 7, 1995, p. A29.

"High Court Backs CIA in Curb on Articles Its Employees Write." *New York Times*, February 20, 1980, p. 1.

"High Court Ends Snepp's Fight to Keep Royalties." *Publishers Weekly*, April 25, 1980, 18, 23.

"Hitler Book Is Banned as 'Insulting' Poland." *New York Times*, October 1, 1933, p. 4.

"History Texts Declared 'Sick.' " *Sonora* [California] *Union-Democrat*, March 12, 1968, pp. 1, 6.

Hitchens, Christopher. "Mind the Gap." *Atlantic Monthly*, October, 2004, 188–193.

Hollobaugh, Dix. "The Wrath of Kanawha." *Des Moines Sunday Register*, February 24, 1980, pp. 1A, 5A.

"Hollywood Tempest Breaks on *It Can't Happen Here*." *Publishers Weekly*, February 22, 1936, 900.

Hoyle Bolick, Sandy. "Book Issue: Pros, Cons." *Asheville Times*, February 20, 1981, n.p.

"Huntsville [Alabama] Public Library Rocked by Mailer Book." *Library Journal*, January 15, 1968, 138.

Hvistendahl, Mara. "China's Three Gorges Dam: An Environmental Catastrophe?" (March 25, 2008). *Scientific American*. Available online. URL: www.scientific american.com/article.cfm?id=chinas-three-gorges-dam-disaster. Accessed January 24, 2011.

"Ideas and Trends: Education, Religion, Privacy." *New York Times*, December 15, 1974, sec. 4, p. 7.

Importation of Publications (Prohibition) Order. Grenada. Statutory Rules and Orders No. 6 of 1989. Gazetted. April 14, 1989.

"Index Index." *Index on Censorship* 14 (1985): 48.

Index on Censorship 6 (November/December 1979): 69; 2 (April 1980): 73.

Inter-American Commission on Human Rights. Report No 2/96, Case 10.325. Grenada. Washington, D.C.: Organization of American States, March 1, 1996.

"Interest Healthy—Up to a Point." [Charlottesville, Va.] *Daily Progress*, January 17, 1988, p. C2.

"International PEN Calls for Government Condemnation of Attacks on Author Orhan Pamuk." *International Freedom of Expression Exchange*, April 6, 2005.

"*It Can't Happen Here* Storm Continues Unabated." *Publishers Weekly*, March 14, 1936, 1,174.

Jarnigan, Bill. "Board, Committee Hear Textbooks Denounced." *Birmingham News*, March 26, 1981, p. 10A.

Jarvis, Richard. "Let Parents See Reading Lists, Trustee to Urge." *Greenville Piedmont*, April 10, 1991, p. 3.

Jiad, Abdula-Hadi. "Obituary: Abdul Rahman Munif." *Guardian* (London), February 5, 2004.

Jones, Sidney. "Release." *Asia Watch* (March 28, 1990).

"Judge Backs Refusal by CIA to Provide Data to an Ex-Agent." *New York Times*, July 21, 1981, p. 11.

"Judge Rules Snepp Violated Contract and Must Forfeit Profits on Book." *New York Times*, July 8, 1978, p. 8.

"Judge Rules That US Can Continue Suit for Agee Book Profits." *New York Times*, April 3, 1980, sec. 2, p. 9.

"The Jungle Vindicated." *Bookman* (July 1906): 481–485.

Kanon, Joseph. "A Woman in Berlin: My City of Ruins." *New York Times*, August 15, 2005.

Kaplan, Steven B. "The CIA Responds to Its Black Sheep: Censorship and Passport Revocation—The Cases of Philip Agee." *Connecticut Law Review* 13 (Winter 1981): 317–96.

Kappel, Tim. "Trampling Out the Vineyards—Kern County's Ban on *The Grapes of Wrath*." *California History* (Fall 1982): 210–21.

"K.C. Libraries Ban *Grapes of Wrath*." *Bakersfield Californian*, August 18, 1939, n.p.

Kegler, Sissy, and Gene Guerro. "Censorship in the South." *Newsletter on Intellectual Freedom* 35 (1986): 29, 56.

Kilborn, Peter T. "Agee Sees Long Legal Fight over Britain's Ouster Order." *New York Times*, January 29, 1977, p. 8.

———. "Another American Told to Quit Britain." *New York Times*, November 18, 1976, p. 11.

King, Seth S. "Book's 2 Pigs Stir Censorship Row." *New York Times*, February 20, 1971, p. 29.

———. "Professor Causes Furor by Saying Nazis Slaying of Jews Is a Myth." *New York Times*, January 28, 1977, p. 10.

Kinsey, Linda. "Books Still Ire, but Okayed." *County Line* (June 12, 1974): 1.

Kipp, Lawrence J. "Report from Boston." *Library Journal* 77 (1952): 1,843–46, 1,887.

Kirtley, Jane E. "The Law Lords Take a Detour: Chapter Two of the *Spycatcher* Saga." *Government Information Quarterly* 7 (1990): 53–58.

———. "A Walk Down a Dangerous Road: British Press Censorship and the *Spycatcher Debacle*." *Government Information Weekly* 5 (1988): 117–35.

Klepp, Lawrence. "In Dubious Battle." *Far East* (April 4, 1995): 37.

Knox, Don. "More Books Challenged in Jeffco School District." *Rocky Mountain News*, October 30, 1986, p. 41.

Kramer, Hilton. "The Soviet Terror Continued." *New York Times Book Review*, June 18, 1978, pp. 1, 28–29.

Kristoph, Nicholas D. "Tiananmen Square." *New York Times*, June 11, 2010.

Kronholz, June. "School Drops 'Anti-American' Book." *Miami Herald*, March 29, 1974, p. 1B.

Krotz, Robert. "Controversy at Glenwood over Censorship of Books." *Des Moines Register*, December 5, 1969, n.p.

Kuhn, Anthony. "Concerns Rise with Water of Three Gorges Dam." National Public Radio. Available online. URL: www.npr.org/templates/story/story.php?storyId=17723829. Accessed January 24, 2011.

Kundera, Milan. Author's Notes in *The Joke* by Milan Kundera. New York: Harper-Collins, 1992.

Kurtz, Bill. "Book Ban Reversed in Racine." *Milwaukee Journal,* June 19, 1984, p. 3.

Landy, Heather. "Protestors Condemn Butz, Holocaust Revisionism." *Daily Northwestern,* May 10, 1994, p. 4.

"Large Attendance at School Board Meeting." *Glenwood Opinion Tribune,* December 10, 1969, n.p.

"Latest Gordimer Novel Banned in South Africa." *New York Times,* September 7, 1979, p. 8.

Lea, Richard. "Plot to Kill Nobel Laureate." *Guardian* (London), January 28, 2008.

Leary, William M., Jr. "Books, Soldiers and Censorship during the Second World War." *American Quarterly* 20 (1968): 237–45.

Ledbetter, Les. "Appeals Court Supports CIA in Blocking Article by Ex-Aide." *New York Times,* September 18, 1972, p. 23.

Lewis, Anthony. "And a Threat to That Freedom: A Court of Appeals Decision on Prior Restraint." *New York Times,* February 16, 1974, p.16.

———. "Don't Look Now. . . ." *New York Times,* January 10, 1974, p. 37.

———. "The Price of Secrets." *New York Times,* August 21, 1980, p. A27.

———. "Security and Freedom." *New York Times,* May 22, 1974, p. 39.

"Lewis Says Hays Bans Film of Book." *New York Times,* February 16, 1936, pp. 1, 35.

Liao Yiwu. "Nineteen Days." *Paris Review* 189 (Summer 2009). Available online. URL: www.theparisreview.org/letters-essays/5929/nineteen-days-liao-yiwu. Accessed January 24, 2011.

"Libel Suit Against Viking Dismissed." *New York Times,* June 21, 1984, sec. 3, p. 17.

Lind, Carol. "Soviets Steal More Than a Glance at U.S. Books on Display in Moscow." *Christian Science Monitor,* September 2, 1981, 1.

Linn, Jennifer. "Censorship Fight Has Just Begun." *Panama City News-Herald,* May 15, 1987, pp. 1A, 2A.

———. "Lawsuit Filed Against Hall, School Board." *Panama City News-Herald,* May 13, 1987, pp. 1A, 2A.

———. "Leonard Hall Bans 64 Books." *Panama City News-Herald,* May 8, 1987, pp. 1A, 2A.

Liukkonen, Petri, and Ari Pesoner. "Abdul Rahman Munif (1933–2004)." Available online. URL: www.hirjasto.sci.fi/munif.htm. Accessed October 25, 2010.

Macrae, John, III. Letter: "The Moscow Book Fair." *New York Times Book Review,* September 4, 1983, p. 30.

Manak, Evelyn H. "Books Pulled off Shelves Again." *Hernando Free Press,* September 16, 1987, pp. 1, 12.

———. "Librarian Not Surprised Books Were Removed." *Sun Journal,* September 16, 1987, pp. 1, 12.

May, Greg. "Hall Challenged: City Protests Categories." *Panama City News-Herald,* May 13, 1987, pp. 1B, 7B.

May, Lucy. "Group Wants Five Books off Schools List." *Greenville News,* January 30, 1991, p. 1C.

———. "Proposal to Ban Some Books Draws Crowd to Board Meeting." *Greenville News,* March 13, 1991, p. 2.

———. "School Board Affirms Policy Allowing Panel to OK Books." *Greenville News,* April 10, 1991, p. 2.

McDowell, Edwin. "Publishing: Reversal of Ruling Troubles Authors." *New York Times*, September 16, 1983, sec. 3, p. 24.

McRae, Lorie. "Seized Book Is Back." *Feliciter*, October 30, 1984, p. 1.

McVicar, D. Morgan. "Disputed Books Go to Reserve Shelves." *Anniston Star*, November 17, 1982, pp. 1, 5A.

McWatt, Jennifer. "Saudis Flock to Bahrain to Buy a Book Banned by Riyadh." BBC Monitoring (January 31, 2006). Available online by subscription. URL: www.monitor. bbc.co.uk.

"Millionth Copy of Book by Hitler Off the Press." *New York Times*, September 28, 1933, p. 16.

Mitgang, Herbert. Book Notes. *New York Times*, August 31, 1988, p. C22.

———. "Crazy Horse Author Is Upheld in Libel Case." *New York Times*, January 16, 1988, sec. 2, p. 5.

Moffat, George. Book 'Ban' Challenged in Roselle." *Newark Star-Ledger*, June 28, 1972, p. 18.

———. "Roselle Will Buy 'Banned' Books and 4 'Balancers.'" *Newark Star-Ledger*, July 6, 1972, p. 20.

Morro, Anthony. "Judge Says He Thinks Ex-Official of CIA Violated Secrecy Pact." *New York Times*, June 22, 1978, p. 12.

———. "Reporters' Notebook: Alarums and Explosions at Ex-Agent's Trial." *New York Times*, June 23, 1978, p. 8.

———. "Trial over CIA Book Raises Rights Issues." *New York Times*, June 19, 1978, p. 15.

———. "Turner, Testifying in Snepp Case, Says Book by Ex-Agent Has Hurt CIA." *New York Times*, June 21, 1978, p. 15.

"Muscogee County, Georgia." *Newsletter on Intellectual Freedom* 58, no. 3 (May 2009): 93.

Mutter, John. "*Grapes of Wrath* Survives Banning Attempt in Vermont Town." *Publishers Weekly*, December 11, 1981, 9.

Naughton, James N. "Panel Backs *Washington Post*." *New York Times*, June 24, 1971, pp. 1, 16.

———. "*Post* Case Opinion." *New York Times*, June 20, 1971, pp. 1, 27.

———. "U.S. Loses in Move to Curb *Post*." *New York Times*, June 25, 1971, pp. 1, 13.

———. "*Washington Post* Restrained: Appeals Court Reversed Decision Favoring Paper." *New York Times*, June 19, 1971, pp. 1, 11.

"Nazi State Church Plan Proposes to Oust Other Faiths and Ban Bible." *New York Times*, January 3, 1942, p. 1.

Newsletter on Intellectual Freedom
13 (1964); 14, 24, 48, 81
15 (1966): 21, 28
16 (1967): 14, 67
17 (1968): 1–3, 15, 19, 20, 22, 39–40, 52, 55, 63.
19 (1970): 30
20 (1971): 5, 27, 44–45, 60–61, 77–78
21 (1972): 103–04, 128, 147
22 (1973): 52, 88, 146
23 (1974): 4, 69–70, 79, 145, 162
24 (1975): 6, 69, 85, 104, 111–12, 120, 139

25 (1976): 34, 37, 61–62, 85–86, 115
26 (1977): 8, 45, 133
27 (1978): 57, 61, 67, 100, 124
28 (1979): 6, 75–76, 81, 85, 110, 141–45, 147
29 (1980): 41, 48, 51, 53–54
30 (1981): 67–68, 73, 74, 92–93
31 (1982): 10–11, 12–13, 18, 33, 58, 59–60, 67–69, 126, 136–37, 149, 155, 156, 166, 170,
     173–86, 195, 197, 215, 221–25
32 (1983): 7, 37, 112, 192–93, 201
33 (1984): 18, 69–70, 75–76, 105, 116, 148, 158, 197
34 (1985): 1, 15, 16, 30–31, 34, 45
35 (1986): 9–10, 21–25, 29, 49, 52, 56, 57, 82, 91, 114, 137, 196–97, 209–10
36 (1987): 29, 32–33, 49, 51, 52, 72, 85–86, 126–28, 168–69, 173–74, 224, 225, 229
37 (1988): 9, 86–87, 99, 105, 122, 139–40, 178–79, 193, 216
38 (1989): 3, 4, 49–50, 121–23, 141–42, 186
39 (1990): 51, 219
40 (1991): 18, 55, 126–27, 130–31
42 (1993): 126–27
43 (1994): 9, 97
44 (1995): 100
46 (1997): 9, 25
47 (1998): 110, 183
48 (1999): 40, 160
49 (2000): 44, 54
50 (2001): 14, 62
51 (2002): 51
56 (2007): 35–36, 271
58 (2009): 93, 155–156

North, William D. "Pico and the Challenge to Books in Schools." *Newsletter on Intellectual Freedom* 31 (1982): 195, 221–225.
"Northwestern Is Thrust into Debate over Academic Freedom." *Minneapolis Star Tribune*, January 10, 1997, p. A9.
O'Donnell, Lynn. "China's Doctor Zhivago out in Cold." *Australian*, July 3, 2000, 13.
Oelsner, Lesley. "CIA Head Loses Appeal to Judge." *New York Times*, January 11, 1974, p. 29.
———. "Judge Backs Publishing of CIA Book." *New York Times*, April 2, 1974, p. 12.
———. "Judge Orders Data in Suit to Justify Deletion in Book on CIA." *New York Times*, December 22, 1973, p. 22.
"Official Removes 'Objectional' Books." *St. Louis Post Dispatch*, March 28, 1973, p. 22A
"OK for *Slaughterhouse Five*." *Racine Journal Times*, June 14, 1984, n.p.
Oliver, Malcolm. "Appeals Court Upholds CIA Secrecy Pact in Snepp Case." *Publishers Weekly*, April 2, 1979, 24, 26.
Omotoso, Kole. "The Necessity of the State." *Black Renaissance* 1, no. 3 (1993): 90–93.
"One Arbitrary Policy Doesn't Justify Another." *Panama City News-Herald*, May 13, 1987, p. 6A.
Pace, Eric. "Cuts That CIA Sought in Book Touch on Official Slips." *New York Times*, April 15, 1974, p. 24.

Palm, Edward F. "James Webb's *Fields of Fire:* The Melting-Pot Platoon Revisited." *Critique: Studies in Modern Fiction* 24 (1983): 105–18.

"Palmyra Board May Reinstate Banned Book." (Lebanon, Pa.) *Daily News,* October 1, 1994, p. 1.

"Parents Request Removal of Books." *Antelope Valley Press,* December 19, 1995, p. A1.

"Parent Wants Vietnam Book Removed from High School Library." *Fort Mill Times,* April 27, 1988, pp. 1, 3.

Pathfinder Press releases. New York. October 19, 1988; March 10, April 5, April 27, 1989; and April 9, 1996.

Pear, Robert. "Plea by Ex-CIA Agent to Restore Passport Is Denied." *New York Times,* January 1, 1980, p. 6.

Peyser, Andrea. "Battles over Book-Bans Getting Dirty." *Tampa Tribune,* May 17, 1987, pp. 1B, 10B.

Pierpont, Claudia Roth. "Found in Translation: The Contemporary Arabic Novel." *New Yorker,* January 18, 2010, 74–80.

Pipkin, Gloria. "Confessions of an Accused Pornographer." *Arizona English Bulletin* (1994): 14–18.

"Poll of Libraries Shows Free Choice." *New York Times,* June 16, 1953, p. 22.

Prescott, Peter S. "The Things They Carried." *Newsweek* (April 2, 1990): 57.

"Pro Books Group Is Organized in County." *Asheville Citizen,* February 14, 1981, p. 7.

Proffitt, Nicholas. "The Mission of Comrade Quan." *New York Times Book Review,* February 12, 1995, pp. 13–14.

"Publisher Scored for Hitler's Book." *New York Times,* August 18, 1933, p. 16.

Puhr, Kathleen M. "Four Fictional Faces of the Vietnam War." *Modern Fiction Studies* 30 (1984): 99–117.

Quisit, Raid. "Court Rejects Case against Rajaa Al-Sanea." ArabNews.com. Available online. URL: http://archive.arabnews.com/?page=1&section=0&article=87886&d= 9&m=10&y=2006. Accessed January 24, 2011.

"Rafferty Finds Two Dirty Words." *San Francisco Chronicle,* May 13, 1966, p. 43.

"Reich and Austria Reach Peace Truce." *New York Times,* July 13, 1937, p. 15.

"Reich Bans *It Can't Happen Here.*" *New York Times,* January 31, 1937, p. 26.

"Restricted List FMHS Library?" *Fort Mill Times,* May 11, 1988, pp. 1, 3.

Reuter, Madalynne. "Fourth Moscow Book Fair: Controversy as Usual." *Publishers Weekly,* September 23, 1983, 14.

Rich, R. Bruce. "The Supreme Court's Decision in Island Trees." *Newsletter on Intellectual Freedom* 31 (1982): 149, 173–86.

Riding, Alan. "Book by American Leads to Charge Against a Turk." *New York Times,* July 21, 2002, pp. 1–12.

"Ridgefield Board Reverses Its Decision to Ban *Boss.*" *New York Times,* April 20, 1972, p. 23.

Rintoul, William T. "The Banning of *The Grapes of Wrath.*" *California Crossroads* (January 1963): 4–6.

———. "The Banning of *The Grapes of Wrath.*" *California Crossroads* (February 1963): 26–28.

"Rock County Librarians United to Battle Would-Be Banners." *Beloit Daily News,* April 17, 1969, n.p.

Roos, Jonathan. "Kanawha's Ban Turns Novel into Best-seller." *Des Moines Register,* March 6, 1980, pp. 1A, 4A.

Rosenbaum, David E. "Judge Bars Book by Ex-CIA Agent." *New York Times*, April 19, 1972, p. 19.

Royko, Mike. "Now, about That Book . . ." *Chicago Daily News*, September 17, 1971, p. 3.

Rubenstein, Joshua. "*The Gulag Archipelago.*" *New Republic*, June 22, 1974, 21–22.

Runkel, David. "Book Controversy in Anne Arundel: Antibusiness, Class-Struggle 'Facts' Hit." *Baltimore Evening Sun*, February 17, 1966, p. D1.

"Russia Makes Gulag Required Reading." *Boston Globe* (September 10, 2009). Available online. URL: http://www.Boston.com/news/world9sep2009. Accessed June 14, 2010.

Salisbury, Harrison E. "Triumph of Boris Pasternak." *Saturday Review*, November 8, 1958, 22.

"School Board Bans Russian Book, Fails to Change Reading." *Burkie* [La.] *Record*, February 3, 1966, pp. 1, 8.

"A School Board Head in Jersey Orders 'Liberal' Books Deleted." *New York Times*, June 18, 1972, p. 50.

"School Board Selects Committee to Review Library Books." *Glenwood Opinion Tribune*, January 14, 1970, p. 1.

"School Censors Hit New York, Ohio, Maryland and California." *Library Journal* 96 (1971): 228–30.

"Schmemann, Serge. "Moscow Bars 49 Books of U.S. Jewish Group." *New York Times*, September 12, 1983, p. A9.

———. "Palestinian Security Agents Ban Books by Critics of Arafat." *New York Times*, August 25, 1996, pp. 1–12.

Schwendener, P. "The Holocaust Didn't Happen." *Reader* 12 (February 1983): 8–14.

Scott, Margaret. "Waging War with Words." *Far Eastern Economic Review*, August 9, 1962, 26–30.

"Seizing Anti-Semitic Book Wrong—Jews." *Edmonton Journal*, September 14, 1984, p. B3.

Selden, Mark. "Agnes Smedley, American Radical." *Monthly Review* 40 (October 1988): 32.

Shaffer, Terry. "Food Chain Lifts Book Ban." *Chicago Daily News*, September 19, 1971, p. 4.

Shaw, David. "History 'Interpretation' Stirs Tempest in Downey." *Long Beach* (Calif.) *Press-Telegram*, February 19, 1968, pp. B1, 4.

Shenon, Philip. "In This Author's Book, Villains Are Vietnamese." *New York Times International*, April 12, 1994, p. A4.

"Sidney Howard Backs Lewis in Film Row." *New York Times*, February 23, 1936, p. 3.

Simmons, Ernest J. "Russia from Within." *Atlantic Monthly* 202 (September 1958): 67–68, 72.

Simmons, Joel. "Film and International Politics: The Banning of *All Quiet on the Western Front* in Germany and Austria, 1930–1931." *Historian* 52 (1989): 40–60.

Simoneau, Duke. "Book Controversy Flares in Nashua." *New Hampshire Sunday News*, March 5, 1978, pp. 1, 18.

Sinclair, Upton. "Is *The Jungle* True?" *Independent*, May 17, 1906, n.p.

———. "The Condemned-Meat Industry: A Reply to Mr. J. Ogden Armour." *Everybody's* (May 1906): 608–16.

Siollun, Max. "Buhari and Idiagbon: A Missed Opportunity for Nigeria." Available online. URL: http://www.nigerdeltacongress.com/barticles/buhari_andidiagbon_a_missed_opp.htm.

"16 Countries Outlaw Reds, Survey Shows." *New York Times*, May 16, 1950, p. 20.

Snepp, Frank. "On CIA Secrecy, News Leaks and Censorship." *New York Times*, March 3, 1978, p. 25.

"South Africa Bans Novel by Popular Africaner." *New York Times*, September 15, 1979, p. 4.

"South Africa Bars Book by American Journalist." *New York Times*, September 19, 1984, p. 24.

"South Africa Lifts Ban on Gordimer Novel." *New York Times*, October 7, 1979, p. 79.

"South Africans Cancel Ban on Gordimer Book." *New York Times*, October 5, 1979, p. 6.

"South Dakota Governor Calls Stores to Ask Book's Removal." *New York Times*, May 1, 1983, p. 132.

"Soviets to Increase All Arms, Fearing Reich and Japan." *New York Times*, January 11, 1936, p. 1.

"A Special *New Republic* Report on Book Burning: Who Are the Book Burners? What Happened in San Antonio, St. Cloud and Boston? Senate Transcript—McCarthy vs. Conant." *New Republic*, June 29, 1953, 7–9.

"Special Report on Nigeria (4): Why General/Buhari/Failed the Coup." *Guardian* (London), September 13, 1985, n.p.

Sproule, J. Michael. "Whose Ethics in the Classroom? An Historical Survey." *Communication Monographs* (October 1987): 317–26.

Stadtmiller, Amanda. "PARC Cancels Controversial Fireside after NU Intervention." *Daily Northwestern*, May 10, 1944, p. 4.

Standbury, Beth. "Parents Air Concerns over Books." *Charlottesville Progress*, October 15, 1990, pp. B1, 2.

———. "Parents Seek Removal of Supplementary Books." *Charlottesville Progress*, September 26, 1990, pp. A1, 12.

Steig, William. Letter: "Steig's Likable Pigs." *New York Times*, March 3, 1971, p. 42.

Steiner, George. "The Forests of the Night." *New Yorker*, June 16, 1974, 78–87.

"Stockwell Settles with CIA to Keep Profits from Book." *Publishers Weekly*, July 11, 1980, 16, 18.

"Support of *Grapes* Ban Is Urged by Farmers Group." *Bakersfield Californian*, August 22, 1939, n.p.

Tanner, Stephen L. "Sinclair Lewis and Fascism." *Studies of the Novel* 22 (Spring 1990): 57–66.

"Textbook Issue Causes Suspension of Morongo Student." *Riverside* (Calif.) *Enterprise*, February 13, 1968, n.p.

"Third Ex-CIA Agent Sued by U.S. for Profits." *New York Times*, March 4, 1980, p. 13.

"365 Days Returned to Maine School Library." *Newsletter on Intellectual Freedom* 31 (1982): 33, 67–69.

Tickell, Paul. "Righting History." *Inside Indonesia* (May 1986): 29–30.

Tolischus, Otto D. "The German Book of Destiny." *New York Times Magazine*, October 28, 1936, pp. 1–2, 23.

Tonkin, Boyd. "From Public Enemy to National Hero." *Independent* (October 16, 2008).

"Tuolumne Education Board Opposes History Text." *Stockton* (Calif.) *Record*, March 12, 1969, n.p.

Turget, Pelin. "Novelist Acquitted after Trial for 'Insulting Turkishness.'" *Independent* (September 22, 2006).

"Turkish Publisher Fined for U.S. Book on Kurdish Conflict." *Agence France Presse,* August 2, 2002.

"Two Books Likely to Stay in LPS Libraries Despite Challenge." *Littleton Sentinel,* June 29, 1989, n.p.

"Unified Bans 5 Books." *Racine Journal Times,* June 12, 1984, n.p.

"Unified Lifts Book Ban." *Racine Journal Times,* June 19, 1984, n.p.

"Unofficial Translation of Turkish Indictment against Abdullah Keskin." Committee to Protect Journalists CPJ News Alert. 2002. Available online. URL: http://www. cpj.org/news/2002/Turkey03apr02na.html.

"Unstocking the Shelves." *Racine Journal Times,* May 27, 1984, n.p.

Updike, John. "Anatolian Arabesques." *New Yorker,* August 20, 2004, 98–99.

"Upton Sinclair Works Banned." *New York Times,* May 18, 1956, p. 23.

"U.S.I.A. in Reversal on *Ugly American.*" *New York Times,* December 6, 1958, n.p.

"U.S. Seeking to Block Former Agent's Book about CIA in Africa." *New York Times,* February 6, 1980, p. 17.

Varney, Mark Nesbit. "A.C.L.U. Watching School Censorship." *West Hernando News,* September 30, 1987, pp. 1A, 3A.

———. "Librarian Beats School Board." *West Hernando News,* September 16, 1987, pp. 1A, 3A.

"Viking, Matthiessen Prevail in Libel Suit." *Publishers Weekly,* January 29, 1988, 314.

"Viking and Matthiessen Win in Price Libel Suit." *Publishers Weekly,* September 1, 1989, 8.

Ward, Bruce. "Carving out Their Own Way: Novel Has Ignited a Debate about Women in Saudi Arabia." *Montreal Gazette,* August 11, 2007.

Warren, Chante Dionne. "Black History Month: History Text Called Incomplete." [Baton Rouge, La.] *Advocate,* February 1, 1996, p. 213.

Watts, Jonathan. "Three Gorges Dam May Force Relocation of a Further 300,000 People." *Guardian* (London) (January 22, 2010). Available online. URL: www. guardian.co.uk/environment/2010/jan/22/wave-tidal-hydropower-water. Accessed January 24, 2011.

Weaver, Warren, Jr. "Justice Department to Sue Author of CIA Book." *New York Times,* February 15, 1978, p. 21.

———. "Justices Let Stand Censorship Order over a CIA Book." *New York Times,* May 28, 1974, p. 1.

Wedel, T. O. "On the Philosophical Background of *Gulliver's Travels.*" *Studies in Philology* 23 (1926): n.p.

Whitman, Alden. "Suppressed China Book Sees the Light Again." *New York Times,* December 10, 1974, p. 55.

Wicker, Tom. "The CIA and Free Speech." *New York Times,* March 18, 1974, p. 37.

Wilson, Raymond J., III. "The Misreading of Solzhenitsyn's *Cancer Ward:* Narrative and Interpretive Strategies in the Context of Censorship." *Journal of Narrative Technique* (Spring 1989): 175–96.

Wilson, Scott. "Disapproval Still Hangs over Saudi Writers." *Toronto Star,* March 19, 2005.

Winer, Todd. "Tangled Web: NU Professor and the Holocaust." *Chicago Jewish News,* October 25–31, 1996, n.p.

Wines, Michael. "For 13th Time, Critic of China Is Barred from Travel Abroad." *New York Times,* March 3, 2010.

Wiskari, Werner. "Guatemalan Author of Anti-U.S. Works Wins Nobel Prize." *New York Times,* October 20, 1967, pp. 1, 44.

Witteles, Ron. "PARC Bureaucrats: We Know What's Best for You." *Northwestern Chronicle*, May 13, 1944, p. 1.

Wolfe Bell, Stephanie. "State Education Board Drops Several Social Studies Books." *Alabama Journal* (March 17, 1981): 13.

Time (October 12, 2007). Available online. URL: www.time.com/time/world/article/0,8599, 1671000,00.html. Accessed January 24, 2011.

Yang, Lin. "China's Three Gorges Dam under Fire." Time (October 12, 2007). Available online. URL: www.time.com/time/world/article/0,8599,1671000,00.html. Accessed January 24, 2011.

Zaleski, Jeff. Review of *The Appointment* by Herta Müller. *Publisher's Weekly*, August 6, 2001, 61.

WORKS DISCUSSED IN THE OTHER VOLUMES OF THIS SERIES

THE BLOUDY TENENT OF PERSECUTION
Roger Williams

THE BOOK OF COMMON PRAYER
Thomas Cranmer and others

THE CARTOONS THAT SHOOK THE WORLD
Jytte Klausen

CHILDREN OF THE ALLEY
Naguib Mahfouz

THE CHRISTIAN COMMONWEALTH
John Eliot

CHRISTIANITY NOT MYSTERIOUS
John Toland

CHRISTIANITY RESTORED
Michael Servetus

*CHURCH: CHARISM AND POWER: LIBERATION THEOLOGY
AND THE INSTITUTIONAL CHURCH*
Leonardo Boff

COLLOQUIES
Desiderius Erasmus

COMMENTARIES
Averroës

COMPENDIUM REVELATIONUM
Girolamo Savonarola

CONCERNING HERETICS
Sebastian Castellio

THE COURSE OF POSITIVE PHILOSOPHY
Auguste Comte

CREATIVE EVOLUTION
Henri Bergson

THE CRITIQUE OF PURE REASON
Immanuel Kant

THE DA VINCI CODE
Dan Brown

DE ECCLESIA
Jan Hus

DE INVENTORIBUS RERUM
Polydore Vergil

DE L'ESPRIT
Claude-Adrien Helvétius

*DIALOGUE CONCERNING THE TWO CHIEF
WORLD SYSTEMS*
Galileo Galilei

DIALOGUES CONCERNING NATURAL RELIGION
David Hume

DISCOURSE ON METHOD
René Descartes

DON QUIXOTE
Miguel de Cervantes Saavedra

DRAGONWINGS
Laurence Yep

ÉMILE
Jean-Jacques Rousseau

ENCYCLOPÉDIE
Denis Diderot and Jean Le Rond d'Alembert, eds.

AN ESSAY CONCERNING HUMAN UNDERSTANDING
John Locke

ESSAYS
Michel de Montaigne

ETHICS
Baruch Spinoza

THE FABLE OF THE BEES
Bernard Mandeville

THE GUIDE OF THE PERPLEXED
Maimonides

HARRY POTTER AND THE SORCERER'S STONE
J. K. Rowling

HARRY POTTER AND THE CHAMBER OF SECRETS
J. K. Rowling

HARRY POTTER AND THE PRISONER OF AZKABAN
J. K. Rowling

HARRY POTTER AND THE GOBLET OF FIRE
J. K. Rowling

HARRY POTTER AND THE ORDER OF THE PHOENIX
J. K. Rowling

HARRY POTTER AND THE HALF-BLOOD PRINCE
J. K. Rowling

HARRY POTTER AND THE DEATHLY HALLOWS
J. K. Rowling

THE HIDDEN FACE OF EVE: WOMEN IN THE ARAB WORLD
Nawal El Saadawi

HIS DARK MATERIALS TRILOGY, BOOK I: *THE GOLDEN COMPASS*
Philip Pullman

HIS DARK MATERIALS TRILOGY, BOOK II: *THE SUBTLE KNIFE*
Philip Pullman

HIS DARK MATERIALS TRILOGY, BOOK III: *THE AMBER SPYGLASS*
Philip Pullman

HISTORICAL AND CRITICAL DICTIONARY
Pierre Bayle

HISTORY OF THE CONFLICT BETWEEN RELIGION AND SCIENCE
John William Draper

*THE HISTORY OF THE DECLINE AND FALL OF THE ROMAN
  EMPIRE*
Edward Gibbon

HOLT BASIC READING SERIES
Bernard J. Weiss, sr. ed.

IMPRESSIONS READING SERIES
Jack Booth, gen. ed.

INFALLIBLE? AN INQUIRY
Hans Küng

AN INQUIRY CONCERNING HUMAN UNDERSTANDING
David Hume

INSTITUTES OF THE CHRISTIAN RELIGION
John Calvin

INTRODUCTION TO THEOLOGY
Peter Abelard

*AN INTRODUCTION TO THE PRINCIPLES OF MORALS AND
  LEGISLATION*
Jeremy Bentham

INTRODUCTORY LECTURES ON PSYCHOANALYSIS
Sigmund Freud

THE JEWEL OF MEDINA
Sherry Jones

THE KORAN (QUR'AN)

LAJJA (SHAME)
Taslima Nasrin

THE LAST TEMPTATION OF CHRIST
Nikos Kazantzakis

LETTER ON THE BLIND
Denis Diderot

LETTERS CONCERNING THE ENGLISH NATION
Voltaire

LEVIATHAN
Thomas Hobbes

THE LIFE OF JESUS
Ernest Renan

MARY AND HUMAN LIBERATION
Tissa Balasuriya

MEDITATIONS ON FIRST PHILOSOPHY
René Descartes

THE MERITORIOUS PRICE OF OUR REDEMPTION
William Pynchon

THE METAPHYSICS
Aristotle

MEYEBELA: MY BENGALI GIRLHOOD
Taslima Nasrin

THE NEW ASTRONOMY
Johannes Kepler

THE NEW TESTAMENT
William Tyndale, trans.

NINETY-FIVE THESES
Martin Luther

OF THE VANITIE AND UNCERTAINTIE OF ARTES AND SCIENCES
Henricus Cornelius Agrippa

OLIVER TWIST
Charles Dickens

ON CIVIL LORDSHIP
John Wycliffe

ON JUSTICE IN THE REVOLUTION AND IN THE CHURCH
Pierre-Joseph Proudhon

ON MONARCHY
Dante Alighieri

ON THE INFINITE UNIVERSE AND WORLDS
Giordano Bruno

ON THE LAW OF WAR AND PEACE
Hugo Grotius

ON THE ORIGIN OF SPECIES
Charles Darwin

ON THE REVOLUTION OF HEAVENLY SPHERES
Nicolaus Copernicus

OPUS MAJUS
Roger Bacon

PENGUIN ISLAND
Anatole France

THE PERSIAN LETTERS
Charles-Louis de Secondat, baron de La Brède et de Montesquieu

PHILOSOPHICAL DICTIONARY
Voltaire

THE POLITICAL HISTORY OF THE DEVIL
Daniel Defoe

POPOL VUH

THE POWER AND THE GLORY
Graham Greene

THE PRAISE OF FOLLY
Desiderius Erasmus

PRINCIPLES OF POLITICAL ECONOMY
John Stuart Mill

THE PROVINCIAL LETTERS
Blaise Pascal

THE RAPE OF SITA
Lindsey Collen

THE RED AND THE BLACK
Stendhal

RELIGIO MEDICI
Sir Thomas Browne

RELIGION WITHIN THE LIMITS OF REASON ALONE
Immanuel Kant

THE RIGHTS OF THE CHRISTIAN CHURCH ASSERTED
Matthew Tindal

THE SANDY FOUNDATION SHAKEN
William Penn

THE SATANIC VERSES
Salman Rushdie

SHIVAJI: HINDU KING IN ISLAMIC INDIA
James W. Laine

*A SHORT DECLARATION OF THE MISTERY OF
    INIQUITY*
Thomas Helwys

THE SHORTEST WAY WITH THE DISSENTERS
Daniel Defoe

THE SOCIAL CONTRACT
Jean-Jacques Rousseau

THE SORROWS OF YOUNG WERTHER
Johann Wolfgang von Goethe

THE SPIRIT OF LAWS
Charles-Louis de Secondat, baron de La Brède et de Montesquieu

SPIRITS REBELLIOUS
Kahlil Gibran

THE STORY OF ZAHRA
Hanan al-Shaykh

A TALE OF A TUB
Jonathan Swift

THE TALMUD

THEOLOGICAL-POLITICAL TREATISE
Baruch Spinoza

THREE-PART WORK
Meister Eckhart

TOUBA AND THE MEANING OF NIGHT
Shahrnush Parsipur

THE VEIL AND THE MALE ELITE: A FEMINIST INTERPRETATION OF WOMEN'S RIGHTS IN ISLAM
Fatima Mernissi

VOODOO & HOODOO: THEIR TRADITIONAL CRAFTS AS REVEALED BY ACTUAL PRACTITIONERS
Jim Haskins

VOYAGES TO THE MOON AND THE SUN
Savinien Cyrano de Bergerac

THE WITCHES
Roald Dahl

WOMEN WITHOUT MEN: A NOVEL OF MODERN IRAN
Shahrnush Parsipur

ZHUAN FALUN: THE COMPLETE TEACHINGS OF FALUN GONG
Li Hongzhi

ZOONOMIA
Erasmus Darwin

WORKS DISCUSSED IN *BANNED BOOKS: LITERATURE SUPPRESSED ON SEXUAL GROUNDS* BY DAWN B. SOVA

ALICE SERIES
Phyllis Reynolds Naylor

ALWAYS RUNNING—LA VIDA LOCA: GANG DAYS IN L.A.
Luis T. Rodriguez

AMERICA (THE BOOK): A CITIZEN'S GUIDE TO DEMOCRACY INACTION
Jon Stewart, Ben Karlin, David Javerbaum

AN AMERICAN TRAGEDY
Theodore Dreiser

THE ARABIAN NIGHTS, OR THE THOUSAND AND ONE NIGHTS
Sir Richard Burton, trans.

THE ART OF LOVE (ARS AMATORIA)
Ovid (Publius Ovidius Naso)

THE AWAKENING
Kate Chopin

BESSIE COTTER
Wallace Smith

BLESS ME, ULTIMA
Rudolfo Anaya

THE BLUEST EYE
Toni Morrison

BOY
James Hanley

THE BUFFALO TREE
Adam Rapp

CANDIDE
Voltaire (François Marie Arouet Voltaire)

CANDY
Maxwell Kenton

THE CARPETBAGGERS
Harold Robbins

CASANOVA'S HOMECOMING (CASANOVA'S HEIMFAHRT)
Arthur Schnitzler

THE CHINESE ROOM
Vivian Connell

CHRISTINE
Stephen King

THE CLAN OF THE CAVE BEAR
Jean Auel

CONFESSIONS
Jean-Jacques Rousseau

THE DECAMERON
Giovanni Boccaccio

THE DEER PARK
Norman Mailer

THE DEVIL RIDES OUTSIDE
John Howard Griffin

THE DIARY OF SAMUEL PEPYS
Samuel Pepys

DROLL STORIES
Honoré de Balzac

DUBLINERS
James Joyce

EAT ME
Linda Jaivin

THE EPIC OF GILGAMESH
Unknown

FANNY HILL, OR MEMOIRS OF A WOMAN OF PLEASURE
John Cleland

THE FIFTEEN PLAGUES OF A MAIDENHEAD
Anonymous

FLOWERS FOR ALGERNON
Daniel Keyes

THE FLOWERS OF EVIL (LES FLEURS DU MAL)
Charles Baudelaire

FOREVER
Judy Blume

FOREVER AMBER
Kathleen Winsor

FROM HERE TO ETERNITY
James Jones

THE GENIUS
Theodore Dreiser

THE GILDED HEARSE
Charles O. Gorham

THE GINGER MAN
J. P. Donleavy

THE GOATS
Brock Cole

GOD'S LITTLE ACRE
Erskine Caldwell

GOSSIP GIRL SERIES
Cecily von Ziegesar

THE GROUP
Mary McCarthy

HAGAR REVELLY
Daniel Carson Goodman

THE HANDMAID'S TALE
Margaret Atwood

THE HEPTAMERON (L'HEPTAMERON OU HISTOIRES DES AMANS FORTUNEZ)
Marguerite d'Angoulême, Queen of Navarre

THE HISTORY OF TOM JONES, A FOUNDLING
Henry Fielding

HOMO SAPIENS
Stanley Przybyskzewski

HOW THE GARCÍA GIRLS LOST THEIR ACCENTS
Julia Alvarez

HOW TO MAKE LOVE LIKE A PORN STAR
Jenna Jameson

IF IT DIE
André Gide

ISLE OF PINES
Henry Neville

*IT'S PERFECTLY NORMAL: CHANGING BODIES,
 GROWING UP, SEX, AND SEXUAL HEALTH*
Robie H. Harris

JANET MARCH
Floyd Dell

JUDE THE OBSCURE
Thomas Hardy

JURGEN: A COMEDY OF JUSTICE
James Branch Cabell

*JUSTINE, OR THE MISFORTUNES OF VIRTUE;
JULIETTE, HER SISTER, OR THE PROSPERITIES OF VICE*
Marquis de Sade

THE KAMA SUTRA OF VATSAYANA
Sir Richard Burton, F. F. Arbuthnot, translators

THE KREUTZER SONATA
Leo Tolstoy

LADIES IN THE PARLOR
Jim Tully

LADY CHATTERLEY'S LOVER
D. H. Lawrence

LA TERRE (THE EARTH)
Émile Zola

LOLITA
Vladimir Nabokov

THE LUSTFUL TURK
Anonymous

MADAME BOVARY
Gustave Flaubert

MADELEINE
Anonymous

MADEMOISELLE DE MAUPIN
Théophile Gautier

THE MAID OF ORLEANS (LA PUCELLE)
François-Marie Arouet Voltaire

MEMOIRES
Giovanni Casanova de Seingalt

MEMOIRS OF A YOUNG RAKEHELL
Guillaume Apollinaire

MEMOIRS OF HECATE COUNTY
Edmund Wilson

THE MERRY MUSES OF CALEDONIA
Robert Burns

MOLL FLANDERS
Daniel Defoe

MY LIFE AND LOVES
Frank Harris

NATIVE SON
Richard Wright

A NIGHT IN A MOORISH HAREM
Anonymous

NOVEMBER (NOVEMBRE)
Gustave Flaubert

THE 120 DAYS OF SODOM (LES 120 JOURNÉES DE SODOME)
Marquis de Sade

OUR LADY OF THE FLOWERS (NOTRE-DAME-DES-FLEURS)
Jean Genet

OUTLAW REPRESENTATION
Richard Meyer

PAMELA, OR VIRTUE REWARDED
Samuel Richardson

PANSIES
D. H. Lawrence

THE PERFUMED GARDEN
Sir Richard Burton, trans.

THE PERKS OF BEING A WALLFLOWER
Stephen Chbosky

PEYTON PLACE
Grace Metalious

THE PHILANDERER
Stanley Kauffmann

POEMS AND BALLADS
Algernon Charles Swinburne

POINT COUNTER POINT
Aldous Huxley

RABBIT, RUN
John Updike

THE RAINBOW
D. H. Lawrence

REPLENISHING JESSICA
Max Bodenheim

SANCTUARY
William Faulkner

SARI SAYS
Sari Locker

THE SATYRICON
Gaius Petronius Arbiter

SEPTEMBER IN QUINZE
Vivian Connell

SERENADE
James M. Cain

SEX
Madonna

SEXUS
Henry Miller

SHANGHAI BABY
Wei Hui (Zhou Weihui)

SIMON CALLED PETER
Robert Keable

1601—A FIRESIDE CONVERSATION IN YE TIME
   OF QUEEN ELIZABETH
Mark Twain

SLEEVELESS ERRAND
Norah C. James

SNOW FALLING ON CEDARS
David Guterson

SONG OF SOLOMON
Toni Morrison

SOPHIE'S CHOICE
William Styron

A STORY TELLER'S HOLIDAY
George Moore

STUDS LONIGAN
James T. Farrell

SUSAN LENOX: HER FALL AND RISE
David Graham Phillips

SWEETER THAN LIFE
Mark Tryon

TEN NORTH FREDERICK
John O'Hara

TESS OF THE D'URBERVILLES
Thomas Hardy

THEIR EYES WERE WATCHING GOD
Zora Neale Hurston

THEN AGAIN, MAYBE I WON'T
Judy Blume

THE THIEF'S JOURNAL
Jean Genet

THIS BOY'S LIFE
Tobias Wolff

THREE WEEKS
Elinor Glyn

TOBACCO ROAD
Erskine Caldwell

TRAGIC GROUND
Erskine Caldwell

TRILBY
George du Maurier

THE TRIUMPH OF DEATH
Gabriele D'Annunzio

TROPIC OF CANCER
Henry Miller

TROPIC OF CAPRICORN
Henry Miller

TWILIGHT SERIES
Stephenie Meyer

ULYSSES
James Joyce

VENUS AND TANNHAUSER (UNDER THE HILL)
Aubrey Beardsley

THE WILD PALMS
William Faulkner

WOMEN IN LOVE
D. H. Lawrence

WOMEN ON TOP: HOW REAL LIFE CHANGED WOMEN'S SEXUAL FANTASIES
Nancy Friday

A YOUNG GIRL'S DIARY
Anonymous

WORKS DISCUSSED IN *BANNED BOOKS: LITERATURE SUPPRESSED ON SOCIAL GROUNDS* BY DAWN B. SOVA

THE ABSOLUTELY TRUE DIARY OF A PART-TIME INDIAN
Sherman Alexie

THE ADVENTURES OF HUCKLEBERRY FINN
Mark Twain

THE ADVENTURES OF SHERLOCK HOLMES
Sir Arthur Conan Doyle

THE ADVENTURES OF TOM SAWYER
Mark Twain

ALICE'S ADVENTURES IN WONDERLAND
Lewis Carroll

THE AMBOY DUKES
Irving Shulman

THE AMERICAN HERITAGE DICTIONARY OF THE ENGLISH LANGUAGE

AM I BLUE?
Marion Dane Bauer

AND STILL I RISE
Maya Angelou

AND TANGO MAKES THREE
Justin Richardson and Peter Parnell

ANNE FRANK: THE DIARY OF A YOUNG GIRL
Anne Frank

ANNIE ON MY MIND
Nancy Garden

ANOTHER COUNTRY
James Baldwin

APHRODITE
Pierre Louÿs

APPOINTMENT IN SAMARRA
John O'Hara

AS I LAY DYING
William Faulkner

THE AUTOBIOGRAPHY OF BENJAMIN FRANKLIN
Benjamin Franklin

THE AUTOBIOGRAPHY OF MALCOLM X
Malcolm X, with Alex Haley

THE AUTOBIOGRAPHY OF MISS JANE PITTMAN
Ernest J. Gaines

BABY BE-BOP
Francesca Lia Block

THE BASKETBALL DIARIES
Jim Carroll

BEING THERE
Jerzy Kosinski

THE BELL JAR
Sylvia Plath

BELOVED
Toni Morrison

THE BEST SHORT STORIES BY NEGRO WRITERS
Langston Hughes, ed.

BLACK LIKE ME
John Howard Griffin

BLESS THE BEASTS AND CHILDREN
Glendon Swarthout

BLUBBER
Judy Blume

BRAVE NEW WORLD
Aldous Huxley

BRIDGE TO TERABITHIA
Katherine Paterson

CAIN'S BOOK
Alexander Trocchi

CAMILLE
Alexandre Dumas, Jr.

THE CANTERBURY TALES
Geoffrey Chaucer

CAPTAIN UNDERPANTS (SERIES)
Dav Pilkey

CATCH-22
Joseph Heller

THE CATCHER IN THE RYE
J. D. Salinger

THE CHOCOLATE WAR
Robert Cormier

A CLOCKWORK ORANGE
Anthony Burgess

THE COLOR PURPLE
Alice Walker

CUJO
Stephen King

DADDY'S ROOMMATE
Michael Willhoite

A DAY NO PIGS WOULD DIE
Robert Newton Peck

DELIVERANCE
James Dickey

A DICTIONARY OF AMERICAN SLANG
Harold Wentworth

DICTIONARY OF SLANG AND UNCONVENTIONAL ENGLISH
Eric Partridge

DOCTOR DOLITTLE (SERIES)
Hugh John Lofting

DOG DAY AFTERNOON
Patrick Mann

DOWN THESE MEAN STREETS
Piri Thomas

DRACULA
Bram Stoker

THE DROWNING OF STEPHAN JONES
Bette Greene

EAST OF EDEN
John Steinbeck

ELMER GANTRY
Sinclair Lewis

END AS A MAN
Calder Willingham

ESTHER WATERS
George Moore

FAHRENHEIT 451
Ray Bradbury

FALLEN ANGELS
Walter Dean Myers

A FAREWELL TO ARMS
Ernest Hemingway

FINAL EXIT
Derek Humphry

THE FIXER
Bernard Malamud

FREAKONOMICS
Steven D. Levitt and Stephen J. Dubner

FRUITS OF PHILOSOPHY: OR THE PRIVATE COMPANION
OF YOUNG MARRIED PEOPLE
Charles Knowlton

GARGANTUA AND PANTAGRUEL
François Rabelais

GENTLEMAN'S AGREEMENT
Laura Z. Hobson

THE GIVER
Lois Lowry

GO ASK ALICE
Anonymous

GONE WITH THE WIND
Margaret Mitchell

GORILLAS IN THE MIST
Dian Fossey

GO TELL IT ON THE MOUNTAIN
James Baldwin

THE GREAT GATSBY
F. Scott Fitzgerald

GRENDEL
John Gardner

HEATHER HAS TWO MOMMIES
Leslea Newman

A HERO AIN'T NOTHIN' BUT A SANDWICH
Alice Childress

HOWL AND OTHER POEMS
Allen Ginsberg

I KNOW WHY THE CAGED BIRD SINGS
Maya Angelou

IN THE NIGHT KITCHEN
Maurice Sendak

INVISIBLE MAN
Ralph Ellison

JAKE AND HONEYBUNCH GO TO HEAVEN
Margot Zemach

JAMES AND THE GIANT PEACH
Roald Dahl

JAWS
Peter Benchley

JUNKY
William S. Burroughs

KING & KING
Linda de Haan and Stern Nijland

KINGSBLOOD ROYAL
Sinclair Lewis

THE KITE RUNNER
Khaled Hosseini

LAST EXIT TO BROOKLYN
Hubert Selby, Jr.

LEAVES OF GRASS
Walt Whitman

A LIGHT IN THE ATTIC
Shel Silverstein

LITTLE BLACK SAMBO
Helen Bannerman

LITTLE HOUSE ON THE PRAIRIE
Laura Ingalls Wilder

LITTLE RED RIDING HOOD
Charles Perrault

LORD OF THE FLIES
William Golding

MANCHILD IN THE PROMISED LAND
Claude Brown

MARRIED LOVE
Marie Stopes

MOTHER GOOSE'S NURSERY RHYMES AND FAIRY TALES
Unknown

MY HOUSE
Nikki Giovanni

THE NAKED APE
Desmond Morris

NAKED LUNCH
William S. Burroughs

NANA
Émile Zola

NEVER LOVE A STRANGER
Harold Robbins

NEW DICTIONARY OF AMERICAN SLANG
Robert L. Chapman
(discussed with *A DICTIONARY OF AMERICAN SLANG*)

OF MICE AND MEN
John Steinbeck

OF TIME AND THE RIVER
Thomas Wolfe

THE OLD MAN AND THE SEA
Ernest Hemingway

ONE FLEW OVER THE CUCKOO'S NEST
Ken Kesey

ORDINARY PEOPLE
Judith Guest

THE OX-BOW INCIDENT
Walter Van Tilburg Clark

THE RED PONY
John Steinbeck

THE SCARLET LETTER
Nathaniel Hawthorne

A SEPARATE PEACE
John Knowles

SISTER CARRIE
Theodore Dreiser

SOUL ON ICE
Eldridge Cleaver

STEPPENWOLF
Hermann Hesse

STRANGE FRUIT
Lillian Smith

STRANGER IN A STRANGE LAND
Robert A. Heinlein

THE SUN ALSO RISES
Ernest Hemingway

TO HAVE AND HAVE NOT
Ernest Hemingway

TO KILL A MOCKINGBIRD
Harper Lee

UNCLE REMUS
Joel Chandler Harris

UNLIVED AFFECTIONS
George Shannon

WE ALL FALL DOWN
Robert Cormier

WELCOME TO THE MONKEY HOUSE
Kurt Vonnegut, Jr.

THE WELL OF LONELINESS
Radclyffe Hall

WHALE TALK
Chris Crutcher

WOMAN IN THE MISTS
Farley Mowat
(discussed with *GORILLAS IN THE MIST*)

*WORKING: PEOPLE TALK ABOUT WHAT THEY DO ALL DAY
 AND HOW THEY FEEL ABOUT WHAT THEY DO*
Studs Terkel

A WORLD I NEVER MADE
James T. Farrell

INDEX

Note: **Boldface** page numbers indicate major treatment of a topic; *b* denotes entries located in the biographical section.